Courtesy of the Atwater Kent Museum, Philadelphia

6/24/85

Keith

Hope you can trace some of your mishpochah in this volume.

Best regards

Norm B.

Philadelphia
The Jewish Publication Society of America

The History of the Jews of Philadelphia from Colonial Times to the Age of Jackson

 EDWIN WOLF 2ND

MAXWELL WHITEMAN

To the Wolf Family of Philadelphia

Pride in your history is pride
In living what your fathers died,
Is pride in taking your own pulse
And counting in you someone else.
                    —Louis MacNeice

From "Suite for Recorders III," in *Ten Burnt Offerings* (1952), Faber and Faber (London), and Oxford University Press (New York).

Preface —
American Bicentennial Edition

Two hundred years ago by a Declaration of Independence the people of the British colonies in most of North America constituted themselves as the free and independent United States of America. It was a bold step; it was a step which influenced and still influences the rise of new governments and new nations.

On July 28, 1776, Jonas Phillips of Philadelphia wrote to an Amsterdam correspondent:

The war will make all England bankrupt. The Americans have an army of 100,000 fellows and the English 25,000 and some ships. The Americans have already made themselves like the States of Holland. The enclosed is a declaration of the whole country.

The enclosure was the broadside of the Declaration of Independence as it was first printed by John Dunlap, Phillips's neighbor on Market Street. The letter was intercepted by the British on its way across the Atlantic. The printed Declaration was clear, crisp, and easily understood. The written letter was in Yiddish. The unsophisticated British intelligence of two centuries ago puzzled over Phillips's harmless message, wrote it off as an unbreakable American code, and filed it. The letter and the broadside are still in the Public Record Office in London.

To descend from the sublime to the mundane, twenty years ago the preface to the first edition of this work was written. Since then a number of additional facts previously unknown or omitted have turned up; a few errors have been brought to our attention.

All these would have changed, added, or deleted a sentence or a paragraph here and there. Basically, however, there is no need for addenda and corrigenda to this reissue of the text. The history as published in 1957 has stood the test of two decades. The only disappointment has been that there are not young historians of the Philadelphia Jewish community who, like those of American academia as a whole, have relegated their predecessors to the polite limbo of "elders."

Sectarian histories usually suffer from a desire on the part of their authors to inflate or apologize for the actions of their fellows by national origin or religion. Dealing with only a segment of the whole, they are inclined to overlook the mainstream of events. Some of the inherent faults of such a history will be found here as well. For this is the story of the Jews of Philadelphia who, during the period covered, were neither a sizable element in the city nor a decisive influence on its history. Yet, it is the story of individuals, many of whom contributed significantly to the progress of Philadelphia, and of a religious group which, from small beginnings, has become an integral and important part of the diversity which is the city's life today. We have attempted to portray the individuals and the group as they emerge from the records available to us. We have tried to place them in the background of their times. If they sometimes seem somewhat larger than life, it is only because we are dealing with a microcosm within a macrocosm, and hence that illusion is created.

So little has been written about the early Jews of Philadelphia that their real contributions as persons and as a religious community have been overlooked. We have tried to show that from the earliest days they were like the other men and women who built our nation: some rich, more poor; some enterprising, many satisfied with little; some pious, others without religious feeling; most of them patriotic, a few indifferent. And even more important, they were what they were: individuals—in this case Jews —clothed in the dignity of citizenship and enjoying the satisfaction of worshiping freely.

This history was originally written as a series of weekly articles which appeared in the Philadelphia *Jewish Exponent* during 1954–55, the year of the American Jewish Tercentenary. Because the research and the writing were done one step ahead of a weekly deadline, much that was discovered later bearing upon a section already published could not be included. This extensive new material was later incorporated, much of the work completely rewritten, and a corpus of notes added. It is now being reissued during the year of the American Bicentennial, but it has not been rewritten. It simply would not have been practical to reset the whole book for the sake of minor changes.

It was once believed that there was no extensive raw material for research on American Jewish history. We are now convinced that there is so much that it would be a lifetime task to gather it. We used major manuscript sources like the Gratz Papers, and yet we cannot claim to have extracted every reference to a Jew or by a Jew contained in those thousands of documents. We examined a complete file of newspapers for each year covered by this history, but we know there are other papers which unquestionably have some details that we have missed. We examined many books of the period, but there are as many others that certainly would produce additional information of interest. A more thorough examination of the tax lists of the city and of the records of deeds will undoubtedly yield new names and facts. There is still much that can be found out about the early Jews of Philadelphia, but we feel that the essentials are here and sufficient details to make this a comprehensive and coherent picture of the people and their religious community.

Wherever possible we have cited original sources for our statements of fact. We may have overannotated, but we found that the lack or inadequacy of notes in most earlier American Jewish histories presented us with our most vexing problem. Statements were made and repeated for which we could not find a shred of evidence, and in many cases we found solid evidence to the contrary. There will be, as in any work of this size, a few errors; we can only hope that they will be very few. Our intent has been to state only those facts for which there is documentary proof.

In gathering the material, we used the resources of many libraries and received valuable help from many people—to all of whom we are most grateful. Some of them have passed away since the first publication of this work: Barney Chesnick of the Library Company of Philadelphia, R. Norris Williams, 2nd, of the Historical Society of Pennsylvania, and J. Solis-Cohen, Jr., former president of the Jewish Publication Society. Others will be able once again to receive our thanks: Nicholas B. Wainwright, director emeritus of the Historical Society of Pennsylvania, through whose courtesy the rich manuscript resources under his care were made freely available; Dr. Jacob R. Marcus of the American Jewish Archives, the dean of American Jewish historians, whose pioneering work was of tremendous assistance; Dr. Solomon Grayzel, former editor of the Jewish Publication Society, under whose watchful eye the first printing appeared; Rabbi Isidore S. Meyer of the American Jewish Historical Society; Dr. Abraham Feldman, formerly with the Department of Records, City of Philadelphia; Dr. David H. Wice of Congregation Rodeph Shalom; and other individuals and institutions mentioned specifically in the notes.

We were indebted to the *Jewish Exponent* and to the Philadelphia Section of the American Jewish Tercentenary Committee for having made available funds through which the time-consuming research for this work was made possible, and to the Jacob R. Schiff Fund for its sponsorship of the first edition.

It is a matter of satisfaction to any authors to find that their work has warranted a second printing. We are grateful to a number of disappointed purchasers who found the history out of print, and to the editor, Publication Committee, and trustees of the Jewish Publication Society for being willing to fill what we hope may prove to be a demand as satisfactory to the publishers as to the authors.

Edwin Wolf 2nd
Maxwell Whiteman

July 4, 1975

Contents

List of Illustrations

The History of the Jews of Philadelphia

Prologue

No history has its beginning at a particular point in time. The history of the Jews of Philadelphia did not begin when the first Jew set foot on the shores of the Delaware. Long before that, the stirring of events in the cauldron of Europe created forces which brought him here, and long before that there were other events which in turn created their successors. As seeds are carried on the wind to sprout and grow into new plants, so individuals are carried on the currents of historical movements to begin a new life in a new location.

It should be realized that, as John Bach MacMaster first pointed out so trenchantly when he named his major work "The History of the People of the United States," history is not the story of individuals, but the movement of masses of individuals. No single tree grew, but a forest. The country was not settled by Captain John Smith or William Penn; they were merely leaders whose claim to fame rests upon the fact that millions of no-names decided to build a home in a new land which they too had believed in. American Jewish history is not the story of Asser Levy or Haym Salomon or Judah P. Benjamin or Rebecca Gratz. They were but a few of many. And it is the many whose story we seek. This is basic in American Jewish history, as it is in all history.

The prelude to the history of the Jews in America is really the history of civilization before that time, but the year 1492 can serve as a point of entry into that continuous stream. Everybody knows the significance of that date in the history of America, but not too many realize its significance for the Jews of the United States. The last day of March, 1492, Ferdinand

3

and Isabella signed the order expelling the great and cultured Jewish community from Spain; and three weeks later they granted letters patent to Christopher Columbus for his voyage of exploration to the Indies. The Jews of Spain were forced to find new homes and new ways of life; and Columbus discovered not the Indies, but America.

Many of the Spanish Jews became Christians, either tentatively or irrevocably. Columbus himself is said by some historians to have come from such a family. Gabriel Sanchez and Luis de Santangel, who obtained for Columbus the financial backing he needed, were certainly among them. And another, Luis de Torres, commanded the first landing party to set foot on the shores of the new world. Many others fled to Portugal, whence, as part of the marriage agreement between Manuel of Portugal and a daughter of the implacable sovereigns of Spain, they were expelled five years later.

A vast, confused movement of harassed people began, which sent as refugees to Italy, Africa and the Ottoman Empire the once prosperous and highly cultured Jews of the Iberian peninsula. Even those who remained as Marranos, or crypto-Jews, were not safe from the Inquisition. A number, believing that their safety was in direct proportion to their distance from the European centers of that dreadful instrument of the Church, sailed away at the very beginning of the sixteenth century and helped establish the new Portuguese colony of Brazil. Other Marranos sought safety in northern lands, particularly the Netherlands, then still a province of Spain, but uneasy under her yoke and at least some distance from the somber dread of the Escorial. A shifting and reshifting was taking place, an upheaval and a resettlement.

At almost the same time another mass movement of Jews was going on. France and England had long since expelled those who had lived there for centuries before. In Germany some communities struggled on through a tenuous existence, always subject to restrictive laws, periodically attacked by the straggling troops and camp-followers of successive crusades, ever at the mercy of frenzied religious fanatics, never safe and never secure. The end of the fifteenth century saw a new eruption of intense anti-Semitism. The false report of the ritual murder of Simon of Trent sowed fresh seeds of hate; the newly discovered art of printing gave wide circulation to old and new polemics against the Jews. Martin Luther, at first friendly, and then bitterly hostile when his pleas for conversion failed, added fuel to the fire. There were new restrictions and new expulsions, and many old German Jewish communities dissolved.

But there was hope for them in the east. In Poland, beginning with Casimir the Great in the fourteenth century, under liberal rulers and a nobility which found them useful, a small number of Jewish traders grew slowly, and then at an increasingly rapid pace, into a great community. More and more German and Bohemian Jews found opportunity, the possibility of earning a livelihood, and freedom to establish synagogues and schools in Poland and its sister principality, Lithuania. It is estimated that the number of Jews in that area grew from 50,000 to 500,000 during the period between 1501 and 1648. It became the largest Jewish community in the world.

Then the kaleidoscope of history shifted, and a new pattern emerged. The Dutch, converted to the new Protestantism, rebelled against Spain, and, finding the Marranos natural allies in their fight for freedom, granted them the right to worship openly as Jews. When the Netherlands was free, a new Jewish community blossomed in Amsterdam. And suddenly, the Marranos of Brazil found that they too were affected by this, for in 1630 the Dutch, at the height of their mercantile expansion, conquered the northern captaincies of Brazil.

There had been Jews, but no Jewish life, in Brazil for over a hundred years. When the Dutch came, they brought a bill of rights, approved by the States-General for such colonies in West India as had been or were to be conquered, which promised that "the liberties of Spaniards, Portuguese and natives, were they Roman Catholics or Jews, will be respected."

As a result most of the Brazilian Marranos shed the forced trappings of their Christianity, and, even more important, several hundred families of descendants of Sephardic Jews who had found asylum in Holland over a century before migrated to the new colony. A large Jewish community—larger than any that would appear again in America for a century and a half—flowered into being.

However, it was only a brief lull in the storm. In 1654 the Portuguese won back Brazil. The same terms were offered the Jews as were granted the Dutch: they had three months to leave the country, or become subject to Portuguese rule—and the

Inquisition. Again there began a flow of Jews, back to Holland, and for the first time in sizable numbers to Dutch Guiana and up through the West Indies, seeking a place to settle and live and work. A small group of these refugees, after having left Recife, were captured by a Spanish ship, which fortunately for them was in turn captured by a French frigate, the *St. Charles.* Finally, in September, 1654, it landed and stranded these penniless fugitives in New Amsterdam.

They were the twenty-three who formed the first Jewish community in the United States. Others, the flotsam and jetsam of the Brazilian settlement, followed them, some going to flourishing Newport in liberal Rhode Island, some stopping off at Surinam or Curaçao or Jamaica, others scattering as individuals along the shores and islands of British America and the West Indies. They were mostly small traders, only a tiny handful succeeding in any worldly sense, but they gradually won themselves a home, tolerance, and eventually rights and privileges too. They organized synagogues following the Sephardic rite where they existed in numbers sufficient to maintain them, but much of their lives was spent trading and travelling far from a *minyan,* so that by necessity among Christians they could not live the lives of the historic religious, scholarly Jew. In all of America there were very, very few Jews by the end of the seventeenth century.

Meanwhile, tragedy had struck in Poland. An uprising of the Cossacks in 1648 threw that land into turmoil, and one war succeeded another, the only common features of which were that, no matter who was fighting whom or for what reason, they all killed Jews. Pogroms and new restrictions weighed heavily on what had been a flourishing Jewish community. Once more a movement started westward, and stragglers from the east gravitated to those places where the Spanish and Portuguese Jews had found havens. Holland was the choicest refuge, for Amsterdam was the richest Jewish community of Europe, but soon under Cromwell the back door of England was opened. At first the Sephardic merchants and then a steady, if small, stream of Jews from Germany and Poland began to settle there. A new flow and a new route opened up. From Poland to Germany—where old communities like Frankfurt, Worms and Hamburg were augmented, and new settlements begun where the authorities begrudgingly granted permission—from Germany to Hol-

land, from Holland to England, from England to America—one
by one, and but rarely family by family—stopping a generation
or two on the way—thousands of Jews from the troubled east
headed west.

After the first wave of Jews of Iberian extraction settled here,
there was little pressure on them to emigrate in numbers from
Europe, for by 1700 they were successfully and prosperously
established in Amsterdam and London and Hamburg. From that
time on comparatively few Sephardim crossed the ocean. On
the other hand, the continued chaos in Poland, the War of the
Austrian Succession, and the aggressive progress of Prussia
through Central Europe kept pushing the uneasy Jews of the
east westward; and in increasing numbers they made their way
to the American frontier: the Levys, the Cohens, and the Isaacs
of New York, the Gratzes and the Franks of Philadelphia, the
Harts of Canada, the Myers of Charleston, and the Sheftalls of
Savannah. It is curious that before American Jewish history
began to be written there had already grown up a myth of the
predominance of Spanish and Portuguese Jews in colonial America. As a matter of fact, by the time of the Revolution there
were far more Ashkenazic Jews in North America than Sephardim.

Yet the myth was based on a germ of truth. All the earliest
congregations of America used the Sephardic ritual, and it was
not until 1795 that the first Ashkenazic synagogue was founded
in Philadelphia. However, the reason is clear. The New York
synagogue and the Newport synagogue were actually founded
by men of Sephardic ancestral heritage, and those who followed
them were not inclined to argue ritualistic points. They accepted
what was there. More important, and as was the case with
Mikveh Israel in Philadelphia, there was a social eclat attached
to Sephardic practice and Sephardic society. In Amsterdam and
in London, through which most of the early immigrants passed,
the descendants of the Marranos were the leaders of the community, the established, the cultured, the integrated Jews.

So it was that in America it seemed better to begin at this level
of society, at least as far as form of worship was concerned, and
throughout the country Sephardic synagogues were joined and
founded by Yiddish-speaking Jews.

The overwhelming majority of the Jews of the United States
came from the same background. The whole pattern of im-

migration has not only been the same, but has been essentially formed by the same people from the same vast reservoir of misery and persecution. The English and Dutch Jews who came to this country in the eighteenth century were the sons or grandsons of Polish Jews, who themselves were probably the sons or grandsons of German Jews, who may well have been descendants of English Jews who had been expelled from England in 1290. It is significant that Sigmund Freud, professionally conscious of the unconscious, who was himself of Lithuanian ancestry, traced his line back to the Rhineland in a similar fashion.

The story of Jewish immigration to the United States is the story of all immigration here. Irishmen, Italians, and Jews all fled from impossible economic conditions. Puritans, Quakers, and Jews all fled religious persecution. The Merchants of the Virginia Company, the Dutch of New Amsterdam, and Jews all sought the adventure and promise of untapped resources and unexplored land. And they came in the same pattern. It was usually a young, unmarried man who first left a village or a family to make his way in the new world. After he was settled, financée, brothers, father, aunts, and grandparents followed. That is how our country was populated.

In the early part of the nineteenth century, during the period of reaction and absolutism which followed the Napoleonic Wars, Jews, who had hoped that the egalitarian principles of the French Revolution heralded a bright, new world freed from oppression, fled to a land where liberty was a fact. In the middle of the century it was the stern crushing of the liberal uprisings of 1848 which sped them westward. In the 1880s it was no longer ideals which stimulated emigration, but the vicious pogroms in Russia, Poland and Rumania which made resettlement no longer a choice but a necessity. And finally, only twenty years ago, Nazi racism, unloosed on the once proud Jews of Germany, drove those who could leave to seek asylum where they could. Each reactionary wave of history has thrown the people it engulfed upon our shores, and these successive waves, from the days of Ferdinand and Isabella to those of Hitler, built the American Jewish community. These are the citizens of the United States. Famines, wars, tyrants, poverty, misery, and hope sent them here, and sent them in great movements of masses, many different people at different times, impelled by forces beyond their control, to seek a common goal.

1

The Earliest Days under Dutch and English Rule

IN 1654, when the refugee Jews from Brazil landed in New Amsterdam, there were only a few Swedish trading posts along the Delaware River. Except for some log-cabins nestling up to their walls, these were simply wooden forts for protection against hostile Indians and enemy traders and for the storage of trade goods. Most of the Indians were comparatively friendly, and the vast hinterland held a rich potential of furs and lumber and other exports which would enrich a European motherland. The Dutch, having consolidated their foothold on Manhattan Island and having expanded their trade north up the Hudson, began to look for new territories to exploit, and the commercial potentials of the Delaware posts and the weakness of the Swedish forces there invited conquest. So, in 1655, in a bold foray up the Delaware, the Dutch seized control of the river, and brought New Sweden within their orbit.

While the struggle for the trade to the south was going on, the Jews of New Amsterdam were engaged in their own struggle with the dictatorial, peg-legged Peter Stuyvesant. The governor did not want them to settle in his little town, and, although they had no money and no place to go, he at first refused them permission to stay. But the Jews were desperate, and they appealed over Stuyvesant's head to his superiors of the Dutch West India Company in Amsterdam, who, after the

9

intercession of resident Jewish stockholders, granted their plea for asylum. It was a bitter Stuyvesant who was forced to obey the orders which came from Holland and let them stay, but thereafter he continued to try to restrict their lives and their activities. Each request for a privilege, which other inhabitants freely exercised, was at first refused; each refusal was appealed to Holland; and each time the governor's intolerant decision was countermanded.[1]

One of these rights, and an important one for people struggling to make a living in a frontier land, was that of carrying on trade. Claiming that under the instructions of February 15, 1655, they had received consent from the Directors of the West India Company to travel, trade and reside, and enjoy the same privileges as other inhabitants, three Jews, Abraham de Lucena, Salvador Dandrada, and Jacob Cohen, requested permission to "travel and trade on the South River of New Netherland," as the Delaware was then known.[2] Stuyvesant and his Council, stubborn in their intolerance, refused the request, but did say that the Jews could send two persons to the South River to dispose of stock they had already shipped there in the hope that they would be allowed to barter it for furs.

Therefore, to liquidate their affairs the three traders late in 1655 sent south two of their co-religionists, Isaac Israel and Isaac Cardoso.[3] They were the first Jews known to have come to the Delaware River Valley; but, since their task was neither happy nor profitable, it may be assumed that their stay was short. They were at Fort Casimir, near the present Newcastle, Delaware, in December when a treaty with the Indians was being negotiated whereby the natives would get more goods for the furs they sold the traders. Israel and Cardoso, who after all were ending a venture and had been denied permission to continue trading, refused to sign it. This displeased Jean Paul Jacquet, the Dutch vice-governor of the Delaware, who wrote they "refused to give their consent and prepared to leave the river and give up their trade, rather than to assist, with other good inhabitants, in maintaining the peace of this highway."[4] Yet, he must have known it was not their choice.

The Directors of the West India Company at home had a more tolerant and more practical attitude towards the Jews than did their governor abroad. They wanted to encourage any hardy souls, Jews or non-Jews, who would brave the wilderness for the greater increase of trade, and so once again, on June 14, 1656, they noted that they had "seen and learned with displeasure" what Stuyvesant had done, and ordered him to permit the Jews, along with the other residents of the Dutch colony, to trade in the rich South River region.[5] This official ruling must have been anticipated, for on March 25, 1656, Joseph d'Acosta was granted permission to send goods for trade down to the Delaware,[6] and in June of the same year Isaac Israel was back at Fort Casimir, engaged in a dispute about some brandy, beaver skins, and cheese paid to Captain Jan Flamman for bringing Israel and his goods to the South River.[7] From then on Jews had free access to the southern territory.

Records of this early period are sparse, and while it may be assumed that the Jews of New Amsterdam took full advantage of the opportunity given them, only a few of the names of those who did have been preserved. In 1657 Isaac Masa (also spelled Mesa and Mara), "a Jew," signed an Indian treaty at Fort Casimir which established fair prices for trade, and a month later appeared before Jacquet and his Council to complain that one Jan Schaggen had sold him a hogshead of tobacco, which, contrary to contract, turned out to be of such inferior quality as to be unmarketable.[8] It is one of the ironies of history that accounts of trouble which entered the records of courts of law were preserved as official documents, whereas those of profitable ventures and amicable intercourse have disappeared in the dust of the past.

It is possible that some of these Jews, or others, who left no trace behind them, stopped not only at the main fort, but came further up the river to the little settlement at Wicaco. If they did so, they were the first Jews to land at Philadelphia; for Wicaco, a tiny group of cabins along the river, near where Old Swedes' Church is today, was the beginning of what later grew into Penn's city. It is intriguing to read that in 1663 "the Honourable Councillor Israel" was in charge of the trading-post at Passayunk.[9] This may have been Isaac Israel the Jew, but since Israel was a last name not uncommon among non-Jews in early Pennsylvania, there is no certainty it was he. If it were, he would have been the first Jew to hold office in the area, and the first Jew to have been in what is now Philadelphia.

Although the invasion of the British, who wrested New Amsterdam from the Dutch in 1664 and renamed it New York, was accompanied by the usual deaths and depredations of war in the Delaware Valley, it also brought a further guarantee of tolerance. A group of Dutch Mennonites, who had set up a community on the banks of the Horekill in Delaware County two years before, which excluded from it "all intractible people—such as those in communion with the Roman See; Usurious Jews; English stiff-necked Quakers; Puritans; foolhardy believers in the Millennium; and obstinate modern pretenders to revelation,—"[10] was wiped out in the name of progress. Furthermore, Sir Robert Carr, the British commander on the Delaware, in accordance with orders from the government at home, declared that "all people shall enjoy the liberty of their conscience in Church discipline as formerly."[11] The transition from Dutch to English rule presented no problem to the Jews. As in New York, under whose jurisdiction it was, the Delaware River region was to be open to all persons who behaved themselves.[12]

It was with the mixed feelings of a Moses leading his followers to a land of promise, and of a land speculator anxious to look at his unknown property, that William Penn sailed for Pennsylvania in 1682. Just the year before he had received a grant of vast, unexplored land, including what had formerly been New Sweden, from Charles II to whom his father, Admiral Sir William Penn, had once lent a large sum of money. To William the son, the grant offered an opportunity to build a new colony where tolerance and freedom, within the limits of his age's concept of freedom, would enable industrious, law-abiding men to flourish in happiness and prosperity and peace.

William Penn was a Quaker, and as such had suffered the rigors of imprisonment for his unorthodox belief; for in late seventeenth-century England all non-conformist creeds were held to be dangerous to the state. The charter and the laws and liberties under which the new province was to be administered were the most liberal ones that had been framed up to that time; but it must be remembered that liberalism in Stuart days was something less than liberalism a century later, and much less than today. Although liberty of conscience was written into the law, which recognized the right of free worship, freemen—the only ones who could vote and hold office—had to own property and profess faith in Jesus Christ.[13]

The question of what treatment Jews would receive in Pennsylvania probably never entered Penn's head, but he was deeply interested in them from a theological point of view. His mentor, George Fox, the founder of the Society of Friends, had written two missionary tracts, *A Visitation to the Jews*, and *A Looking-Glass for the Jews*,[14] which urged those people to see the error of their ways and accept the divinity of Jesus, and Penn would have shared his leader's sympathetic concern for their salvation. As a religious man and himself a prolific writer of theological treatises, he respected the Jews' background, and at one time suggested a Hebraic frame of government for his province.[15] Yet he could not accept what he interpreted as their present stubbornness.

He was certainly influenced by the contemporary messianic interest in the conversion of Jews; for some British visionaries believed that England was destined to be the New Jerusalem, and that if the Jews of the world were gathered there and as a body accepted Christianity, the millennium would come. This mystic idea was further strengthened by the belief, held by many throughout Europe, that the Indians of America were the lost ten tribes of Israel.[16] This theory was one that many in Pennsylvania would have accepted, for Gabriel Thomas in *An Historical and Geographical Account of Pennsylvania*, published in London in 1698 as a kind of promotional pamphlet to attract settlers to the new province, wrote:

The Natives, or first Inhabitants of this Country in their Original, are suppos'd by most People to have been of the Ten Scattered Tribes, for they resemble the Jews very much in the Make of their Persons, and Tincture of their Complexions; they observe New Moons, they offer their first Fruits to a Maneto, or suppos'd Deity, whereof they have two, one, as they fansie, above (good,) another below (bad,) and have a kind of Feast of Tabernacles, laying their Altars upon Twelve Stones, observe a sort of Mourning twelve Months, Customs of Women, and many other Rites to be toucht (here) rather than dwelt upon . . .[17]

Whether Penn's avowed intent to deal honestly with the Indians was a tribute to their supposed distinguished ancestry, or reflected merely his Quaker ideals and the sound principle that in peace trade could prosper, is an unanswerable question. But his determination to permit all kinds of people to settle on his lands was effectively carried out in practice.

From the few caves built along the Delaware on the site of the City of Philadelphia, still unsurveyed in 1682, the town grew rapidly into a fair, neatly laid out, green city of stocky, red-brick houses. At first the new settlers were predominantly

Quakers; soon, however, a large group of German pietists came to the colony and settled in Germantown. The records show that in the early days there were also inhabitants of French, Dutch, Scotch-Irish, Danish, Swedish and Finnish origin.

As the resources of the land were exploited and as trade began to grow, Philadelphia spread and prospered. There was an atmosphere of easy tolerance which looked with favor on anyone who lived honestly, worked hard, and succeeded by the sweat of his brow or the ingenuity of his brain. It is likely that there were Jews here during these first two decades of Pennsylvania history, but no written record of their presence survives. The earliest possible evidence of a Jew in Philadelphia is an entry in the ledger of William Trent, one of the leading merchants of the city, of an account with a Jonas Aaron, or Aarons, in 1703.[18] Nothing is known about Aaron, not even positively that he was a Jew; for in this era when biblical names, both first and last names, were common, it is difficult to tell, without additional information, whether a particular name was borne by a Jew or a Christian.

While it had long been supposed that individual Jews had been in Philadelphia, staying perhaps days, weeks or months, to transact their normal business in the early decades of the eighteenth century, only recently has proof of their presence been discovered. In the old receipt book of the Quaker merchant, Thomas Coates, who had come over with Penn when his colony was first established, are the records of six Jews from New York and the West Indies who were in the city between 1706 and 1719.[19] On April 27, 1706, Joseph Monteyro[20] acknowledged the receipt of £10.10.5 "for a hogshead of mellassoz" which he had sold to Coates; in June, still in Philadelphia, he was paid the same sum for more molasses; and in July he sold the Philadelphian a bag of cotton. He was back in town early the next spring, and then his dealings with Coates seem to have stopped.

A second Jew, Eleazer Valverde, from Barbados[21] was in Coates' counting-house late in 1706; two years later a third, Samuel Peres,[22] received from the Quaker full payment for a bag of cotton and all his other accounts; and in August, 1714, Jacob Pinedo[23] was in town. A much more important visitor was Abraham Haim de Lucena,[24] the minister of Shearith Israel in New York, who in addition to his religious duties was actively engaged in the career of a busy merchant. He came down from New York eight times from the beginning of 1715 until the middle of 1719. At one time he got in trouble with the authorities, because on October 28, 1718, he petitioned the Pennsylvania Council seeking the return of goods seized by officers for non-entry and praying for relief "on account of his poverty and numerous family."[25] On his last recorded trip he probably traveled with his friend Daniel Gomez, whose father was the founder of the largest and most influential family in the Jewish community of New York during the eighteenth century and whose brother Mordecai was married to de Lucena's daughter.[26] Gomez, who had also been doing business with Coates for four years, received the settlement of his account just a week before de Lucena did. It is a curious coincidence that Daniel Gomez, one of the first Jews to come regularly to Philadelphia, came again, then an old man, as a refugee from the British during the Revolution. With other patriotic New Yorkers he fled to the safety of an American-held city, and there in 1780 he died and was buried in the cemetery of Mikveh Israel.

Scattered records of trade are all there is to chronicle about Jews in Philadelphia during its early days; but they do show that merchants from established Jewish communities in British America were accustomed to visit the city. No doubt there are similar entries in other, similar ledgers, still unread, in various archives. These meager facts throw some light upon the attitude of non-Jews towards Jewish merchants. Philadelphia was essentially a merchant town, and ships from its docks plied regularly to other trade centers along the coast, in the West Indies, and in Europe. In these older ports Jewish merchants were to be found, and trade with them was as usual and as little to be commented on as trade with any other merchants. Mercantilism had no time for prejudice.

An example of the esteem in which some Jews were held by their non-Jewish correspondents can be seen in a letter of the Philadelphia merchant Jonathan Dickinson, the account of whose providential rescue after being shipwrecked on the coast of Florida while coming from Jamaica became one of the more popular colonial American tales of adventure.[27] Dickinson did business with a number of Jamaican Jews,[28] but he had particular regard for the venerable Moses Jeshurun Cardoso.[29] When late in 1719 Cardoso sent a Negro slave, Sarah, to Dickinson in Philadelphia to sell, the Philadelphia merchant, "Calling to mind ye Date of Acquaintance, Being more yn forty years past, thy Character and Age," promised to do everything he could in Cardoso's interest, and did, even to supplying Sarah with warm clothes so that her health would not suffer during the cold Pennsylvania winter.[30] Jews were no strangers to Philadelphians even before Jews settled permanently in the city.

Nor were their language, religion, and rites unknown in Penn's city. Much has been written about the study of Hebrew by the clerics of New England; little about the considerable interest of intelligent laymen in that ancient tongue. In Virginia the landed gentleman, William Byrd of Westover, began each day's entry in his diary, with almost monotonous repetition, "I rose at 7 o'clock and read a chapter in Hebrew and 200 verses in Homer's *Odyssey*."[31] But even more interesting was the considerable study which Penn's agent in Pennsylvania, James Logan,[32] devoted to the Hebrew language, Jewish history and Jewish rites and customs. During almost the whole first half of the eighteenth century he was the most influential man in Pennsylvania, and certainly the most learned. A Quaker, born in Ireland, Logan was living in Bristol with his father who had moved there to take charge of a Friend's school, when Penn set out for his second visit to Pennsylvania in 1699. Penn urged young Logan to accompany him as his secretary, and he went.

One of the most capable men in the province, Logan was also Penn's most faithful friend and personal agent. He was soon appointed Secretary of the Province, and served in that key post from 1701 to 1717. At first a clerk to the Governor's Council, within a year he was made a voting member. Between 1736 and 1738, he served, in the absence of a governor, as chief executive of the Province. He was elected Mayor of Philadelphia, commissioned as a judge of the Court of Common Pleas, and in 1731 appointed chief-justice of the Supreme Court. Logan was a busy executive and administrator. He made a fortune in land investment and in trade with the Indians. But he was also an intellectual with insatiable curiosity.

How he acquired the knowledge he did seems a miracle to our less encyclopaedic minds and our more hurried times. He was a jurist whose charges to juries were held in such high repute that Franklin printed one of them. He was a botanist, a friend of John Bartram, and the writer of a pioneer work on the fertilization of corn. He was an astronomer who bought an unfinished work of Halley and worked out the incomplete tables himself. He was a mathematician who ordered Newton's *Principia* when it was a novelty, and made his own notes and corrections. And he was a linguist. Latin and Greek of course he had acquired in grammar school, and he kept them up so that he was able to write both languages with astonishing fluency. French and Spanish he picked up from reading with the help of grammars and dictionaries. Then came Hebrew.

He had gotten the rudiments of the language from his father at the Bristol school, but there was no one in Philadelphia who could teach him the advanced knowledge he sought. Hebrew had been a required language at theological seminaries like Harvard for years, but no such seminary existed in Philadelphia at the time. And it was required of prospective clergymen for the same reason that Logan wanted to learn it. It was the language of the Bible, the language behind the King James version, behind the Vulgate, behind the Septuagint. For a religious man, for an intellectually curious one—and Logan was both—what more fascinating subject could there be?

So Logan began studying Hebrew seriously. He bought himself the dictionaries, grammars and syntaxes of Buxtorf,[33] Leusden,[34] Robertson[35] and others, and pored over them, studying the alphabet, learning how to read and write the letters, acquiring a vocabulary and the syntax, and finally learning how to read and write in sentences.

He bought himself Hebrew Bibles and Hebrew prayerbooks, and read them and made notes in them. When he was more fluent, he added a *Shulhan Arukh*[36] and the great six-volume edition of the Mishna with the Maimonides and Bertinoro commentaries.[37] In fact, Logan gathered together in Philadelphia in the first half of the eighteenth century one of the largest collections of Hebraica which existed in frontier America.[38] It was certainly the best collection that a private person owned outside academic halls, and remained so for many years.

These volumes, together with Logan's whole library which once rested in Stenton, his large house in the middle of woods and pastures on the fringe of the section of the city which bears his name, are now in the Loganian Library, held in trust since 1792 by the Library Company of Philadelphia. In that collection too, is the most compelling evidence of Logan's real mastery and interest in the language, a little note-book in which he compiled, in beautifully formed Hebrew letters, a Bible vocabulary, setting down each word, the location in the text, its meaning in Latin, and its Hebrew root.[39]

There is no doubt that the Hebrew language was one of his real interests. In 1724, he wrote to his friend Thomas Story in England that his daughter Sally was industrious with the needle,

but is this moment at the table with me (being first day [Sunday] afternoon and her mother abroad) reading the 34th Psalm in Hebrew, the letters of which she learned very perfectly in less than 2 hours time, an experiment I made of her capacity only for my Diversion, tho' I never design to give her that or any other learned Language unless the French be accounted such.[40]

The interest in Hebrew was passed on, and of course was picked up by others—possibly through Logan or independently. Through his books, also in the Library Company, we know that Isaac Norris, Jr., who married Sally Logan, was somewhat learned in the language. A noble sixteenth-century Hebrew printing of the book of *Isaiah* has his Latin version written on interleaved pages, and a handsome folio Hebrew Bible was also his.[41] This interest was important, for a respect for the language of the people of the Book went far towards creating an acceptance and respect for the people themselves in this new, frontier colony.

One of the first of these to come and settle down was Isaac Miranda, of whom more records have survived than of any other Jew who lived in Philadelphia in the first quarter of the eighteenth century. It is significant that, although born a Jew, he had become a Christian, thereby acting in accordance with a pattern that had been and was to be repeated over and over again in the history of the United States, and of the world.

A Jew, alone and without family ties, coming into a place where there were no, or at best extremely few, other Jews, frequently found it both difficult and impractical to maintain his traditional religious practices. There was no *minyan* for services; there was no *kosher* meat; there were no fellow Jews to look askance at lapses.

Many of these lonely individuals, like Miranda, formally abandoned their Judaism; life for them was easier so. Others never accepted baptism, but married non-Jewish wives—there were no Jewish women about, and these men had the normal urges for wives, families, and homes—and by default, as it were, permitted their children to grow up in their mother's faith, not realizing that the Talmud had long ago decided that a maternal faith had precedence.

Isaac Miranda, said to have come from Italy, arrived in Philadelphia sometime between 1710 and 1715. He entered the Indian trade, which James Logan, not long before had learned was the most profitable business in Pennsylvania, and settled in the heart of the Indian country, on Conoy Creek, now Lancaster County, before the organization of the town of Lancaster.[42] That he became successful is evidenced by an entry in the account book of Thomas Chalkley,[43] one of the great early Quaker merchants of Philadelphia, which shows that in 1720 Miranda bought himself a pair of silver candlesticks with a pair of snuffers and a stand for them. It is amusing to read the record of one of his ventures to gain that wealth. When Chalkley shipped a cargo "on board ye Trine Hope for Antigua May 24, 1720," among many others who had part shares in the venture, Miranda is listed as owning "5 barrells of pork."

Up the ladder he climbed, and in 1723 he was sent by the Governor to negotiate some arrangement in connection with a mine beyond the Susquehanna.[44] Either under orders or anxious to prove himself a capable agent, he apparently negotiated contrary to the interests of other settlers.

But they had a friend in James Logan, and he, factually and without malice, referring to Miranda as "an apostate Jew or fashionable Christian," warned a correspondent against his actions. Exactly what he had done, or what resulted, the records do not show. Again, seven years later, there were complaints on the frontier against his treatment of the Indians,[45] but even in Pennsylvania where Penn had thought he had established a pattern of fairness and honesty towards the original owners of all the land, most Indian trade was based upon the gullibility and childish wants of the primitive people, who happily gave valuable furs for mirrors and rum and blankets.

Apparently Miranda traded as hard and as shrewdly as his fellows on a wild frontier; perhaps because of this he gained a measure of respect. In 1727 he was an "Agent to Receive and Collect the Perquisites and Rights of Admiralty,"[46] and in July of that year he was named deputy judge of the Court of Vice-

Admiralty of the Province of Pennsylvania.[47] He was the first "Jew" to hold office in the Province; it should be remembered that, although he could take the oath of office on the faith of a true Christian, his contemporaries continued to refer to him by his origin.

But his tenure of office was short, for before the end of the year he was dismissed because he refused to carry out the orders of his superior, the Vice-Admiralty judge, Joseph Brown, in a case which seems to have involved corruption.

Perhaps his acquaintance with James Logan on a more personal level dates from this time, for it was about then that Logan secured from him several books, one a *Sepher haGilgulim*,[48] a mystic work on the *Zohar*, and the other a Spanish manuscript to which were added Portuguese poems in memory of Jewish martyrs of the Inquisition.[49] On a fly-leaf of the latter Logan wrote:

This is a Dialogue between a Jewish Doctr or Rabbi and a Christian about the Christian Religion composed (I think in Morocco) in Spanish by the Jew from whence we may certainly conclude how ye dispute is made to issue. It has divers Singularities in it and especially of the Jewish nations wch render it a Curiosity worth preserving. It belonged to Isaac Miranda a Jew by Education, who tore out the first pages or first twelve leaves of it. I read it over in 1735.

Logan was obviously more interested in the fact that he had had a Jewish education than that he had become a Christian. Christians he saw every day, but a Jew, a man who knew Hebrew, was, no matter his character or personality, a man who could add fuel to Logan's mental fires.

Miranda's books give evidence of his cultured Jewish background. His desire for social advancement comes to the fore in his will,[50] which left to his heirs two houses in Philadelphia, silver plate, furniture, books, a farm in Lancaster County, and several thousand acres of land, but which made special and liberal provision for young James Hamilton, the son of the great freedom-of-the-press lawyer, Andrew Hamilton, if that coming young man would marry his daughter, Mary Miranda. James Hamilton became lieutenant-governor of Pennsylvania, but he did not marry Mary.

If the first Jew the early Pennsylvanians got to know was both fashionable and an apostate, they at least heard of others who were neither. It is surprising how many references to Jews throughout the world occur in the *American Weekly Mercury*, the first Philadelphia newspaper.[51] Most of them were incidental, such as the gruesome account of "Mr. Gomez the Jew," the owner of a large part of the cargo of the *Greyhound*, out of New York, who was killed and cut up into quarters by the Spaniards in Cuba when the ship put into a port there. He was Jacob, the brother of Daniel Gomez, who had been doing business in Philadelphia some years before. Of great importance—there were still no newspapers in New York then—was the advertisement carried in the issue of October 17, 1723, of the school of Mr. John Walton, late of Yale College, which although established on Broad Street, near the Exchange, in New York, sought students from Philadelphia for courses including not only the three Rs, but "the Greek and Hebrew Grammars."

This is the earliest notice of the teaching of Hebrew made in Philadelphia, albeit the course was given in New York, and it was printed at the very same time that the famous convert Judah Monis was making his debut as Professor of Hebrew at Harvard.[52]

The undercurrent of popular interest in Hebraic culture was a continuing feature of colonial life. As early as 1693 Hebrew words had appeared in a book printed by William Bradford,[53] the pioneer printer of both Pennsylvania and New York; and Samuel Keimer, for whom Franklin worked when he first came to this city, in his almanac, A *Compleat Ephemeris for the Year of Christ 1726*, printed a "brief introduction towards learning the Hebrew and other Tongues."[54] This included a full Hebrew alphabet, the first to be published in Philadelphia. It has been claimed, because he wore a full beard and is said to have observed the Sabbath on Saturday, that Keimer was a Jew.[55] It is now definitely known that he was a communicant of the Church of England, however eccentric his appearance or observances may have been. Yet, it is interesting that, in a publication intended for so wide and so popular a circulation as an almanac, a Philadelphia printer in the 1720s would have thought it of sufficient general interest to print a Hebrew alphabet, together with the fundamental rules of Hebrew pronunciation.

2

The Beginnings of a Philadelphia Jewish Community

PHILADELPHIA in the 1730s was already a city of considerable size and importance. Thousands of immigrants, chiefly from England but also from other European countries, were year after year making the perilous journey from the Old World to the young and welcoming metropolis, whose economic foundations were rooted in its fertile soil and the rich resources under its control, and whose commerce was expanding rapidly. As in all times economic prosperity acted like a magnet. Intellectual progress too was being made through the contributions of Benjamin Franklin, who had just set up his own press, and was beginning to make his mark in the political life of Pennsylvania.

He and his friends of the Junto had in 1731 organized the first subscription library in America. Two newspapers, one of them his own provocative *Pennsylvania Gazette*, were appearing at least once a week. The Quakers were losing their numerical strength, and the conformist Protestants were becoming predominant. The city with its safe tidewater port was acting as a funnel for goods from the vast hinterland of Pennsylvania, and the number of ships loading at its docks was increasing from month to month. It had long since ceased to be a collection of huts in a wilderness; its population was now nearly 13,000.

To this growing center of trade and population Nathan Levy came as early as 1735, for on July 1st of that year he supplied his ship *Dispatch* with beer from a brewery in which Isaac Norris was a partner. He seems to have made yearly trips; the following July he put Norris beer aboard the *Abbot*. Levy must have liked what he saw of Philadelphia, and some time in 1737 he settled there permanently with his family and his brother Isaac.[1] He had made the "voyage" from New York where he had been born in 1704 and where his father, Moses Levy, was an established merchant, long active in the Jewish community and in 1730 an officer of Congregation Shearith Israel. From him Nathan had received both his business and his religious training. The year he arrived Franklin reported a news item from Germany to the effect that "the Jews there are in great consternation," for in ten days they were to be banished from Berlin.[2]

From Germany the elder Levy had earlier taken the already familiar route to London, remaining there awhile before proceeding to New York. Indeed, the tales of horror reported in the Franklin press during the 1730s[3] were cause enough to force others to undertake the same long journey. In the fall of the same year that Levy arrived, Franklin wrote with more than casual interest about Jews, not the comparatively few whom the German traveler to America, Von Reck, reported seeing,[4] but those of antiquity. An article in the *Pennsylvania Gazette* read: "The Jews were acquainted with several Arts and Sciences long e're the Romans became a People, or the Greeks were known among the Nations". Continuing his lengthy disquisition on Saul and David, he reflected:

If the Greeks had been acquainted with the Songs of Moses . . . or the Romans had ever known the Odes of David . . . they would never have spoke of the Jews with so much Contempt, as a rude and barbarous People; at least I am persuaded their Poets would have conceived a much better Opinion of them, when they found them so far exceed anything that their own Nations had ever produced. I believe I might fairly challenge all the Antiquity of the Heathens, to present us with an Ode of more beautiful Sentiments, and greater Elegancy than this Lamentation over Saul and Jonathan . . . there is scarce anything of God or Religion in it. David the mere Man was a sublime Poet, and God made him a Prophet.[5]

Such an article helped to create a sympathetic atmosphere in the Philadelphia to which the first Levys came, and soon thereafter they entered the hubbub of colonial trade. In Franklin's now musty and yellowed *Gazette* for January 3, 1738, we find the first documentary evidence of their activity: "A likely young Negroe Man to be sold by Nathan and Isaac Levy, fit for Town and Country."[6] Like other enterprising colonials they had located as close to the waterfront as possible. Their first address was "Front street, not far from Pemberton's Wharffe."

Colonial economics had its own specifications. In Pennsylvania slavery was never popular—in fact some of the Quakers, like Anthony Benezet, fulminated against it—but cheap labor was necessary and, where Negro slaves did not supply the need, redemptioners, or indentured servants, took their place. From 1730 to the end of the century the propaganda of ship-owners and their agents brought hundreds upon hundreds of redemptioners to Philadelphia. In the first years of their business the Levy brothers were frequent participants in the trade of placing servants with masters for a given number of years in payment of their passage; but, aside from the occasional sale of a Negro slave, the Levys never ventured as heavily in the slave trade as did other merchants along the Atlantic seaboard.[7]

By the summer of 1738, putting to good advantage the mercantile connections of the older New York Levy and his English associates, they were well on their way towards securing a firm business foothold. Yet before Nathan Levy had the opportunity to establish himself solidly, tragedy struck him, a tragedy which, though personal, influenced the religious establishment of the Jews in the city. One of his children died.

Life without the rituals of his religion was bearable for a Jew, if circumstances prevented his practise of them, but burial in unsanctified soil was not to be thought of. Hence it was that in many communities, before a synagogue—before any other community project—a Jewish cemetery was the first step towards religious identity. Levy, faced with the choice of burying his child in the cemetery of Christ Church or in the Strangers' Burying Ground, decided in a positive Jewish spirit to seek ground which could be called Jewish to cover his dear one's remains.

Consequently, on September 20, 1738, he made application for a private place apart in which to bury his child. His request was granted by the Proprietor, Thomas Penn, who permitted him to buy "a small piece of ground lying on the North

Side of Walnut Street," between Eighth and Ninth Streets, to be "enclosed with a Fence of Boards."[8] The little plot of ground was then in open country—for the built-up city had not yet eaten up the fields to the west—and there was buried the first Jew known to have died in Philadelphia.

It has been believed up to the present time that Levy first applied for a burial plot on Spruce Street between Eight and Ninth, but this did not take place until two years later, on September 25, 1740, when he was concerned, not with an emergency, but with the establishment of a permanent family cemetery.

Then, at the instruction of Thomas Penn, the official surveyor of the Province, Benjamin Eastburn, plotted a sketch for the now historic site on Spruce Street, the first piece of hallowed ground to be used by the community of Jews in Philadelphia.[9] It may be assumed that upon the purchase of this larger plot the body of the Levy child was reinterred there. In later years, what had been intended for private use became the Jewish communal cemetery.

The Levy brothers—Nathan and Isaac—worked hard at their business, and their four-year partnership brought them success. At least one other Jewish business man was on the scene. George Miranda, son of the "apostate" Isaac, was now a shopkeeper. He had returned from an expedition in Western Pennsylvania, trading with the Shawnee and Mingo Indians, to settle down to a quieter life on Philadelphia's Second Street, "over against the Sign of the George."[10] But the Levys were an economic rung above shopkeeper Miranda. They were merchants, and the title, "merchant," commanded an added respect which colonial semantics well recognized.

The scope of their activities is revealed in the local newspapers of the day. Philadelphia's two papers never had more than ten or twelve advertisements an issue, ranging from a few to twenty lines; but in many cases they contain the only surviving records of tradesmen, shopkeepers, merchants and ship movements. They were not designed for the city alone, but circulated in the backwoods and in contiguous and distant colonies, and this geographical distribution was kept in mind by the colonial entrepreneur when he bought his space.

All of this was familiar to the Levy brothers, and, as an advertisement in the *Pennsylvania Gazette* of August 31, 1738, shows, they offered what would appeal to a large clientele.

> *Just Arrived from London*
> *In the Brigt. Pennsylvania Packet,*
> *Henry Harley, Master*
> *Now Lying at Pemberton's Wharffe:*
>
> A Parcel of likely Servants, most part Tradesmen; whose Times are to be disposed of, by said Master, or Messrs. Nathan & Isaac Levy.
>
> Also, Imported in the said Vessel, and to be dispos'd of by said Levys, sundry Sorts of Goods, viz
>
> All Sorts of London Nails from 3d. to 30d. Saddlery Ware, Brass, Copper and Tin Ware, striped & plain India Blankets, rose Blankets, Ruggs, blue and red Duffields, long and short Bays, broad-Cloths, Strouds, half-Ticks, Kerseys & Plains, Druggets, Frize, Plush, felt Hats, star Gartering, Shot, and bar Lead, best Powder, best of Trunks, Copperrass, Alum, London Glew, Shalloons, Calimancoes, variety of Stuffs, Calicoes, Muslins, Iron Potts, and sundry Sorts of other Goods.

Dry goods of qualities and types now unknown, and hardware—the two colonial essentials—were their main stock, but they at one time offered "Very good Raisins" in a one-line advertisement[11] which suggests a willingness to try an untouched market. One could search for a long time to find another advertisement for raisins, an exotic commodity in 1740 Philadelphia.

That same year marked the arrival of two other New Yorkers, David Franks and his brother Moses, whose mother was Nathan Levy's aunt.[12] Like the Levys, they too were American-born, and had been reared in the Sephardic Congregation Shearith Israel by their father Jacob, an orthodox Jew, who—again like the Levys—had come to America from London, but stemmed from Germany or lands farther to the east. Levy, however, was David's senior by seventeen years, and was already an established merchant in 1740, so he became the teacher and guide in mercantile affairs to the Franks brothers. This pattern of help and guidance to newcomers became a regular part of Philadelphia Jewish life.

Neither the Levys nor the Franks had to be concerned with George II's Naturalization Act,[13] for they had been born British subjects. Unhampered by restrictions, the Franks brothers, like the Levys a few years earlier, established their own partnership. By the spring of 1741 they were conducting business "at their store at the widow Hannah Meredith's on Front Street,"[14] but their partnership was brief, and soon thereafter Nathan Levy and David Franks combined to form the first major Jewish company in Philadelphia.

Levy and Franks, their firm name, were both diligent and enterprising. Nathan Levy's English connections were very useful, but now they were further strengthened by Moses Franks, who set sail for London to join up with his older brother, Naphtali, who was already established there. A trusted agent in a foreign port could spell the difference between success and failure. He was responsible for selling the goods shipped to his care, and for buying the goods shipped back.

Colonial commerce was not without its difficulties. The scarcity of hard money—gold and silver coin—was a constant problem in the colony. Provincial paper was subject to fluctuation, and a Pennsylvania pound could be sold only at a discount in London. The need to establish an equitable rate of exchange was faced by the Philadelphia businessmen in the fall of 1742. Seventy-four merchants, shopkeepers and interested persons met with the object of establishing a standard rate of exchange for three years. Nathan Levy and David Franks were among them.[15] This constituted the first known participation of Jews in the general civic affairs of Philadelphia.

Meanwhile, the shipping interests of the firm expanded. Ships, hired or registered in their names, sailed regularly from Philadelphia to London and back. All these ships did not belong to Levy and Franks, but many certainly did, and some registrations specifically mentioned them as owners. For instance, on March 10, 1744, Nathan Levy and David Franks appear as owners of the schooner *Drake*, built in Philadelphia; in 1745 they are noted as co-owners of the *Sea Flower*, of 30 tons, built in Connecticut; for many years the well-known *Myrtilla*, "250 tons burden, 10 guns and 20 men," was registered in their name; and in 1746 and 1750 the ships *Richa* and *Phila*, carrying the name of Franks' sisters, appear as theirs in the shipping record.[16]

Levy and Franks were fortunate; almost all their sea-faring ventures proved safe. Twice a year the *Myrtilla*—Richard Budden, master—sailed for London with colonial exports and returned with valuable manufactured goods which the growing colony demanded in ever-increasing quantity. In addition, at least once a year a cargo of East India goods consigned to Levy and Franks would be landed on the bustling Philadelphia wharf.

Cargoes in those days were shared, many men entering into the costs and proportionately sharing the profits. Frequently the ship captain himself was interested financially, and his integrity was an important asset to any colonial mercantile "adventure." In the spring of 1747, the brig *Richa* brought just such a jointly-held cargo to Philadelphia, and many merchants shared in the European and India goods she carried in her hold. While the *Richa* remained at dock at "Hamilton's Wharffe," her captain, Benjamin Burk, announced that he would sail again in six weeks for London; meanwhile, arrangements for loading an export cargo could be made with Levy and Franks.[17] The procedure of joint ownership was applied as frequently to export as to import; and both were of equal importance to the colony. Philadelphia required a balance of trade not only with her sister colonies but with the mother country as well.

Eastern Pennsylvania's limestone soil enabled her to become an important agricultural region. Rich, fertile farms yielded a variety of grain, and fed an abundance of cattle. Unfelled forests supplied a plenitude of timber, and the natural ores were turned into iron in the forges and furnaces of the province. All of these products were most desirable for export purposes; few ships left Philadelphia's thriving port without them. Timber made perfect ballast for the slender sea-craft and it was required for His Majesty's naval stores. Wheat, corn, and meat products came down regularly from Lancaster to the Delaware River waterfront.

The young partners did not limit themselves to shipping and importing staple commodities, or dealing with the common cargoes of sugar and rum from the West Indies. Freight and passage to London could be arranged through them. Wholesale and retail goods could be bought at their warehouse. English sail cloth, sweet almonds, medical kits for nautical or domestic use, all sorts of India goods, English cordage by the ton and such a variety of dry goods and hardware that their lengthy listings would be ended with a note that other things "too tedious to mention" were also available.[18]

There could also be obtained at either their store or their warehouse "Advices," that is to say, the news and the money and commodity quotations from all the European capitals, for the reliable Captain Budden brought with him European newspapers, as up-to-date as the winds and waves permitted.

By 1746, the firm had a store at Front and Water Streets. In 1751 they gave it up and rented the largest house on Second Street near Walnut,[19] the property of Isaac Norris, Jr., who had become one of the wealthiest of all the merchants of Philadelphia, and had just the year before been elected Speaker of the Provincial Assembly.

Norris was responsible for one of the most valuable imports that ever came on a Levy and Franks ship, or on any other. In late August of 1752 there arrived on the faithful *Myrtilla*[20] a bell—the famous Liberty Bell[121]—which had been ordered for the State House on the occasion of the fiftieth anniversary of Penn's Charter of Liberties for Pennsylvania. As Speaker of the Assembly it had been Norris' responsibility to make the purchase and the arrangements for its transportation from England. He was also personally responsible for the motto which was cast on it—"Proclaim liberty throughout all the land, unto all the inhabitants thereof."[22] Norris was a profound student of the Bible, not only in English, but, like his father-in-law, Logan, in the original Hebrew as well. Some years before Logan had said of Norris, "if he had as much skill in ye Greek as he has in Hebrew he would merit the general reputation of a Learned man."[22a] It is fascinating to imagine that the prophetic and inspiring text from Leviticus struck a sympatic note in his mind as he read it in his own large Hebrew Bible, which is still preserved in the Library Company of Philadelphia.[23]

What happened to the foreign imports after they reached the Philadelphia wharves? Philadelphians alone could not absorb the immense quantities of merchandise that poured in from all the English ports of the eighteenth-century world. Competition was as sharp then as it is today, and many colonial merchants fell by the wayside because they could not regularly find an outlet for their wares. For this reason, the Bayntons, Whartons, Drinkers, and Shippens began to develop western trade, tapping in return that rich source of furs. Here again much of colonial enterprise depended upon the stability of one's connections. The Shippens had relatives and stores in the Lancaster outpost, and Levy and Franks, quickly realizing the importance of the West, found the perfect representative in Joseph Simon, who had become the leading merchant of that town.[24]

Lancaster was the tip of a western arc which fanned out

from Philadelphia, encompassing an area which was rapidly absorbing large numbers of newly arriving German and Scotch-Irish immigrants. In the absence of a developed colonial manufacture these new arrivals constituted a rich market for every conceivable item in the register of eighteenth-century commerce, particularly the tools to build homes and the implements to till the soil, the textiles to make their clothing, and the few luxuries they could afford. In reaching them, the road from Philadelphia to Lancaster was rutted by the coaches and wagons of the Shippens and Levy and Franks.

Through their combined enterprises the community grew rapidly. To the west of Lancaster lay the perilous roads to distant Fort Duquesne, later Pittsburgh, and the heart of the Indian fur country. Lancaster, therefore, fed both east and west, and from this point the first steps for the "western" expansion of Pennsylvania began. The Simon-Levy-Franks consortium became one of the major factors in the western trade. Indian trade goods began to fill more and more of their invoices.

It was because of his interest in the safety of the trade routes both by sea and by land that Nathan Levy in 1743 had joined in a petition to the King asking that a militia be raised in Pennsylvania.[25] This was the earliest participation of a Philadelphia Jew in an effort for the common good. But the question of a militia, the organization of citizens into a military troop, was a hotly debated one in Philadelphia. The Quakers in line with their pacifistic doctrines strongly opposed it, and others were satisfied to let sleeping dogs lie. It was not until French and Spanish privateers appeared in Delaware Bay and raised havoc there in the summer of 1747 that, at the effective call of Benjamin Franklin, a volunteer company of Associators was formed who pledged themselves to the defense of the city. The defense of the western roads and posts remained an unsolved problem for many years.

During the next two decades many Jewish newcomers joined the handful who formed the nucleus of the Philadelphia community. Either socially or commercially most of them were associated with Levy and Franks. In 1739 Israel Jacobs had arrived from London, and he lived to observe the growth of the city for the next seventy years.[26] Mathias Bush, taking advantage of the Naturalization Act, swore allegiance to the King, "on the Old Testament only," in the spring of 1749.[27] About this time, too, came Moses Mordecai, the first of his distinguished family to arrive in America.[28] He had been born in Bonn in 1707, and had come west after spending some time in England. By 1745 Solomon Heim Bonn and Midrach Israel were settled here.[29] Isaac Rodriguez Santino is found selling "dry goods of all sorts, very cheap for ready money" from his store in Chestnut Street.[30] Naphtali Hart Myers, who later became the head of the Great Synagogue of London, was preparing to enter business with Benjamin Levy, who was to marry Nathan Levy's daughter.[31] The first Gomez to take up residence in Philadelphia—the brother of Daniel and of him who was cut up by the Spaniards—was Benjamin, who sold his West India goods from "his house, below the Draw-bridge, next door to Captain Edgar's."[32]

With two exceptions, these are the Jews of whom we have records in the documentarily barren decades of 1730–50. One was the family of Sampson Levy, Sr., who was a step-brother of the other Levys.[33] He, like Miranda, became a Christian, and was a member of St. Peter's Church, although, also like Miranda, he was referred to as "a Jew" by his contemporaries. His firstborn son, Nathan, who does not seem to have survived childhood, was circumcized by Jacob Moses in New York,[34] but his other sons, Sampson, Jr. and Moses, who later distinguished themselves at the bar, never considered themselves Jews nor took any part in the Jewish life of the city.

The other exception was the family of Israel Israel, a man who later became prominent in Philadelphia, being an ardent patriot during the Revolution and an ardent Jeffersonian after it. Because of his Jewish-sounding name early historians assumed that he was a Jew, and in an account of the Grand Masters of the Grand Lodge of Pennsylvania he was referred to as an "Israelite in whom there was no guile." Yet, his tombstone, with the inscription, "A Christian patriarch, firm in faith," argued so strongly against it, that Morais was convinced that his Jewish blood derived from distant ancestors.[35] The fact is that Israel was the son of Michael Israel, who "professed to be a Jew outwardly," and Mary Paxton, an Episcopalian, and that "upon serious Petitioning of your tender loving Mother, on whose Breast you lay yet and were about a year old" Israel was baptized in 1746 by the Reverend Henry Muhlenberg, who many years later wrote an account of the conversion in infancy for Israel himself.[36]

However, Michael Israel, the father, seems to have had no strong connections with his fellow-Jews, and his children, Israel, Abigail and Joseph, were all brought up in their mother's faith and within the circle of her friends. Yet, since Muhlenberg said he was a professing Jew, it is possible that, early in his life in America, Michael Israel may have joined with others to pray on solemn or memorial occasions. He most certainly was the Midrach Israel who as a Jew took his naturalization oath on the Old Testament only in 1752.[37]

With increasing numbers, Jewish life began to take on a communal aspect, with Nathan Levy playing a leading role as the observant Jews banded together for worship. Tradition holds that they held religious services in a house on Sterling Alley (which ran from Cherry to Race Street between Third and Fourth) some time in the mid-1740s.[38] The services were probably conducted entirely in Hebrew from a prayer-book imported from Europe. It seems unlikely that Sephardic prayers in Portuguese or Spanish would have been used, for at least half of the participants would not have understood them, and English was not yet available to them in printed form.[39] They had no *hazan*, nor even a *shohet*, for documents of a later date indicate that whatever ritual slaughtering was done, was performed by each man for his own use.

Barnard Jacobs, the itinerant *mohel*, did not come upon the scene for at least another fifteen years, so that even the fundamental ceremony of circumcision was performed by practised laymen in accordance with Jewish law. It is known, for instance, that in the larger community of New York in the 1760s Benjamin Gomez circumcised his nephew.[40]

It should be stressed that although this group of Jews joined together for worship, and were probably augmented on special occasions and high holidays by their co-religionists from Lancaster and travellers and solitary Jews from other towns nearby, they did not establish a congregation in any formal sense. Mikveh Israel grew out of this loose association, but its regular life as a congregation did not begin until some decades later. The early Philadelphia *minyan* had no name, no rules or constitution, and no officers or clerical leader.

Only a few details of the social life of that early Jewish community are known. The Maryland physician, Alexander Hamilton, who toured north in 1744, observed one Jew sitting with the coffee-house crowd, and noted also that "One Levy there played a very good violine" at Philadelphia's music club.[41] The winter of 1748 inaugurated one of the outstanding social events of colonial Philadelphia, the Assembly Ball, which offered dancing and cards.[42] Fifty-nine leading citizens of the city took part in the exclusive entertainment. A warehouse on Water Street at the "far side of the draw-bridge" served as the social center. It was not held that year only, but became an annual function and continues to the present day. Sampson Levy, then still a Jew, and David Franks, who married into an Episcopalian family, and whose sister Phila had eloped in 1742 with the socially very prominent Oliver Delancey of New York, each paid his annual fee of £3 and enjoyed the fellowship of the colonial gentry. Joseph Marks has been cited as the third man of Jewish origin who took part in the first Assembly, but nothing Jewish about him except the sound of his name has been uncovered to bear out the statement.[43] Nathan Levy, who was equally "society," did not attend, for in the winter of 1748 he was in London and did not return until the following spring with a fresh cargo of goods.[44]

David Franks had gained general acceptability in Philadelphia society, and in 1748 his position may even have been considered enviable by those who sought social standing. He had married Margaret Evans, daughter of Peter Evans, Philadelphia's Registrar of Wills, in 1743. In 1757 he became a member of the Library Company of Philadelphia,[45] and in 1762 of the very exclusive Mount Regale Fishing Company, to which Benjamin Levy also belonged.[46] Yet his attitude to the Jewish community was ambivalent. His children, born between 1744 and 1760,[47] were all baptized at Christ Church, while he continued his annual contributions to Shearith Israel in New York and even attended services there on occasion. The belief that Franks himself became a Christian is untrue.[48] He was totally cognizant of Jewish affairs in both cities and took more than a passing interest in the communal activity of his orthodox business associate and relative, Nathan Levy. His personal reading interests at this time, judging from the few books surviving from a large collection, were in the field of biblical and Jewish antiquities.[49]

As Levy passed on to Franks his knowledge of commercial affairs, so he handed down his leadership in religious affairs to the receptive Mathias Bush. Seven years after the 1740 cemetery grant, Nathan Levy had made another plea for additional land for his burial plot, but this the proprietors refused. In the fall of 1751 he was forced to warn "unthinking people" against using the cemetery wall for target practice and desecrating the tombstones.[50] Undaunted by this lack of respect and the previous refusal, he made still another attempt to get a larger plot, and was at last successful in the summer of 1752. Thirteen years later, as the Jewish community added to what had been a private tract, his heir in Jewish communal life, Mathias Bush, requested the Pennsylvania land office to re-survey the ground and provide additional space.[51]

One of the early Philadelphia Jews, Benjamin Gomez, soon left for New York to join his family, some of whom came to town during the Revolution when they were forced to flee the British; but most of the others settled in Philadelphia. They were the Jewish community which took root and grew. But Nathan Levy lived only to see the planting of the seeds of Jewish life.

He died on December 23, 1753, and the two obituaries written after his death, gave witness to the esteem in which he was held by his fellow-citizens, Jews and non-Jews alike. The first obituary notice of a Philadelphia Jew was more than the usual, passing comment on the death of a well-known merchant. Franklin, who knew Levy as a regular advertiser and a family man, wrote sympathetically in his *Gazette:*

> On Friday last died, of an Apoplectick Fit, Mr. Nathan Levy, an eminent Merchant of this City. The fair Character he maintain'd in all his Transactions, the cheerful and friendly Disposition that constantly appear'd in him, make his Death much lamented: And the prudent and affectionate Manner in which he conducted himself in his domestick Capacity, renders the Loss irreparable to his Family.[52]

A Jewish obituary, which survives in manuscript, the earliest Hebrew document known to have been written in Philadelphia, has a more biblical flavor:

> The crown has fallen from our head; the splendor vanished from our midst. Woe, woe, he passed away and our heart within us is crushed by grief. Our Sabbath is steeped with mourning. The exalted and wealthy Nathan, son of Moshe ha-Levi, died on the eve of Sabbath, and was buried on Sunday. The Lord has given; the Lord has taken away; blessed be the name of the Lord.[53]

It is not known who composed this lament, nor the Hebrew acrostic which was inscribed on Levy's tombstone, but one of those early Philadelphia Jews, possibly Mathias Bush, was somewhat learned in Hebrew letters.

Nathan Levy died intestate, but letters of administration granted to his wife Michal, his partner David Franks, and his son-in-law Benjamin Levy have appended an inventory of his estate which gives evidence of his wealth and cultural interests.[54] He owned tables of mahogany, a walnut card-table, a "Pier Looking Glass walnut tree fram'd & gilt" valued at the high figure of £12, glass-painted pictures, a blue and white china service, no less than two-and-a-half dozen wine glasses, silver trays, tankards, spoons and other plate with a total value of almost £63, and damask table cloths and napkins. These, with many more articles of furniture and household goods, were what any successful merchant might have left.

Much more unusual was a "Violin & Case," evidence that Nathan was the Levy whose playing Dr. Hamilton heard. But Levy was a cultured man in more ways than one. The inventory includes a long list of books which he owned, almost without exception serious works. In his collection he had Rapin de Thoyras' standard *History of England;* the most influential philosophical work of his age, John Locke's *On Human Understanding;* Plutarch's *Lives;* the best pre-Johnson English dictionary by Bailey; the popular, exhaustive encyclopaedia of Chambers; a few books on mathematics; a few law books, including the *Laws of Massachusetts;* one book of poetry, Prior's *Poems;* dictionaries in Dutch, Latin, Spanish, "Lingua Franca," and French; de Retz's *Memoirs;* curiously enough a *Confession of Faith;* and Wollaston's deistic *Religion Delineated.*[55] These titles are all listed individually, but, apparently because the Hebrew type baffled the appraiser, there are lumped together in addition what was for the time and place a sizable collection of Hebraica. According to the inventory Levy owned a "Bible, in Hebrew, Greek & Latin," a "Hebrew & Latin Dict," "22 Hebrew Books," and "8 Spa: Hebrew Books." Thirty-two Hebrew works would have been found in few, if any, other private libraries in colonial America.

3

The Gratzes Assume Leadership

SIX weeks after the death of Nathan Levy, Barnard
Gratz arrived in Philadelphia.[1] He had been born in Langendorf,
in Upper Silesia, about 1737, the son of Solomon Gratz, who
died while Barnard was still a boy. Conditions for Jews in his
native town were almost unbearable: their entry into business
and trades was severely restricted; special taxes were crushing;
even the right to marry was given to only a limited number.
Frederick the Great, who had just seized the territory from
Austria, added—in the name of enlightenment—his own, new
discriminatory laws. It was impossible for the oldest brother,
Hyman, who had taken in the fatherless brood, to continue to
support them under such conditions. So, in his early teens,
Barnard was sent out into the world to shift for himself.[2]

Fortunately for the Gratz family, a cousin, Solomon Henry,
the son of Solomon Gratz's sister, had already gone to London
and had succeeded in the export trade sufficiently to be able to
take in young Barnard and teach him the ways of a merchant.
For four or five years he worked in Henry's counting-house,
learning how lumber and sugar and furs were turned into pounds
sterling, and pounds back into manufactured goods, and of course
learning English. Henry was doing business, with, among others,
David Franks of Philadelphia, and the opportunities in America
seemed to offer such a good future that he made arrangements
for young Barnard to go over and work out his apprenticeship at
the western end of the trade with Franks.

36

Already, Jacob Henry, Solomon's younger brother, had gone to the colonies, so Barnard would not be without friends.[3] In 1754 Jacob was in Lancaster, when arrangements were made to extend the credit of the Pennsylvania fur traders who had been caught by the outbreak of the French and Indian War on the Ohio. Henry was discouraged by what seemed to be the end of that lucrative trade, and, shortly after his cousin Gratz had entered the employ of Franks, went back to London. But Henry had made connections which would be valuable to his cousin.

By February 1, 1754, Barnard Gratz was at work in the big Norris House on Second Street, getting £21 a year salary as a clerk for Franks.[4] The pattern was repeating itself. A young immigrant was being taught the business by an already integrated *landsmann*. What Franks had learned from Levy he was prepared to pass on to Gratz; and, to encourage him and sharpen his wits, the older merchant permitted his young assistant to put some of the stake he had got from Solomon Henry into joint ventures which promised well.

To widen his experience he was sent on trips to New York to the elder Franks, and was charged with the job of settling the estate of an unrelated Henry Benjamin Franks of Mount Holly, New Jersey. He invested his own capital in business with Benjamin Moses Clava of Gloucester, New Jersey, with whom he had dealings from 1755 to 1769; and the records show that the ad hoc firm of Clava and Gratz sold trinkets to the Widow Hannah Moses, above whose store Barnard boarded.[5]

The most practical and informative experience that Barnard had in his first few years in America was the opportunity to observe the turmoil in trade caused by the war for colonial supremacy between the French and English. Even before major battles had begun, Indian depredations of pack trains, the banditry of white marauders who took advantage of the un-settled conditions, and bloody massacres which drove the frightened backwoods traders east brought about a temporary collapse of the Indian trade.

David Franks and his Lancaster associate Joseph Simon lost heavily, while their friends, the Lowrey brothers and George Croghan, who had through their Indian connections been largely responsible for opening up the great western trade, were ruined. In a spirit of friendship and understanding, Simon and Jacob Henry, acting for David Franks, as surviving partners of Levy and Franks, waived interest from July 6, 1754, on a mortgage they held on the plantation of Colonel Lowrey.[6] With the capture of Fort Necessity by the French there was fear the war might bankrupt all those concerned in the western trade, but the need for the supply of troops suddenly offered new opportunities.

Through the connections of their family in London, David Franks and his father, Jacob, in New York, became the official agents and contractors for the British Army in North America. With their associates they handled over £750,000 of provisioning contracts during the period of the war.[7] In Pennsylvania, where sutlers were needed badly, an offshoot firm of William Plumsted and David Franks acted as representatives for the Crown. One of their more important contracts was to round up the supplies which General Braddock needed as he marched his troops across Pennsylvania. Not many colonials were willing to permit their wagons to be requisitioned to lumber along with the soldiers over the difficult and dangerous country from Lancaster to Carlisle to Fort Bedford to Ligonier to Fort Pitt, and the agents worked hard to get enough carts and enough provisions to keep the army moving. Braddock's defeat, July 11, 1755, was not only a military blow, but a commercial disaster for the agents. For years after the war, Plumsted and Franks were trying to unravel the accounts of the ill-fated expedition.[8] In 1758, when Washington marched again, this time to capture Fort Duquesne, he ordered from Franks some supplies for his troops and, for himself presumably, such items as two English pack saddles, "a travelling letter-case, with stands for ink, wafers, &c," "a pair of light shoe-boots, round toes, without linings, and jockey tops made of thin, english calf-skin, by the enclosed measure," a trunk to go under his field-bed, and half a dozen china cups and saucers.[9]

However, the business of handling "Stores, Provisions and other Necessaries" during the war did not prevent David Franks from engaging in other enterprises, the pounds and shillings of which Barnard Gratz was carefully entering in his employer's account books. Maritime insurance,[10] soap-manufacturing and tallow-chandling, or candle-making, were a few of his widespread interests. By 1757 he was in partnership with Michael Moses, a professional tallow-chandler, for whom he supplied the capital. As Benjamin Franklin's father and brothers had found, it was a good business when the quality of the goods was kept up. The firm of Franks and Moses was maintained successfully until the latter's death in 1769, when the Bushs took over his interest, and they continued "making, vending, and selling soap and candles" until 1773, when Nathan, Mathias Bush's son, put the business up for sale.[11]

All the other Jews in town did not do so well. Jacob Henry, with his usual hard luck, had been robbed on his way from Breslau to Amsterdam, and had arrived in Philadelphia again in 1757 without a penny of his own, but hopeful. "Christian merchants who knew his skill in goods for the American market," as his brother later wrote, advanced him a merchandise credit of about £3000, so he brought with him a "neat assortment of European and East India Goods,"[12] which he promptly placed on sale in a rented store on Water Street near the busy High Street wharf.[13] Poor Henry, his health failing, could not meet the competition, and he soon left for New York. Somewhat later he came back to Philadelphia, and then entered into a series of restless movements and assorted business ventures, up to Newport, to New York again,[14] and finally back to his starting point on the Delaware. He never settled down.

Much of colonial Jewry was similarly on the move. In 1758 Benjamin Levy and Naphtali Hart Myers dissolved their partnership, and Myers set off for London.[15] As one left, another replaced him; Abraham Judah,[16] the first Jew known to have lived in Wilmington, Delaware, was busy at the same time liquidating his business there so that he could move to Philadelphia. His brother, Benjamin,[17] was doing the same in Georgetown, Maryland. Both became residents of Philadelphia. Isaac Levy, junior,[18] had opened his own shop on Front Street, and Miranda was now in partnership with one M'Pherson, handling West India goods.[19] Two relatives of Gratz, Henry and Levy Marks, also moved to town. The former manufactured starch "in the English and Polish" manner, and the latter became a gentlemen's tailor.[20] All these men did business regularly with each other, and with Jews of other cities, as well as with non-Jewish merchants everywhere.

On November 20, 1758, Barnard Gratz wrote in Yiddish to his cousin, Solomon Henry:

I likewise heard my brother Michael is coming back from the East Indies, which I am very sorry for. I should be glad to know his reason for returning. I don't know what advice to give him that would be for the best of his interest, as I do not know his disposition. If he could content himself with living in that country, or else living here at Mr. David Franks' in my place, [he might do well,] as I intend to leave him next spring, as I've wrote for a cargo to Mr. Moses Franks by direction of Mr. David Franks. With their assistance, I believe I could get him my place where he could learn the business of this country by staying with him two or three years, and he might do a little business for himself, as he has some money of his own. The place requires honesty, industry and good nature, and no pride, for he must do everything pertaining to the business. So if you and he think he is capable of the last— I have no doubt of his honesty—and he has a mind not to be stubborn but to take advice after his arrival, I would advise him to come by the first vessel in the spring. I would assist him as far as is in my power as a brother.[21]

Michael, younger than Barnard, had been a rolling stone, and a source of worry to his family. Sent off by his eldest brother, as Barnard had before him, he went to Berlin where, in spite of good sponsorship, he had failed completely. From there, with other letters of introduction, he had gone to Amsterdam, where his lack of success had been consistent. Finally, he too went off to London to place himself under the tutelage of the reliable Solomon Henry. When he was ready to be sent off on his own, with a small capital to invest in trade goods, he sailed east instead of west, hoping to profit in the growing English trading posts of India. There, too, he failed, and in 1758 turned up again in London, with no plans and no prospects.[22]

No doubt Henry felt it was time for a closer relative to take the responsibility for young Michael, described as a dandy, who bought himself fine breeches and silver buckles in spite of his lack of a well-filled purse to go with them. Off Michael went to Philadelphia,[23] where he found a clerkship in David Frank's establishment awaiting him. Barnard, as he had planned, had gone into business for himself "near the Queen's Head" in Water Street, and a large cargo secured through Franks represented his debut as a merchant.[24] After a short time Michael joined with him to form the long-lived partnership of B. and M. Gratz.

In 1760 Barnard Gratz was twenty-three years old, and his mind turned to matters other than business. On one of his trips to New York he had become acquainted with the family of the late Samuel Myers Cohen, whose daughter Richea he courted and married. Another sister, Rebecca, had already married Mathias Bush, and their brother married the daughter of Lancaster's Joseph Simon, so that business relationships already established were cemented fast through family ties. A third sister, Elkalah, was married to the New York silversmith Myer Myers, and their intertwined cousins and in-laws included many of the most prominent Jewish families of the country.[25]

The growing population of Jews in Philadelphia, with young married couples as anxious as they are today to establish a communal and religious life in which their children could find roots and a background, was no longer content to worship according to minimum *minyan* standards. Plans were in the air for a synagogue. Ailing Jacob Henry dipped his quill in frozen ink to write from New York on January 7, 1761, that he had heard the happy rumors.

> . . . I am told there is Great and mighty News with you, at Philadelphia— that the Building of a [Shul] is actually Resolved on, and according to my intelligence, is to be put in Execution with the utmost Vigor. This is news! I cou'd hardly have though[t] 7 month ago, that the Same would be Talk'd of this 24 Years, to come, tho' it Convinces me eternity is niegh at hand, for I have been my Self very neigh eternity Twice Since my Absence from you. Pray Barnard if your time permitts (wch I make no Doubt ys time of the year) lett me Know who is at [the] head of this Grand undertaking, with a short Skatch of the plan, whether the [Shul] is to be Hambro, Pragg or Poland Fation. For my part [I] think it will be best after the old mode, of Pennsylvania. The same Seemingly Suites every Body.[26]

Two months later Henry died, so that he never knew that the plans so warmly spoken of came to nought, at least for the time being. However, it is most significant to note that in asking about the kind of service planned he assumed that it would be an Ashkenazic one. Yet at the same time, facetiously to be sure, he expressed his inclination towards a native one, presaging the "Minhag Amerika" of the next century.

Gradually, however, a degree of formality did enter into the religious life of the Philadelphia community, even though they had no house of worship of their own. For the High Holy Day services in 1761, Joseph Simon of Lancaster, Mathias Bush, Moses Mordecai, Barnard Gratz, Moses Heymann,[27] and Meyer Josephson[28] of Reading, in a formal receipt, acknowledged that they had "borrowed and received a Scroll of the Law" from Congregation Shearith Israel in New York. They borrowed it "in order to fulfill the Biblical injunction 'The Book of the Law shall not depart from thy mouth'," and they promised "to return it without any let, plea or excuse whatsoever."[29] It may be assumed that with a *Sefer Torah* on indefinite loan in Philadelphia, religious services became more regular. There was even a communal employee; Michael Gratz's account book for this period records a payment to a *shamash*, or beadle.[30]

Although Hebrew was the language which non-Jews assumed the Jews were familiar with, it was Yiddish which most of these men used in their private correspondence or in personal notes and business letters. A very considerable number of colonial American Yiddish letters has survived in the Gratz papers.[31] Such a letter from Meyer Josephson to Michael Gratz in 1763 told him that he was leaving Reading for Lancaster to spend Yom Kippur, and thanked him for sending "one pair of Tefilin."[32] More than once Michael himself gave evidence of his adherence to religious practices by hastily closing a letter on Friday evening before the beginning of the Sabbath.[33]

His cousin, Jacob Henry, had reflected the same kind of concern for his religion. His will, the first known Jewish will probated in Philadelphia, contains the earliest bequest to a Philadelphia Jewish institution.[34] Miranda's will was that of a Christian, and Nathan Levy had died intestate, for only letters of administration of his estate are recorded. Henry bequeathed £10 Pennsylvania currency to the Philadelphia cemetery and £20 to the synagogue, not in New York, but in his native village, Weiwelwisch, near Langendorf, in Silesia. His executors, David Franks and Mathias Bush, faithfully carried out its provisions. It is interesting that, in spite of Franks' position on the fringe of religious life, observant Jews did not hesitate to rely upon him in matters pertaining to Jewish and even synagogal life.[35] This remained true until Franks' death late in the century.

A consciousness of their position in the total community was also beginning to make itself felt among these Philadelphia Jews. Mathias Bush in 1761 made a contribution of £10—half of Barnard Gratz's annual pay while he worked for Franks—to the Pennsylvania Hospital.[36] His was the earliest Jewish contribution to that infant institution, the first hospital in the American colonies, which Franklin had founded only a few years before. In its sister institution, the Academy and College of Philadelphia— later the University of Pennsylvania—Abraham Judah, fresh from Wilmington, registered his son David in 1760. The same year John Franks enrolled his son, David Salisbury Franks. As time went on, there were matriculated in the same Academy Moses

Franks, the merchant David's son, in 1761, Sampson Levy's son Moses in 1764, and Nathan Levy, Benjamin's son, in 1768.[37]

Some of these men had prospered as a result of the English victories at sea during the war now drawing to a close. In 1760 Abraham Judah, with non-Jewish partners, registered two brigantines taken from the French by privateers. John Franks and an associate from Halifax took title to a sloop similarly captured the same year; and in 1761 Samuel Levy renamed and entered the snow *Charming Betsy* which the private man-at-arms, *War Hawk*, had seized from the French.[38] The war had hurt trade, but to some there were recompenses.

An interest in international affairs, together with a spice of missionary zeal, brought forth the appearance of the first book by a Jewish author to be published in Philadelphia. On the occasion of Frederick the Great's crushing defeat of the superior Austrian forces in Silesia, Rabbi David Hirschel Frænckel had delivered a sermon in the Berlin synagogue celebrating the victory. The sermon had actually been written by the youthful Moses Mendelssohn, and in an age which relished a fine homiletic style (and, curiously enough, looked upon Frederick as a liberal monarch), this was deemed worthy of translation and publication. It appeared first in William Bradford's *American Magazine* in June, 1758, was promptly reprinted in German by Franklin's former partner, Anton Armbruster,[39] and then reprinted in English again in 1763.

In the later Philadelphia edition, the publisher Andrew Steuart added a special introduction to the "Christian Reeder." "The lesson of divine Providence," he wrote, "is proof despite the severe treatment and persecutions which they incurred at the hands of Christian governments" that the Jews "have Patriotic Sentiments." Therefore, Steuart implored "all Christian people to pray yet more earnestly for the conversion and Restoration of this once happy nation, and treat them with kindness in all their Dispersion."[40] But when the great Lutheran pastor Henry Melchior Muhlenberg offered some missionary tracts to a Philadelphia Jew—probably Moses Levy or David Franks—he was told, "The most representative men in the city, with whom I associate, admit that their Messiah . . . was an impostor. Give your writings to these gentlemen. I have no intention or time to read them."[41]

In Quaker Philadelphia there was tolerance for all. But in business matters Quakers were inclined to be clannish. One example of a warning to others not to meddle in affairs of their people has survived in a note from the trustees of William Griffits to Isaac Levy. They informed him that he should not institute proceedings against the bankrupt, for such "cruel prosecutions of some merciless creditor" would be completely out of order.[42] Apparently Levy had no intention of doing so, and never did take the legal steps which would have been his right as a creditor.

While bankruptcies were not uncommon, the notices of them in the newspapers were not as frequent as those advertising for knowledge of runaway slaves and indentured servants. Less usual, but rather more exciting, was the news of some business rascality. When stocky, black-haired Myer Levy absconded with a wagonload of unpaid-for merchandise from Spottswood, New Jersey, in 1761, reportedly heading for Philadelphia, a reward for his apprehension was posted in the press. David Franks, Barnard Gratz, and Moses Heymann were among the ten merchants, Levy's creditors, who joined in offering the reward.[43]

The times were beginning to become more restless in the colonies. What had been a British trading outpost in the west was growing into a new country. Trade and population had both increased phenomenally. A new era was in the making, and in Philadelphia, Jew and non-Jew alike were to be affected.

All too frequently political contentions and economic upsets bring forth anti-Semitism. The Pennsylvania election for the General Assembly in 1764 was hotly contested. In a bitter fight, which produced scurrilous pamphlets, cartoons and newspaper articles by the dozens, Benjamin Franklin and his running-mate, Joseph Galloway, were defeated by a slim margin. The whole province was in a turmoil about the charges and counter-charges which had run the gamut from larceny to lechery. In the midst of this battle of words, which lasted long after the votes had been counted, there appeared the earliest known instance of an anti-Semitic article in the Philadelphia press.

The German vote had been wooed by both parties, for with this group lay the balance of power. The Quaker party, through the German printer, Christopher Saur of Germantown, had given wide publicity to Franklin's unfortunate criticism of the German immigrants—"Should the Palatine Boors be suffered to swarm into our settlements, and by herding together establish their language and manners, to the exclusion of ours?"[44] To counteract this and show how his party had really helped the Germans, Ludwig Weisz, a notary public and scrivener, seeking to lay down a false scent, sent in a vicious article to the pro-Franklin paper, the *Staatsbote*:

I have unquestionably been a declared enemy of the Jew landlords. As long as I saw a group of these terrible people make false claims and purchase land for a small sum of pocket money, then set upon German plantations and not question the resulting ruin of ten or twenty German families, I placed myself in the way of such people. I prevailed upon them with God's assistance so that my honest and industrious countrymen were not deprived of their means and they still live where they previously lived and they lost not one inch of land that the Lord our God has bestowed upon them. By doing this I punctured a wasps-nest.[45]

Like most of the statements made during the heat of the campaign and immediately thereafter, this one was not intended to appeal to men's reason. There are no records which bear out Weisz's contention, and neither before nor after was the charge repeated. If he had been referring to Joseph Simon, the largest Jewish landowner in the Pennsylvania-Dutch country, he would have made little headway among the Germans who respected their "principal merchant"; the Reverend Thomas Barton of Lancaster described him as "a worthy honest Jew."[46] The Jews who were regular readers of the German press made no comment, but Henry Miller, the publisher of the series of controversial letters of which this was only one, received so many complaints about the undignified pen-warfare that he decided to eliminate it from his columns. In the future, he warned, polemics of such a character would have to be printed as a special supplement, and be paid for by the writer.[47]

The Stamp Act crisis which followed on the heels of the election evoked another slur upon the Jews. In this instance, however, it would seem that the anti-Jewish tone was the unthinking result of the cultural background which still looked upon Jews in the abstract in medieval terms of scorn. Resistance to the Stamp Act, which went into effect November 1, 1765, was so bitter and so intense that those few who were willing to obey the law were hunted out and persecuted. The colonists were determined to show a united front against the tax. One recalcitrant citizen from near Philadelphia, who refused to pay a debt with unstamped paper, was immediately brought before a kangaroo court, and, according to the newspaper report, the crowd who came to watch the fun voted the following action:

Vote 1. That this Man is not a Christian.
Vote 2. That he ought to be of some Religion.
Therefore 3dly, Voted, That he be a Jew.
Whereupon, Resolved, That he be circumcised.[48]

The horse-play so terrified the poor creature that he begged forgiveness and was permitted to make a confession of faith in opposition to the Act.

This was, however, a comic interlude in a serious drama which marked the beginning of the American Revolution. In point of fact, the Jews of America—and those of Philadelphia, in particular —were just as zealous in their opposition to the Stamp Act as were the non-Jews. The colonies were at the crossroads of their existence. They had developed not only trade, but manufactures as well, and they were fast becoming economically independent of the mother country. The English goods which Nathan and Isaac Levy had offered for sale in August, 1738, had been necessities for colonial America. The cargo offered by Bernard Gratz in the fall of 1759 contained more luxuries than basic tools.[49]

In the sale of one commodity the firm seems to have been a pioneer. Most spirits were imported from Europe, but in 1765 the Gratzes received a request from a merchant in Montreal for a new, typically American liquor—

I did goen now to Setle me hear to Set op a Distill house of all Sortes of Cordiales, and as I am Informed that by you is Destillet a Sort of English Brandy from Corn, So I take me the Liberty to inquire of you could send me 4 pipes of them for a Reasoneable pris.[50]

This is one of the earliest references known to bourbon whisky.

The wares of the earlier shipments were now being manufactured in Pennsylvania and New England. Colonial enterprise was branching out into world trade which began to impinge upon the former predominance of England. From the plantations of the South the Gratzes received rice and tobacco in exchange for gin and butter.[51] Bar iron was shipped to England,[52] and scythes to Canada.[53] Food stuffs which funnelled into the port of Philadelphia from its encircling farmlands went by sloop to the West Indies.[54] The islands sent their products of sugar, molasses, coffee and spices back to the colonies. Molasses was turned into New

England rum and became the key commodity of the famous triangular trade in slaves. The rum went to Africa; slaves went to the West Indies; and so it revolved. Throughout the early 1760s David Franks participated in this trade, as a typical advertisement indicates:

> To be sold, on board the Schooner Hannah, lying in the River Delaware, very near Mr. Daniel Cooper's Ferry, West New Jersey, opposite the city of Philadelphia, A Cargoe of Likely Negroes, Just imported in said Schooner, directly from the coast of Guiney.[55]

At each port American ships made profits which flowed back into the colonial economy.

The colonists, particularly the colonial merchants, looked upon the measures of Parliament as an attempt to hold down this surging mercantile growth. Great Britain, on the other hand, desperately needed additional revenues to pay for the expensive war she had just won. A tax on colonial imports seemed like an easy way to get them. The Stamp Act, which placed an impost on paper, was merely a single measure in a total policy of getting more money from the American colonists; but it lit the spark of open rebellion. To combat it patriotic organizations were founded all along the Atlantic seaboard. The merchants of Boston banded together to boycott English imports with a formal Non-Importation Agreement, and they urged the merchants of other cities to join with them in this gesture of commercial retaliation. The Jews stood solidly with their fellow-citizens, when on October 25, 1765, it was resolved in Philadelphia to import no more English merchandise until the act was repealed.

There were hardly a dozen merchants among Philadelphia's approximately twenty-five known Jewish families in 1765, but there were nine or ten Jewish signatories to the Philadelphia Non-Importation Agreement.[56] Mathias Bush and the Gratz brothers affixed their signatures, Michael Gratz arriving just in time after having escaped shipwreck on his way back from the West Indies.[57] The two related and one unrelated Levys—Benjamin, Sampson, and Hayman, Jr.—joined them, as did Joseph Jacobs and Moses Mordecai. Joseph Simon's partner, Abraham Mitchell, possibly a Jew, but never positively identified as such, was among the group. And David Franks, who was absent from the city at the time,[58] signed the document as soon as he returned. The participation of so many Jews—and Jews were still an almost insignificant fraction of the total population—foreshadowed the patriotic role they would later play in the fight for independence.

One of the more interesting signs of organized Jewish life appeared as the result of Michael Gratz's business trip to the West Indies in 1765. He returned to Philadelphia with ideas about a new export commodity, *kosher* meat! The West Indian islands had for years depended upon import for their foodstuffs, and Pennsylvania had been supplying much of the demand, particularly meat and fats. It was the ingenious Michael who recognized the advantages of sending *kosher* meat and fat which the large Jewish settlements in the islands would prefer to any other shipments.

To meet ritual requirements, the meat could not be sent fresh, for the trip exceeded the three days allowed by law for fresh meat; besides, fresh meat was not usually shipped in colonial days. Hence authorization had to be obtained approving the slaughtering and manner of preparation, so that the barrels of beef would be acceptable to the ultimate consumers. The nearest religious authority, Abraham I. Abrahams, was at Shearith Israel in New York, and from him was obtained in 1767 a Hebrew *hekhsher*, or certificate,[59] declaring that the Jews of Barbados could eat the contents of the barrels sent by Gratz. This is believed to be the earliest American *hekhsher*. Blank forms were then made out in English, similar in content, for Curaçao, and it may be presumed wherever else Gratz shipped his meat:

> I testify by This That I have kill de Meat & Examine the same as Being Sohet this Plaice that in consideration of that all our Brothers the House of Israel may Eat of the Same In witness thereof I sign my Hand, Philadelphia the ————— 17—.[60]

Once proper licensing had been secured, some one was required to perform the work entailed. The careful slaughtering, the boiling and salting of the meat, and the proper packing of the huge chunks in kegs made it possible for the food to reach the warm islands without danger of contamination—bacterial or ritual. It would seem that in Philadelphia individuals received the instruction necessary, and most of them did the butchering for themselves and their families. Wealthier families might have employed some one to do it for them, but there is no record at this early date of a communal *shohet*. However, it is known that the small community of Lancaster did employ one, or at least the patriarch Joseph Simon did. In 1768 he was having trouble getting someone to slaughter for him, and his nephew Levy Andrew Levy wrote Michael Gratz asking for help.

Moses Lazarus is going to leave our family, my Uncle pay'd him off yesterday, he says your Brother advised him to go to Rhode Island, can that man who boarded at Moses Mordecai be spared, and if he would come to live with us my uncle will allow him the Sallery of £20 pr year and what other percusits in case makes him business with our family, is only to kill meat for us and to teach the Children, if none to be had at Phila. its my Uncles request will write to New York & Endeavr. to get him a Sober man if possible, or as soon as you can. . . .[61]

Apparently, no permanent employee was forthcoming; for, some months later, Simon, who may well have provided some of the meat for the Gratz export trade, wrote Barnard Gratz that Mr. Solomon, a long-time resident of Lancaster, would no longer slaughter for him—he had probably done it on a temporary basis to help out—and could he, Simon asked Barnard, depend on Mr. Simmons coming up, or would Barnard get a man from New York.[62] Barnard sailed shortly thereafter to England, so the result of the inquiry is not known.

This was only one of the close inter-relations between Philadelphia and the back-country to the west. While the Jewish community in the city was small, those in the towns of Lancaster, Reading, Heidelberg and York were smaller still, and to a large extent they had to pool their Jewish resources. One of these was the *mohel*, or circumciser, Barnard Itzhak Jacobs. A resident of Heidelberg and a shopkeeper by trade, Jacobs acted as ritual surgeon for the whole area. Almost half a century before the Methodist circuit riders were covering the same territory, Jacobs was riding horseback through Pennsylvania to perform the covenant of Abraham wherever a Jewish family was blessed by the birth of a boy.

Jacobs first appears in 1759 in partnership with Jacob Levy, "residing on the Millcreek Road, five miles above Conrad Weiser's Tavern," which was two miles from Tulpehocken in Lancaster County.[63] He was apparently a good friend of Weiser, the most skillful Indian interpreter on the Pennsylvania frontier, for in 1761 Jacobs publicly defended his character against the accusations of one Frederick Robel.[64] The Jew's reputation for fair dealing led to his being chosen as the manager of the Millcreek Church lottery, and, although he was later accused of embezzling some of the funds, he denied the charges flatly[65] and he was vindicated so completely that the city of Lancaster erected a plaque to the memory of the Jew who made possible the building of one of the first churches in the area. There is no doubt that his fluent Yiddish made him completely at home with the Pennsylvania Germans, who referred to him in friendly fashion as the "Jew Rabbi."

While never a permanent resident of Philadelphia, Jacobs was intimately a part of its Jewish religious life, and he was a subscriber to Mikveh Israel in 1782.[66] He was affectionately called "the Bear" by his friends, a play on his name Barnard. His record book, still preserved at Mikveh Israel, bears his name in square Hebrew characters on its vellum covers. Within the book, neatly executed illustrations of the surgical instruments he used precede his statistical records. The individual entries, each headed by the salutation, "Mazel Tov," list the names of many of the future prominent Jews of Philadelphia for whom he performed his skillful service as soon after the prescribed eight days following birth as he could make the necessary journey—Nathan Levy of Lancaster, Joseph and Reuben, sons of Elijah Etting of York, Solomon, the son of Philadelphia's Levy Marks, the sons of Michael Gratz, and Jacobs' own son, whom the proud father circumsised in 1770. Jacob Mordecai, born in Philadelphia in 1762, who knew the *mohel*, wrote in this unusual record book which came into his possession that it shows that in spite of "the scattered residence of the Jews and removed as they were by distance neither trouble or expense were regarded in procuring a Molle."[67]

Mordecai's father, was the Moses, who had settled in Philadelphia about 1750. Before he entered the brokerage business in which he prospered, Moses Mordecai sold orange and cinnamon water with some success in Philadelphia, but with none at all when he tried to send his wares to New York.[68] More successful was the tailor Levy Marks. By outfitting whole families, such as the Quaker Pembertons, together with their servants and slaves, he made a good living, and in 1767 was able to afford a redemptioner servant.[69] Marks also attained the distinction of being the first known Philadelphia Jew to become a member of the Masonic order; he had been raised to the Third Degree in Philadelphia Lodge No. 2 in June, 1762.[69a] The advertisements for runaway redemptioners show that other Jews too were able to afford help: Benjamin Levy, Michael Moses, and of course the prosperous David Franks.[70] And tax lists give evidence that a few others were, if not rich, at least well off, like the innkeeper Israel Jacobs, who paid for having a horse and two servants,[71] and John Franks, who owned a cow.[72]

Population mobility, however, kept changing the faces of the community. Isaac Abraham, of whom nothing else is known, advertised in 1760 for the owner of a sorrel filly, which strayed on to his plantation in Upper Merion, to come and take her away.[73] David Salisbury Franks, a cousin of David Franks, bought a handbook to learn German in 1762 while he was living in Germantown,[74] but after French Canada was opened up to the British he went to Montreal. Jonas Phillips, who later settled here, was in town briefly as early as 1764 to do business with the merchant Richard Morris.[75] Isaac Lyon decided that his future lay in the West Indies, and, in mid-August 1767, after advising "all Persons that have any demands against him to bring their accounts," left for Jamaica.[76]

Those that left were replaced by others. Joseph Cohen came to work as a foreign clerk for the Gratz brothers in 1768.[77] The same year Abraham and his son Ezekiel Levy[78] arrived with their Polish-speaking, German-reading families, and set up as small traders. Mordecai Levy[79] added to the confusing, but unrelated, number of Levys in town. And, of course, the up-country Jews, Simon and Levy Andrew Levy from Lancaster, the "Yorker" Ettings, and others, came regularly to Philadelphia on business and for the religious holidays.

The numerical growth brought new activity. If there was any but whispered gossip among the Jews at the marriage of Abigail Franks, David's daughter, to the very prominent Andrew Hamilton, it has not survived. Isaac Miranda must have stirred in his grave, for it was this heir to Bush Hill that he had sought for his daughter Mary. Socially, the wedding was one of the main events of 1768,[80] but for the Jewish community it could have meant little, for the Franks children had all been brought up in their mother's faith and among their mother's friends.

It was somewhat different a year later when Michael Gratz became engaged to Joseph Simon's daughter, Miriam. Business connections had led to the courtship, and the ties between the Bushs, Simons, and Gratzes were now further strengthened. There was considerable concern as to how the ceremony would be performed, since there was no one in either Lancaster or Philadelphia qualified to conduct a Jewish wedding. Fortunately, Barnard Gratz, hurrying to New York to catch a ship leaving for London, was able to make arrangements there for a *hazan* to come down for the occasion.[81] For a fee of £10, which covered the cost of hiring a horse and of a *misheberach* at the wedding, the New York *hazan*, young Gershom Seixas, with a letter of recommendation from his father to Joseph Simon,[82] rode to Philadelphia in company with David Franks, just returning from settling his father's estate.

David Franks, now a respectable member of the British-American gentry, would not have attended the wedding which took place on June 20, 1769,[83] for, with an atavistic return to the faith of his fathers, he was rigidly observing Jewish mourning customs. Barnard Gratz, with pressing matters abroad which required his attention, could not attend it either. Yet, it was certainly an event which most of the rest of the Jewish community celebrated.

Barnard had gone to London primarily to see Solomon Henry and make arrangements to develop the firm's regular trade between Philadelphia and London; but new regulations being decreed by Parliament were presenting new difficulties. Moses Franks told him, he reported to Michael, "that by act of Parliament there is but 12 Jew Brokers allowed to act in that station as brokers and that he would be very glad to serve me in anything that would be to my advantage."[84] That was all to the good, but otherwise trade was in a parlous way. The Townshend Acts had been passed, taxing chiefly lead, paper, glass and tea, and they brought forth renewed opposition in the colonies. A second Non-Importation Agreement was drawn up and signed. Barnard wrote from London on October 31, 1769, to report on the effect of the boycott there:

> As for times being bad I make no manner of Doubt as they are here as bad as possible—there can be if one had cash here just now to purchase goods they might make themselves at once, there is evrey Day sales by Publick Oction or vendue, but all the people most thinks the acts will be Repealed as all the Tradesman and Manufacturers are a'crying out about it, they have nothing to Do, and all give the americans Right to stick out for their liberty—[85]

The situation in Philadelphia was not much better, and Mathias Bush, who had just signed the second Non-Importation Agreement, adding his Hebrew initials to the signature,[86] sent news from home which must have crossed Gratz's letter in mid-ocean:

Trade in America is very dull, which I leave you to judge when exchange is from 47½ to 50 per cent, owing to the scarcity of money. The goods shipped from Great Britain since last April are all stored, by which means woolens are scarce. Our collector has seized 40 odd pipes of wine belonging to John Ross, merchant. The sailors found out the informer. They rolled the informer in tar and feathers and paraded the streets with him.[87]

Against this background of political consciousness the tiny Jewish community of the 1760s expanded. It now numbered approximately one hundred men, women and children, and was predominately of central European, or Ashkenazic, origin. New families were growing up, in spite of the appalling mortality rate characteristic of colonial America. Almost one out of every three infants died before reaching childhood. Smallpox carried away many, as it had Franklin's son. Barnard Gratz's first-born daughter died before she was two.[88] Moses Heymann, who had conducted his business near Second and Race Streets for five years, succumbed after a brief illness in 1765.[89] Isaac Levy, Jr.,[90] Michael Moses and the first of the Sephardic Pereyras to come to Philadelphia died a few years later.[91] These deaths caused more than personal sorrow; they created a community problem.

To meet it, Mathias Bush during the summer of 1765 made application for additional land to use as a cemetery. By order of the Proprietors, the Spruce Street lot of Nathan Levy was re-surveyed, and land contiguous to it was granted for that purpose.[92] That this was intended for communal use is clear from the will which Michael Gratz drew up about this time, in which he bequeathed five pounds "towards the support and repair of the Jews Burying Ground in Philadelphia."[93]

In this (happily premature) will Michael further left his cousins Henry and Levy Marks ten pounds each "as mourning." Nathan Levy, Jacob Henry and the Jews who died after them were probably remembered in the memorial prayer, duly recited according to custom. It was to assure this for himself that Michael Gratz left money to his cousins. This is significant, for it gives evidence that the Philadelphia Jewish community was no longer just a *minyan*, or quorum, of Jewish worshippers, but, probably from 1761 when the first Torah was brought to the city, a congregation holding regular services. The unofficial head of the congregation, still without a name, was certainly Mathias Bush, since the Gratzes, who shared his religious zeal, were generally "on the road" for extended periods of time.

Bush was concerned about other matters too, matters closely tied to the Jewish community. Emanuel Lyon, late of London, acquainted the public through an advertisement in the *Pennsylvania Gazette* of February 16, 1769,

> that he intends to teach a few gentlemen the Hebrew Language, in its Purity, either at his Lodgings, at Mr. John Taylor's in Front Street, at the corner of Race Street, or at their respective Houses.[94]

He had two competitors, John William Kals and Philip Keyl, both itinerant teachers, who traveled around Pennsylvania and New Jersey conducting their classes in Hebrew for "gentlemen of learning."[95] Lyon was the first Jew, however, to offer Hebrew lessons in Philadelphia.

As an educator he was not a success, and so he turned to business, at which he succeeded no better. Unable to adapt himself, and somewhat erratic, within a short time he had had to pawn his clothes and his other earthly possessions. In six months he had become a communal charge. Rachel Moses, in the absence of any organized charity, did her best to set him on a proper course. She redeemed his clothes, paid his debts, and tried to provide vocational and personal guidance. Lyon was a hopeless case. In despair she appealed to the Reverend Richard Peters, Rector of the Episcopalian Christ Church:

> Your Charitable friendship to Emanuel Lyon, a Jew is Praiseworthy. . . .
> I am a Jew and has no Rabbin to apply to here, you are a Christian minister of approved character—on your account and lest you should suffer loss by him I shall wait some time in hopes you may bring him to reason.[96]

With dignity she signed her neatly written letter in Hebrew and English. It was to no avail; later events showed that the educated Emanuel Lyon was a rogue.

Bush too must have tried his hand with Lyon, for to his letter to Barnard Gratz he added the note, "Pray prevent, if it is in your power to hinder any more of that sort to come."[96a] Settled and integrated Jews were always proud and jealous of their situation, and always afraid that less respectable Jews might upset what they looked upon as the delicate balance of tolerance. It was likely that problems of this nature, in the absence of a well-regulated synagogue, spurred the responsible Jews of the city to attempt a consolidation and unification of their numbers.

Before Barnard Gratz left London for home in October, 1770, an English cousin, Andreas Henry Groth, wrote him from Exeter, expressing the hope which he shared with many English merchants, "that the Colonies may keep firm in their resolutions, so as not to give away their freedom and become like the Irish."[97] The Boston Massacre, which had taken place in March of that year, had already firmed those resolutions, and Gratz returned to a Philadelphia still growing, but seething with political problems.

It was a Philadelphia, too, in which a Jewish community, augmented almost monthly, was beginning to act in a communal fashion. In 1768 there had come to town one Jacob Musqueto, with a letter from the president of Shearith Israel in New York.[98] He had arrived there from the Dutch West Indian island of St. Eustatia, and had thrown himself upon the mercies of the synagogal charity fund, asking that he be sent to the Barbados. New York kept him for a while, and then shipped him off to Michael Gratz, "requesting he would Collect Sufficient among the Yahudim at Phila. as would defray the Expence" of sending him on to his destination. Were the Philadelphians to find themselves three or four pounds short, the New Yorkers would make it up. Although this curious itinerary of the wandering Musqueto seems strange, a very logical explanation of it appears. Isaac Lyon—or De Lyon, formerly of Philadelphia—recommended that Jacob Melhado of Kingston write Michael Gratz to ask him to forward some letters to St. Eustatia.[99] For, he explained, it was very difficult to convey letters from Jamaica to any of the Windward Islands, since few ships made the journey between islands. Musqueto, wanting to get from St. Eustatia to the Barbados, only a few hundred miles apart, found it quicker to go by way of New York. He knew that he could rely upon his fellow Jews to help him on his way; it was more economical for them to pay a passage than to support an object of charity.

The kind of inter-community relationship which helped Musqueto also existed in other philanthropic activities. In 1761 London's Haim Mudhay appealed to American Jews for emergency help when a great earthquake partially destroyed the city of Safed in Palestine, and money was forthcoming.[100] Thereafter, a special fund for Palestine was established, and Benjamin Gomez, then of New York, became its treasurer.

Philadelphia, too, soon became known as a community which would contribute to such a cause, and in 1763 to "Mr. Michael greths at Filadelfia" there came by way of London two printed letters from Palestine, appealing for funds for Hebron.[101] Although Gratz and others may have answered that appeal with donations, the earliest record which exists of a communal contribution is of 1770. That year, once more for the Congregation of Hebron, which maintained itself largely with funds raised from Jews all over the world, Philadelphia contributed £13.-10.0.[102] It is an interesting indication of the comparative wealth of the three main Jewish communities of North America that on this occasion New York raised £32.1.6, and Newport £25.12.0 This was probably the first national Palestine appeal in American history.

It was not long, however, before the Jewish community of Philadelphia surpassed that of Newport in numbers, wealth and influence. A constant influx was swelling the population. By 1770, Lyon Nathan, formerly of Reading, had established his residence in the city. He offered a hundred dollars reward for the capture of two men who attacked him "near the Robbin Hood Tavern four miles from this city," and took from him "295 pounds, in which were 40 half-Johannes, 4 Spanish Dubloons, 2 Pistoles, some Silver, 10 fifty Shilling bills, 12 thirty."[103] A short time later Abraham Franks, "Tobacconist and Snuff-Manufacturer, of London," advertised the best manufactured goods of the kind at his new store on Water Street.[104] David Levy, from Upper Hanover Township, a colonial suburb, lamented in the press over a "much harressed and abused" stray horse which he hoped its owner would reclaim.[105] Isaac Lyon, still unsettled, returned from Jamaica and opened a general store, only to fail in 1772,[106] and be forced to turn over his assets to creditors. Israel Phillips was unjustly committed to jail for possessing goods said to have been stolen, but made his escape from the constable.[107]

While the Jewish population increased, it was still measurably small, small enough so that we can trace the coming and going of individuals. Yet, little is known of most of these but their names, a fleeting appearance in an advertisement, a document, or a letter. As in times past, Jews were fleeing from intolerable situations to seek refuge and a home where numbers of their co-religionists had settled and become integrated. "In almost every packet from Holland, Jews are brought into this kingdom, who beg their passage, and are set on shore without sixpence in their pockets," the *Pennsylvania Packet* reported over a London date-line. England was outraged by the "indigent wretches," and legislation was introduced to prevent the destitute human cargoes from being landed.[108]

The only way that many could make their way to America at all was to go as indentured servants, to enter into a contract for a stipulated period of years in service in exchange for their passage. Many of the Germans who had come down the Rhine, and sailed from Dutch ports in the pre-Revolutionary period, had been forced to pay for their passage in this manner. In 1772 Isaak Benjamin and Michael Levy landed in Philadelphia as indentured servants and another indentured Jew, Isaac Heuman (Heymann), arrived on the ship *Howe* out of Rotterdam.[109]

Although this same year Joseph Abrahams moved on to try his luck elsewhere,[110] several other Jews appeared on the Philadelphia scene for the first time. Aaron Levy, of Aaronsburg fame, who may well have passed through Philadelphia on his way west, is recorded as buying a lot in the newly laid out frontier town of Sunbury, Northumberland County.[111] From France came tough, young Benjamin Nones to begin his American career as a petty trader.[112] And from Ireland came the peddler Isaac Jacobs.[113]

Jacobs turned out to be one of a plague of scoundrels with which the Jews of the area were temporarily afflicted. In July 1771, Manuel Josephson had written Michael Gratz from New York cautioning him about "a rogue named Levy Marks [not the Philadelphia tailor of the same name], who came to your place with the Widow Jacobs from St. Eustatia."[114] He had a substantial lot of goods from Josephson on commission, and disappeared. Four months later Joseph Simon from Lancaster warned the Gratzes of a man who had turned up there claiming relationship with Levy Andrew Levy,[115] and who, with a companion he called Bailey, had been begging and swindling his way through the countryside. Simon added that he thought "Bailey" was a Jew too.

There is more than a hint to the identity of these two in an advertisement which appeared in the *Pennsylvania Gazette* in July, 1772, offering a reward for Isaac Jacobs and Emanuel Lyon, "Jew pedlers," who defrauded sundry merchants in the city.

Isaac Jacobs will probably pass, in the country, by the name of Jacob Isaac; he was born in Germany, is a short thick set man, of a fair complexion, wears his hair short, which is of a very light colour, and much curled; came from Ireland about 2 years ago, and has since followed the business of a pedlar. Emanuel Lyon was also born in Germany, is about 5 feet 10 inches high, of a dark complexion, wears short black curled hair, almost bald on the top of the head; he was for some time concerned in the soap business in this city, in partnership with Peter Baker; pretends to be a great scholar, and to be well versed in the Hebrew Tongue.[116]

Mathias Bush, who had tried to help Lyon before, must have shaken with indignation when he read his paper. It was bad enough for a Jew to be fleeced by a Jew, but the harm spread wider when a non-Jew was the victim. The older Jewish inhabitants had worked hard and honestly. Bush could boast of his own ship, the *Priscilla,* built and launched on the Delaware.[117] Michael Gratz, for whom success in America had not been predicted, had just acquired the *Rising Sun* from Hays and Polock of Newport;[118] about the same time Solomon, his first child, was born.[119] They were now well-established, ship-owning Philadelphia merchants; men with positions and families. They were rooted in the city.

These men were also the leaders of the Jewish community. When Joseph Simon had written the Gratz brothers about the itinerant rascals, he addressed them as "the honorable congregational heads." The Jews of Philadelphia had outgrown the home on Sterling Alley in which they worshipped; they had outgrown the loose informality of their religious organization. On Thursday, July 30, 1771, the *Pennsylvanische Staatsbote* carried the following news item, in German, of course:

On last Saturday in Cherry Alley in this city was opened the first Jews-synagogue, and Jewish divine services were there held.[120]

This announcement, not previously noted, marked the beginning of a settled, permanent, religious community of Jews in Philadelphia.

Cherry Alley was a little, cobble-stone street, about fifteen feet wide, which began at Third Street and ran west between

Race and Arch. An occasional tree threw some shade against the two-story brick houses in which some of the congregants lived. There were but few shops along its short length, for while it was surrounded by the business district it was not part of it. It was in this area around the new synagogue, a few blocks north of High Street and a few blocks west of the Delaware, that the first Jewish community settled itself.

Now, of course, there was need to equip the synagogue. The loaned scroll had to be replaced by a permanent one. Barnard Gratz, who was taking the lead in these matters, promptly wrote to his friend Michael Samson of London:

> In regard the *sefer torah* have only to say and to lett you know that we have the one you mentioned to me, that did belong to Mr. Jonas Philips from New York, from Mr. Myers, as Mr. Philips order'd, for which you will be kind anough to pay Mr. Philips for it. I suppose he will not charge too much for it, as he asked me but seven guenes, I think, for it. But shuld he ask something more now, you must pay him. Mr. Myers of New York, I heard, told somebody he thinks it will be nine guenes, but hope Mr. Philips will lett it goe for the price he asked me for it, as above. However, I leave this to you to agree with him.
>
> You need not to send the silver *yad* [pointer] I mentioned to you before, as we had one made a present for the *shool* from New York. And shuld be glad if you would be kind anough, after paying Mr. Philips for the *sefer torah*, and if mony anough in your hands, you would pay Mr. Jacob Barnett seventy-five shillings sterling for some *tefillot* he sent me hear . . .[121]

It was to be some time before scribes qualified to produce a Scroll of the Law settled in America; but the *rimonim*, the silver crowns which decorated the Torah, were American-made. Myer Myers of New York, one of the leading silversmiths of the country and a close friend of the Gratzes with whom they stayed when they were in New York, fashioned them with great artistry. He had already made crowns for both the New York and the Newport synagogues. On January 26, 1772, they were sent on to Michael Gratz with a note from their maker, "The bearer, Mr. Aarons, is kind enough to take the *rimonim* with him, which hope he will deliver you, and that they may meet your, and the contributers approbation."[122] They are still in the possession of Mikveh Israel.

Myer Myers was not the only Jewish craftsman of the period. In the *Pennsylvania Packet* for May 17, 1773, Lazarus Isaac inserted the following advertisement:

LAZARUS ISAAC
Glass Cutter and Engraver upon Glass,

At the house of Mrs. Mary Wood, nearly opposite to Mr. John Elliot's Looking-Glass Store in Walnut-street, Philadelphia

Being just arrived by Capt. Sutton from London, takes this method of acquainting the publick in general, that he undertakes to cut and engrave on glass of every kind, in any figure whatsoever, either coats of arms, flowers, names or figures, to the particular fancy of those who may please to employ him: Patterns of his work may be seen at his dwelling. He cuts upon decanters a grapevine or other flower, with a label containing the name of the wine, &c. for 1s., tumblers for 6d. each, wine glasses for 2s. per dozen, and the stems cut in diamonds at 2/6 per dozen. He returns his thanks to those gentlemen and ladies who have been pleased to favour him with their custom, and hopes for a continuance of the same, as he will use his utmost endeavor to give satisfaction to his employers; and as he is a stranger he hopes for the patronage of the publick.[123]

Isaac (or Isaacs) did not stay on Walnut Street long, for his craft was not a common one in the colonies, and the infant glass industry needed him. Less than a month later, William Henry Stiegel hired him as a cutter and flowerer,[124] and he went to work for that now-famous maker of flint glass at the Elizabeth Furnace in Lancaster County. There is no doubt that Isaac was a Jew, for the contract which he made with Stiegel bears his signature in Hebrew, Lezar bar Yitzhak, *Sgl* (the three letters recording his levitical descent); he apparently could not yet write English. It has not heretofore been known that the charming flowers, leaves and other decorations found on some of the finest examples of the precious Stiegel glass were the productions of a skilled Jewish craftsman. It is also of interest to note that Meyer Josephson in 1765 had acted as the distributor in Reading for glass from the Elizabeth Furnace.[125]

The synagogue was growing, but organization lagged behind. In the preceding decades its leaders had been those who felt a deep interest in religious ceremonies and customs, but they had not bothered themselves with formalities or regulations. Nathan Levy and Mathias Bush had acted as individuals on behalf of a formless community, but now the more energetic and more methodical Gratzes assumed the leadership in a larger group.

Since a synagogue room had been obtained, there must have been some semi-corporate body, with a name, to effect the lease. However, the earliest surviving record of such a body is that of February 22, 1773,[126] when at a meeting of the "Mahamad, Kahal Kodesh Mikve Israel," it was "resolved unanimously that in order to support our holy worship and establish it on a more solid foundation" money should be collected for the "uses of the Synagogue, now established in the city of Philadelphia." Pledges were to be made payable annually for a three-year period. Barnard Gratz subscribed £10, Michael Gratz, the same amount, Levy Marks the same, Solomon Marache and Henry Marks both £5, Levi Solomon £4, and Mordecai Levy £3.

This list of subscribers included most of the officers of the congregation. For at this time—the time when it is believed the name Mikveh Israel was adopted—Barnard Gratz was the *parnass*, or president, Solomon Marache the *gabay*, or treasurer, and Michael Gratz, Henry and Levy Marks, Moses Mordecai, Mordecai Levy, and Levi Solomon, members of the *adjunta*, or board of directors. The organizational structure was patterned after that of the sister congregation in New York and the mother congregations in Amsterdam and London. Marache, who had begun his career in New York in 1749 as an orphaned apprentice under contract "to learn the Art, Trade and Mystery of a Merchant" from a full-fledged merchant,[127] did not long remain as treasurer, for early in 1774 business called him to Lancaster.

A letter which he wrote his president shortly after his removal reveals a fascinating side of the inner life of the Philadelphia community.

Agreeable to my promise, have completed the Synagogue accots, I assure it is taken infinite deal of pain to state them in a compleat and regular method, as I possibly could, so as to render them easy for any one that may pursue the same plan. I hope they may be approved of, which be assured will afford me pleasure. They have been ready some time, but as the Books Mr. Henry Marks was pleased to send me are of such size, that they would not admit of putting them in a Portmanteau, I kept the favor of Doctor R. Boyd to put them in his Trunk, who will be good enough to deliver them to you.

Enclosed you will find the state of Receipts & Disbursements during the time I had the Synagogue accounts under my care. Balance due to the Tsedaka £1.5.9 which dont doubt will be found right on examination.

Please to the above last charge in the amt. of £1.12.6 is for Punch & Wine had of Israel Jacobs for the use of the Synagogue; you have his private account with me herein for your government.

I have also stated Mr. Mordecai Levy's account with the Synagogue (for your personal & government) up to the 14 of November 1773. Balance due from him (after yourself and Israel Jacobs have paid him) £4.5. I think the account is so plain that you will understand it readily, he wanted his account properly adjusted, therefore have sent it will be a President (precedent) him after to state his accounts.

It will afford me much pleasure to hear that your congregation flourishes; my wishes attend them as a community, & yourself as an individual . . .[128]

The membership lists of pre-Revolutionary days and the trunk of precious records that Dr. Boyd brought back to Philadelphia have not survived. We know nothing about the duties or salary of "Wolf the beadle" who was an employee, possibly the first, of Mikveh Israel; nor who succeeded the original officers. Michael Gratz may have taken over the treasurership from Marache, for Lancaster's Levy Andrew Levy inquired of him to "know what I owe to the *shool*."[129] And, in his brother's absence, he certainly acted in his place. Marache only hinted at a social life by his reference to punch and wine, and the *tsedaka,* or charitable fund, gives evidence of some organized charitable activity. Of more significance was the fact that the Jews of Philadelphia considered themselves "a community."

About the time Sol Marache moved to Lancaster, an energetic New Yorker unobtrusively moved with his family to Philadelphia, and entered the dry goods business.[130] He was Jonas Phillips, who before 1773 had already led a varied, if not rugged, life in his efforts to maintain his ever-increasing family. Two years earlier, when Barnard Gratz had written to London to secure ritual articles,[131] Jonas Phillips had been the New York agent who helped make the arrangements.

As a young man, hardly twenty years old, he had left his native Hesse, where the Jews were subject to discriminatory taxes, were excluded from crafts, and were restricted in their trade. He followed the well-worn path of emigration—first to London, where he anglicized his name from Feibush to Phillips, then in 1756 to Charleston, South Carolina, in company with his first employer, the indigo expert, Moses Lindo, on board the *Charming Nancy*. Three years later as a freeman in Albany he was bartering all sorts of goods for furs, and trading with the soldiers moving northward to Canada. Finally, he settled down for a while in New York.[132]

In 1762 he came to Philadelphia and married Rebecca Mendez Machado, the daughter of the former *hazan* of Shearith

Israel.[133] The following year, back in New York, the first of his twenty-one children was born. Like the twelve children of Michael Gratz, most of Phillips' offspring survived. But to provide for so many mouths was a man-sized task. Phillips tried hard, but found success elusive. He failed at business in 1765, and in desperation accepted the poor-paying post of *shohet* for Shearith Israel. For four years he worked as a communal employee at the annual salary of £35, trying his hand at trade on the side to augment his meager income. New York, however, was not lucky for him, and by the middle of 1773 he moved permanently to Philadelphia. Slowly, fortune began to smile on him, and Jonas Phillips gradually emerged as one of the post-Revolutionary leaders of the Philadelphia Jewish community.

Side by side, those Jews who were not members of the professing group had a life of their own. The Franks family, with growing and adult children, maintained its Assembly Ball status. To one charmer, young, socially prominent Joseph Shippen early in 1774 paid tribute in his "Lines written in an Assembly Room:"

> With just such elegance and ease
> Fair charming Swift appears;
> Thus Willing, whilst she awes, can please;
> Thus Polly Franks endears.[134]

Polly, less well-known than her alluring sister Rebecca, died before the year was out. "Her remains were interred," the newspaper sadly reported, "in Christ Church burying ground."[135] The family of the apostate Sampson Levy also maintained their status in the city. Moses, a son of Sampson, was now practicing law, having graduated from the Academy of Philadelphia in 1772.[136]

Benjamin Moses Clava of Mount Holly never took an active part in the communal or religious affairs of his co-religionists, although he always maintained close commercial relations with them. He was much like David Franks. He had married out of the faith—with a Christian minister officiating—but he knew Hebrew, and after he moved to Philadelphia for good, in the fall of 1774,[137] he kept up his friendship with the Gratzes and others.

No amount of sociological explanation can better describe the situation of Jews who, like Clava, lived most of their lives in isolated areas than the words of Levy Andrew Levy of Lancaster, lamenting his own situation. Late in his life he expressed a desire to:

remove to a place where a congregation of our Society [was] and that I might bring up my children as Jews—this my Dr. Sir is a part of my troubles & which I often consider of, for a family to be Remote from our Society is shocking. The Almighty I hope will be my guide and Protector, in him I place my trust and hope, forgiveness should I be drawn against my will to a strange Place, that my capacity cannot afford me to keep a Person to kill [meat according to ritual] for me. This place has been my first residence in America for nearly 38 years.[138]

It was not an easy problem to solve.

William Murray, the Scotch-Irish Indian trader who had worked with and for the Gratzes in the west for many years, could well appreciate the conditions of living or travelling through the lonely wilderness, which the Gratz brothers did frequently themselves. He complained good-naturedly to Barnard about Michael's refusal to do business on the Sabbath and holidays, and in one letter written to his Jewish associates from Pittsburgh, in May, 1773, he joshed them, at the same time giving an eloquent picture of what frontiersmen had to face:

I arrived here last Monday and am in hopes to leave this wretched place tomorrow, or Monday at farthest . . . I cannot have it in my power to transgress the Mosaic law by eating swine's flesh here. Not an ounce of it can be had in this beggarly place, nor indeed of anything else . . .[139]

When Barnard left for Pittsburgh three years later for an extended stay, he went with supplies to meet the challenge which the wild country offered to his Judaism. The Gratzes had the tenacity and resourcefulness to overcome obstacles which others, with equally good intentions, never were able to muster.

4

A Group of Jewish Merchants Help Open up the West

IN the spring of 1776, while the colonies were seething in the heat of the latest political developments, Barnard Gratz packed his saddlebags for a long journey. His destination was that "beggarly place," Fort Pitt, on the wilderness frontier of Pennsylvania. He did not plan to stay there long, for he hoped to be back in Philadelphia in time for Passover, just a few weeks away. Not only was he unable to return for the holiday, but he scarcely had time to write and tell Michael of it. Instead, an associate, Charles Matheson, performed the duty in friendship for Barnard, saying "as your brother could not write by this opportunity, this being the Holy Days, he desired me to let you know that he is well."[1]

Months passed before Barnard, now representing a major interest of the brothers, had time to report in detail the treaty which had been negotiated with the Shawnee and Delaware Indians. It was vital business which was being transacted at Fort Pitt almost to the day that the handbills of the Declaration of Independence were being circulated in the streets of Philadelphia. Yet, these affairs at Fort Pitt were merely the latest development in a long and complicated series of treaties, contracts, assignments, deeds and promises involving the great expanse of undeveloped territory in the west, which had begun the year Barnard arrived in America.[2]

As he had seen in the early part of 1754, the rich western trade with the Indians had been abruptly cut off. The outbreak of the French and Indian War on the frontier, the pillaging of the traders by the Indians, the defeat of Washington at Fort Necessity, and the loss of control of the area forced the American colonials to withdraw. A number of the friends and associates of Joseph Simon and David Franks lost all their goods, and faced ruin.[3] The war ended the first phase of British expansion in the west.

In 1756 Benjamin Franklin had first suggested his scheme to develop the west by splitting it off from the seaboard colonies and forming it into new colonies under separate control.[4] He had the imagination to foresee the benefits of such a scheme to England and to get the backing of Philadelphia mercantile interests to make it viable; but successive stolid ministries in London studied the plan, postponed action, and finally permitted the idea to lapse by default. What was unreal and unimportant across the ocean was the life work of Indian traders and merchants in Pennsylvania. They could not wait for the delays of governmental procedure; they sought a goal and gained it by immediate and definitive action.

When the peace treaty which ended the war in 1763 forced the French to abandon their claims to the area between Fort Pitt in western Pennsylvania and Fort Chartres in the Illinois territory, the opportunity for a renewed surge westward presented itself. Led by George Croghan, the "Prince of Pennsylvania Traders," the men who went into the wilderness to barter trade goods for furs assembled stocks and set out. Two main companies were their suppliers: Baynton, Wharton and Morgan of Philadelphia; and a Lancaster-based and Philadelphia-connected consortium of Simon, Trent, Levy and Franks, in which William Trent handled most of the liaison between the traders and the merchants, Joseph Simon and Levy Andrew Levy managed the Lancaster end of the business, and the firm of Isaac Levy and David Franks handled affairs in Philadelphia.

Then suddenly, disaster struck them again. As Franks wrote Michael Gratz, "The Indians have begun a war near the Forts; killed and taken several people and traders, and Levy is a prisoner."[5] Pontiac, chief of the Ottawas, taking advantage of the still unsettled conditions in the Ohio territory led an attack against the English traders. Some were massacred; others escaped; but all lost their merchandise to the plundering Indians. Simon, Trent, Levy and Franks, who like the other merchants had let the traders have their goods on credit, were the hardest hit. They figured that their losses were almost a third of a total that reach the staggering sum of about £86,000.[6] It was not a sum of money that even a wealthy firm could afford to lose, and so plans were drawn up to petition the government in London for compensation.

The "Suffering Traders of 1754" and the "Suffering Traders of 1763" at first decided to work cooperatively, for some men had lost goods on both occasions, and others, involved in one or the other of the debacles, had bought up claims or had had them signed over to them. Early in 1764 George Croghan was sent over to England to cooperate with Moses Franks in presenting the case of all the traders to the authorities in England, but his pleas were in vain.[7] Then William Trent was given a power of attorney to handle the total claim of the "Suffering Traders of 1763," which was consolidated into corporate form as the Indiana Company, with shares issued in proportion to the losses. In February, 1765, Trent presented the petition of these men to Sir William Johnson, with the suggestion that he obtain from the Six Nations a grant of land to pay for the spoliation. With the help of Croghan, Johnson began what were always long drawn-out and tortuous negotiations with the Indians. These ended finally and successfully in November, 1768, with a treaty at Fort Stanwix, by which the Iroquois made an extensive cession of land, west of the Alleghenies and south of the forks of the Ohio, in what is now West Virginia. At the same time Croghan received a personal grant of land in the Mohawk Valley.

Sir William Johnson, however, refused to bring pressure on the Indians to give compensation for the losses of 1754, which he said were the result of French-inspired aggression. Consequently, a group, including David Franks and Benjamin Levy, who were "the legal representatives of the Indian traders who were the real sufferers in the year 1754," wrote to the influential Moses Franks of London, David's brother, offering him a one-ninth share in their claims if he would handle their case.[8] By now, the overlapping of claims, the purchase by speculators of the shares of the original sufferers, and the assignment of interests to men like Governor William Franklin, who were presumed to have influence with the administration abroad, had complicated the whole matter to such an extent that it almost defied unravelling. A further disconcerting factor was the fact that Virginia claimed the same area which had been granted to the "Suffering Traders of 1763." Conflicting claims, interlocking interests and new speculative land companies all were seeking official status in London.

Meanwhile, western trade was booming once more. How extensive a business this was can be judged from an invoice made out in March, 1765, to George Croghan at Fort Pitt by Simon, Levy and Company.[9] "Sundries for the Use of the Indians," totalling over £2000, included such items as black-and-red striped blankets, scarlet cloth, "1 Scarlet Westcoat Laced with Silver," shirts plain and ruffled, silk handkerchiefs, "19 Dozen Jews Harps," beads, tomahawks and axes, looking-glasses, 36,400 black wampum and 24,100 white wampum, silver arm bands, wrist bands, earrings and bells. It was a potentially very lucrative business. When payments for the goods were made by Croghan during the next two years, it was David Franks in Philadelphia who signed the receipts.

Up to this time the Gratz brothers had not been very active in the western trade, and had been hardly affected by the Indian depredations. They had had some small dealings in furs, but their commercial activity had been oriented to coastwise trade and West Indian shipments, which seemed safer and more lucrative. But when the reaction to the Stamp Act and successive Non-Importation Agreements put an end for the time being to trade with England, the import and export business all but dried up. The Gratzes were forced to look elsewhere to invest their capital and direct their energies.

Their close family ties with Joseph Simon of Lancaster and his associate, Levy Andrew Levy, drew them towards the west. When William Murray, an old friend of the Franks family, prepared to leave Carlisle for Fort Pitt in 1768 to organize what he fondly believed would become the "inland colonies," he turned his business in Philadelphia over to the Gratz brothers,[10] so that he would have a reliable home base for his extended operations. At the same time, B. and M. Gratz, as the firm was now known, assembled trading goods, then difficult to obtain because of the reduced imports, and outfitted the pack train which was headed west.[11]

This was their first active participation in the western movement, and in the summer of 1768 their first large "cargo" of goods reached the Ohio on its way to Fort Chartres and the isolated Illinois country. There Murray, with and for the Gratzes, began extensive trading at the posts of Fort Chartres, Kaskaskia, and Cahokia. It was simple trade, but important; Michael Gratz wrote to Murray at the end of August, 1768:

If opportunity offers down to you, we shall send you some shoes, stockings, etc., on our joint account this Fall yet; but if no opportunity offers from Fort Pitt down, we shall be obliged to defer till early in the Spring, before which time we hope to hear from you what sort of goods will best answer with you, that we may send you such as answer best and give you good profits.[12]

If there was little excitement in the counting-houses of Philadelphia, it was vastly different in the outposts of civilization where the traders brought in their furs and bought their supplies. Days before Murray reached Kaskaskia, George Gibson and Captain Henry Prather had bought a fine consignment of bear, raccoon, deer, silver fox and wildcat skins from Baynton, Wharton and Morgan.[13] When Morgan learned that these were purchased for Simon and the Gratzes, his firm's bitterest rivals, he flew into a rage and attacked Gibson. Prather intervened, and soon had Morgan pinned to the ground.

As the latter reported afterwards, "He soon convinced me that his strength was as much superior to mine as mine to a fly." But no sooner was Morgan released than he sprang back to attack, this time barely escaping with his life.

George Morgan had gone out to the Illinois country, hoping to control the new colony, which had been proposed by George Croghan in 1766. But he proved a poor representative. He antagonized Croghan and his fellow-trader James Rumsey. He overstocked with costly goods which could not be sold on the frontier; and he lost both trade and influence to Murray. By 1771, the firm of Baynton, Wharton and Morgan failed in the west, and their remaining goods were sold to David Franks for almost £10,000, a very considerable sum of money in those days.[14]

Part of the confusion which exists today concerning the affairs in the west is due to the fact that different *ad hoc* companies handled various ventures. Sometimes a shipment belonged to Gratz and Murray; sometimes it was Frank, Simon and Trent's; sometimes a special group was formed to handle a special situation, as when the Baynton, Wharton and Morgan goods were bought. Then Franks, the Gratz brothers, Murray, Rumsey and Alexander Ross organized as Franks and Company to market these particular items. However, in almost all of these "adventures" one or more of the Philadelphia Jewish merchants played a part.

Their share in the opening of the west cannot be over-emphasized. It was their confidence in the potentials of the new market, and their willingness to invest in its development, that paved the way for traders and settlers.

Among the "Indian Traders" who obtained licenses from the state in the pre-Revolutionary period were Moses Abraham in 1765, Joseph Solomon Cohen, Benjamin Wolf and Abraham Levy in 1772, Jacob I. Cohen in 1773, Ephraim Abraham in 1774 and Lyon Nathan in 1775.[15] They dreamed dreams of a vast Anglo-American empire beyond the Alleghenies; and they took west the goods needed to build it.

Meanwhile, in London, the Board of Trade was besieged with requests to approve the grants and purchases made. In 1768, Samuel Wharton and William Trent had been sent over to London to oversee the interests of the Indiana Company. The following year Barnard Gratz crossed the sea to observe the situation and, at the same time, personally to represent George Croghan, who had received a large tract in the Mohawk Valley in New York by one of the stipulations of the Fort Stanwix treaty. He had assigned nine thousand acres of it to the Gratz brothers, so Barnard and Michael's own interest was involved.[16]

Wharton and Trent had appealed to Lord Hillsborough, Secretary of the Colonial Office, for recognition of the land claims and had gained the support of the influential London banker, Thomas Walpole, for a plan for a new company which would buy from the British government some millions of acres of the land granted by the Indians at Fort Stanwix. With the active participation of Benjamin Franklin, then acting as the agent for Pennsylvania in England and on behalf of his son who had been assigned shares in the Indiana Company, a scheme was worked out to combine the Indiana grants and the new Walpole Vandalia Company into an overall Grand Ohio Company.[17] A list of

investors who put money into the new venture shows that
Franklin, on behalf of himself, his son William, and Joseph
Galloway, paid in £600, and that Moses, John and Naphtali
Franks subscribed £800.[18] At a meeting held at the Crown and
Anchor Tavern in London on December 27, 1769, which Franklin attended as did Naphtali Franks, the Grand Ohio Company
was formed.[19] It is possible that Barnard Gratz was present as an
observer. His father-in-law Joseph Simon and his friend George
Croghan had a considerable stake in the company, for Wharton
and Trent were able to secure a proportionate number of shares
for the "Suffering Traders of 1763."

But the British government, in spite of backing for the scheme
on the part of individual ministers, did not look with much favor
on this kind of western expansion. It did not want "inland
colonies" beyond the reach of British troops; it was having difficulty enough in Boston and New York and Philadelphia—within
the range of the guns of British ships—where Parliament's right
to tax the colonies was being openly challenged. In London the
spokesmen for this welter of claims and companies were making
their pleas to men who kept postponing final action. Even
Croghan's title to the lands he had received at Fort Stanwix was
not clear, and Barnard Gratz in 1773 petitioned for official confirmation of the deeds he had accepted from Croghan in payment
of a debt of almost £12,000.[20]

Although negotiations in London concerning western lands
could hardly be said to be progressing promisingly, the merchants
of Pennsylvania had high hopes and kept expanding their plans
and their trade. Simon and John Campbell, who as a firm had
become the chief merchants of Pittsburgh, were laying plans for
a town to the southwest, later to become Louisville. Kentucky,
still part of colonial Virginia, was gradually being explored and
settled.[21]

Other large scale settlements were being drawn up for the
Illinois country. On July 5, 1773, Murray, B. and M. Gratz's
partner, held a council at Kaskaskia with the chiefs of the
Kaskaskia, Peoria, and Cahokia tribes at which the Indians
granted to the Crown or to the Illinois Company, as the law
might require, a huge tract of land, including approximately the
southern half of the present states of Illinois and Indiana. Murray
carefully complied with all the requirements of the law—open
council, the absence of "strong liquors," and satisfactory pay-

ment—and after the treaty was recorded at Fort Chartres in
September, the land belonged to the Franks-Simon-Gratz combine. The original shareholders included David Franks and his
son Moses Franks, his brother and nephew Moses and Jacob
Franks of London, David's connection William Hamilton, Joseph
Simon and Levy Andrew Levy of Lancaster, Simon's Pittsburgh
partner John Campbell, Barnard and Michael Gratz, their partner
William Murray, the other members of "David Franks and Co.,"
who operated the new Illinois Company stores, and a few others
with whom all of these men were connected.[22]

On the frontier, far from the intrigues of London, there had
been assurance that not only the Grand Ohio Company would be
chartered, but the new venture as well. Writing from Pittsburgh
in May, 1773, where he was assembling a huge shipment of goods
for use at the treaty and for stocking the trading posts, Murray
brought the Gratzes up-to-date on the news from the west:

> . . . I was yesterday at Mr. Croghan's who informed me that the New
> Colony [Vandalia] was fixed, Trent immediately expected and the Gover-
> nor to be over in June. Mr. Croghan is empowered by the Proprietaries to
> grant land and build houses &c at this place, which they are assured, will be
> twelve and three-fourths miles out of Pennsylvania.
> By his letters he is informed that the Administration intends to send a
> battalion to the Illinois country, as they have at last found it to be the master
> Key to Canada . . . Mr. Croghan also assured me that Lords Camden and York
> personally confirmed to them the opinion respecting Indian titles when
> Croghan was last in England. So courage, my boys. I hope we shall be satis-
> fied for past vexations attending our concern at the Illinois. If troops are sent,
> we cannot fail doing something worthy our attention. . . .[23]

However, land purchase from the Indians and government
sponsorship did not provide the settlers with clear title. In the
case of the western lands, particularly those of the Indiana, now
Grand Ohio Company, there were the claims of Virginia to be
considered. This colony looked upon all the land west, as far as
it extended from its coast line, as her territory, and land warrants
in what is now West Virginia had been given to the Virginia
militiamen—including George Washington—who had fought in
the French and Indian War. To avoid difficulties, David Franks
and his associates, in April, 1774, petitioned Governor Dunmore
of Virginia to take the Illinois Company under his wing. Franklin
in London had already convinced the Virginians to lump their
claims into the Grand Ohio scheme.

The petition of Franks set forth the:

motives of extending the British trade into the Indian country, and by
equitable, fair, and open dealing to bring over the natives to a due sense of a
peaceable and well regulated commerce, as well as to avert the evil consi-
quences that might ensue to his Majesty's good subjects from the great
numbers of irregular and lawless emigrants that are about seating themselves upon the lands of the natives, without having obtained the consent
of those natives and natural proprietors to the making of such settlements,
which irregular and unlicensed incroachments might very probably be
productive of Indian insurrections and depredations, the fatal consequinces
of which have been experienced by many thousands of his Majesty's subjects. . . .[24]

David Franks was a keen analyst and a good prophet. Three
weeks later Murray wrote to Barnard Gratz that a distressing
report:

which I cannot believe true, has reached us that 38 or 48 Indians have been
killed by white people on the Ohio, but the intelligence is only verbal. Not a
word from J. Simons or any other person at Fort Pitt. If this intelligence
be true, it would be much against us and greatly endanger my scalp. I hourly
hope to hear that the report is void of truth.[25]

Murray had been delayed on his trip, because he had been held
up by Michael. He had begun the letter with a complaint:

Little, very little indeed, has been done here to expedite my going hence;
and now, as the Devil will have it, you must be informed forsooth, that Moses
was upon the top of a mount in the month of May—consequently his followers must for a certain number of days cease to provide for their families.

They might have been more fortunate if Shevuos had come a
bit later.

But the truth was soon confirmed by John Campbell, writing
to Michael Gratz from Pittsburgh.[26] The family of the Indian
chief Logan had been massacred, and the frontier was ablaze.
Cresap's, or Lord Dunmore's, War, as the incident is known in
history, set the Indians on the warpath, and, howling for venge-
ance, they drove the settlers and traders back to the forts. In
August, 1774, Michael wrote his brother who was in New York
that:

Messrs. Simon & Campbell will Keep all the Goods that was sent up for the
Illinois Concern, & Suppose all Sold before now, as they had all the Business
up at Pittsburgh for the Virginia Milicia Troops, and even want now more.[27]

It was years before Virginia paid them for the supplies.

Michael, who was trying hard to get the Assembly, busy with more critical affairs, to honor their bills, wrote Barnard out west less than a month before the Battle of Bunker Hill:

> ... I am told it is said here by one of the first members of that House, whose name is Mr. Patt. Henry, one of the Delegates also, that if the Government lets the Assembly sit, all those accounts will be allowed and paid.[28]

Unfortunately for the Gratzes, Patrick Henry, John Randolph and the other influential Virginians had more pressing decisions to arrive at.

Western trade and expansion did not just happen. They required vast sums of money—for these men paid the Indians for the land they secured—and constant attention to details of supply, demand, transportation, and relations with the Indians. "The wampum is come to hand," Robert Campbell wrote Barnard Gratz from Pittsburgh in July, 1775:

> No part of it is yet disposed of, notwithstanding our treaty is this day ended with the Mingo and Delaware Indians. The Shawanese did not come in according to appointment, which causes some uneasiness here; however, hope all will yet be well.[29]

The following year, while others were still negotiating about the Ohio lands with the Virginians attending the Continental Congress in Philadelphia, Barnard had to go out to Pittsburgh to see that the war against Great Britain did not unsettle the Indians. Not only did he not get home for Passover in the spring, but he was still tied up negotiating a new Indian treaty, when Michael in Philadelphia at the end of July, 1776, wrote him:

> I should have sent more b[ead] wampum which I have by me, but as you don't say if they will answer or not, must defer it at present. ... No doubt you will stay now till after the treaty with the Indians is over, which I hope will be before Rosh Hashono, so that you can be with us for the Holidays.[30]

Barnard was unable to get home for the Holidays as Michael had hoped. Major Butler, who had carried the letter to Barnard, promptly returned to Philadelphia with his answer to Michael, containing a request, in Yiddish, that his prayer-books for the High Holydays be sent west by the next post-rider.[31] It was with a deep feeling for his religion that Barnard Gratz, a lone Jew with prayer-book in hand, that autumn of 1776, betook himself to some quiet room in the western trading post, faced east, and recited the traditional *musaf:*

removed far from our country, so that we are unable to perform our duty in the habitation which thou hast chosen . . .

Independence had been declared. The whole country was engaged in a bitter war for freedom. Such goods as were available were desperately needed by the under-equipped Continental troops. Negotiations in London on behalf of charters and grants had become meaningless. Once again war put an end to Indian trade and western expansion.

5

The Fight for Life, Liberty and the Pursuit of Happiness

THE restlessness which had been created in America by the Stamp Act had grown as the blind statesmen of England decreed one tax measure after another for the colonies. "Taxation without representation" became a bitter slogan for the colonists seeking relief from the injustices imposed upon them by a ministry across the ocean. Franklin in London tried to point out the harmfulness, the futility, of discriminatory taxes and repressive measures, and sought every means to close the ever-widening gap between America and the mother country.

With some hesitation the merchants of the colonies banded together to make economic reprisals through Non-Importation Agreements. Unrest and dissatisfaction spread rapidly through the land. When troops quartered in Boston to keep the peace and enforce the acts of Parliament opened fire in the streets and killed some inhabitants of the city, a wave of resentment swept along the coast from New Hampshire to Georgia. When tea was shipped into Boston harbor from London, in accordance with the law granting a monopoly in that commodity to the East India Company, the ship carrying it was stormed and the tea dumped into the sea. A sympathetic wave of resistance warned off tea-ships about to dock in New York, Philadelphia and Annapolis.

In the autumn of 1774 representatives of all the seaboard

colonies, except Georgia, came together in Philadelphia to plead with Great Britain to right the wrongs being done and to consult with each other as to what steps should be taken to better the situation. Room was found for the First Continental Congress in Carpenters' Hall, off Chestnut Street near Fourth. Philadelphia, a midway point between north and south, became the focal center of a unified effort to seek peace but obtain redress. But events were moving too quickly. The British looked upon the Congress as a sign of open rebellion, and further restrictive measures, rather than conciliation, were offered as answers to its petitions. Revolution needed but a spark to ignite the land, and on April 19, 1775, it came when the British fired on a group of colonial irregulars at Lexington.

Post riders carried the news south as fast as men could ride. In Philadelphia, where delegates from now all thirteen colonies were meeting soberly, the outbreak of the war changed Congress from a consultative, advisory body into a government. Lexington and Concord were followed in June by the Battle of Bunker Hill. A Continental Army was created; George Washington was made its commander-in-chief. Money had to be raised; supplies had to be obtained; a whole people had to be mobilized for war.

Prior to the War of Independence Jews could not participate in the political life of the province, nor were they allowed to hold office, for the Christian test oath still had to be sworn to. Only Isaac Miranda, who had embraced Christianity, had held a political post.[1] Yet, the trend for fuller freedom inherent in the Revolution promised much. The American Jews were far from uninterested in what was going on, and their correspondence was patriotically flavored with references to American liberties and American rights. They were zealous participants in the movements to counteract the Stamp Act and the Townshend Acts, and loyal supporters of the decisions of the Continental Congress.

A change in the economic aspect of the Philadelphia Jewish community had taken place as a result of the steady immigration. There were now Jewish cordwainers, soap and starch makers, glaziers, tailors, peddlers, and other petty tradesmen and artisans. A tiny Jewish proletariat formed a nucleus within the larger colonial proletariat. Less evidence of their activity survives because, unlike the merchants, few of them had to attach their names to formal documents or advertise extensively in the press.

A sign hanging over a door and a good, word-of-mouth reputation brought them the business they needed; and their small transactions were handled in cash.

It was these men who formed the backbone of the community, and while few emerged as individuals of civic importance, as a group they identified themselves as Jews and Americans. They were probably no more—and no less—observant than the average Jew in twentieth-century America. Many of them joined the synagogue, but the unaffiliated presented the same problem which they do today. That was, and is, a part of American life in which there is no established, or state, religion. People were free to join a church, or not join one, as their consciences dictated, and, since prior to the Revolution in Philadelphia there were only eighteen churches, exclusive of the synagogue, or one to every 2,200 persons,[2] it is obvious that many other Philadelphians had no religious affiliation.

Yet, even though all the Jews did not become members of the religious community, the increasing number of those who did hastened the development of communal functions. The traditional *tsedaka*, or charity fund of the synagogue, was available for emergency aid to the poor or the sick. *Kosher* meat was a religious need and children required a Jewish education; so, on June 18, 1776, Michael Gratz "for and in Behalf of the Jewish Society" engaged Abraham Levy to be helped by his son in the three-fold capacity of "a Jewish Killer, Reader in the Synagogue & to Teach Six Children the Art of Reading the Hebrew Tongue" at an annual salary of £30 and board and lodging.[3]

More important events were stirring in Philadelphia that month than the hiring of the first communal teacher-cum-*shohet*-cum-*hazan*. The Continental Congress was in session in the dignified, red-brick State House on Chestnut Street. Ten days before Gratz had contracted for Levy's services, the resolution for independence had been placed before the delegates from the thirteen colonies. Thomas Jefferson was busy writing the draft of a declaration on the second floor of a house at the corner of Seventh and Market Streets, which would one day house the store of Michael Gratz's sons.[4]

Before the Declaration was signed the pro-American activity of many Jews had been apparent. Benjamin Levy, who had left Philadelphia after 1769 for Baltimore, and whose patriotic actions dated from the Non-Importation Agreement of 1765, was appointed by Congress to issue bills of credit from Maryland.[5] In the spring of 1775, he wrote to Major, later General, Gates, offering to keep him as informed of recent events as possible, because "your Sentiments are so generous and liberal in favor of America, that if you had no other Merit that alone would lead me to gratify you in every intelligence in my power."[6]

Mordecai Levy, who, like some others in Philadelphia, had wavered about the extreme position taken by Congress, made up his mind in July, 1775. He signed a full retraction of his former views, and pledged his allegiance to the new American Congress:

Whereas I have spoken disrespectfully of the General Congress, as well as of those Military Gentlemen who have associated for the defence of the liberties of America, I now take this opportunity of declaring, that my conduct proceeded from the most contracted notions of the British constitution and of the rights of human nature. I am sorry for my guilt, and am ashamed of my folly. I now believe all Assemblies to be legal and constitutional, which are formed by the united suffrages of a free people; and am convinced that no soldiers are so respectable, as those citizens who take up arms in defence of liberty. I believe that Kings are no longer to be feared or obeyed, than while they execute just laws; and that a corrupted British Ministry with a venal Parliament at their heels, are now attempting to reduce the American Colonies to the lowest degree of slavery. I most sincerely wish that the counsels of the Congress may always be directed with wisdom, and that the arms of America may always be crowned with success. . . .[7]

At the very end of June, 1776, David Salisbury Franks asked the Provincial Congress of New York for permission to proceed on to Philadelphia. As he wrote later when he petitioned for a government position,[8] he had settled in Montreal in 1774 and had been successful as a merchant. In the spring of 1775, he suffered "a short tho' rigorous imprisonment" on account of his attachment to the cause of America. When the troops of General Montgomery, on the ill-fated attempt to conquer Canada, took Montreal in November, 1775, Franks did everything he could to help them, and advanced the Americans both goods and money.

When Quebec was attacked, General Wooster appointed him paymaster of the workmen of the Montreal garrison, and again he advanced his own funds to help the cause. Finally, when the bedraggled army retreated from Canada, Franks joined it as a volunteer and made his way south. An officer and the chairman of the Albany Committee of Safety certified that "the said Franks is a friend to the American cause,"[9] and he was allowed to go to the capital city, where he had been born and where he was to re-establish his residence after the war.

He must have arrived at about the time the Declaration of Independence was read to the assembled crowd in the State House square. The printer Dunlap had rushed the text to his shop, and handbills of the solemn and momentous declaration which promised life, liberty, and the pursuit of happiness to all the inhabitants of the land were eagerly bought by the enthusiastic citizens of the new United States of America. Jonas Phillips, whose store was "in Market-street, near Mr. Dunlap's Printing office,"[10] bought one as soon as it was available and, to show his friend Gumpel Samson of Amsterdam what was going on in Philadelphia, enclosed it with a Yiddish letter. He was anxious to have some money forwarded to his mother in Europe, and it was necessary to circumvent the British blockade, so he sent off his request by way of the Dutch island of St. Eustatia. With pride he described the situation:

The war will make all England bankrupt. The Americans have an army of 100,000 fellows and the English 25,000 and some ships. The Americans have already made themselves like the States of Holland. The enclosed is a declaration of the whole country. How it will end, the blessed God knows....[11]

The letter was received and forwarded from St. Eustatia in September, but it never reached Amsterdam. It was intercepted by the British, who thereby received their first official printing of the Declaration, but the Yiddish puzzled them. They assumed that it was a secret code, the key to which they did not have, and both the printed broadside and Phillips' harmless letter were filed away, with other seized mail from the rebellious colonies, in the Public Record Office in London.

The day that independence was declared, Congress appointed Franklin, Adams and Jefferson a committee "to bring in a device for a seal of the United States."[12] It was Franklin who suggested a design stemming directly from the Holy Scriptures:

Moses standing on the shore, and extending his Hand over the Sea, thereby causing the same to overwhelm Pharaoh who is sitting in an open Chariot, a Crown on his Head and a Sword in his Hand. Rays from a Pillar of Fire in the Clouds, reaching to Moses, to express that he acts by Command of the Deity. Motto, *Rebellion to Tyrants is Obedience to God.*[13]

Jefferson amended this only to show the Israelites passing through the Red Sea. And the committee as a whole brought in a report suggesting that this scene be on one side of the seal, with a heraldic device on the other.[14] More pressing business intervened; the report was tabled, and nothing further done until finally, in 1782, another committee brought in the designs of the present seal. It is of more than passing interest to realize that the authors of the Declaration considered themselves the political descendants of the ancient Hebrews, and had wanted to perpetuate that idea in their country's seal.

The independence which the Declaration brought was a principle which needed implementation. The provinces, now states, had to revise their colonial forms of government to spell out and put into effect the freedom which was theirs. A convention was convoked in Pennsylvania to draft a new constitution, and on September 10, 1776, a proposed form was published.[15] Section 6 allowed anyone who had reached the age of twenty-one, and who was a resident and freeman, to vote after taking the oath of allegiance. Section 10 spelled out the oath in the words, "I do believe in one God, the Creator and Governor of the universe." Nothing was said about specific forms of religion; nothing was implied.

Pennsylvania, however, was not yet ready to accept so liberal a code. Sections 6 and 10 were immediately subjected to severe criticism. Philadelphia's Tory paper, the *Evening Post*, carried a long letter condemning the provisions which would allow Jews or Turks to

become in time not only our greatest landholders, but principal officers in the legislative or executive parts of our government, so as to render it not only uncomfortable but unsafe for Christians, which I hope every American would wish to prevent as much as any other national slavery.[16]

Another writer in the same Tory sheet tried to establish a precedent for his objections:

William Penn, in his Declaration of Rights, says, that all persons, who also profess to believe in Jesus Christ, the Saviour of the world, shall be capable to serve this government in any capacity. This was a bar against professed Deists, Jews, Mohamedans, and other enemies of Christ, which is now removed if the declaration, section ten, remains unaltered.

The author observed that all religions have equal "Privileges" in Pennsylvania, but exhorted the ministers of the gospel in Philadelphia to speak out "and remind the members of the Convention that they ought to give a testimony to their Christianity." Should they not, he concluded, "Wo unto the city! Wo unto the land!"[17]

This, of course, was a narrow view, and an unrealistic one. A

professed Deist, Tom Paine, had provided the inspiration for independence in the fiery words of *Common Sense;* Jews had already died for the patriotic cause; and as far as anyone knew
there were no Mohammedans around. The Quakers and Lutheran
leaders, who spearheaded the protest under the leadership of
Pastor Henry Melchior Muhlenberg, wielded enough influence
to be effective. Protestantism, as the unofficial religion of the
new state, was successful in reserving political rights for those
who adhered to its doctrines.[18]

In the legislative council only one protest was raised against
the churchmen. Wise, old Benjamin Franklin, who had always
believed in full freedom of conscience, objected to any civic
limitations of a religious nature.[19] But in spite of his objection
the wording of the oath was changed to "I do acknowlege the
Scriptures of the Old and New Testament to be given by Divine
Inspiration."[20] To satisfy Franklin, it was agreed that no other
religious test would be given, but by this oath Jews were excluded from office under the first constitution of the state of
Pennsylvania. It was not until the end of 1783 that the Jews of
Philadelphia protested against the discriminatory section, and in
the new constitution of 1790 the disability against them was
removed.

The political problems confronting the Continental Congress
—and, as of July 4, 1776, the Congress of the United States—
would have defied solution by more experienced hands. However, the additional problems of organizing an army and fighting
a war presented extraordinary difficulties which harassed the
delegates from day to day and month to month. One of these,
and among the most pressing, was the desperate need for military
supplies of all kinds—blankets, shoes, guns and powder.

Supplies were being requisitioned in all quarters of Pennsylvania. From distant Northumberland County, Aaron Levy had
already furnished sundry goods in accordance with an Assembly
resolution.[21] Michael Gratz was instructed by the Committee of
Safety in Philadelphia to bring to the city a "quantity of Blankets
and other Woolen Goods said to be proper for covering and
Cloathing the Troops now raising for the Continental Service."[22]
Levy Marks petitioned Congress seeking the job of superintend-
ing the manufacture of army uniforms,[23] and Manuel Josephson
did secure for the army "guns, cutlasses and bayonets."[24] Levy
Andrew Levy in Lancaster wrote apologetically to Major Ephraim Blaine that he could not supply either shoes or blankets—

If I had known that the country-made blankets, which are thin and light, would have done, I might have got a few; others not to be had.[25]

Barnard Gratz, still at Fort Pitt in September, 1776, was approached by Colonel Mackay on the same subject—

As you have a quantity of blankets and leggings-stuff on hand, and I find that the people will stand in great need of them, I have thought proper to send Lieutenant McDowell to look over them.[26]

As urgently as they were needed, many of the supplies were not easy to dispose of in the war-confused and dislocated market. Connecticut's chemist, Samuel De Lucena, prior to his arrival in Philadelphia, had acted on the urgent plea of Congress for the manufacture of salt-petre and the location of sulphur, both essential for gunpowder.[27] Three years later, in 1779, he presented his petition to Congress seeking compensation for the work he had done; but it was read, referred to committee, and finally rejected.[28] Joseph Simon, who had outfitted several companies late in 1775[29] with a better known and less theoretical commodity—the famous Pennsylvania rifles which he manufactured with his partner, the gunsmith William Henry, at Lancaster—two years later had to seek customers. "Perhaps the Virginia delegates will buy my rifles," he wrote Barnard Gratz who had been conducting negotiations with them.[30] One hundred and twenty rifles were for sale at the same price which the Philadelphia Council of Safety had paid for them.

Michael Gratz, early in the fall of 1776, had taken another short trip to the south, and on his way home learned from his Philadelphia clerk, Alexander Abrahams, "the disagreeable news of our people being obligated to evacuate Long Island, with considerable loss on both sides."[31] The next day, September 3, 1776, Nathan Bush sent him a colorful description of the battle and told him how

our people retreated from Long Island with all their cannon excepting two large ones which they left spiked up. . . . I imagine we shall soon have a visit from them [the British] here through the Jerseys.[32]

It is significant to note that these Jews had so thoroughly taken up the American cause that all their references were to "our people."

Solomon, a brother of Nathan Bush, was already in the Pennsylvania Militia. He "distinguished himself in the Public Service, especially in the Winter of one thousand seven hundred and seventy-six, when the service was Critical & Hazardous."[33]

A year later, as Nathan Bush had guessed, General William Howe did advance on Philadelphia, but from the south rather than through the Jerseys. The ill-equipped, weary army of Washington had paused along the winding banks of Brandywine Creek, not far from Philadelphia, hoping to halt the invaders' march towards the capital city. The superior British forces drove the Americans back, and in the course of the retreat Solomon Bush "was dangerously Wounded in a skirmish between the Militia and the Advance of the British Army," in Goshen Township, Chester County.[34]

In November, 1777, he wrote from Chestnut Hill to his friend Henry Lazarus telling him of his situation.

I suppose you heard of my being wounded the 18th of Septr when with difficulty was brot home in a most deplorable condition with my thigh broke, and the surgeons pronounced my wound Mortal. Seven days after, the Enemy came, who treated our family with the utmost respect. They did not take the least trifle from us, though our neighbors, the poor Tories, lost everything. Howe's march this way has made many W[h]igs.

I was conceal'd after the British Army came here 22 days and shou'd have Got Clear but a Vilian gave information of me when I was waited on by an officer what took my Parole. When I wrote a line to the Commanding Officer letting him know of my being a prisoner and requesting a Surgeon which he imedeatly comply'd with and was attended every day during their stay at this place. I am thank God getting better and have the Satisfaction to have my Limb perfectly Strait, my wishes are to be able to get Satisfaction and revenge the Rongs of my injured Country. I wish you joy of our Troops to the Northward and hope to tell you New York is ours before long—the shiping is not got up to Philadelphia though this is the 9th time of their attacking the Fort; there is a Cannonade whilst I am writing; shou'd they not be able to Carry the Fort their stay in Philada will be short . . .[35]

While Bush was writing his letter, General Howe was comfortably ensconced in the rebel capital which had fallen to him. The last American stronghold, Fort Mifflin, fell before Lazarus could have gotten the letter. All the known Whigs who could afford to do so fled the city. Congress had departed precipitately for Lancaster, and as many of the Jewish patriots as were able to leave followed them there, or close by to York.

One, Barnard Solomon, who had decided to stay in Philadelphia, did not do so long, and when he suddenly disappeared the British offered five guineas reward "for information leading to his apprehension."[36] At least eight other Jews with their families stayed on during the occupation: Jonas Phillips, who boldly kept advertising in the two Tory newspapers which appeared in

Philadelphia,[37] the aging Moses Mordecai, Sol Marache, Solomon Aaron, Joseph Solomon Cohen,[38] and Israel de Lieben,[39] who had preceded Abraham Levy as the synagogue factotum, and David Franks and his clerk Patrick Rice. It is speculative, in the absence of documentation, to state that such of these Philadelphians as had patriotic records remained behind to prevent the desecration of the synagogue at the hands of the British, a sacrilege which had occurred at Shearith Israel in New York. One thing is certain, if the military had known of Jonas Phillips' letter, his safety would not have been worth what "continentals" were fast becoming. Nor would the British have looked with trust upon young Jacob Mordecai, then clerking for David Franks, who said that as a twelve-year-old he had dressed up and with school-companions been part of a guard of honor which welcomed the First Continental Congress to Philadelphia.[40] Only one Jewish newcomer arrived with the British. He was Alexander Zunz, a Hessian, who travelled with Howe's army, remained in Philadelphia during the occupation,[41] and left to settle in New York where, as *parnass* of Shearith Israel, he managed the affairs of that dwindled congregation during the war.[42]

It was during this time that the ragged, barefoot, but heroic, American army spent the winter at Valley Forge. It was the lowest point in the fortunes of the new country. Philip Moses Russell, who had enlisted as surgeon's mate in 1775 under General Lee, became mate to Surgeon Norman of the Second Virginia Regiment then encamped at Valley Forge. During the unforgettable winter of 1777–78 Russell gave, as Washington is said to have written in commendation of his services, "assiduous and faithful attention to the sick and wounded."[43] The sick were so many, the doctors so few, that Russell himself developed a serious illness as the result of the strain of working during these long, cold months, and he had to leave the army in 1780.[44]

Bush, still a prisoner and not recovered from his wound, had to report regularly to the British. One day while receiving medical attention at the enemy headquarters, he saw a civilian agent transmitting messages from a spy in Washington's army. As quickly as he could, he reported that important information back to Washington through General John Armstrong.[45] Still on parole in 1779, he appealed to the federal Board of War for financial help, and, when it was not forthcoming, to the Supreme Executive Council of Pennsylvania.[46] They recommended that in view of his distinguished service he be given pay and rations equal to his rank, that of a major. But more honor came quickly, for at the end of October, 1779, Bush was made a lieutenant-colonel,[47] the highest rank attained by an American Jew in a combat unit of the Continental Army.

Meanwhile, in Philadelphia, the British were endeavoring to win doubtful residents to their side, and, clumsy as they were in this delicate kind of persuasion, they did have a measure of success. A number of Philadelphia merchants had stayed on in town, and to a greater or lesser degree most cooperated with the occupying army. Among these was David Franks. Ostensibly he was neutral, but his social connections, his business associates and his relatives were either of the British gentry or members of the military, like his brother-in-law General Oliver De Lancey. All the pressures pushed him over towards the Tory side. His daughter, the youthful, beautiful and capricious Rebecca, extended a warm, welcoming hand to the handsome officers of Howe's army, just as she and the other Philadelphians had done but a short time before to the equally charming, but not so resplendently accoutred, officers of Washington.

Before Howe had reached Philadelphia, both sides had taken a good number of prisoners. American prison stockades were set up in the Pennsylvania towns of Easton, Reading and Lancaster. In the late winter of 1775, at the request of Congress, David Franks was appointed to provide for them,[48] and early the next year Washington suggested that, if Franks would expand his activity by appointing a deputy to take care of the prisoners in Massachusetts, "It will save me much time and much trouble."[49] When, in June, 1777, Congress appointed Elias Boudinot Commissary-General of Prisoners, responsible for the welfare of both British and Americans, Franks became his subordinate.[50]

However, his position was complicated by the fact that he also received the agency, through the London firm of Nesbitt, Drummond and Moses Franks, of supplying the British troops, and, because of this, General Howe deemed it expedient to appoint him also supplier to the English prisoners.[51] His associations in carrying out these functions were of such a varied and extensive nature that it is not easy to get a clear picture of them. No one man, and no one firm of merchants, could possibly have provisioned all the prisoners. The British prisoners located at Lancaster formed one of the largest groups, and to take care of them

Franks appointed Joseph Simon as sub-contractor. Another center was at York, and for that locality another Jew, Myer Hart, one of the founders of Easton, became agent.[52] This was perfectly legitimate business, recognized and approved by Congress which at first permitted the payment by the British to be made in bills of credit, but later in the war, to maintain the stability of the depreciating Continental currency, demanded that such payment be made in specie.[53]

This regulation roughly shook the tight-rope of Franks' position. His sub-contractors each furnished his own capital, and expected to be reimbursed by Franks who in turn was supposed to collect from the British authorities. His own funds as well as his friends' were involved.

As early as October, 1776, he requested permission to go to New York with his clerk Patrick Rice—a Jew in spite of his name—to adjust his claims against the British.[54] They were allowed to travel across the country and through the enemy lines with the specific stipulations that they "give their parole not to give any intelligence to the enemy, and that they will return to this city." After all, it was to the advantage of the United States to get the money the British owed into the American economy. But Franks could not get all the specie he needed for his extensive operations, and his financial position continued to weaken. He was considerably indebted to his Lancaster and Easton agents, and by 1777 he was unable to meet their demands.

Notes and bills would not do. Joseph Simon, warned about the congressional resolutions, in January, 1778, wrote Elijah Etting in York, where Congress was then sitting, asking him to speak to some of the members of Congress about the problem and the difficulties of getting paid for the supplies.[55] A few months later he, officially Deputy-Commissary of Prisoners, was called by General Gates to appear before the Board of War to answer charges made by Elias Boudinot, Commissary-General of Prisoners, concerning payment in other than specie.[56] Finally, when one of his agents in Frederick Town also received a summons, Simon told Franks that he would have to be paid legally or he would decline to act any longer on his behalf.[57]

If David Franks was having business troubles, he was at the same time enjoying a social triumph. Howe and his men, fortified and secure from American attack, were taking advantage of their situation to indulge themselves in unmilitary pleasures. Never had Philadelphia been so gay. There was a constant succession of balls, parties, teas and amateur theatricals. Yet all these were but a prelude to the climax of the season, the famous—or, as General Anthony Wayne saw it, infamous—Meschianza.

The atmosphere of the not-too-staid Quaker city had so seduced General Howe that he kept postponing his main business, the prosecution of the war. The War Office at home recalled him to answer charges of inefficiency, but he could not afford to lose face in the city he had captured by leaving furtively; so an elaborate festivity was arranged as a farewell party on May 14, 1778.

It was fancifully patterned after a medieval tournament. Major John André, who had painted Rebecca Franks' portrait in 1775 while he was a prisoner on parole in Philadelphia, and Captain Oliver DeLancey, Jr., her first cousin, were the directors of the fête. A procession of ornamental barges, weighted down with British officers glittering in gold and scarlet, floated slowly down the Delaware to the Wharton estate in Southwark, a mile south of High Street. There a fine lawn had been prepared as a tourney field, with a pavilion at each end to shelter the charming maidens of Philadelphia for whose honor the knights would joust. In one sat the seven ladies of the Knights of the Blended Rose, who chose as their queen Miss Auchmuty; in the other were those of the Knights of the Burning Mountain, who gave their accolade to Miss Rebecca Franks. She wore a polonaise dress of white silk, open in front to the waist, trimmed with black and white sashes and edged with black. Over her face was a veil covered with spangles and edged with silver lace, and on her head a towering edifice, in the fashion of the time, filled with a profusion of pearls and jewels. Before these Queens of Beauty the Knights dashed back and forth in splendid pageantry, clashing spears against shields with a brave sound. The fiesta started late in the afternoon, continued with a banquet held in a hall of many mirrors, and ended with dancing and revelry which lasted until the dawn of the next day.[58]

With this blaze of glory, the British departed from Philadelphia. Washington had crossed over into New Jersey, and was clearing out the British between New York and Philadelphia. The initiative was in his hands, and fat Sir Henry Clinton was forced grudgingly to order his troops out of their comfortable quarters to resume the war.

On July 7, 1778, Barnard Gratz had the pleasure of writing his brother, Michael—then at Williamsburg on land affairs—the happy news that the British had left Philadelphia "and since gott beat in the Jerseys in a Battle they had with General Washington who commanded in person."[59] As soon as Michael received the letter he passed on to his wife Miriam, still with their children at Lancaster where they had fled, "the good news of our old city being again in our possession, to which place I expect to convey you at my return in a very short time."[60]

With the Americans back again, David Franks found himself in serious trouble. As a resident during the occupation, and with a daughter who showed herself so prominently in the good graces of the British Army, he was under suspicion. To make matters worse, he was forced by his financial difficulties to try to communicate with the British in New York to get paid for the supplies which he had provided for their prisoners. A letter which he wrote on October 18, 1778, to his brother Moses in London, enclosed in one to Captain Thomas Moore, of General De-Lancey's Regiment, in New York, was intercepted. Congress immediately took cognizance of the matter and passed a resolution stating:

That the contents of the said letter manifest a disposition and intentions inimical to the safety and liberty of the United States; and that Mr. Franks, having endeavoured to transmit this letter, by stealth, within the British lines, has abused the confidence reposed in him by Congress to exercise within the jurisdiction of these States, the office of commissary to the British Prisoners.

Therefore, Congress ordered that General Benedict Arnold, Commander-in-Chief of the American Army in Philadelphia, arrest and jail Franks, that he be stripped of his office, and that Sir Henry Clinton be asked to nominate "a proper person" to take over the supply of prisoners.[61] It was Washington himself who notified the British general that Franks had been relieved.[62] Joseph Simon promptly suggested to the War Board that he believed he would be "able to give satisfaction and on as good terms as any other person whatever."[63]

Apparently Franks languished in jail for only a week.[64] In April, 1779, he was tried before the Supreme Court of Pennsylvania "on a charge of misdemeanor in giving intelligence to the enemy at New York."[65] After an all-night deliberation the jury brought in a verdict of not guilty. The case, the verdict, and the principles of trial-by-jury in war-time became the subject of a heated controversy. The *Pennsylvania Packet* of April 29, 1779, carried an account of the case, the full text of the intercepted letter, and a bitter, anonymous attack upon the verdict and the jury by Timothy Matlack,[66] Secretary of the Executive Council of Pennsylvania, who some weeks later admitted his authorship.

The contents of the intercepted letter had not been known until the recent discovery of the newspaper in which it was printed and, as there printed, it seems rather innocuous. David Franks discussed his business affairs and quoted at length the current prices in Philadelphia for various kinds of commodities and merchandise. It contained no intelligence which could aid the enemy, although they may have received comfort from the fact that supplies were so scarce that prices had skyrocketed. One ill-advised comment had a pro-British tone. In mentioning that William Hamilton had been acquitted of treason, Franks continued, "People are taken and confined at the pleasure of every scoundrel. Oh, what a situation Britain has left its friends."

However, Franks was not without his friends. A letter, "To the Public" in the same paper two weeks later, began:

> The malignant attempts of some late publications, to blacken the characters of Mr. David Franks, and of the Jurors who sat upon his trial, must excite the indignation of every friend to his country, every friend to trial by Jury, and every lover of good order in society.

The anonymous writer, "A. B.," pointed out that Franks was supplying the British prisoners by resolve of Congress, and that he had to tell his brother that due to the sudden rise in prices he could not afford to supply rations at the former rate. As for the unfortunate expression about the friends of Britain:

> it is charging our enemies with ingratitude and want of humanity, who by all the arts of cunning and deception, by denouncing vengeance against their foes, and promising protection to their adherents, seduced some to join them.[67]

Clearly, there was doubt at the time about Franks' loyalty, but also strong belief in his integrity. He seems to have been placed in an impossible position by the job that Congress asked him to do. But General Charles Lee did not hesitate to begin a bantering friendship with Rebecca Franks[68] when he retired to Philadelphia after the Battle of Monmouth, and her friendship with Nancy Paca, the young wife of the Maryland delegate to Congress, remained unaltered.[69]

Moses in London, who had gotten news of his brother's imprisonment, did his best to help. He wrote Sir Grey Cooper, pleading that he instruct Sir Henry Clinton, Moses Franks' American schoolmate, to get David exchanged for another prisoner.[70] Of that there was no need. David Franks was freed, but he was suspended from office and was faced with the insuperable task of collecting the moneys still due him.

The Supreme Executive Council of Pennsylvania read a petition from him in January, 1779, requesting that he and his clerk be permitted to travel through the lines to New York to settle his accounts.[71] The Council, wary of Franks' reputation, referred it to Congress, who granted it in part.[72] Patrick Rice was given a pass.[73] He was unable to accomplish anything, and so Franks continued to plead that he be allowed to go himself and he was consistently refused.[74] Meanwhile, in England, the contractors referred the matter to the Lords of the Treasury, who referred it to Sir Henry Clinton in New York, who procrastinated by sending the claim back to England again.[75] Franks found it was difficult to carry water on both shoulders.

Hopeful of being able to salvage some funds from his interest in western lands, he helped bring together the combined Illinois and Wabash Company with the old Indiana Company. On June 2, 1779, David Franks, as president of the new, enlarged Indiana Company, called a meeting of the proprietors "at the sign of the Indian Queen," next door to Barnard Gratz's office.[76] But although subsequent meetings were held the following year as well, there was little harvest to reap in land.

In December, 1779, the Council again found cause to suspect him as an enemy of the American cause and placed him under surveillance.[77] He had, in fact, smuggled a letter to Major André in New York from Elizabeth Town, asking his friend from the days of the occupation, then Adjutant-General of the British Army, to help Rice get some money from the Headquarters. Again, early in October, 1780, he was arrested under an act "to apprehend suspected persons."[78] Poor Franks was still trying to collect his British bills, but the Executive Council could not be sure that that was all he was doing. Finally, they decided not to let Franks go to New York, but to make him go. By resolution of Council on October 6, 1780, David Franks and William Hamilton were ordered to leave the state and give security in the amount of £200,000 that they would "not return again to any of these United States during the continuance of the present war."[79] Unlike that of other Tory sympathizers, Franks' property was not confiscated, nor was he subjected to maltreatment by the mob. He was, however, forced to sell some of his bulkier possessions, such as his library.[80] His Jewish associates were disappointed in him, and without specific comment, their former warm tones, as expressed in correspondence, now became chilly and cryptic.

Behind the British lines in New York, Franks continued to work hard to adjust his accounts. He was still able to write frequently to his favorite daughter, Abigail Hamilton, in Philadelphia.[81] He showed no rancor at his changed situation, and his genial manner remained the same. In spite of his experience he did not forget his patriot friends. In one letter to Abigail, he asked her to communicate with the *mohel*, Barnard Jacobs, to ask that he send some money to Lancaster's Nathan Levy, then a prisoner on a near-by British prison ship.

Frolicksome Rebecca, banished with her father, had no need to concern herself with Jewish associates, if indeed she had any. A "Jewess" only to those who knew her father, she had British tastes and was subject to Episcopalian influences. In 1782, Rebecca married a dashing English colonel, later to become General Sir Henry Johnson, and after the war she went to live permanently in England. It is reported that, when Winfield Scott met Lady Rebecca Johnson in England a few years after the War of 1812, she said to him, "I have gloried in my rebel countrymen! . . . Would to God, I, too, had been a patriot!"[82]

The evacuation of Philadelphia by the British was not only a turning point in the American Revolution, it was an important influence upon American Jewish history. Congress returned to the capital city. American Jewish soldiers and patriots from other cities which were in British hands began to pour into the seat of liberty. The port was reopened; the river cleared of obstacles; and the commerce so vital to the new nation resumed.

General Benedict Arnold, upon entering the city in June, 1778, issued a proclamation ordering all persons who had public or private stores left behind by the enemy to make returns of them to the Town Major. This important document and his other proclamations, which were circulated throughout the city in handbill form, were signed "By his Honor's Command, David S. Franks, Sec."[83] New York's Hayman Levy had seized some of this abandoned property, which he was directed to turn over to the military.[84]

Once again David Salisbury Franks was back in his native city, this time as one of the conquering heroes of the American army, aide to Arnold, the commanding-general of the Continental troops in Philadelphia. Exactly what his relationship was to David Franks, the merchant, is not clear. He may have been a distant cousin, but there was no close association between them; and if David Franks' patriotism was in question, there was no doubt at all about David Salisbury Franks' devotion to the revolutionary cause.

After his return from Canada, he had served with the Northern Army until after the surrender of Burgoyne at Saratoga, in October, 1777. When the French fleet under Comte d'Estaing arrived in American waters, Franks, with letters of recommendation from the Board of War, the French ambassador Gérard, and Silas Deane, one of the American commissioners to France, joined it off Sandy Hook. He remained with that fleet, which was blockading Howe in New York, until he was called by duty to Philadelphia to serve as a major in the Pennsylvania Line, attached to the staff of General Arnold.[85] One of his more unpleasant duties was to appear as a witness at the court-martial of Arnold, when he was charged, but acquitted, of having shut up the shops in Philadelphia, "while he privately made considerable purchases for his own benefit."[86] It was at this time that the impetuous young officer formed part of the mob which stormed the house of the patriot-lawyer, James Wilson, because he had had the fortitude to appear as attorney for a group of accused loyalists. Franks, with other rioters, was arrested, brought before the Supreme Executive Council of Pennsylvania, held in £2000 bail, but—because of the temper of the times—eventually pardoned by a general amnesty.[86a]

This, however, was but part of his adventurous career. In 1779, he went as a volunteer to Charleston and became an aide-de-camp to General Lincoln; but before the fall of that city to the British he was back again in Philadelphia. There, in September, he was treated by the famous Dr. Benjamin Rush, who in the credit side of his ledger patriotically wrote, in lieu of a fee, "Given in consideration of his being a Contil. Officer."[87] Like most of the soldiers of the Revolution, he was, as the war dragged on through the spring of 1780, badly in need of money. So he applied to Joseph Reed, president of the Executive Council of Pennsylvania, to find out if he were not considered entitled to the Emoluments granted by the Honorable House of Representatives of this State to the Officers of the Continental Army Subject thereof . . . As many Officers of this State now in this Place can vouch; I have made Sacrifices and that everything in my Power was done for them, while in Canada, and that my good Offices and Purse were ever open to them, at a time when they had neither friend or money[88]

His military position put him in close association with many important personages. To Baron von Steuben at West Point he forwarded a special sum of $4000, a "Bundle of Plumes & Cockades," and the compliments of Mrs. Morris and "the Lady's of your acquaintance in Philadelphia."[89] He kept General Washington informed of military events, and had sent him the unhappy news of the Conway Cabal on July 4, 1778:

This morning a Duel was fought between Generals Cadwalader and Conway, the latter was shot through his head and 'tis supposed will not recover.[90]

In August of 1780 he was again Arnold's aide-de-camp at the Robinson's House headquarters, near West Point. Only a month before Arnold's flight, Franks was busy conducting routine affairs on his behalf—several horse thieves were turned over to Colonel Lamb and some seamen were requested to transport flour to Albany.[91] The treasonous desertion of Arnold at the end of September put both his aides, Colonel Varick and Major Franks, in a ticklish position, and they were both arrested on October 2, 1780.[92]

The very next day they were tried by a court-martial, and honorably acquitted. Arnold himself, after his treason had become known, wrote Washington,

In Justice to the gentlemen of my Family, Colonel Varick and Major Franks, I think myself in honour bound to declare, that they as well as Joshua Smith, Esq. (who I know is Suspected) are totally Ignorant of any transactions of mine that they had reason to believe were injurious to the Public.[93]

Washington himself was convinced, and wrote General Heath, "The Gentlemen of General Arnold's family, I have the greatest reason to believe, were not privy in the least degree to the measures he was carrying on, or to his escape."[94] But people gossiped, and Franks, from camp at Bristol where he had been returned to duty under orders from the Supreme Executive Council of Pennsylvania, had to make a public statement in the newspapers:

The extraordinary conduct of my late General has given rise to suspicions in the breasts of my countrymen, which are a direct attack upon my integrity, and sensibly wound my feelings as a man of honour and a whig: many surmises void of truth and replete with malevolence, have been industriously spread abroad, and with such success, that the judgements of those inclined to think favourable of me have been thereby misled; assertions without proof have been received as established facts, and my reputation on this account injured and aspersed.

. . . I must here remark, as argumentative of my innocence, and also to shew the sentiments of my honourable council, as to the several reports and insinuations respecting me, "that I am ordered after examination, by them to return immediately to the army under General Washington" . . . Can the supposition of treason or disaffection on my part, be admitted, and the adjudication of that honourable body be reconciled? No: either Council believed me Criminal or they did not; if the affirmative, the impropriety of that order is obvious; for camp is a very improper place for traitors, or persons even suspected of treason or disaffection; if they did not, their conduct is explicable, and to be accounted for on just and rational principles. . . .[95]

However, Franks was not completely satisfied with this kind of exoneration. He was anxious to have his record publicly stated, as it had been in the case of Colonel Varick. After personally seeing General Washington, he again wrote him:

I had here nothing but a Name unspotted I trust, until Arnold's baseness gave the Tongue of Calumny Grounds sufficient to work upon against any one unhappily connected with him.[96]

To satisfy the staunch patriot, Washington ordered a Court of Inquiry to review his case at West Point, and on November 2, 1780, he was officially and completely exonerated.[97] Some years after, Franks was promoted to Lieutenant-Colonel.[98] He and Solomon Bush, both native Philadelphians, were the only Jews from the area to rise to high military rank in the Continental army.

Yet, Washington's army had need of more than officers. Jews, anxious to fight for a cause they believed in, or willing to fulfill their military obligations like others, joined the militia to serve as needed in the field or, as most Americans between sixteen and sixty, in what amounted to a home guard. Before the British took Philadelphia, Jacob I. Cohen, Solomon Aaron and Ephraim Abraham were enrolled in a company of the Northern District City Guards.[99] By the beginning of 1779, both Cohen and Aaron had made their way south and joined Captain Lushington's "Jew Company" which fought in the bitter South Carolina campaign.[100] They may have been joined by Ezekiel Levy,[101] the son of the *shohet*, who turned up at Charleston in time to get into action. Abraham Levy, probably another than Ezekiel's father had been wounded first at Valley Forge, in the Third Regiment under Colonel Craig, and, later transferred to the Artillery, had his ankle so badly crushed when a gun carriage fell on it in 1781 that he limped the rest of his life.[102]

A few months after the Americans re-occupied the city, Jonas Phillips was mustered in as a private in Colonel William Bradford's Battalion of the Philadelphia County Militia.[103] Solomon Myers Cohen and his brother Myer, fugitives from the British in New York, joined the Upper Delaware Ward Fifth Battalion shortly after they arrived in Philadelphia.[104] Lyon Moses,[105] Lazarus Levy,[106] Isaac Moses,[107] Benjamin Judah,[108] and others shouldered rifles, studied Baron Von Steuben's official drill regulations, and stood prepared to defend the city should the enemy threaten.

As the war progressed, and Charleston and Savannah fell to the British, other Jews who had distinguished themselves sought safety in Philadelphia. The veterans of the Carolina campaign began to drift into the city. Jacob I. Cohen, who had been here before, stopped off in Richmond to enter into partnership with Isaiah Isaacs and then came on to be a kind of resident buyer for the firm.[109] Some, like Abraham M. Seixas who, when he took his oath of allegiance to the State of Pennsylvania on May 31, 1782, was described as "formerly an officer in the Militia of Charlestown, South Carolina, lately arrived in this city, Mercht,"[110] stayed only temporarily. Such another was Mordecai Sheftall, of Savannah, who with his son Sheftall had just been freed from a prison-ship. He had been Deputy Commissary General of Issues in the State of Georgia, and "the wants of the army in that quarter led him to make advances for their support when no Continental money was sent by Congress for the support of troops there," as he told Congress shortly after his arrival in Philadelphia.[111] His "long and painful captivity" had reduced him to desperate circumstances, heightened by his having a wife and four children left in Charleston, "deprived of every means of subsisting," and he asked for a settlement of his accounts; he was still petitioning as late as 1792.

While Sheftall was still in Philadelphia, in December, 1780, his eighteen-year-old son was honored with a special assignment by the Board of War.[112] Sheftall Sheftall's mission was to take the sloop *Carolina Packet* through the British blockade under a flag of truce to deliver money and food to the American prisoners there. The young Flag Master accomplished his task successfully and returned to the city late in the spring of 1781.

But the Sheftalls were not to become Philadelphians. On the other hand, Bordeaux-born Benjamin Nones, who had apparently been in the city briefly before, was to make it his permanent home. Nones had made a particularly gallant record in action, fighting "in almost every action which took place in Carolina,"[113] and brought with him from the siege of Savannah a glowing testimonial from his superior officer, Captain Verdier of Pulaski's Regiment. Verdier from Charleston in December, 1779, had certified

> ... that Benjamin Nones has served as a volunteer in my Company during the campaign of this year and at the siege of Savannah, in Georgia, and his behavior under fire in all the bloody actions we fought, have been marked by the bravery and courage which a military man is expected to show for the liberties of his country and which acts of said Nones gained in his favor, the esteem of General Pulaski as well as that of the officers who witnessed his daring conduct.[114]

Still another veteran with distinguished service decided shortly after the war to make Philadelphia his home. Isaac Franks, the son of the New York merchant Moses B. Franks, had been taken prisoner on September 15, 1776, when the British captured New York, while he was serving in Colonel Lesher's Volunteer New York Regiment. After three months he escaped, rejoined the army near West Point, served as Forage Master there, was commissioned an ensign in the 7th Massachusetts Regiment on February 22, 1781, and held that post until he resigned because of ill-health in June, 1782, at which time he settled in Philadelphia.[115]

The Jews of America had travelled a long road from that day in 1655 when Asser Levy and Jacob Barsimson had petitioned Governor Stuyvesant for the right to bear arms.[116] They now possessed "inalienable" rights, including that of fighting for their country. Dr. Benjamin Rush, in one of his many observations on this war period, remarked "that many of the children of Tory parents were Whigs, so were the Jews in all the States."[117]

6

Haym Salomon in Philadelphia

P HILADELPHIA, with Congress busily con-
ducting the government of the nation, was not only the capital
city, but, as the British Navy asserted its power on the seas, the
chief seaport safely in American hands. Boston, isolated in the
north, remained in the possession of the Continentals; but New
York, Newport, Charleston and Savannah all fell to the British.
An influx of patriots from the occupied cities flowed into Philadelphia, making living quarters in the town almost impossible
to secure, and with the others came an increasing number of
Jewish refugees. Weary soldiers, affluent merchants reduced to
penury—although there were a few with wealth—many who
possessed nothing but their tested patriotism, filled the city.

From New York came the largest number, for the Jews of
that city left almost to a man rather than stay and live under
British rule. It was difficult to abandon the neat, firmly established synagogue. Yet, their principles and the fight for independence were more important to them, and their known
revolutionary sympathies would have made life, with the British
in power, dangerous, if not impossible.

Hazan Gershom Mendes Seixas had moved the scrolls and
other ritual property first to Stratford, Connecticut, and then,
on June 6, 1780, to Philadelphia.[1] Some members of the large
Gomez family, "staunch friend to freedom," always active in
Shearith Israel and at one time its heaviest contributor, chose
to surrender a fortune rather than stay under Tory rule. Isaac
Moses fared somewhat better, managing to salvage a considerable

98

part of his assets. Even while he was available for duty as a private in the Pennsylvania Militia, he subscribed £3000 "in Pennsylvania Currency payable in gold or silver" to an emergency fund established in July, 1780, to supply the army with provisions.[2]

The tax lists of the later years of the war give some indication of the comparative wealth of the residents of Philadelphia at that time. Isaac Moses was the wealthiest Jew. His property was appraised in 1780 at £115,200,[3] which was considerably less than the prominent merchant Samuel Powell, whose holdings were valued at £639,900,[4] but was more than Michael Gratz's £92,200, Benjamin Seixas' £33,200, Moses Nathan's £39,400, and Solomon Myers Cohen's £30,000.[5] That Moses continued to do well into the next year is evidenced by the fact that his tax was then based on the deflated figure of £2,904,[6] compared to Robert Morris' £8,764.[7] Except for Michael Gratz, whose real estate slipped to £615,[8] most of the others seem to have held their own or done better.[9] The appearance of new names from year to year, and the emergence of a more successful—or in a few cases less successful—business, tell the story of the Philadelphia Jewish community as it grew.

Samuel Judah, his wife and twelve children might have found temporary comfort in New York, but they preferred the free air of Philadelphia.[10] He was listed as a "gentleman" in the 1780 tax list roll, and died the next year. Jonas Phillips and Solomon Marache were still here, the latter as a purveyor of "Firkins of excellent Irish butter."[11] Benjamin, the brother of *Hazan* Seixas, entered business with Hayman Levy as soon as the British left Philadelphia.[12] However, one of the most important additions to the Philadelphia community was Manuel Josephson, a New York merchant who had begun his career in America as a sutler in the French and Indian War in 1757.[13] A man with considerable knowledge of rabbinic lore, he had long been associated in business with the Gratzes, and after the war remained in Philadelphia, becoming one of the leaders of Mikveh Israel.

The list of New Yorkers is lengthy, but those who came from the South were of equal importance. Sheftall, Da Costa, Sasportas and their kin had already made their mark in their own states, and their contributions as part of a religious group during a few years' life in Philadelphia became significant.[14]

A Georgian who arrived late in October, 1780, only sought at first the safety of the city. He visited his friends, the Georgia delegates to Congress; and they, among them George Walton who had signed the Declaration four years before, presented him with a character reference:

> This may certify, that Mr. Coshman Polock merchant, has been a citizen of the State of Georgia, for many years past; that he gave early demonstrations of his attachment to the American cause, by taking an active part, has been in several engagements against the enemy, when he behaved himself with approbation; that he is now to be considered as a refugee of the said State, and is entitled to every indulgence usually given to sister States to persons of his description.[15]

Just as Benjamin Levy, the old Philadelphian who had moved to Baltimore, had offered Robert Morris sanctuary and a home when the British took Philadelphia,[16] so now another signer of the Declaration was doing what he could to help a Jew in the same fashion.

As frequently in war-time, there was a rash of marriages. This natural tendency towards matrimony during an era of crisis was intensified by the fact that young Jewish men and women from several cities were gathered together for the first time. Benjamin Seixas married Hayman Levy's daughter, Zipporah.[17] Philip Moses arrived from Charleston, and soon after met and wed Sarah Machado, the step-daughter of Israel Jacobs.[18] In 1778, Jacob Hart married Leah, the daughter of Lyon Nathan,[19] and the following year Dr. Isaac Abrahams took as his wife her sister Rachel.[20] The Englishman Simon Nathan, who came to Philadelphia by way of New Orleans, Havana, and Richmond, wooed and won the *hazan*'s sister, Grace Seixas, shortly after he settled down.[21] These weddings and others, as well as the presence in town of numbers of already married couples from other cities, account for the fact that many Jews, later prominent in New York and elsewhere, were technically native-born Philadelphians.

A few Jews came to town only for short periods to conduct necessary business with Congress, as did the distinguished merchant of Newport, Aaron Lopez, who in February, 1779, was concerned with an appeal for the recovery of his schooner *Hope* which had been seized by Connecticut privateers.[22] One such visitor was somewhat of a rolling-stone. Abraham Forst, "Mercht., lately arrived in this City from Eustatia," who took his oath of allegiance on August 16, 1780,[23] was treated by Dr.

Rush in September, 1781; and by the next year, instead of paying his doctor's bill, he had "Run away to London."[24] A number of Jews, both temporary and permanent residents, called on the famous physician for his help, and his ledger for 1779-82 contains many entries, like "Mordecai Sheafter [Sheftall] a Jew from Georgia," "Mr. Josephson Jew Markt. St.," and "Moses Cohen Jew in front Street."[25]

However, of all the Jews who sought asylum in Philadelphia during the Revolution, the most distinguished was the man who had little to say in all of the many languages at his command. His genius in discounting foreign notes and converting them into spendable cash helped the worried government out of one of its many difficulties. If Haym Salomon had not escaped the British, his life would have been as worthless as the fiat continental currency. He arrived in Philadelphia in 1778 penniless, and shortly thereafter, with diligence and devotion, helped chart the course of the country's finances.

If the Jews of Poznan province, who were able to recall Haym Salomon, would have known that on Yom Kippur eve in the year 1785, and forever thereafter, as a mark of his distinction a Sephardic *hashcabah*, or memorial prayer, would be chanted in his honor,[26] they would have shaken their heads in disbelief. They might have asked why he, who knew little Hebrew beyond his prayer book, warranted such recognition—the first in its history—in a synagogue in Philadelphia, where he had lived only a few years. As a Jew, Salomon received the reverent immortality which befitted the dignity of the synagogue. As a man who became intimately involved in the first wartime finances of the United States, he has been immodestly glorified. His consistent patriotism was in itself strong enough not to require the unhappy falsification of history.[27]

Salomon was born in Lezno, Poland, in 1740, of poor parents. The Prussian acquisition of the town gave it the German name of Lissa. Poland during the eighteenth century gasped for freedom, but continued to heave between the Prussian west and Russian east. The Jews desired to live as freely as Poland herself wished to be, but the Poles gave little thought to the aspirations of their Jewish fellow-sufferers. A weak, disintegrating country, which persecuted its Jews, fought bravely but hopelessly for its own freedom, and finally was swallowed up by its more powerful neighbors.

It was not alone the oppressiveness and uneasiness of the

times which dispersed many of the Jews of Lezno. In 1767 the city was partly devoured by a fire which destroyed many of the wooden shacks of the Jewish section, forcing the homeless to flee to other nearby towns or distant lands.[28]

Almost nothing remains to tell us of Salomon's Polish background. The legend that he had associated with Pulaski and Kosciusko in the Polish fight for freedom has no foundation in fact. Poland did not seek Jewish help in her conflict with Russia, nor was it willing to extend to Jews the rights that would have enabled them to participate in it. In America, the three Poles emerged as leaders in a common cause, but no documentary evidence exists to show that Salomon even knew Pulaski, who was killed in the South Carolina campaign in 1779.

There is but one record of Salomon's contact with Kosciusko,[29] who, however, did not become active in the Polish independence movement until after his service in the American Revolution.

The fogginess of myth which has obscured the course of Salomon's life before he came to America hides as well the facts of his career after his arrival. It is known that he brought with him a knowledge of several European languages, acquired in the various countries in which he had traveled, and enough experience in European commerce to be able to solve the mysteries of foreign exchange. The exact date of his arrival in New York is not known, but it would seem to have been some time around 1775.[30]

Neither is it known how he first earned a living. If he followed the pattern set by other immigrants from Europe, he would have worked as a clerk or assistant for one or another of the Jewish merchants of the city. In the summer of 1776 he is described in a document as "a distiller,"[31] and that may well have been his old country trade, for Lezno had earned a local distinction for brewing and distilling.

Before he could develop this venture, the fast-moving events of the war drew him into its vortex. For a short time in 1776 he was a sutler to the American troops at Lake George, where he went with a recommendation that he had "hitherto sustained the Character of being warmly attached to America."[32] It is probable that his sympathies lay with the Americans from the start, yet there is no record showing that he belonged to the pre-Revolutionary Sons of Liberty. He never joined Shearith Israel either, for before he had had a chance to establish himself in New York, the patriotic congregation broke up for the duration of the war.

Again the evidence is not detailed, but it is certain that by 1776 Haym Salomon had irrevocably cast his lot with the patriots. Shortly after the British occupation of New York in the autumn of that year, he was arrested as a spy by General Robertson, and confined in the dread, military prison, the Provost.[33] Soon after, as Salomon later explained to Congress, he was released "by the Interposition of Lieut. General Heister who wanted him on account of his knowledge in French, Polish, Russian, Italian &ca. Languages," and he was turned over to the Hessian commander to act as purveyor of commissary supplies.[34] In this position he worked quietly, performing his tasks for the British, while at the same time he helped French and American prisoners with money and with plans for their escape to the American lines.

He was, however, permitted to continue his business, now apparently a very profitable trade in ships provisions. Advertisements in the first half of the next year show Salomon located at various addresses on old Broad Street between the Post Office and the City Hall in New York, offering "ships bread and rice" and other supplies for "Captains of Ships and others."[35] During his peculiar and dangerous respite he had married Rachel, the fifteen-year-old daughter of Moses B. Franks. Abraham I. Abrahams, who had prepared Michael Gratz's Hebrew *kosher* certificates ten years before, now turned his quill to engross the traditional *ketubah*, or marriage certificate, which was duly signed and witnessed on July 6, 1777.[36]

Ezekiel, his first son, was born on July 28, 1778, and even this added responsibility did not prevent Salomon from working as best he could for the American cause. While interpreting for the Hessians, he tried to propagandize them into desertion. But before his son was two weeks old, the British got wind of his actions and issued orders for his arrest.

In some undetermined manner Salomon made his escape, and, leaving his family and all his material possessions behind him, he successfully crept through the British lines, crossed New Jersey, and reached Philadelphia and safety two weeks later.[37]

He promptly appealed to Congress for such work as would enable a patriot to support himself, but this was the least part of his petition. After recounting his own personal experiences—and this is one of the extremely few documentary sources for his life up to this time—Salomon emphasized the unhappy plight of a Monsieur Demezes, a French prisoner "now most barbarously treated," so that this Frenchman, fighting for the Americans, might be quickly placed on a prisoner-exchange list. He ended his plea:

Your Memorialist has upon this Event most irrecoverably lost all his Effects and Credits to the amount of Five or six thousand Pounds sterling and left his distressed Wife and a Child of a month old at New York waiting that they may soon have an Opportunity to come out from thence with empty hands.[38]

Congress, beyond referring it to the overworked Board of War,[39] took no action on the petition, which told the story of genuine sacrifice, and which, moreover, placed primary emphasis on the needs of another.

Nothing that can be substantiated has survived to give us a picture of Salomon's life in Philadelphia from his arrival in the late summer of 1778 until late in 1780.[40] With foreign money in the form of bills and drafts coming into Philadelphia as a result of the loans negotiated by Franklin and others in Europe, there was opportunity for a broker who knew foreign exchange. It seems logical that Salomon with his European financial background should have chosen this field in which to support himself, and by 1781 he had established himself firmly. Meanwhile, in some unknown fashion, he had managed to get his wife and son to Philadelphia, and the Salomons kept increasing their family year by year.

His first advertisement in the Philadelphia press on February 28, 1781, modestly noted there were "A few Bills of Exchange on France, St. Eustatia & Amsterdam, to be sold by Haym Solomon, Broker."[41] Unlike some of the other refugee New Yorkers who were able to secure offices, counting-houses, or modest shops, Salomon was at first without benefit of his own place of business. He stated in his notice that he would:

attend every day at the Coffee-House between the hours of twelve and two, where he may be met with, and any kind of business in the brokerage will be undertaken by him.

A month later, when he had added English bills to his list, he announced that in addition to his midday attendance at the Coffee-House he could be "met with at Jacob Mier's in Front-street, next door to Stephen Shewell's, facing Pewter-platter-alley, in the forenoon and afternoon."[42]

Salomon's newspaper advertisements trace his transition from an humble and obscure businessman to the authorized broker to the Office of Finance. In July, 1781, he offered "Bills on Holland, France, Spain, England, St. Croix, &c.", stated that he would sell "on commission, Loan-office certificates, and all other kinds of merchandise," and gave evidence of his rise up the mercantile scale by referring to "his office in Front-street, between Market and Arch streets."[43] Yet, the bustling Front Street Coffee-House remained the center of his activity, for there, amid the hubbub, smoke and ale, bills of exchange and merchandize were bought and sold by the merchants who used that tavern as their Bourse.

On May 10, 1781, Robert Morris was appointed the first Superintendent of the Office of Finance, a pre-Constitution Secretary of the Treasury. He found the country's credit low, its need for funds great, and its financial affairs in a muddle. He proceeded with imagination and administrative skill to arrange the money matters of the government so that the needs of the army and the new government could be met. And one of his main problems was to turn the foreign bills of exchange, which the United States was receiving in the form of loans, into usable cash without losing so much in discount that the loans failed in their purpose.

Morris needed a broker with two assets: an understanding of European finance and an unimpeachable credit. Haym Salomon had both. He had found a secure niche in commercial Philadelphia, and the Philadelphia merchants had learned to respect him. When Robert Morris "agreed with" Salomon to assist him, he already found that he was working officially for the French Army, converting its government bills into hard cash, which in turn was used to buy supplies for its troops. Morris' diary entries are the key sources of information for Salomon's relationship with the Office of Finance. The first of more than a hundred of the references to Salomon there, on June 8, 1781, reads:

I agreed with Mr. Haym Salomon the Broker, who has been employed by the officers of his most Chris'n Majesty to make sale of their Army and Navy Bills to assist me.[44]

There were in Philadelphia at the time some twenty-five brokers of whom two were Jews, Moses Cohen and Haym Salomon.

Why the French, now America's chief ally, chose Salomon from this number to handle their affairs is not known.[45] Previous investigators have been misled into writing that Salomon actually negotiated the French loans. The fact is that he was employed as a trusted agent of the French government for the most logical of reasons; he understood their language, and he understood the complications of Franco-American finance. Morris' choice of Salomon was also logical. He would have as his agent the man who was at the same time the agent for the government with whom the United States was most financially involved. Or, could Morris, who was a member of Congress, have recalled Salomon's letter of August 11, 1778, asking for help for the French patriot Demeze, and an opportunity to serve Congress?

The main fact was that Haym Salomon was a devoted patriot. An interesting observation on this fact and on the position of Jews in Philadelphia is contained in the autobiography of the prominent lawyer, Peter Stephen Du Ponceau. There, speaking of the notorious Tory physician, Abraham Chovet, Du Ponceau wrote his recollections of a meeting between Salomon and Chovet:

> Being one day in the Coffee-house, just after the news of the capture of Lord Cornwallis at York Town had been received, he [Chovet] was accosted by a Jew Broker of the name of Solomon who in a rude manner went up to him and said with a sneer, 'Well, Doctor, I presume you know that your friend Lord Cornwallis is taken with all his army.' 'Do you believe it?' said Chovet. 'To be sure, I do,' replied the Jew. 'Well, my good friend, I can only tell you that you had better believe in Jesus Christ, that will save your poor soul from a worse fate than that of Lord Cornwallis, if, as you say, he has been captured.' The laughers were not on the side of the Israelite.[46]

Writing these reminiscences in 1837, Du Ponceau significantly added, "At this day it would be a cruel sarcasm; but people at that time were not so liberal as they are now. The Jews were yet a hated and a despised race."

The fall of 1781 was a decisive one in American history. With much effort supplies had been obtained for the final campaign in Virginia. The French fleet sailed south, and the French troops joined the Americans already there. On October 19, 1781, Cornwallis surrendered to Washington at Yorktown. The fighting war was over, but the financial battles continued. A more subtle enemy—inflation—plagued the former colonists, and maintained a hidden war when British guns had been silenced. Continental currency, English counterfeits, Pennsylvania paper bills and the like from each of the new states circulated at unequal values and with no gold or silver to back them.

In the face of speculators, who worked in quiet but consistent opposition to the vital interest of the United States, Haym Salomon undertook the task of selling on the Philadelphia market bills of exchange and government notes for the highest price obtainable. Morris and Salomon had agreed that his commission would not exceed one-half of one percent, which was Salomon's total profit on each transaction; and this at a time when other Philadelphia brokers were charging from two to five percent.[47] On December 31, 1781, "when our finances were, in a crisis, almost desperate," as Peletiah Webster wrote five years later,[48] the Bank of North America was established by Congress to provide credit for the government and a regularized channel for money. A thousand shares at $400 each were issued; Isaac Moses bought one, and Haym Salomon two.[49]

Small as his commission was, Salomon must have made up for it by volume, for his advertisements which began appearing with increasing frequency told of an enlarged business. In the *Pennsylvania Packet*, which came out three times a week, Salomon's advertisements appeared nineteen times from January to July.[50]

The week of July 12, 1782, Robert Morris observed in his diary that:

This Broker has been useful to the public Interest and Requests leave to Publish himself as a Broker to the Office to which I have consented as I do not see that any disadvantage can possibly arise to the public service but the Reverse and he expects individual Benefits therefrom.[51]

Consequently, a week later, Salomon announced himself with a new title, and described what had become, by then, manifold activities.

Haym Solomons,

Broker to the Office of Finance, to the Consul General of France, and to the Treasurer of the French Army, at his Office in Front-street, between Market and Arch-streets, Buys and Sells on Commission.

Bank Stock, Bills of Exchange on France, Spain, Holland and other parts of Europe, the West Indies, and inland bills, at the usual commission. He buys and sells Loan Office Certificates, Continental and State Money, of this or any other state, Paymaster and Quartermaster Generals Notes; these and every other kind of paper transactions (bills of exchange excepted) he will charge his employers no more than One Half Per Cent for his Commission.

He procures Money on Loan for short time and gets Notes and Bills discounted.

Gentlemen and others, residing in this state or any of the united states, by sending their orders to this Office, may depend on having their business transacted with as much fidelity and expedition as if they were themselves present.

He receives Tobacco, Sugars, Tea, and every other sort of Goods to Sell on commission; for which purpose he has provided proper Stores.

He flatters himself, his assiduity, punctuality, and extensive connections in his business, as a Broker, is well established in various parts of Europe, and in the united states in particular.

All persons who shall please to favour him with their business, may depend upon his utmost exertion for their interest, and part of the Money Advanced, if required.[52]

In August, 1782, Morris delivered to Salomon a wagon receipt for twenty dry hides sent from South Carolina, and asked him to sell them to the best advantage of the United States, and also requested that he do the same with a "few Casks of Pott Ash or Pearl Ashes," which were government property.[53] In the same sultry month, James Madison wrote his fellow-delegate to Congress, Edmund Randolph:

I cannot in any way make you more sensible of the importance of your kind attention to pecuniary remittances for me than by informing you that I have for some time past been a pensioner on the favor of Haym Salomon, a Jew Broker.[54]

This was a side of his business which brought Salomon thanks, but no money. Yet, he understood the difficulties of Madison and others who were serving their country at great sacrifice to themselves.

The pattern repeated itself, and other names appear in his ledger—General St. Clair, Baron Steuben, his fellow-Pole Kosciusko, General Mifflin, Edmund Randolph, Colonel Mercer, James Wilson and James Ross.[55] Madison had to return to this well, and again to Randolph he wrote:

The kindness of our little friend in Front Street near the Coffee-House, is a fund which will preserve me from extremities, but I never resort to it without great mortification, as he obstinately rejects all recompense. The price of money is so usurious that he thinks it ought to be extorted from none but those who aim at profitable speculations. To a necessitous delegate he gratuitously spares a supply out of his private stock.[56]

It is noteworthy that the "Jew Broker" had become "our little friend." But chances are that neither Salomon nor Madison noticed the change; both were occupied with more serious matters.

Salomon's activity now embraced all the usual phases of brokerage. His services, if not the best in America's largest city, were apparently the most reliable; his endorsement on a note made it "undeniable." When the sudden exhaustion of American funds drawn on French loans left many bills of exchange worthless, Salomon announced that all such bills bearing his endorsement would be guaranteed.[57] Even then the signature of Haym Salomon was worth a good deal of money.

Like other brokers, he expanded his interests into the field of real estate, and the valuable square "bounded by Chestnut, Walnut, Seventh and Eighth streets" was but one of the many city and country properties which were placed with him for sale.[58] As far as existing evidence shows, none of this was owned by Salomon. He did have some property in the northern part of the city, but its location is not now known. In spite of the fact that his purse was open to Jewish charities, the general welfare, and individual patriots, his name was entered on the delinquent tax list for this property in 1784.[59] Paradoxically, in this year, the last of his life, the volume of his businesses moved steadily forward.

Merchants and brokers who had achieved success moved their families as quickly as possible from the bustle of Front Street commerce to homes more in keeping with their financial standing. Salomon, more unassuming, lived in the same building where he conducted his business. The family lived above and behind the office, and their quarters, if not spacious, were appointed with a suggestion of newly-acquired luxury. Mahogany furniture and silver-plate helped fill the two rooms used for the living space of a family, now grown to five persons.[60] A horse and chaise met the needs of comfort and transportation. This was not fancy living for one to whom great wealth has been ascribed. Compared to lesser known Jews, who had neither five years' residence in Philadelphia nor Salomon's financial ability, he had not acquired much in worldly goods. Simon Nathan, after four years, could boast a "handsome, genteel House, Garden and Stables in Arch-Street . . . known by the name of Rock-Hall."[61] The closest Salomon could come to an eighteenth-century mansion was the agency for the sale of the famous Slate Roof House, where William Penn had lived in 1700.[62]

In the spring of 1784, Salomon planned further to expand his business by opening a New York branch. He entered into partnership with young Jacob Mordecai in a venture which added to all the other services he had offered that of auctioneering.[63] The announcement of this plan, differing considerably from the usual American advertisement of the period, contained a summary of Salomon's previous patriotic and business activities:

> A desire of being more extensively useful, and of giving universal satisfaction to the Public, are among his principal motives for opening this house, and shall be the great leading principle of all its transactions. By being Broker to the Office of Finance, and honored with its confidence, all those sums have passed through his hands which the generosity of the French Monarch, and the affection of the Merchants of the United Provinces, prompted them to furnish us with, to enable us to support the expence of the war, and which have so much contributed to its successful and happy termination; this is a circumstance which has established his credit and reputation, and procured him the confidence of the Public, a confidence which it shall be his study and ambition to merit and encrease by sacredly performing all his engagements. . . .

There was hardly a newspaper in Philadelphia—in English, French or German—which did not carry the full-column advertisement of which the foregoing was a part.[64]

Meanwhile, the semi-official Bank of North America had to meet its need for additional capital with a second subscription. In addition to Salomon both for himself and on behalf of the Dutch firm, De Heyder, Veydt & Co., other Jewish merchants, now in a better position to participate, added their support. Sol Marache, representing his firm of Spencer and Marache, Moses Cohen, and Solomon Lyons, all bought shares.[65] But at this juncture in its tenuous existence as the clearing house for national funds the Bank of North America was suddenly threatened—and with it the solvency of the nation—by the petition of a private group seeking a charter for a new, competing bank, the Bank of Pennsylvania.[66]

Morris received the unpleasant news from his agent, and on February 10, 1784, he recorded in his diary:

> Haym Salomon informs me that Edward Shippen and others chosen President and Directors of a new Bank lately instituted in opposition to the National Bank have presented a Petition for a Charter of Incorporation.[67]

A bitter struggle ensued. One bank was struggling for existence and for national credit; a second bank, organized for personal profit, could, in the unstable economy, bring destruction to both. There was no doubt where Salomon's loyalties lay, and his support of the Bank of North America and opposition to the Bank of Pennsylvania in the Coffee-House evoked a vicious attack upon him and his fellow-Jews by one of the petitioners for the new bank, Miers Fisher.

Miers Fisher was a Quaker lawyer, who prior to the Revolution had attained considerable distinction. During the war, his Tory sympathies led to his detention in a Virginia camp for like-minded exiles. When he returned to Philadelphia after the war, he, together with other members of his well-established mercantile family, began to reassert their former influence in the affairs of the city. Not primarily interested in its effect on the United States, Fisher vigorously supported the establishment of the new bank, and in the Assembly of Pennsylvania made a sensational plea on its behalf, which, although the original cannot now be located, seems to have been largely an attack on "Jew Brokers."

The reply to Fisher's attack, a counterattack upon him, and at the same time a defense of the Jews of the United States—the first of its kind to appear in this country—was signed "A Jew Broker." Its author could have been any one of the seven Philadelphia Jews then in the brokerage business,[68] but internal evidence would seem to indicate that it was written by one, who served as spokesman for all—Haym Salomon. But it was more than Salomon, linguist though he was, would have been able to write alone. Not too well disguised was the co-authorship of the editor of the paper in which it appeared, Eleazer Oswald of the *Independent Gazetteer*, whose curdling adjectives, anti-Quakerism, and strong patriotic views sing clearly through the whole article. Oswald's friendliness with Jews was no secret; Moses Cohen was a close associate of his and had known him since the battle of Monmouth where Oswald lost a leg.[69] Yet, the article was equally against the Bank of Pennsylvania and everything that institution stood for. It was a gamey polemic of a period when controversial writing was an art.

The article, which appeared in the paper of Saturday, March 13, 1784, is too long to be printed in full, although as a significant one in American Jewish history it deserves such treatment. It was addressed to Miers Fisher, Esquire:

I must address you, in this manner, although you do not deserve it. Unaccustomed as you are to receive any mark of respect from the public, it will be expected that I should make an apology for introducing a character, *fetid* and *infamous*, like yours, to general notice and attention. Your conspicuous *toryism* and *disaffection* long since buried you in the silent grave of *popular* oblivion and contempt . . .

. . . Unhappy and disappointed man! Once exiled and excommunicated by the state, as a *sly, insudious enemy;* severed and detached from the generous bosom of *patriotism* and *public* virtue: *Shunned* and deserted by *faithful*

friends, in whom you once so safely trusted; Since, debarred and prevented
from *your practice* by rule of court, as an attorney at the bar . . .

But whatever claims of mercy you may demand, on these accounts: Whatever I should think, were I to judge of you as your *personal* enemy in *private*
respects: Yet the *forward* and unexampled advances and steps you have lately
taken in the concert of *public* affairs: The high-cockaded air of *fancied* importance you now assume: The petulant, discontented humor you have manifested for establishing *a new Bank:* Your longings and pantings to approach
our *political vineyard,* and blast the fruits of those labors for which you
neither *toiled nor spun;* and more particularly, the indecent, unjust, inhu-
mane aspersions, you cast so indiscriminately on the Jews of this city at large,
in your arguments of Wednesday week, before that honorable Legislature of
the commonwealth: These circumstances, if my apprehensions are right, pre-
clude you from any lenity or favor, and present you a fair victim and offering
to the sacred altar of public justice. . . .

You not only endeavoured to injure me by your unwarrantable expressions, but every other person of the same *religious* persuasion I hold, and
which the laws of the country, and the glorious toleration and *liberty of
conscience* have allowed me to indulge and adopt. The injury is highly crim-
soned and aggravated, as there was no proper reason or ground for your
invectives. The attack on the *Jews* seemed wanton, and could only have been
premeditated by such a base and degenerate mind as your's. . . .

Permit me, then, with this view of things, to take notice of these terms of
reproach and invective, which, considering you as a friend to good manners
and decorum, you have heaped on our nation and profession with so liberal
and unsparing a hand. I am a Jew; it is my own nation and profession. I also
subscribe myself a Broker, and a Broker too whose opportunities and knowledge, along with other Brokers of his intimate acquaintance, in a great course
of business, has made him very familiar and privy to every minute design
and artifice of your *wiley colleagues* and associates. I exult and glory in reflecting that we have the honour to reside in a *free* country where, as a people,
we have met with the most generous countenance and protection, and I do
not at all despair, notwithstanding former obstacles, that we shall still obtain
other privilege that we aspire to enjoy along with our fellow-citizens. It also
affords me unspeakable satisfaction, and is indeed one of the most pleasing
employments of my thoughtful moments, to contemplate that we have in
general been early uniform, decisive whigs, and were second to none in our
patriotism and attachment to our country!

. . . Having only ventured to give an account of the leading characters who
compose the new Bank, allow me in conclusion to rectify an error of Mr.
Fisher's, who publicly declared, 'the Jews were the authors of high and unusual interest.' No! the Jews can acquit themselves of this artful imputation,
and turn your own batteries on yourself. It was neither the *Jews* or *Christians*
that founded the practice; but, *Quakers,*—and *Quakers* worse than *Heathens,
Pagans* or *Idolators;* men, though not Jews in *faith,* are yet Jews in *traffic;*
men abounding with avarice, *who neither fear God, nor regard man.*

Those very persons who are now flattering themselves with the idea of a
new Bank, first invented the practice of discounting notes at five per cent. I
have retained an alphabetical list of names as well as the other Brokers, and
can specify persons, if necessary. In the language of *Naphtali* to *David,* I have

it in my power to point at the very *would-be* Directors, and say, "*Thou art the man.*" I can prove, that it were these people, unwilling to venture money in trade during the war, who first declined letting out money on the best mortgage and bond security. . . .[70]

The controversy did not end with this; it continued for many months thereafter. The "Spectator," in answer, thought he "could discover worse than a Shylock's temper remaining in the hearts of those despisers of Christianity," hinted that "no Jew Broker," but the peg-legged editor of the *Gazetteer* wrote the attack, and referred to an "air balloon, of a large construction, to convey him and all the Jew-Brokers, to New-Scotland, where they will be abundantly more thought of, than in Pennsylvania."[71] The writer was alluding to a balloon ascension which had been scheduled to take place on the Fourth of July, 1784, for which subscriptions were asked. The most prominent citizens of the city joined in the fund raising, and Haym Salomon, Benjamin Nones, and Jonas Phillips were listed as receiving subscriptions at their various places of business.[72]

But the bank controversy went bitterly on. Seven months later, when Salomon was confined to bed with his final illness, "A Whig," still smarting under the restoration of privileges to Fisher, punned that "this discontented party . . . might *mire* every point of the revolution, if not restrained in the first instance of *fishering* to some sense of submission."[72a]

The incorporation of the Bank of Pennsylvania was defeated, but Fisher was not only successful in maintaining his position, he bettered it; later he became a director of the very bank he had opposed. Yet, his anti-Jewish feeling crept into an account of Philadelphia written by the French traveller, Brissot de Warville, who in 1788 on a visit here relied upon Fisher for certain of his observations, among them the vicious canard:

. . . and this will explain the common saying that you so often hear repeated at Philadelphia, that the Quakers are so cunning that the Jews themselves cannot live among them. Usurious Jews can never live among economical men, who have no need of borrowing at enormous interest; for a similar reason a seller of pork cannot live among Jews.[73]

It is small wonder that Robert Morris pleaded with Tom Paine to write a pamphlet on the Bank of North America and its opponents.[74] There, most effectively, the author of *Common Sense* upheld what Haym Salomon had worked so hard to establish, and castigated those Tories who were enriched, rather than impoverished, by the Revolution.

7

The Organization of Religious Life and the Building of the First Synagogue

THE American Revolution not only created a new nation, but it profoundly influenced the Jewish community of Philadelphia. Political equality and complete religious freedom evolved gradually but surely. The Jewish population had grown from slightly over one hundred in 1765 to three times that number in 1775, and the direct impact of the war brought refugees to Philadelphia from all the colonies. By the time of Cornwallis' surrender, six years later, there were almost two hundred families, or approximately one thousand Jews, crowded into the city.[1]

Hazan Seixas, when he arrived in Philadelphia on June 6, 1780, bringing with him the ritual property of the New York congregation,[2] had noted that the rented synagogue quarters were small, but it was the experienced laymen from the other states who stimulated the reorganization of the congregation and the construction of the first synagogue building. Indirectly, too, the Revolution spurred the religious life by inspiring the communal leaders to organize themselves in a broader and more definite manner. The outcome, a new synagogue and a congregation with formal rules and regulations, was of a national character rather than purely a local accomplishment. The same Jews who had fought the British guns or refused to remain under the British yoke in occupied cities were now directing their energies to establishing a permanent religious home in Philadelphia.

The matter came to a head on March 17, 1782. The oldest extant minutes of the congregation record a memorandum signed by Barnard Gratz, Hayman Levy, Jonas Phillips, Benjamin Seixas, and Simon Nathan, as the *adjunta,* or board of directors, stating that they thereby formed themselves into "a Congregation to be known and distinguished by the name of Mikve Israel in the City of Philadelphia."[3] That same day the original members of that congregation signed their names to a list.[4] And Barnard Gratz and Solomon Myers Cohen were immediately authorized to negotiate the purchase of an old bake-house and lot on Sterling Alley within sight of the rented quarters on Cherry Alley, now Cherry Street.

The New Yorkers, drawing upon their experience in the administration of Shearith Israel, recognized that at this juncture a formal organization had to be created. With Isaac Moses as *segan,* or acting presiding officer, a meeting was held on Sunday, March 24, 1782, to receive the report of the committee appointed to secure a new site. Before that pressing business was presented, Moses observed that, although it had been decided to buy a piece of ground, the congregation had no established rules; their officers had no legal powers; and their determinations were not binding on the members. To correct this situation he offered a resolution that those present should agree "That in order to promote our Holy Religion, and Establish a Proper Congregation in this City," they form themselves into a congregation, and bind themselves "One to the other that we will assist if required, to form a Constitution, & rules for the good Government of the Congregation, and strictly abide by the same."[5]

He thereupon suggested that new officers be properly elected, and he forthwith divested himself of his own office. The other members of the old *adjunta* followed suit. A chairman pro tem, Charleston's Isaac Da Costa,[6] was appointed, and the meeting proceeded to act. It was decided that the congregation should be administered by an elected *parnass,* or president, and five *adjuntas.* A penalty of £10 was set for the refusal to serve as *parnass* if elected, and one of £5 for refusal to serve as an *adjunta.* Isaac Moses was promptly elected *parnass,* and the five former *adjuntas* formally reinstated.

The first obligation of the new officers was set as the preparation of a "Code of Laws" which would be read publicly on the
first and second days of the approaching Passover holidays. Any
persons not present at the March 24th meeting, who wanted to
join the congregation, could make application for membership
within fifteen days after the publication of the laws. This initial
action was felt to be too restrictive, and the clause was changed
at a subsequent meeting to allow absentees to sign the membership list and become members automatically. At the same time
two *gabayim,* or treasurers, were added to the officers: Solomon
Myers Cohen for the *tsedaka,* or congregational charity fund,
and Simon Nathan for the important building fund.[7]

Once the formal framework had been set up, the matter of
the new synagogue site came up for discussion. It was then discovered that it would cost as much to repair and enlarge the old
building on Sterling Alley, which Cohen and Gratz had already
bought from Robert Wall, as it would to erect a new one.
Consequently, the officers were authorized to go ahead with
the more ambitious plan.[8] Contracts were promptly made with
carpenters and masons.[9] Mordecai M. Mordecai, who had been
a resident of Easton as early as 1760,[10] was assigned the important
task of preparing letters in Hebrew to secure the approval of the
London and Amsterdam synagogues for the design of the building. At last, the "mighty news" which had excited Jacob Henry's
imagination in 1761 was about to become a reality.

However, all did not proceed smoothly after the brave beginning. The Jews then in Philadelphia were far from affluent; most
of them had lost much when they voluntarily left their businesses
in British hands to go into exile. The funds did not pour in over-
abundantly, although at the first try sixty-one subscribers pledged
£897,[11] of which Haym Salomon promised better than one-third
of the total. This was only a year and a half after he had become
a war-time broker, and how he managed to make such a substantial contribution—which he had difficulty paying on time—remains incredible. Others gave too—Jonas Phillips £144, Isaac
Moses £96, Hayman Levy £73, and Michael Gratz £57—and
still others in much smaller amounts, which reflected their ability
and a genuine spiritual interest in the project, and which as a
start seemed to promise success.

Almost as soon as the project had gotten under way, notice
came from Joseph Cauffman—apparently not a Jew—the landlord

of the Cherry Street house where the congregation was occupying a rented second-floor room, giving them notice to vacate immediately.[12] The short notice compelled Jonas Phillips to apply for an extension, which in view of the positive building program, was granted. But then another, more serious problem presented itself. The ground on Sterling Alley, intended for the synagogue, adjoined that of the Reformed German Congregation and, when notice of the Jews' plans came to its attention, objection was raised by the German church on the ground that a synagogue next door would "disturb" them.[13]

It was strange that a sect which had itself been persecuted in Europe showed so little tolerance of others in a land which had given it freedom and peace, for it was representatives of a similar group that had ardently supported the Christian Test Oath of 1776. They had not yet learned to share religious freedom with others; nonetheless, some years later the Reformed Church of Aaronsburg was to receive a plot of land for its church as a gift from Aaron Levy, a member of Mikveh Israel.[14] The Jews of Philadelphia, while they must have been hurt, maintained their dignity and showed no animosity. A series of letters sent to the church, expressing their surprise that a neighboring synagogue "should in the least Disturb you," and declaring their desire "to live in friendship with our Neighbours," offered to sell the ground to the church for what it had cost, £540.[15] The letters remained unanswered.

During the time the congregation awaited a reply from the church a better site had been offered them, but exhausted funds prevented their making an immediate purchase. The subscription moneys had been spent on the first lot and were committed to the building. On April 25th the congregation was called together to resolve the problem: to build in spite of the church opposition or to find the money for the new lot. It was the energetic Isaac Moses who had suggested that, if they could raise the necessary £300 within the next few days, they should do so; and it was decided that, in order to accomplish it, following an old Jewish custom, the four cornerstones and the two doorposts be sold to the highest bidders in return for prayers and synagogal honors.[16] Jonas Phillips bought the first cornerstone for $100, Isaac Moses the second for $75, I. Mordecai the third for $60, Michael Gratz the fourth for $75 and the right-hand doorpost for $30, and Isaac Da Costa the left-hand doorpost for

$30.[17] A total of $370 was thus promised, and the purchase of the new lot was authorized.

At last the work on the building could proceed. On the north side of Cherry Street, about midway in the block from Third Street to Sterling Alley, around the corner from the German Reformed Church which had been so unfriendly, half a block from the Zion Lutheran Church at the corner of Fourth and Cherry, only a square from the first Methodist Church established in America at the corner of Third near Vine, and just as near to the Friends' Arch Street Meeting, the first synagogue building in Philadelphia began to rise. With fitting ceremony on 7 Tamuz 5542—June 19, 1782—the cornerstones,[18] and nine days later the sills and doorposts,[19] were laid, with blessings asked for the generous men in whose names they were dedicated.

By modern standards it was a tiny edifice, being described by the building committee—consisting of Barnard Gratz, Benjamin Seixas, Gershom Seixas and Jonas Phillips—as "thirty feet from East to West and Thirty Six feet from South to North."[20] After Phillips had pointed out that space should be left in the rear for the future addition of a school house, a ritual bath, and a residence for a *hazan*,[21] the synagogue was placed about in the center of the lot, 35 feet from the street. On each side were two alleyways, one to the east for women, and one to the west for men.

Phillips, who seemed most concerned with the details, insisted upon a rabbinic opinion on the necessity of having the door on the west side, for aesthetically he would have preferred it to open on Cherry Street.

Religious custom prevailed over architectural preference,[22] and those who passed along the street saw a solid, almost square, typical Philadelphia, red-brick building, no doubt with white-painted trim, hardly distinguishable in style from those surrounding it. The contract with the builders, which gives the details of the construction, called for

. . . Eight square windows of twenty four lights each, of Ten by Twelve Glass, and two of ten by thirteen in the first story, and nine Windows of ten by thirteen in the Gallery, of sixteen lights each, the sashes for all the windows to move up and down, with proper weights, pullies and shutters, to have one outside Door, which is to hang double, and two inside doors, a plane place in the nature of a Portico of Eight feet by six, to be boarded with a winding stair Case in it, with a door at the top or bottom, . . . the seats for the men to be one set against the wall, all round the Backs to be boarded, three feet above the seats, with a caping sufficient to lay a book on, three plain rows of seats in the Front part of the Gallery, and two Rows of Seats in the sides, for the women, with a narrow strip of board to rest the back against, passages to be in the rear of the seats, the fronts of the Galleries to be panneled, and have proper caping, with six columns to support it, and in the Tuscan order, the seat for the president of the said Synagogue to be made large enough for four Persons to set in, without inconvenience, to be armed and plain on each side, and pannel'd in the back and Front, and to have a plain Canopy over it, supported by two small columns, in the same order as the Other six pillars, the platform for the Reader to be nine feet six inches, by seven feet nine inches, railed and banistered with proper pedestals, in the usual form, The Platform for the Ark to be seven feet by Eight feet, with two steps to the Ark, and to be rail'd, and banister'd with proper pedestals in the usual form also; the wooden work to be pine.[23]

Inside, off-center on the east wall, was the *hechal,* or ark containing the scrolls of the Law, decorated with branches against a stucco background. It was on the sides that the congregants sat, and, as in similar Sephardic synagogues, facing the ark was the *tebah,* or reader's table, so that the *hazan* led the services with the congregation on either side. Around the north, west and south walls ran the women's balcony. The pattern was that already established in both Newport and New York.

Knowing that the funds already raised in Philadelphia would be insufficient to take care of all the building costs, the congregation looked abroad for further help. A letter of appeal went to the wealthy Newport residents, Jacob Rodriquez Rivera and Aaron Lopez, who had just returned to their own city.[24] Another letter to Lancaster, and a similar one, written in Hebrew, to the old, established congregation in Surinam were sent off;[25] but the general tone was that of one written in English to the co-religionists of Cap François, St. Thomas, and St. Croix:

A small number of our Brethren, who having during this colamitious War fled here from different Parts for refuge, in conjunction with those in this city undertook to build a place of Worship, that we might meet to offer up our Prayers to the Holy God of Israel, having hitherto substituted a room for that purpose, from which we were compelled to move by the owner.

Our ability to compleat the building is not equal to our wishes, from many recent losses, we are under the necessity to ask assistance of our absent Brethren amongst them, we look up to *you,* & the rest of our Brethren with you, not doubting but you'll readily contribute to so laudable an undertaking—

We pray the Almighty Father of the Universe, The Lord God of Abraham, Isaac & Jacob, to take you all under his Holy Protection, & Grant you Long Life—Health & Happiness.[26]

This kind of solicitation of older congregations was, and has remained, one of the accepted means for a new congregation to get financial help. Frequently, aid was forthcoming; at other times, unbeknownst to the petitioner, the hopefully rich uncle turned out to be poorer than the struggling youngster and completely unable to help.

The financial difficulties of the congregation remained critical enough to plague the Philadelphia Jews for some years to come, and to create friction among them. Isaac Moses, Barnard Gratz, Hayman Levy, Jonas Phillips, Benjamin Seixas and Simon Nathan had signed a bond for the purchase money, which long remained unsettled.[27] The bake-house and its twenty-eight foot lot on Sterling Alley were offered for sale by Moses and Phillips at public auction on July 1st, but apparently it was not then sold.[28] Over a month later, at the foot of an advertisement of a shipment of miscellaneous French goods, just imported by Jonas Phillips for sale at his store on Market Street between Front and Second Streets, appeared a notice that the Sterling Alley property was still for sale, "the terms of payment to be made easy."[29]

Meanwhile, as the work on the synagogue building progressed, it was necessary to equip it with ritual objects. One *Sefer Torah* was already in the possession of the congregation, and now the *adjunta* applied to Moses Gomez to borrow his scrolls and ornamental crowns for use on the day of dedication. Jonas Phillips, who had his own scroll, announced his intention of consecrating it on that day; Haym Salomon presented his scroll as an outright gift. Solomon Myers Cohen supplied a new cloth for the *hazan's* reading desk.[30] Abraham Mendes Seixas presented a silver *habdalah* cup.[31] And later Captain Philip Lyon gave the congregation a glass lustre.[32] The women busied themselves conducting a subscription which netted £13.7.4 for curtains for the Ark, a silk cloth for the reader's desk, and covers for the scrolls.[33] The only items which had to be purchased out of congregational funds were additional crowns for the scrolls and the oil-lamps which burned perpetually before the ark and in memory of the dead.[34]

Hazan Seixas carefully prepared the plans for the consecration, which was to take place in September, so that the dedication would be conducted before the High Holy days. A special prayer for General Washington and the United States was composed in Hebrew and English.[35] And an invitation went off to "his Honour, the Vice-President, and the Honourable, the Executive Council of the Commonwealth of Pennsylvania."[36] The congregation, it stated, who ever "profess'd themselves liege subjects to the Sovereignty of the United States of America," would be honored by their presence at the dedication. Two days before the ceremony Jonas Phillips had been elected *parnass*, and he together with the new *adjunta*—Michael Gratz, Sol Marache, Simon Nathan, and Solomon Myers Cohen—signed the letter.

The joyful event took place on Saturday, September 13, 1782. At three o'clock, the Jews of Philadelphia solemnly but happily met "at the old shull" to recite the afternoon prayers. After the *amidah*, the president of the congregation announced the *mitzvoth*, or honors for the ceremony: the opening of the synagogue door, the opening of the ark, and the carrying of the scrolls. The procession left the Cauffman house, walked across Cherry Street, and "without any band of musick" approached the new building.[37]

Haym Salomon, as the largest contributor, was at its head, and to him fell the honor of opening the door. After appropriate blessings, the line of congregants entered the building and made the first of six *hakafoth*, or circuits around the *hazan's* reading desk, with the honored members bearing the scrolls. They all chanted the *Baruch Haba*, following it with the customary Psalms, the members having been warned on this occasion "to be particularly carefull not to raise their Voices higher than the *Hazan's* who will endeavor to modulate his Voice to a proper Pitch so as only to fill the Building."[38]

At the end of the seventh circuit, the scrolls were placed in the ark. Then the service proceeded with *Hanothen*, or prayers for "His Excellency the President, and Hon'ble Delegates of the United States of America in Congress Assembled, His Excellency George Washington, Captain General and Commander in Chief of the Federal Army of these States," the General Assembly of Pennsylvania, and the friends and allies of the nation.[39] Finally, *misheberach*, or blessings, were asked for all those who had contributed generously to the subscription fund which had made the building possible. At last the Jews of Philadelphia had their own place of worship.

Almost as soon as the synagogue was dedicated, Mikveh Israel and the Jewish community of Philadelphia faced a crisis. Just as the war had brought many Jewish refugees to Philadelphia, so peace and the evacuation of the British from the occupied coastal cities drew them home again. This gradual, but drastic, reduction in the Jewish population naturally created problems for those who were left. As soon as the British left Savannah, the Sheftalls, Polocks[40] and Sarzedas[41] began the long trip back to Georgia. Charleston welcomed its Moses', Da Costas and Sasportas'. New York's Shearith Israel called home its many members, including the influential Isaac Moses, Myer Myers, the Gomezes and others.[42] Most of the New Englanders had already left. In 1783 and through the following year the exodus continued.

The status of the *hazan*, Gershom Mendes Seixas, was part of this pattern. Everyone knew that he would eventually return to his former congregation in New York, but no one seemed prepared to face that eventuality. As Philadelphia's first spiritual leader, he could not easily be replaced.

It is an interesting commentary upon the religious life of the community to note that Gershom Mendes Seixas, a third-generation American, who had already served the New York community with distinction and who was an acknowledged leader, was not a rabbi in the European or modern sense. He was not a *hakham*, a learned man, such as ministered to the congregations of Europe. He was a minister in a new American sense, respected by Jews and non-Jews alike for his spirituality and eloquence. With only a native background, Seixas was able to control the *minhag*, or form of service, but he did not have—nor ever laid claim to—the knowledge of rabbinic law which was possessed by some of the Ashkenazic Jews who had come directly from European Jewish centers. Through his influence Mikveh Israel continued using the Sephardic prayers, introduced earlier by Nathan Levy, and continued through the efforts of Sol Marache, although they were strange to the overwhelming majority of Ashkenazic Jews who in the last two decades of the eighteenth century formed the membership of the congregation. Seixas chanted the services, but the technical problems of orthodox life had to be resolved by authorities abroad, or by one of the few learned laymen in Philadelphia.

Realizing full well that Seixas would leave, although it was not openly discussed at the meetings of the congregation, the Gratzes began to look around for a successor to him. As soon as political conditions permitted, Moses Myers, a New York friend and business associate of the Gratz brothers, went to London on behalf of his firm of Isaac Moses and Co. To him the Gratzes had entrusted a confidential mission of solicitation and inquiry, and he wrote them, with a cynical twist, of the results:

> I have presented your Petition from the Parnass & Adjunto but people don't Incline to be charitable. Should therefore anything of same nature happen your way, you must treat it in same coin: however I hope in this the Synagogue is paid for, & as I suppose you will get rid of the Yorkers, you'll have it to yourself—shall I send you a Hazan & a Haham, plenty here for each man serves himself—I am really sorry to see our Religion so much on the decline in this country, tis really Incredible; me thinks you'l say when have you grown so religious—I was always so but did not take the Methods of Shewing it, that others did—enough of this or I shall forget being in London.[43]

Actually, the English community was as impoverished by the war as were the Americans. Immigrants from Germany and Poland were making urgent demands on the communal resources, and there was little left to spare. Among these newcomers would certainly have been many who had the qualifications for the position in Philadelphia, but with no date set for Seixas' departure, the Gratzes did not press the matter.

The New Yorkers, however, their congregation formally reestablished, were pressing for their *hazan's* return, and by the end of 1783 it had come to a matter of terms, for Seixas was not completely happy about the situation at Shearith Israel. He wrote to Hayman Levy, and told him that he was not sure he could give or get satisfaction.

> . . . In the first place I am unacquainted with the Spanish and Portugueze languages which have ever been used since the first establishment of the synagogue. Secondly, I am informed that many parties are form'd (and forming) to create divisions among the reputable members of the congregation, by which means a general disunion seems to prevail instead of being united to serve the Deity, consonant to our holy law. And, thirdly, as I have now a family to provide for, I cannot think of giving up this place till I meet with some encouragement from you that my salary will be made equivalent to what I receive here, . . .[44]

Agreement, nonetheless, was satisfactorily reached, and Levy wrote the Philadelphia congregation, when they expressed some indignation, that "those who have been obliged to take up their residence in Philadelphia while this place was in the power of the British, always expected Mr. Seixas would return."[45] On

February 15, 1784, the *hazan* had given notice of his intention to leave Philadelphia at Passover.[46] He felt that he was giving the *adjunta* sufficient time to provide the congregation with another *hazan*, but Mikveh Israel complained bitterly to its sister congregation in New York that the notice was short.[47] The complaint availed them nought, but Levy, the *parnass* in New York, hinted that "the Gentn. who now officiates here" might be willing to come to Philadelphia were he approached.[48]

He was; and he came. Reluctantly, Mikveh Israel accepted Seixas' resignation, and speedily engaged the man who had substituted for him at Shearith Israel since the post-Revolutionary reconstitution of the New York congregation.

The second *hazan* of Philadelphia was Jacob Raphael Cohen, believed to be a native of the Barbary States whence he emigrated to London.[49] There he became a *mohel*, and acquired training in the leading of prayers. With this experience, he settled first in Quebec, and, when Shearith Israel in Montreal sought a *hazan*, Cohen accepted that post, becoming, late in 1779, the first Jewish minister in Canada. After the war he moved to New York, and finally in 1784 to Philadelphia, where he served faithfully as *hazan* until his death in 1811.

Fortunately, one important functionary of the new synagogue, a full-time *shamash*, or beadle, had been engaged. Three candidates for the post, Lyon Nathan, Mordecai M. Mordecai, and Abraham E. Cohen, all with adequate experience, had offered their services. The *adjunta* chose Nathan, who had come to Philadelphia in 1770, and then spelled out the terms of his employment. In addition to his annual salary of £37.10, the *shamash* was to receive his *matzoth* free. His duties were

to keep the shull and everything belonging to it clean and in good order, he is to make all the candles—light them when they are wanted, and see them properly put out. He is to attend whenever there is prayers, and see the shull secured afterwards . . . He is to see that the lamp is kept constantly burning. He is to attend all circumcisions, wedding and funerals, which are according to our religion, and no others.[50]

Almost the same duties had been prescribed by Shearith Israel in 1768.[51] Nathan did not long hold the position. Less than a year later he resigned, and Cohen was chosen in his place.[52]

Of course, the community also needed a *shohet*, or ritual slaughterer, but this presented no problem. Abraham Levy, who had replaced the controversial Israel de Lieben, whose qualifica-

tions had been the subject of inquiry by the Gratzes when he
came to Philadelphia to practise his calling in 1774, was an accepted slaughterer. And so were the religiously trained Mordecai
M. Mordecai and Mordecai Levy,[53] the latter of whom was now
serving the synagogue.

However, in Lancaster the old difficulty about which Joseph
Simon had written Barnard Gratz in 1768 again cropped up.
They had no qualified *shohet*. This time Barnard Gratz helped
out by giving a certificate to Solomon Etting, then at the minimum age of eighteen set by law, to practise *shehita* for his own
use only, according to the procedure which Barnard had taught
him. The certificate, the first of its kind in which an American
granted such a license to another American, was also signed by
Aaron Levy of Aaronsburg.[54] Had Joseph Simon, who had instituted the action, affixed his signature as well, it would have
constituted the formal licensing by a *Beth Din*, or religious
court; but for some reason he did not.

Life in America, as has been noted before, was not easy for
a religiously orthodox Jew. Burial, circumcision, marriage, *kosher*
food, services and ceremonies—all were important parts of Jewish life that had to be planned for and worked out for each
individual and each new community. There were other more
recondite matters of religion too, which for want of numbers
and organization were overlooked or disregarded in the early
days, but which in the atmosphere of a formally constituted
religious body began to assume great importance.

The observance of the Sabbath, which had been a personal
matter theretofore, then became part of the synagogue discipline.
In 1782, Ezekiel Levy, a dry goods merchant of Philadelphia,
was on a business trip to Baltimore.[55] There he was seen shaving
by a Baltimore Jew, Isaac Abrahams, who felt it his duty to
report the infraction to Mordecai M. Mordecai, who in turn
passed on the news to the head of the synagogue, Jonas Phillips.
Formal charges were instituted against Levy by the *adjunta* of
Mikveh Israel, but for lack of evidence they were dismissed.[56]
Phillips, one may be sure, would not have allowed the case to
pass by if he had been satisfied that the evidence was sound, for,
like the Gratzes, he was a faithful observer of the seventh day.
In 1793, when he was called into court as a legal witness on a
Saturday, he permitted himself to be fined £10 rather than be
sworn in on the Sabbath, and so break the Commandment.[57]

Up to this time too, the technicalities of the marriage laws had not concerned the few, unorganized Jews of Philadelphia. However, with the new feeling of corporate dignity, these became matters of concern to the community. In May, 1782, when the building plans were occupying the thought and energy of the leaders of Mikveh Israel, two poor women, Hannah Levy and the Widow Mordecai, applied to the charity fund for money to pay their rent. In spite of the pressing need for funds for the new synagogue, the women's request was granted.[58] At the same meeting of the board, note was taken of the application of Jacob I. Cohen of Virginia for membership in the congregation. A few weeks later, Cohen requested permission to marry the widow of Moses Mordecai—she who had just been helped with her rent.[59]

This presented a delicate problem to the *adjunta*. Esther Mordecai had been Elizabeth Whitlock, a Christian, who had embraced Judaism prior to her marriage with Mordecai. According to rabbinic law, a Cohen, of priestly origin, could not marry either a proselyte or a divorcee. On this occasion only the first point was involved. Cohen was told privately by Manuel Josephson of the restriction, but then the congregation insisted upon a formal statement from the prospective bridegroom, so that they could just as formally advise him that the *din*, or law, forbade a Cohen from marrying "a woman situate as the widow Mordecai is."[60]

Several meetings of the *adjunta* were devoted to this difficult case. Finally, after Gershom Seixas had asked what course he was to follow, two more meetings were held the same day, and a letter of instruction was given him:

> In answer to your letter of the 24th of August, we now inform you that you are not to marry Mr. Jacob Cohen to Mrs. Mordecai. Neither are you to be present at the wedding, and you are hereby strictly forbid, to mention said Cohen or his wife's name in any respect whatsoever in the synagogue.[61]

It is interesting to note that the *hazan* acted as an instrument of his board, and not himself as the interpreter and administrator of religious law. The directive was further strengthened by informing the membership that anyone participating in the marriage would be subject to censure or punishment. Cohen defiantly married Esther Mordecai a few days later, and narrowly escaped the only threat of excommunication by Mikveh Israel. It is not known who performed the ceremony. Jacob Cohen a few years later moved to Richmond, but lived to return with honor, and twenty-eight years later became the president of the congregation.

Another case, some years later, showed a more conciliatory attitude on the part of the synagogue officials. Moses Nathans, who had been active in synagogue affairs, was living with a woman, not a Jewess, out of wedlock, and she had had three children by him, two of whom were boys. In 1790, over the objections of the strict Manuel Josephson, he had fought for the right to have the *hazan* circumcise one of the boys.[62] Three years later, Nathans petitioned to have his mistress converted and to be permitted to marry her according to Jewish law.[63] In 1784 a similar application to Shearith Israel had been flatly refused because of a constitutional provision,[64] but Mikveh Israel had no such prohibitory clause.

This "Business of importance to Jewdaism" was difficult to resolve, and "having fully considered with Pain that there was no Haham or Beth Din appointed in any congregation on this Continent," the *adjunta* directed Benjamin Nones, then *parnass*, to write to the *Beth Din* of London for a judgment.[65] What its reply was is not known, but the marriage records of Mikveh Israel show that a Moses Nathans was wedded to a Sarah Abrahams—an appropriate name for a female convert—in May, 1794,[66] almost a year after the request was first made.

There are no extant documents relating to divorce among the Philadelphia Jews prior to 1800. However, there was a case of an unusual conditional *halitzah*, or leviration, the release of obligation to marry a brother's widow. On that occasion, the bride-to-be, Mathias Bush's daughter Eleanor (Elkalah), removed the ceremonial shoe from the foot of Georgia's Sheftall Sheftall, who promised that he would grant her a formal leviration within three months after his brother's death by which she would be freed to marry whom she pleased.[67] The record books are barren of other information, but the shoe, an essential artifact in the ancient ceremony, is still treasured at Mikveh Israel. There may have been some feeling between the orthodox Sheftalls and almost apostate Bushs which resulted in this pre-marital agreement. Moses hinted at it in a letter to his father asking permission to marry:

. . . I called on his [Dr. Solomon Bush's] Sister who was at his house—and there beheld the object of my Love; whereupon entering into a Conversation with her, and asking her Similar questions as I had ask'd the Doctor made Similar replys; she declared that her affections for me were the same & that she was ready to Convince me of it by going with me now or whenever I thought most Convenient to Georgia; . . . in my former letter I mentioned something respecting her Religion which I think proper to Explain, bad Examples are very apt to be Catching and as she frequently comes to town to her Brothers she may possibly come into some of his mode of Living . . .[67a]

It has generally been assumed that there were not men with a sound knowledge of rabbinical law in eighteenth-century America. While it is true that there were no ordained rabbis nor any accepted authorities such as were to be found in most of the established Jewish communities of Europe, there were—at least in Philadelphia—a few men with good, orthodox, scholarly backgrounds who were capable of rendering assistance in those cases which, being of a religious nature, could not properly be referred to the civil courts. Some of these were referred to Europe, but the letters setting forth the situations and the problems, as well as the cases handled by the Philadelphians themselves, show how surprisingly learned some of these men were. Perhaps it should not be surprising, for a man like Isaac Da Costa had received a good training under *Hakham* Isaac Nieto in London, and others had probably attended schools and *yeshivoth* in Europe before their emigration. The fact is that they were not professional rabbis or scholars, and yet for laymen they were well-grounded in the traditional Jewish law.

Such a one was Mordecai Moses Mordecai, a native of Telshi in Lithuania.[68] It was he who had brought the Sabbath-breaking charges against Ezekiel Levy. But in 1784 he found himself in trouble with the congregational authorities. A niece of his in Easton, Judith, the daughter of Myer Hart,[69] had fallen in love with a Christian, Lieutenant James Pettigrew, and they had been married by an army chaplain in May, 1782, without her father's knowledge or consent.[70] Thereupon he had closed his door to her, but, with a child on the way, the girl's mother was anxious to effect a reconciliation between the father and his daughter. So she asked her brother-in-law Mordecai, "a man who is well learned in Jewish law," to come to Easton to help settle the family problem.[71]

What happened thereafter became a matter of serious contention. Only one fact was agreed upon—that the father had become reconciled. Barnet Levy,[72] also a brother-in-law of Mordecai and a resident of Easton, being in Philadelphia one day, told some members of Mikveh Israel, including the *parnass* Simon Nathan and Benjamin Nones, that he had been present when Mordecai remarried the couple according to Jewish law, and that he, Levy, had actually signed the *ketubah*, or marriage contract, as a witness. Mordecai was ordered to appear before a congregational court to answer the charge, and was found guilty of performing an act contrary to Jewish law.

Mordecai was indignant, and sent Barnard Gratz and his fellow-officers a lengthy letter in Yiddish, interspersed with citations in Hebrew.[73] In this statement filled with rabbinic arguments, he attacked the ad hoc court on the basis that the members of it were neither experts on marriage law nor rabbinic law, that he had not been permitted to face the witness against him, and that Levy's evidence was invalid, because he was a single witness, whereas the law called for two, and because he was a Sabbath-breaker and a violator of the food laws and hence incompetent in a Jewish court. He further objected to the manner in which the case was heard—"I must conclude that they have resorted to the laws of Spain and Portugal, the laws of the Inquisition. The witnesses are kept behind closed doors, and they testify in secret session." Citing the law with scholarly dignity, Mordecai asked the officers to reconsider his case, and begged Gratz "for the sake of our boyhood friendship" to intervene on his behalf. The leaders of the congregation were seriously perplexed by the problem presented to them.

Perhaps feeling that these men could not understand his Yiddish sufficiently well, he addressed them once more toward the end of October,[74] and when they failed to see the matter his way, he sent them a poorly written, but colorful, letter in English, insisting that the *Beth Din* which judged the case did not know the law.[75] An ultimate decision was postponed by the urgency of other affairs which affected the congregation, particularly the unpaid bond for the synagogue land,[76] and Mordecai's case hung over until the spring of 1785.[77]

As they began once more to debate the rights and wrongs of this particular case, another knotty problem required solution. Benjamin Moses Clave, Barnard Gratz's old New Jersey partner, died in Philadelphia. He was not a member of the congregation, although a year before, fearing that he was about to die, he called in several Jews and recited the *viddui*, or confession of faith; and he had been married to a non-Jewess by a Christian minister. The question was: should he, or could he, be buried according to Jewish custom?[78] One group in the congregation at first insisted upon a *Din Torah*, or legal interpretation, from Holland.[79] They had just instructed Joseph Wolf Carpeles and Manuel Josephson to write to the rabbis of Amsterdam and The Hague about the still unresolved case of Mordecai. But another group, somewhat more realistically, felt that an immediate decision would have to be made. After all, the corpse could not be kept unburied until an answer came from abroad. Consequently, the decision was left up to a panel of experts, consisting of Carpeles, Josephson and Moses D. Nathans. It was their judgment that Clava should be buried in a corner of the cemetery, without ritual washing, without a shroud and without a ceremony.

In spite of the fact that disobedience to this judgment would bring upon the transgressor exclusion from the religious functions of the synagogue, Mordecai M. Mordecai once again opposed his judgment against that of the congregation. He not only attended the body to the grave, but washed it and clothed it.

The matter was too serious for the congregants of Mikveh Israel to handle, and so they authorized Carpeles and Josephson, as those most capable of presenting so complicated a matter, to include all their problems in a *she'elah*, or request for an interpretation, to be sent to a recognized authority abroad.[80] It is noteworthy that on this occasion the Sephardic congregation of Mikveh Israel addressed its query to Rabbi Saul of "the Ashkenazic Community of Amsterdam."

A copy of the original letter,[81] telling of Mordecai's supposed action in Easton and his known action in Philadelphia, has survived. With apologies because it was not written in Hebrew, the letter was composed in Yiddish—"German" its writers called it— a non-Slavic Yiddish, with a curious incursion of French and Alsatian words. However, it showed a grasp of rabbinics which makes it apparent that Carpeles was certainly the most Jewishly learned man in America at the time, and Josephson almost his equal. The *responsum*, or religious opinion, of Rabbi Saul has not been found,[82] but a compromise was effected at least in the Easton affair. An agreement was made with the girl and her husband whereby the boys born to them would be brought up as Christians, and the girls as Jews. A genealogy of the family shows that today the descendants on the male side are Christians, and most of those on the female side still Jews.[83]

The problem, as Carpeles and Josephson pointed out, was more than a matter of personalities.

> The matter touches the very roots of our faith, particularly in this country where each acts according to his own desire; unfortunately, many marry Gentile women, some even who are Kohanim [of the priestly tribe], and make poor excuses for themselves. [They are] completely irreligious people who profane the name of God publicly; all this has to be seen to be believed. The congregation here has no power to discipline anyone except for the minor punishment of excluding them from a ritual quorum. Nevertheless, these evil people pay no heed and come to the synagogue, because according to the law of the land they cannot be excluded. Therefore, the duty and the need are great to make an impression on the public in a matter where the congregation has jurisdiction, and to close the breach as much as possible.[84]

This appeal to higher authorities abroad was not restricted to the Jews of America. The absence of rabbinical authority in America did indeed force the Philadelphia community to address queries to such large communities as Amsterdam and London, but other religious groups were also dependent theologically upon their mother churches abroad. Even after the Protestant Episcopal Church parted formally from the Church of England, the Americans took their lead from the actions of English churchmen. The Lutheran pastor, Muhlenberg, regularly sent back notes and queries, full of sectarian problems, to Halle in Germany. Young Francis Asbury, founder of the Methodist Church in America, felt in constant need of counsel from the great English leader, John Wesley. And after the war, the Catholics of the United States petitioned Rome for the appointment of an American bishop. Most of the religious bodies of the new nation were still tied to the theological apron-strings of Europe.

It is all the more remarkable, therefore, that the co-author of the *she'elah* to Holland, Manuel Josephson, should have been accepted as an authority by other Jews in America. He had a small library of rabbinic literature, which he probably imported from Europe, as he did the works of the popular Anglo-Jewish author, David Levi, whose books he sold.[85] His European correspondents addressed him in Yiddish, but he wrote English and Hebrew with almost equal facility. In 1785, he was elected presi-

dent of Mikveh Israel.[86] When Haym Salomon died and left
his widow and children an estate which contained barely enough
to pay the outstanding debts, Josephson personally aided the
widow.[87] He reached that point of social and economic standing which successive Philadelphia Directories described as "a
gentleman."

He also had the distinction of owning the only *shofar*, or
ram's horn, used in the High Holy Day services, in Philadelphia. But, at one period, when he was having some difficulties
with his successors in the administration of Mikveh Israel, he
told them, when they requested his horn for the High Holy
Days in 1793, "that the Parnass the Juntas and the whole Congregation might be Damd. & that he would not send the
Sophar."[88] Personal feuds and internal dissension—much of which
blew off like fog—were not uncommon in the Jewish community
of Philadelphia in its early days.

It was very differently that Josephson had answered a letter
addressed to him by Moses Seixas of Newport at the end of
1789. He had already written his sister-in-law Mrs. Judah of that
city "relative to some of your Congregational Matters and
Ceremonies," and it was in answer to Seixas' comments on
that original letter that Josephson wrote again, spelling out
rules and practices, "literally just & conformable to our Oral
Law as deduced & digested from scripture, and by no means
matter of Opinion of my own." Knowledge of Hebrew was
at such a low ebb in Newport that they had been reading the
Torah portion from a printed text with vowels, instead of
from a manuscript scroll without them. Josephson pointed
out that this was wrong, even if the scroll lay on the table
next to the book.

> You say Mr. Rivera reads Hebrew perfectly, surely then it can't be so
> mighty a task for him to read from the Sepher a few chapters occasionally
> . . . especially when it can be done so easily by means of a Prompter.

Blowing the *shofar* evoked special comment from Josephson.

> There is no law on blowing the shofar when there is no shofar, and it
> is better to use a cracked one, instructions for the repair of which exist, than
> none at all, but it is better not to blow it than to have such a holy function
> performed by a person whose character is in disrepute.

The long, detailed letter is in fact the first expression of an
American mode of service, based upon age-old laws, traditions and

interpretations, but adapted to circumstances. Josephson summed up the situation which was to exist for many years as far as organized religious life in America was concerned—"as to our North American congregations, not much can be said in that respect as in reality they have no regular system; chiefly owing (in my opinion) to the smallness of their numbers."[89]

Although Newport's status economically and as a community of Jews was declining, it is significant that a Sephardic congregation—the only one in America the members of which were still predominately of Iberian extraction—did not hesitate to consult on religious technicalities an Ashkenazi, albeit the president of a sister Sephardic congregation. Actually, Josephson was then the best authority on the continent. By the last decade of the eighteenth century, the prejudices which existed in Europe between the proud descendants of the Marranos of Spain and Portugal and their co-religionists from Central Europe had disappeared in the United States. Trade, marriage, and the leaven of American democracy had wiped out most of the distinctions. European ancestry was not a matter of much concern anywhere in the country; it was not until somewhat later that American ancestry began to assume social significance.

One other instance may be given of Americans solving a problem according to Jewish custom without recourse to civil or foreign authorities. This time the case was reported by Carpeles alone. He had appeared in Philadelphia some time about 1783, originating from Prague,[90] and he only remained in the city three years. In 1784 he was called in by Haym Salomon to help him untangle a knotted skein.

Salomon had been asked by Rabbi David Tevele Schiff of London to help settle a claim against an American which originated in Poland.[91] Jacob Abraham, of Lissa, believed himself entitled to part of the estate of Ephraim Abraham, "late of the State Virginia Merchant," which was in the hands of Jacob I. Cohen, then in Philadelphia.

Instead of resorting to the civil courts, Salomon and Cohen agreed to submit the dispute to a traditional Jewish court of arbitration. Carpeles represented Salomon, and Simon Nathan, the *parnass* of Mikveh Israel, Cohen. Both parties signed a bond for £2000, as a guarantee that they would accept the decision of the arbiters. Cohen was ordered to pay what was due the heir, and Carpeles, in Salomon's name, wrote a full account of the proceedings to Rabbi Schiff.[92] The affair is significant as the earliest recorded instance of a Jewish court of arbitration in the United States.

Haym Salomon was by this time well-known in Lissa. Like others who prospered in America before and since, he felt a deep obligation towards his relatives in Europe. The war years and his temporary impoverishment had prevented him from sending any help to his family in Poland, but soon after the war ended, in January, 1782, he made efforts to contact them. To Gumpel Samson, a relative of Jonas Phillips and the agent in Amsterdam for many of the American Jewish merchants, Salomon sent off a draft for the staggering sum of £1000 which was to be transmitted to the Salomon family in Lissa. This is the first evidence that Salomon was a man of means, although the sum probably reflects more his selfless generosity than a vast capital.

This attempt to help his folks proved to be a worrisome experience, for no reply was forthcoming from the usually reliable Samson. Impatiently, Salomon then asked his Franco-American connections in Nantes, the firm of Watson and Cossoul, to try to trace his personal bill of exchange.[93] He was naturally enough exceedingly anxious to hear from his family and to be assured that the money had arrived safely. Later, when no news had yet arrived, Salomon tried another channel. This time he asked his friend Eleazer Levy, whose West Point land had been "borrowed" by the army, to write his correspondents to see what they could learn.[94]

At last, in the spring of 1783, Salomon finally heard from his parents. His insistence and devotion were rewarded with a whole packet of letters. But strangely enough, Salomon whose success had been due to his knowledge of languages, though he could read Yiddish, was unable to turn his quill to the cursive flourish of Hebrew script. There were plenty of Jews in Philadelphia who could have done it for him, but, perhaps for personal reasons, he asked Israel Myers of New York to help him. Under care of Eleazer Levy, he sent his parents' letters to Myers, requesting him "to answer in the best manner you can and according to the directions that Mr. Levy will give you." His postscript was revealing:

Please to mention to my father the difficulty that I have laboured under in not having any learning, and that I should not have known what to have done had it not been for the languages that I learned in my travels, such as

French, English, etc. Therefore would advise him and all my relations to have their children well-educated, particularly in the Christian [western] language, and should any of my brother's children have a good head to learn Hebrew [I] would contribute towards his being instructed.[95]

Once contact had been made, Salomon's reputation as a man of great wealth spread quickly among his relatives in Poland. His business as a broker had indeed made his name known in banking houses throughout Europe and North America; but to the poor folks at home the fortune of their rich, American kinsman was magnified far beyond the fact. Begging letters began to pour in to him, and he was compelled to answer them much in the fashion that he wrote to an uncle in England in the summer of 1783:

> Your bias of my riches are too extensive. Rich I am not, but the little I have I think it my duty to share with my poor father and mother. They are the first to be provided for by me, and must and shall have the preference. Whatever little more I can squeeze out I will give my relations, but I tell you plainly and truly that it is not in my power to give you or any relations yearly allowances. Don't you nor any of them expect it. Don't fill your mind with vain and idol expectations and golden dreams that never will nor can be accomplished. Besides my father and mother, my wife and children must be provided for. I have three young children, and as my wife is very young may have more, and if you and the rest of my relations will consider things with reason, they will be sensible of this I now write. . . .[96]

Salomon further warned his uncle against coming to America. His *yihus*, or ancestry and scholarly background, he told him, would be worth very little over here, for "*vinig yidishkayt*" was in the nature of the country. But he tempered the tone of the letter by sending him six guineas, and informing him that Samson had fifty more for him in Amsterdam.

Like Salomon, the Gratzes too had been concerned about their relatives in the old country. Before the war, they had sent some money to Silesia through Solomon Henry,[97] and in 1784 they got word from him that the distress among their relatives there was terrible. "Since that tyrant King of Prussia deprived them all of the distillery," he wrote, "I am under the necessity to support my brothers."[98] Fortunately, at that time Henry was able to help; the Gratzes for the time being were land rich and cash poor.

Important as these personal benefactions were to individuals, even more important was the need for some communal fund for use in Philadelphia. The unsettled times of the post-Revolutionary inflation were bringing strangers to Philadelphia, looking for work or passing through the city on their way to greener pastures. The free resumption of trans-Atlantic shipping was bringing new immigrants again from Europe. Among these were, of course, Jews.

Traditionally, Jews always took care of their co-religionists in trouble or in need; and the Jews of Philadelphia, even though their congregation was in financial difficulties, were determined to do what they could. In those days, a Jew in a strange city went straight to the synagogue for help. Hence, it was logical that the new society should have been organized by and in Mikveh Israel. There always had been a *tsedaka*, or synagogal charity fund, which used freewill offerings for the relief of the poor; but in 1783 the need was felt for a specialized branch of the fund. As a result the Ezrath Orechim, or Society for Destitute Strangers—the first Philadelphia Jewish charitable organization, and the earliest one in America whose records have survived—was created, with Jacob I. Cohen as its president, Isaiah Bush its secretary, and Haym Salomon its treasurer.[99]

It was an eighteenth-century version of a combined HIAS and Traveler's Aid Society. Itinerants received from fifteen shillings to a pound, with only the obligation of promising "to repay when in my power."[100] This was characteristic of Jewish charity. The recipient was not demeaned by what he was given; he was able to accept it as his by ethical right. All that was required of him was a signature acknowledging that the money had been received from the *tsedaka*. These signatures, incidentally, reveal a high degree of literacy on the part of the Jewish immigrants. There were very few who signed "X his mark;" occasional names were in Hebrew; more were in roman or German script. Simon Rivera, a poor French boy, appealed to the society for clothing.[101] Two "gentlemen" from Poland, for whom there was not enough money available, were sent on to New York by a private subscription.[102] Mordecai Moses was sent to Charleston.[103] Two Jews, arriving as bond servants on board a ship from Hamburg which docked on the afternoon before Yom Kippur, were redeemed from servitude.[104] A special subscription was taken for this pious emergency, for the funds needed were far greater than were usually laid out.

An unusual contributor appeared on the books in 1791. Non-member David Franks, now past seventy, and returned from his brief exile in England—his wife dead and buried at Christ Church

—offered one pound on the occasion of Rachel Gratz's marriage to Solomon Etting and ten shillings a few months later in honor of the nuptials of Moses Sheftall.[105] Franks, though he never joined the synagogue, now had nothing but professing Jews for friends. The records also show that the young physician of distinguished ancestry, David de Isaac Nassy, who came to Philadelphia from Surinam, and ministered to the sick during the yellow fever epidemic, was a regular contributor to the charity fund from 1792 on.[106] Of course, the members of the congregation made frequent donations, on happy and sad occasions, to mark births, deaths, marriages and holidays. Haym Salomon was one of the most generous, and, rather pathetically, among the last gifts from him were eighteen shillings, then a little later £3.12 for "Prayers when sick," sent in the last months of his life, and finally £13 from his widow for the year's *hashcaboth*, or prayers for the dead.[107]

The records do not always differentiate between the *tsedaka* and the Ezrath Orechim, but there is no doubt but that the latter was maintained as a separate function of Mikveh Israel for some years. After the death of Salomon and Bush's departure for South Carolina in 1785,[108] the president and treasurer of the congregation continued the work of the society, with the help of others among whom Benjamin Nones was most active. All the accounts seem to have been kept by him. He and Moses Cohen asked the executors of Salomon's estate to pay "unto Mr. Manuel Josephson Presidt. of the Jewish Synagogue of this City" £15 which was "the Property of the Society called Hezrat Orechim."[109] Eventually, the society was reabsorbed into the *tsedaka* and disappeared as an entity.

The accounts which were kept of the two funds supply valuable data relating to unsynagogued Jews and strangers temporarily in the city,[110] as well, of course, as information about members of Mikveh Israel and sister congregations. Funds came from the distant West Indies, and from many in the coastal cities who had been members of the congregation during their war exile. Yet, lest it appear that Philadelphia only received, it should be noted that the records of Nidche Israel of Barbados show that contributions came there from Philadelphians,[111] and the Gratzes, Jonas Phillips and others regularly sent donations to Shearith Israel in New York.[112]

The Jews of Philadelphia, struggling desperately to pay for

their new synagogue, must nonetheless have had a considerable reputation for wealth in Jewish circles abroad. Just at the time of their worst financial crisis, they received a visit from two Palestinian messengers, seeking funds directly, rather than through New York or Newport. The story of the first such visitation in Philadelphia is incomplete. They consulted with the officials of Mikveh Israel, but the only record of their stay is a scrap of paper dated 1788, with the entry, "for the 2 Turks their baggage £-2.6."[113] We know of the unusual, foreign solicitors chiefly from the *Pennsylvania Packet* of August 16, 1788, which is, incidentally, an outstanding example of an editor's friendliness towards Jews:

> A correspondent says that two Jews, one of whom is a person of distinction, have lately come to this city from Jamaica, and who have not long ago been at Hebron, which is about 30 miles from Jerusalem, and which is their usual place of residence. Their object is to collect subscriptions for some of their brethren, who have been enslaved by the Turks for not producing a certain tribute at an appointed time. There are some who remember, that upon the failure of the payment of this tribute the Jews at Hebron were seized upon once as slaves by their cruel and insulting oppressors the Turks. It would be a laudable instance of generosity and magnanimity in the Christians to contribute according to their ability, as well as the Jews, for the purpose of relieving the oppressed. It has been said, that mercy is twice blest; that it blesses those who receive and those who give.[114]

Individual Jews may have contributed to this worthy cause, but the congregation corporately was in no position to do so.

The financial problems of Mikveh Israel continued to be a source of worry to the leaders of the congregation, and the cause of serious friction between some of them. Jonas Phillips in particular felt aggrieved. He, together with Isaac Moses and a few others, had signed bonds for the purchase money for the synagogue lot. These were, as he several times pointed out,[115] really obligations of the synagogue; and, when he and the others were pressed by their creditors for payment, they appealed for help. Phillips refused to turn over the deeds and other papers until he was repaid,[116] and apparently kept them until 1791, when his accounts with the congregation were straightened out. He even hired the non-Jewish lawyer, Moses Levy, to represent him against the congregation.[117] In June, 1786, matters were so desperate that Phillips sent word that the sheriff had called on him and given him until five o'clock in the afternoon to pay his note. "I hope you will not leave me in the lurch," he wrote the *parnass,* "if you do it will be a piece of injustice done to your Injured present Jonas Phillips."[118]

The complicated arrangements that had to be made to meet payments falling due, the collection of subscription promises, the claims of the men who had advanced money on the congregation's behalf—all the struggles of a young, and far from affluent, religious group—fill the minutes of Mikveh Israel. Yet, these difficulties did not discourage the Jews of Philadelphia. Squabble and scrape they might, but they were determined to care for their religious needs, and expand they would if that proved necessary.

One of these needs was a supply of *matzoth,* unleavened bread, for Passover. The first specific mention of *matzoth*-baking occurs in the minutes of March 16, 1784. At that time the *adjunta* agreed that ten barrels of flour were to be provided for the use of the congregation and the poor. The baker was to keep an account of the quantity each person took and what payment he made, and any flour or money that the baker was short would be made up by the congregation. The *shamash* was to be in attendance at the bakery until all the congregants had baked their *matzoth;* Michael Gratz was to act as *mashgiach,* or inspector of the baking, to see that the ordinances of Passover *kashruth* were observed.[119] Every precaution was taken to see that the *matzoth* would be prepared according to ritual law. The law required that special implements and utensils be used for Passover food; that too was taken care of. George Goodman was the baker who worked for the congregation in these early days.[120] They had the joiner Andrew Van Witter make them a "New Table at Bakehouse,"[121] and the cabinet-maker David Evans, who in 1776 had made benches for "the Jew Synagogue," supplied them with other articles. In his Day Book is an entry on April 8, 1786, "Ordered by Michael Gratz, small planed boards, on which to make cakes for the Passover for Jewish Congregation,"[122] and the next year a "New Charity Box" was constructed by him.[123]

This careful and pious observance of their religion did not escape the notice of the Christian community. A letter, signed "A Protestant," who may have been the religious poet and minister, Charles Crawford, which appeared in the *Pennsylvania Packet* on December 23, 1784, rather unseasonably chided his co-religionists for their levity and lack of solemnity on Good

Friday. "That day in my opinion ought to be observed, if possible, more holy than the Sabbath," he wrote. "The Jews set us an example; who, at the time of their passover, refrain from the tempting gain of lucre during the course of almost a week."[124]

The Jews themselves realized that in America they not only had the right but also the duty to be as religious as possible.

> It having pleased the Almighty God of Israel to appoint our lot in this Country, The Rulers whereof He has inspired with Wisdom, and a benevolent disposition toward us as a Nation, whereby we enjoy every desirable privilege and great pre-eminence far beyond many of our Brethren dispersed in different Countries & Governments—and in order to manifest our gratitude for those peculiar favors & blessings, we ought in a very sincere manner observe a strict & close adherence to those Laws and Commandments, ordained by him and delivered to our Master Moses of blessed memory, which have been handed down to us in a regular succession to the present time. . . .[125]

So read the preamble to a petition for the building of a *mikvah*, or ritual bath, addressed to the officers of the congregation in 1784.

A *mikvah* had been first spoken of in the spring of 1782, at the time the synagogue was being planned, when Jonas Phillips pointed out that space for one should be on the lot. It had also been the concern of the Gratz brothers. Michael, in April, 1785, wrote Barnard, who was in New York, asking him to try to arrange matters with Isaac Moses, "Pray take care of the Shilah affair that it may be in a way to get it settled, as the people have want to build a habrah and mikivay."[126] That same month, when meetings were concerned with the lack of money to pay the *hazan* and interest on the loans, the taking of subscriptions for building the bath was approved.[127]

Drafted by those early experts in rabbinic law, Carpeles and Josephson, the petition set forth the horror felt by the orthodox at not having a bath for their women. It was with a kind of hell-fire-and-damnation fervor that the petitioners pointed out that the lack of a bathing place "for the purification of Married Women at certain periods" forced the Jews of Philadelphia to break a religious law, which act was "highly Criminal to both Husband & Wife."[128] To get the bath-house erected, these pious Jews offered to subscribe new building-fund moneys; and once it was built, they promised "that every married Man will use the most persuasive and other means, to induce his wife to a strict compliance with that duty so incumbent upon them." By 1786, the new building was up, and Josephson was appointed its "overseer."[129]

It is an interesting commentary upon the life of the early Philadelphia Jewish community that, although ritual practices were observed by individuals haphazardly and in accordance with the particular individual's piety, the religious practices of the formal congregation became increasingly more intense, better defined and more orthodox. Mikveh Israel employed a professional fire-maker, a *Shabbas goyah*, to keep the fires going in winter and the candles lit on the Sabbath.[130] The candles themselves were carefully made of *kosher* wax. The *shamash*, Abraham Eleazer Cohen, who had succeeded Lyon Nathan, made them as part of his duties.[131] When Cohen died in 1785, *Hazan* Cohen made them for a while,[132] but when he could not mould the candles, the work was done out of the synagogue by one of its pious members, Ephraim Hart.[133] The *hazan* also took over the work of the now-aging *mohel*,[134] Jacobs, and, until a new specialist, Wertheim, appeared on the scene, performed circumcisions for the Jewish community. The Reverend Jacob Cohen, as he was referred to by the Philadelphians, was a very busy man, and a man of all Jewish work, for in addition to everything else he also was responsible for the ritual slaughtering for the members of the congregation, in which he was assisted by Mordecai Levy, who was so dedicated that he left his entire estate to the congregation.[135]

However, provision for all these religious matters did not meet the total requirements of Mikveh Israel. There were still the children and their education to take care of. So, in addition to the *mikvah*, a tiny *hebrah*, or Hebrew school, was constructed behind the synagogue building. The duty of teaching children was not included among the original duties of the *shamash*, but according to Abraham Eleazer Cohen it was his principal one, for in his will, which left the synagogue £50, he described himself as a "schoolmaster" rather than a beadle.[136]

The records relating to elementary education in the synagogue are scant, but there is no doubt but that it was modestly provided for. It is not likely that Hebrew in advanced form was taught, except privately, but ample evidence has survived to show that most of the native Philadelphians acquired enough of the language to wear into tatters their sturdy calf-bound prayer-books. The second generation Bushs, Gratzes, Phillips' and Ettings acquired their Hebrew in this city.[137] Their knowledge was in contrast to the almost complete ignorance of some of the earlier American Jews, who had to rely on transliterated texts or Pinto's translations which had appeared in 1761 and 1766.[138] The Pinto version had not been a great success, for nineteen years after its publication his *Prayers for the Shabbath, Rosh-Hashanah, and Kippur* was advertised for sale by Eleazer Oswald, the Philadelphia publisher and bookseller.[139]

Both *Hazan* Cohen and his son Abraham—not to be confused with the beadle—also taught Hebrew from their Cherry Alley residence. In 1790, Abraham advertised publicly that he would give lessons in Hebrew, and also Spanish.[140] At last the wayward Emanuel Lyon had a competent successor. But on the stylish side of town, Cohen had a competitor who had preceded him in the field. A non-Jew, James Kidd announced in the papers that he was about to open a grammar school on the west side of Second Street near Spruce, where, among other subjects, young gentlemen would be instructed in the rudiments of Hebrew, and would be able to peruse and compare Bibles "both with and without points."[141]

The interest in Hebraic studies remained unabated in America, and the Jews were still looked upon by many Christians as people who were "once the darling people of the Almighty." In 1788, the representatives of these people were sorely in need of mundane assistance. As a result of the additional buildings— the ritual bath, the school-house, and a better roof for the synagogue—the treasury was bare. All subscriptions had been exhausted; membership fees were hardly adequate to cover either the small charity disbursements or the salary of the beadle. The salary of the *hazan*, paid quarterly, had to be raised in advance to guarantee his continued services.[142] Mikveh Israel was dangerously approaching the brink of bankruptcy.

There is no full record of what went on in the critical years between September 4, 1785, and June 28, 1789, for there is an unexplained gap in the minutes of the congregation covering this period. It can be guessed that there may have been embarrassing creditors' suits and threats of—if not the actual appearance of—the sheriff. The only surviving document which gives evidence of the desperation of the good Jews of Philadelphia is also the best evidence of the esteem in which they were held by their non-Jewish fellow-citizens.

At the end of April, 1788, and for some time thereafter the *hazan* and members of Mikveh Israel undertook a series of visits to the leading men of the city.[143] With them they took a document containing a dignified plea for help.

To the Humane, Charitable, well-dispos'd People
The Representation and Solicitation of the good People of the Hebrew Society in the City of Philadelphia, commonly call'd Israelites—
Whereas the religious Order of Men in this City, denominated Israelites, were without any Synagogue, or House of Worship untill the Year 1780 when desirous of accommodating themselves, and encouraged thereto by a number of respectable & worthy bretheren of the Hebrew Society then in this Place (who generously contributed to the Design) they purchased a Lot of Ground, & erected thereon the Buildings necessary & proper for their religious Worship. And whereas many of their Number at the Close of the late War, return'd to New York, Charleston, & elsewhere their Homes (which they had been exiled from, & obliged to leave on account of their Attachment to American Measures) leaving the remaining few of their Religion here, burthen'd with a considerable Charge consequent from so great an Undertaking. And whereas the present Congregation, after expending all the Subscriptions, Loans, Gifts, &c., made the Society by themselves, & the generous Patrons, of their religious Intentions to the amount of at least £2200 were obliged to borrow Money to finish the Buildings & contract other Debts that is now not only pressingly claim'd but a Judgment, will actually be obtained against their House of Worship, which must be sold unless they are speedily enabled to pay the sum of about £800—And which from a Variety of delicate & distressing Causes they are wholly unable to raise among themselves. They are therefore under the necessity of earnestly soliciting from their worthy fellow Citizens of every religious Denomination, their benevolent Aid & Help flattering themselves that their worshipping Almighty God in a way & manner different from other religious Societies, will never deter the enlightened Citizens of Philadelphia, from generously subscribing towards the preservation of a religious house of Worship. The subscription paper, will be enrolled, in the Archives of their Congregation, that their Posterity may know, & gratefully remember the liberal Supporters of their religious Society.[144]

The congregation has not to this day forgotten its pledge: that document, with the names of those who subscribed to it, is cherished as one of the most precious treasures of Mikveh Israel.

The bold signature of Benjamin Franklin is at the head of the list of the Christian gentlemen who gave their help. The old philosopher and patriot, then an octogenarian but still active as the president of the Executive Council of Pennsylvania, had had a long history of tolerance and love of his fellow-men. One of his maxims was: "Avoid all discourse that might tend to lessen the good opinion another might have of his own religion;" and in his *Autobiography*, speaking of his contribution to a certain church, he added, "My mite for such purpose, whatever might be the sect, was never refused."[145] He gave £5 to Mikveh Israel in that same generous spirit.

Together with his name on the list appear those of Hilary Baker, one of the aldermen of Philadelphia and later a distinguished Jeffersonian and friend of Benjamin Nones; William Bradford, the Attorney-General of Pennsylvania; Thomas McKean, a signer of the Declaration of Independence and later governor of Pennsylvania; David Rittenhouse, the scientist and astronomer; Thomas Fitzsimons, the leading Catholic layman of the city, one of the drafters of the Constitution and the first president of the Philadelphia Chamber of Commerce; a Rush; a Biddle; and an Ingersoll. The total amount of money raised from these friends was not—it is true—very large, but it heartened the Jews of Philadelphia. Somehow they managed to save the synagogue, at least for the time being.

But it was only for the time being. The need for £800 still existed a year later. Having exhausted the charity of Jews and non-Jews alike, the congregation turned to what had proved in the eighteenth century to be the most practical way of raising money for charitable and religious institutions—a lottery. Christ Church steeple and a large proportion of all the churches in Pennsylvania had been erected or improved by funds obtained from the profits of lotteries. In February, 1788, Mikveh Israel, had applied to the General Assembly for permission to set up one to pay the amount due upon the synagogue building.[146] No action was taken at the time; but two years later the request was acted upon favorably. Even as the decision was being reached, Dickinson College in Carlisle and the city fathers seeking to build a "city hall" for Philadelphia were appealing to the gambling instincts of the public in the same way.[147]

Shortly after the enabling act was passed on April 6, 1790,[148] there was prominently advertised a lottery for raising the sum of £800 "to enable the Hebrew Congregation in the city of Philadelphia to extricate their House of Worship from its present incumbrances."[149] The managers appointed by law were Manuel Josephson, Solomon Lyons, William Wister, John Duffield, and Samuel Hays, all of Philadelphia, and Solomon Etting, of Lancaster. The tickets, signed by Josephson, received wide distribution. In Philadelphia both Jewish and non-Jewish merchants had them for sale. Etting was the Lancaster agent, and Isaac

Moses sold them from his Wall Street office in New York. When this store was broken into in September, ninety-five of the Mikveh Israel lottery tickets were stolen, and those numbers were announced as cancelled.[150]

The advertising appealed not only to charitable instincts but to commercial ones as well:

> . . . It is to be hoped, that all pious persons of liberal sentiments will encourage it, especially as there is no blanks, of course the risk is inconsiderable: and although the low prizes are less than the price of a ticket, yet the adventurers do not lose the whole of their disbursements (as is the case in most lotteries) while for the small sum of two dollars and one-half, which they do venture in this, they have the chance of drawing a prize of 1000 dollars, or even 1400 dollars, besides the satisfaction of having contributed to an object so pious and meritorious.[151]

After several minor delays, due, the managers said, to the wide circulation of the tickets throughout the states, the drawing was held at the Court-House in Market Street on October 19, 1790.[152] As was customary, the state lent two small lottery wheels for the purpose.[153] Who won the grand prize, the records do not show. For Mikveh Israel, the turn of the lottery wheels marked the end of a crisis which had threatened its very existence.

∾ 8

The Struggle for Civil Rights

LATE in the spring of 1783 the citizens of Philadelphia received a rough shock. The streets were full of mutineering soldiers who had left their encampments near the city and marched into town to present their demands to Congress. They were not being paid, and they were angry. Hurriedly, in June, Congress stole out of the city and established itself in Princeton.[1] With it, of course, went the considerable amount of business that a capital city attracts. The Philadelphia merchants and professional men were greatly concerned, and in July petitioned Congress to return to Philadelphia.

The address, drafted by Tom Paine,[2] then acting as clerk of the Pennsylvania Assembly, cited the support given by these men to Congress in the past, and offered continued loyalty, even in the matter of taxes, which hurt. Eight hundred Philadelphians signed the memorial, and of these ten were Jews—Moses Cohen, Isaac Moses, Jonas Phillips, Haym Salomon, Moses Levy, Sol Marache, Isaac Franks, Seymour Hart, Isaac Levy, and Jacob Simpson.[3] The fact that Congress later moved from Princeton to Annapolis was no reflection upon the patriotism or sincerity of the Philadelphians. The further fact that Jews participated in the petitioning was definite evidence that they consistently considered themselves part and parcel of every phase of the life of the city.

But every phase of that life was not yet open to them. The formal treaty of peace with Great Britain, which Franklin had been shrewdly negotiating in Paris, was finally signed on September 3, 1783. Even as that happy news reached Philadelphia, the *adjunta* of Mikveh Israel was considering what to do about a political, rather than a religious, problem.[4] Although the Jews had devoted much time, money and energy to their own internal, communal and religious matters, they were at the same time living busy lives as American citizens, and their status as Americans and Pennsylvanians was very much the concern of the congregation.

The Jews had always been anxious to share in the equalities for which they had fought in the Revolution. They had been disappointed in 1776, when the new constitution of Pennsylvania included a restrictive oath. During the war the matter had remained dormant, but with peace the hurt rankled anew. Gershom Seixas, who had evidenced his active patriotism when he fled with the scrolls of Shearith Israel from British-occupied New York, was particularly concerned. He was, after all, the minister of a congregation which included residents of most of the states as members, so that his concern was national in scope.

With this in mind, Seixas bought himself a copy of the official printing, which had been issued in Philadelphia in 1781, of the constitutions of all the states, together with the Declaration of Independence and the Articles of Confederation. These he studied carefully, and at the end of each separate constitution he made a note pointing out the rights and limitations of Jews under the then current codes.

This volume, recently discovered in the collection of the Rosenbach Foundation, is the earliest study known to have been made of the civil liberties of the American Jew. At the end of the Pennsylvania constitution Seixas wrote:

No Jew can be a member of the General Assembly (of the Representatives of the Freemen) of Pennsylvania, as appears by the 10th Sect. of the above Constitution on acct. of the Declaration that it requires should be made, & Subscribed before he takes his Seat. But there is no impediment of a Jew, being an Officer of either Judicial, Executive or Military Departmts. as p(er) Sect. 40. of the above Const. Philada. 13th Janry. 1783.[5]

Seixas felt that this was a matter which required action. In November, 1783, the injustice of the civil restrictions in Pennsylvania was presented to the *adjunta* of Mikveh Israel for consideration. Since the Council of Censors, a curious body whose duty it was to assemble to decide whether there had been any infringements upon the fundamental law of the state, was sitting, it was decided that, as patriots and professing Jews, the members of Mikveh Israel should present to the Council a special memorial containing their grievances.

A general meeting of the congregation was called to approve the action,[6] and by December the petition, requesting equal rights, was in readiness. Gershom Seixas, as minister, Simon Nathan,[7] as president, and Asher Myers,[8] Barnard Gratz, and Haym Salomon, as members of the board, "in behalf of themselves and their bretheren Jews, residing in Pennsylvania," signed the memorial. It pointed out that, although the Jews in Pennsylvania were but few in number, a declaration by the state that "liberties are the rights of the people" might attract others from countries where they lived under restraint. The memorialists pointed out that Jews were not particularly anxious to seek office, but looked upon a disabling clause preventing them from holding one as "a stigma upon their nation and religion."[9]

The heart of their complaint was this religious discrimination.

The Jews of Pennsylvania in proportion to the number of their members, can count with any religious society whatsoever, the whigs among either of them; they have served some of them in the continental army; some went out in the militia to fight the common enemy; all of them have chearfully contributed to the support of the militia, and of the government of this state; they have no inconsiderable property in lands and tenements, but particularly in the way of trade, some more, some less, for which they pay taxes; they have upon every plan formed for public utility, been forward to contribute as much as their circumstances would admit of; and as a nation or religious society, they stand unimpeached of any matter whatsoever, against the safety and happiness of the people.

All they could ask was that, if the Council recommended a convention to revise the constitution, it would bring the memorial to the notice of that convention. The Council considered it on December 23, 1783, and tabled it.[10]

The petition appeared, in whole or in part, in three Philadelphia newspapers.[11] Eleazer Oswald, always a good friend of the Jews, added his own editorial comment in the *Independent Gazetteer:*

It is an absurdity, too glaring and inconsistent to find a single advocate, to say a man, or a society is Free, without possessing and exercising a right to elect and to be elected.[12]

A correspondent in the *Freeman's Journal,* who wrote "as a friend to the State of Pennsylvania and as a friend to Christianity," said that he thought a sufficient oath would be: "I believe in one God, the creator and governor of the universe, the rewarder of the good and the punisher of the wicked."[13]

The whole question received a most unusual turn at the hands of the Reverend Charles Crawford. In 1784, he reprinted George Fox's old missionary tract, *A Looking-Glass for the Jews*, with a new preface. In it he appealed to the Jews, as Fox himself did, to heed the call to conversion, but he also chided his fellow-Christians for their ill-treatment of the Jews. He pointed out that Christian prejudice might well "have a tendency to confirm them in their disbelief." His real plea, however, was for the removal of religious tests in states where they existed.

I conceive that the drawing of a political line between us and them has a tendency to prevent their conversion, that the unlimited toleration of them has a tendency to bring them over to the gospel, and therefore the unlimited toleration of them is the cause of God.[14]

Crawford's psychology was more perceptive than he could have realized. A large percentage of the descendants of those eighteenth-century Philadelphia Jews—once political and social prejudice against them disappeared—did in fact become Christians. As had already occurred in the case of the children of Sampson Levy, Sr., and David Franks, intermarriage and full acceptance were to beguile many away from their ancestral faith.

To Jonas Phillips, as stubbornly principled in maintaining synagogue discipline as he was in seeking civil rights, this would not have occurred as a probability. When the representatives of the thirteen states were meeting in Philadelphia, during the hot summer and early fall of 1787, as a Constitutional Convention to draft a new frame of government for the United States, Phillips remembered what had happened in Pennsylvania eleven years before. In an attempt to secure for American Jews what had been withheld from Pennsylvania Jews, he addressed to the Convention a vigorous expression of their desire to share fully in the democracy of the land.

His petition pointed out that the test oath in the Pennsylvania constitution was in contradiction to the statement on freedom of conscience in the bill of rights which was prefixed to that constitution, and begged the Convention not to include such an oath in the new federal constitution:

... then the Israelites will think themselves happy to live under a government where all Religious societies are on an Equal footing—I solicit this favour for myself my children, posterity, & for the benefit of all the Israelites through the 13 united states of America.[15]

Phillips sent off his plea on September 7, 1787, not knowing, since the meetings of the Convention were held in secret, that two weeks earlier—on August 20th—the delegates had passed Article Six, which declared that no religious test was to be required of office-holders.[16]

Even this broad statement was not considered strong enough by the first Congress which met under the new constitution, and when the amendments to that constitution, known as the Bill of Rights, were passed on September 25, 1789, the first of them declared that Congress shall make no law respecting an establishment of religion.[17] For the first time in the history of the world an organic law of a nation emphatically stated the principle of religious freedom and the separation of church and state.

The citizens of Philadelphia were fully conscious of the great social significance of the new constitution. A city-wide celebration was held to mark its ratification by the State of Pennsylvania. Triumphal arches and bunting decorated the streets. A grand procession, led by state and city officials, with ingenious floats representing all the trades and professions—butchers, farmers, sailors, printers, blacksmiths, cobblers—followed by children from the various schools, dignitaries from every segment of the city's population, the militia and the fire companies, paraded for hours along the cobble-stone streets. Among the paraders were "the Clergy of the different Christian denominations, with the rabbi of the Jews, walking arm in arm."[18] As Benjamin Rush wrote after the event:

Pains were taken to connect Ministers of the most dissimilar religious principles together, thereby to shew the influence of a free government in promoting christian charity. The Rabbi of the Jews, locked in the arms of two ministers of the gospel, was a most delightful sight. There could not have been a more happy emblem contrived, of that section of the new constitution, which opens all its powers and offices alike, not only to every sect of christians, but to worthy men of *every* religion.[19]

Such equality had been written into the constitution, and it was the equal right of all to the benefits and prerogatives of democracy which the procession symbolized. But equality is a rather vague philosophic concept; practical consideration and respect are its more warmly effective handmaidens. The parade went from Spruce Street north along Third—passing only half a block from the synagogue—to Callowhill, and then west to the old estate of the aristocratic Hamiltons at Bush Hill. On the lawn before the mansion a plentiful collation was spread on tables to refresh the weary marchers.

The arrangers of the fête, with a thoughtfulness that gives evidence of their high regard for their Jewish fellow-citizens, prepared a special *kosher* table for the Jews who came to celebrate the day and "could not partake of the meals from the other tables." There, as Naphtali Phillips who participated in the event as one of the school-children recollected eighty years later, they had "a full supply of soused salmon, bread and crackers, almonds, raisins, etc.," prepared under the charge of an old cobbler named Isaac Moses, "well known in Philadelphia at that time."[20] That table was a homely sign of the position of the American Jew. Nowhere else in the world would public acknowledgment of his religious practices have been given on such a voluntary, friendly basis.

To wind up the day, as was customary at that time, a long series of formal toasts were made to General Washington, liberty, the constitution, and "to the clergy of almost every denomination united in charity and brotherly-love—may they and their flocks so walk through life!" A round of artillery greeted each toast, and each round was answered by a discharge from the ship *Rising Sun*, anchored in the Delaware River, the vessel which Michael Gratz had bought in 1770[21] and sold sixteen years later.[22] Long after tired little Naphtali had gone to bed that night, the *Rising Sun*, moored out in the river, handsomely illuminated in honor of the great festival, winked to the late celebrants.

While these statements with regard to religious tests applied to the federal government, they did not change, or interfere with, the laws of the individual states.[23] Hence it was of great importance to the Jews of Philadelphia that a convention was called in 1789 to draft a new constitution for the state. Once again Jonas Phillips, on behalf of the congregation, sent a letter —the contents of which are not known, but may be guessed— and it was received on December 31, 1789, and ordered to lie on the table.[24] This time, however, there was no question but that the limiting oath would be changed. The fourth section of the Bill of Rights, as adopted in 1790, provided:

That no person who acknowledges the being of a God, and a future state of rewards and punishments, shall, on account of his religious sentiments be disqualified to hold any office or place of trust or profit under this commonwealth.[25]

Atheists were still not free to hold office, but at length the last official discrimination against Jews in Pennsylvania had come to an end.

Already, the United States of America was under way with its new frame of government. George Washington had been sworn in as the first president, in New York, on April 30, 1789. Throughout the country church groups—the Quakers, the Protestant Episcopal Church, the German Reformed Church, the Lutherans, the Roman Catholics—prepared messages of congratulations to the new president upon his assumption of office. The Jews moved rather more slowly, and it was not until June, 1790, that the *adjunta* of Shearith Israel sent a letter to Philadelphia which they had also written to the other congregations in the country:

We are desirous of addressing the President of the United States in one general address, comprehending all the congregations professing our holy religion in America, as we are led to understand that mode will be less irksome to the President then troubling him to reply to every individual address.[26]

They asked all their correspondents to send in a draft of what they thought ought to be said in this the first attempt to speak on behalf of all the Jews of the nation. But a united voice it was not to be. Because of the time that had elapsed between the inauguration and the New Yorkers' letter, the congregation in Savannah, "without any previous notice," had gone ahead on their own. "We do not consider ourselves well treated by the Georgians," Isaac Moses and Solomon Simson wrote their other co-religionists in the United States.

Moses Seixas, answering for Congregation Yeshuat Israel of Newport, felt it would be improper for them, "so small in number," to address the President before the Legislature and other large bodies in Rhode Island did, but castigated Shearith Israel and other congregations who could with propriety have sent congratulations sooner for having delayed so long. Rather sternly he wrote:

... it was incumbent on you from your Local situation, & as being the Eldest Congregation within the United States of America, to have form'd that

System, & transmitted it to the Other Congregations, when no doubt they would have chearfully coincided therein, but for you to procrastinate a measure (which was eagerly embraced by all Publick Bodies) for a Year, without taking the least notice thereof, it might, & would readily be supposed, that you did not mean to pay any attention thereto, or if you did it was to be done on contracted principles—[27]

Savannah's letter had gone off over a year before.[28] The draft of the joint address seemed to be making no progress in New York. Consequently, on August 17, 1790, when Washington made an official visit to Newport, the congregation there presented an address of their own.[29] In November, Charleston rather impatiently asked what had happened to the draft that they had submitted to Shearith Israel.[30] Then Philadelphia, not having heard any further news, told Isaac Moses that they had prepared an address, and were going to present it to the President on the occasion of the removal of the capital from New York to Philadelphia.[31] That at last crystallized the affair. The *parnass* of Shearith Israel sent Josephson drafts he had received from Charleston and Richmond, and agreed that the Philadelphian should go ahead with his plans.[32]

On December 13th, Manuel Josephson took the "Address of the Hebrew Congregations in the cities of Philadelphia, New York, Charleston and Richmond" to President Washington, "had the honor to present the same to him in person, and was favoured with his answer."[33] He assured the officials of the New York congregation that he had "made it a point to inform the President verbally, the reasons of your Congregation's seeming remissness in not having paid their respects before; and he appeared perfectly satisfied." The letter had been largely prepared by Josephson, who signed it on behalf of all the congregations, and, with apologies for having been "prevented by various circumstances" from adding their congratulations before, continued:

The wonders which the Lord of Hosts hath worked in the days of our Forefathers, have taught us, to observe the greatness of his wisdom and his might throughout the events of the late glorious revolution; and while we humble ourselves at his footstool in thanksgiving and praise for the blessing of his deliverance; we acknowledge you the Leader of the American Armies as his chosen and beloved servant; But not to your sword alone is our present happiness to be ascribed, that indeed opened the way to the reign of Freedom, but never was it perfectly secure, till your hand gave birth to the Federal Constitution, and you renounced the joys of retirement to seal by your administration in Peace, what you had achieved in war.[34]

Washington, who had already replied to Newport—stating that the government gives "to bigotry no sanction, to persecution no assistance"[35]—and to Savannah,[36] now penned to the other four Jewish communities an equally sincere expression of thanks.

The liberality of sentiment towards each other, which marks every political and religious denomination of men in this Country, stands unparalleled in the history of Nations. The affection of such a people is a treasure beyond the reach of calculation; and the repeated proofs which my fellow Citizens have given of their attachment to me, and approbation of my doings, form the purest source of my temporal felicity. The affectionate expressions of your address again excite my gratitude, and receive my warmest acknowledgment . . .[37]

The struggle for group recognition was parallelled by the efforts of at least two Philadelphia Jews for individual consideration. The demands of veterans for special treatment from the government for whom they had fought has been a part of American life ever since the days when the soldiers of Washington's Virginia Militia, after the French and Indian War, were faced with the difficulties of picking up the broken strands of civilian life. It has also been a part of American life to recognize the justice of those demands and, in one way or another, to compensate old soldiers for the economically unproductive periods of time they spent in the military defense of their country. In colonial times, and thereafter for many years, one of the chief rewards offered to these men was land, for in the early days the colonies, then the states, and eventually the federal government, were money poor but land rich. Washington and his fellow-militiamen received such grants of wilderness land in what is now West Virginia from the colony of Virginia for their service in the 1750s.[38] After the Revolution a similar offer of western lands was made to qualified veterans, but the only Philadelphia Jewish soldier who seems to have applied for and received his allotment of four hundred acres was David Salisbury Franks.[39]

However, Franks and many other veterans had more ambitious plans for themselves. One of these was Colonel Solomon Bush, who had managed to scrape together enough money to make a contribution to the synagogue building of Mikveh Israel.[40] He was still somewhat incapacitated by his wound, and like scores of other former officers was eager to secure a government position. His appeal to Congress in 1780 for the post of secretary to the Board of Treasury went unheeded.[41] Nor was he more successful in 1784, when he applied to the Supreme Executive Council of Pennsylvania for the position of Health Officer of the Port of Philadelphia.[42] Bush seems to have picked up some medical knowledge at some time during his career—perhaps a smattering while he was convalescing, and certainly somewhat more during one of his later stays in London—and, although he was not professionally a physician, he was, in conformity with the loose standards of the eighteenth century, accorded the title of "Doctor."

By the time Colonel Bush finally received the pay that was due him from the Pennsylvania Council,[43] he had already begun to make a place for himself through his own exertions. In 1781, by the appointment of Moses M. Hays, he had been made Deputy Inspector-General of Masonry for Pennsylvania.[44] Within a few years he was chosen Grand Master, and had occasion, as "Solomon Bush, Grand Elect, Perfect and Sublime Knight of the East and Prince of Jerusalem, Sovereign Knight of the Sun and of the Black and White Eagle, Prince of the Royal Secret, and Deputy Inspector General and Grand Master over all Lodges, Chapters, and Grand Councils of the Superior Degrees of Masonry in North America within the State of Pennsylvania," to address a letter to the head of the brotherhood, Frederick the Great of Prussia.[45] Such prestige and position, even in the egalitarian Masonic Order, would have been impossible for a Jew in Frederick's domain. The *Pennsylvania Packet* carried a story over a London dateline, in which a Jewish merchant at Constantinople was quoted as writing, "Our people are in a most deplorable situation; we are forbid to write to our brethren either in Prussia or Germany on pain of death,"[46] and another one later the same year reporting that Frederick had issued an edict drafting all the Jews to fight against the Turks.[47] It is doubtful that he recognized a son of a German-Jewish immigrant behind the elaborate Masonic titles.

In Philadelphia there were a large number of Jews who took an active part in Masonic affairs. Many of the refugees from British occupied cities had apparently joined lodges in the cities from which they had come, and in June, 1781, at a meeting of the Sublime Lodge of Perfection of Philadelphia, at that time composed only of Jews, there were noted as present: Bush in the chair; Isaac Da Costa, "Grand Warden, Grand Inspector General for the West Indies and North America;" Simon

Nathan, "Deputy Grand Inspector General for North Carolina;" Samuel Myers, "Deputy Grand Inspector for the Leeward Islands;" Barnard M. Spitzer, "Deputy Grand Inspector for Georgia;" Benjamin Seixas, "Prince of Jerusalem;" Moses Cohen and Myer M. Cohen, "Knights of the Sun;" and Joseph M. Myers, "Grand Secretary *pro tem.*, Inspector for Maryland."[48] In Lodge No. 2, A. Y. M., others are noted as members, Isaiah Bush and Benjamin Nones in 1783, and Moses Cohen, Haym Salomon and Solomon Etting in 1784.[49] Even the volatile Abraham Forst turns up in Masonic records, and his appointment as Deputy Inspector General for Virginia in 1781, attested to by Bush and others, is said to be the oldest document of its kind which has survived.[50]

In November, 1788, Solomon Bush announced that he was shortly to leave for Europe, and at that time resigned as Grand Master of the Sublime Lodge of Perfection.[51] He went on a special mission on behalf of American Masonry and was instrumental in bringing about fraternal relations between the Pennsylvania Grand Lodge and the two rival Grand Lodges of England, Ancient and Modern.[52] However, he was able to be of service to other than his Masonic brothers. England, still smarting from the loss of her American colonies, was determined to maintain her rule of the seas, and for her growing navy she needed sailors, and ever more sailors. On the home islands press-gangs were busy shanghaing young men for service afloat, while at sea and in British ports American ships were being brazenly stopped and searched and American sailors, claimed as British subjects, seized and impressed into the navy. This same affront to her citizens' rights, which the United States later answered by the War of 1812, her lack of strength and the inadequacies of her diplomatic service could not cope with at this time.

In July, 1789, an American ship commanded by Captain Watson was seized and part of its crew impressed. Bush, then in London, was shocked when he heard the news, and, since no American authority existed in England prepared to intervene, he took it upon himself to protest vigorously to the British government. Within a month his untiring efforts proved successful. Bush had already written to Washington congratulating him upon his election and telling him of the misfortune which had befallen the American sailors.[53] Now, elated with his accomplishment, he wrote again to inform the President of the happy outcome of the affair:

. . . I took the liberty to mention to your Excellency the seizure of the Ship Commanded by Capt Watson belonging to New York, and am happy to say by a spirited exertion, and due representation, the Ship is again liberated. From this event and a number of American Seamen daily comeing to this Metropolis it points out the necessity of a Minister or Consuls being appointed for the United States. From my Connection in the Kingdom, I think it wou'd be in my power to serve my Country shou'd they think proper to confer a diplomatic Appointment on me. Believe I do not speak from Interested or pecuniary principles, as I will undertake to serve my Country from the same principles I step'd forward to the field.[54]

General Claiborne, who was in London at the time, even before Bush's efforts had been crowned with success, had written Washington suggesting his appointment as consul, because "the situation in which he stands in point of Business, and respectability of Society, seems to give him an exclusive opportunity of discharging the Duties of the Office with justice to his own Country, and satisfaction to this."[55]

The case of Captain Watson had been one of the earliest instances of the search of an American vessel in port, but by the next year the practise had become so frequent that Washington sent Gouverneur Morris from France to warn the English that a continuance of it might provoke serious consequences. In answer to Bush, Washington thanked him, but discreetly said nothing about a diplomatic appointment.[56]

However, the return of "Dr. Bush" to his native city was deemed of sufficient importance to warrant a notice in the paper,[57] and not long after his return, his marriage to Nancy, the daughter of the prominent Christopher Marshall, Jr., was announced.[58] Like that of a number of the Jewish revolutionary soldiers, Bush's Judaism was gradually shed. Within less than ten years after he had made his contribution to the building fund of Mikveh Israel, he was totally assimilated in the Christian community. But his status as a veteran looking for a dignified post was still the same. During the yellow fever epidemic in 1793, while he was at Alexandria, he asked Washington to appoint him Naval Officer for the Port of Philadelphia,[59] and after he had returned to Whitemarsh and while the seat of the government was in nearby Germantown, he renewed his request.[60] This time he got Congressman Muhlenberg to second his plea,[61] but nothing came of it. He was no more successful two years later when he was bold enough to petition for the cabinet post of Postmaster-General of United States, when Timothy Pickering gave up that office to become Secretary of War.[62] Bush never obtained a government post, but on a local level he remained a person of consequence, taking part in the "Grand Inquest of Montgomery County," which passed a resolution condemning the Pennsylvania Legislature for having raised its own salaries.[63] In 1795, Solomon Bush died, and in his will he gave instructions that he should be interred in the Burial Ground of the Society of Friends.[64]

What Bush had done on a governmental level to free American seamen had already been done on an individual basis by Israel Jacobs. The Barbary powers, like the British, were taking maritime law into their own hands; but, instead of impressing seized seamen, they enslaved them. Such victims, popularly known as "Algerine captives," could only obtain their freedom by the payment of ransom. The Philadelphia Quaker, James Joshua Reynolds, master of the ship *Rising States*, had been captured by two Algerian cruisers off Lisbon, and held in captivity from 1784 to 1788. "His redemption was effected," a news-story reported, "by means of one John Jacobs, a Jew, he accidentally fell in with: he had a brother named Israel Jacobs, at Philadelphia, who transacted for his ransom with his friends, which was fixed at 6400 dollars which they paid."[65] The guns of Decatur's ships eventually put an end to that form of international kidnapping.

Effective American representation in Europe, the need for which Bush had underlined, together with respect for the armed power of the United States, was to come a decade later. Meanwhile, another Philadelphia Jew, David Salisbury Franks, came closer than Bush to a diplomatic career, although his aspirations too were never fully realized. After the investigation of Franks' military association with Benedict Arnold and his complete vindication, Robert Morris sent him, in July, 1781, as an official courier with dispatches for John Jay at Madrid and for Benjamin Franklin at Paris.[66] Franks seems to have been one of those men—enthusiastic, willing and devoted to his country—who nonetheless had the misfortune continually to get himself in trouble.

No sooner had he landed in Spain than the captain of the ship which brought him to Europe complained to Franklin that Franks had not paid for his passage. John Jay from Madrid assured his colleague that it was not the major's fault, for Morris had engaged to pay for him, and hence it was the government's, not Franks', responsibility.[67] The Americans in Madrid were most favorably impressed with the official courier, and Jay's assistant, William Carmichael, sent him on to Paris with a most enthusiastic letter of recommendation to William Temple Franklin who was acting as his grandfather's confidential secretary.

This will be delivered you by Major Franks, whom I recommend to your notice & *particular* civilities not only as a worthy honest active Officer, but for reasons which I am going to mention—Your Grandfathers Enemies yours & mine, have endeavored to injure you all in their Power in the Circles which they frequent at Philadelphia. The unfavorable impressions & prejudices conceived hastily in the Capital extend to the Provinces & altho' interiorly we may dispise Malevolent & Injust calumnies, we owe to ourselves every honest endeaver to remove them. The Major is received favorably in all the polite Circles in Philadelphia & is generally known in every State of the Union & equally so in the Army. I give you this hint, because I own I wish to make him, as Lord Chesterfield expresses it your *Puff*. . . .[68]

Perhaps even more likely to assure Franks a warm reception in Paris was a letter of introduction to Benjamin Franklin from his daughter Sarah Bache.[69]

It is quite apparent that the dashing major enjoyed Paris. Later, he lightly complained to Temple Franklin that he had not mentioned Madame Nicholson or the Comtesse de Monturier— "the last you know shot me thro the Heart, pray tell her that there is still a small suppuration from the Wound."[70] It can well be imagined that Franks was not at all anxious to leave the gay life of the French capital and return home; but official business was official business, and there were dispatches which had to go back to the States. So, early in December, he set off to Brest with instructions to deliver a letter at Bordeaux on his way.

For almost six months thereafter Franks seems to have been involved in what was almost a comedy of errors. As he "was going Express, had not time to loose, had rode 400 miles, was tired & wish'd to push on," he gave the letter he was supposed to have delivered himself to his landlord at Bordeaux, and when word got back to Paris that it had not reached his destination, the courier was in trouble.[71] Even before his carelessness was reported, he—so far as can be determined, innocently—was creating difficulties for the busy, old American minister to the French court.

Upon his arrival at Brest, Franks was arrested by the Town Major. Indignantly he sat down to write of his plight not only to Temple Franklin, but to his distinguished grandfather as well. He had behaved as an officer should, presenting his credentials to the authorities immediately upon his arrival, but he was picked up "on the Public Walk when it was most crowded with People," almost immediately thereafter released, and then the following evening "taken out of the Play House" and put under arrest. He wrote:

> . . . I could not do more than I have done, he (the Town Major) has now my Commission, my Passeport, my Letters of Credit & of recommendation with Mr. W. T. Franklin's last letter to me ordering me to Brest. How they will operate I cannot at Present determine, but in the mean time you will allow with me my worthy Sir that I have great Reason to be *offended* at the treatment I have met with. . . .[72]

To Temple he added that living at Brest was expensive, and that he would need more money while waiting for passage to America.[73]

Franklin was not terribly upset by the news; he apparently had formed his own opinion of Franks' temperament, and in a calm manner assured him that the security of an important port like Brest was not only vital to France, but to the United States as well. It was the duty of the officers there to make careful inquiries about strangers who appeared. In a gentle but chiding manner, the philosopher-diplomat wrote the young major:

> A Man may be sensible of his own Integrity, of his Consequence, & of the Respect due to it, but it does not follow that all the World should be sensible of the same at first Sight of him. The French are naturally so civil to Strangers, that I am apt to suspect you have inadvertently committed some Indiscretion, that has drawn upon you the Treatment you complain of.[74]

So far as expenses were concerned, Franks could draw on him for fifteen *Louis d'or*.

Poor Franks! He felt he had to vindicate himself. He told Franklin first that he had received a letter from John Jay, who thought he ought to go back to Spain before he returned to the States—"I am persuaded he has something of Consequence *more* to send to Congress & wishes for a confidential Person to entrust it to—" and then that his treatment was the result of a plot.[75] He developed his theme at some length in a second letter, assuring Franklin that he thought most highly of the French, but felt he had "not been in any way treated as a Subject of a Country in Alliance with that Nation." What had occurred, he had discovered, was because "a woman of infamous Character

had influence enough with them to make me further suspected
& to continue those suspicions to this Moment." "Permit me to
add," he continued, "that *I have been guilty of no Indiscretion.*
. . . I am now of an Age not to be liable to many indiscretions
& I have too great a Regard to my Country & to myself to fall
into any while in France."[76] Franklin probably smiled patiently;
he had just received a letter from a man asking what he knew
of Franks and what the Minister thinks he might have done
with a carriage which had been obligingly lent him.[77]

The longer he was held up at Brest waiting for a ship, the
more Franks wanted to stay in Europe. Jay kept urging him to
come to Madrid. When Lafayette passed through the town, he
told Franks he had some dispatches for Jay "which he was
anxious lest they should be inspected if sent by a common
Hand." Should he come back to Paris to pick them up, he
asked.[78] Winter turned into spring. Franks went from Brest
to L'Orient to Nantes, and still he had not sailed. In May, he
asked that orders be issued so he could travel with the Duc de
Lausanne and the Prince de Broglia who, having been forced
back by a storm, were getting court requisitions for space on
the next ship going to America.[79] By summer Franks was home,
in his own eyes and apparently those of the government, a
seasoned diplomatic courier.

In his absence, through some inadvertence, his commission
had been permitted to lapse; and, after reapplying for it, he
remained in the army until January, 1783.[80] At that time he
became one of the original members of the newly formed
Pennsylvania Society of the Cincinnati, the first veteran's organization in the United States, composed of officers who had fought
in the Revolution.[81] His distinguished service and engaging
manner had made him valuable friends, and when Jefferson was
preparing to leave for France in 1783 to help negotiate the
Treaty of Peace, he took Franks "into his family."[82] For several
months Franks was constantly in attendance upon Jefferson,
acting as his amanuensis and confidential messenger. The statesman apparently liked Franks, but gave a shrewd characterization
of him to Madison:

He appears to have a good enough heart, an understanding somewhat
better than common, but too little guard over his lips. I have marked him
particularly in the company of women where he loses all power over himself and becomes almost frenzied. His temperature would not be proof

against their allurements were such to be employed against him. This is in some measure the vice of his age but it seems to be increased also by his peculiar constitution.[83]

However, Jefferson passed on to Madison an anecdote "which is related to me by Major Franks who had it from Doctr. Franklin himself."[84] The trip with Jefferson came to nought. Even as Franks had made his last-minute plans to sail and sold his horses which were stabled in Philadelphia,[85] news of the signing of the provisional treaty reached the United States, and Jefferson's mission was cancelled.

Meanwhile, another friend tried to help him. Robert R. Livingston, who had been one of the committee appointed to draft the Declaration of Independence and who had just resigned as Secretary of Foreign Affairs, wrote to Elias Boudinot, President of Congress, in June, 1783, recommending that Franks be named a vice-consul in France.[86] The letter was accompanied by a testimonial "from a Number of respectable Merchants."[87] "As he acquitted himself with great Propriety of the commission with which he was charged in Spain," wrote Livingston, "and as it is desirable to place the Business of the United States as much as possible in the Hands of Americans, . . . I flatter myself Congress will see no Impropriety in making the Appointment."

Congress may have seen no impropriety in the matter, but it saw no urgency either. As Livingston noted also, Franks having wasted time in attendance upon Jefferson was unpaid and unemployed. Finally, over a year later, Congress found something for him to do. He was sent to Europe with a copy of the ratification of the Definitive Treaty, which, Franks later wrote, "I had the honor of delivering to our Ministers in Paris, where I remained ill of a Fever, which prevented me going to Holland."[88] Franks seems to have found France a congenial place to live. Mrs. Gibson, who knew him there, noted that "He was respected and welcomed wherever he went, for his social humor and manly candor."[89]

Once more he entered into the Gallic spirit of Paris, introducing to Temple Franklin a Madame de Villeneuve, "one of the most perfectly amiable Women I have the pleasure of being acquainted."[90] Once more he spent more money than he had, and had to apply to young Franklin for help to straighten out his affairs.[91] And this time he seems to have been embroiled in some fracas the only record of which is a letter from Jonathan

Williams to Temple Franklin, saying, "I heard there was some affair in the Palais Royal, in which it was supposed Franks was concerned," and hoping that Temple had not been mixed up in it.[92]

It was undoubtedly this kind of behavior which made Thomas Barclay hesitant about appointing him to the vice-consulship at Marseilles. A French "gentleman of character and ability" had been holding that office, but Franks came to Barclay in Paris and told him that Congress had issued new regulations insisting upon such posts being filled by American citizens. Franks having applied in the light of the new rule, Barclay told Boudinot, he did not think himself justified in refusing him, and so was going to give him his commission.[93] As a result, Franks remained at Marseilles as vice-consul until the spring of 1786, during all of which time, as he later complained to Congress, he received no pay.[94] This time, because "disappointment in my expectations of remittances from America has brought me into great distress," he appealed to Jefferson, then Minister at Paris, for a loan.[95] Jefferson responded that his own financial condition at the moment was far from good, but his account book shows that in September, 1785, he advanced Franks 200 francs.[96]

Once again, new employment was found for him. He was called from the south of France to act as secretary to the American delegation negotiating a peace treaty with the Emperor of Morocco.[97] Then, in his now almost professional character of treaty courier, he took the completed pact around to the various ministers in Europe for their signatures. From North Africa he went first to John Adams in London, back to North Africa, up to Madrid, then to Jefferson in Paris where he repaid his loan and presented his friend with some Moorish coins,[98] and finally back again to London.

When the treaty was duly signed, it was entrusted again to Franks' care to deliver to John Jay, then Secretary of State, in New York. Upon his return to America in 1787, Jefferson suggested him for some new appointment in terms so vague that nothing came of it, calling him once more "light, indiscreet, active, honest, affectionate."[99]

Franks, however, was certainly an active man, and his services were deserving of reward. He asked Washington to make him consul-general in France to succeed Thomas Barclay who was leaving;[100] but, instead, another odd-job was found for him. He was ordered out to the frontier to act as secretary for another mission, this time one treating with the Creek Indians.[101] Washington, to whom a report of the proceedings was made, spoke of Franks in his diary in November, 1789, in that connection. His unabashed protagonism of the federal government was recorded in another private journal of the day. The western land enthusiast, the Reverend Manasseh Cutler, wrote down a description of a political tête-à-tête he had had with Franks and Colonel John Armstrong, whom he called "high Bucks and affected as I conceived to hold the New England States in contempt." They made his Yankee blood rise when they cast reflections on Rhode Island's reluctance to adopt the Constitution, and on Shay's Rebellion which had broken out in Massachusetts, and there ensued a war of words, "in which the cudgels were taken up on both sides; the contest as fierce as if the fate of empires depended upon the decision."[102]

Franks' military friends, his proven devotion, his unceasing petitions, and the connections he had in high places availed him nothing. His personal resources were exhausted. Those to whom he had loaned money were unable to repay him, and he himself was once again in Jefferson's debt. The fire of enthusiasm for a glamorous career was gone when he last wrote Jefferson apologizing for the delay in his repayment.[103] His next-to-last post was some connection with the French-financed Scioto Land Company which hoped to exploit the Ohio lands. It must have been a slight connection, for we only know that the Executive Council of Pennsylvania in November, 1790, lent him four tents "for the use of the French emigrants who are going to Sciota."[103a]

And then Franks went home to Philadelphia and was happy to settle down in the responsible, but not exciting, post of assistant cashier to the Bank of the United States.[104] For three years he worked faithfully in the bank, and died in 1793, stricken by the yellow fever.[105] Although he had been *parnass* of the Montreal congregation in his younger days, he had no religious affiliation at the time of his death. It is noteworthy that in all the correspondence to and about both Franks and Bush the fact that they were Jews does not seem to have been mentioned.

～ 9
Economic Life after the Revolution

FOR a period during the last decades of the eighteenth century Philadelphia was the richest, most important city in the United States. Together with its satellite suburbs, like Northern Liberties, Southwark and Germantown, it had a population in 1790 of more than 42,000 persons. Following Penn's original checkerboard pattern of streets, neat rows of brick houses had spread south, west and north from the center of the city where High (now Market) Street ran bustling down to the Delaware. It had handsome public buildings and churches, impressive and beautiful beyond those of any other city on the continent. And from 1774 until 1800, except for a few interludes, it was the capital of the United States.

Delegates to Congress, and later members of the House of Representatives and Senate, boarded in neat homes within walking distance of the State House on Chestnut Street. President Washington lived in an elegant house, "119 High Street," almost on the fringe of town on Market below Sixth, which became the center of an aristocratic social life so grand that the liberal Democratic-Republicans wondered if a court had not been established in America. The rich, Federalist merchants of Philadelphia delighted in the trade, the distinguished visitors and the aura of importance that flowed into the once staid Quaker town. The financial hub of the country was Hamilton's Bank of the United States on South Third Street. The wharves on Front Street, facing the offices and stores of some of the largest merchant houses of North America, had never been busier.

From the moment the British evacuated Philadelphia, the city's port, as the only major one except for isolated Boston open to the Americans, became a beehive of activity, and offered opportunities for merchants and mariners, as well as stevedores, carters, laborers and coachmen. Ships were built, chartered, bought, sold, loaded and unloaded. Blockade running, necessary to bring in supplies, was lucrative when successful. Privateering was not only legal, but officially encouraged by the new government. Prizes, the seized ships of the enemy, were most desirable spoils of war, and their cargoes were desperately needed for the struggling American economy. Long before there was an effective American navy, Yankee privateers waged a daring war of attrition against the British over the whole North Atlantic.[1]

At least six Jews, who were then living in Philadelphia, participated in this activity during and after the Revolution, for this form of legalized piracy continued on the open seas even after Cornwallis' surrender at Yorktown. Isaac Moses was the most active.[2] He either owned or bonded eight ships, alone or in partnership with Benjamin Seixas, Sol Marache, the merchant-financier Robert Morris or Matthew Clarkson, who later became mayor of Philadelphia. Michael Gratz was engaged jointly several times with Carter Braxton, a signer of the Declaration from Virginia,[3] and they were sometimes lucky and sometimes lost money. The Gratzes' old ship, the *Rising Sun*, fitted out with guns and captained by Stephen Decatur's father,[4] ploughed the dangerous waters. Abraham Sasportas, with a fellow-Frenchman, François LeBoeuf,[5] braved the English-patrolled West Indian waters to bring in French goods for the local market.

The entrepreneurs, Moses Cohen and Samuel Judah, during the war offered for sale an equipped "fast-sailing top-sail Schooner," loaded with fifteen hundred pounds of scarce Irish beef[6]—an obvious prize—probably intended for the British army. On the crowded Delaware waterfront, amid the brigs, sloops and schooners where the Cohen-Judah vessel was docked, Jewish laborers could offer the services of their hand-drawn carts, or work good hours as stevedores unloading cargoes.

All this merchandise and all the manufactured goods and commodities that came into Philadelphia from other parts of the continent, from the West Indies and, at first rarely—but with the peace in increasing quantities—from Europe, had to be bought, sold and channeled into the hands of merchants for resale to consumers. Commission agents were the key men in these transactions. They traded in every conceivable kind of goods, sold at wholesale or retail, and acted as the conduits through which flowed the economic blood of the nation.

A workable method of handling all kinds of goods, property and bills of exchange and credit was essential to the building of the new economy, the more so since it was plagued with inflation, speculation and a confusing variety of state currencies, each of different value and changing almost from day to day. To the Jews of Philadelphia belongs much credit for having organized commission or brokerage houses to fill that need. Until the country's business and commerce settled down in the last decade of the eighteenth century under Alexander Hamilton's direction, the Jewish brokers played a leading role in the economy.

The first of these was Moses Cohen, who opened up his office to trade on a most comprehensive scale. His notice in the *Pennsylvania Packet* on May 28, 1782, contains the announcement of the first employment agency introduced into the city, which he rather grandly called an "Intelligence Office," and it further shows the wide extent of his business.

> The Subscriber having observed the great and general utility of an Intelligence Office in populous and trading cities, begs leave to inform the Public, that he has opened an Office for that purpose, at his house on the east side of Front-street, eight doors above Market-street; where persons wanting to purchase or sell Goods or Property of any kind—such as, houses, farms, lots, horses, carriages, ships, bills of exchange, continental or state certificates, &c. may enter and dispose of their respective articles at a moderate premium; secrecy, if required, may be depended on. Clerks, gardeners, coachmen, nurses, chamber maids, cooks and servants of every description may enter their names in said Office, after paying Eighteen-pence; the same sum is to be paid by persons who are accommodated with servants by means of the Office; nothing charged for enquiries which prove unsuccessful.[7]

This thrived so well that, in September, Cohen told the public that he had had to hire a clerk and was forced to raise his listing fee to two shillings and sixpence.[8] At the same time he divided his business into two departments, and spoke of a "Broker's Office," in addition to the "Intelligence Office."

His good fortune continued through the inflationary aftermath of the war, and early in 1783 he opened a store on Second Street between Chestnut and Market, "One of the best stands in this city," where he was prepared to receive all sorts of merchandise for sale on commission.[9] The brokerage office remained on Front Street. Cohen pioneered in an all-embracing kind of office which dealt in anything that was salable. Haym Salomon, who had started out handling only notes, bills and foreign exchange, soon followed Cohen's pattern and developed it to an unequalled level. And others quickly entered the field and tried hard to compete in a highly competitive business.

Among these were Isaac Franks and Benjamin Nones, both battle-scarred veterans of the war, of whose military careers any American would have been proud. Both had settled in Philadelphia before the peace, and by the middle of 1782 both had opened brokerage offices in the heart of the business section of town. Franks was only twenty-three years old when he embarked on his business career, near Moses Cohen on Second Street,[10] and Nones only twenty-nine when he opened his office "in the House occupied by the Widow Laboyteaux" on Front Street.[11]

Once Isaac Franks entered the field, he followed the general course already set by his predecessors. His first advertisement suggests that he had carefully studied the methods of others, and his manner and appeal were those of an old hand rather than a novice. In a month he enlarged his scope to include virtually every item of brokerage, differing from the others in that he noted he was "conversant in the Laws of Exchange and Barter."[12] Occasionally, also, he dealt in Negro slaves,[13] one commodity which Haym Salomon, for all his versatility, seems never to have traded in. Franks developed real estate to a high point and numbered among his clients such distinguished Philadelphians as William Bradford and Dr. Benjamin Rush.[14] He used the term "stock and exchange broker" before it was generally accepted,[15] and in 1789 he became the first Jew to be commissioned as a notary public by the state.[16] Parenthetically, it should be noted that, although Franks was Haym Salomon's brother-in-law, the two do not seem to have been close.[17] It is possible that Franks' marriage to a Christian and his complete separation from the synagogue may have been factors in the estrangement. He was never a member of Mikveh Israel, and his children were brought up in their mother's faith.

Nones was not as successful as his competitors. Before opening a brokerage office he had been doing miscellaneous business with the French merchants of the city whose language was his own, but in 1782 he combined his resources with those of Myer M.

Cohen, and the partners, dealing extensively in French, Spanish and Dutch bills of exchange, became one of the band of Front Street brokers.[18]

It was just at this time that Nones became involved in a bitter, public controversy with Abraham Levy and his son Ezekiel, which flared up in the public press, raged bitterly for a little over a month and died out without enhancing the reputation of either side. The argument began with a statement signed by Nones apologizing for having been rude in demanding, in the public street,[19] the payment of a debt due him by Abraham Levy. Ten days later Nones inserted a lengthy letter in the same paper which had published his statement vehemently attacking Levy. According to him, Levy had bought some goods from him, promised to pay immediately, kept postponing payment, sent his son to offer cash at a discount, and finally had agreed to let Nones have the money if he would write out an apology which, under the circumstances and only because he needed the money badly, Nones had done. He had never imagined that Levy would publish it in an attempt to injure his reputation, and, since he did, Nones wanted to tell the whole story. In extremely bad taste he concluded his letter by observing that only Levy's age protected him from his, Nones', just resentment:

> Were it not for this consideration, I should certainly shave that beard, which induces many people falsely to imagine him a distinguished member of our congregation, in which his ignorance disqualifies him from holding the humblest office.[20]

This kind of public airing of dirty linen was not conducive to good public relations, and an anonymous correspondent, presumably a non-Jew, called both Levy and Nones to task for their lack of tact.

> You are unhappily involved in a quarrel which, in my opinion, is equally disadvantageous to yourself and your antagonist. Neither of you is sufficiently acquainted with the English language, to understand the essays published in the name of the other. You must both have the assistance of interpreters, and wholly rest your reputations on their knowledge and fidelity. . . .
>
> The propriety or impropriety of the reflections made by Mr. Nones on your beard, on your ignorance in religious matters, and on your supposed incapacity in your congregation, can be determined but by men, legally appointed, in conformity with your church discipline, for the discussion of such subjects. You may rest assured that no Christian, for the sake of settling your dispute, will be at the trouble of studying the talmud, the commentators upon it, together with the books of controversy which relate to your re-

ligious ceremonies and customs. And it is clear to me that, without a competent knowledge of all those abstruse matters, it is impossible for the most sensible and upright men to do you justice. You should refer those points to the proper judges in your congregation.[21]

With absolutely no anti-Semitic overtones the moderate observer suggested that the two parties submit their dispute to arbitration by four merchants of the city.

Ezekiel Levy, on his father's behalf, was not willing to let matters be decided so sensibly. He again brought the matter to the public's attention by denying Nones' statements and answering his personal abuse of his father with other personal abuse of Nones.[22] This once more roused Nones, and he rushed back into print with a long story of how, on another occasion, the Levys had bilked him of a commission.[23] Protesting that it was "entirely foreign to my profession, and repugnant to my inclination, to become a newspaper disputant," Ezekiel Levy promptly denied Nones' story and produced a statement from Joseph Mercier, "a respectable merchant in Philadelphia," who had been involved in the transaction, to refute the allegation.[24]

A second time an anonymous writer, in a letter to the editor Oswald, chided both parties. One wonders if some other member of Mikveh Israel was not attempting to shame the disputants from further public argument which was doing neither any good and might well prove harmful to the other Jewish merchants in town.

For some weeks past, the public have been amused with the most insignificant controversy between one Mr. Abraham Levy and a Mr. Nones; if you are well paid for inserting such pieces, none others can be well pleased with such entertainment.

The chief topic of this controversy, and more particularly on the part of Mr. Abraham Levy, hinges on a terrible apprehension of his character, and credit suffering, as the parties are foreigners, and have very little knowledge of the English language. I wish both parties to be informed, that character, and credit, are, and have different meanings, which Mr. Levy, or his writer introduce as synonimous terms and meanings, for a man's credit may be extensive, and his notes pass as current as those of the bank, when at the same time his character will not admit the minutest inspection.

It was illiberal in Mr. Nones to drag his antagonists beard into the contest, as it certainly has no affinity to any matter of their dispute, and though as I am informed Mr. Levy's beard entitles him to no more dignity with his brethren than the beard of a menonist: Yet far from any degradation (which probably was Mr. None's intention) it is esteemed meritorious and commanded by their legislator in Leviticus, Ch. 19, v. 27.[25]

The final riposte was delivered by Nones, who produced a

statement from his partner, Myer M. Cohen, to the effect that his story about the commission due and never paid was correct.[26] The congregation at the time was too busy with its own financial problems to take official cognizance of the affair. The whole thing died down as quickly as it had begun, and as far as is known there were fortunately no repercussions which might have been a threat to the reputations of Levy's and Nones' co-religionists. A year later, for no reason connected with the earlier trouble, the partnership of Nones and Cohen was dissolved, and a new firm, Benjamin Nones and Company, was announced in the "Factorage and Broker Business."[27]

The period was one of movement and change, and the brief Nones-Cohen partnership was typical of the reshifting and resettling process. This was intensified by the exodus from Philadelphia of the Jews from other states, which, as we have seen, became a problem in synagogal life. Abraham Sasportas dissolved his partnership with Le Boeuf as soon as the British evacuated Charleston and he could return home.[28] The looseness and informality of business relations were also evidenced by the brief association of Abraham Forst and Joseph M. Myers, which lasted only a month.[29] The new firm of Lazarus Barnett and Lyon Moses, both fresh from Amsterdam, who described themselves as transacting "the business of a Dutch Broker," was dissolved the same year it was formed.[30] Barnett turned out to be an unhappy failure, who fled his creditors,[31] and Moses had to work most assiduously to reestablish himself on his own.[32] None of these brokers became rich. Even the capable Haym Salomon, who died intestate in January, 1785, left assets which barely covered his debts consisting of notes which he had guaranteed, and the executors of his estate were hard put to provide sufficient money from his tangled affairs to enable his widow and children to live in even the most modest fashion.[33] The *Independent Gazetteer*, which only the week before had carried his advertisements in English, Dutch and French, printed the following obituary:

Thursday last, expired, after a lingering illness, Mr. Haym Salomons, an eminent Broker of this city; he was a native of Poland, and of the Hebrew nation. He was remarkable for his skill and integrity in his profession, and for his generous and humane deportment. His remains were yesterday deposited in the burial ground of the Synagogue, in this city.[33a]

Within less than two years his widow married David Heilbrun,[34] perhaps as much through need as by choice.

Another sign of the marginal status of many of the Jewish businessmen was their frequent removal from one address to another. In two years Isaac Franks had three addresses: first on Second Street, then on the south side of Market between Second and Third, and finally—a sign of conservatism or contracting business—his dwelling-place on Third Street between Market and Arch.[35] Moses Cohen combined his two earlier establishments in one, at the corner of Second and Chestnut, moved in 1784 to Second Street opposite the Friends' Meeting, and moved again in 1786 to the corner of Front Street and Elfreth's Alley.[36]

With but a few exceptions all the brokers and merchants carried on their activities in a small area bounded by Chestnut north to Race, and Front west to Fourth. There was, however, a definite trend of the Jewish houses northwards. Whereas in 1782 Benjamin Seixas had his dry goods store, where he sold "Spermaceti Candles, Bohea Tea, Allum, Ginger, and Madeira Wine," on Chestnut Street[37] and Samuel De Lucena his brokerage house in Norris's Alley (now Sansom Street),[38] in 1784 Lyon Moses opened up on Race between Third and Fourth Streets,[39] in 1790 Moses Homberg became the proprietor of the Franklin Tavern at the corner of Second and Race,[40] and the same year Solomon Lyons advertised as a broker at 109 Race Street.[41]

The state and national financial crisis continued to make the conduct of normal business extremely difficult. Pennsylvania, in order to meet the requirements of its share of the interest on the national debt and to pay the debts due citizens of the state by the United States, framed a funding bill in 1785 to raise the necessary money. The townships of the county of Philadelphia each elected delegates to participate in a discussion of the proposed bill. Among those who met in Germantown to consider this important issue was Colonel Solomon Bush, who, with the distinguished Dr. George Logan and three others, was named on a committee to revise the proceedings.[42] This was the first instance of a Philadelphia Jew taking part in a civic function in the new government.

The funding bill was passed, and the new Pennsylvania paper money which it authorized was issued. This new currency was to replace the older miscellaneous moneys circulating in the state in an attempt to stabilize the rate of exchange. As soon as the new money appeared, Jewish brokers and merchants either altered their standard advertisements in the newspapers or inserted new ones supporting its issue and advocating its acceptance. Cohen, Phillips and Franks each emphasized his willingness to accept the new tenor.[43] Haym Salomon had the year before in his reply to Miers Fisher advocated it on principle. But there were many other Philadelphia merchants who refused to accept it except at a discount.

This led to rampant speculation, and instead of stability there resulted a state verging on chaos. Competitive moneys issued by neighboring states were of different values; stock and funded certificates, government loan certificates, foreign notes, all added to the confusion of the exchange system; and the stocks of the newly-formed land companies became speculative favorites. After 1785 bankruptcies began to increase in frequency. Extended credit, as in the former days, was almost non-existent. Hard money—specie—spoke the loudest in any transaction. A merchant's credit could be impugned overnight by a slighting remark or a passing rumor, and Moses D. Nathans and Solomon Lyons, both of whom suffered in this manner, had to resort to a public announcement to assure their creditors that they were willing and able to make payment.[44]

Simon Nathan ran into a bit of unpleasantness with Thomas Jefferson. The Virginia statesman had bought some wine from him and, in that money-scarce era, had agreed to pay for it in tobacco. After the payment was made, Jefferson sent off a highly indignant letter to Nathan pointing out that he had made two errors in his calculations, both in his own favor, one in setting the price of the tobacco and the other in figuring out the difference between Pennsylvania and Virginia currency.[45] It was not easy to make the multiple calculations that even a simple transaction required.

Most of the Jews in town managed to keep their heads above water; but it should be noted that the financial crisis of the congregation took place during this financial crisis of national credit. Samuel Hays, who advertised that "By a long residence with the late Mr. Haym Salomon, he has acquired a perfect knowledge of this business,"[46] weathered the storm, as did Isaac Franks, Moses Cohen, Moses D. Nathans, and those three pillars of Mikveh Israel, Solomon Marache, Manuel Josephson and Jonas Phillips. However, the power of the unseen, uncontrollable, economic tide swept more than three hundred Philadelphians into bankruptcy between 1787 and 1791, and among these were four Jews, Manuel Noah,[47] Simon Nathan, Benjamin Nones and Moses Homberg.[48]

The frenzy of the situation was best described by Dr. Benjamin Rush, a careful observer of many things that took place in Philadelphia. In the unrestrained language of a diarist he described the city in 1791 as "a great gaming house." And he continued:

> A young Broker from New York who made 10,000 dollars, lost his reason. I attended him with Dr. Barton at the City tavern. Major McConnell (his wife told me) had made between 30,000 & 40,000 dollars in one month by buying and selling Script. The great speculators became talkative & communicative—or dull—sullen—silent & peevish. Gen'l Stewart who had just begun to deal in Script said he could not sleep at nights.—Never did I see so universal a frenzy—Nothing else was spoken but Script in all companies—even by those who were not interested in it.[49]

A few days later the scene again impressed itself on Rush. The "mania had increased;" merchants, grocers, shopkeepers, clerks and apprentices left their jobs to speculate. "Two brokers, Maj. [Isaac] Franks & a Mr. Anderson," told the doctor, "they had made between 2 & 3000 dollars before one o'clock."[50] Even though an earlier land speculation in which Rush had joined with Isaac Franks in taking quarter shares in an 18,400 acre tract of Pennsylvania land had been attended with nothing but trouble,[51] Rush once more took a plunge, and noted that two shares he had bought for $450 one morning sold for $315 to $320 apiece by night. Rush's personal friendliness to Jews and his own excursion in the market did not prevent him from chastising Solomon Lyons, "a Jew broker," for dealing shrewdly,[52] as unfortunately many prominent non-Jews were doing too in those days of speculative frenzy.

With the exception of Manuel Noah, the Jews who had been bankrupted made satisfactory comebacks. Simon Nathan moved to New York, and slowly re-established himself.[53] Moses Homberg resumed his career, as noted, by purchasing the Franklin Tavern, where he also sold dry goods until his death in 1793.[54] Benjamin Nones showed real resilience by returning to his old stand on Front Street, where he offered all kinds of merchandise, including furniture, "an elegant Collection of Books, Instruments, and Anatomical Plates," at the same time reopening his brokerage business at his home on the opposite side of the street.[55] Thereafter and for decades to come he was favorably remembered by the other merchants of the town.[56]

The Jews had worked hard to maintain their good standing. They did not want it jeopardized. The *Independent Gazetteer* of October 9, 1784, had carried a warning in the form of a letter "from an Israelite in London to a gentleman in this city," that "several of our society, who, after disgracing their brethren by acts of the most atrocious villainy" had embarked for America. "I trust," the letter continued, "as the Jews of Pennsylvania have ever supported the character of honest men, that these men may not prejudice their reputation."[57]

Among the Jews who enjoyed this high general reputation was Manuel Josephson, one of the leaders of Mikveh Israel, who remained in Philadelphia when other New Yorkers like Isaac Moses returned to their liberated city. Without fanfare he established himself "on the southside of Market-street, two doors above the Conostogo Waggon," as a general commission merchant.[58] If Franklin's homely axiom, that two removes were equal to a failure, contained the germ of truth, Josephson's maintenance of his store on Market Street through the years spelled solid prosperity. The esteem in which he was held was evidenced by the fact that his word was considered by non-Jews of such weight that, in a case where the facts were disputed, his statement of the case was published as a clinching proof.[59]

Solomon Marache, long in partnership with Joseph Spencer, dissolved the association in 1788,[60] opened up a boarding-house,[61] and began to dabble in the land speculations of Robert Morris and John Nicholson. After the Pennsylvania Population Company was formed in 1792 to develop land in the Lake Erie region, Marache became its secretary.[62] When Nicholson began buying up tracts in Westmoreland County for the North American Land Company, Marache and his wife, Mary, sold him eight hundred acres.[63] So close was this relationship that the Maraches named one of their sons Nicholson. These children, however, were brought up as Christians, for it seems that Marache, like others, after his marriage to a non-Jewess withdrew from his active participation in the synagogue he once so enthusiastically supported.[64]

This was not true of another of the chief supporters of Mikveh Israel, nor of his children. Jonas Phillips, who had already shown his mettle as a patriot and a fighter for religious freedom, was also succeeding in the world of business. He was a persistent advertiser in the Philadelphia press, and from his store, first on Market Street near the Court House, and after 1790 on Second Street above Arch, he offered for sale a wide assortment of items ranging from dry goods and groceries to furniture and real estate.[65] Phillips was just as outraged by economic restrictions as he was by religious ones, and he was not the kind of man to give up without a fight. When he decided to include auctioneering, which he had done before he joined the militia, among the services he offered, he found that the new laws of the state restricted the number of auctioneers within the limits of the city. This restriction he deemed unfair, and so he promptly petitioned the Pennsylvania Assembly in his own interests and those of the public at large, stating that any citizen should be allowed "to open a store for the sale of goods by public auction."[66] The Assembly pigeon-holed the petition, eighteenth-century style, by ordering it "to lie on the table." Annoyed by this infringement upon his economic freedom, Phillips moved back to New York. There he promptly applied for, and received, a license "to act and officiate as and to be, one of the publick vendue masters and auctioneers of New York City."[67] But the ties he had in Philadelphia called him back after a few years, and he resumed his fight for the right to auction. In the course of several years he petitioned again and again, protesting against the monopoly of auctioneering and the unconstitutional structure of the law, complaints against which, he said, "have resounded from every quarter." Phillips felt it was "his Interest as a Citizen to Remonstrate against, and as a part of the Body politic to condemn" such a regulation.[68] Eventually, the law was corrected.

Meanwhile, however, Phillips had assured his own success as "a vendue master" in an unusual and imaginative way. He conducted auctions across the river, outside of the city limits, and to attract buyers printed and distributed handbills announcing that he kept a coach on hand near Front Street on "Vendue day," which would drive his customers, who needed transportation, to the Upper Ferry, near where Spring Garden Street crossed the Schuylkill River, "where Town and Country Shop Keepers, Pedlars, and others, will find to their interest to attend his sales."[69]

There was in Phillips a streak of stubborness which continually manifested itself, and there was also the economic pressure of a very large family which kept goading him on. The stubbornness he carried beyond the grave, for, when his intermittent feud with the congregation was reopened shortly before his last illness, he withdrew from membership in Mikveh Israel[70] and forbade his remains to be buried in their cemetery. After his death in 1803, his body was shipped to New York and interred in the burial ground of his old congregation, Shearith Israel.[71]

His children were now, some of them, of marriageable age, and in 1785 his daughter Zipporah married Manuel Noah, who had come to Philadelphia from Mannheim by way of England.[72] Noah was a small tradesman, lacking both ability and responsibility. He failed in business a year after his marriage, and after some time disappeared without a trace, leaving his wife with a young son and daughter. When Zipporah died in Charleston in 1792, the boy Mordecai Manuel Noah was sent to his grandfather in Philadelphia, and that boy, destined to become the most flamboyant figure of American Jewry in the early part of the next century, was brought up by Jonas Phillips,[73] whose spiritual son he really was. It is now known that Manuel Noah, the father, left the country in 1797 and returned to Philadelphia in 1816, when he reapplied for membership in Mikveh Israel,[74] but by then his son was well launched on his career.

During the post-Revolutionary period, when others were having troubles of one kind or another, the Gratz brothers were struggling to realize something from their vast land interests. In July, 1787, Congress passed the Northwest Ordinance, by which federal control of the lands west of Pennsylvania and north of the Ohio River was established. This was the resolution of a long and complicated dispute about the ownership of those lands, which continued even thereafter into the Supreme Court of the United States.[75] Virginia had claimed that they were hers by original charter, by exploitation just before the outbreak of the Revolution, and by reconquest under George Rogers Clark in 1778. Both New York, through cession of lands to her by the Six Nations, and Connecticut, also by original charter, entered their counterclaims. The land companies—Ohio, Vandalia, Indiana, and Illinois and Wabash—all asserted their rights to various sections of the country obtained through treaty and purchase.

The struggle for ownership had been a hotly contested one, and it was only after the Virginia legislature in the autumn of 1783 agreed to cede its claims, following similar acts on the parts of New York and Connecticut, that the issue became capable of solution.[76] In all of this, David Franks, Levy Andrew Levy, the Gratz brothers and Joseph Simon, as owners of shares in various of the companies and as assignees of other interests, were deeply involved. In 1774 the Gratzes had formed part of the syndicate which bought up a large part of what they planned as a new town at the Falls of the Ohio, eventually to become Louisville.[77] They worked diplomatically to make friends of and influence the legislators of Virginia at the time when that state seemed to hold the key to the west. They took over the interests of the man who was chiefly responsible for the whole westward expansion, George Croghan, and advanced money to that then virtually destitute pioneer.

The issues involved concerned the whole future development of the United States, and there was a sharp conflict in Congress and in the state legislatures between national, state and personal interests. It was important to have men of influence and of unquestioned patriotism on your side, no matter which particular group you were part of. And the Gratzes throughout the whole period associated themselves with all parties who might influence the eventual decision.

In December, 1779, when the Illinois and Wabash Companies were united, George Ross, a signer of the Declaration of Independence, was chosen as president of the combined company, and Barnard Gratz was made its secretary.[78] James Wilson, the distinguished lawyer, later succeeded his fellow-signer Ross.[79] Benjamin Franklin continued his connection with the Indiana Company, of which David Franks was president for a short time before he was exiled,[80] and Michael Gratz represented the interests of Simon and Levy and the estate of Robert Callendar at a meeting of the company which was held at the Indian Queen in the spring of 1783.[81]

But it was in Virginia that the key to the situation lay. There Richard Graham of Dumfries, the brother-in-law of George Mason, who was the most influential figure in the whole Virginia land controversy, was so friendly that he passed on to Michael Gratz confidential information with regard to the Assembly's determination to sell lands in the west.[82] He even

offered to buy some for him with the profits of a joint privateering venture. As a gesture of goodwill, and of course as
part of their business, B. and M. Gratz, in partnership with
John Gibson at Pittsburgh, sold supplies to George Rogers
Clark, then setting out on an expedition intended by Virginia
to capture Detroit.[83] Repayment was slow; Gibson was bankrupted,[84] and the Gratzes three years later were paid in "transfer tobacco."[85]

Land of questionable title and notes with land of questionable
title for security were not promising assets. And in the post-
Revolutionary period, first one and then another of the grandiose
schemes which had promised so much were being wiped out
by decisions of Congress or the states. There was as yet no
federal law and no constitutional government to bring order
to the complicated situation. Petitions were unsatisfactory,
and suit was difficult.

A parallel was provided by the action of Simon Nathan on
July 13, 1781. He had been unable to collect a debt due him
by the State of Virginia,[86] and so with a court order issued
by Pennsylvania he attached property of Virginia then in Philadelphia. Virginia promptly protested to the Supreme Executive
Council of Pennsylvania, that as a member of the

Union with this and other United States of America . . . [it] cannot or
ought not to be in any respect held to answer in the courts of Justice of any
other State, nor reduced to the alternative of yielding its property to a
claim made by any individual.[87]

The Attorney-General ruled in favor of Virginia, and established a precedent which helped Virginia triumph over the land
companies when, later, she appeared against them in the Supreme
Court of the United States. In 1791 Edmund Randolph of Virginia told Michael Gratz he would not give him an opinion on
his claims against Virginia or the United States, but would be
willing to give an opinion and enter suit on his claims against
Pennsylvania.[88] It took a constitutional amendment and several
decisions of the Supreme Court to establish a satisfactory method
of procedure in such matters.[89]

Meanwhile, the Gratzes were far from affluent. On May 1,
1789, Michael Gratz petitioned the City of Philadelphia for permission to act as a broker. In it, rather pitifully, this "old Citizen of Philadelphia who has resided therein upwards of thirty
years," stated that he

(owing to the Late Revolution among other Causes) has Sustained Considerable injuries, and is at Present without any fixed Employ, or Business, to Preserve that Decent Support for his numerous family of Ten young Children, which he trusts he has hitherto Done, with Reputation and Credit. [Therefore, since he was] A man long Acquainted with Business, and well versed in Mercantile Transactions and who knows, he Presumes, the Particular Duties of the Profession or Calling of A Broker,

he requested a license.[90] This was to supplement what Gratz's income was from the general store which the brothers still maintained at 107 Sassafras (now Race) Street.[91]

There were, however, some good assets and the "gloomy cloud which has hung over us," of which Miriam Gratz wrote to her brother-in-law Barnard, did lift.[92] They were not negotiable at the time, and the Gratzes were not in a position to play a leading role in helping to solve the financial troubles of Mikveh Israel. It has seemed curious that they were not larger contributors to the new synagogue, but the fact is now revealed that their years of financial troubles coincided with those of the congregation, and that their fortunes began to improve at about the same time as did the congregation's.

The good assets were lands in Virginia, New York and Pennsylvania. The title to those in Virginia had eventually been confirmed by the state, for they had been secured by direct purchase and were not part of any land company holding. They lay in that part of western Virginia which in 1792 was formed into the new state of Kentucky, and consisted of tens of thousands of acres.[93] John Campbell advertised his "Proposals for laying of a Town at the Lower Falls" in 1784, with Barnard Gratz as his Philadelphia agent.[93a] Michael Gratz in 1795 entered into negotiations with Stephen Austin, then in England but later one of the founders of the Texan Republic, to sell the land to colonists or land promoters abroad.[94] Some of it was sold to Robert Morris' fantastic North American Land Company,[95] but some was retained, and a quarter of a century later Benjamin Gratz moved to Kentucky to take charge of the family interest there.

The New York land was a vast tract along the Mohawk Valley, which had been acquired from George Croghan long before the Revolution and had been obtained by him in turn as part of his personal share in the settlement made with the Indians at Fort Stanwix. On this tract Michael Gratz founded Gratzburg,[96] and he may have sold a portion of it to James Fenimore Cooper's father for his settlement, Cooperstown.[97] The Pennsylvania land consisted of many scattered pieces in the central and western part of the state which had been bought by the Gratzes from time to time, or obtained as collateral on notes taken from Croghan and others.[98] It may have been some of these for which Michael Gratz acted as agent, when Levy Andrew Levy announced the sale of miscellaneous tracts, including 36,000 acres in Indiana, in 1784.[99]

But Michael had even better assets—his sons.[100] Two of them, Solomon, the first born, and Jonathan, had died young; but Simon, born in 1773, and Hyman, three years younger, were being educated to follow in the footsteps of their father and uncle. The English commercial textbooks, which were their first business guides,[101] were studied and used with the same thoroughness with which Barnard and Michael had pored over theirs at Solomon Henry's London counting-house. And the American-born Gratzes followed the same kind of apprenticeship away from home with a relative as had their elders. At first, Simon Gratz, with the impatience of youth, complained that he was doing all the work for his Philadelphia master and getting none of the credit.[102] Then he went to work at Lancaster for his grandfather, Joseph Simon, where he learned well all that able pioneer merchant could teach him.[103]

Simon's training was completed at a time when he was called upon to take over some of the responsibilities of the older firm of B. and M. Gratz. First Barnard's health began to fail, and he spent more and more time in Baltimore with his daughter Rachel Etting. It was clear that he relied heavily upon his nephew, whom he affectionately called Simmy, and their brief correspondence reveals a mutual, mature respect.[104] When Michael suffered a stroke late in the century, Simon and Hyman were ready to assume the management of the family's affairs.

Their life was to be complicated by several matters which had taken place before they took control of the scattered Gratz interests. David Franks, who had gone over to England to secure compensation for his supposed loyalty to the crown, had received scant reward, and in 1786 was actually apprehended by the King's Bench for debt to one Amos Hayton.[105] He then conveyed to Tench Coxe and Isaac Hazelhurst, in payment of that debt, his interest in a mortgage given by William Trent to Franks, Simon and the Gratzes. The mortgage was on

7,500 acres of land in south-eastern Pennsylvania. After he returned to Philadelphia, still almost destitute, he was helped out by the Gratzes, and, with the forgetfulness of old-age and desperation, assigned to them this same interest in the same mortgage. Since the mortgage had become delinquent in interest payments, and apparently without the knowledge of the other parties, Joseph Simon foreclosed and bought back the tracts in 1790.

When Simon's estate was settled after his death in 1804 his two heirs, Bilah [Bell] Simon Cohen and Leah Simon Phillips, received the land. There had been bad blood between Michael Gratz and his sons on the one part and their father-in-law and grandfather respectively on the other before the old man's death, and this continued to the next generation. A suit was instituted, and the case of Gratz vs. Cohen dragged on for almost half a century, until finally adjudicated by the Supreme Court of the United States in 1850.[106]

The other problem was some land in Virginia which had been given by Solomon Henry of London to his nephew, Joseph Joachim Henry. Joseph Henry had come over to Philadelphia in 1785 and lived with his uncles, Barnard and Michael Gratz.[107] Early in 1793 he died and was buried in the Mikveh Israel cemetery, where his uncle Jacob Henry had been interred in 1761. News of his death and his estate eventually reached Joseph's father, Jonas Hirschel Bluch (that being the name he adopted) in Langendorf, and he apparently wrote to the Gratzes asking for an accounting.[108]

When no answer was forthcoming, Bluch assumed that the Gratzes were dead, and in 1797 addressed a plea for information to the "High-Mighty Lords, Supreme Lords of the Republic of America in Philadelphia." The young Gratzes were considerably embarrassed when this was delivered to President Adams, and then "politely handed us by the Speaker of the House of Representatives." They immediately sent a statement of the estate, with drafts representing the income from it, to their uncle, explaining that Barnard and Michael had retired from business some years before, and begging him not to write to the authorities again, since "any letters directed to us and put on board a vessel bound to any port in the United States, will reach us safe."[109] S. and H. Gratz, now well-known merchants, had just bought from the estate of Jacob Hiltzheimer the building at 232 (later 700) Market Street, where Thomas Jefferson had boarded in 1776 and where he had written the Declaration of Independence.[110]

Among the minor assets of the Henry estate was one lot in the town of Aaronsburg which Aaron Levy had given Henry.[111] In 1786 Levy had laid out the town on a tract which he owned, located in Penn's Valley, almost in the exact geographical center of the state, and offered lots in it for sale by a widely advertised lottery.[112] He foresaw its eventual development as the capital city of Pennsylvania, a future which it never realized. During the time when Robert Morris and his associates of the North American Land Company were pyramiding land purchases into speculative stock holding companies, Levy acted as agent for Morris in the area of Northampton County, where he lived.[113] He bought land on his own account, as well as investing in a few of the companies.[114] At length, sometime in the early 1790's, he decided to move to Philadelphia and retire from active business.

When the land boom collapsed in the last years of the century, Levy was in trouble. He had plenty of land but no cash. So, the story was told, he made an arrangement with Simon Gratz to turn over his holdings to him in return for an annuity.[115] Aaron and Rachel Levy had had no children, consequently Levy virtually adopted young Simon Gratz, gave him a full power of attorney, and made him his sole heir.[116] To the Gratz lands the young financier added the Levy lands. The second generation of Gratzes was on its way to reputation, success and communal service.

Between the close of the Revolution and the end of the century, the Jews of Philadelphia had become an integral and significant part of the life of the city. In the busy commerce of the capital, they competed with the non-Jews and offered their services to all. The directories show that in this period there were ten Jewish brokers and forty Jewish merchants and shopkeepers active in Philadelphia. These were the men of "high visibility," who advertised in the newspapers, who were leaders in the synagogue, who prospered publicly, or just as publicly failed. The social gradations of the day described Aaron Levy and Solomon Lyons as "gentlemen," the Pragers, Michael Gratz and Samuel Hays as "merchants," and Abraham Phillips, Moses Nathan and Levy Phillips as "shopkeepers."[117]

These, however, were the minority of the Jewish community. Most of their co-religionists depended upon more humble ways to earn their livings. A wide variety of occupations and of handicraft trades numbered Jews among them, and these occupations and trades were encouraged by the great need for domestic manufactures to replace those formerly supplied by Great Britain during the colonial days.

In the absence of a factory economy, these were largely home industries, and it may be assumed that women and children helped the head of the household make or sell his wares. Myer Marks was a hatter;[118] Abraham Cohen made trunks;[119] Moses Judah, "Embroiderer from London," announced that he worked in gold, silver and silk for ladies and gentlemen at his lodgings in Elfreth's Alley;[120] Isaac Katz was a cooper;[121] John Moss, also newly arrived from England, advertised that he engraved designs on glass;[122] Jacob Myers[123] and Michael Katz[124] fashioned leather goods; and Isaac Moses was, as noted, a shoemaker.[125] Homberg and Carpeles entered a partnership as innkeepers, and after Carpeles left Philadelphia,[126] Homberg alone took over the management of the Franklin Tavern at Second and Race Streets. Sol Marks had a haberdashery shop;[127] Isaac Marks sold watches;[128] Henry Moses was a saddler and coachman;[129] Louis Van Amring was a grocer;[130] and J. Rodriquez Pereyra[131] and Solomon Raphael[132] were licensed peddlers. In the United States a man was free to do what he was capable of doing, without let or hindrance from the officials of the land, and it was this economic fact—as much as political and religious freedom—which kept attracting new immigrants from Europe.

The peddler was an important functionary in American life. Before the days of mail-order houses which reached into isolated farms, before all the modern means of transportation which brought the customer to the store, a large percentage of the population bought what they needed from a man who came to their door with his stock-in-trade on his back or in a little cart. As the United States expanded westward from the big cities of the coast, the peddler's role became increasingly important, for it was he alone who supplied the small settlements before they were large enough to support a country store of their own.

In Pennsylvania peddlers were required to have licenses, and Solomon Raphael received one duly signed by Benjamin Franklin in his capacity as President of the Executive Council of the state.[133] The career of Raphael is typical of that of the many Jewish peddlers who followed him throughout the first half of the next century. He appeared in the synagogue records as a man whose knowledge of English was poor. When he requested permission to be married by the *hazan* in 1788, he wrote:

> To the anerable the presedent and the genthelman jountay weer as I have pramis mie selleff in mattarimony whit one gall the dogter of Mr. Barent Jacob in the norderen Libberthies in Philladelpia and y would bie werry happay that your anerable Budday would order to mr Jacob Kahan as gasan at the Congragashis of mikvy Israel to give mie goupa and kadousin agins dousday . . .[134]

But his license was a key to a livelihood which required no specialized skill, little money, and only a limited ability to speak the language of the country. By hard work—and trudging the streets of a city or the forest paths of the frontier was hard work—a peddler could earn enough—and with the great American virtue, thrift, save enough—to set himself up in business as a small shopkeeper. Five years after he received his license Raphael was entered in the *Philadelphia Directory* as a "dealer in watches,"[135] and in 1795 he was a "coffee-house keeper."[136] Such was a peddler's progress.

In spite of the number of craftsmen and mechanics among them, the Jews tended more to petty trade and shopkeeping. And for very sound reasons. First, they had been forbidden by law in many European countries from which they came to own land, to work in any but a very few of the handicraft trades, to engage in any but a very few kinds of business. They came to America with fewer skills and more limited experience, through no choice of their own, than their non-Jewish fellow-immigrants.

Secondly, they found that learning a trade was incompatible with their religious observance. A mechanic had to go through a long period of apprenticeship, boarding with his employer and working long hours at the employer's convenience. For a Jew to do this meant sacrificing *kashruth* and probably breaking the Sabbath. Had there been a whole community of Jewish employers, as there was by the end of the nineteenth century, they could have worked for a Jew and remained religiously Jewish. But the American-Jewish community of the 1790's could still be numbered by households, and the opportunities for employment by a Jew were few.

That factor, too, may account for the small number of Jews who came to the country as indentured servants, although there were some. On the other hand, a significant percentage of the early German and Irish immigration consisted of indentured servants. A story told about Aaron Levy of Aaronsburg highlights the problem. One day before the Revolution, when Levy had come into Philadelphia from the west, he was walking past the house of the rich merchant Samuel Chew, and saw there a young girl scrubbing the steps and crying. When he asked her what troubled her, she told him that it was Saturday, and she was a Jewess and a bond-servant, and so forced to work on the Sabbath. Levy paid Chew the girl's redemption money, and married her.[137] In view of his own experience, it may be assumed that Levy treated with due consideration his own indentured servant, Isaac Solomon, who in 1788 bound himself for four years in return for his passage money from Rotterdam.[138] In 1801 two non-Jews advertised for two runaway German servants with the obviously Jewish names of Levy Hirsh, "much addicted to telling vague stories about Hamburgh and Amsterdam," and Nathan Gerson.[139] But such cases must have been rare.

Because it had not been part of his background, the Jew lacked the craft feeling which others brought with them to this country. Those Jews who, as we have seen, came here with varied skills had acquired them chiefly in the more emancipated centers of Amsterdam or London. They had no ancestral pride in their craft as did others who came from generations of blacksmiths, or ironmongers, or tinkers, or weavers, and few of them passed on to their children the training they had received.

Frequently, the metamorphosis from craftsman to merchant took place in one generation. A glass engraver like John Moss did not remain long at his trade after his arrival in 1796. He turned to the more lucrative field of import business, which laid the foundations of his wealth and communal standing.[140] On the other hand, an exception to this general rule was Naphtali Phillips. Like most of his brothers, he turned away from the mercantile activities of his father Jonas, although in 1795 he appeared in the directory as a "merchant" at 86 North Second Street.[141] But shortly after, he went to work for David Claypoole, copublisher of the *Pennsylvania Packet*, where he learned the trade of printing and the profession of journalism. Naphtali later became the first Jewish publisher of an American newspaper.[142]

~ 10

Glimpses of Jews in the Contemporary Scene

IN the spring of 1788 the Jews of Philadelphia, like Jews elsewhere in the English-speaking world, must have scanned their morning paper eagerly for news of the well-publicized boxing match between Humphreys and the great Jewish pugilist, Daniel Mendoza. On May 2, 1788, the *Pennsylvania Packet* carried an almost blow-by-blow description of the encounter which had taken place at a country spot outside London. Alas, Humphreys won. But, the report objectively declared that it had been the Jew's fight all along, until he sprained his ankle.

The Jew, in the early part of the contest, exhibited a great share of the *vis comica* in his aspect; for whenever his opponent missed his aim, he laughed at him with a conscious superiority of his defence. . . . In the abatement of the exquisite skill displayed in the conflict we must observe that Mendoza acted unworthy of himself, for when he closed in with Humphreys, he screwed his nose, and thrust his knuckles in his eye. This he did, as report says, by way of retaliation; for his antagonist, conscious of his superior strength, frequently endeavored to frustrate the skill of his adversary, by closing in upon him. . . . The victory of Humphreys, is rather to be imputed to the accident of Mendoza's straining his ankle, the anguish of which made him faint, than to the effect of the last blow, however well placed.[1]

A year later, the young Phillipses and their friends were heartened to learn that Daniel's cousin, Aaron Mendoza, had trounced one of Humphreys' pupils; "his adversary's eyes, according to the technical expression, were completely buttoned up."[2]

It is surprising how much news of Jewish interest appeared in the Philadelphia press of the day. Dunlap, in his *Packet*, printed reports from Galicia, St. Petersburg, Stuttgart, Danzig, London and Paris, as well, of course, as items sent from New York, Charleston and the West Indies. Most of these were friendly and complimentary, and played no small part in creating the cordial atmosphere which existed in Philadelphia. There was a high compliment intended in a story about a drought in Kingston, Jamaica, which the Philadelphia editor chose to print:

> The Jews in and about Kingston, impressed with a sense of the common danger, are endeavouring to avert the impending evil, by fasting and prayer two or three days in a week, while the joyous profession of christianity intoxicated with luxury and dissipation, invigorate themselves with ale and rhenish, and tacitly bid defiance to the "wars of elements and the crush of worlds."[3]

Such a news item was neither isolated nor infrequent. The Jewish community of Kingston was referred to several times, including praise for their charitable contributions[4] and an account of the dedication ceremony of the new synagogue in 1788.[5]

However, Dunlap considered more newsworthy events which pointed up the surging interests of the day, the spread of the doctrines of freedom, liberty and equality. In his long reports of the debates of the New York Assembly—still incidentally, unstudied by Jewish historians—he printed a section of the discussion on Sunday and Sabbath laws, in which it was argued:

> Suppose a Jew should say, you offend me by working on the Saturday, and for which he will say he has a positive command; why has he not as good a right to a law to prevent his sect being disturbed, as any other sects in the community? They, by the constitution, are to enjoy equal rights and privileges.[6]

And, following the same theme of religious rights, Dunlap included the sensational pleas of the Jesuit priest, Abbé Gregoire, who, against the protest of the French clergy, demanded that the delegation of French Jews be permitted to voice their protests before the National Assembly in 1789.[7] The achievements of the French Revolution were weighed in America and its libertarian progress regularly noted. "No people will be greater gainers," the *Daily Advertiser* commented, "than the Jews, by the declaration of the Rights of Man in France. In that country, they were formerly not merely treated as the most abject of the human race, but in many cases actually put upon a level with the brute creation."[8]

All American denominations were heartened by the subsequent news that "a number of Methodist Priests are daily expected in Paris, a church having already been purchased; and the Jews will shortly open their synagogues. In short, religious liberty reigns in France, and will sooner or later extend itself over the whole universe."[9] There was pride in eighteenth-century America in the seemingly millenial impact of the Revolution upon the world.

Yet, not all the Philadelphia press was so seriously concerned with the Jews. Benjamin Franklin Bache, the grandson of the great Franklin, used them rather facetiously to make an editorial point. When the Quakers of Philadelphia, with other religious groups, petitioned against the theater which was flourishing in the city, Bache attacked their stand by citing a parallel which of course was pure fiction:

We are informed by a correspondent that the class of citizens denominated Jews, propose at their next Sabbath meeting in the synagogue to appoint from among the elders, a committee to frame and draw up a memorial which will be presented before Congress, praying "An act for the utter destruction throughout the United States, of that filthy race of Quadrupeds called Swine." They ground their claim upon equal justice with another class of citizens who have lately presented a petition for the restriction of Play-houses &c. They are themselves prohibited the privilege of eating Pork, and surely have as just a right to debar their fellow citizens the sensual gratification of partaking exclusively of so *nice a dainty!*[10]

Four Jews—Samuel Hays, Mark Prager, Jr.,[11] Isaac Franks and Michael Prager—were among the earliest subscribers to the new Chestnut Street Theater in 1792.[12]

If occasionally there is some evidence in the newspapers or in letters of the attitude of non-Jews to Jews, there is little which has survived to tell us what Jews thought of their fellow-countrymen. Consequently, a scrap here and a scrap there have significance. Such a one was the notice placed in the papers by Levy Andrew Levy, back in 1778, seeking a Lancaster public character and odd-job helper, the deranged Blizzard McGruder, who had strayed away.[13] Most such notices were stern, but exactly the opposite was the case in this situation. Levy asked whoever might find McGruder "not to treat him with harshness or severity," and his description of the servant's attire, clothes fit for a merchant, showed that he had been given consideration unusual for lunatics in the eighteenth century.

This approach was seldom found in advertisements for either runaway slaves or indentured servants, and few of them carried "an agate snuff-box set in silver, and a silk pocket handkerchief," as did McGruder. The Reverend Jacob Cohen's short, teen-age, bound girl wore a spotted jean jacket, a striped linsey petticoat, a spotted coarse shawl and a black wire-framed bonnet, when she ran away, and he was forced to offer a dollar's reward for anyone who would bring her home or take her to the gaol.[14] The Jews who could afford them had both servants and slaves. The Quakers were the only people who as a religious denomination opposed the institution of slavery. Yet, many of the Jews in time were influenced by the arguments of the Quaker-sponsored Pennsylvania Society for Promoting the Abolition of Slavery, and did manumit their slaves.

The first formal abolition society was organized in Philadelphia in 1774, but the Revolution interrupted its work, and it was not until 1787 that it was reconstituted and enlarged with Benjamin Franklin as its president and Benjamin Rush as its secretary.[15] The Society quickly created an atmosphere in the city which more and more looked upon slavery as an evil and an injustice. Men who had owned slaves began to free them in increasing numbers through conviction or moral suasion. Rush, a non-Quaker, had held two slaves when he first became active in the abolition movement; but in 1788 he set them free, because he was convinced that slavery was "contrary to reason and religion."[16] On the other hand, Solomon Bush, one of the first Jews to join the Society, never owned or sold a slave.

In Newport, the Lopez and Rivera families had traded extensively in Negroes;[17] Sarzedas and Sasportas in the plantation South were dependent on slave labor.[18] Yet, the metamorphosis of Benjamin Nones in Philadelphia shows well the influences of Philadelphia abolitionism. After recovering from his business losses, Nones acquired a Negro man and a female indentured servant, who frequently plagued him by running away.[19] But by 1793, perhaps through his association with the liberal alderman, Hilary Baker, he not only freed his own slave, but appeared at least ten times as a witness or participant in the manumission of others.[20] Israel Jacobs[21] and Philip Moses Russell[22] liberated their slaves in 1784, with the synagogue's controversial figure, Mordecai M. Mordecai, serving as witness for the latter.

Even David Nassy, whose ancestors had built a whole colony based on slave labor in Surinam, came under the sway of Philadelphia humanitarianism, and "set free from slavery" his two personal slaves shortly after his arrival in town.[23] His act was witnessed by Sol Marache, whose name appeared several times in the records of the Society. The procedure followed by Nassy, as well as Samuel and Solomon Alexander,[24] Samuel Hays[25] and Isaac Pesoa,[26] differed from full and outright liberation. They registered their slaves so that they would be manumitted according to law, but they reserved the right to hold them as indentured servants for a specific period of time.

The scope of the activity of Philadelphia Jews in this movement can be measured by the manner in which they changed the opinions of a number of French Jewish refugees who fled the Negro revolts in Santo Domingo in 1793. The Moline family, who had escaped the blind wrath of the aroused Negroes of the island, brought with them to Philadelphia their own slaves branded with the Moline name. Within a short time after they had reached the safety of Philadelphia they came in company with their compatriot Benjamin Nones before the Society to give these slaves complete freedom.[27] And furthermore, Solomon Moline was so completely converted that he in turn appeared in a like role with another Frenchman straight from the horrors of Cap François.[28]

The record books of the Pennsylvania Society carry many an entry in which Jews figured as principals or witnesses. The hatter Moses Myers freed his Negro man David Anderson for the "faithful service heretofore to me rendered."[29] And no major communal movement would have been complete without the participation of Jonas Phillips. His responsibilities with the Society first concerned the property of New York Isaac Moses, on whose behalf in 1790 he acknowledged formally

that a certain Negro named Bill of the age of thirty or thereabouts . . . hath obtained his full and absolute freedom and emancipation and is now free and emancipated to all intents and purposes.[30]

Three years later Phillips manumitted his own slave, Phillis, allowing her to be purchased by her husband and set free at the same time.[31]

Of course, not every Philadelphian considered slavery an evil, and not every Jew did either. Isaac Franks, who had sold slaves from time to time, is not known to have liberated his own sixteen-year-old girl, Bell.[32] Michael Gratz kept Negroes as personal house-servants, and at least one of them took over the complete operation of his *kosher* kitchen.[33] Barnard Gratz's slave took his master's paternalism so seriously that he refused to allow himself to be sold on the block when sent to Lancaster for that purpose.[34] He was tough and recalcitrant, and probably aware that he might not fare as well under changed circumstances. Barnard was informed that he had had to be shackled and was being held in jail until word was received what to do with him. There is no record that he was sold; perhaps Barnard was impressed with his determination to remain with him.

A quite different attitude was held by Barnard's son-in-law, Solomon Etting. He was an early subscriber to Mikveh Israel, and during a brief Philadelphia residence married Rachel Gratz. Shortly afterwards the whole family moved to Baltimore.[35] In 1794 Etting became a member of the Standing Committee of the Republican Society of Baltimore,[36] and in 1797 he, with his father-in-law and others, unsuccessfully petitioned the Maryland House of Delegates to place the Jews, insofar as civil rights were concerned, "upon the same footing with other good citizens."[37] But he carried his interest in human equality beyond his self-interest as a Jew. In a border state with strong leanings toward slavery, he joined in the formation of the Maryland State Colonization Society, and by 1831 was both a manager and a member of the executive committee of that pro-Negro organization,[38] which propagandized on behalf of the establishment of a state in Africa for freed Negroes.

Many in Philadelphia were convinced that the flood of fugitives who poured into town from the rebellion-wracked West Indian islands was responsible for the disastrous epidemic which swept the city in the fall of 1793.[39] On Rosh Hashanah of that year, there was a great fire on Second Street.[40] Ordinarily it would have been considered a major catastrophe, but Philadelphia was then in the throes of a horror more devastating and more frightening. Yellow fever was raging through the streets of the city, killing men, women and children at first, when the epidemic began in August, in twos and threes, then by the dozens, and, as the plague grew worse, by the hundreds. The disease was known and recognized, but no doctor understood its cause, and none had a specific, effective treatment.

The city, state and national governments shut up their offices in town. For a month a volunteer Committee "To transact the whole of the business relative to mitigating the sufferings of those that are or may be afflicted" was the actual governing body of the city.[41] Trade was at a standstill. Those who could packed up and left for more salubrious parts. Those who stayed were concerned only with nursing the sick and burying the dead. The doctors, most of whom heroically remained, were frantically trying to do the best they knew how for more people than they had time to visit. A public hospital was established by the Committee at the Hamiltons' old mansion at Bush Hill to care for the scores of those who would otherwise have been left helpless. In September, 1400 deaths were recorded; by the end of the month the average number of deaths per day reached 70; and on October 11th the staggering total of 119 was recorded.[42]

The leading physician of Philadelphia was Dr. Benjamin Rush, and, with sincere confidence in what he considered to be the best scientific judgment, he was treating the sick with violent purges and drastic bleeding. To his amazement, although some of the sick recovered, a high percentage died in spite of his treatment.[43] While many of the other doctors in town, who were his colleagues in the College of Physicians or had been his students at the University of Pennsylvania, followed his regime, and stoutly supported its efficacy, there was a group of physicians, chief of whom was the Frenchman, Jean Devèze, who had seen other similar epidemics in the West Indies and who recommended stimulants and quinine, cleanliness, rest, fresh air and a light diet as the best therapy.[44] A controversy over the cause of the fever, how to avoid it, and the care and treatment of those infected, raged in the newspapers, by word of mouth and in pamphlets. Nothing was settled, and but little learned by the time the cold weather came along and killed the anopheles mosquitoes which, all unknown in those days, had carried and spread the fatal fever. With the first frosts the yellow fever epidemic of 1793 came to an end.

During the few tragic months of its duration, David de Isaac Cohen Nassy had been ministering wisely and well to the stricken citizens of Philadelphia. A scion of the greatest Jewish family of Surinam, Nassy had come to Philadelphia in 1792.[45]

That he was a trained and respected scientist by then is best evidenced by the fact that, within a short time after his arrival, he was elected a member of the American Philosophical Society,[46] the first Jew, except for the Georgia convert and expert on silk culture, Joseph Ottolenghe,[47] to be so honored. He was also the first Jewish physician in a professional sense to practice medicine in Philadelphia. "Doctor" Solomon Bush may have treated patients, but he was not a trained physician. And, in the academic years of 1790–91 and 1791–92, Moses Sheftall, Mordecai's son from Georgia, had been a student of the famed Dr. Rush,[48] but he, the first Jew to receive a formal medical education in America, returned to Savannah after his schooling.

Dr. Nassy was one of the proponents of Devèze's methods of the treatment of yellow fever. He too had observed the fever in the Caribbean and felt that Rush's measures were more harmful than helpful, and proved it, to the satisfaction of the "French" school, by post-mortem examination.[49] He visited Bush Hill, which was under Devèze's care, and lavishly praised the Frenchman's clinical genius.[50] Prescribing the same mild treatment, which the Committee's patients were so successfully receiving there, Nassy himself was accorded "a monopoly of praise" by the merchant John Welsh, who noted that Nassy seemed to lose scarcely any of his patients, whereas those treated with Rush's calomel and jalap only occasionally recovered.[51] The statistics bore out Welsh's praise. From August 28 to October 10 Nassy visited 160 patients; 117 had yellow fever, and of them he lost only nineteen.[52] Furthermore, of the nineteen, he saw eleven only after they had been treated with Rushite medicines by other physicians.

As the fever began to lose its deadliness, doctors, journalists and other observers set about writing their accounts of the Philadelphia epidemic. One of these was Nassy, who wrote originally in French and had his report published both in that language and in English. His *Observations* was the first American Jewish medical publication.[53] In other chronicles of the deadly months, statistics were printed and lists of those who died were set down, with indications of the victim's religion. It is amazing how few Jews seem to have succumbed.

There is not a mention of the epidemic in the minutes of Mikveh Israel, at a time when most of the literate survivors of the plague hastened to put down their observations. The *ad-*

junta, which met only twice during the critical period, was gravely concerned with Josephson's insulting reply to their request for a *shofar*.[54] It is undoubtedly true that many of the Philadelphia Jews, like other inhabitants of the city, had fled. Yet, it was largely the well-to-do who could afford to go elsewhere, and most of the Jews were not that, nor did they have relatives scattered in outlying sections as did many other Philadelphians.

The Gratzes were fortunate. Barnard Gratz, living with his daughter in Baltimore, wrote Michael, who was at Lancaster with his father-in-law, begging him not to go to Philadelphia for Yom Kippur, because shocking accounts of the fever were circulating—"110 was buried last Sunday & the Doctors will not attend the sick as it is so Mortil."[55] From Easton, Judge William Bradford, there on judicial circuit, wrote, "It is an enemy that must not be opposed but avoided." On September 25, the Judge noted the arrival of Jacob Cohen, who had remained in town until after Yom Kippur, and then left for the "high and healthy country" of Easton to be with his daughter, the wife of local shopkeeper, Michael Hart:

> The Jewish Rabbi arrived from Philada yesterday—He says he staid till most of his congregation had fled or were diseased & then thought it was his duty to fly also. Many were striving to get out of Town, and he confirms the fact which we heard before that on Friday, Saturday & Sunday the dead were numbered at 340.[56]

Moses Homberg, David Franks, David Salisbury Franks, Rachel, the wife of Myer Hart, formerly of Easton,[57] and probably a few others whose names are not known died of the fever. On October 7th Dr. Rush told his wife that David Salisbury Franks had died that day "at Mr. Kean's under the care of a French physician, deserted by all his former friends—so much so that he was buried in the Potter's field."[58] But two days later he corrected the final statement with the news that "Honest Jno. Thompson" had prevented a pauper's burial, and "obtained a grave for him in Christ Church burying ground."[59]

The fact remains that, proportionately, very few Jews succumbed. Among the experts who filled the newspapers with advice for the avoidance of the disease—fire cannons in the streets; carry camphor around your neck; bathe in vinegar—one recommended the high standards of cleanliness as practiced among the ancient Jews and set forth in the regulations of

Leviticus.[60] However, it is doubtful whether orthodox adherence to religious law protected those Philadelphia Jews who lived in one of the sections of the city where the toll was heaviest. Was it possible that their low mortality rate was due to the fact that they preferred to be treated by the Jewish doctor, David Nassy?

Washington had left the city for Mount Vernon on September 10th,[61] but he returned in November after the danger of infection no longer existed.[62] However, even then it seemed unwise to move back to the center of the crippled town, for who knew but that the fever might flare up again. The suburb of Germantown, higher and healthier, offered itself as a safer place to establish the seat of government, at least for a while, and so President Washington looked around for a house there. Isaac Franks, who had sought safety in Bethlehem, had a fine dwelling on Main Street in Germantown,[63] and, since it was then unoccupied, the President asked if Franks would rent it to him. He was honored to do so, and, as a result, a temporary presidential residence was set up. The curious bill for the two months' occupancy included not only the rent at $66.66 but an item for transportation for Franks and his wife from Bethlehem to put the house and furniture in order to accommodate the President, $2.50 "Cash paid for Cleaning my house and putting it in the same condition the President rec'd it in," $6 damage done to a "large double Japan'd waiter," and the cost of a few missing items such as a flat-iron, a large fork and three ducks.[64] In spite of what would seem to be an overly-detailed bill, Washington rented the house again the following summer.[65] He at least thought that Franks was a fair landlord.

Franks had married Mary, the daughter of Captain Samuel Davidson, in 1782, a month after he resigned his commission as ensign in the 7th Massachusetts Regiment.[66] He was now moving in higher social circles, and his position as Washington's landlord certainly helped him maintain his status. When the Pennsylvania Militia was called out to march to the western part of the state to put down the Whisky Rebellion, the Governor appointed Franks Lieutenant-Colonel of the 2nd Regiment of the Philadelphia County Brigade.[67] It was as a result of this appointment that he became generally known in the city as "Colonel" Franks. After his return to Germantown, he became secretary of the school board,[68] and was made a Justice of the

Peace,[69] and it was there in 1802 that Gilbert Stuart painted his portrait which he presented "to friend Isaac Franks as a token of regard."[70] In spite of the fact that Franks was a contributing member of Mikveh Israel in 1782, he ceased all connections with the Jewish community thereafter.

Some time after Stuart painted his portrait Franks moved upstate. From there he maintained the friendship he had formed with Dr. Benjamin Rush during the hectic days of his brokerage career. For a while he was not doing well financially, and in 1803 he asked Rush to renew a note in the expectation that he would be able to sell some of his Northumberland lands.[71] However, things got worse, and in 1810 from Ephrata he wrote his physician friend rather pathetically:

I must inform you, that some time since in consequence of the unceasing pressure of two of my exorbitant and vindictive creditors, whom you well know, And rather then put my Person in their power, I have been compelled to take the benefit of the Insolvent Acts.[72]

He assured Rush that he had discharged his debts in full, had been privileged to have a private hearing where he received "honorable attention" from the judge, but that nobody, not even his children, knew of his action, and he begged Rush to have "the goodness to burn this letter." Its main point was a plea for Rush's help in getting him a clerkship in the Mint, or perhaps in the Custom House "under Genl. Steel, who knows me as a revolutionary officer."

A fascinating series of letters from Franks to Rush dealing with his health has survived, curious in that Franks, suffering from various ailments, described his symptoms in detail and asked Rush, who for many years had taken care of him and his family, to prescribe for them at long distance—which he did. He first complained of an "excruciating pain about my right loin, or kidneys, bladder, and testicles, attended with colic and bleeding."[73] And the following year surmised that he had a stone, which diagnosis he found to be correct, for a week later he had the pleasure of informing his physician that he discharged a large stone, the size of which he indicated with a drawing of its outline.[74] Early in the winter of 1812 he once again consulted his doctor by long distance, this time setting down pages of clinical self-observations about what seems to have been flatulent dyspepsia, gravel, and infected gums.[75] When Rush offered suggestions for a treatment, Franks wrote back after seven weeks that they had done no good, and would Rush be good enough to prescribe something else.[76] The best that the most famous American physician of the period could offer was garlic and spirits of turpentine, and a blister to the arm. Benjamin Rush died the following year, but Franks lived on, continuing to apply for government posts,[77] and continuing to be disappointed, until he was finally made Prothonotary of the Supreme Court of Pennsylvania in 1819,[78] which position he held until his death three years later.[79]

Franks' friend, Benjamin Rush, was a man whose genuine feeling for his fellowmen had moved him to the forefront of many of the humanitarian undertakings of the city. He was active in the anti-slavery movement; he was an advocate of temperance; he was one of the leaders of the group trying to reform prisons; he was interested in a number of educational institutions. And, as he wrote his wife, "I love to be in the way of adding to my stock of ideas on all subjects." So, having attended Mrs. Phillips in a professional capacity,[80] he eagerly accepted an invitation to attend the wedding of Jonas Phillip's daughter Rachel to Michael Levy of Virginia. His description of the marriage ceremony, which is contained in a letter to his wife of June 27, 1787, is the only description of an eighteenth-century American Jewish wedding which has survived.

At 1 o'clock the company, consisting of 30 or 40 men, assembled in Mr. Phillip's common parlor, which was accommodated with benches for the purpose. The ceremony began with prayers in the Hebrew language, which was chaunted by an old rabbi and in which he was followed by the whole company. As I did not understand a word except now and then an Amen or Hallelujah, my attention was directed to the haste with which they covered their heads with their hats as soon as the prayers began, and to the freedom with which some of them conversed with each other during the whole time of this part of their worship. As soon as these prayers were ended, which took up about 20 minutes a small piece of parchment was produced, written in Hebrew, which contained a deed of settlement and which the groom subscribed in the presence of four witnesses. In this deed he conveyed a part of his fortune to his bride, by which she was provided for after his death in case she survived him. The ceremony was followed by the erection of a beautiful canopy composed of white and red silk in the middle of the floor. It was supported by four young men (by means of four poles), who put on white gloves for the purpose. As soon as this canopy was fixed, the bride, accompanied with her mother, sister, and a long train of female relations, came downstairs. Her face was covered with a veil which reached halfways down her body. She was handsome at all times, but the occasion and her dress rendered her in a peculiar manner a most lovely and affecting object. I gazed with delight upon her. Innocence, modesty, fear, respect and devotion appeared all at once in her countenance. She was led by her two bridesmaids under the canopy. Two young men led the bridegroom after her and placed him, not by her side, but directly opposite to her. The priest now began to chaunt an Hebrew prayer, in which he was followed by part of the company. After this he gave to the groom and bride a glass full of wine, from which they each sipped about a teaspoonful. Another prayer followed this act, after which he took a ring and directed the groom to place it upon the finger of his bride in the same manner as is practised in the marriage service of the Church of England. This ceremony was followed by handing the wine to the father of the bride and then a second time to the bride and groom. The groom after sipping the wine took the glass in his hand and threw it upon a large pewter dish which was suddenly placed at his feet. Upon its breaking into a number of small pieces, there was a general shout of joy and a declaration that the ceremony was over. The groom now saluted his bride, and kisses and congratulations became general through the room. I asked the meaning, after the ceremony was over, of the canopy and of the drinking of the wine and breaking of the glass. I was told by one of the company that in Europe they generally marry in the open air, and that the canopy was introduced to defend the bride and groom from the action of the sun and from rain. Their mutually partaking of the same glass of wine was intended to denote the mutuality of their goods, and the breaking of the glass at the conclusion of the business was designed to teach them the brittleness and uncertainty of human life and the certainty of death, and thereby to temper and moderate their present joys.[81]

Dr. Rush went upstairs after the ceremony to inquire for the health of Mrs. Phillips, who had fainted from the heat and the weakness of a previous illness, and found the bride and groom sipping a bowl of broth together. The proud mother, who was recovered, explained that they had fasted since the night before, and, as the Doctor left, pressed upon him a piece of cake for Mrs. Rush, an old New York friend of the bride's mother, the former Rebecca Machado. Commodore Uriah Phillips Levy was the son of the young couple married in Philadelphia that early summer day in 1787.

Again in 1792 this physician, blessed with an insatiable intellectual curiosity, was witness to a Jewish ceremony of a different kind in the Phillips house. In his commonplace book Rush again left a detailed account of it.

This day agreeably to an invitation I attended the circumcision of a child of eight days old of Jonas Philips. There were above 30 persons, all Jews except myself, at the ceremony. The men only witnessed it. The women remained upstairs 'till the operation was completed and the child returned to the mother. The ceremony began by chanting from a Hebrew Book in which the Priest led. The company followed standing with their hats on. Two held candles lighted, one a forceps, one a knife, and three a glass of wine each. After chanting 5 minutes the Priest took the child and placed it on the knees of one of its brothers, who with a sash on sat on a table with a pillow in his lap. The Priest then drew forward the foreskin and secured it with his silver forceps, and then suddenly cut off the skin. He afterwards tore the inner skin with his fingers and trussed it backwards so that nothing appeared but the naked glans penis. He now put his lips to the wound, and sucking some blood from it spit it into one of the glasses of wine. After this he springled Dragon's blood on the wound, and a little wine, and then covered it with lint wet with Balsam Copaira, over which he spread a plaster of wax and oil. During the whole of the process, the chanting was continued to drown the cries of the child. When the ceremony was finished, and the child returned to its mother, all the friends of the family went up to her and saluted her. The women upstairs showed great marks of distress and sympathy during the performance of the ceremony. Mrs. Nones said she rejoiced that her last child was a girl, as it thereby escaped the dreadful operation. An ingenious Physician, a Jew, who attended the ceremony told me that Jews in consequence of the loss of the foreskin were less subject to be infected with the venereal disease, and when they received it, escaped all the troublesome symptoms which were connected with the foreskin, as phimosis, paraphimosis, chancres, etc. After the whole was ended, the company sat down to a splendid and plentiful breakfast. The heat of the day was 84°.[82]

The "ingenious Physician" was, as Rush elaborated in his entry of the next day, David Nassy, who then came to see him, and presented him with a copy of his history of Surinam.[83] He and the Philadelphian chatted about the state of the world and religion in general, which was one of Rush's favorite subjects, and Rush discovered that "he thought with Dr. Franklin that it was best to believe, but that it seemed very improbable that the Supreme Being should give a preference to any one nation such as it was said he has given to the Jews."[84] Nassy was an advanced free-thinker, a Deist, Rush noted, but men could be Deists "and yet be warmly attached to the forms of the Sects in which they have been educated," he continued.

This conversation had taken place the year before the yellow fever epidemic, and a few months later Nassy called him in consultation on the illness of Benjamin Nones.[85] In 1793 Rush, embittered by the attacks of the French physicians on his treatment of the disease, was not charitably disposed towards any of them, and, obviously referring to Nassy, but not mentioning his name, he wrote in 1793 that "the French physicians" were falling into disrepute, and added,

one of them (a Jew) does not even feel the pulse of his patients. Upon being offered a hand for that purpose by a Mr. Morrison, he said, "no—no. I never

feel the pulse; that is the way the Philadelphia physicians catch the disorder."
This man died on the 3rd. day.[86]

Morrison well may have been one of those Nassy lost who had
already received Rush-recommended treatments before he was
called in.

Dr. Isaac Nassy stayed on in Philadelphia for about a year
after the epidemic, and, early in 1794, he notified his patients
that he was moving from the house of Mr. Somerkamp, Druggist, on Market Street to 105 North Third Street, where he has
for sale "several Chymical and Chirurgical instruments, Analyp-
tics, Wines, Cordials, Ratafiats, Elixers, syrups, &c."[87] Just about
the time he moved, he presented a paper on botany before the
Philosophical Society,[88] and a few months later, sending notice
that an indisposition would prevent him from attending a meeting, he offered to subscribe to a fund to move Peale's Museum
into the rooms of the Society.[89] When he announced his intention of returning to his native Surinam the following year, he
promised to carry out any studies there that the Society might
desire, for the country contained "rare products, which are the
more interesting for scientists because they are little if at all
known, since the country has not been visited by knowledgeable
travellers."[90] It is interesting to note that Nassy had become an
American citizen during his stay, and he told a Providence correspondent that he felt sure his citizenship would protect him
against privateers on his way home.[91] When some years later,
back in Surinam, he published his *Lettre sur les Juifs,* a defense
against current Dutch publications which urged disabilities upon
the Jewish community, he puffed his own work as "a specific
application of the great principles of liberty and equality of
which the United States gave the first example to the world,"
and sent copies to both the Philosophical Society and the Library
Company in Philadelphia.[92]

From time to time Nassy remembered Mikveh Israel with a
contribution, and his colleague, Dr. Moses Sheftall of Savannah,
also maintained his ties in the city. Loyal to his teacher, he wrote
Dr. Rush in 1795 praising his treatment of the yellow fever.
After dilating at some length upon Rush's greatness and his
spirit of forgiveness towards his detractors, Sheftall came to the
point of his letter. He would like Rush's influence in Congress
to help him secure the post of visiting physician for the Port of
Savannah—

My recommendations having been laying for some time in the hands of my
Brother in Law Doctor Bush, to whom I have wrote, requesting him to
deliver them to a Mr Baldwin a member of the House of Representatives
from this State; if you can serve me, I shall ever gratefully acknowledge it.[93]

After Nassy left there was not another Jewish doctor in
Philadelphia until 1800. That year Abraham Solis, also formerly
of Surinam, and lately from Boston, where he was characterized
as an "Interpreter of Foreign Languages,"[94] informed the public
"that he will be happy to practice in the medical profession, he
is regularly acquainted with."[95] About Solis nothing else is
known, and the earliest Jewish doctor to set up a permanent
practise in town was Manuel Phillips, one of Jonas' sons.[96] At
this period it was only a small number of native-born sons of
established Jewish families who sought a professional career.
There was not the positive desire—so marked a hundred years
later—on the part of Jewish parents to see their children enter
a field which they considered distinguished and above their own
station. Consequently, only a few Jews drifted into medicine.

In the field of law, the story was much the same. Moses and
Sampson Levy, both Christian-bred, had been admitted to the
bar before the end of the Revolution,[97] but no professing Jew
became a lawyer in Philadelphia until Zalegman Phillips, Manuel's
brother, was graduated from the University and was admitted to
the bar in 1799.[98] Again, those who followed his example were
few. Beginning in 1810, other second generation American Jews—
Joseph Simon Cohen, Benjamin Gratz, and Elijah Gratz Etting—
entered the legal profession,[99] but it was to be a good many years
before there was more than a handful of Jewish lawyers in the
city.

If there were not many Jewish lawyers, there was not much
Jewish crime either. When arrangements were made for the
prisoners at the Walnut Street Gaol to receive religious min-
istrations according to their faiths, the Board of Inspectors remembered that they should also provide for the services of a
Jewish minister,[100] but they found there was nothing for him
to do, because there were no Jewish prisoners. Nonetheless, in
1797 several Philadelphia Jews did ask the Board to make sure
that such Jewish inmates as there might be would not be required
to perform any duties which might interfere "with the observance of what they conceive to be a religious duty."[101]

The Reverend Jacob Cohen was, of course, the only Jewish

minister in town, and he was accorded recognition equal to that of clergymen of other sects. When the elite Young Ladies Academy, situated near the synagogue on Cherry Street,[102] was opened in 1788, the Jewish *Hazan* was among ten other ministers of various denominations who were appointed visitors and examiners.[103] He served in that capacity for several years. There never existed in America the medieval background of superstition and prejudice against the Jews which even in a newly rationalistic Europe affected the relations between Jew and non-Jew. Here, although there were occasional overtones of inherited hatreds, the Jew was basically a fellow-American of a different religion.

11

Politics in an Era of Consolidation

"T HE affairs of this country are in a violent par-
oxysm,"[1] President Washington wrote to his old friend Charles
Cotesworth Pinckney late in the summer of 1795. The honey-
moon of Washington's first administration was over; his second
was beset with the rising tide of dissension within the country.
Hamilton's financial program had aided chiefly the rich—the
shipowners, the merchants, the manufacturers and the speculators. Jay's treaty had conceded much to the English, but hurt
the Southern planters. The tax on whisky had aroused the
western farmers and provoked an insurrection in Pennsylvania.
Opposition to the increasingly pro-British, strong central government policies of the administration began slowly to gather
strength and form.

International difficulties added to the confused situation. France
and England were at war with each other, and on the seas both
nations were seizing American ships. The French, under a revolutionary government which had come to power in the Reign
of Terror, were more aggressive, and within the next few years
there was undeclared war between the French and the Americans
in the West Indies.

Washington, anxious to preserve American neutrality, warned
of entangling alliance, but he and the Federalists who supported
him were outspoken in their sympathy for the English and in
their fear of the influences of anarchy and atheism which they
believed might be the exportable products of the French Revolu-

tion. In 1796 John Adams, a staunch Federalist, was elected to the presidency when Washington declined a third term, and with his followers strongly entrenched in Congress continued the policies of the previous administration.

Jefferson, who had emerged as the leader of the opposition, was at the same time elected vice-president, and during the next four years party lines were sharply drawn, as the bitterness between the two American points of view mounted. Jefferson and his Democratic-Republicans had the backing of the farmers, the frontiersmen of the West, the old states-rights opponents of the Constitution, those who believed that the French Revolution had dealt a blow to tyrannical monarchy, and miscellaneous groups like the Irish-born Americans who were doing all they could to help the rebels in Ireland throw off the British yoke. These "democrats," as they were scornfully called by the Federalists, were suspicious of the autocratic and aristocratic tendencies of the Washington-Adams-Hamilton faction, who seemed more and more to be favoring the few instead of the many.[2]

In the last five years of the eighteenth century the United States was plunged into a political conflict which left neither participant nor bystander unscathed. In Philadelphia, still the capital of the nation and the chief stage of political life, one of the targets of the partisan invective which flooded the newspapers of the day was the *parnass* of Mikveh Israel. Anti-Semitism, used against non-Jew as well as Jew, became one of the weapons of the Federalists; but before the battle ended the Jew emerged with dignity.

Before Washington's second term had ended, a number of political societies were organized whose opposition to the administration was so outspoken that the President suggested that they were a menace which the government should annihilate by force if necessary.[3] Both in Philadelphia and New York, the quaint old Society of the Sons of St. Tammany, which had been started before the Revolution, was reactivated to counteract the efforts of the pro-British Sons of St. George. In Philadelphia another anti-Federalist group, the Democratic Society, was

founded on the purest principles of civil liberty, and of respect and attachment to the constitution and laws of their country; unbiased by any party views, and actuated solely by patriotic motives, at a time when the most momentous concerns agitate the public mind.

Less piously, but more practically, the Society declared its opposition to the "noisy declamations of pretended Patriotism" and the "proscriptions of Aristocracy under the Masque of Federalism."[4]

Within a few years other societies, with similar programs and similar views, added their weight to the original two. Stephen Girard, the prominent merchant of French descent, David Rittenhouse, second only to Franklin as Philadelphia's greatest early scientist, Caesar A. Rodney, whose uncle had signed the Declaration of Independence, General Peter Muhlenberg, who fought in some of the bloodiest battles of the Revolution and was the spokesman of the Pennsylvania Germans, Dr. George Logan, the Quaker agriculturist, and the famous Dr. Benjamin Rush were a few of the leading members of the Philadelphia societies, whose membership, however, was largely composed of workingmen.

Few membership lists of these political groups have survived, so that it is impossible to give a complete picture of the Jewish participation in them. However, the first Jewish member of the Democratic Society of Philadelphia noted was Lancaster-born Solomon Marks, Jr.,[5] who was active from 1794 until 1797, when he moved from the city. Benjamin Nones, who played an important role in the reconstituted Tammany Society, was also a member of the Democratic Society, and possibly of the French Society of Friends of Liberty and Equality, which drew its adherents from men like himself, Americans of French origin.[6]

Tension increased in Philadelphia as the Federalists began to insist upon a declaration of war against France. In the alleged interests of national security they determined to silence the opposition. A mob—incited by such articles as one urging its readers to treat him "as we should a Turk, a Jew, a Jacobin, or a dog"[7]—was formed to attack the shop of Benjamin Franklin Bache, the editor of the violently anti-Federalist *Aurora*.[8] Then he was accused of being treasonously in the pay of France. When that charge was found to be untenable, the administration forces arrested Bache for "libelling the President & the Executive Government, in a manner tending to excite sedition, and opposition to the laws." He was defended by Alexander J. Dallas, Secretary of Pennsylvania, and Moses Levy, then a leading radical Democratic lawyer.[9] While the case was pending, and because a conviction seemed doubtful, Congress in 1798 passed the infamous Alien and Sedition Acts, which were the most repressive, reactionary laws ever placed on the statute books of the United States. By them the President was given the power to deport "dangerous" aliens; it was made more difficult for new arrivals to become citizens; any person who wrote or spoke against the President, Congress or the Federal Government was subject to a five-year prison sentence and a fine of $5,000. Instead of ending the opposition, the Acts merely added fuel to the fire of its fury.

One unforeseen, uncontrollable intruder was to interrupt the bitter political fight. A second plague of the yellow fever swept Philadelphia during the late summer of 1797.[10] By the end of the first week of September, 1,400 residents had boarded up their homes and fled the city's disease and politics. President Adams found refuge in Braintree, Massachusetts. The Secretary of State moved to Trenton, the Secretary of War personally to Downingtown, and his offices to the Falls of Schuylkill.[11] Most of the Philadelphia Jews who could leave went to Lancaster, and from that city and other towns in the surrounding area money for relief was sent to Philadelphia to combat the disease and alleviate the sufferings of the afflicted. The Philadelphia refugees of Lancaster, as a group, contributed $720, and individual Jews there—Samuel Hays, Aaron Levy, Hyman Marks, Aaron Joseph and Solomon Gottshalkson—added $134 more.[12] Only two Jews, Myer Hart and Nathan Barnett, are listed as having succumbed in Philadelphia.[13]

The fever was too strong a foe for eighteenth-century medicine or political debate to overcome. When a third plague hit the city hardly a year later, Benjamin Franklin Bache fell victim to the fever before he could be made the first victim of the Alien and Sedition Acts.[14] His assistant, William Duane, married Bache's widow, took over the *Aurora*, and inherited the wrath of the Federalists.[15] This time, before they left the city, Simon and Hyman Gratz donated one tierce of rice to the sufferers,[16] and then from Lancaster joined with other Philadelphians once again to make up a purse to send back home.[17] Dr. Rush was as busy with his purges and bleeding, jalop and calomel, in the second and third epidemics as he had been in the first. And chiefly because he was at the same time a politically active Democratic-Republican, he was accused of mortal blood-letting by the vitriolic English journalist William Cobbett, writing under his well-known pseudonym "Peter Porcupine."[18]

Although at one point in the battle of words which ensued, the Federalist *Gazette of the United States* reported with vicious intent that "Duane was once a Jew Cloathsman in London, from which occupation, his *integrity* expelled him," and that he "passed in London under the name of Jew Aine,"[19] William Duane was a spirited Irishman. He would have been furious to have realized that it was the son-in-law of Philadelphia's late David Franks, Lt. Col. Henry Johnson, who was at that moment quelling the Irish rebels at New Ross.[20] But Duane was also a dedicated opponent of the Alien and Sedition Acts and of the Adams administration, for which he was harassed, and, finally in March, 1800, ordered to appear before the Senate of the United States to answer a charge of having uttered seditious opinions. When, after further denunciations of the Senate and its actions, he scorned the order, a warrant was issued for his arrest. Immediately, Duane went into hiding, all the while continuing to put out his paper and to attack his attackers.[21]

The anti-Semitism which inevitably followed the anti-French, anti-Negro, anti-Irish, "America First" propaganda of the Federalists was aimed first at a non-Jew, the American-born Christian Moses Levy. Levy, together with Joseph Hopkinson and Jared Ingersoll, had represented Dr. Rush in his libel suit against Cobbett. The suit was won, and Cobbett was required to pay $5,000 damages.[22] Smarting under this indignity, the sarcastic Peter Porcupine moved to New York and launched a new journal, *The Rush-Light*, the main purpose of which was to blackguard those with whom he disagreed politically and medically. In the second issue of the new periodical he loosed a quill to hit a Jew, and struck instead, as he well knew, a good Episcopalian.

> Moses Levi, one of Rush's lawyers, had the charity to suggest, that I, being a *royalist*, might possibly have hoped, by discrediting the Doctor's practice, to increase the mortality amongst the *republicans!* Such a diabolical thought never could have been engendered but in the mind of a Jew! But honest Mosey seemed to have forgotten that I could not possibly want to kill *myself*. I cannot for my life, however, muster up anything like anger against a poor devil like Moses; he did not believe a word that he said; he vash vorking for de monish, dat vash all.[23]

Levy had no need to defend himself; Cobbett's smear had merely been part of his attempt to divert attention from the real issue. Shamelessly, in another number of *The Rush-Light*, he continued his mocking references to "Levi the Jew."[24] It is interesting that Rush gave £38.15s worth of medical services to Moses Levy "for prosecuting Wm. Cobbet & Jno. Fenno."[25]

Moses Levy was not the only non-Jew who became the butt of the Federalists for his supposed Jewishness. Israel Israel was called "a Jewish Tavern Keeper, with a very Jewish name," who was "chosen one of the Senators of this commonwealth for the city of Philadelphia solely on account of his violent attachment to the French Interests."[26] Israel certainly had a very Jewish name, but it happens that he was even less of a Jew than Levy.[27] However, he was a man of strong democratic principles.

On July 30, 1800, he joined with others like Benjamin Rush, Peter Stephen DuPonceau, Cyrus Bustil, Benjamin Nones and a large number of artisans in an evening meeting of the Democratic Society of Philadelphia. The meeting was promptly reported in the Federalist *Gazette of the United States* as having been attended by

the very *refuse* and *filth* of society . . . men of the most infamous and abandoned characters; men who, are notorious for the seduction of *black innocence*, who have more than once been convicted in open court of wilful perjury.[28]

The account singled out some of the participants for special insults. Israel was mentioned in the abbreviated form of I-S-L. The barb about "black innocence" was thrown in the direction of Rush, who was then, among other civic offices, president of the Pennsylvania Society for Promoting the Abolition of Slavery. Bustil, a leading Negro, was referred to in slighting fashion as "Citizen Sambo." The anonymous "Observer," who described the meeting, used the kind of slander and abuse characteristic of the crudest partisan writing of his day. For his final blow he chose "Citizen N—— the Jew." When the meeting was ending, before the collection plate was passed—he wrote—Nones said, "I hopsh you will consider dat de monish ish very scarch, and besides you know I'sh just come out by de Insholvent Law." The reported reply was, "Oh, yes, let N—— pass." It was obvious that the writer was not trying to tranliterate Nones' French accent which was the only one he had; Nones was being insulted because he was a Jeffersonian and a Jew.

Among the many who attended the meeting—leading citizens, professional writers and keen politicians—there were others who might have chosen to answer one of the vilest attacks on the

Democratic-Republicans which had up to that time appeared. But it was Benjamin Nones who replied for himself, for his fellow-Jews, for the "respectable citizens" present that evening, and for the spirit of the times. As soon as an appropriate statement had been drafted, Nones appeared with it at the office of Caleb P. Wayne, the publisher of the *Gazette*, and requested that his rebuttal be published.[29] Wayne tried to evade the issue by vague promises, but, when pressed, flatly refused. Nones was not to be put off. He promptly had printed a broadside circular with his defiant letter to the editor of the *Gazette*, and it was distributed on the streets of Philadelphia.[30] Then he turned to Duane, still a fugitive from the Senate warrant, and sought its re-publication in the *Aurora*, the newspaper upon which Jefferson reposed the hopes of republicanism.

Duane needed no urging to blast once more the forces which were threatening his own personal liberty, and, as he and other Democratic-Republicans believed, the liberties of all Americans. He featured the letter of Nones,[31] which still rings clear today as the credo of a liberty-loving American Jew.

... I am accused of being a *Jew*, of being a *Republican*, and of being *Poor*.

I am a Jew. I glory in belonging to that persuasion, which even its opponents, whether Christian, or Mohamedan, allow to be of divine origin—of that persuasion on which christianity itself was originally founded, and must ultimately rest—which has preserved its faith secure and undefiled, for near three thousand years, whose votaries have never murdered each other in religious wars, or cherished the theological hatred so general, so unextinguishable among those who revile them. A persuasion, whose patient followers have endured for ages the pious cruelties of Pagans, and of Christians, and persevered in the unoffending practice of their rites and ceremonies, amidst poverties and privations; amidst pains, penalties, confiscations, banishments, tortures and deaths, beyond the example of any other sect, which the pages of history has hitherto recorded ...

But I am a Jew. I am so; and so were Abraham, and Isaac, and Moses and the prophets, and so too were Christ and his apostles; I feel no disgrace in ranking with such society, however, it may be subject to the illiberal buffoonery of such men as your correspondents.

I am a *Republican!* Thank God, I have not been so heedless and so ignorant of what has passed, and is now passing in the political world. I have not been so proud or so prejudiced as to renounce the cause for which I have *fought*, as an American, throughout the whole of the revolutionary war, in the militia of Charleston, and in Polaskey's legion, I fought in almost every action which took place in Carolina, and in the disastrous affair of Savannah, shared the hardships of that sanguinary day, and for three and twenty years I felt no disposition to change my political any more than my religious principles. And which in spite of the witling scribblers of aristocracy, I shall hold sacred until death, as not to feel the ardour of republicanism . . .

I am a Jew, and if for no other reason, for that reason am I a republican. Among the pious priesthood of church establishments, we are compassionately ranked with Turks, Infidels and Heretics. In the *monarchies* of Europe we are hunted from society, stigmatized as unworthy of common civility, thrust out as it were from the converse of men; objects of mockery and insult to froward children, the butts of vulgar wit and low buffoonery, such as your correspondent, Mr. Wayne, is not ashamed to set us an example of. Among the nations of Europe we are inhabitants every where; but citizens no where *unless in republics.* Here, in France, and in the Batavian republic alone, are we treated as men and as brethren. In republics we have *rights,* in monarchies we live but to experience *wrongs.* And why? because we and our forefathers have *not* sacrificed our principles to our interest, or earned an exemption from pain and poverty, by the direliction of our religious duties, no wonder we are objects of derision to those, who have *no* principles, moral or religious, to guide their conduct.

How then can a Jew but be a Republican? in America particularly. Unfeeling and ungrateful would he be if he were callous to the glorious and benevolent cause of the difference between his situation in this land of freedom and among the proud and privileged law-givers of Europe.

But I am *poor;* I am so, my family also is large, but soberly and decently brought up. They have not been taught to revile a Christian because his religion is not *so old* as theirs. They have not been taught to mock even at the errors of good intention, and conscientious belief. I trust they will always leave this to men as unlike themselves, as I hope I am to your scurrilous correspondent.

I know that to purse-proud aristocracy poverty is a crime, but it may sometimes be accompanied with honesty even in a Jew. I was a bankrupt some years ago; I obtained my certificate and I was discharged from my debts. Having been more successful afterwards, I called my creditors together, and eight years afterwards, unsolicited, I discharged all my old debts. I offered interest which was refused by my creditors, and they gave me from under their hands without any solicitations of mine, as a testimonial of the fact, (to use their own language) "as a tribute due to my honor and honesty." . . .

I was discharged by the insolvent act; true, because having the amount of my debts owing to me from the French republic, the differences between France and America have prevented the recovery of what was due to me, in time to discharge what was due to my creditors. Hitherto it has been the fault of the political situation of the two countries that my creditors are not paid. When peace shall enable me to receive what I am entitled to, it will be my fault if they are not fully paid . . .[32]

If Nones and Duane were vigorous in throwing down the gauntlet by publishing the spirited letter "To the Printer of the Gazette of the United States," the Federalist press was no less eager to pick it up. Alerted by the circulation of the broadside, the *Philadelphia Gazette*, the same day that the Nones statement appeared in the *Aurora*, parodied Nones' defense. "I am a Jew—thank God for that," began a letter signed "A Jacobin—Ironically," "But I am no Democrat, thank God for that *also*." It was a piece of sardonic impudence, the theme of which was that if the original reporter was "ironical," as Nones claimed, then he was using a mode of speech in which the meaning was contrary to the words, and hence that Nones had nothing to complain of.

Benjamin boasts of his *rank* with Moses and the Prophets. He felt no *disgrace* in *their society,* but he forgot to tell us whether these worthy gentlemen were not *disgraced by his!* Benjamin reviles the Christian religion, and talks of religious wars, and of bigoted contempt, most loquaciously!—Benjamin wants an office—*and that accounts for it!*[33]

The presidential campaign of 1800 was on. Worried by the growing popular support which seemed to be swinging toward Jefferson, the Federalists began to woo the votes of Roman Catholics, Jews and others with whom they had shown little sympathy. Jefferson's free-thinking religious principles and his support of the French Republicans earned him the epithet of atheist, and his supposed anti-religious views were used against him wherever his opponents thought they might be effective. As Joseph Bloomfield, who was running for the governorship of New Jersey, wrote, Jefferson was branded an infidel because he was not a fanatic who thought that the Quaker, the Baptist, the Methodist, or Christians of any other denomination should pay the pastors of other sects; because he did not think "a Catholic should be banished for believing in transubstantiation, or a Jew, for believing in the God of Abraham, Isaac and Jacob."[34]

In that hectic month of August, 1800, the Rev. James Abercrombie preached a Federalist sermon in Christ Church and St. Peter's Church.[35] The *Aurora* took notice of it with a shower of abuse, because it had associated Jefferson with atheism and monarchy.[36] In reply the *Philadelphia Gazette* introduced a new ruse to catch the attention of Jews and others. A letter was published, signed "Moses S. Solomons, Second-Street, Philadelphia," which rallied to the defense of Abercrombie.

Having heard that there were several objections to Mr. Jefferson for his disbelief in the importance of *Christianity*, I gave myself little trouble on a subject with which as a follower of Moses and the Old Testament, I had little to do: but since the abuse offered to Mr. Abercrombie, I have examined the merits of the question; and find, that Mr. Jefferson in his Notes on Virginia, by making a belief of twenty Gods or even NO GOD unimportant, has struck *at all religion!* Therefore, Mr. Abercrombie will be considered as engaged in a COMMON CAUSE, and should he be persecuted for advocating religion, GENERALLY he will find friends who would risk as much as any of the Christians in defense of a God and of his Holy Religion, against any who would revile his name by their pretended *doubts* of a belief in his existence: for, Sirs, we all abhor the very name of an Atheist.[37]

On the face of it the letter seemed innocuous enough, but Duane was as sharp as he was fiery, and five days later, thanks to a "presiding member of the Jewish community," he was able to denounce the letter as a forgery. Benjamin Nones was back in the fray. Under the title, "A Prop for Parson Abercrombie," the editor of the *Aurora* wrote a full exposé, noting that he saw through the imposture at first glance because

No person of the Jewish church could object to a man who was the avowed advocate of universal toleration? no Hebrew could be hostile consistently to a man, who in the very introduction to the Declaration of Independence, declared *all men equal,* and implores a *Divine Providence.*[38]

Furthermore, his investigation had shown that nobody named Moses S. Solomons lived on Second Street, that no Jew by that name was known in the synagogue and that "there were only two Hebrew families of the name of *Solomons* in the United States, all of whom were known, and none of them named as in this *forgery*."

To cap his case and show up the "imposition which was attempted to be put upon the public, and the delusion upon the minds of that ancient and persecuted people," Duane applied to the synagogue and obtained from his friend Benjamin Nones a formal statement, signed only "A member of the Hebrew Church."

The duty I owe to the Hebrew congregation, of which I have for several years been a *Parnass* (or president) to inform our fellow-citizens, and the United States in general, that the publication in Brown & Relf's paper of the 5th inst. signed by *Moses S. Solomon,* North Second-street, is an imposture, intended, no doubt, to answer certain political ends incompatible with the discipline of our people. I therefore feel it incumbent on me as a real, and not a false *"follower of the Mosaical law"* to declare, and authorize you to publish that no such man as *Moses S. Solomon* has *ever been,* or is now a member of the Hebrew congregation of this city, and I pledge myself to prove by the records of our society *now in my possession,* that there is not at this time in

Pennsylvania, a person of that name, attached or belonging to the Hebrew congregation.

In the heat of the election even such a comparatively minor matter as this was magnified into an issue by the newspapers of both parties. The *Philadelphia Gazette* noted that Duane had produced "a certificate, *without a name*, to prove there is *no Solomon* among the Jews," but, he continued, "let the Jews speak for themselves."[39] The original Solomons letter had been re-printed in New York, and the *Gazette* proudly carried praise from "A Christian" of that city, who wrote:

It shews us the opinion which the Jews entertain of Mr. Jefferson's creed as to religion, and their determination to consider those who oppose his election as engaged in a common cause with them . . . The testimony of Mr. Solomons is the more valuable because he is a Jew.[40]

With the heading "Forgery & Federalism," Duane reprinted the New Yorker's letter adding a sly note that it was really un-necessary to "advert to our detection of the forgery."[41] Religion was very much in the election. The *Aurora* shouted about "hypocritical professors of religion" and "pulpit politics." The Solomons letter was proving an effective weapon against Aber-crombie and the *Gazette*, and Duane succeeded in getting a statement from the minister that he condemned the fabrication.[42] In the end, the Solomons letter would seem, like most political canards, to have hurt its authors more than it helped.

On October 14, 1800, the election took place. Jefferson was elected the third president of the United States, and for the first time, what was to evolve into the Democratic Party came to power. The new president saw to it that his editor friend Duane was cleared of all charges against him.[43] The Alien and Sedition Acts were repealed by the new Congress. Benjamin Nones con-tinued active in politics, and early in 1802 became the "Father of the Council" of the Tammany Society.[44] A few years later the once "insolvent debtor" was named examiner of insolvent debtors.[45] But poor he remained; he tried hard to recover his losses, which were estimated in a list of the "French Spolia-tions"[46] at 22,383 livres, and at the time of his death his estate amounted to only $100.[47] Yet Nones, in asserting his own right to political views, had asserted the rights of all American Jews to full and equal citizenship.

Thomas Jefferson, in his inaugural address on March 4, 1801, declared that he regretted that the political convulsions and turmoil of the Old World had spread to the New, and that it would be his object to replace with harmony the strife and intolerance that had attempted to root themselves in American soil.[48] The new president dismissed many of the Federalists who held administrative posts, partly to remove from the government their autocratic influence and partly to reward his own loyal followers. One of these, Reuben Etting, who in 1798 had become the first Captain of the militia company, the Baltimore Independent Blues,[49] was chosen to fill the post of Federal Marshall for the District of Maryland.[50]

Etting, then living in Baltimore with other members of his family, who settled there after they had left York and temporarily resided in Lancaster and Philadelphia, had in 1794 married Frances Gratz, the daughter of the old pioneer,[51] Michael. At the end of the eighteenth century the Gratz-Etting family was the major part of the Jewish community of Baltimore and certainly the most dynamic members of it. Etting's federal appointment was for them more than a political reward; it was recognition of the status of a Jew in a state where Jewish rights were still proscribed.

Perhaps without full consciousness of its significance, Jefferson by his appointment delivered the first blow against the disabilities of Maryland Jews. The state constitution, like the earlier one of Pennsylvania, permitted only those to hold state offices who affirmed the divinity of both the Old and New Testaments. As early as 1797, Solomon Etting, Barnard Gratz and others had petitioned the House of Delegates "praying to be placed upon the same footing with other good citizens," but this and numerous subsequent petitions were tabled or defeated until 1824, when finally an act permitting Jews to hold office in the state was passed.[52] Reuben Etting, in 1804, moved back to Philadelphia and stayed there while his son Elijah Gratz Etting was attending the University of Pennsylvania, from which he was graduated in 1812.[53] Reuben almost immediately became active in the political life of the city and seems to have been, for a while at least, successful as a merchant at 251 Market Street and, four years later,[54] as an auctioneer.

The Jews of Philadelphia and elsewhere were not specifically seeking political office; they merely sought the *right* to vote and to seek such office. In Pennsylvania this right was theirs, and, with the beginnings of a two-party system, the Jews at a grass-root level worked for and supported the party of their choice. Benjamin Nones had not incurred the enmity of the Federalists because he hoped for an office, but merely because he was working for the opposition party.

A curious document of some interest appeared in the Philadelphia newspapers the year after Jefferson's inauguration. It told of the vision of Nathan Ben Ashur, whom the inhabitants of Vermont, where he was reputed to live, called the "Hermit of the Mountain," and who was described as "evidently of Jewish extraction," for he kept all the rites of the Jewish religion.[55] The vision, perhaps a political fiction, described in biblical language the appearance of Jefferson as "The Genius of America." Whether Nones and other Philadelphia Jews were impressed by the oracles of the mysterious recluse is not known, but they would have been more practically impressed by the fact that Nones received one of the five coveted appointments for the post of Notary Public made by the Governor of Pennsylvania.[56]

As an adjunct to this appointment, Nones also became a state-authorized interpreter of French, Spanish and Portuguese.[57] His office was close by the old Custom House at No. 29 Chestnut Street, and there he handled and affixed his seal to a great number of foreign maritime documents, passports and citizenship papers which passed over his desk for a quarter of a century. On the side, he transacted the business of a ship broker.[58]

The pride of Pennsylvania was in its devotion to religious and civil liberty, and in its liberal franchise. The state boasted of its large number of naturalized citizens, which exceeded that of any other state,[59] and the Jeffersonians were eager to give free instruction to immigrants for obtaining their citizenship papers. Much of this work passed through the hands of Benjamin Nones. Both the Federalist press and the Democratic newspapers, in spite of the political differences between them, emphasized its importance. One Federalist writer commented on the Catholic petition before the British parliament, lavishly praising the American constitution which recognized no religious distinctions,[60] and another gave a running account of the attempts of the French Jews to secure full citizenship rights and privileges.[61]

In this atmosphere, it is most interesting to observe that the Episcopalian Levy brothers remained Jews in the mind of the whole community. A story, written much later about an event of this period, shows how prevalent this opinion was.

About fifty-five years ago there was an eccentric lawyer in Philadelphia named William S. Blair. On one occasion he and Moses Levy Esq. who was of Hebrew origin tho' a Christian by profession, were opposed to each other in a case. Blair having made a mumbling speech, Levy in his reply said that the counsel's oration reminded him of an epic poem which begins in the middle. Blair in the concluding speech said that tho' his learned friend had likened him to the author of an Epic poem, he could not perceive any resemblance between himself and Homer, but that the Jury would probably agree with him in likening his learned friend's argument to the Hebrew, which begins at the latter end.[62]

Although originally the brothers had been supporters of Jefferson, by 1805 Sampson was running on the Federal ticket in a local election.[63] Moses, the younger of the two, had become Recorder in 1802,[64] and his charge to the jury, as presiding magistrate in the Mayor's Court in 1806 in the famous Shoemakers' Case—the beginning of American labor law—is of great importance in the history of labor,[65] but not in American Jewish history. It is interesting, however, that there were no anti-Semitic overtones when both houses of the state legislature, dominated by the Democrats, passed a bill to prevent the Recorder from practicing in any court of law, in retaliation for the verdict in the Shoemakers' Case that the defendants were "guilty of a combination to raise their wages." The Federalist governor, Thomas McKean, vetoed the bill, and it was not passed over his veto.[66]

When Jefferson, considering Moses Levy for the post of Attorney-General in his second cabinet, had asked Albert Gallatin to inquire fully "Into the legal knowledge, judgment, and moral and social character of Levy,"[67] Gallatin answered that he had found it hard to obtain much information about him.

As a lawyer, he is superior to Dickerson, and would, I presume, do tolerably; still he is but second rate, and as a statesman, and in some degree member of your cabinet, I do not think he would do. Nor if his practice be, as it is presumably, worth six or seven thousand dollars, is it probable that he would give it up for the place of Attorney General, and exchange Philadelphia for Washington.[68]

It may also have been Moses Levy's newly acquired conservatism which colored Gallatin's judgment.[69]

Under a friendly administration the spirited journalism of William Duane grew in influence, and his warm feeling for Jews became known beyond Philadelphia. The *American Eagle* of Easton, on July 6, 1805, published a sporting tale which attacked simultaneously Duane and his Jewish friends.

A crazy Jew, Moses of Lancaster, was set on by federalists to pelt Governor M'Kean with stones if he met him on the street. Moses did so. In order to pacify this crack-brained fellow the governor dubbed him with a sham title of General. It proved effectual. Moses afterwards shook hands with the governor and was no more his opposer. It would be good if the governor would do the same to the Moses's of this county, nay of this state, then would there be peace throughout Duane's tribe.[70]

Of course, there were far too few Jews in all of Pennsylvania to make the question of a "Jewish" vote of any significance whatsoever. And, the facts were that, although there were records of more Jewish Jeffersonians than Jewish Federalists, a few of the most influential Jews of Philadelphia were to be found in the latter party.

At a pre-election meeting of the Federalist Friends of the Constitution in 1806, Joseph Gratz[71] was appointed to the Committee of Vigilance for the Middle Ward of Philadelphia and thereafter both he and his brother Hyman served frequently for that party.[72] The members of such a committee were actually watchers at the polls, but in the early nineteenth century this was a position of distinction in the party, and members of the Rush, Rittenhouse and other prominent families, as well as the candidates for office themselves, served on these committees. While Moses Myers of Norfolk was protesting against the British attack on the American ship *Chesapeake* in the early summer of 1807,[73] young Jacob Gratz, destined to be the most politically successful of the family, was delivering an oration on patriotism at the graduation exercises of the University of Pennsylvania, from which he was receiving his degree.[74] Jacob in later years was elected first a State Representative, and then a State Senator.[75]

Each successive year witnessed a small, but increasing, number of Jews in the city's political life. Possibly the most influential of them, although he does not seem to have figured in the public eye, was retired Aaron Levy of Aaronsburg. Simon Snyder, an old and close friend of Levy from Northumberland County, was emerging as the spokesman of the Jeffersonians in the legislature, where he served for eleven years from 1797, during four of which he was Speaker of the Assembly. After Levy moved to Philadelphia, the close friendship was maintained, and a series of letters from Snyder to Levy shows the warmth which existed between them.[76] Snyder added popular Jewish expressions to his vocabu-

lary, and occasionally sent Mrs. Levy some *drink gelt* in ap-
preciation of particular kindnesses.[77] When Snyder's church
needed hymn books, he asked Levy to buy them for him,[78] and
when a friend of Levy needed a political favor, Snyder was
happy to do what he could[79]—and all this in spite of the fact
that Aaron Levy was a staunch Federalist. Snyder's banter on
political subjects appears throughout the correspondence. In
reference to the Banking Bill, being debated in 1804, Snyder
wrote:

> You are as wrong about Banking as you are in your political opinions gen-
> erally—when I see you I hope to be able to convince you. I know I shall have
> Mrs. Levy on my side for she also knows you are always wrong.[80]

Households were split in those days too, for Snyder maintained that Rachel Levy "was all along a good democrat."[81] In
1808, Snyder defeated McKean for the governorship, and this
good friend of the Levys remained governor until 1817.

In the election of 1808, when James Madison was running for
the presidency and Snyder for the governorship, eight Jews were
active in four of the city's fourteen wards in support of their
Democratic-Republican ticket. On the city committee of the
Democratic Young Men for Simon Snyder was the youthful,
energetic Mordecai Manuel Noah.[82] Then twenty-three, Noah,
back living with his grandmother Phillips, had just finished writing his first play, *The Fortress of Sorrento*. This play, despite its
amateurishness, expressed the libertarian views of the Jeffersonians and Noah's admiration for the vigorous Democrats of this
city.[83] His participation in the 1808 election marked the beginning of a political career which was to reach its peak in New
York a few decades later.

Also a member of the Democratic Young Men was David B.
Nones,[84] following in his father's footsteps by supporting Mathew
Carey. He maintained his interest in the old Chestnut Street
Ward until business took him to the island of St. Croix. Reuben
Etting worked as a Jeffersonian in the Middle Ward,[85] while in
the same district, his brother-in-law Joseph Gratz threw his
support to the Federalists. The second generation of the Phillips'
family, notably Zalegman and Dr. Manuel,[86] were consistent
Democrats, and twenty years later Zalegman distinguished him-
self as one of the earliest Jacksonian Democrats of Philadelphia.
For the same party in 1808, Samuel M. Solomon was a mem-

ber of the Committee of Vigilance in the Chestnut Street Ward
and Isaac Lyons in the Lower Delaware.[87] A year later Abraham H. Cohen, the *shohet*, assumed the same responsibility for
the Federalists in the Dock Ward.[88] When there was a three-
way fight in a local election in 1810, A. Myers Cohen and Henry
Solomon were active in the Federalist camp;[89] Michael Levy
worked for the Whigs, and Isaac Nathans, Isaiah Nathans,
Isaac Abraham and Isaac Rodrigues helped the Democrats.[90]

The Jews as a group did not create, and were not looked
upon as, a political or economic problem. Individual Jews played
their roles in the life of the community, but they were not
numerically of high visibility. On the other hand, the Irish were
beginning to come into the country in large numbers, and in
Philadelphia as elsewhere in the nation the rumblings of an
anti-Irish, anti-Catholic feeling began to be heard. This feeling
was to erupt into hate movements and violence before the century was half over; but even in the early 1800's the undercurrent
of resentment against the growing immigration of impoverished
Irish peasants was in the air.

In Philadelphia the most eloquent spokesman for his own
people was Mathew Carey, but Carey was not the protagonist
of Irish Catholics only; he was a humanitarian and a liberal who
looked upon America as a refuge for all the oppressed, upon
the immigrants as a boon to the growth of the land, upon the
unfortunate as persons who should be helped, and upon economic poverty as a blight which should be eradicated by constructive measures. In addressing the Irish Catholics of
Philadelphia in the pages of the *Aurora* in 1808, Carey wrote:

> Remember, Catholics, that the majority of you left your beloved country
> from oppression and persecution, left your friends and relations to seek an
> asylum in some foreign region: But providence guided you to the happy
> shores of Pennsylvania, where you found peace, liberty and freedom, and not
> forced to the wars as you were in your own country, to fight for the honor
> of the royal crown, that has loaded your ancestors with crowns of thorns,
> and placed them on the lists of proscriptions, like the Jews, for ages past . . .[91]

The problems of one minority group have always been those
of another, but not always have the members of different minori-
ties remembered it.

Against this background, the famous case of Jacob Henry, a
Jew of North Carolina, is noteworthy.[92] In 1809 Henry had
been re-elected for the second time as a representative of Carteret

County in the North Carolina House of Commons, and in the following year a motion was introduced to refuse him his seat on the ground that he denied the divine authority of the New Testament. During the debate, significantly, he received the support of two prominent Catholics, the Attorney-General and a fellow-member of the House. The speech which Henry himself delivered on liberty of conscience was so impressive a statement of American principles, not only for Jews but for all denominations, that it was immediately reprinted by almost the entire American press, and later included as a forensic classic in the oratorical text-books so popular at the time.[93] The motion to unseat Henry was defeated. To the Jews of Philadelphia who followed the incident in their own newspapers,[94] the result must have been a satisfactory confirmation of their own happy experiences in the political life of the city. They were becoming, by participation, a part of the American way of political life.

12

The Establishment of a New Synagogue and Religious Rules and Problems

THE separation of church and state which was written into the Constitution of the United States was the expression in legal and philosophical form of the pattern of American life. Since the people had been free to choose their own form of religion, there was to be no established national church in the nation, and no religious test was to be required for the holding of office. The people had sought diverse ways of worship and were following diverse theological tenets with such enthusiasm that there grew up a bewildering variety of native sects. Revivalism, or evangelical Protestantism, spread from the coastal cities and found fertile ground in the backwoods communities. Churches reflecting new views, nonconforming to their nonconformist origins, sprang up where no religious edifice had been built before. American individualism, furthering the cause of democracy, was making its way felt.

Mikveh Israel had come into existence and had constituted itself as a formal congregation within that framework of democratic diversity. No national or international body, civil or religious, had brought pressure upon the Jews of Philadelphia to organize themselves. They had voluntarily come together and made their own rules to govern their religious life. There did not even exist at that time a national, Jewish, co-ordinating body, such as had been created by the Episcopalians, Presbyterians, Lutherans, Quakers, and other religious groups, to develop American codes of worship, write American prayerbooks and make religious decisions on behalf of all their communicants in the country. All the Jews had—or needed—was a heritage of religious practices which they adapted to their new environment.

In New York, Shearith Israel had had a century's experience, and while no organizational relationship existed between the Philadelphia and the New York congregations, the personal relationships of the leaders of the two groups was so close that many of the regulations which had been satisfactorily introduced by the older congregation were taken over by the younger one. But American life and American law did not make it compulsory for Jews, or any other Americans, either to participate in or to stand aside from religious practices. The law of the land did not enforce the law of the synagogue as it did in most countries of Europe. The Jews of the United States did not live in a religious enclave within the larger community; they were an integral part of the total citizenry.

This fact presented a problem to the Jews of America who, since their expulsion from Palestine, had been accustomed to a tightly circled life designed to protect them from their persecutors and preserve their faith. This community living, a combination of religion, law and custom, had been one of the factors which made possible the seventeenth-century miracle of Jewish survival. It had been a necessity for so long that it was a part of Jewish life, and to those freshly come from Europe it seemed essential to Judaism. And then suddenly in America they were faced with freedom, and the old laws and old customs had to be moulded to fit the new situation of democratic life. It was the same kind of change which transformed the Church of England into the Protestant Episcopal Church of the United States.

The concept of Mikveh Israel was to be found in the two words prefixed to its name, *Kahal Kadosh*, the Holy Community. The community was not only to provide a place of worship for the Jews who wanted a synagogue, but also, in a European sense, to bring all the Jews of the city under its religious jurisdiction. But, from the outset, it was realized that willingness to accept this jurisdiction was purely voluntary, and that punitive coercion was limited to a withdrawal of religious rights and privileges. Like the Quakers, who read members of their society out of the meeting for not observing its rules, the *adjunta* of Mikveh Israel determined to legislate against Jewish backsliders.

On Rosh Hashanah, 1792, a lengthy resolution was read to make all the Jews who attended that Holy Day service fully aware of the decisions of the community. The most important problem facing the congregation was lack of financial support, so it was declared that those persons who professed Judaism and received the benefits of the synagogue, such as *kosher* meat, the services of a *mohel*, and birth, marriage and burial rites under its auspices, and did not contribute to its support:

shall be deemed as not belonging to our society either in public or private nor shall they be noticed in any concerns peculiar to the Rites and Ceremonies thereof on any occasion whatever; and in case of Death of themselves or any of their family residing within their dwelling—they shall not be entitled to the aid or attendance usual on such occasions from any Person belonging to the congregation.[1]

This was the greatest punishment that could be meted out to a believer, for it was tied to eternity.

Lack of support was, however, only part of the problem. Infrequent synagogue attendance, Sabbath-breaking and intermarriage plagued the community even more. All were direct expressions of the seductively free American environment, although they were not new to Judaism. If a member married out of the faith, he was subject to expulsion from the congregation, and yet intermarriage continued. When the same penalty was suggested for Sabbath-breaking in three successive constitutions within a quarter of a century, it was three times voted down.[2] In his answer to the charges of separation made by a Dutch anti-Semite, the physician and scientist Dr. David Nassy made an interesting comment on this phase of the Philadelphia Jewish scene in the mid-1790's:

there are the Maraches, the Amrings, the Cohens, the Hombergs, the Wallachs, the Solises and several other families lawfully married to Christian women who go to their own churches, the men going to their synagogues, and who, when together, frequent the best society.[3]

There were few Jews in the city who fitted Mrs. John Warder's description of Mark Prager, "a Hebrew who left England a year or two since and now disclaims all title to his religion."[4] His position had become such that Washington dined with him when he was in town for the Constitutional Convention.[5] Nor were such as the Levy brothers, Sampson and Moses, second-generation American Christians, more than a handful as yet. Even old David Franks had taken an oath as a Jew on the Five Books of Moses near the end of his life.[6] The community was still young, with far more unmarried men than eligible Jewish girls. American-born sons of immigrants were assuming leadership, and a fresh group of newcomers was drifting in from Europe. The heady air of America was working on them. They had full freedom of conscience; they felt their destinies lay in their own hands.

These newcomers—almost all of them Dutch, German, and Polish Jews—not having participated in the evolution and development of Mikveh Israel, were not entirely satisfied with the Sephardic *minhag* which was strange to them. They had the residency requirements for membership in what was then beginning to be called the Portuguese Hebrew Congregation, and, perhaps to assure themselves and their families a religious burial, they contributed to that synagogue; but by the middle of the last decade of the century they came together as a *minyan* for their own Ashkenazic services. It must have been men like Abraham Gumpert, Abraham Moses,[7] the Dutchman Lion van Amring and others who formed the separate—and second—Jewish congregation which the careful French observer, Moreau de Saint-Mery, noted in his journal as being in existence during his stay in Philadelphia in 1795.[8]

The history of the organization of Rodeph Shalom, which was an outgrowth of this Ashkenazic *minyan*, is neither clear nor complete. It struck at the attempt of the older, organized synagogue to function as a religious *kahal*, but it was not a secession like that of Bnai Jeshurun from Shearith Israel in New York which took place thirty years later.[9] The carefully kept minutes of Mikveh Israel do not even vaguely suggest a difference which would have led to the formation of a dissident group. There was no hint of social snobbery which would have denied the newcomers full membership in the congregation under the terms of its constitution.[10] What apparently happened was that by 1795 there were enough Jews in Philadelphia who wanted to say their prayers "according to the German and Dutch Rules" to form a congregation of their own, and in the free land of America they could do it without bitterness or recrimination.

From the very beginning the German Hebrew Society, as it was known, was the expression of an independence based on ritual. Many later new synagogues in the United States were formed as a result of a personal, social or ritual revolution from within; the new Philadelphia group was a formation from without. In perspective, Philadelphia becomes distinguished by being not only the sole city in the eighteenth century to have two synagogues and the first American city to have an Ashkenazic one, but also one of the very few cities in this country to grow in that manner without a bitter, intra-communal struggle.

The German Hebrew Society began as an orthodox congregation in a manner but little different from Mikveh Israel half a century earlier. Its metamorphosis from a simple *minyan* to a full-fledged congregation was more rapid, because it had the benefits of increased immigration and the precedent of another synagogue before it, but its problems were little different from those of its predecessor. There are hints that in 1796 this new group had its own *mikvah*, or ritual bath.[11] However, the first definitely recorded act of its organizers was the purchase of a plot of land in Kensington as a cemetery, and the deed for this ground, dated November 23, 1801, is the earliest document in the archives of Rodeph Shalom.[12] The guarantors of the purchase stated that they were holding the land in trust "for the Hebrew Tribe or Nation of and belonging to the synagogue to which they, the said guarantors, now belong," the mention of an existing synagogue corroborating the observation of Moreau de Saint-Mery, although the formal congregation was not organized until the following year. It is interesting to note that four of the six signers of the deed had had previous contact with Mikveh Israel. Isaac Marks' name appears in the marriage records for 1797 when he wed Hetty Hart;[13] Aaron Levy, Jr., was connected through his uncle Aaron Levy of Aaronsburg;[14] and both Abraham Gumpert and Abraham Moses were on the contributors' list for 1799-1800.[15] Only Lion van Amring, who was mentioned by David Nassy in 1795, and Isaiah Nathans do not appear in the records of Mikveh Israel.

On October 10, 1802, the founders formally "dedicated our new German Shul, and named it Rodeph Shalom."[16] The first constitution of the new congregation was written in Yiddish, with an English translation added at the time. This—in addition to the form of services—was one of the significant differences between the two groups; the use of Yiddish at Mikveh Israel was limited to correspondence, but its minutes and rules were from the beginning written in English. At Rodeph Shalom formal government with officers and regular meetings was instituted, but like Mikveh Israel before the Revolution there was no *hazan*. The members served as their own readers. With regard to other services, those of a *shohet* and a *mohel*, the German congregation depended upon its Portuguese sister, and for many years the names of German congregants appear regularly as contributors in the records and account books of Mikveh Israel.

If the governing body of Rodeph Shalom had anticipated a reduction in the problems of adherence and religious practice when they set up a form of worship more familiar to its members, they quickly learned that it was the environment and not the forms which had created those problems. As early as 1810, they constitutionally forbade attendance at a separate *minyan* or at any other congregation,[17] thereby restricting the principle of independent choice which had brought them into being. Of course, it was as much financial difficulties as the desire to maintain a specific form of worship which prompted the restrictive measures. But not even constitutional provisions could prevent the fluctuation of membership between the two congregations. By 1825, after the completion of Mikveh Israel's second structure, a large portion of the original German congregation had swung over to the older one,[18] which by then had begun to acquire a social prestige which its rugged eighteenth-century founders would have found strange. It was only as new, foreign-language-speaking immigrants, not entirely at home with the by-then-Americanized Germans of a generation before, arrived that Rodeph Shalom received the infusion of new blood which enabled it to survive and grow.

Matters of *kashruth*, the upkeep of the cemeteries, the general lack of Jewish education and the growing need to counteract the influence of Christian missionaries both divided the Jewish community and brought it together. From both congregations arose adjunct organizations, like mutual-aid societies. Intra-communal philanthropic groups were formed which were the pioneers of present-day institutions. Jewish women, freed from old-world restrictions, expressed their independence beyond the periphery of the synagogue to display for the first time in America their unique gifts. In the arts, sciences, professions, businesses and trades active members of the Philadelphia Jewish community participated in the formation and development of some of the most important American secular institutions centered in this city. Although Jewish religious life, under the constant pressure of integration, retrogressed somewhat, the first three decades of the nineteenth century witnessed the progress of Jewish organizational growth which enabled succeeding generations, sons of immigrants and immigrants themselves, to build and further expand.

Within this period Mikveh Israel, still the dominant force within the community, also underwent a fundamental change. The first indication was the election of Naphtali Phillips, at the age of twenty-five, as the first American-born *parnass*[19] and the adoption of a new constitution which he drafted. Shortly afterwards, Phillips went back to his native New York, there to become *parnass* of Shearith Israel.[20] But, thereafter and for decades to come, his brothers, the young Gratzes, the Phillips' the Marks' and the Nathans', second- and third-generation American Jews, dominated the life of the congregation.

With a Jewish education which was completely native, they managed to acquire a working knowledge of the fundamental elements of religious forms, services and rituals, without any real training in Jewish lore or law. Considering how limited their Jewish learning was by modern, or by then contemporary European, standards, their devotion to Jewish life was all the more remarkable. The older generation with a European background had passed away; Barnard and Michael Gratz, Mathias Bush, Jonas Phillips, Manuel Josephson and Haym Salomon were dead.[21] The community was to be led by the first generation of Jews ever to have been born in a democracy.

The Sephardic contribution to early synagogal life in Philadelphia lay, not in numbers of congregants of Portuguese descent, but in a tradition of organization, of rules and regulations, which dominated Mikveh Israel and produced a form of prayer, a method of government and a system of keeping records. The keeping of minute books, accounts, receipts, correspondence and the registers of vital statistics, which enable the modern investigator to trace with accuracy the religious life of the period, owe their origin to the standards introduced by Gershom Mendes Seixas and his fellow New Yorkers from Shearith Israel, and their maintenance by his successor Jacob Raphael Cohen.

It was a provision of the constitution of the congregation that the records be kept in a professional style,[22] not for the sake of future researchers, but out of respect for orderliness and the written word. Birth, marriage and death were within the orbit of the synagogue, and as a traditional part of Jewish life it was doubly important to keep circumcision records and *ketubah* books. Since there was no health office that legally required such records, those of the synagogue, as of other denominations, comprise the only ones which give the basic facts about the people.

With the same feeling for order, Seixas in 1782 wrote out in full regulations for worship, the occasions for special prayers, the hours when the morning and afternoon services were to begin daily, *shaharit, minhah,* and *arbit,* the services for the Sabbath and Holy Days, the order of the reading of the *Torah and haftara,* the dressing of the scrolls, and the order in which they were to be read, so that all of them would be used.[23] His minutely prepared instructions were followed faithfully in later years by Cohen, Carvalho, and Keys, as well as by the intermediate, temporary *hazanim* of the first three decades of the nineteenth century. Seixas even compiled a *luah,* or calendar and table of the time of sunrise and sunset in Philadelphia,[24] for no printed calendar for Jewish usage was printed in the United States until Lopez's of 1806.[25] A similar set of rules for religious worship was prepared in 1810 by four members of Rodelph Shalom who met at the house of Abraham Gumpert,[26] but they of course outlined Ashkenazic practice. Mikveh Israel followed the western calendar,[27] Rodelph Shalom the Hebrew one.

These instructions for the conduct of worship, practiced in Europe for centuries, were the precursors of the constitutions of both congregations. Mikveh Israel's first code of laws of 1782 has not survived, but many of its provisions are known because they were recorded in the minutes for reading aloud on Sabbath or on the High Holy days. Its second constitution, of 1798, exists in manuscript in the congregation's archives, and those of 1813, 1823 and 1824 were issued as printed pamphlets.[28]

The first organizational need was a governing body which consisted of a *parnass,* a *gabay,* and three *adjuntos;* by 1824 a regular secretary and a fourth *adjunto* were added.[29] They were all elected at the first regular meeting of the congregation, the Sunday preceding Erev Rosh Hashanah.[30] The congregation as a whole at first met once every three months, and then twice annually, before the New Year and the Sunday preceding Erev Pesach.[31] The *adjunta* met monthly in the early days, and later as the occasion required.[32] In the hands of the officers and *adjunta* were rather full powers to conduct all the affairs of the congregation and to rule upon all its problems, both administrative and religious.[33] A special meeting could be called by the *parnass*, the *adjunta*, or any at first four, and later ten, members of the congregation.[34] Those who declined to serve in office when elected were subject to a sliding scale of fines.[35]

Membership at first was open to all Jews residing in Philadelphia and the two adjoining districts of Northern Liberties and Southwark who paid three dollars and signed the constitution.[36] The same sum was required of subscribers, not residents, who came to the city for the High Holy days.[37] An applicant had to make a written request for admission to the *adjunta* and was usually recommended by one or two members. For instance, in 1812, a year after he had arrived in Philadelphia from London, Hyman Polock was certified by his wife's cousin, Aaron Levy, Jr., and Isaiah Nathans, both of whom by then had left Rodeph Shalom to join Mikveh Israel, as being of "right honest Industry and religious."[38]

In 1813 residency requirements began to be introduced. A man had to have lived in the country for six months before he could apply. And at the same time it was provided that members could not become electors until after two years, except that the son of an elector, American-born and of age, could become an elector as soon as he became a member.[39] It was this provision that enabled second-generation sons of electors to assume office at an early age. Ten years later the provisions were stiffened; it was then necessary to be a resident of Pennsylvania for four years, a seatholder for two years, and a resident of Philadelphia County for one.[40] In 1798 the admittance fee was set at $3, raised in 1813 to $5, raised again in 1823 to $20, and in the following year lowered to $10, at which time the four-year Pennsylvania residence was changed to three.[41]

The procedure was strictly adhered to. Moses Lopez of Newport could not become a member until he had established a three-year residence.[42] When finally admitted to membership he was so elated that he presented the congregation with a specially constructed chair to hold the ewer and basin for the ritual washing of the *Kohanim*. Carved on the back of the chair are two hands, with thumbs touching and fingers separated, according to the manner of the priestly blessing. Dr. Lopez, as he was known, must have fared well at his profession of dentist and bleeder to have been able to afford so elaborate a gift.[43]

Rodeph Shalom did not have such affluent members, nor did its constitutions contain provisions which increased rather than decreased the difficulty of affiliating with the synagogue. As many of its members transferred their allegiance to Mikveh Israel, possibly as much because of the inadequacy of successive rented synagogue quarters and the lack of a *hazan* as for reasons of social prestige, which then as now was a motivating factor, the German congregation needed new members badly and continually. When the congregation was formed in an established manner in 1802, the members prepared Articles of Association, which were found to be inadequate as an instrument of government by 1810, at which time a new set of rules was drawn up.[44] Mikveh Israel enjoyed the benefit of the wisdom of two generations of the Phillips family in their successive efforts at drafting constitutions and by-laws. Jonas Phillips dominated the first constitution; Napthali Phillips helped to draft the second; and the lawyer Zalegman Phillips was largely responsible for the later ones. Rodeph Shalom did not have the advantage of such experienced hands, and its early constitutions, which were written in Yiddish, do not have the polish and are not as definitive as those of its elder sister.

In 1812, however, Rodeph Shalom was the first congregation in the city and state to receive a charter as a corporate body from the Commonwealth;[45] Mikveh Israel did not apply for one until 1824,[46] although the matter had been discussed and a memorial to the Assembly ordered to be drafted as early as 1784.[47] The German congregation established its own system of records, which in 1810 were kept in Yiddish, in 1820 changed to English, and in 1830—reflecting the change in membership—in German. The more informal group introduced a kind of congregational government to suit its needs, but the influence of the older congregation can be seen in the use of the Spanish term, *junto*, to describe its board, which consisted of a president, sometimes called *parnass*, a "cashier," and two associate members.[48] The president had to be married, thirty years old, and a member of the congregation and a resident of the county for three years.[49] The cashier also had to be married, and in addition a "man of reputed good character, who has never failed in making payments by Bankruptcy or has taken the benefit of the Insolvent

Act."[50] Mikveh Israel presumably did not have to worry about such things, but its treasurer, Hyman Gratz, who served from 1824 to 1856,[51] went through bankruptcy shortly after he was elected.

To become a member of Rodeph Shalom there was no residency requirement, merely a six-month waiting period.[52] There was no set entrance fee, but an annual subscription fixed by the officers was expected, from which cash offerings made during the year could be deducted.[53] The main difference between the two constitutions lay in the fact that the members of the German congregation were not affluent and were chiefly recently-arrived immigrants, and so the provisions of its code were adjusted to meet those situations. Although synagogue honors were auctioned off to the highest bidders in both synagogues,[54] and in Mikveh Israel first- and second-class seats were sold,[55] there was a provision at Rodeph Shalom that those too poor to meet established fees of not less than four dollars a year could appeal their case and receive the same *mitzvoth* as anyone else.[56]

In 1820 the congregation apparently found difficulty in collecting money due it from members and drew up a set of by-laws to spell out procedures.[57] One new rule is of special interest. Persons wanting to become members did not have to apply in writing, but could call upon any member of the board, who would have power to admit him.[58] On the other hand, if resignations were not submitted in writing, the persons would be liable for their subscriptions.[59]

To be sure, Rodeph Shalom's need for funds—without a *hazan* and with no synagogue building to maintain—was not great, but they did need money for their rented quarters and later for Rabbi Lippman's tiny stipend. In 1808 the Hebrew German Society petitioned the state legislature for permission to conduct a lottery for the purpose of buying ground and building a synagogue.

Unfortunately, times had changed since Mikveh Israel had been granted a similar request. After a committee reported: "That they have the suggestion under consideration and are of the opinion that the prayer ought to be granted," and at the same time took the liberty to suggest "that all places of worship should be built at the expense of a more moral system than that proposed by lottery or some other gambling system or institution," the application was voted down.[60] Nonetheless, Mikveh

Israel in 1806 had also petitioned for permission, had gotten it,[61] printed up a broadsheet announcing grandiose plans for a $100,000 lottery,[62] and went ahead with repairs to their building. Then they found themselves in trouble. With the money spent—fortunately only a fraction of the advertised $100,000—the majority of the commissioners appointed to conduct the lottery refused to serve, and the congregation was forced to apply once more to the Assembly for help, which eventually they got.[63]

Many of the early records of Rodeph Shalom were destroyed by a fire in 1839,[64] so the exact history of the many changes in its place of worship is not known. However, it is believed that services were held at the beginning of the nineteenth century in a building on Margaretta Street below Second. They were moved from there in 1820 to No. 1 Bread (now Moravian) Street; again the following year to Church Alley between Second and Third; by 1830 to No. 7 Pear Alley (now Chancellor Street); and within the next ten years successively to No. 15 Vine and to the south side of Cherry above Fifth.[65]

As can be seen, most of these locations were within a few blocks of Mikveh Israel's synagogue, in a neighborhood where most of the Jews of the city were living so as to be within easy walking distance of their synagogue. An apt commentary on the unsatisfactory nature of these temporary locations—though perhaps not intended as such at the time—was the sign over the entrance to the stairway leading to the synagogue room on Pear Street, above a turner's shop, on which a Hebrew passage from Genesis (28.17) was painted, which, according to the recollection of Jacob Ezekiel, read, "How awful is this place; this is none other but the House of God."[66]

Both congregations had a provision that the president might give a sum not exceeding five dollars to any sick or poor person.[67] There were other welfare provisions in the Rodeph Shalom constitution to be mentioned later;[68] these were not deemed necessary at Mikveh Israel. Nor was Mikveh Israel seeking new members aggressively. Rodeph Shalom was. It passed a resolution calling upon all newcomers to the city to state their preference as to which of the two congregations they wanted to belong.[69] In this manner the board of Rodeph Shalom extended itself to reach unaffiliated immigrants.

As far as Sabbath-keeping was concerned, Mikveh Israel did

not raise the point officially,[70] although internally it was a matter of concern. Rodeph Shalom policed the situation by making it obligatory to attend Friday night and Saturday morning services by levying a fine for absence, which was excused only in case of sickness or travel.[71]

By and large, observance was left to the individual, but the Sunday Law of 1794 worked against Jewish observance. To conform both to it and to his own religion, a Jew would have had to keep two Sabbaths. In 1816 Abraham Wolff was convicted under the act for performing "worldly employment on the Lord's day commonly called Sunday." His lawyer, Zalegman Phillips, argued logically that the Fourth Commandment said that one should labor six days and keep the seventh as a holy day, and that since Wolff had observed the Sabbath on Saturday he was not breaking the divine law by working the other six days. The court did not interpret the commandment as broadly as Phillips, and Wolff, like Jonas Phillips twenty-three years before, was subjected to a fine because his Sabbath came on Saturday.[72] Much later, William J. Duane told the story:

Joseph S. Cohen, Esq., when Prothonotary of the Supreme Court of Pennsylvania for the Eastern District, was found one Sunday morning at work in his office in "the row." Objection having been made to such conduct, he said, "Sunday is *dies non ju.*"[73]

If lack of support financially and lax observance of religious laws were problems, they were far overshadowed by that of intermarriage. Six months after Moses Nathans married the convert Sarah Abrahams in 1794, the *adjunta* of Mikveh Israel received the following request:

Gentlemen,
Permit one who has not the happiness to be Born a Jewess & Favoured immediately from the God of Israel as you are to Request your Attention to my Particular Case & trust that nothing has been or shall be Wanting on my part to Render me worthy of being Admitted an Associate of your Congregation & to become a Jewiss, this I ask not as a Favour, but as a Right feeling as I do this—of living up to the Divine precepts of the Bible—I am & willing to Submit to such Ceremonies as are Necessary to obtain this my demand, the greatest of all my Worldly wishes & may the God of Abraham, Isaac & Jacob take you under his Holy Protection & Instill into your minds to do what is Just & Right in his Sight & Grant a Speedy Answer to this the Petition of your—

Humble Friend,
Anna Barnett.[74]

In the course of the coming half century both Philadelphia congregations were to receive many similar applications. Dr. Jacob R. Marcus has estimated that ten percent of the Jews in the cities before the end of the eighteenth century married non-Jews, and that proportion was maintained; the percentage in country towns and villages was tremendously higher.[75] Intermarriage did not, of course, always mean that the Jew gave up his own religion, but it frequently meant that the children of the marriage were brought up as Christians. David Franks never denied his own Judaism, but his indifference towards it permitted his children to be baptized. Isaac Franks completely disassociated himself from the Jewish community after making a single contribution to Mikveh Israel the year he married, and in his will he urged his children to be good Christians.[76]

In a number of instances a non-Jewish woman, either before or after marriage, asked for the privilege of being converted, as did Anna Barnett. Yet, there was some hesitancy about granting permission for such a conversion. European injunctions against conversions, particularly those adopted by the Anglo-Jewish community,[77] still influenced the thinking of many Jews. During medieval times it had been a crime to judaize, and later it seemed wiser not to stir up resentment by doing it, so there was both doubt and reluctance on the part of the American Jewish community concerning the whole matter. Also, there was suspicion that in many cases it was expediency rather than conviction which motivated the request. The problem was a thorny one, because in practice a number of devoted synagogue members went through a civil ceremony and then applied for conversion on behalf of their wives, followed by *kidushin,* or a religious marriage ceremony.

Traditional Judaism never sanctioned mixed marriages, and, although constitutional strictures were introduced to prevent them, both congregations had to modify their articles to condemn only those marriages which were not in conformity with a rather elastic synagogal law. As has been mentioned before, there were more unmarried Jewish men in Philadelphia than available single Jewish girls, so that traditional law had to be relaxed to meet the demands of nature and realism. In 1798 the second constitution of Mikveh Israel provided that any Jew who married a person of another religion would forfeit his membership in the congregation and not be entitled to religious rights and privileges.[78] This provision must have been found to be unrealistic, for in 1805 the *hazan* was merely ordered not to convert or marry any Jew to a Christian woman "without consent and approbation of the Parnass."[79]

The irregularities resulting from such a procedure presented still other problems. One premarital conversion carried out by the Philadelphia congregation was not recognized elsewhere. Sophie Deacon, who became Mrs. Sarah Nathans by a civil ceremony, had been converted by *Hazan* Carvalho in 1816,[80] and with her husband sailed to England. Later they sought to be remarried with Jewish rites, but her certificate at that time—eight years later—was subjected to doubt, and the London authorities refused to sanction the wedding. Isaacs wrote imploringly to the Philadelphia congregation, requesting that they reissue a copy with signatures that could be easily recognized as genuine, or file an acceptable, authorized statement before the British consul or the local merchant John Moss, whose name was well-known and respected in England.

> Do for Heavens Sake, my Good Sirs, comfort the Uneasiness of mind, the want of the solemn ceremony of marriage has occasioned, and send me per return of Packet an attested abstract from your Register Books of the Synagogue of the Particulars of that event, with the Names of the then present.[81]

Some years later, a conversion and marriage performed in Philadelphia by the itinerant Reb Hayim, without prior permission from the *parnass* and *adjunta,* was questioned. A religious court of Rodeph Shalom hailed him before it and ruled that no convert should be made in the future unless the act were approved by a special meeting. The offender was suspended from the congregation until word could be obtained about Reb Hayim from Bnai Jeshurun in New York.[82] The status of poor Abraham Cuyk, who was the groom, was not resolved for two years, at which time it was agreed that everything would be all right if his children were circumcised and raised as Jews.[83]

Benjamin Nones, who had been authorized to write to the London *Beth Din* on "Business of importance to Jewdaism" in connection with Moses Nathans' request,[84] was himself faced with a similar situation in his own family more than twenty years later. His son David had married a Spanish girl in St. Croix, and when they returned to the United States in 1818 the father, as "Sworn Interpreter of Foreign Languages," submitted to the *adjunta* a translation of his daughter-in-law's request for conversion. One rather suspects that Nones not only translated but originated the phrases,

> Having reflected for many years on the Holy and primitive religion of Moses which I have observed in all its forms as if I had been born of the same religion, I have now determined and it is my proper will and wish without any body's advise to Embrace the same with all my heart.[85]

After her conversion, Anna, now appropriately Hannah, Nones, had her three sons circumcised,[86] and then finally she and her husband asked permission to be married "with Hoopah & Kaydooshin."[87] That permission was granted provided that Nones could procure a proper person to perform the ceremony, for the congregation was then without a *hazan*.[88]

The most curious instance of the complications which could occur concerned the application of Joseph Aarons for membership in Mikveh Israel in 1826. A letter from the "German and Hebrew Congregation of Kingston, Jamaica" had preceded him, setting forth his religious disqualifications because of his father Jacob's marriage, or lack of marriage, to the daughter of the late David Mendes Alvares.[89] The *adjunta*, although desirous of "preserving inviolate our holy laws," declared themselves unable to see the religious distinction between a *mamsor* and a legitimate child so far as the innocent offspring was concerned.[90] And, since even the report of an illegal connection, which dated from 1744, was based "altogether on report and hearsay evidence," they agreed to permit the whole Aarons family within the synagogue.

An exception was made so far as Aarons' daughter Rachel was concerned, for she had been married to Alexander Fleish by a Christian minister; but even they would be admitted if they would repent and be properly married. It is interesting that three well-integrated American Jews—Zalegman Phillips, Samuel Hays and John Moss—made this decision on the part of the congregation, and Isaiah Nathans, himself married to a convert,[91] argued Aarons' case before the *Beth Din*.

A recently discovered memoir throws some light on a case of a different kind.[91a] In 1806 Abraham Haim Cohen, the son of the *hazan*, married Jane Picken. Because of his position as his father's assistant the marriage came close to creating a scandal. However, the bride-to-be permitted herself to be converted, and in her story describes "the Jewish baptism" which took place in one of

Philadelphia's rivers where the congregation put up a small building for that purpose. About the time Cohen left the city to accept a post in Richmond, his wife, unbeknownst to him, reverted to Christianity, and seems clandestinely to have given her children Christian instruction. Her memoir is chiefly the story of the death at the age of eight of the Cohens' son, Henry Luria, who as he was dying called upon Christ. The book was obviously of a missionary nature, but except for its curious mysticism it does contain a rather sympathetic picture of the life of a one-time convert to Judaism.

When a woman married out of the faith, with almost the single exception of the controversial girl from Easton in the previous century, she and her children were lost to Judaism. There were few applications for conversion from men prior to that of the Johnson family and the well-known Warder Cresson, which took place somewhat later. One of these is of unusual interest, for there has survived a Hebrew certificate of conversion. The convert, who adopted the ritual name of Jacob bar Abraham *Abinu*, but whose original name is not known, was circumcised by Dr. Manuel Phillips and took a ritual bath in the presence of three witnesses, the performance of which ceremonies was attested to by Phillips, Jacob Lippman and Solomon Mordecai.[92] With the document is another Hebrew certificate by Naphtali Phillips stating that his brother was "well known to me to be a *Mohel* and qualified to perform the covenant of circumcision."[93]

Sensational instances of intermarriage, where one of the partners embraced Christianity, upset the Jewish community very much. If New York society had been distressed by Dr. Nicholas Schuyler's choice of a Jewish bride, Shinah Simon, her father Joseph Simon and his friends were no less heartbroken by her action. Although there is no specific mention of it, Simon seems to have torn her from his life as he would have ripped his clothing upon the loss of a relative by death. This marriage, and the tension it caused, were given considerable thought by Shinah's niece, Rebecca Gratz, and may have affected the course of her own life.

The story is told that during his last illness, in 1804, the ninety-two-year-old Simon was nursed skillfully and tenderly by his granddaughter Rebecca. Calling her to him one day, he asked what he could do to repay her love. Her eyes brimming over with tears, young Rebecca answered, "Grandfather, forgive Aunt Shinah." Touched, the old man pressed her hand, and in a broken voice said, "Send for her." And so the Lancaster pioneer forgave his estranged daughter, gave her his blessing, and died in her arms.[94] It was just at this time that Rebecca herself made a difficult decision.

Rebecca Gratz never spoke of it, and the story of her young love has come down through the recollections of others.[95] It seems that in her late teens or early twenties Rebecca entered into a close friendship with Samuel Ewing, the son of the Provost of the University of Pennsylvania and one of the most promising young lawyers in the city. She went with him to the City Dancing Assembly on Washington's Birthday in 1802.[96] The friendship ripened into love; but when the question of marriage arose, both felt that the devotion of each to his or her own religion made that impossible. Solemnly, and doubtless tearfully, they agreed to part. Ewing is reported to have told Miss Redman, whom he married in 1810, that he had deeply loved Rebecca Gratz and that only the difference of their religions separated them. Rebecca, as is well known, never married, and a passionate nature, which might have found its fulfillment in love and maternity, was sublimated and changed into the restless energy of her philanthropic altruism. When Ewing, married to another and the father of a family, died tragically at the age of thirty-nine in 1825, Rebecca Gratz came quietly into the room where his body lay in its coffin, placed three white roses on his breast, put a miniature of herself next to his heart, and left as proudly and silently as she had come in. This was the stuff of which Victorian novels were made, but it was more than a hopeless, romantic love. It was the conflict in the heart of a beautiful and intelligent woman, dedicated to her own religion—at the cost of her happiness.

With a detachment she never actually possessed, Rebecca Gratz wrote to her dear friend Mrs. Ogden Hoffman in 1817, speaking about a fictional story of intermarriage which she had just read:

I believe it is impossible to reconcile a matrimonial engagement between persons of so different a creed, without requiring one or the other to yield— in all instances we have heard of in real life, this has been the case and where a family of children are to be brought up, it appears necessary that parents should agree on so important a subject. I have known many Jews marry

Christian women, whose wives became strict conformists to the rites of our religion—and Jewesses married to Christians who have entered the church, as in the instance of my Aunt Schuyler—one instance similar to Montevieia I have heard here—but the parties lived very unhappily—little jealousies were continually occurring, and at length when the husband died the widow and her daughters returned to her family & the synagogue while the son was put in the navy, and quite estranged from the family. The poor fellow is also dead, but had he survived the division of interests and sentiments would have broken up the harmony of feelings that should subsist between such relations . . .[97]

When, two years later, Rebecca's own youngest brother Benjamin, who had moved to Lexington, Kentucky, became the second of the family to marry a Christian,[98] she was at first shocked and unhappy. But Maria Gist was a person so sympathetic to Rebecca that she agreed from the time of the marriage "not to remember that there is a difference of opinion on any subject between us,"[99] and Maria Gist Gratz became one of her closest friends and most trusted confidantes. It is significant that, although Benjamin Gratz was buried as a Jew,[100] his children were brought up in their mother's faith. Simon, the oldest of the second-generation Gratzes, wrapped his matrimonial life in secrecy. He had seven children, but whether he was married to their mother is not known.[101] That the children were brought up as Christians is evidenced by the fact that one daughter, Louisa, who had been active in the Jewish community, officially embraced Judaism after 1851.[102] Simon, while his children were growing up, served as an officer of the congregation, and his liaison was not mentioned in the community. Jacob too had a wife or mistress, and left a son,[103] but the other two brothers, Hyman and Joseph, never married.

The problem which the synagogue faced was impersonal, but it was little different from that of the Gratzes. Intermarriage was usually the first step away from Judaism, but in a society where the synagogue had no control over outer influences it could only try its best to exert moral suasion upon affiliated Jews. Both congregations were seriously faced with the problem in the later 1820s. Since synagogal law did not in practice prevent intermarriage, and since the provisions of the constitution were flouted more and more, the emphasis within the congregations was shifted away from prohibitions to procedural rules for proselytism and marriage. In 1826 Rodeph Shalom decreed that, except for Aaron Dropsie, no member who had been married to

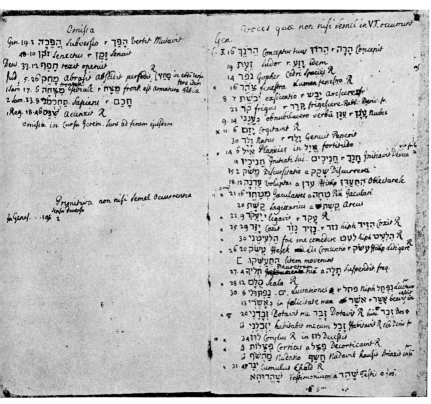

1. James Logan's Manuscript Hebrew Vocabulary, *ca.* 1725

BIBLIA
HEBRAICA·CVM
NOVO DOMINI NOSTRI
IESV CHRISTI
TESTAMENTO,

EORVNDEM LATINA INTERPRETATIO
XANTIS PAGNINI LVCENSIS,

BENEDICTI ARIÆ MONTANI Hifpal.& quorundam aliorum collato
ftudio, ad Hebraicam dictionem diligentiffimè expenfa.

Accefferunt huic editioni,

Romanæ Correctionis in LATINIS BIBLIIS editionis vulgatæ iuffu Sixti V. P.M.
recognitis, Loca infigniora obferuata,& denuo aucta ex vetuftis manufcriptis
exemplaribus à FR. LVCA BRYGENSI, Ecclefiæ Cathedralis Audomaropoli-
tanæ Theologo & Decano: Cum rerum copiofo Indice,& Chronologia ab or-
be condito vfque ad Saluatoris noftri paffionem.

נדפס שנת שׁעׁח על ידי כאפא אילן פה

גנווא

2.   Isaac Norris, Jr.'s Hebrew Bible

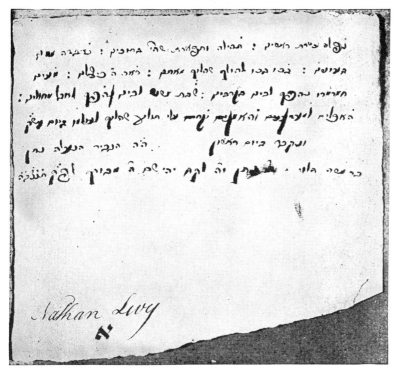

3. Obituary of Nathan Levy, 1753

4. Circumcision Book of Barnard Itzhak Jacobs, *ca.* 1765

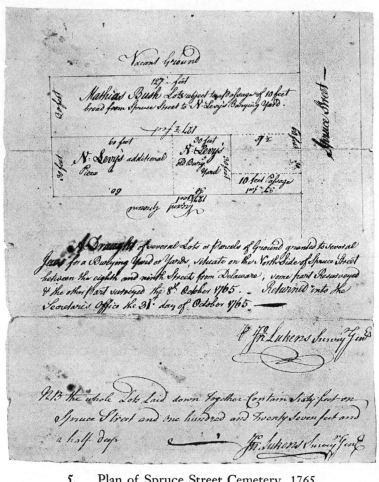

5. Plan of Spruce Street Cemetery, 1765

6a. Rebecca Gratz   6b. Rachel Gratz Moses   6c. Israel Jacobs
6d. Rachel Levy

7.   Michael Gratz

After original by Thomas Sully

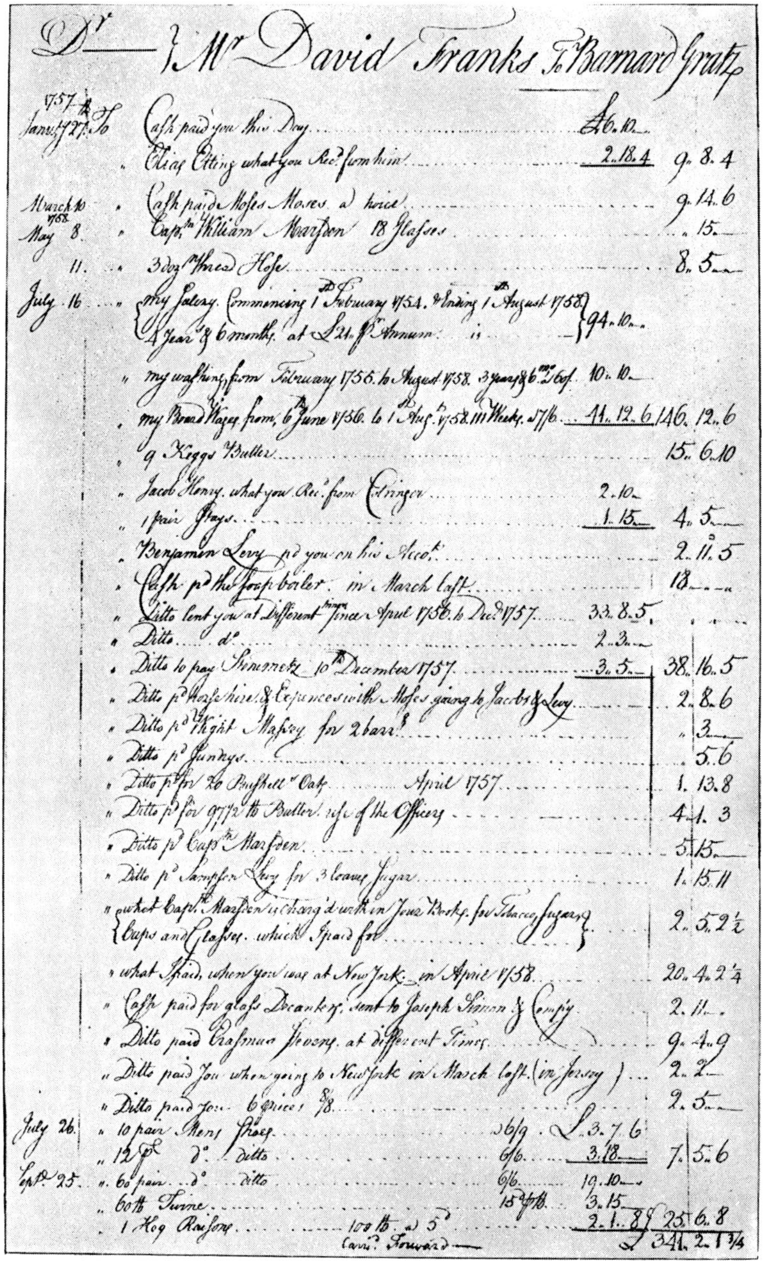

Dr } Mr David Franks To Barnard Gratz

1757 Janry 27.	To	Cash paid you this Day	£6.10..	
	"	Elias Etting what you Recd. from him	2.18.4	9.. 8. 4
March 10	"	Cash paid Moses Moses a twice		9. 14. 6
1758 May 8.	"	Captn. William Marsdon 18 Glasses		.. 15..
11.	"	3 doz. thread Hose		8.. 5..
July 16	"	my Salery Commencing 1st February 1754. & Ending 1st August 1758 4 Year & 6 months at £21. pr. Annum is	94. 10..	
	"	my washing from February 1756. to August 1758. 2 years & 6 mo. 26/	10.. 10..	
	"	my Board Wages from 6th June 1756. to 1st Aug. 1758. 111 Weeks 7/6	41. 12. 6	146. 12. 6
	"	9 Keggs Butter		15.. 6.10
	"	Jacob Henry what you Rec. from Etringer	2. 10..	
	"	1 pair Stays	1. 15..	4. 5..
	"	Benjamen Levy pd you on his Accot.		2. 11. 5
	"	Cash pd the Soap boiler in March last		18.. ..
	"	Ditto lent you at Different times since April 1756. to Decr 1757	33. 8. 5	
	"	Ditto ... do	2. 3..	
	"	Ditto to pay Stinmetz 10th December 1757	3. 5..	38. 16. 5
	"	Ditto pd Horse hire & Expences with Moses going to Jacobs & Levy		2. 8. 6
	"	Ditto pd Night Massey for 2 barrl.		.. 3..
	"	Ditto pd Sundrys		.. 5. 6
	"	Ditto pd for 20 Bushell Oats April 1757		1. 13. 8
	"	Ditto pd for 97½ lb Butter use of the Officers		4. 1. 3
	"	Ditto pd Captn. Marsden		5. 15..
	"	Ditto pd Sampson Levy for 3 loaves Sugar		1. 15. 11
	"	what Captn. Marsden is Charg'd with in Your Books for Tobacco, Sugar, Cups and Glasses which I paid for		2. 5. 2½
	"	what I paid when you was at New York in April 1758		20.. 4. 2¼
	"	Cash paid for glass Decanters sent to Joseph Simon & Compy		2. 11..
	"	Ditto paid Erasmus Stevens at different Times		9.. 4. 9
	"	Ditto paid You when going to New York in March last (in Jersey)		2. 2..
	"	Ditto paid You 6 pieces 8/8		2. 5..
July 26.	"	10 pair Mens Shoes 6/9	£3. 7. 6	
	"	12 pr. do ditto 6/6	3. 18	7. 5. 6
Septr. 25.	"	60 pair do ditto 6/6	19. 10..	
	"	60 lb Twine 15 d/lb	3. 15	
		1 Hog Raisons 100 lb a 5	2. 1. 8	25. 6. 8
		Carrd. Forward		£341. 2. 1¾

8. Account of David Franks with Barnard Gratz

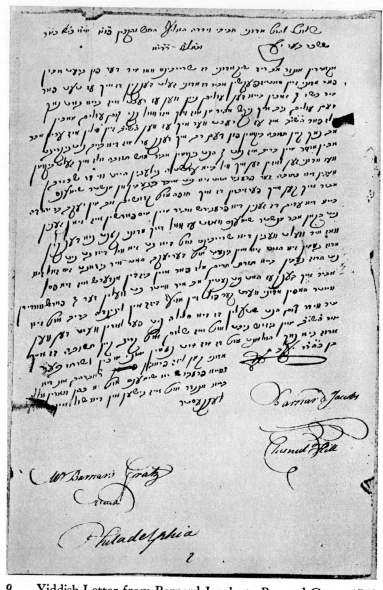

9. Yiddish Letter from Barnard Jacobs to Barnard Gratz, 1768

Mr. Joseph Simons   Philada. April 3d. 1760.

Sir
    Yr. favr. pr. post I recd. I shall send you the
Barril Muscovado Sugar as allso the Loaf Sugar pr first
oppe.; shall write to Mr. Franks tomorrow abt. the
Wampum. Ive recd. the £86.3.9 from the Comiss.ro
& pr. the Copper-smith £69.12 yr. Recet. the officer
of the Virginia Regimt. I could not meet with, have
showeing the Note to Coll. Byrd & he told he would see
abt. it that the men shall pay it, I am with Regard
                          Sir Yr. Most Humble Servt.
                              Barnard Gratz

My Complements
to yr. wife & family &
Mr. Levy & a. Levy & should
be Glad of his Jornall Dureing
the Campaing

10.   Letter from Barnard Gratz to Joseph Simon

Fort Pitt March 23d 1765 —

George Croghan Esqr —

To Simons Levy & Compy Dr

For Sundrys for the Use of the Indians —

37 pis Strouds	12/4	£444
17 pis Half Thicks	£4.10	76.10
2½ pis French Match Coats	£15	37.10
2 pis Do 40 yd Each	£12	24
3 ¾ pis English Match Coats	£11	41..5
15 pis Black Striped Blankets	£10	150
10 Do Red Striped Ditto	£11	110
14¾ yd Scarlet Cloth	24/6	16 — 72
22¼ yd Do Napt	20/	22..5
5 yd Imbroived Serge	3/6	17.6
65 Blankets & Match Coat Coats	20/	65
55 Cloth Ditto Diff.t Colours	25/	68..15
1 Scarlet Westcoat laced with Silver		3..
4 yd Callico	5/	1
4¼ yd Chints	10/	2..2..6
29 fine Ruffd Shirts	25/	36..5
82 Callico Shirts	12/	49..4
7 Plain White Shirts	10/	3..10
4 Do Smaller	5/	1
16 Checkerd Shirts	12/	9.12
139 Half Ruffled Shirts	11/	76..9
Carried Over		£1238..5..7½

11.   Record of Indian Goods sold by Simon, Levy and
Company to George Croghan

12. Manuel Josephson

After original by Jeremiah Theus

13a. Jonas Phillips   *13b*. Rebecca Machado Phillips
13c. Reuben Etting   *13d*. Frances Etting

So that they were, declared Adjuntas Elect, for the time speci=fied in One of the above Resolutions; all whom are to be Publicly proclaimed in the Synagogue on the Morning of the 1st day of Pesah ensuing,——

Moved & Seconded; whether the Old Building, on the Lot Bought for the use of a Synagogue; should be repaired & put in order for a place of worship, or should we agree to Build a new One? And on Examination of the diff.t Estimates of the Repairs of the Old Building, and those for Building a new one; and finding that a new Build.g would not Cost much more than the repairs of the old one; It was Resolved N.C that a new Syna=gogue be built; and now that the Parnass & adjuntos are Elected; who are Authorized to Transact that Business, and which is recommended to their Care & attention.

Isaac DaCosta. Chairman

Benj.n Seixas
Emuel Gratz
Simon Nathan
Hayman Levy
Gershom Seixas

Jonas Phillips
Isaac Moses
Samuel DeLucena
Israel Jacobs

Abm. Levy
Barnard Gratz
Moses Cohen
Bernd. Mrs. Spitzer

Jacob Mordecai

Mordecai Sheftall
Jacob Myers
Coshman Polack
Manuel Josephson

Jacob Hart
Ezekiel Levy
S.d Marache
Henry Murrey
S.n Myers Cohen
Lyon Nathan
Hayim Solomon

14.   Record of the First Meeting of the Reorganized Congregation Mikveh Israel, 1782

15. Expenditures and Receipts of the First Synagogue Building, 1782

The Miswot for opening the היכל. Zemirot. Kadish. & Aftora
for Sabbath to be publish'd — & begin the Prayers for Sabbath as usual,
the Congregation to be particularly carefull not to
raise their voices higher than the Hazan's, who will
endeavor to modulate his voice to a proper Pitch
so as only to fill the Building —————

His Excellency the President. & Honble Delegates of the United States ויתן וגו
of America in Congress Assembled — His Excellency George Washington
Captain General & Commander in Chief of the fœderal Army of these
States, His Excellency the President, the Honble Executive Council
& Members of the General Assembly of this Commonwealth, & all Kings
& Potentates in Alliance with North America: מלך מלכי וגו

מי שבירך וג את כל הקק הזה מקוה ישראל מיא קדושים ותוכס ה שנדרו ריאס
לבנות הקרקע ולבנות עליו דית הכנסת הזאת/שכאנו מחנבי ומקד ד'היים
לעורדת ה הקניע ואן ... הא אלקי ... תלכם עלים וג

בפרק מב יען בר אמן אור יהושע את מבני הבנות לשא דית הכנסת המא מי שעירך

צדק עזי את הקהבניה תחת המזוזות בקבן צדיעים והלבן
the first three named are debunct — הרשום דד'ת הכנסת הזאת מי שעירך

שעישו את העמודים צדית הכנעת הזאת
Farewell $ the Levis, one is dead, the rest are now married men — מי שעירך

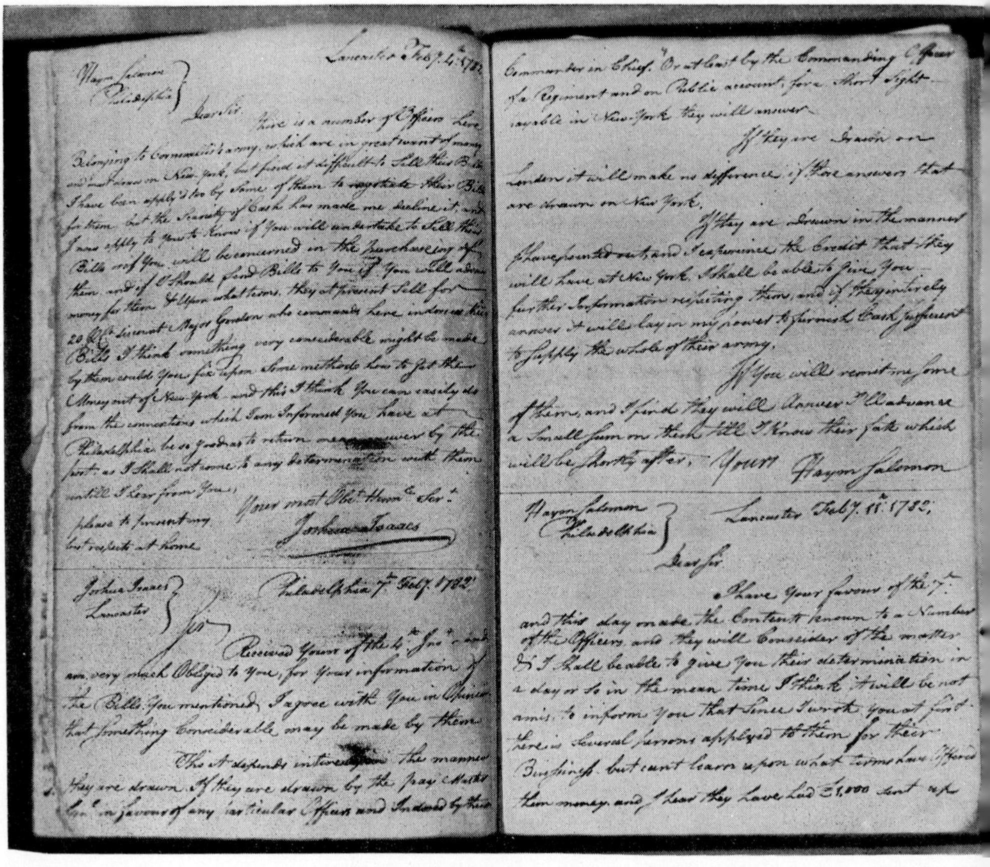
Haym Salomon
Philadelphia

Lancaster Feby. 4th 1782

Dear Sir

There is a number of Officers here Belonging to Cornwallis's army, which are in great want of money and have drawn on New York, but find it difficult to Sell their Bills I have been apply'd too by Some of them to negotiate their Bills for them but the Scarcity of Cash has made me decline it, and I now apply to You to Know if You will undertake to Sell them Bills or if You will be concerned in the purchasing of them and if I Should Send Bills to You if You will advance money for them & Upon what terms, they at present Sell for 20 [illegible] discount Major Gordon who commands here indorses their Bills I think Something very considerable might be made by them could You fix upon Some methode how to get the Money out of New York and this I think You can easily do from the connections which I am Informed You have at Philadelphia be so good as to return me an answer by the post as I Shall not come to any determination with them untill I hear from You.

Your most Obed. Hum. Ser.
Joshua Isaacs

please to present my best respects at home

Joshua Isaacs
Lancaster

Philadelphia 7th Feby. 1782

Sir

Received Yours of the 4th Ins.t and am very much Obliged to You, for Your information of the Bills You mentioned, I agree with You in Opinion that Something Considerable may be made by them

This it depends intirely upon the manner they are drawn If they are drawn by the pay Master Gen.l in favour of any particular Officers and Indorsed by their Commander in Chief, Or at least by the Commanding Officer of a Regiment and on Public account, for a Short Sight payable in New York they will answer

If they are drawn on London it will make no difference if those answers that are drawn on New York.

If they are drawn in the manner I have pointed out, and I experience the Credit that they will have at New York I Shall be able to give You further Information respecting them, and if they intirely answer it will lay in my power to furnish Cash Sufficient to supply the whole of their army.

If You will remit me some of them, and I find they will Answer I'll advance a Small Sum on them till I Know their fate which will be Shortly after, Yours Haym Salomon

Haym Salomon
Philadelphia

Lancaster Feby. 11th 1782,

Dear Sir

I have Your favour of the 7th and this day make the Content known to a Number of the Officers and they will Consider of the matter & I Shall be able to give You their determination in a day or so in the mean time I think it will be not amiss to inform You that Since I wrote You at first there is Several persons applyed to them for their Bushiness but can't learn upon what terms have Offered them money and I hear they have had £1,000 Sent up

17. Haym Salomon's Letter Book, 1782

18. French Loan Note, Payable to Haym Salomon

To the Hebrew Congregations in the Cities of Philadelphia, New York, Charleston and Richmond.

Gentlemen,

The liberality of sentiment towards each other, which marks every political and religious denomination of men in this country, stands unparalleled in the history of Nations. The affection of such a people is a treasure beyond the reach of calculation; and the repeated proofs which my fellow citizens have given of their attachment to me, and approbation of my doings, form the purest source of my temporal felicity. The affectionate expressions of your address again excite my gratitude, and receive my warmest acknowledgment.

The Power and Goodness of the Almighty were strongly manifested in the events of our late glorious revolution; and his

19.   George Washington's Letter to the Hebrew Congregations

his kind interposition in our behalf has been no less visible in the establishment of our present equal Government. — In war he directed the Sword; and in peace he has ruled in our Councils. — My agency in both has been guided by the best intentions, and a sense of the duty which I owe my Country. — And as my exertions have hitherto been amply rewarded by the approbation of my fellow Citizens, I shall endeavour to deserve a continuance of it by my future conduct.

May the same temporal and eternal blessings which you implore for me, rest upon your Congregations. —

G. Washington

of Philadelphia, New York, Charleston and Richmond

To the Humane, Charitable, and well disposed People

The Representation and Solicitation of the good People of the Hebrew Society in the City of Philadelphia commonly call'd Israelites.

Whereas the religious Order of Men in this City, denominated Israelites, were without any Synagogue, or House of Worship untill the Year 1780 when desirous of accommodating themselves, and encouraged thereto by a number of respectable & worthy bretheren of the hebrew Society then in this Place (who generously contributed to the Design) they purchased a Lot of Ground, & erected thereon the Buildings necessary & proper for their religious Worship. And whereas many of their Number at the Close of the late War, return'd to New York, Charleston, & elsewhere their Homes (which they had been exiled from & obliged to leave on account of their Attachment to American Measures) leaving the remaining few of their Religion here, burthen'd with a considerable Charge consequent from so great an Undertaking. And whereas the present Congregation, after expending all the Subscriptions, Loans, Gifts &c made the Society by themselves, & the generous Patrons of their religious Intentions to the Amount of at least £1000 were obliged to borrow Money to finish the Building & contract other Debts that is now not only pressingly claim'd but a Judgment will actually be obtained against their House of Worship, which must be sold unless they are speedily enabled to pay the sum of about £800 — And which from

a variety

20. Mikveh Israel Subscription List Signed by Benjamin

a Variety of delicate & distressing Cases they are wholly unable
to raise among themselves. They are therefore under the
necessity of earnestly soliciting from their worthy fellow Citizens
of every religious Denomination, their benevolent Aid & Help,
flattering themselves that their worshipping Almighty God
in a way & manner different from other religious Societies will
never deter the enlightened Citizens of Philadelphia, from
generously subscribing towards the preservation of a religious
house of Worship. The subscription paper, will be enrolled in
the Archives of their Congregation, that their Posterity may
know & gratefully remember the liberal Supporters of their
religious Society.

Philadelphia April 30th 1788

Franklin and Other Non-Jews

Haym Salomon,

Authorised Broker to the Office of Finance, &c. has now to dispose of at his OFFICE in Front-Street (where he transacts, in the most extensive manner, every branch of business relative to his profession)

BANK STOCK.

THE various sorts of Certificates, Notes, &c. issued by the public; Bills of Exchange upon France, Spain, Holland, England, Denmark, Hamburgh, &c. and the principal West-India islands; and can draw bills upon most of the principal places on this continent.

He receives every species of Merchandize to sell upon Commission; for which purpose he has provided proper stores; and procures freight for vessels. Any person residing in this or any of the United States, who will send their orders to his office, may depend on having their business transacted with as much fidelity as if they were themselves present.

He flatters himself his assiduity, punctuality and extensive connections in his business, as a Broker, are well established in several parts of Europe, and the United States in particular.

All those who shall please to favour him with their business, may depend upon his utmost exertions for their interest, and part of the money advanced, if desired.

Haym Salomon, Broker,

To the Office of Finance,

HAVING procured a licence for exercising the employment of an AUCTIONEER in the city of New York, has now opened, for the reception of every species of *Merchandize*, his House No. 22, Wall-street, lately occupied by Mr. *Anthony L. Bleeker*, (one of the best stands in that city) and every branch of business, which in the smallest degree appertains to the professions of

Factor, Auctioneer & Broker,

will be transacted in it with that fidelity, dispatch and punctuality which has hitherto characterised his dealings. The house, in point of convenience and situation, is exceedingly well calculated for the different kinds of business abovementioned; and he thinks it almost unnecessary to assure those who may favor it with their orders, that the strictest attention shall be paid to them, and the utmost care and solicitude employed to promote their interest.

The nature of his business enables him to make remittances to any part of the world with peculiar facility, and this he hopes will operate considerably in his favor with those who live at a distance.

A desire of being more extensively useful, and of giving universal satisfaction to the Public, are among his principal motives for opening this house, and shall be the great leading principle of all his transactions. By being Broker to the Office of Finance, and honored with its confidence, all those sums have passed through his hands which the generosity of the French Monarch, and the affection of the Merchants of the United *Provinces*, promoted them to furnish us with, to enable us to support the expence of the war, and which have so much contributed to its successful and happy termination; this is a circumstance which has established his credit and reputation, and procured him the confidence of the Public, a confidence which it shall be his study and ambition to merit and encrease, by sacredly performing all his engagements. The Business will be conducted upon the most liberal and extensive plan, under the *Firm* of HAYM SALOMON and JACOB MORDECAI.

Philadelphia, May 7, 1784.

Haym Salomon,

COURTIER de Change & du Bureau des FINANCES,

AYANT obtenu la permission d'exercer la charge de *Maitre d'Encan* dans la ville de New-York, vient d'ouvrir ses magazines pour la reception de toutes sortes de marchandises, dans la maison ci devant occupé par Mr. Anthony Bleeker, situé dans Wall-street, No. 22, une des meilleures situations de la ville pour les affaires, ou il exerce les emplois et professions de FACTEUR, MAITRE D'ENCAN et COURTIER, et transige avec la fidelité, la promptitude & la ponctualité, qui ont jusqu'ici caracterisé ses operations, & qui ont etabli sa reputation tant en Europe qu'en Amérique toutes sortes d'affaires ayant le moindre raport avec les differentes branches.

La maison par sa situation et par sa commodité est extremement propre aux differens genres d'affaires ci dessus mentionnées, et il croit qu'il est presque inutile d'assurer ceux qui voudront bien l'employer, qu'il donnera tous ses soins et toute son attention à leurs affairs et à l'avancement de leurs intérêts.

La nature & l'etendue de ses affaires, le mettent dans le cas de pouvoir faire des envois et des retours dans toutes les parties du monde, avec une facilité particuliere, ce qu'il croit devoir operer en sa faveur avec les personnes qui demeurent dans des lieux eloignés.

Le desir de se rendre de la plus grande utilité et de donner au public toute espèce de satisfaction sont les principaux motifs qui l'induisent à ouvrir cette nouvelle maison, & ce même desir sera toujours le grand principe qui dirigera toutes ses operations.

Etant depuis longtems honoré de la confiance de Messieurs les Chefs du Bureau des *Finances*, dont il est le Courtier, il a eu entre ses mains toutes les sommes que la generosité du Monarque de France, et l'affection des Negociants des Provinces Unies les ont engagé à avancer aux Etats Unis, qui nous ont aidés à soutenir les depenses de la guerre et qui ont contribué à son succes & à son heureuse fin—C'est cette circonstance qui a etabli son credit & sa reputation & qui lui a procuré la confiance du public, confiance qu'il s'efforcera de meriter de plus en plus, en remplissant fidelement tous ses engagements.

Les affaires de la dite maison se conduiront sur le plan le plus liberal & le plus étendu sous la raison de HAYM SOLOMON & JACOB MORDECAI. à Philadelphie, le 7 May, 1784.

Wanted to hire, a convenient

dwelling house, with three rooms on a floor, a good yard, &c. for which a generous price will be given. Enquire at Messrs. *Ingrahams* store in Front street, between Market and Arch streets.

August 31.

Benjamin Nones & Co.

BROKERS.

ACQUAINT their friends, and the public in general, that they intend carrying on the Commission, Factorage and Brokers business in their various branches, at the house of Benjamin Nones, in Front street, next door to the Post-Office, and formerly occupied by Mr. Philip Syng. Where they have provided stores for the reception of all kind of Goods to sell on commission; will purchase on the shortest notice and most advantageous terms, all kind of merchandize or produce, for such as please to employ them as Factors. Buy and sell Bills of Exchange on France, Spain, Holland, and other parts. Likewise Loan-Office and other Certificates, State and Continental Money, &c.

They flatter themselves that by steady attention, secrecy, punctuality and dispatch, which shall be their earnest endeavours, to give general satisfaction to such as please to employ them in all or either of the above branches.

Lion Moses, Broker,

BEGS leave to acquaint the Public in general, and his friends in particular, that he carries on the business of BROKERAGE in all its various branches, at his house in Race-street, opposite the King of Prussia tavern, between Third and Fourth streets. Negociates bills of exchange on Europe, the continent of America, or the West-Indies, loan office and state certificates and notes, takes goods for sale on commission, buys and sells houses, lands, shipping, &c. Those that please to employ him may depend on the strictest punctuality, dispatch and secrecy. It will be his constant study to merit the confidence of a discerning Public, and will gratefully acknowledge all favors conferred on him. May 17. stu.

Philadelphia, Aug. 23.

Isaac Franks, Broker,

At his OFFICE on the south side of Market-street, between Second and Third-streets, two doors below the Presbyterian-Meeting, Philadelphia,

BUYS and sells on Commission, all kinds of Merchandize, Bills of Exchange, Continental Loan-Office Certificates, State Money, Officers and Soldiers Certificates, and every other kind of Paper Security of the United States, or of any particular State: he procures Money on Loan, discounts Notes, Bonds and Bills of all sorts; Lets out Money; disposes of, and purchases Real Estates, and every other kind of transferable property; he procures Freight or Charter for Vessels, at the shortest Notice; and transacts every other kind of Business as a Broker, with fidelity, care and dispatch.

He has for SALE, a Variety of

Well assorted MERCHANDIZE,

Wholesale and Retail, upon easy Terms for Cash or Public Securities. Feb. 6.

TO BE SOLD.

The following Tracts of unimproved LANDS, lying and situated on the river Kiskimenitas, in the county of Westmoreland, about 20 miles from Fort-Pitt.

No 1 FIFTY-EIGHT Acres—*The Point*; this tract is in the fork of the Alleghany, and Kiskimenitas rivers, it is all a rich bottom, and commands a fine prospect. (Patented)

No. 2. Two hundred and eighty-six acres, and 20 perches—*The Farmers Delight*, mostly rich bottom; the path from Fort-Pitt to Kittanning crosses here. (Patented)

Two hundred and seventy eight acres and 3 perches—A survey adjoining *Farmers Delight*, good wheat land and meadow. (Warrant)

No. 3. Three hundred and fifty one acres and an half—*The Three Bottoms*; on this tract, there is upwards of 100 acres of fine bottom, the remainder good wheat land, and a coal bank. (Patented)

No. 4. Five hundred acres and a quarter—*Warren's Sleeping Place*; about 300 acres exceeding rich bottom, fit for hemp, tobacco, corn and meadow, fine timbered, a great part of which Locust. (Patented)

Seventy acres and three-quarters—A survey adjoining *Warren's Sleeping Place*, rich, good wheat land. (Warrant)

No. 5. One hundred and forty-three acres and an half—*Black Legs*; this tract is mostly rich bottom, a good spring of water, good timber, and a delightful prospect. (Warrant)

(Note. The following tracts by special order of survey.)

One hundred and fifty acres—A survey adjoining *Black Legs*: good upland.

No. 6. Two hundred and forty acres and an half—The greatest part of this tract is a bottom, formerly an Indian town; on it there is a good mill seat.

No. 7. Two hundred and twelve acres and an half—An old Indian Town, nearly all a bottom, fit for hemp, tobacco and Indian corn.

No. 8. Nine hundred and twenty five acres—*The Upland Bottom*; good upland, fit for wheat, a considerable quantity of meadow ground, good timber and water.

No. 9. Two hundred and thirty acres and 120 perches—Very rich upland, well adapted for wheat.

No. 10. Two hundred and forty acres—Good upland, and adjoining No. 9.

The river on which these Lands are situated, is about 30 perches broad, navigable the greatest part of the year for small craft, having a water carriage from each tract to Fort Pitt, the Falls of the Ohio to New Orleans. Likewise, a fine range for cattle.

Any person who inclines to purchase, may know the terms by applying to WILLIAM NICHOLS, Merchant, Philadelphia, and to EPHRAIM BLAINE, Esquire, for any further description of the quality.

Philadelphia, August 17, 1784. 3wlhf.

Just Imported, and to be Sold by

Onfray Painniere,

At his Store the west side of Front-street, five doors above the Drawbridge,

SUPERFINE and second broad-cloths, plushes, cassimers, Silesia cloths, prunellas, silk ribbons, gauzes, silk stockings, thread, cotton and woolen ditto, silk gloves, lawns and cambricks, silk handkerchiefs, taffities, chintzes, linen and cotton handkerchiefs, sewing silk, cotton stripes, threads, oznaburgs, sail-cloths, small cordage, twine, writing paper, stuff for curtains, ticken, white and brown linen, Britania and Laval linen, delf ware, nails, salt, lampblack, red and yellow oacre, copperas, claret in hogsheads and boxes, Port wine in pipes and quarter pipes, Malaga and Champaigne in boxes, cordials and sweet oil in boxes, brown sugar of the first quality in hogsheads and barrels.

IMPORTED BY

Kuhn & Risberg,

In the Ships Susanna and Friendship, from Amsterdam; the Ship Pigou, from London, and other late Vessels from England and France, *A large Assortment of* MERCHANDIZE; among which are the following: and now Opening on SALE at their STORE the north side of Market-street, between Fourth and Fifth streets, for Cash, Tobacco, Bills of Exchange, or short Credit,

CASSIMERS, Ratteens, shalloons, tammies and durants.
Camblets, calimancoes, sattinets and lastings.
Moreens, damask, masqueradés, crapes, and dorsiteens.
Sagathies,
7-8 and yard wide Irish linens,
Brown and white Irish and Russia sheetings.
Ravens duck.
German oznaburgs.
Lubec rolls.
Dowlasses.
Platillas.
German bedticks.
6, 7. 9 and 10-4 bedbunts.
Harlem stripes & checks.
Russia diaper,
Damask and diaper tablecloths, plain and fringed.
White and coloured threads,
Harlem lace, tapes and bobbins.
Superfine dark & light ground chintzes.
Printed cottons and callicoes.
Mens, womens & childrens brown & white thread hose.
Womens cotton ditto.
Mens plain and rib'd, white and coloured, silk ditto.
Leghorn and chip hats.
A large assortment of silk, linen and cotton handkerchiefs.
Mens brown and white thread and fine coloured linen gloves,
Womens white kid and coloured jean ditto.
Womens silk mitts and gloves.
Blond and thread laces and edgings.
Mens, boys and childrens castor and felt hats.
Morocco leather.
Mens Morocco slippers.
Childrens ditto shoes.
A large assortment of the most fashionable black & white gauzes.
Tiffanies.
A variety of the most fashionable gauze, tiffany, millenet and kenting handkerchiefs and aprons.
Sewing & marking silks.
Twist and trolly.
Yellow canvas.
Ferrits and nonsoprettes.
Silk, thread and cotton stay laces.
Bindings and gartering.
Broad and narrow ribbons.
Millenet lawns & kentings.
Mock and bordered Marseilles quilting of the newest figures.
Linen & cotton checks.
Holland stripes.
Furniture checks and callicoes.
Fine worsted damask dit.
Drab jeans and fustians.
Prussian & Dutch cord.
Coloured Marseilles quilting.
Superfine white India jeans.
Printed jeans & jeanetts.
Nankeens.
Flowered drawboys.
Dimothies.
Tricklets.
Cross-overs.
Italian, or hat-band crapes.
Ell-wide India persians.
Plain & figured modes and manteas.
Persians and sarsnets,
Batavias.
Mens silk caps, single and double.
6-4 Humhums.
Long lawns.
Plain, striped, corded and cross-barred muslins.
Dressed dolls.
Sadlers web.
Hair cloth or chair seating.
Gilt leather trunks in nests.
Pocket looking glasses.
Silver watches.
Temple and common spectacles.
Horn and ivory combs.
Dutch quills, wafers & sealing-wax.
German slates and pencils assorted in cases.
Writing paper.
Bibles, testaments and spelling books.
German scythes & draw knives.
Moyland wheelstones.
Coffee mills.
Black pepper.
Mace, cloves, nutmegs and cinnamon.
Brimstone & copperas.
White and red lead in small casks.
Spanish white & brown in tierces.
Yellow oaker ditto.
Prussian blue and vermilion.
Gold and silver leaf.
White and yellow metal ditto.
Saltpetre in small casks.
Antimony.
Juniper berries in hogsheads and barrels.
Aniseeds.
Liquorice.
Nuhrenberg toys assorted in cases.
Fine hyson and gunpowder tea in canisters.
Best hyson, green, souchong, &c.
Bohea tea in quarter chests.
Queen ware assorted in crates.
Glass ware do. in chests.
Iron wire.
Brass kettles in nests.
F & FF gunpowder.
Shot and bar lead.
Nails.
Window glass.
Sweeping, cloaths and shoe brushes.
Long pipes.
German Reel, &c.

With a Variety of other Articles suitable to the Season. A few Pair—

Elegant Pier Looking-Glasses,

of the very latest Fashion. 2wtf

Map of the United States,

JUST Published and to be Sold by DAVID C. CLAYPOOLE, an elegant coloured Map of North-America, describing the United States, generally, and also each particular State.

Jones and Foulk[e]

Have for SALE, at their STORE in Market-street, between Third and Fourth streets,

A general Assortment of Goo[ds]

Imported in the last Vessels from London [and] Amsterdam: among which are, a large [Quan]tity of

German DOWLA[S]

Which they will sell very reasonable by the [piece] or smaller Quantity. ep[tf]

Just imported in the last Vessels from Londo[n and] Bristol, and to be sold by

Adam Zantzinger

At his Store in Market, between Third [and] Fourth streets, a neat Assortment of

Dry Goods, Hardware, Cutle[ry,]

Brass Desk Furniture, Sadlery, &c. &c.

Which he will dispose of very reasonable b[y the] quantity, and receive in payment, good tob[acco], rice, flour, bar and pig iron, or any other [pro]duce. eptf.

For SALE by

LACAZE and MALLE[T]

At their STORES in Water-street between [Arch] and Race streets,

CLARET in hogsheads,
Ditto of superfine quality,
Old Medoc ditto in boxes of 12, 24, and [50 bot]tles,
White and Red Burgundy in bottles,
Sherry in quarter casks,
A few pipes of the best Teneriffe wine,
Old Cognac Brandy in boxes of 12 bottles [each],
Sweet Oil in boxes,
Old English Beer in hogsheads. ALSO,
A large assortment of Dry Goods.
One hundred and sixty tierces of best Car[olina] RICE, just arrived in the ship Philadel[phia], captain Strong, from Charlestown.

For sale, a cargo of Havanna box SUG[AR], just arrived.

Just Imported in the last Vessels from Nant[s, and] to be sold on reasonable Terms for C[ash or] short Credit, by

P. D. Robert,

In Water-street, three Doors above Market [street],

BOHEA and hyson tea,
Chintzes and calicoes,
Madder,
Old Bourdeaux claret in bottles,
White Burgundy wine in barrels;
Also, a large Assortment of DRY GOODS [to be] sold at low Prices; viz.

Several kinds of broad and narrow cloth, [shal]loons, plushes, velvets, corduroys, silesia [...] cassimer, calimanco, buckram, camblets, [...]bines, prunella, sattinet, everlasting, flo[wered] flannels, linens, black silk stuffs, silk stock[ings,] kenting, gauze handkerchiefs and aprons, pr[inted] handkerchiefs, superfine cotton tufted cov[erlids] adorned with ribbons and fringes, and va[rious] other articles.

Likewise, several musquets and pistols, [...] barrels, twine, &c. June 28. [...]

THE PARTNERSHIP of WILLIAM [and] JAMES MILLER, being dissolved b[y the] death of William Miller, all persons [who] are anyway indebted to the said Partnership [or] to the Estate of William Miller, are request[ed to] discharge the same as soon as possible; an[d] those who have any demands against the Partnership or Estate, are desired to bring [them] in to the subscribers for settlement.

JAMES MILLER,
JOHN MILLER, junr. } Administr[ators]

Philadelphia, August 29, 1784.

JAMES MILLER still continues the Bu[siness] at his store in Front-street, the corner of Gr[...] alley, between Chesnut and Walnut streets, [and] has for Sale a general Assortment of M[ER]CHANDIZE, and expects a large Importa[tion] by the first Vessels from Europe. eptf.

Wanted to Rent,

To enter upon immediately,

A Small convenient house, in the neighbo[ur]hood of the city vendue, either in a pu[blic] street, or one of the alleys. It must consi[st of at] least three rooms and a kitchen, or part of a ho[use] where boarding may be had in the family, [situ]ated as before mentioned. Enquire of the Pri[nter].

Twenty Dollars Reward

RAN-AWAY yesterday, the 15th instan[t, a] German SERVANT, named WILLIA[M] ANTON METZ, a smart looking fell[ow,] square built, of a middling size, about 28 [years] of age, dark, short hair, pitted with the sm[all] pox, a remarkable blemish in one of his e[yes,] writes a tolerable good hand, speaks French, [He]brew, and a little English, much addicted to [drink]ing, by trade a butcher, and has some pretensi[ons] to the limner's or painter's business: had on [and] took with him, two good London brown c[loth] coats, one of which is lapelled, with fashion[able] white metal buttons, two pair new buck[skin] breeches, two pair Flanders ticken trowsers [and] coatee of the same, several shirts ruffled at [the] bosom, a white dimothy vest lapelled and fring[ed,] plated buckles, with sundry other articles; [he] arrived last June in the Ship Washington, [captain] Dale, from London. Whoever secures the [said] Servant in any gaol, and gives information [to] the Printer hereof, shall be intitled to the ab[ove] reward and reasonable charges.

N. B. All masters of vessels and others, [are] forbid carrying off or harbouring the said Serv[ant] at their peril. Philadelphia, Aug. 16, ep[tf]

PHILADELPHIA: Printed and sold by DAVID C. CLAYPOOLE, on the south side of Market-street, the third house [east] of Second-street, where Advertisements, &c. are thankfully received for this Paper.

21. *Pennsylvania Packet*, September 4, 1784

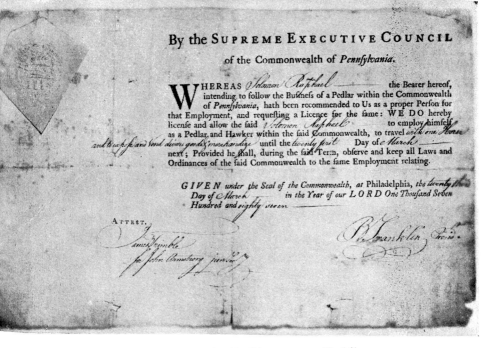

22.   Solomon Raphael's License as a Peddler

23. Promise of *Halitzah* given by Sheftall Sheftall, 1791

OBSERVATIONS

ON THE

CAUSE, NATURE, and TREATMENT

OF THE

EPIDEMIC DISORDER,

PREVALENT IN PHILADELPHIA.

BY D. NASSY, *M. D. Member of the American Philofophical Society, &c.*

[Tranflated from the French.]

———

PHILADELPHIA:
Printed by Parker & C°. for M. Carey;
Nov. 26,—1793.

24. First Medical Work by an American Jewish Physician

25.   Child's Hebrew Horn-Book, 1809

תורה נביאים וכתובים

BIBLIA HEBRAICA,

SECUNDUM ULTIMAM EDITIONEM

JOS. ATHIAE,

A

JOHANNE LEUSDEN

DENUO RECOGNITAM,

RECENSITA VARIISQUE NOTIS LATINIS ILLUSTRATA

AB

EVERARDO VAN DER HOOGHT,
V. D. M.

EDITIO PRIMA AMERICANA, SINE PUNCTIS
MASORETHICIS.

TOM. II.

PHILADELPHIÆ:
CURA ET IMPENSIS THOMÆ DOBSON EDITA EX ÆDIBUS LAPIDEIS
TYPIS GULIELMI FRY
MDCCCXIV

26.   First Hebrew Bible printed in America, 1814

כהנים
קק
מקוה ישראל

27.   *Habdalah* Cup and Basin for *Kohanim:* Cup presented by
Abraham Mendes Seixas, in 1781; Basin presented by Raphael De
Cordova, in 1816

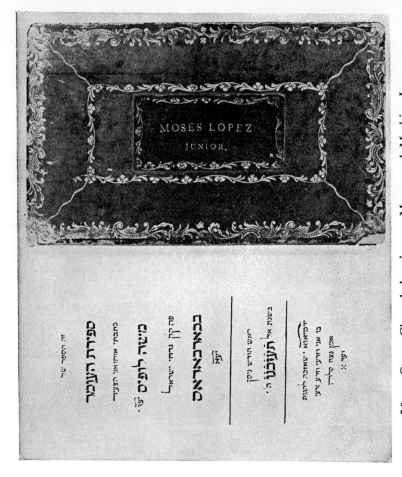

29. *Omer* Chart belonging to Moses and Mathias Lopez

28. The Chair of Elijah

30.   David G. Seixas

Gift of the Author

TALES

3176.

FOR

LEISURE HOURS.

By Jonas B Phillips Esq

Around the cheerful hearth now seat yourselves,
And I will read you tales of love and war;
Of ages past, and days in which we live,
And suited likewise, for the grave and gay.
Good friends, extend to me your kind attention,
I humbly trust they will requite your hearing.
                    Winter Evenings—A Poem.

PHILADELPHIA.
ATKINSON & ALEXANDER, PRINTERS.

1827.

31.   First Work of Fiction published by a Philadelphia Jew

בית הכנסת
לקק"ק מקוה ישראל
יעא"
בשנת התקמ"ב
בנין חדש לבדיקה הבית
בשנת התקפ"ב

Founded A.M. 5542, 6 year of the
Independence of the U. S. of America
Enlarged and Rebuilt A.M. 5583

32.   Cornerstone of the Second Mikveh Israel Synagogue

33. Second Synagogue of Mikveh Israel

a non-Jew could share in the honors and privileges of the synagogue, and any member, who after that time did so, would forfeit his membership.[104] In a most unusual provision in the agreement by which Dropsie was given special status, it was agreed
that his son should be given no religious education until he was
old enough to make his own choice.

There is no exact record of the number of Jews who continued to act contrary to religious law, but the newspapers of
the period announced mixed marriages with significant frequency,[105] a goodly number of them performed by Christian
clergymen who apparently did not insist upon premarital baptism. In the face of this apparently irresistible trend and after
much bitter debate within the congregations, Mikveh Israel
modified its approach,[106] and Rodeph Shalom withdrew its punitive provision three years after it had been introduced, and ruled
that if members raised their children as Jews they were not to
be expelled.[107] The effect that this leniency had was more evident
after 1830, when applications increased for the circumcision of
boys and the ritual immersion of girls who were the children of
mixed marriages.

In addition to the difficulties within the fold, there appeared
on the scene what loomed as a very serious threat to the Jewish
community from without. Converted Jews in the role of missionaries were not new. The Reverend Charles Crawford made brief
reference to one, whose name is not known, in the late eighteenth
century:

Some of the Jews scattered through the world are of the opinion that some
of the Indians are the descendants of the ten tribes. There was a learned Jew,
the son of a Jewish Rabbi, or a Rabbi himself, who was converted to Christianity, and who preached with some applause in various parts of Great-
Britain, sometime before the year 1787. About this time he came over to
Philadelphia, where the religious people were considerably struck with the
decency of his behaviour. He said that many of the Indians in America were
the descendants of the ten tribes. He said his design was to go and live among
them (he went first among the Chickasaws I believe) to learn their language,
that he might teach them the Gospel, and proceed with them in person to
Jerusalem; . . . He died a natural death, it is supposed some little time after
being among the Indians.[107a]

Of course, this man affected the Jews of Philadelphia not at all,
but in 1823 the Philadelphia branch of the American Society for
Meliorating the Condition of the Jews was established,[108] thus
bringing into the city a militant missionary organization which

had been founded in England and brought to America by an apostate German Jew, Joseph S. C. F. Frey. In spite of its rather innocuous-sounding name, the organization's prime objective was the conversion of Jews to Christianity. But, while the Reverend Dr. Frey, stopping in Philadelphia on his tour from Maine to Georgia, inveighed against "the present degraded state of Jewesses" as compared to those of the Bible,[109] it was chiefly Protestants who came to hear him and not, as he had hoped, Jews. However, in that day of evangelical movements the Society made a considerable stir in the community. Christians were exhorted to join this cause and did; Jews were fearful lest the propaganda which was arousing missionary zeal among their neighbors might also arouse prejudices of a less pious nature.

This possibility did not escape "An Episcopalian," who vehemently criticized the supporters of the Society in the *Philadelphia Gazette* of March 18, 1824:

> In a country such as ours, where political and religious liberty are not only established, but identified with its existence, one might be led to suppose, that not a vestige of intolerance and fanaticism could be found; since their votaries can promise themselves no rewards either in church or state for their "labors of love"—yet sorry I am to say that this is not wholly the case.
>
> I have been led into these remarks from having heard it gravely announced from the pulpit of one of our churches, that a meeting of the Ladies' Society for converting the Jews was to be held, &c. A *what*, asked I of myself—a meeting of the Ladies' Society for converting the Jews? How in the name of all that's reasonable, and in what manner are the Ladies to convert them? . . .
>
> Permit me here to ask, what means are to be used by those Ladies towards the attainment of their object? Are they merely to be a contributing or collecting Society, to raise a fund to pay Missionaries to convert the Jews abroad? If this be all I am content, for that is quite innocent, and simple; it has been often tried and has done very little harm—But if this Society has resolved itself into an association for the conversion of our citizen Jews, then here is the serpent's sting, here is the *intolerance* which I deprecate, and here is an insult offered to a respectable part of the community. What, let me ask, would Episcopalians think and feel should a society be established amongst the Quakers or Friends, whose object was to induce them to lay aside their Liturgy and no longer use 'vain repetitions but to worship in spirit and truth' . . .[110]

After some years of much smoke but little fire, the Society, having failed to convert any but a single Jew here and there, died out. But it had a constructive effect on the Jewish community. Like many other malevolent forces arrayed against them, the Society brought to the Jews a renewed consciousness and pride in their Judaism. It brought forth the establishment of the first American Jewish periodical in New York, which was published by Solomon Jackson to answer the charges of conversionist literature.[111] American Jews began to read more extensively about Judaism, and to write about it. In Philadelphia, the latent threat of the Society brought about an increased concern with Jewish charities, and particularly with Jewish education, which men like Carvalho and Keys had tried to promote in their congregation with comparatively little success.

13

The Religious Functionaries and the Religious Practices of the Community

IN the 1798 constitution of Mikveh Israel the positions of *hazan, rabbi, shohet* and *shamash* were specifically mentioned,[1] for these were the posts which were necessary for the religious life of an organized community. The *hazan* was the chief religious leader, who acted as reader at services, conducted weddings and funerals and was recognized by the non-Jewish community as the "minister" of the synagogue. The *rabbi*, not necessarily the same person, was the teacher of the young; the *shohet*, the ritual slaughterer who supplied the community with *kosher* meat and fowl; and the *shamash*, the caretaker of the synagogue and its ritual objects, and a general factotum. For some years before 1800 the first three offices were combined in the person of Jacob Raphael Cohen, aided by his son Abraham Haim.

His rapport with the *adjunta* was of the utmost importance, for the *parnass*, with his governing associates, controlled the *hazan's* activities beyond the mechanical performance of his duties. The board had the final word which allowed or forbade the *hazan* to perform a marriage, accept a convert, conduct a funeral, oversee *shehita*, or act as *mashgiah*, or inspector of the preparation of *matzoth*. This control reflected the autocratic pattern of the Sephardic congregations of London and Amsterdam, but in America it was gradually relaxed.

The board found it a comparatively simple solution for the *hazan* to fill the first three posts when possible. The congregation during this period of transition, from the adoption of the constitution to the War of 1812, was not in a position to afford separate and additional employees. This was the period of Cohen's service in Philadelphia. He does not appear to have been a scholar, but rather a simple man devoted to the obligation of being Jewish. He was meticulous in synagogal administration, and kept complete records of all the marriages, circumcisions deaths and memorial prayers which he conducted from the time of his English residence in 1776 until his death, providing thereby a rich statistical portrait of the Jewish community to which he ministered. He held no contract at Mikveh Israel, and his salary was dependent, not on the treasury, but on a regularly raised subscription fund.[2] The responsibility for slaughtering meat according to ritual was his without additional compensation. Starting much lower, his annual salary reached a high of $400,[3] about half of Seixas' in New York,[4] and Cohen had to make frequent requests to be paid on time.

In 1800 Cohen requested a leave of absence to go to Easton to stay with his daughter because of ill health.[5] During his absence another *shohet* was temporarily appointed, and his pay was deducted from the *hazan's* salary. "My present emoluments are so small that they will admit of no deduction," Cohen rather pathetically wrote the congregation, "Therefore I will during my inability appoint a proper Person with your permission to kill for the Congregation."[6] That person was, of course, his son who was fully equipped, so far as training was concerned, to do the work. It was not an uncommon practice to keep such duties within a family, both for convenience as well as for financial reasons.

Both father and son were also the first Hebrew educators under the new government. They provided the basic elements of prayer-book Hebrew for the children of the congregants[7] and the son, from 1790 on, taught Spanish and Hebrew professionally to those who wanted special tutorial guidance.[8] This combination of work, carried on by the father-and-son team, was not a fully satisfactory situation. Cohen needed more money to support his family, but the congregation was reluctant to increase his meager salary, because its resources were still limited. When Cohen threatened to resign, he was persuaded to remain on in his dual capacity as *hazan-shohet*.[9] But by 1804 Cohen's health was so impaired that it was difficult for him to handle the large animals required for beef and veal, and, when the subscription funds did not permit his salary being paid on time, he advised the congregation that he would be compelled to stop slaughtering after the High Holy days.[10]

It was at this time, or perhaps a bit earlier, when there was some question of Cohen's carrying on as *shohet*, that he entered into a verbal agreement with the *parnass*, Isaac Pesoa, which was written down in the form of an unsigned contract. According to it, the congregation was to pay Cohen $250 a year, for which he would carry out the following duties:

. . . that he doth appear in a *Decent* & Suitable manner in the Shool evry friday afternoon & in a Devote Manner read the Prayers Suited to the Occasion with, or without *Minian*.

that he doth appear in like Manner at a Suitable hour evry Shabas Morning & perform the Service of the day with, or without Minian—without *hurrying* over the Service or Parasah, & fully impressed with the Dutys of his *Sacred* & holy office—That evry Roshodesh & holidays the Shool to be opened & Service in the like Manner performed, That the Shool shall be opened evry Saturday afternoon & evening & service performed with or without Minian—

that the Hazan when requested shall attend & say prayers for the Sick without fee or reward except at the Optian of any Individual. that he also attends Funerals & Berits in like Manner when requested, that he also attends & performs Service for those who may have Yortside (when intitled to the Same) & that he also Attends at the houses of those who may have occasion to keep Shiva (or 7 Days). that he will not during the present term of this Engagement kill any Beast or Beasts or in any Way act as *Shochet* or interfere with that business; that for evry five Kegs of Beef or less Quantity put up for Exportation he shall be Intitled to 50/100 for such Certificate requisite & for any quantity above 5 Kegs he shall receive 1$—

that he doth attend & have or cause the Lamp *Always* and the Candles occasionally lighted in the Shool & the same kept constantly cleaned fire made in the Stove in the inclement Season when fuel shall be in Store for such purpose & the lights otherways attended to & that the Windows & doors shall be *nightly* secured the Achol locked & the Key thereof kept by him & in evry respect the Shool to be kept Clean & in *Decent* order & as further compensation for such services he (the said Parnass) in behalf of the Congregation promises that he shall live in the house he now occupies free from rent charge Tax or Duty & that he shall also be allowed 10 Dollars for Wood & 10 Dolls for Matzas during said Year, . . .[11]

The relinquishment by Cohen of the work of a *shohet* was an emergency for the congregation, and Simon Gratz was authorized to procure a new slaughterer for the Jews of Philadelphia.[12] Aaron Levy of New York's Shearith Israel, to whom he turned, recommended Isaac Lazarus, "a perfect stranger in this place, and without any money in his pocket," but with a certificate of his ability to perform *shehita* granted to him in Europe.[13] Levy had had him examined in his craft by the New York *shohet* and by Jacob Hart, "an old and respectable member of our society,"[14] and had his certificate scrutinized by Gershom Seixas' son-in-law, Israel Baer Kursheedt, who reported that it was a good one and that he knew "the signature to be from a respectable person." When he arrived, Gratz himself examined the applicant, but there was at first trouble because Cohen refused to deliver up the ritual knives and punches which were the congregation's property.[15] That was straightened out,[16] and Lazarus was finally hired.

The new *shohet* did not long fill the post. In July, 1805, he informed the *adjunta* that he would leave unless he were paid $300 a year;[17] he left. Again the problem of finding a replacement was in the laps of the officers,[18] and once again they turned to Jacob Cohen, who told them he would continue to work as *hazan* and *shohet*, if the congregation would pay him $400 a year together with the perquisites of fire-wood and *matzoth*, or as *hazan* alone for $250.[19] Benjamin Nones and Moses Nathans convinced the aging minister that $300 was fair, and, again "in consideration of a number of members who would not eat of any other meat but that of his killing," he accepted.[20] Once more he found himself unable physically to carry on,[21] and once more in 1807 Lazarus was hired under a formal agreement by which he was paid $200 and was to take orders from no one but the *parnass*.[22] Apparently, one of the problems was that there were too many persons who considered themselves a better authority on *shehita* than the *shohet*.

In September, 1811, Jacob Raphael Cohen died. His temporary successor was his son, who accepted the post until a permanent *hazan* could be obtained.[23] The younger Cohen made his offer as a measure of thanks to the synagogue for granting a continuation of his father's salary to his widowed mother and for extending to them the privilege of living rent-free in the house provided for the *hazan*. The temporary arrangement met the needs of the congregation, but, in spite of Cohen's request that they provide themselves with a *hazan* "as early as possible,[24] it soon assumed a permanent character. Abraham H. Cohen, who was performing his services with the same dignity as had his father, in the course of time asked that he be recognized as *hazan* and not as a mere factotum. He requested a salary of $600, since, as he put it, the necessity of engaging in other pursuits to supplement his income would detract from the dignity of his religious office.[25]

He rejected a counter-offer, but his decision to resign in 1815 seems to have been influenced as well by what he considered a personal slight.[26] The synagogue, out of respect for the late *hazan*, had permitted Abraham Cohen to give his father precedence in the order of the *hashkaboth*, or memorial prayers for the illustrious dead, which were recited at the beginning of every month. After three years there was a revision in the form of the service, changing the order and the frequency of the recitation. Considering it to be an act of disrespect towards the memory of his father, Cohen had refused to officiate until the right of making the monthly *hashkaba* was restored.[27] The *adjunta* took his request seriously, but not personally, and requested an expression of opinion from the aging Gershom Mendes Seixas. The wise elder did not perhaps wish to enter in the middle of a quarrel, and he sent an incomplete *responsum* to the effect that with the coming holiday

let it suffice to say that the ensuing Ros Hodes [new month], is absorbed in Rosh Hashana [new year]—consequently, we, in New York, do not make the Ascabot, usually said on Rosh Hashana.[28]

He promised a fuller review of the case, which because of his failing health was never sent, but referred the congregation for guidance to the *Ascamoth*, or synagogal rules, which he had drawn up during his ministry in Philadelphia. Cohen was not satisfied with the decision or the salary offered him, and so brought to an end his voluntary career as a functionary of Mikveh Israel. The impact of this minor difference resulted in two divergent changes; the number of *hashkaboth* was reduced,[29] and an increase in salary was projected for future *hazanim*.[30]

Meanwhile, Cohen's brother-in-law, Abraham Forst,[31] became the official *shohet*. However, the same trouble which had produced difficulties before continued to do so. Forst, as his work increased with the increase in the size of the community, in 1813 applied for a raise,[32] and pointed out the way in which the additional money could be obtained.

I would mention that could any means be adopted to oblige the German congregation to contribute towards supporting the supply of the meat of which they partake (and frequently to the inconvenience of the members of ours) it would be but justice.[33]

The German congregation had been dependent on Mikveh Israel in many ways, but it was not yet in any position to assume communal financial responsibilities. Nothing came of Forst's suggestion, although later joint control of *shehita* was established.

In 1824, when Joel Angell offered his services as *shohet* to Rodeph Shalom in hopes of serving both congregations, a *Beth Din* of three, consisting of Simon Gratz and Isaac Phillips for Mikveh Israel and Wolf Benjamin for Rodeph Shalom, examined him.[34] Service to both congregations had been given from the beginning by Jacob Cohen's successor as *mohel* for the community, Alexander Wertheim, originally from Holland and lately of Baltimore.[35] A competent circumciser, he worked faithfully in the city until his sudden death in 1830.

After Abraham H. Cohen left its service, Mikveh Israel decided that Emanuel Nunes Carvalho was the man who would best suit them.[36] Carvalho, originally from London, had had seventeen years of experience in three congregations. He had served Congregation Nidche Israel of Barbados from 1799 to 1808, when his erratic conduct as a pedagogue compelled him to leave for the United States.[37] For the next three years he had taught at New York Polonies Talmud Torah, and earned a considerable reputation as an educator.[38] From there he was called to act as *hazan* for the distinguished old Congregation Beth Elohim of Charleston, and during his three-and-a-half years' tenure of that post he brought his abilities to bear chiefly in teaching the children and establishing decorum in the services.[39] However, he did get in trouble with the congregation on one occasion, when he refused to do the bidding of the *adjunta*. They suspended him, and according to Mordecai Manuel Noah, who was in Charleston at the time, Carvalho

. . . collected a rabble composed of all the vagrant Jews & had a petition signed by them to give him redress, this petition was handed the Parnass who could not act upon it being in express violation to the constitution. Mr. Carvalho in person aided and abetted the confusion and riot which took place in a short time, the whole meeting parnass & all were battling with clubs & bruising boxing etc. during which his reverence & brother & friend Lipman came off with a few thumps . . .[40]

It was a temperamental but gifted man who came to Philadelphia to accept a temporary appointment in October, 1815. He must have already started work on his *Key to the Hebrew Tongue*, which was published here that year for the use of his pupils in Philadelphia,[41] the first Hebrew grammar written by a professing American Jew. It should also be noted that Carvalho's sermon on the death of Gershon Mendes Seixas in 1816 was the first one known to have been delivered in a Philadelphia synagogue, and definitely the first to have been printed.[42]

He adapted himself quickly to a form of service which differed only slightly from that to which he had been accustomed in Barbados and Charleston. And soon his zeal as an educator made itself evident, when he suggested "the teaching gratis any children of indigent parents, belonging to the congregation."[43] In the spring of 1816 Carvalho received an appointment for five years,[44] and in the fall an increase in salary from $800, which had been first agreed upon, to $1000, the increase to compensate for the fact that the *hazan's* house was in a state of disrepair.[45]

The prestige of his previous experience enabled him to obtain a contract which Jacob Cohen had never been granted, and a salary more than double that of Cohen or his son, without the performance of *shehita*. The position of *hazan* was beginning, both financially and so far as respect for the office was concerned, to assume the status of that of a Christian minister.

Unfortunately, almost as soon as the synagogue was again operating smoothly the sickly Carvalho died.[46] His death was a severe loss to Philadelphia Jewry, for he had brought to the city the kind of Jewish learning which had become rare in this country and was not easily replaced. From 1817 to 1824 Mikveh Israel struggled on with acting readers. They disregarded such unsolicited applications as that of Moses Haim Morpurgo[47] and the anonymous J.M.S., who sang his own qualifications as reader, circumciser, and blower of the *shofar*, in a Hebrew acrostic poem.[48] And again letters were sent to various congregations elsewhere seeking help in finding a man for the office. This time Mikveh Israel found itself competing with Shearith Israel, for in 1816, during Carvalho's incumbency in Philadelphia, Gershom Seixas had died in New York. Shearith Israel was also sending letters about the country hoping to attract an eligible *hazan*.[49] The problem was no different and the appeal no less urgent in Charleston,[50] Savannah or Richmond.

From the time that Moses L. M. Peixotto gave up mercantile pursuits to become Seixas' successor in New York until the arrival there of Jacques Judah Lyons, Shearith Israel was served by a succession of *hazanim*.[51] Mikveh Israel's similar experience, until the arrival of Isaac Leeser in 1829, was typical of that of other American congregations. Abraham H. Cohen served once again on a temporary basis,[52] and part of the interim period in Philadelphia was filled with men who were competent readers, like Hartwig Cohen of Charleston[53] and Jacob Bensadon,[54] but not men of great learning or wide experience. For the High Holy days Isaac B. Seixas[55] and Eleazar S. Lazarus[56] came from New York to assist in the services, and both of them were offered a permanent appointment. Seixas, who had been ministering in Richmond, was described as one who "does not possess a Grammatical Knowledge of the Hebrew language," but this lack was not apparently considered a major shortcoming by old Jacob Mordecai, a professional educator and competent Hebraist, who further wrote, "We should relinquish this gentleman with much regret, indeed were we deprived of his services, our synagogue must be closed."[57]

The difficulty was not that the congregations wanted a man of great learning, but that they could not find even qualified readers willing to serve for the modest pay given to *hazanim*. The shortage was national.

Meanwhile the membership of Mikveh Israel kept increasing, and—with its uphills and downhills—so did that of its sister German congregation, still too poor to be concerned with a pretentious choice. For years they had had their services conducted by lay readers, much in the same manner that Mikveh Israel had done in colonial days. Mayer Ullman, who helped prepare the by-laws of 1810 which made no provision for a paid *hazan*, was the first known *baal tefilla*, or leader of the services.[58] In 1818 Abraham Levy stipulated in his membership application that he would join only with the understanding that he would conduct the services on Sabbath and holidays.[59]

One year later, Levi Ancker made the serious proposal that a regularly paid reader be obtained for the congregation, and a subscription for his maintenance be started.[60] The first *hazan* of Rodeph Shalom was another arrival from Charleston, Rabbi Jacob Lippman.[61] Of course, it was not expected that he would serve the congregation full-time, for it could only pay him an annual salary of $50, so Lippman kept a second-hand clothing store on the south side of South Street and further added to his income by acting as *mohel* when Dr. Alexander Wertheim was unavailable.[62] He also acted as *shohet* for the German congregation, and in 1822 charges were brought against him for not being qualified for that work, which, after due and proper investigation by "competent gentlemen" acting as a *Beth Din,* were found to be unjust.[63]

Services could go on with lay readers, but the whole religious life of the community depended upon an adequate supply of ritually clean meat. It must be realized that at this time the observance of *kashruth* was not merely a matter of conscience; it was an accepted and very important part of the daily life of the Jews of Philadelphia. Consequently, it loomed large on the community's horizon. The *shohet* did not work alone, but on the spot with the butchers, like John Hentz, George Waltman, and Samuel Runner, who supplied the animals, served as assistants in the slaughtering, and sold the properly stamped meat to Jewish customers.[64] Arrangements for a meat supply at established prices had been in effect with local butchers for many years. Zalegman Phillips told Daniel Solis in 1832 when his contract as *shohet* was renewed,

As to the prices that is a matter you must regulate yourself with the butchers but it is due to the Congregation to say that they must not suffer by your asking more than the butchers were accustomed to give your predecessors.[65]

The *shohet* was instructed to be present at all times with the butchers until the meat was punched and sealed, and doubts or complaints about the thoroughness of his work laid him open to an examination of his character and conduct. An anonymous complainant in 1822 told *Parnass* Zalegman Phillips that gossip which he had just heard in New York about the habits of Forst made him blush and shudder. It was reported, he wrote, that Forst was too weak, and, because of the "stimulus of Ardent Liquors," unfit to do proper justice to the office.[66] A formal investigation of the charges found there was no evidence to support them.

In 1830, when Daniel Solis became the congregational *shohet,* Phillips made a careful investigation before permitting him to enter upon his work. Although Solis had been examined in New York only fifteen months before, Phillips sent him back to his brother Naphtali, then *parnass* of Shearith Israel, asking that he be re-examined, since he had never slaughtered for a community before.[67] A New York committee, consisting of Joseph B. Seixas, Joseph Samuels and Phillips, returned a certificate that they had examined Solis "on the knife & in the dinim relative to the Scheta & Bedeka, & find him perfect therein," but they warned that, since he was a young man, he should frequently review the *dinim*, or laws.[68] They did not apparently know that the law expected such a review to take place regularly.

The seven years between the death of Carvalho and the arrival of Abraham Israel Keys was not a period of dormancy in the congregation. No sooner had Carvalho died than the first plans for a new synagogue were spoken of, and by 1818 a subscription list was in active circulation.[69] As the imposing structure approached completion, it became a matter of pride to have a regular, qualified *hazan* to grace it. Again Isaac B. Seixas was offered the position, and he refused it.[70] A little later, Eleazar S. Lazarus of New York, anxious for the honor, also refused the post, because he would not accept a contract "unless it be during good behaviour and with a salary not extravagant but sufficient."[71] During this period in both congregations laymen performed wedding ceremonies, and within two days in December, 1823, Levy Phillips of Mikveh Israel married the "amiable and interesting Miss Rachel Agnes," daughter of Gershom Seixas, to Joseph Jonas of Cincinnati, and Wolf Benjamin of Rodeph Shalom married Anna Marks to Lewis Allen.[72]

Finally and almost desperately, Simon Gratz in June, 1824, wrote a promotional letter to Abraham R. Brandon at Bridgetown, in Barbados, setting forth the great advantages of the city of Philadelphia in general and the position of *hazan* at Mikveh Israel in particular, hoping that his glowing picture would persuade Abraham Israel Keys to come north.

The character you give us of Mr. Keys fully meets our views in that of a *Hazan*, and we hope you will succeed in inducing him to accept the terms which we offer, and that his residence in this Khal will be agreeable and happy to himself and family. You know the character of our people in this City and I believe if he comes he will meet with a brotherly reception. Our City for health and convenience yields to none perhaps in the world, and the price of living most moderate! House rent is low, a very genteel and suitable one for Mr. Key's family, which you state to be small may be had for about Five Hundred Dollars, fuel is greatly reduced in price owing to the great abundance of Stone Coal in the vicinity and which is getting into general use, it sold the last year at $8 pr ton delivered and is expected to be much lower the succeeding years—wood is reduced in price nearly 5 pr bh good oak now at $4 & hickory at 5½ Dolls per Cord—

The Salary of the *Hazan* of this Congregation, One thousand Dollars per Annum—perquisites derived from Matona's, the extent of these must depend always on the *Hazan* himself, if he meets the approbation of the Khal (individually) no doubt, they will be handsome. Those also derived from Marriages and Barits—Medical attention always gratis—teaching the hebrew will most probably yield from Three to five thousand Dollars per annum.—

As in our former letter we stated that the Synagogue was nearly finished, we now have the satisfaction to say that the building is completed, and we are all desirous of having it dedicated at as early a period as possible, and we hope if Mr. Keys accepts the Station that his engagements with your Khal and his other concerns will permit him to reach this place by the next new year . . .[73]

The Cohens would have been amazed to hear how much money could be made in Philadelphia teaching Hebrew; there are no other indications that such a fantastic sum, even by modern standards, could be so earned. It would be charitable to believe that Gratz, accustomed in his business life to dealing with large sums, habitually thought in terms of big business. In any event, Keys accepted the call,[74] and came to Philadelphia with a letter of recommendation from Barbados.[75]

The character and conduct of Keys, who could intone the prayers with dignity and impressiveness, was described in contrasts by Rebecca Gratz in a letter to her brother Benjamin in Kentucky:

I do not believe he is a learned man—nor indeed a very sensible one—but he is a good Hebrew scholar—an excellent Teacher, and a good man, he is moreover very popular with the congregation and reads the prayers in a manner as to make his hearers feel that he understands and is inspired with their solemnity—perhaps his usefulness is not lessened by his diffidence—he is modest and unassuming, which suits the proud, the ignorant & presumptious —these require most reformation and he is so respectable on the Tabah that he gives general satisfaction . . . Mr. K. has had a congreagtion which only required him to perform his shool duties—now that he is among more intelligent people he too will feel the necessity of study—he has a wife and three clever children and when he gets over his West Indian indolence he will shew what he can become—one very important talent he certainly possesses—he is a good Hebrew teacher—yesterday one of his pupils read a bar mitzvah portion very handsomely altho' he had only a few weeks instruction.[76]

Such a man helped contribute to the gradual change that came over the community. Where once it had been difficult to find a *hazan* or a *shohet* who could carry out the ritual duties of his office adequately and without causing too much dissension, it

now became important to secure someone of character and
ability rather than mere technical skill. While the lay leadership
of the synagogue continued to exercise full control over the congregational matters, there was an inclination to seek a clerical
leader who would have greater competency in Judaism as such.
The whole question of the Jewish education of the children of
the city was still handled on an individual tutorial basis, and the
position of rabbinical teacher, mentioned in the constitution of
1798, was never given serious communal attention. Joseph Andrews, who married a daughter of Haym Salomon, knew Hebrew
well and advertised himself as a teacher.[77] And Abraham Eleazer
Israel, for years both the scribe and the *shamash* at Mikveh
Israel, taught from time to time.[78]

The first concrete step taken by either of the synagogues to
provide for general Jewish education was in the autumn of 1824,
when the *adjunta* of Mikveh Israel said they would appoint

a rabbi to the Congregation and allow him such compensation as they shall
think proper for the instruction of every poor Israelite who shall by them be
recommended & he shall teach the Hebrew language grammatically as also
the laws and ceremonies of the Jewish religion, he may also take scholars
on such reasonable terms as he may think proper.[79]

That was a worthy idea, but it was not implemented as it was
framed, for by the next year the *adjunta* declared officially what
had already been the practice, that it was the duty of the *hazan*
to do the teaching. In both congregations, at the end of the first
quarter of the century, most of the time, energy and money of
their members was being devoted to the new buildings that were
being erected or talked of being erected, but both were on the
eve of a greater spiritual growth.

Unfortunately, we have virtually no records of Jewish life or
Jewish practices outside of the synagogue, and even there the
minutes are full of the divergence from the norm rather than of
everyday life. For instance, the only early reference to a *bar
mitzvah* is a brief one, to that of Joseph Gratz. Barnard Gratz in
1798 mentioned in a letter to his nephew Simon that he was
"sinceerly sorry for been Dissoppointed of Injoyment of Jose
bar mitzwa hope he performit well in Reading his parsha."[80]

Rebecca Gratz occasionally in her letters refers to the Passover,
but in a philosophical rather than a descriptive fashion, as to her
brother Benjamin:

... The 10th of April is Passover—would I might expect you to keep it with us, when you went away I did certainly hope to see you at that time—you must at least let me know where you will be at that period—on Thursday next is Purim no longer a mirthful festival with us—it passes away without celebration—but more solemn feasts are more permanently observed. It is difficult to fix a time to be happy and tho' we feel grateful for the deliverance this feast commemorates as nothing is required of us but to be glad and merry, we are not always able to do so.[81]

One rather imagines that in less elegant Jewish homes both Purim and Passover were celebrated more joyously.

In any event, *matzoth*, the main symbol and special food of Passover, was supplied to both rich and poor under the auspices of the synagogue.[82] For years the baking had been done on synagogue premises,[83] but when the old buildings were torn down in 1822, professional, non-Jewish bakers were employed. One such was Bladen's Biscuit Bakery, who prized the business and whose successors in 1834 asked Mikveh Israel for a continuance of its patronage based on the satisfactory performance of previous years.[84] Rodeph Shalom supplemented its synagogue-made *matzoth* with some bought from Thomas Watson.[85] It was not until 1840 that the Jews entered the *matzoth*-baking business commercially in New York,[86] and shortly thereafter that one established himself in Philadelphia.[87] However, during this whole period the Philadelphia congregations sent overseers to the bakeries to be assured that all the proper ritual regulations were being adhered to. There was no law preventing individuals from making their own, and Jacob I. Cohen, who could afford his own special baking utensils, considered them important enough to make special provision for them in his will.[88]

His will, and those of other Jews, usually made mention of the testator's ritual objects. Cohen presented his pentateuchal scroll and a manuscript of the Book of Esther to the Richmond congregation, just as Haym Salomon and Joseph Simon of Lancaster[89] had enriched Mikveh Israel by giving theirs to the Philadelphia congregation. When Congregation Bnai Jeshurun was forming in New York in 1825,[90] Salomon's son Haym M. asked for its return, and thereby precipitated a stir in Philadelphia. The Torah, which he claimed

was lodged in the Philadelphia shule as our property, had in Consequence of being unopened for the long time while the Shule was rebuilding so dimned the Ink of its writing that in many places it has become quite obscure.[91]

Parnass Zalegman Phillips replied that the Torah was "in very good order, is frequently used and requires no alteration and amendment," but that the claim that it was Salomon's property after nearly forty years was "as novel as strange."[92] Salomon asked for an official statement from the *adjunta*, which he got to the effect that the scroll was Philadelphia's.[93]

Salomon took his defeat in very bad grace, and let loose a blast at Mikveh Israel and its members, which, if more than venom, painted a rather dreary picture of religious life there since his father's time.

> ... I need not remind you how indifferent after his death his survivers were in keeping up a regular attendance on the shull. It is well known that for years scarcely a minyon at the proper times of service & many respectable persons were not seen in shule more than once in a year. ... The Lord, I fear is taking his countenance from off us in america—I mean as it regards the govts of the old shules both in New York & Phila so disgusted have numerous true followers of our faith become with the management both temporal and spiritual here that on the Sabbath eve not more than three heads of families are sometimes found to join in prayer with the reader of the old shule on friday night.
>
> It has been stated to me that it is only since the breaking down of the former building with you that the people have renewed their attention to our divine worship in Phila. ... .[94]

Things were really never that bad. There was a strong feeling of loyalty to the congregation even though synagogue attendance may have left much to be desired. When a Torah, the donor of which is not known, was deposited in the *hechal*, or ark, at Mikveh Israel in 1815, a special broadside was printed listing the order of service on the occasion and specifying the Psalms to be sung during the seven circuits around the synagogue.[95] At the end was an anonymous acrostic poem in Hebrew, spelling out the name of the congregation. Others too donated ritual objects. David M. Phillips sent a "Mantle, Cover, & Pharasha for the Seapher."[96] Before Moses Lopez had given the chair for the *Kohanim*, Raphael De Cordova presented a silver basin to be used in the hand-washing ceremony, apologizing that he did not have a ewer to go with it.[97] Michael E. Cohen, the merchant, who was the official *shofar*-blower for several decades, had a new ram's horn fashioned, which he gave when the new building was opened.[98] Alas, poor Rodeph Shalom was concerned, because it was "disrespectful for the Holy of Holies to be covered with a plain curtain," and a special subscription had to be raised to buy a suitably elegant one.[99]

It must have been Mikveh Israel's rich and curious ritual art which Hyman Gratz showed with pride to several Christian ladies whom he brought to the synagogue. At the same time, with a complete disregard for religious conventions, he took a scroll out of the ark and displayed it to the visitors. His influential position as *gabay* did not prevent him from being severely reprimanded by Michael E. Cohen for committing so unforgivable a profanation,[100] but it did protect him from official censure, and no further mention of the incident was made.

No such visitation to the ritual bath is noted, and the scant and occasional references to it hardly present an adequate picture of it. Both congregations officially, if not all their congregants, were concerned with facilities for the ritual cleanliness of the daughters of Israel. When a group of Jews organized Rodeph Shalom, they diverged from the standard pattern of American Jewish life. It was not a cemetery which became their first communal undertaking; it was a ritual bath.[101] The reasons for their haste are speculative, but only a short time earlier that vigorous protestor, Jonas Phillips, threatened to remove his children from the Mikveh Israel *heder*, or school, adjoining the *mikvah* unless the prevailing stench was taken care of.[102]

A regulated water system and adequate sewage disposal did not come to Philadelphia until the construction of the waterworks in Center Square and the laying down of water-pipes after 1800. The Gratzes and Cohens joined with their fellow-citizens to petition for their installation.[103] The *mikvah* may have been easier to keep clean thereafter, but a protest of *Hazan* Cohen was in much the same language as Phillips' earlier one.[104] The troubles continued, and in 1814 a committee was appointed to inquire into the expense of making the needed repairs.[105] Some twenty years later, and perhaps before, conditions were such that the *mikvah* was not used, and the certificate of the conversion of Hannah Johnson states that she "went in the Delaware River and took a Bathing according it's required by the Mosaic Law."[106] For the upkeep of the *mikvah* that Rodeph Shalom rented a nominal charge was made; but the Sephardic congregation recorded no fees for the use of its bath.[107]

If the *mikvah* was considered important to Jewish life, the cemetery, as the gateway to eternity, was even more important.

In Philadelphia, as in many cities and towns across the country, it was the first tangible evidence of a religious community. As noted before, Nathan Levy bought the first Jewish burial ground, in which his child was buried in 1738.[108] Two years later he secured another and larger piece of ground on Spruce Street, and there in 1742 the second Jewish interment took place.[109] After Levy's death, Mathias Bush applied for and received from the Proprietors of Pennsylvania an additional grant in 1765 "for the Jewish nation forever,"[110] and the year after the Battle of Yorktown the lot was further increased by Michael Gratz.[111]

Because the religious organization in the community was until 1782 informal, these various additions to the cemetery were considered by some members of the families which made them to be for individual or family use. However, each application for new ground reflected the organic increase of the Jewish population of the city, and during the colonial period any Jews who died in Philadelphia were buried in the Spruce Street plot. By the end of the Revolution, the burial land was a piece which ran from Eighth to Ninth Street on the north side of Spruce, and northwards from Spruce 130 feet, approximately to where Manning Street is today.

When Mikveh Israel was formally constituted, the *adjunta*, under the authority of the constitution, appointed five trustees— Joseph Simon, Manuel Josephson, Barnard Gratz, Solomon Lyons and Samuel Hays—to hold jurisdiction over the burial ground,[112] but this formality did not clear up the old claims of individual, rather than communal, ownership. In 1791 it became necessary to call upon the dissident David Franks, as the only surviving witness to the original application, to establish the fact that it had been Nathan Levy's intention not only to provide sanctified ground for the burial of his family but also for "the same to be a trust for a burial place for the interment of Hebrews" as such.[113] His attestation related to the conveyance to the synagogue of the land Gratz had bought, with the proviso that a separate Gratz reservation be maintained. It was a strange paradox that the only Jewish witness to establish the synagogue's right to the original land was Franks, whose peculiar fate was to deny him a final resting place in the cemetery.

The daughter of Nathan Levy, long since a resident of Baltimore, returned to Philadelphia in 1793 to make sure that a plot was available for her and her husband in the event of their death. When that was assured her, she intended to release to the synagogue trustees her right to all the other ground remaining from the original grant.[114] Somehow or other the documents containing the Gratz and Levy cessions of ownership were temporarily lost, and the inability of the trustees to produce them led to some bitterness. When Rachel and Benjamin Levy, the daughter and son-in-law of Nathan, died in Baltimore, they were, contrary apparently to their own earlier expectations, buried in an Episcopalian cemetery.[115] And in 1812, three years after Benjamin's death, his daughter Hetty wrote to Simon Gratz requesting that she be reimbursed for the Levy family cemetery rights.[116] Actually, the matter had been settled in principle in 1793, but since the release had not been signed, Hetty Levy placed her claim in the hands of Moses Levy, and threatened suit.[117] Nothing came of the affair, and the matter remained closed.

After the deaths of Michael and Miriam Gratz, resolutions were introduced, in 1813, to establish an exclusive area in the cemetery for the burial of members of the Gratz family in accordance with the earlier proviso.[118] It was not until thirteen years later, however, that a resolution was approved permitting the erection of a physical barrier to complete the separation,[119] thereby setting apart the only family plot in the Spruce Street Cemetery, where in the course of time more than twenty-five members of the Gratz family were buried. It is interesting to note that, under similar circumstances, such requests for exclusiveness after death were not granted by the more aristocratic Shearith Israel, and there are no private reservations to be found in its old Chatham Street Cemetery.[120]

By an act of the legislature in 1828 all the private claims were consolidated, and Mikveh Israel was given full title to the ground.[121] At the same time, the congregation was permitted to rent or sell off any excess land. An unused plot at the corner of Ninth and Spruce was thereafter rented to supplement congregational income.[122] The whole western section from Schell Street to Ninth was sold prior to the Civil War to the Society of Friends,[123] and the eastern part went to the Pennsylvania Hospital, which erected on it the Lying-In Hospital. Today, the oldest Jewish landmark in Philadelphia runs north and south from Manning to Spruce, and east and west from Darien to Schell.

Of course, all matters respecting the management of the cemetery lay in the hands of Mikveh Israel, but an unofficial *hebra*, or burial society, composed of *adjunta* members,[124] occasionally referred to before 1800, oversaw all funeral arrangements, *tahara*, or the ritual preparation of the corpse, burial and the allotment of graves. It was this group which decided who might be buried and where.

In 1789 a small house was erected on the grounds, where the *tahara* took place, and in 1814 a more permanent structure was built.[125] After the funeral ceremony, the house was used by a "watcher" who stood guard, according to congregational rules, to prevent vandalism or body-snatching.[126] This watch was maintained two nights in the winter and three in the summer. The practice—perhaps because of the propinquity of the Pennsylvania Hospital—began in Philadelphia earlier than in New York, where it was not until 1845 that a professional "watcher" was hired after an outbreak of vandalism[127] which never seems to have occurred on Spruce Street, possibly because of the precautions. There are records of the removal of the remains of one family for burial elsewhere, which must have been performed in accordance with Jewish practice, which permits disinterment only in unusual circumstances.[128]

The rules which governed burial privileges were carefully observed. Suicides were relegated to a section near the fence, but there is the record of only one such case prior to 1830, which is as well the only early instance of a post-mortem performed on the body of a Jew.[129] Those who intermarried, or did not marry according to Jewish law, or never went to synagogue, were either interred at the fringe of the holy congregation of the dead,[130] or were refused burial anywhere within the sacred confines. The request of a mother to bury her son, the child of a mixed marriage, was turned down,[131] but such rejections were not frequent. There is the curious story of a Negress, who had worked for the Marks family and who had scrupulously observed Jewish rites and Jewish holidays. When she died her employer asked permission to have her buried in the Spruce Street Cemetery. The request was understandably refused; but, it is told, that nonetheless Marks and a few friends broke into the graveyard and buried her there near the gate.[132] The poor, newcomers and transients of the Jewish faith were never sent to the unhallowed ground of Potter's Field. Impoverished members of the congregation or those without kin were regularly buried at the expense of the synagogue.

All graves at Spruce Street were supposed to have been marked, but many of the Jews of the city were unable to afford a lasting tombstone, and hence nothing remains to tell where they were buried except the carefully kept records of Mikveh Israel. Some gravestones—a few of marble—have survived of the more affluent, with inscriptions in English, Hebrew, French, Spanish and Portuguese. Two *hazanim*, Keys and Carvalho, were honored by having their tombstones erected and paid for by the congregation.[133] Today, those marbles and the remaining stones lie row on row under the trees which during the years grew up in the plot.

The appearance of the cemetery underwent several changes in the course of years. Originally fenced in by boards, a low brick wall was erected in 1751 to keep out vandals.[134] There is an account by an eye-witness that the British executed army deserters against this wall when they occupied the city in 1777.[135] In 1803 a new and higher wall replaced the one of colonial brick.[136] Wrought iron gates were added, and a sandstone marker erected telling of the cemetery's origin. So it appears today.

William J. Duane remembered a story about it, which must have taken place in the 1820s. In his collection of anecdotes, he wrote the following:

Dr. Chapman and some friends were passing up Spruce Street near the Jewish cemetery, when they observed a light under the gate. "I wonder what that light is," said one. "An Israel-light," said the Dr.[137]

In 1801, the second Jewish cemetery in the city came into existence,[138] when the Jews of Rodeph Shalom decided that they wanted their own burial place as well as their own kind of service. Very little is known of this Kensington plot, but the records of the congregation show that—of course, without the title difficulties encountered on Spruce Street—the general rules and regulations governing its use were the same in both congregations, and the Jewish burial laws and traditions were zealously guarded. Like the Blockley Cemetery of the Society of Friends,[139] that of Rodeph Shalom was in the suburbs, and hence exposed to casual vandalism.

Ten years after its founding a fence was built to keep out

desecrators,[140] but the Jews found that cemeteries in outlying sections were subject to all kinds of indignities. Sagging wooden fences were not much protection. Neglect, pillage and desecration continued and grew worse, when after thirty years the congregation bought a new burial ground in the Jacksonville section. A committee in 1850 reported on the "most deplorable situation" which they found in Kensington, noting particularly that hogs had forced their way in among the receding mounds and pushed over weakened tombstones.[141] The committee commented also that the burying ground in Jacksonville was rapidly deteriorating too. Exactly what was done is not known, and the first Ashkenazic cemetery seems to have disappeared and been forgotten.

~e 14

The First Communal Philanthropic Organizations

THE tendency of immigrants in a new land to look for help from others who had come from the same country is as old as human nature. Amid strange surroundings one seeks the comfort of the familiar. In British America during the eighteenth century, when a frontier land was being populated by immigrants, this understandable desire of men to seek out and live with others of the same cultural and linguistic background helped shape the colonies. Benjamin Franklin at midcentury was worried because the Germans were clustering together in Pennsylvania, speaking their own language, following their own customs, and shunning the Anglo-Saxon culture of the majority.[1] Yet, it was inevitable that such cultural pluralism should exist. Newcomers and foreigners not only had deep emotional ties which bound them to the ways of their fathers, but they needed guidance in establishing themselves, and then the assurance that understanding friends would help them in the times of emergency. It was to their own people that they turned.

The early congregations of the country, from the time that the Jews of New Amsterdam were permitted to remain, provided that their poor should never become public charges,[2] had taken care of their co-religionists from the *tsedaka* fund. And in Philadelphia a special synagogal charity, the Ezrath Orechim, had been created to help immigrants and transients. That pattern of help was not new in Philadelphia. In 1748 the Scots of the city, "meeting frequently with our Country People here in Distress, more especially Travellers, and transient Persons, who are not entitled to the publick Charity," had formed the St. Andrew's Society for mutual aid.[3] Scotsmen or the descendants of Scotsmen were eligible for membership. They contributed an initiation fee and annual dues, which were to be used for the relief of impoverished members or fellow-Scots.

In 1772 a group of Englishmen organized the Society of the Sons of St. George, for the same purposes and in the same manner. However, the preamble to its constitution explained the distinctively American motivation behind its formation:

National *Attachments* and *Prejudices* are for the most Part idle and unnecessary; and when they operate so far, as to make us injure or despise Persons born in a different Country from ourselves, they are indeed very reprehensible. But although national Distinction should on most Occasions be avoided, yet the Necessity of forming the present Society is *one Proof,* that on *some* Occasions it may answer the best Purposes.

. . . And this, not for the Purposes of keeping alive any inviduous *national Distinctions,* which ought particularly to be avoided between the different Nations which compose the British State of America, where all the Freemen (from wheresoever they originally migrated) are Brethren, Friends and Countrymen, but merely that unfortunate Englishmen, and especially those who are strangers in America, may know where to apply for Countenance and Assistance.[4]

This too was a mutual-aid society, which contemplated "that any member of this Society may at some future period (however flourishing or easy his present situation in life) be plunged into distress by unavoidable accidental misfortune."[5] Very modern in philosophy seems the provision in the 1840 *Rules* that the managers of the society should not give charity to any persons receiving public poor relief, "unless such relief shall appear to them insufficient."[6]

It is interesting that, although only one Jew was a member of the New York St. George Society,[7] in Philadelphia there were at least ten.[8] Abraham Lindo,[9] who may have been a relative of the Charleston indigo expert, and Joseph Ricardo,[10] who may have been connected in some way with the great British economist, both joined in 1792. During the early years of the next century five of the Moss family became members—John,[11] Samuel,[12] Jacob,[13] Joseph L.[14] and Joseph Moravia[15]—and three other Jews as well, John Moss' son-in-law Isaac B. Phillips,[16] Lyon J. Levy,[17] and Rodeph Shalom's religious leader, Wolf Benjamin.[18] John Moss was one of the group who signed the charter of the society in 1813 when it was incorporated by the state, and for four years he served as a steward. His son, Joseph L. Moss, succeeded him in 1830, and in 1839 the then prominent merchant, Lyon J. Levy, was also placed on the board. Similar in purpose and organization was a French Benevolent Society of which Benjamin Nones was on the steering committee in 1793.[19]

The first Jewish mutual-aid society differed somewhat from these others. Assurance of a Jewish burial with Jewish rites had been a primary concern of Jews for thousands of years. It was to provide for this—financially and religiously—that the *hebra kadisha*, or burial society, had been formed in the Jewish communities of Europe, and as an institution it was several centuries old by the eighteenth century.[20] In America it grew up within the synagogue, and, although by 1785 there was a distinct, functioning Hebra Gemilut Hasadim at Shearith Israel in New York,[21] in Philadelphia the functions of such a society—praying by the side of the corpse, preparations for burial, the funeral itself, and the *minyan* of mourners after it—remained in the hands of the congregation's *adjunta*, who also acted as overseers of the cemetery. The first three constitutions of Mikveh Israel do not suggest an independent society, its responsibilities being understood to be those of the congregation as a whole.

The 1810 constitution of Rodeph Shalom, however, speaks clearly of some of the functions later assumed by a society for the visitation of the sick and a burial society. Article 15 provided that, when a report was received that a member of the congregation was sick, "the Presiding Officers or Junto shall draft two of the members, whose duty it shall be to sit up and attend such sick members all night."[22] Article 16 ordered that two members of the congregation should be sent to bring back the body of any member who died not further than eighty miles from the city.[23] Actually, in 1809 Benjamin Levy, the brother of Aaron Levy, Jr., had died "among the Goyim, 100 miles from here," and his brother had had the body exhumed and reburied in the cemetery of Rodeph Shalom.[24] Finally, article 17 stated that no more than one dollar should be charged to any member or subscriber for a burial plot.[25]

The transition from an accepted synagogal responsibility to a burial society to a mutual-aid society was one of normal growth. By the time the first separate *hebra* was formed in 1813, there were about twenty self-help societies in town. Even a formal Negro organization, the Friendly Society of St. Thomas' African Church, had preceded it.[26] A small number of synagogued Jews had become active in some of these other groups. John Moss, as we have seen, was active in the Society of the Sons of St. George, and in 1796 Naphtali Phillips served as secretary of The Philadelphia Society for the Information and Assistance of Persons Emigrating from Foreign Countries.[27] As the societies grew they influenced each other. Most of the non-Jewish societies assisted their members "in distress," provided for their widows and orphans, and in special cases gave help to non-members of the same national origin. The Jews had much the same objects in mind.

When the Hebra Shel Bikur Holim Ugemilut Hasadim, or Society for the Visitation of the Sick and Mutual Assistance, was organized in 1813,[28] it was the first extra-synagogal Jewish organization to appear on the Philadelphia scene. It grew out of Mikveh Israel; its first members were all members of that congregation; and it did request the sanction of the synagogue and permission to raise funds at services, which were unhesitatingly given.[29] But it functioned separately with its own officers and its own treasury. To join, one had to belong to Mikveh Israel, and if a member of the *hebra* joined another congregation he lost his membership in the society.[30] This provision was changed in 1820, realistically, in accordance with the rapidly changing make-up of the Jewish community[31] to permit non-members of Mikveh Israel to join. Any member marrying contrary to Jewish laws or acting immorally was subject to expulsion.[32] Applicants had to be twenty-one years of age, an indication that American, rather than religious, standards of maturity prevailed.[33] However, in accordance with actuarial logic, an applicant for membership who was over sixty had to pay a life subscription of $30 in three annual installments, and he was then entitled to full benefits, but was excused from the required watch with the sick or the dead.[34]

Two dollars was the regular entrance fee, and the monthly dues were twenty-five cents.[35] Nothing was to be paid out until the capital of the society reached the sum of $200,[36] and it was to be maintained at that figure. This was increased to $400 in 1824.[37] No member was compelled to watch over another who was ill with a contagious disease. Such patients were provided with a professional nurse, as in the case of Jacob Bensadon who was cared for at $8.25 a week by Lyon Jacobson.[38] Sick strangers could be granted aid up to the sum of five dollars, and more if the officers so decided.[39] In 1821 Jacob Simpson was given the lump sum of $25.[40]

A whole series of fines was set up, as in most early institutions, Jewish and non-Jewish alike, ranging from $5 for refusing to serve as president to twenty-five cents for being absent from a meeting, for not attending a fellow-member's funeral, or for not participating in a *minyan*.[41] However, *Kohanim* were to be relieved from attendance with the sick at the first sign of approaching death, for it was contrary to religious law for a member of a priestly family to be in the presence of a corpse.[42]

The benefits were many. A member confined to his house by an illness certified to by a physician received $5 a week for four weeks if he had a family, and $3 if he did not, and thereafter he would get whatever—not to exceed $5—the officers might decide. The widow of a deceased member received $25, and another $20 for funeral expenses. Should a man die and leave children but no widow, relief up to $25 could be granted at the discretion of the officers. Any member was entitled to get $10 for the funeral expenses of any member of his family.[43] In the case of the death of a member or one of his family, the officers of the society were required to provide a watch until the funeral, which all the members were expected to attend, in addition to participation in the morning and evening prayers during the period of mourning.[44]

The guiding spirit and the first president of the Society for the Visitation of the Sick and Mutual Assistance was Jacob I. Cohen, who had returned from Richmond to Philadelphia in 1806. The other officers were Isaiah Nathans, Joseph Simon Cohen,[45] Isaac B. Phillips and Aaron Levy, Jr. All these men were at the time members of Mikveh Israel, but it was characteristic of the flow of members from the German congregation that both Nathans and Levy had been among the founders of Rodeph Shalom. Another sign of the mixed nature of the "Portuguese" congregation was the fact that, although all prayers for the sick and the dead were to be conducted according to Sephardic custom, references to memorial anniversaries and the seven-day mourning period were in the Ashkenazic terms of *yahrzeit* and *shiva*.[46] In 1830 the constitution was revised by a committee consisting of Levi M. Goldsmit, Hyman Polock, and Judah L. Hackenburg, but the changes were in details and wording only.[47]

Jacob I. Cohen, after a short term of office, was succeeded in the presidency by Abraham H. Cohen,[48] but it was certainly the old soldier of the Revolution who initiated one of the early suggestions for an action which had nothing to do with the purposes of the organization. In the fall of 1814, towards the end of the War of 1812, the president of the *hebra* was instructed to confer with the *parnass* of the congregation on the possibility of jointly tendering a sum to the committee for the defense of the city.[49] Alas, lack of funds prevented the Jewish institutions from making the patriotic gesture. The only request for aid which the *hebra* seems to have turned down, once it got a solid financial base, was in 1826 when money was sought for the aid of the imprisoned Jews of Morocco and denied on the grounds that, according to the rules of the society, it could not give funds for that purpose.[50] However, during the Civil War the society did make a handsome contribution to military medical aid.[51]

The first public evidence that the *hebra* gave of the fraternal feeling which was a regular part of the various Jewish and non-Jewish brotherhoods in later years was on the occasion of the death of *Hazan* E. N. Carvalho. Although it was required at the funeral of any member, a motion was passed at a special meeting on March 20, 1817, that the *hebra* "attend the funeral in a body and wear crepe on the hats on the occasion and that the members attend at minyan morning and evening during the shibiya."[52] The death of the "venerable president," Jacob I. Cohen, at the age of eighty in the autumn of 1823 stirred even greater attention within and without the Jewish community. Then, too, the entire *hebra* in mourning crepe and "the large concourse which attended his remains to the tomb, testified the general regret at his decease," as one newspaper feelingly reported.[53]

While the *hebra* was basically a burial society, it did provide an economic prop for its members through mutual insurance features. The Society for the Visitation of the Sick and Mutual Assistance continued on for many years, but as the original members attained financial success the character of the society changed. The funds not needed any more by the members themselves were used for non-members who did need help and for general philanthropic purposes.

By 1863, when the society celebrated its fiftieth anniversary and honored Hyman Polock,[54] its only surviving founder and a former president, it had become a small, general charity, and shortly thereafter quietly disappeared. But as other immigrants came into the city from all parts of Europe, new *hebroth* were formed, served their basic purposes as burial and mutual insurance associations, and then gradually changed, as did the first one, into more general fraternal or philanthropic institutions.

By the end of the eighteenth century there existed in addition to the mutual-aid societies in Philadelphia a number of charitable institutions, many of them either initiated or managed by the philanthropically-oriented Society of Friends.[55] As early as 1713 the Quakers had opened the first almshouse in the city, and in 1732 the municipality established its own poorhouse, where the poor, the sick and the insane were gathered together. Thirty-five years later that institution moved to large buildings on the block from Spruce to Pine and from Tenth to Eleventh Streets, officially called the Almshouse for the Relief and Employment of the Poor, but popularly and euphemistically known as the Bettering House. This was the major charitable resource of Philadelphia for many years.

As long as the Quakers were permitted to dominate its administration, the Bettering House was run along humanitarian lines, but it was at best a place to which the unfortunate could be sent so they would not offend the sensibilities of the stolid citizens by their presence on the streets. This, together with miscellaneous church and small private charities, took care of the city's poor during the colonial period, but the steady rise in the population of Philadelphia during the Federal era—there were approximately 80,000 persons in the county in 1800—produced a need for more relief agencies. At the same time there was a burgeoning of evangelical reform movements, against intemperance, against slavery, for prison reform, for world peace, for universal education, and, of course, for the more immediate purposes of providing care for orphans, deaf mutes, the blind, unmarried mothers and the poor.

There spread throughout American society a consuming desire to "better" people, and it found its outlet in a host of new organizations and in the changing philosophy of the old ones. In

1803 the administration of poor relief was changed; the city was divided into districts with an officially appointed Guardian of the Poor responsible for relief in each area. Direct, indoor relief was almost abandoned, and the binding out of the clients as apprentices substituted.[56] Church groups, which had maintained their own charity programs as Mikveh Israel had done, formed larger and more comprehensive agencies.

Many of these new benevolent societies were sectarian, and most of them militantly evangelical as well. For instance, the Female Hospitable Society for the Relief and Employment of the Poor provided that the visiting committee should "administer spiritual as well as temporal relief," and "use every prudent means to bring back lost sheep to the fold of Christ."[57] Political and social liberation had broadened the participation of Jews in the life of the city beyond the synagogue and its activities, but the basic nature of many of the new charitable organizations prevented Jews from participating in their work. When genuinely non-sectarian groups were formed for a worthy philanthropic cause, the Jews seemed to have hastened to forward them. Hence, it is not surprising to find Naphtali Phillips active in an organization whose object was parallel to that of the Ezrath Orechim, but helped any immigrant in need.[58]

The participation of Jewish women in non-sectarian organizations was particularly impressive. Almost thirty years had passed since Rachel Moses had written to the Reverend Richard Peters asking for help in reforming the wayward Emanuel Lyon.[59] It was no longer necessary to go beyond the Jewish community for such aid. In the early decades of the century the synagogues and the Bikur Holim were able to take care of the comparatively few Jews who needed their help. The time had come when Jews were prepared to extend their philanthropic energies into a wider sphere. Eight Jewish women—Mrs. Miriam Gratz and two of her unmarried daughters, hardly twenty years of age, with still another daughter Richea, now Mrs. Hays, and Deborah Cohen with her daughter, and the wife of Jonas Phillips, and an unidentified Miss Levy—were all among the original members of the Female Association for the Relief of Women and Children in Reduced Circumstances, when it was founded in 1801.[60]

For Rebecca Gratz it was her first communal undertaking, one to which she devoted the driving energy that characterized her entire career. Although the Association was originally financed with $500 raised, but not needed, for the relief of the yellow fever victims of Baltimore, it soon needed funds for a "souphouse," or public kitchen. This sum was raised through the efforts of its twenty-three women members, of whom a third were Jewish; and Rebecca Gratz, who later became one of its managers, was responsible for raising the second largest amount.[61] The Association believed in giving relief in the form of food and clothing rather than in money,[62] and this policy was carried over into the first Jewish charitable agency.

Happily, Rebecca Gratz was an enthusiastic master of the art of letter-writing, and so she has left delightful and detailed accounts of her work in the several societies to which she devoted most of her life. One of these, the Orphan Society, or Asylum, of which she was a board member from its inception, and secretary from 1819 until her death in 1869, was founded in 1814.[63] Its seat was the Presbyterian Church, and its founding was marked by a sermon preached by the Reverend William White, the dean of Philadelphia's clergy,[64] but its administration and functioning were non-sectarian. In reply to a query in a newspaper, asking whether other than Presbyterians were admitted to the Asylum, it was stated:

> that no distinction was ever made by the managers in the admission of children into the Asylum, on account of the religious persuasion of the children, or their parents—that the members of the institution embrace a variety of the religious denominations of our city—and that the religious services at the Asylum are performed by ministers of the Episcopalian, Baptist, Methodist, & other societies, indifferently—in a word, that the charities of this truly benevolent institution have never been circumscribed by sectarian limits—[65]

Yet, later Rebecca Gratz was to comment that Christian sectarian jealousies were so strong that the ladies of the Asylum refused to permit one of their wards to go into service in a Unitarian household, but would gladly have permitted her to enter Miss Gratz's.[66]

The earlier liberal principles attracted whole-hearted support from members of the Jewish community. Although Rebecca Gratz's participation was such that after her death it was recorded that "To her energy and ability, during the struggling infancy of the Society, and to her admirable administration of its expenditures, much of its prosperity is due,"[67] the activities of her Jewish co-workers, heretofore overshadowed, should not be passed by. The women of the Cohen, Moss, Phillips, Nones, Moses, and Levy families were hardly less active in the formative years of the Asylum,[68] and it is noteworthy that members of both the Jewish synagogues took part in its work. Simon and Hyman Gratz were life subscribers, as was John Moss, and later Joseph Gratz.[69] All of these and many others were constant and regular contributors of money and supplies.

Among the Gratzes it was virtually a family project, with Master Henry Etting donating several popular juveniles,[70] Simon Gratz sending a wagon-load of hay and eight bushels of potatoes,[71] and Rebecca giving a bedspread, bedstead and bench.[72] These good people even solicited contributions from out-of-town friends and relatives, like Mrs. Isabella De Leon of Charleston and Michael E. Levy from Havana.[73]

The progress of the Orphan Society was interrupted by a catastrophe on January 24, 1822, when a fire destroyed the asylum and twenty-three of the orphans were burned to death.[74] The press both praised and blamed the managers, and Rebecca Gratz, deeply disturbed by the tragedy, wrote her sister-in-law, Maria Gist Gratz, of her distress:

> You have heard of the most dreadful calamity we have experienced in the destructive fire of the Orphan Asylum, and I am sure have sympathized with our distress—poor little souls how sad their fate! One would scarcely think it possible such a total destruction could take place in so rapid a manner, there was not an article of any thing saved, except what was round the bodies of those who escaped—we have taken a house in Market Street between Schuylkill and Center Square, until an Asylum can be rebuilt. The whole state takes an interest in our misfortune and as much money is already raised as will completely reinstate every pecuniary loss—but the heart-rending circumstance of so many having perished—will create a new anxiety, in the breast of the managers which while it deepens the interest takes off much from the satisfaction of their labours—they have been much abused—as public feeling rather than judgment operates on the first occurance of a fatal accident—but while sensible they were not neglectful of any duty—they can only write their regrets . . .[75]

The terrible misfortune and the damaging criticism did not impair the efforts of the Society's supporters, Jews and non-Jews alike. Jacob Gratz and Joseph Moss were on the citizens' committee to rebuild the Asylum and their interest and contributions continued unabated,[76] and Rebecca Gratz, as secretary, drafted a letter to the Senate of Pennsylvania asking for financial help, which was granted in the amount of $5000.[77]

Meanwhile, the Jews of the city were taking care of their

own largely through the *tsedaka,* or charity funds, of the synagogues. Sporadic requests, increasing in frequency as the years went by, came in for emergency help. Before Passover in 1814 Aaron Levy, Jr., appealed to Benjamin Phillips for "something out of the Charity box" on behalf of poor old Mr. Solomon who did not have "a spoon or a plate to eat with or off of."[78] The following year, a Mrs. Levy, blind and destitute, was sent up to Philadelphia by the Jewish community of Charleston for medical assistance with nothing but a letter of introduction to the "officers of the Synagogue."[79] The response to her plight was immediate. Rodeph Shalom made up a subscription list, and $44 was raised after the case was called to their attention by Mikveh Israel. Shortly after Mrs. Levy's case was taken care of, Hirsch Mendelson, sixty-six years old and afflicted with palsy, petitioned the Portuguese Congregation to help him get to a hospital "or to any other place they shall think proper so as I might recover the use of my limbs again."[80] On another occasion, a stranger in town, "being one of your profession," asked Hyman Marks, *parnass* of Mikveh Israel, for assistance "to that which I may be able to get a subsistance by,"[81] and another stranger, with the distinguished name of Montefiore, applied to him because his trunk was being held by a boarding-house for "a small debt of six dollars."[82] It was a matter of pride for the Jews to see to it that these co-religionists did not have to apply to public or non-Jewish charities for help, except, of course, for hospitalization.

Fortunately in Philadelphia, from 1752, the needy sick could get hospital care at the Pennsylvania Hospital and later at the Almshouse. Furthermore, in 1786 the Philadelphia Dispensary was founded to afford relief to the poor who were not eligible for hospitalization. The Dispensary provided a staff of volunteer attending doctors who kept regular hours at the clinic. The members paid one guinea a year for the privilege of having one patient at a time under care, or two guineas for two patients, and they acted as their own investigators, sending along the patients with a note of recommendation for medical care.[83]

The Dispensary was the first institution to take advantage of the self-help societies, for as it grew it began to accept contributions not only from philanthropic individuals but from the mutual-aid societies, which thereby became entitled to medical care for their members. In the annual report of the Dispensary for 1815, there were listed as contributors, among others: the Scots

Thistle Society, the Friendly Sons of St. Tammany, Richard Allen for Bethel (African) Church, Samuel Craig for the Union Society of Journeymen Taylors, and A. H. Cohen, "President for the Society for Hebra Biken Chotem and Gemelut-Hassadein."[84] As soon as the Dispensary established a northern branch in 1816 in the district of Northern Liberties, to which area Jews were moving in increasingly large numbers, Jonathan, sometimes known as Jonas, Horwitz, was appointed an attending physician.[85] Horwitz thereby became the first Jewish doctor to receive a semi-public post in the county. That Jews needed and used the services offered by the clinic is evidenced by the fact that, shortly after its organization, the Female Hebrew Benevolent Society was officially informed by the Bikur Holim that it was a contributor "to the Dispensaries of the City & Northern Liberties & that the Gabay will procure medical aid from those institutions for any person recommended by their Society."[86] In the same year, 1820, Dr. Alexander Wertheim, who had been *mohel* to both congregations since 1810, became a city health officer;[87] and Dr. Isaac Hays, only a few years out of the Medical School of the University of Pennsylvania, offered his services as a physician to the Bikur Holim.[88] The City Dispensary recognized his status by appointing him an attending physician in 1822.[89]

After the close of the War of 1812, the pauper class in Philadelphia greatly increased. Although the existing private charities were doing what they could to relieve distress, many citizens felt that their kind of dispensation of charity was not only insufficient but confirmed the poor in their situation. A committee was appointed by a town meeting in February, 1817, to investigate the causes of poverty and to suggest plans for improving the situation. They found that the most improvident were the Negroes and the Irish immigrants, as well as the intemperate and the day laborers. They summarily dismissed unemployment as a factor, and judged that a solution to the problem lay in moral "improvement." As a result, the Pennsylvania Society for the Promotion of Public Economy was created, one of whose purposes was to teach the poor "to cherish a regard for moral and religious obligation."[90] This was typical of the period.

Hard times continued for about five years, and severe winters —in 1820-21 the Delaware River was frozen over—added to the misery of the poor.[91] The story is told that on a stormy day in the autumn of 1819 two Jewish "ladies of benevolent instincts" were greatly affected by a tragic case which was brought to their attention, and thereupon resolved to ask their fellow-Jewesses to do something to relieve the poverty which existed among a small number of Jewish families in the city, who had no particular charity to help them.[92]

The result was the Female Hebrew Benevolent Society, the first separate, charitable organization founded by Jews in Philadelphia and the oldest Jewish charity in the United States which has remained in continuous existence.[93] Inevitably, as the size of the Jewish community increased, there were more Jews who found themselves incapable of adjusting to American economic life, others who met with calamitous reversals and more who needed some help while they were adjusting to their new environment. A few such there were in 1819.

To the ladies of Mikveh Israel, faced that winter with the problem of care for one or two such destitute Jews, it was a matter of communal pride to provide a specific agency through which those particular cases and future ones might be taken care of by Jews. Rebecca Gratz, then a spinster of thirty-nine, with her experience in the Female Association for the Relief of Women and Children in Reduced Circumstances and the Philadelphia Orphan Society, was able to guide the Jewish women in their work. In its scope the Society was an over-all welfare agency. During the first year of its operation, the visiting committee, who looked upon the funds elicited by charity as a sacred trust, rejected two cases, because they were unwilling to help the idle and improvident, but spent $41.30 to help one indigent family "who are frugal, industrious and grateful."[94]

The work that they decided to undertake and the manner in which it was to be carried out were similar to those of non-Jewish agencies. They divided the city into districts, and each lady was to be responsible for her own area.[95] They screened their cases personally, for there was no professional help in social work then. They provided the needful support for the worthy "pensioner," as the recipient of charity was called, spelled out in terms of necessaries, but not money. The poor could not be trusted to spend wisely or well. If this seems today a lady-bountiful kind of Victorian charity, familiar to most of us through Dickens, imperfect in planning and execution in the light of modern social theories, it was yet characteristic of its day.

However, the Society went beyond dole. A traveller's aid was provided to give "sojourning Israelites" clothing or small sums of money.[96] A visiting-nurse program was envisioned in sick visits, with professional help volunteered by two Jewish physicians, Doctors Manuel Phillips and Isaac Hays.[97] Volunteer recruitment was planned by asking that those who were willing to attend the sick or to help with the last rites of the poor register with the Society. An employment bureau was projected by having seamstresses seeking employment referred to the Society.[98] Even a means of providing a Jewish education for the children of indigent families was anticipated, but not for the time being implemented.[99] And the age-old Jewish ethical concern for the dignity of the recipients was evidenced by the provision that a select committee should administer relief secretly to those who had seen better days.[100]

In 1820 Mrs. Rebecca M. Phillips[101] was First Directress, Mrs. Bell Cohen,[102] Second Directress, Mrs. S. Bravo,[103] Treasurer, and Miss Rebecca Gratz, Secretary. With the exception of members of the Gratz, Moss, Phillips and Peixotto families, few contributors gave more than the minimum subscription of two dollars,[104] but it is noteworthy that in the first list of subscribers the largest single gift, $150, was the benefaction of a non-Jew, Joshua Byron, through his executor Richard Milne.[105] The Female Hebrew Benevolent Society remained under the direction of the women of the leading families of Mikveh Israel, and, as years went on, most of its funds were bestowed upon gentlewomen in reduced circumstances, a charity which the confidential nature of its records permitted it to grant gracefully and with dignity to the recipient.

Only a few years later, in the late spring of 1822, in the rooms of Rodeph Shalom in Church Alley, a second charity was organized to extend to non-members of the *hebra* certain of its benefits and to care for the Jewish poor on a scale which the good ladies of Mikveh Israel could not be expected to match.[106] Although the records do not give us details, it seems likely that the few Jewish poor in Philadelphia were German or Yiddish-speaking Jews, and perhaps the "Portuguese" ladies were faced with language difficulties in the execution of their missions. There would have been no lack of foreign language speaking Jews in Rodeph Shalom. However, the United Hebrew Beneficent Society, although fostered by that congregation, was from the beginning a community-wide organization.[107] The first minute-book of the Society, which was available as recently as 1940, cannot now be found; hence the story of its earliest activities can only be reconstructed from an unpublished history written then,[108] and the printed constitution and by-laws of 1829.[109]

Its purposes and programs were markedly similar to those of the earlier women's society. The society's funds were to be used for the following purposes:

1. Relief to the poor and sick of the Jewish persuasion. 2. To procure attendance, medicine, &c. for such sick as are unable to provide for themselves; and in case of death, to bury them with decency. 3. To bind poor children apprentices to mechanical trades, with the concurrence of their parents or guardians. 4. Whenever the funds will admit—to encourage the acquirement of the Holy Tongue among the children of the members of our persuasion.[110]

Its members, men this time, were to investigate needs to prevent imposition through false representation.[111] Help was given in cash and kind. From the Bikur Holim it took the provisions that members should visit the sick and attend the funeral and mourning prayers of a deceased member, but most of its work was to be purely charitable.[112]

Of particular interest was the regulation that it was the responsibility of the Board to see that any child bound as an apprentice should be bound so that he could keep the Sabbath and Holy Days and otherwise adhere to Jewish religious practices "as nearly as possible." Furthermore, they were to inquire into the moral character of the master and his capacity to teach his trade, and thereafter "exercise a kindly guardianship" over the child.[113] This was the germ of a foster-home program, and part of the philosophy of gainful rehabilitation which was motivating many of the more progressive agencies of the city. An unusual provision was that, whenever practical, Jews, and no others, should be employed to dig the graves of deceased members or poor Jews buried at the society's expense.[114]

However, while the *hebra*, as late as 1829, turned down a motion "to accept any applicant without his belonging to the Portuguese congr.,"[115] the Beneficent Society from the beginning was willing to open its membership to any Jew residing in

Pennsylvania, provided that he was not married "otherwise than according to the Jewish rites."[116] An entrance fee of one dollar was set; annual dues were four dollars; and a life membership could be obtained for forty dollars.[117] A list of the members in 1829 shows that the society was composed of men from both the Portuguese and the German congregations, so that it was in fact the first broadly communal organization established by the Jews of Philadelphia.[118] From the United Hebrew Beneficent Society by direct descent, as a result of mergers and changes of name, has evolved today's Jewish Family Service.

In the first year of its operation, the society received a total of $469.64 in subscriptions, and spent $127.82 on relief in the form of wood, groceries and cash.[119] Like the Bikur Holim before it, the Beneficent Society joined the Philadelphia,[120] the Northern, and Southern Dispensaries.[121]

In spite of what today seems like small sums spent for a city-wide charity, it should be realized that the needs at the time were equally small. Mathew Carey noted that the seven most prominent benevolent societies of Philadelphia in 1828 had received only $1,069 and disbursed $3,740.[122] There did not exist, and did not appear for many years, a body of Jewish poor. They were not as a group habitual drunkards, confirmed beggars, or malingerers; apparently no Jews applied for admittance to the city poorhouse.[123] Charity was necessary on an individual and usually temporary basis. Yet, the importance of the new agency to the Jewish community can be judged by the stature of its leaders. In 1829 the president of the Beneficent Society was Zalegman Phillips, then one of the leading Jews of Philadelphia, who was serving also as the *parnass* of Mikveh Israel, and its vice-president was Wolf Benjamin, who had been president of Rodeph Shalom.[124]

The relationship between the Jewish societies in Philadelphia was not only non-competitive, but gave evidence of being co-operative. As noted, the Bikur Holim offered medical aid to the Female Hebrew Benevolent Society, and later the Beneficent Society appealed to both of the other organizations for help in a situation which it found itself unable to cope with. A family of small children had been deserted by the father, and the Beneficent Society, whose funds were temporarily exhausted by other charitable work, asked the two other societies to come to the family's rescue, lest the children be neglected as Jews and be brought up under the auspices of some other agency as Christians.[125] Experience was being gained by the Jewish community in philanthropic organization; patterns were being created which were to prove valuable guides in future years.

In addition to the intra-city co-operation, there existed also inter-communal aid in the form of help in building new synagogues and in raising funds for Palestinian messengers and overseas relief. Before it had a synagogue of its own, Rodeph Shalom responded to appeals for building funds from other cities. In 1811 $52 was sent to Beth Shalome in Richmond,[126] and in 1827 $100 to Bnai Jeshurun in New York, America's second Ashkenazic synagogue.[127] The appeal of the New Yorkers, who had seceded from Shearith Israel two years before, was a typical request, such as was to be received more frequently as new congregations sprang up all over the country.

> The German Jews in this city are mostly emigrants who have escaped from the persecution of the old world and are now enjoying freedom and comfort under the protection of the Laws of the United States. Their means are very limited and wishing their place of Worship to be paid for and the Congregation free from debt, they have resolved to throw themselves upon the liberality of their Brethren throughout Europe and America.[128]

Likewise, in 1817 the century-old building of Shearith Israel had been replaced by a new one, and then Mikveh Israel came to the assistance of its sister congregation.[129]

Locally, a situation existed which had no parallel in the United States. When Mikveh Israel in turn wanted to erect a new house of worship, the customary appeals were circulated through the states and West Indies and, among others, Congregation Nidche Israel of Barbados responded with a handsome contribution of $500.[130] However, the local population provided the major part of the funds. This time it was the individual members of Rodeph Shalom, rather than the congregation as a body, who offered financial help to their fellows.[131] If there were differences between the forms of prayer in the two congregations, there was little jealousy. Still unable to erect their own synagogue despite several feeble attempts, the congregants of Rodeph Shalom were willing to help financially when the Portuguese Congregation needed it. But the building was a drain upon the treasury of the older synagogue, and when the new congregation of Cincinnati appealed to it for synagogal funds, the appeal had to be turned down by the *adjunta,* who, however, urged that individual contributions be forwarded promptly.[132] Joseph Andrews sent $20.[133]

So exhausted had Mikveh Israel's treasury become in 1825, that the Sephardic congregation again had to state apologetically that no funds were available to be forwarded to Jerusalem when Jacob David Ickertul of London solicited "aid for our unhappy Brethren in the Holy City."[134] A year later another petition, this time from the Jews of Morocco, also had to be turned down.[135] On the other hand, Rodeph Shalom, without the responsibility of an elegant building, was able to send its contribution directly to Jerusalem.[136] There was no direct nor regular liaison with the Jewish communities in the Mediterranean; occasional contacts barely kept the American community aware of their existence. Yet, in 1840 it was to be the infamous Damascus incident which was to stir American Jewry into its first serious effort at united action.

15

War and Politics

THE series of events, which had begun when Solomon Bush intervened in London for impressed American seamen in 1789, reached its climax in the summer of 1812. Having insolently boarded American ships at sea and taken off American seamen for a period of years, the arrogance of the British reached a new height when the frigate *Leopard* fired on the American *Chesapeake* in 1807. The punitive American Embargo Act, which Jefferson imposed on a rather reluctant nation, hurt the economy of the United States more than it did Great Britain, and the more lenient Non-Intercourse Law, which succeeded it, levelled first at both England and France and subsequently at England only, did nothing to persuade the English to cease their sea-marauding.[1]

In 1808 Madison was elected to succeed Jefferson, and in the congressional election two years later, a majority of "War Hawks" was elected, convinced that the United States must fight to protect her rights. On June 18, 1812, Congress officially declared war on Great Britain. The outbreak of hostilities was received resentfully. The New England states, with an opposition which almost led to secession, bemoaned the use of their state militias. The Federalists were the backbone of the anti-war element in the country, and, before actual fighting began, they sponsored "peace" societies. The Middle Atlantic states were more cooperative, but there too the anti-administration forces organized peace groups, one of which in Philadelphia Moses Levy headed.[2] Another, the "Young Men of the City and

County of Philadelphia, Friends to 'Peace, Union and Commerce,' and those opposed to the measures of the present administration," included Jacob Gratz and Joseph Simon Cohen, fresh from law school, as representatives of the South Ward, and Henry Solomon, the brother-in-law of Zalegman Phillips, from the Cedar Ward.[3]

Although England was deeply involved in a war with Napoleon, Britannia, whose Nelson had but a few years earlier broken the naval power of France and Spain, still ruled the waves, and she looked upon the tiny American navy with undisguised contempt. For more than two decades the Americans, almost supinely, had permitted their ships to be boarded and searched. They had far fewer ships than the British, but the American frigates were sturdy and their captains well-trained. The Atlantic seaboard had been a natural training ground for seamen. Out of the ports from Bangor to New Orleans a flourishing coastal trade was carried on; West-Indiamen regularly sailed south; the Yankee clippers were becoming frequent visitors to the China seas; fishing fleets and whalers went out on long voyages wherever their prey called them. From these seafaring enterprises came the sailors who manned the ships captained by Perry, Hull, Decatur and Bainbridge. There were many like Uriah Phillips Levy, who had begun their careers as cabin-boys on a merchant ship and, by the time the war broke out, were grown, able-bodied seamen.

While the country was busy weighing the advantages of peace and the possible results of war—some praising, some condemning President Madison's declaration—young Gratz Etting, Reuben's son, delivered the outstanding address at the commencement exercises of the University of Pennsylvania, choosing as his theme that fateful summer a vindication of the "character of the United States against the calumnies of foreign writers."[4] His uncle, Jacob Gratz, who five years earlier had delivered another patriotic address on a similar occasion, was already deeply involved in civic and political activities.[5] A few months before, he had been one of the city representatives who joined with the University in condoling with the citizens of Richmond on the calamitous fire which had destroyed the theatre and taken many lives.[6] Politically, Jacob and his brother Joseph supported the Federalists,[7] but Gratz Etting followed in his father's footsteps by being a firm adherent of the administration. However, when war began in earnest, most of the members of the Gratz-Etting family joined one of the armed services. And Rebecca, ever a careful observer of important events, wrote to her brother Benjamin of the first national fastday, proclaimed by the government in late August of 1812.[8]

During the American Revolution some Jews fought in almost every land campaign against the British. Nothing is known of their possible participation on sea, except the mention made by Dr. David Nassy that there were Jewish sailors in the tiny Dutch fleet which joined the coalition against the English in 1780.[9] It was during the War of 1812 that the American Jewish sailor emerged, and that sailor is exemplified in the career of Uriah Phillips Levy.

Benjamin Rush had attended the wedding of Levy's parents at Jonas Phillips' house back in 1787, and before Rush died in 1813, Levy, then twenty-one, was an officer in the United States Navy. Pulled as many other young Americans were by the lure of the sea, Levy in 1802 had begun his adventurous sixty years as a sailor by running away to sea as a cabin-boy at the age of ten.[10] Two years later he came back to Philadelphia still determined to be a sailor, and his father apprenticed him to John Coulton, one of the city's leading ship-owners, who sent him aboard one of his fleet. When the embargo in 1807 choked the port of Philadelphia with idle ships, Coulton had his apprentice-lad go to a school for navigation conducted by an ex-lieutenant of the British Navy. As soon as the embargo was lifted, and trade was resumed, Levy was off again.[11]

In those days, when French and British press gangs were harassing American ships, certification of American citizenship was the most important paper a seaman could own. Levy carried his "protection" from the Port of Philadelphia, attesting to his native birth. But even with this he did not escape impressment. In 1809, while on shore-leave on Tortola, in the British Virgin Islands, he was captured by a press gang from the British ship *Vermyra*, and against his will was forced to serve aboard her for a month until he was released. During that time Captain Scovil of the *Vermyra* invited him to surrender his American citizenship and accept a British commission; but the lad refused the flattering offer. Another time, while Levy was serving on Coulton's ship *Rittenhouse*, it was boarded by a French privateer, its cargo confiscated, and the unharmed crew left with the empty vessel. They took it to Turks Island, put on a cargo of salt, shortly afterwards foundered, and, after drifting aimlessly in an open boat for five days, landed safely on one of the Bahamas.[12]

In rapid succession Levy rose from second-mate to first-mate to master. On the eve of the war, hardly out of his teens, he became captain and part-owner of the *Washington*. In January, 1812, on one of his first trips out in command, his crew mutinied. They seized a cargo of $2,500 of gold and fourteen cases of Teneriffe wine, and Levy barely escaped with his life. He made his way back to the States, and with another ship and a determination to bring the mutineers to justice he scoured the Caribbean. On St. Lucia he finally found them. One of the criminals was hanged, another sentenced to life imprisonment, and Levy's honor was redeemed.[13]

While on this retributive expedition, Levy received his commission as a sailing master in the United States Navy. Later in life he explained why he had chosen to apply for that post:

... I sought this particular position in the belief that my nautical education and experience would enable me to render greater service to my country in this post, than in that of a midshipman—the grade in which the Naval Service is usually entered. The latter was a more conspicuous and attractive place and it presented the only sound prospect of early promotion. But a sailing master is indispensable ... and in battle he is as much exposed ... I felt therefore, that in giving up, in the hour of public danger, an eligible position in the Merchant Service for one in the Navy affording little prospect of promotion, and little gain, I furnished the best proof ... of love to my country.[14]

Levy's commission followed by four months that of the first Jewish naval officer in the War of 1812, Levi M. Harby of Charleston. Two other Philadelphia-born Jews followed them: Ezekiel, the son of Haym Salomon, and Joseph B. Nones, the son of Benjamin.[15] But before either Salomon or Nones was commissioned, Levy had already witnessed the war at sea. In June, 1813, he was assigned to duty aboard the *Argus*, which was to take William Crawford to France to enlist that country's aid once more against England. Having dropped its distinguished passenger at L'Orient, the *Argus* began its short but exciting career as the scourge of England. In the tradition of John Paul Jones, the American warship carried the fight into the home waters of the English, attacking shipping in the Channel and the Irish Sea with such success that insurance rates were raised and the British cruisers recalled for protection. During those bold forays Levy was promoted to the temporary rank of lieutenant and assigned the task of boarding, destroying, or taking over captured ships. One of the prizes, the *Betty*, was so valuable that Levy himself was ordered to take it to a French port. On this mission he escaped by two days the battle between the *Argus* and the *Pelican*, in which the American ship was overpowered and her captain and most of the crew killed. However, if Levy escaped death, he did not get off scot-free. The *Betty* was recaptured before it reached a safe harbor, and her master and crew were taken prisoners. For sixteen months they were to endure the hardships of the dread Dartmoor prison.[16]

While Levy was suffering at Dartmoor, where a number of other American Jewish prisoners of war were incarcerated,[17] his cousin, Mordecai Manuel Noah, was captured together with several other Americans off the Spanish coast, and taken aboard a British warship.[18] In the five years since he had made his debut in Philadelphia politics, Noah had written a play and published a critical work on Shakespeare.[19] But his main drive was political. In 1811 he stopped in Baltimore long enough to see his uncle Naphtali Phillips to get his aid in securing some consular post, those he mentioned as most attractive to him being somewhere in North Africa, Bayonne, Nantes, or Riga.[20] Almost immediately he was offered the position of consul for the United States at Riga, but the outbreak of hostilities between France and Russia at just that time made the possibilities of building a career in the Baltic port seem slight, and so Noah turned down the appointment.[21]

Shortly afterwards he established himself at Charleston, where, clamoring loudly for American rights, he became an ardent advocate of war, even to the point of fighting a duel for his views.[22] He apparently was travelling back and forth between Charleston and Philadelphia, for some time in 1813 he received the complimentary title of "Major," which was voted him at an election of Philadelphia militia officers, which meeting, he later reported with glee, "was attended only by himself and two other persons."[23] The administration recognized that so staunch a supporter of its policies and so consistent a defender of American honor would be most useful in North Africa, where the Algerines for years had been pulling tail-feathers from the American eagle by capturing ships and holding their crews for ransom. Successive punitive naval expeditions had not put an end to the piracy. In April, 1813, Noah was appointed consul at Tunis, a post which this time he eagerly accepted.[24]

His first instructions were to treat for the release of American prisoners held at Algiers by Barbary pirates. But before he even passed the Straits of Gibraltar he was himself taken prisoner by a British man-of-war, sailed to England, and there detained for two months before he was permitted to continue on his way.[25] Noah and Levy, both grandsons of that colonial stalwart Jonas Phillips, led exciting, adventurous lives, one on land, the other on sea. They were both born Philadelphians, but their lives were of national rather than local interest, and their roles as members of the Philadelphia Jewish community ended as their main careers began. When Noah returned to America after the war, he moved to New York; Levy remained in the Navy.

In the spring of 1813 when Levy and Noah were both on their way to capture, the war became an immediate, real threat to the seaboard cities of the United States. Philadelphia was in imminent danger of attack. A committee was organized to plan a defense of the Delaware River, the bay and the adjacent waters, and to implement the plan a special subscription fund was instituted. For the practical needs of defense, Benjamin Nones, always active in affairs patriotic and political, and as ardent a supporter of Madison as he had been of Jefferson, joined with a number of other soldiers of the Revolution over forty-five years of age to form a company "for the purpose of assisting measures of defense." When these veterans chose the venerable General John Steel as their captain, Nones was elected second lieutenant.[26]

With the possibility of the British fleet appearing off Cape May any day, the opposition to the war vanished. The Gratzes and the other Federalists joined with their political opponents to do what they could to prepare against invasion. Simon Gratz was chosen to represent the Middle Ward in raising funds for the committee of defense,[27] and no better choice could have been made. For fifteen years, from the time of the yellow fever epidemic of 1798[28] to the Society of the Cincinnati's Washington Monument fund in 1811,[29] he had represented that busy area in most of its philanthropic, civic and commercial enterprises. From the first year of the war, Simon and Hyman

Gratz, in partnership with Charles Wilkins, supplied great quantities of saltpeter for the manufacture of gunpowder obtained from Mammoth Cave, which they owned.[30] The chroniclers of the history of that natural wonder made a most interesting observation on the part which it played in the war.

> Emphasis should be laid on the fact, not mentioned in any history of the United States, that our War with Great Britain, in 1812, would have ended in failure on our side had it not been for the resources so abundantly furnished by American caverns for the home manufacture of saltpeter at a time when by a general embargo we were wholly cut off from foreign sources of supply.[31]

But the Gratzes also fought. Jacob served during the campaign of Mount Bull as a member of the exclusive First City Troop, the only Jew to be admitted to that socially elite body.[32] His brother Joseph joined another cavalry unit,[33] and young Benjamin set aside his law books to volunteer first in the same unit, and then in the handsomely accoutred Washington Guards, becoming a first lieutenant before the end of the war.[34]

The many loose military associations and militia companies created for the duration of the war made it possible for some of the citizen-soldiers to divide their time between civic and military duties. Hence, while he performed his part-time service, Joseph Gratz was able to remain active in politics. During the election of 1813 he became secretary of the Middle Ward,[35] and Henry Solomon of the Cedar Ward,[36] both supporting the Federal-Republicans. In the interests of the same party Joseph Simon Cohen and Abraham Cohen were busy in the South Ward,[37] and Samuel Moss in New Market Ward.[38] This year the only active Democrat was Reuben Etting, who ran for the minor post of Judge of Elections in his brother-in-law's district, and lost.[39]

Those who were in the regular army and served far from the city had no such opportunities. This was particularly true of Isaac De Young, later the owner of a Philadelphia general merchandising store, a forerunner of the department store.[40] This Dutch-born Jew, who had come to this country at the very beginning of the century with his father, a former diamond agent for the Crown of France, enlisted at the age of sixteen in the Third New Jersey Heavy Regulars. He fought in a number of the major northern battles, Sackett's Harbor, Queenstown, Frenchtown, Fort George, Stony Creek, Lake Champlain, Oswego, Chippewa, and others. In the Battle of Lundy's Lane he was shot in the thigh when he made a bayonet charge with his company against the British Grenadiers.[41]

The story is told that at Fort George, De Young was on guard duty when Colonel, later General, Winfield Scott went out to inspect the picket lines. On his return the Colonel tried to pass the guard, was commanded to halt and give the countersign, and when protesting that he was the Colonel, failed to do so, was made prisoner and held until recognized. De Young stayed in the Army until 1817, when he settled permanently in Philadelphia.[42]

David G. Seixas, one of the sons of the *hazan*, who had just moved to the city where his father had ministered during the Revolution, gave up a modest metal and crockery business to enter the service.[43] Jacob De La Motta, who had received his medical education under Dr. Rush at the University of Pennsylvania, and was then back in his native Charleston, was appointed surgeon in the Second Artillery Regiment.[44] Manuel Phillips, like De La Motta, became a surgeon in the regular navy.[45] His brother, Benjamin I. Phillips, designed uniforms for a local guard unit of which he was a member[46] and two other brothers, Joseph[47] and Aaron,[48] also volunteered. Mordecai Lyons was in the 9th Company of the State Guards.[49] Joshua Moses, merchant and importer, became a major in the 2nd Battalion of the 1st Brigade of the Pennsylvania Militia,[50] in other units of which Abraham and Samuel M. Solomon served.[51] Meanwhile, the sons of Benjamin Nones impatiently waited until they would be old enough to do something for their country.

The triumphant ringing of the bells of Philadelphia, "as they never rang before," to celebrate the victory of the *Constitution* over the *Guerriere* in the summer of 1812 had fired fifteen-year-old Joseph B. Nones with a consuming desire "to enter our Navy, and participate in its glory."[52] Already an older brother, Solomon B., had received a political appointment from the Jefferson administration, that of consul-general in Portugal, and now Benjamin Nones was willing to use his influence to help another son. As Joseph wrote in his autobiographical notes, Nones senior

applied for a midshipman warrant for me—which was promised "the first opportunity offering," as the Navy department was then overloaded with similar applications—time ran on till the latter part of January 1814—but no warrant came. At that time a lady friend of my mother [Mrs. Eliza Parke Custis, of the Washington family], was spending a few weeks under my paternal roof—and being a lady of great influence with our government determined to procure the warrant for me.

Within a month the successful Mrs. Custis was back in Philadelphia with Joseph's commission.[53]

He was ordered to report for duty at New York to Captain Argus of the corvette *John Adams,* which was preparing to carry his father's friend Henry Clay, and John Quincy Adams, Albert Gallatin and the other commissioners to Ghent to negotiate a peace with Great Britain. He accompanied the diplomats on their mission which ended happily in the Treaty of Ghent, which was signed in December. Later, Nones was in the fleet commanded by Decatur in the last stage of the Algerine War, when the naval hero finally forced the Barbary States to pay for the American ships they had taken and give up all future demands for "tribute." On July 2, 1821, Nones resigned his commission, and entered the import trade in Philadelphia. For the remainder of his long life he was a keen observer of naval events and contributed many articles on naval history to the *Army and Navy Journal* and other periodicals.[54] Another brother, Abraham B. Nones, who had joined the First Pennsylvania Volunteer Infantry,[55] switched from a military career to a diplomatic one. In 1826, during the administration of John Quincy Adams, he was appointed consul-general to the province of Zulia in Venezuela.[56]

Even while the American commissioners were in Europe seeking to bring an end to the war, Philadelphia was suddenly alarmed by a fear of invasion based upon a real threat. The Americans had successfully demonstrated their fighting ability on the sea and land, on Lake Erie and Lake Champlain, at the Battle of the Thames in Canada and at Chippewa and Lundy's Lane along the Niagara front where De Young served. But in August, 1814, the British Navy, having chased the smaller American defending force into hiding, landed an expeditionary force in Chesapeake Bay, and took and burned Washington. A subsequent attempt to capture Baltimore, the following month, was frustrated by the heroic defense of Fort McHenry in which some forty Jews participated,[57] and which inspired Key to write *The Star Spangled Banner.* The citizens of Philadelphia were galvanized into frantic attempts to strengthen the city's defenses.

Rebecca Gratz, who worried like a mother over the hardships to which her brothers were exposed in the army, and the dangers which they might be called on to face, gives a good picture of the local scene in a series of letters to her brother Benjamin at "Washington Barracks, Kennett Square:"

. . . I thank God we are at home again—tho hastened to it by alarm and danger. We found Jo here on a short visit but he return'd to camp this morning and we feel forlorn without you and him. I hope it will be in your power to come home for a short visit too—your military zeal is very fine but I hope your wishes will not prevail—an armistice would be more glorious to the country than all the laurels its heroes can gather . . .[58]

You write, My dear Ben, of marching with as much enthusiasm as if you were a veteran soldier animated by success—while we look with horror on the possibility of such an event—you may easily imagine our trepidation on hearing of the gigantic strides made by the war in the short period of our absence . . . Jac has become an indefatigable soldier, but found a day's work at the fortification rather too severe. He has complain'd of burnt arms and shoulders ever since Wednesday. I hope you will take the best means to make yourself as comfortable as a camp life will admit of. The clothes you sent home are exchanged—do let us know what else you want. I am afraid to send anything that might encumber you, but would take the greatest pleasure in preparing whatever would contribute to your convenience. I sincerely hope we shall see you ere long but shall not attempt to visit you. Jacob has the pistols you wrote for to be repaired but will send them by the next opportunity if they are not finished in time for this. Gratz [Etting] will give you all out-doors information and you must accept the love and prayers of all within. Next Thursday and Friday is Roshoshana—we talk of passing it at Bloomfield . . .[59]

We live rather a dull life without you and Jo in which, however, we share but the common lot. Phila. streets are completely deserted except by the few military companies who parade of an afternoon. Jac bids me tell you he fears their company will fall through—they are dividing it for a marching company—the Capt. will not go—and they have only thirty signatures. He is very anxious to effect its marching—but is less sanguine of success than when I last wrote. For my part, I cannot regret it, he is not very fit for a soldier's life tho' I trust in the hour of need would be able to do his duty. Could you not get some business to bring you home for a day or two? say from Saturday to Monday—that you may feast and fast with us on the approaching Great day [Yom Kippur]. We long to see you again and if Sally was well enough should certainly pay you a visit at Wilmington. It seems very tantalizing that you should be so near and conveniently but for us in vain . . .[60]

Benjamin and Joseph were rather enjoying their experience. They were with other young Philadelphians with whom they were on the most friendly terms. The diary of Thomas Franklin Pleasants, who was a captain of the 3rd Company of the Washington Guards, is sprinkled with references to the Gratzes and their cousins Joseph Simon Cohen and Henry Etting. Written during the days when Philadelphia was threatened and the militia companies forming, they indicate a total acceptance of the young Jewish men—

In the afternoon J. Gratz and I played chess . . . Invited to dine with Gratz and Swift—Biddle on guard. In the evening Gratz, Montgomery and I went to see Ingersoll and talked about the formation of a regiment.[61]

The fortifications on which Jacob Gratz worked so enthusiastically, stripped to the waist in the hot summer sun, that he put himself *hors de combat* for a few days, were hastily constructed defenses for the city. While Rebecca was writing her brother, private funds were being collected from Philadelphians to expedite the work. In the earliest located list of contributors, John Moss, who had enlisted as a private in the militia,[62] headed the names with one of the largest contributions.[63] As more donations came in during the emergency and were published in the daily press, the gifts of other Jews were noted.[64] Jacob I. Cohen, heading the newly organized Society for the Visitation of the Sick, proposed a contribution to the fund, but the society's tiny treasury made it "inexpedient" at the time.[65] Fortunately, the breastworks along the Delaware were never shelled; the British never attacked Philadelphia. Within a few months news of the peace arrived, and the President declared a day of general fasting and prayer to be observed on January 12, 1815. Mikveh Israel responded to a motion, introduced by Simon Gratz, "that the Parnass be requested to direct prayers to be said in the synagogue," and that there "be an appropriate discourse delivered in Hebrew and English."[66]

The city of Philadelphia had supplied, according to one contemporary estimate, about two thousand men to the regular army and private companies.[67] Approximately forty of this number were Jews, and they represented slightly less than one-third of the estimated male Jewish population of the city between the ages of seventeen and forty-five. Most of the young men who joined one or another of the services were American-born Jews, men who had become integrated in American life. Yet, like Uriah Phillips Levy and Mordecai Manuel Noah, they were proud of being Jews and fought to be respected as Jews. Their careers and their position as Americans and as Jews in the armed forces, in politics and in civic life smoothed the path for the new influx of Jewish immigrants which began to flow to America at the end of the Napoleonic Wars which came to a close almost coincidentally with the War of 1812.

With the war successfully concluded, Americans could settle down to their domestic politics and problems. Great figures dominated the scene and the issues. Daniel Webster of New Hampshire and Massachusetts at first opposed a protective tariff and later became its most vigorous and eloquent supporter on behalf of the North's new industries. John Calhoun of South Carolina at first followed the new Jeffersonian ideal of favoring the manufacturer equally with the agriculturist, and then, as King Cotton began his reign in the South, the avowedly partisan Southerner switched to an advocacy of free trade. John Randolph, the old, vitriolic irreconcilable, insisted that the South should secede rather than accept any limitation on slavery, which for the first time was becoming a national issue. Henry Clay, as a perennial possibility for the presidency, assumed the role of the great compromiser. And in Philadelphia all the national ferment spilled over into local politics and local problems.

The Jews of the city had become integrated into the functioning of the American two-party system. Many of them remained consistently faithful to one party, and a number changed their allegiance from one to another, as the party and its principles changed. The Solomons, Gratzes, Phillips', Cohens, and Ettings kept their appetite for the politics which they had sampled as soon as they had come of age. For the Solomons and the Ettings Philadelphia was only a temporary home, and they maintained their interest in the affairs of that city only until the "Jew Bill," removing Jewish disabilities, finally passed the Maryland legislature,[68] when most of them moved back to Baltimore whence they had come.

In 1811, the year in which Benjamin Gratz had received his degree from the University of Pennsylvania,[69] a semi-political society with Federalist leanings, the Washington Association of Philadelphia, had been founded. It attracted to its membership many of the young lawyers of the city, who hoped that political connections would become sound assets in a legal career, among whom were Gratz and Henry Solomon. The latter became its secretary two years after it was founded,[70] and a few months later his brother-in-law, Zalegman Phillips, sponsored his admission to the Philadelphia bar.[71] Other young native-born Jews also decided to follow the legal profession, and in 1815 Benjamin Gratz, who was later elected vice-president of the Washington Association,[72] was admitted;[73] the next year Joseph R. Ingersoll stood sponsor for Gratz Etting;[74] and in 1819 William Meredith, a close associate of Simon Gratz, moved the admission of Nathan Nathans.[75]

After his father's death, Nathans had been placed under the guardianship of Meredith,[76] who took seriously the responsibility for seeing that his ward was brought up as a Jew. He must have been specific in that connection, for the master of the school in which Meredith placed young Nathans wrote him:

> . . . I had feared lest there might be some difficulties on account of the peculiarities of his religious sentiment, & the regulations of my school relative to the observance of the Christian Sabbath; but I am happy to say there is none. He is permitted to observe his own Sabbath, & of his own accord, without any requisition from me he has regularly attended with the other young gentlemen under my care at the Church in which I preach. . . .[77]

Nathans may have been willing to conform outwardly, but he was fully conscious of his Jewishness, and he suggested to his guardian that it might be better to have himself prepared for the University of Pennsylvania rather than Cambridge University, where he felt there might be "some difficulty about my religion."[78]

The same pattern of choice of party, crossing family lines, which had existed earlier still persisted. The Gratzes were working on behalf of the Federalist cause in the stylish Middle Ward.[79] On the other hand, their ardently Democratic brother-in-law, Reuben Etting, not only continued to work at a ward level, but in 1816 actually ran independently for the office of sheriff in the city election.[80] He conducted a newspaper campaign for almost three months, and then on the eve of the election, without warning or explanation,[81] Etting withdrew his candidacy.

Locally, there were few exciting events during the second administration of Monroe other than the activity centering around the new synagogue of Mikveh Israel and the efforts of Rodeph Shalom to get a secure foothold, but two national events took place which were to influence the lives of all Americans. In 1820 the Missouri Compromise was pushed through Congress, by which Missouri was admitted to the Union as a slave state, Maine as a free state, and slavery was barred from all the rest of the Louisiana Purchase north of what was to become Arkansas. The first split had occurred in the fabric of the Union. And in 1823 President Monroe announced that any attempt by any

European power to extend its territory in the Western Hemisphere could not be looked upon "in any other light than as the manifestation of an unfriendly disposition toward the United States." As a result of the Monroe Doctrine, the Americas were to be permitted to shape their own destinies without European interference.[82]

Europeans were, however, to influence the future of the United States in a different way. The reactionary Holy Alliance of Spain, Russia, Austria and France, against whom Monroe's warning had been directed, had frozen the liberal yearnings of the peoples of Europe with an icy repression. From Germany in particular, a mass immigration began to flow westward, and the conditions which caused it were noted frequently in the press of Philadelphia. At first, the numbers were few, but as the years went by they grew to such proportions that, by mid-century, New York contained more Germans than any city in the world except Berlin and Vienna, and Milwaukee became virtually a German town.[83] Among these Germans were, of course, some Jews, for conditions which were bad for Christians in Germany were intolerable for Jews. As the *Philadelphia Gazette* noted in 1823, in the little town of Toplitz Jews were restricted to the very worst section and were subject to a curfew, and in the domain of the Duke of Saxe-Weimar, "in a family of Jews devoted to trade, *only one of the sons is allowed to marry!*"[84]

The combination of forces exerted by the growing immigration—the number of immigrants who entered the country increased ten-fold from 8,385 in 1820 to 84,066 in 1840[85]—and the physical expansion of the country westward made its mark on the Jewish community of Philadelphia. It was not to be for another twenty years until the full weight of numbers was to be felt, but in these earlier days of the flow a pattern was created which remained. The increasing number of foreigners who needed help brought into being more and larger immigrant-aid societies and relief agencies. The Female Hebrew Benevolent Society and the United Hebrew Beneficent Society were their forerunners.

Some of these newcomers passed through Philadelphia, received help and advice, and moved on. Most of their names are not recorded, for they were birds of passage, but a few of them, and some of the members of settled Philadelphia families who sought opportunities away from home, are known.

Meanwhile, those who stayed in Philadelphia were involving themselves more and more in the political life of the city. The names of many who worked for the Federal-Republicans were listed,[86] but Duane, in reporting the Democratic meetings, almost invariably stated that the lists of those who attended were too long to print, and so only the names of the most active Jewish Democrats have been preserved.[87]

Henry Solomon, who had been active early and long, became the first Jew to be elected to a municipal office in Philadelphia. In 1817, by a majority of two to one, he was a successful candidate for the Common Council.[88] Two years later, he sought an even more important post, that of one of the five city representatives to the state legislature, but that time he lost.[89] Win or lose, there was no need for him to deny his religion or sacrifice his principles. It is noteworthy too that among the men whose Federalist activity is known, there were a number who had been naturalized only a few years before. Unhampered by any restrictions, German Jewish, Irish Catholic and English Protestant immigrants all rushed into the hurly-burly excitement of acting like an American citizen as soon as they became one.

The pride which Pennsylvania took in its comprehensive political rights, as distinct from those granted in other states, was in marked contrast to the freedoms granted their inhabitants by the rulers of Europe. Even in England, which boasted of its liberal constitutional monarchy, Lionel Nathan de Rothschild, who was elected to Parliament in 1847 and year after year thereafter, was not permitted to take his seat until 1858, because of the age-old restrictions upon a Jew's right to hold office.[90] Nor was there pressure on American Jews of a deceptive enlightenment which moved them to accept conversion, as did German Jews like Heinrich Heine, to obtain the kind of status the Christians held.

The majority of Americans looked with vague hopes upon the rise of the new missionary societies, but stood fast by the basic principles of American democracy. An article on the persecution of Jews in Europe and the possibilities of conversion through tolerance, reprinted in Philadelphia from a Baltimore paper at the time when the "Jew Bill" was being debated in the Maryland Assembly, sets forth the general feeling of the times:

We hope, nay trust, that it is reserved for this young republic, around whose head new constellations are continually breaking out, to show to the older governments of Europe an example worthy of their imitation. A Jew here may worship according to the tradition of his fathers, and be revered and respected, where government is administered by the hands of Christians—he is in almost every other state than this, eligible to office, capable of rising to the highest dignity without renouncing the religion of his ancestors—if he does renounce it from such a motive, he is a base and detestable hypocrite, and would make a worse Christian than a Jew. . . .[91]

If newspaper comment is a guide to contemporary opinion, the frequency with which articles of such a nature appeared is evidence of the early nineteenth-century American's concern for religious and political freedom. It was easy to condemn proscriptions abroad, noted one writer, referring to the Maryland debate:

But why talk of Europe? In a certain part of the United States, the Jews are deprived of the right of holding offices, and the attempt to place them on a footing with other citizens has been so strenuously resisted that it will probably fail.[92]

As the country looked around for a successor to James Monroe, a new kind of political figure emerged, Andrew Jackson, "Old Hickory," a backwoods, popular candidate, a self-made man with a military reputation and a log-cabin background, and a Westerner from Tennessee. Washington, Adams, Jefferson, Madison and Monroe had all been cultured gentlemen in the European mold. Jackson was the rough, indigenous product of the American frontier. He symbolized a new aspect of the Democratic Party, quite different from the statesmanship and theoretical republicanism of Jefferson and his followers. Jackson was not merely the spokesman for the farmers, the pioneer settlers, the soldiers and the artisans; he was one of them.

In 1824 there were four candidates for the presidency, all of them bearing the label of Democrat-Republican—Jackson, John Quincy Adams, William H. Crawford and Henry Clay. Nationally the Federalists had disappeared into limbo, and their successors, the Whigs, had not yet crystallized into a party. However, at a local level factional splits had taken place, and in Philadelphia one of the first to align himself with the Jacksonians was Zalegman Phillips. As he wrote four years later, boasting of his dedication to the cause of Jackson:

. . . Fellow-citizens my predilections for Jackson, are not of late date. I am proud to say that I was one of his first and earliest supporters in the state of Pennsylvania. In the year 1822 I openly avowed my sentiments, not only in opposition to John Quincy Adams, but in favour of Andrew Jackson. During the campaign of 1823 and 1824, I took an active and I trust not an inefficient part—my every exertion was used by my pen, by my personal services and according to my means by contributing that mite for the general good that was due from every citizen in the republic. I aided in procuring the first *Democratic* meeting that was held in Pennsylvania, in support of General Jackson; The 5th of November 1823 was indeed a proud day for the advancement of sound principles. There was on that day a meeting of upwards of one thousand *Democrats* of the city and county of Philadelphia, Jacob Holgate Esq. was Chairman and I was Secretary at that meeting. . . . I repeat fellow-citizens that that was the *first Democratic* meeting held in Pennsylvania, and was one that gave tone to the burst of feeling in favour of General Jackson throughout the state, which indentified him with the *Democratic* party of the state, which secured him not only the whole electoral vote of the state, but carried along our sisters New Jersey, Maryland and North Carolina, and served to fix the minds of thousands of our hesitating fellow-citizens of other states so strongly, as is now evinced in the honourable support which Jackson is receiving from the great Democratic States of Virginia, New-York and Georgia. . . .[93]

The spirited interest of Phillips and his friends led to the organization of the Hickory Club, which celebrated the anniversary of Jackson's victory at New Orleans for the first time on January 8, 1824. Modern Jackson Day dinners are the successors to that occasion. With Phillips in that Democratic company were David G. Seixas, also an original member of the Hickory Club, and Nathan Nathans, who delivered one of the toasts at the first celebration.[94] The next year it was Seixas' turn to propose a toast, and in an unpolitical vein, based on his experiences as a pioneer teacher of deaf-mutes, he offered his glass to "Benevolence the God-like attribute of man."[95]

In spite of the efforts of the Jacksonians, the General was defeated in the election. He won a plurality in the Electoral College but not a majority, and, when Clay threw his votes to Adams in what the followers of Jackson termed a sell-out, John Quincy Adams was elected president. It is interesting to note that Benjamin Gratz was during his whole life an ardent supporter of Clay, and his youngest daughter Anna married one of the great Kentucky statesman's grandsons.[96]

The political enemies of Phillips were not satisfied with the defeat of his candidate, and he was subjected to some mean anti-Jewish abuse. As an outstanding criminal lawyer, the president of Mikveh Israel, and a man of distinctive, but outmoded, dress, Phillips attracted much attention in the city. A new generation of Americans saw him saunter from his Chestnut Street office in the direction of the synagogue near Third and Cherry, his hair tied colonial-style in a pig-tail, wearing knee breeches, buckles on his shoes and lace collars and cuffs. But his ideas were as fresh as his clothes were old-fashioned. It had been thought that the defeat of Jackson would be followed by the dissolution of the Hickory Club,[97] and that Zalegman Phillips would cease his activity as "the *Agent* and *Treasurer* of the *fraternity* at Dandy Hall," ironically named. When the Jacksonian party gained, rather than lost, adherents as a result of Clay's bitterly attacked stratagem, Conrad Keller, a local tinplate worker, tried to undermine Phillips' reputation in a circuitous, libel-proof manner. He began his public letter by asserting that Phillips was his friend, and that he, Keller, had loaned him money, which was never repaid, and he continued maliciously:

> But I do most solemnly aver, that I *never asserted* that Mr. Philips was a Gambler or a Swindler; or that he borrowed my cash, never calculating at the time to refund it;—and further I do declare that I never did give the most distant intimation, that when a *Jew* can take the advantage of a Christian, he glories in his success—and that it was common among them, after such an event, to exclaim, "*I have crucified a Christian!*"[98]

It was strange that politics seemed to bring forth isolated, and apparently, a-typical, bursts of anti-Semitism. However, Keller was a weak tool compared to William Cobbett and his earlier professional blackguardism. His anti-Semitism was still not forgotten in the United States, although he had been living in England for a quarter of a century, and one editor noted that old Cobbett "has within these few years, evinced a terrible dislike to Jews—he omits no opportunity to vent his spleen upon them."[99] Very unlike Keller's post-election pettiness were the quoted excerpts from Mordecai Manuel Noah's *New York National Advocate*. He was now firmly established in New York as a dramatist and newspaper publisher, and his editorial comments—Noah was always a vehement Democrat—sparkling with controversy, were frequently reprinted in the Philadelphia press, and frequently attacked.[100] But in March, 1825, after the inauguration of Adams, it was all good-will and harmony. Said the *United States Gazette* of his political agility:

> Mr. Noah of the New York National Advocate, is at his old business, hunting up "crumbs of comfort" in his defeat, finding something in the new President and his appointments to like, and little to condemn. Such a man is worth a regiment of querulous Atrabilarious, yellow faced knaves, who quar-

rel with every one pending an election, and with *themselves* after it. Mr. Noah should have a pension from all lovers of order, as a most worthy pattern of zeal in the cause he adopts, and resignation to the results of his undertaking. A plan of such a disposition, would do more towards maintaining republican institutions, than a host of brawling office seekers, who are continually harping (like *harpies*) upon the peoples' rights. . . .[101]

It was a newsworthy item when Noah passed through the city of his birth. If there were those who disliked his politics and his polemics, there were few who could ignore so colorful a figure.

The occasional sporadic sniping at men of high visibility like Phillips and Noah was hardly significant against the background of general respect for the Jewish Philadelphians and their accomplishments. The attack on Phillips was published the day after the new synagogue was consecrated, and, amid the expressions of praise and the expositions of religious freedom which filled the papers, the cacophonic outburst was forgotten. One of the newspapers, which highly extolled the religious ceremony, apologized because neither it nor any other paper had mentioned the fact that "clergy of *all* denominations" had been presented to General Lafayette, who had observed on the occasion "that such an assembly of brothers, could be witnessed in no other part of the world."[102]

Lafayette's triumphal tour of the United States in 1824-25 was one of the great events of the first half of the nineteenth century. In an outpouring of patriotic sentiment, Americans came by the thousands to honor, to see, to hear and to shake the hand of this brother-in-arms of the immortal Washington, as he visited one city after another. An early invitation had been sent by the old Rhode Island soldier, Joseph Wheaton, and in thanking him for it, but postponing acceptance, Lafayette also thanked Wheaton "for the introduction of Lieutenant Levy, an amiable young man, and worthy representative of the American Navy."[103] It is not likely that the great Frenchman met Levy again when he finally came to the States, for shortly after his arrival Lieutenant Uriah Phillips Levy, U. S. N., sailed with Commodore Rodgers on a three-year cruise in the Mediterranean.[104]

When Lafayette came the first time to cheering Philadelphia, thousands gathered to hear him on the hallowed soil of Independence Square. On a second visit, Benjamin Nones, one of the last surviving Jewish soldiers of the Revolution in Philadelphia, joined with other veterans of the city on July 22, 1825, to meet and celebrate with the French hero.[105] Nones' son, Abraham, was then serving his country in a different fashion. By appointment of John Quincy Adams he was filling the post of consul of the United States at Maracaibo.[106]

On July 4, 1826, two men who had exactly fifty years before drafted the Declaration of Independence and had served their country as presidents, John Adams and Thomas Jefferson, both died. The whole country went into mourning and nation-wide services were held to solemnize their passing. Mikveh Israel, like other religious bodies, held special services, and the congregation resolved that they

in common with the rest of their fellow citizens deeply regret the loss their Country has sustained in the deaths of Thomas Jefferson and John Adams and that as a tribute of respect to their memories, the Parnass be requested to have the Synagogue opened tomorrow morning at 7 o'clock for divine worship, and cause it at that time to be hung with black as on the 9th day of Ab [the anniversary fast recalling the destruction of the Temple].[107]

Even before the old leaders had died, representatives of a new political era were preparing to assume leadership. New faces as well as old ones appeared at the polls to urge electors to vote for the candidates of their party. As the Democrats consolidated themselves behind Jackson and pushed out into opposition the more conservative members, internal struggles took place. Nathan Nathans, the young lawyer, found himself in the middle of one of these. He had been elected to represent the Democratic citizens of the township of Roxborough at a meeting of the county delegates to be held in February, 1826.[108] The opposition attacked him personally as a self-seeker and the Roxborough Democratic meeting as unrepresentative of the party. After a few weeks of public argument in the press, Nathans won out, and not only went to the county meeting, but was there chosen as a teller to supervise the balloting.[109]

The successful merchant, John Moss, retired from active business, and began to devote himself more and more to civic and political affairs. In the Locust Ward he was first active on behalf of the Federal-Republicans,[110] but later switched to the Democratic Party, which in 1828 elected him to the Common Council on the Jacksonian city ticket.[111] When the cause of Greek independence gained sympathy and support in the United States, and supplies were collected for those brave rebels against Turkish tyranny, it was the brig *Tontine*, which belonged to the

Moss family, that sailed from Philadelphia with $16,000 worth of provisions for the Greeks.[112]

As the presidential election of 1828 approached, it was obvious throughout the country that it would result in an overwhelming victory for the Jacksonians. Zalegman Phillips, who had been working consistently on behalf of the General for six years, thought that he deserved nomination for an important office. In a strong appeal "To the Electors of the Second Congressional District of the State of Pennsylvania," he set forth his claim to a seat in Congress.[113] The *Democratic Press* was sympathetic to this "Original Jackson Man," but it pointed out that the delegates had been chosen to nominate John Lisle, and not Phillips or any other candidate, no matter how worthy.[114] Zalegman Phillips' bid for political office came to nought, but his zeal for the party never diminished. The Phillips family remained the leading Jewish Democrats of the city, and years later Zalegman's son, Henry M., became one of the close political associates of George M. Dallas who emerged as the leader of the party in Pennsylvania, and was elected Vice-President of the United States in 1844.

Other men in increasing numbers began to receive the recognition that was due their services, position and capabilities. Joseph Simon Cohen was the Federal-Republican candidate for the City Assembly in 1829, and lost by only a few hundred votes.[115] At the beginning of the year the Select and Common Councils elected the Directors of the Public Schools, the forerunner of the present School Board, and among the thirty-six then chosen were Benjamin Etting and Michael E. Israel.[116] At a slightly later meeting of the Councils they chose the six members of the Board of Health, among whom was John Moss.[117] More and more the Jews of Philadelphia were to share with their fellow-citizens responsibility for the management of the civic institutions and boards.

❧ 16

Authors, Actors and Patrons of the Arts

PHILADELPHIA was the book-publishing center of the United States. Its people had the reputation of being the most cultured in the country, and the English visitors, who came with increasing frequency to tour the cities of the rising nation and then went home to write unflattering accounts of the barbaric behavior of the Americans, usually paid a grudging compliment to the public buildings, the library, the theaters and the society of Philadelphia. There was still a strong Quaker influence which somewhat moderated the extravagances of dress and behavior that marked high life in George IV and Beau Brummel's England, but the growing wealth of the merchant princes found expression in a rich native cultural life, strongly influenced, however, by the latest standards of London and Bath. And the belles of the city were renowned, not only for their beauty, but their scintillating conversation as well.

Some of the Jews took part in this general cultural life, but there was, outside of the synagogue, little Jewish cultural activity. The Philadelphia Jews of the eighteenth century had not produced a single book of Jewish interest, and only two temporary residents, Ottolenghe and Nassy, had written anything at all that was published in book-form.[1] The only work which represented religious writing was Fraenckel's sermon on Frederick the Great, of European origin and issued under Christian auspices.[2]

303

After 1800 and before the arrival of Leeser in 1829, about a dozen items of specific Jewish interest made their appearance, but with the exception of a Hebrew grammar by *Hazan* Carvalho,[3] a Hebrew Bible and a reprint of Rabbi S. I. Cohen's *Elements of Jewish Faith,* these were organizational publications of one sort or another. Cohen for a short time seems to have brought a little light to the Philadelphia Jewish scene. Once more it is Rebecca Gratz who gives us a glimpse of a fleeting attempt to organize what twenty years later was crystallized in the Hebrew Sunday School Society. In 1818 she wrote to her close friend, Mrs. Ogden Hoffman:

> . . . I have been "chewing the cud of sweet and bitter fancy" at home. Most generally have been sometimes engaged with my sisters families, and sometimes trying to be useful among the Orphans and have added a new employment to my usual occupations in the study of the Hebrew language.
>
> A young Gentleman of good education in the sacred language lately arrived here who was desirous of opening a school in the congregation & applied to my brothers on the subject. There are many children in our family whose parents wished to have taught and I proposed an afternoon class at our house and myself as a scholar. Elkalah Cohen, Maria & Ellen Hays and the little ones to the number of eleven joined us and we have been for the last month declining pronouns &c. with as much zeal as success. Our teacher is a German and not sufficiently acquainted with the English to conduct a large school with facility. But I expect we shall make out very well, if he continues here long enough to take us thro' the grammer. He published in Richmond last year a little tract, which you may perhaps have seen as they were sold at some of the book stores in N.Y. called "Elements of Jewish faith." If you have not, I will send you a copy when the opportunity offers, as I think you will be pleased with the explanations of the decalogue—and it contains nothing that could be offensive to you.[4]

Cohen apparently did not stay in Philadelphia, and the pattern of Jewish cultural life in the city remained unchanged. The lack of real accomplishment in Jewish fields and the lack of consuming interest was due in measure to the small size of the community, to the absence of scholars with the time and enthusiasm to devote to scholarship, and to the direction of the energies of individuals towards establishing themselves and becoming American.

In a way, it was also a reflection of American life, for, in spite of native promise, not even the most patriotic Americans considered that they had produced an equal to the popular Lord Byron or the still anonymous author of *Waverley* and *Ivanhoe.* English plays were in more demand than those by native authors.

The United States was too busy growing and getting strong materially to have more than a nascent interest in its own artistic and cultural resources. A culture of necessity preceded a culture of study, reflection and artistic creation. So it was with the American Jewish community.

For their prayer-books and religious literature the Jews turned to importations from abroad, the bi-lingual works of David Levi of London, the standard Sephardic manuals of Amsterdam, and, to satisfy the needs of the Ashkenazic immigrants, similar works from the centers of German learning.[5] Individuals such as Cohen or Emanuel Nunez Carvalho, whose sermon on the death of Seixas, delivered in both Hebrew and English, was printed in the English version,[6] were not representative of the Philadelphians. The polemics and confutations, intended to combat the assaults of the missionaries, and the first American Jewish periodical were written in New York, as had been the first pre-Revolutionary English prayer-book and as was the first Hebrew-English prayer-book in 1826.[7]

Philadelphia had taken the lead in other fields—philanthropic societies, the fight for religious rights, and the establishment of a second synagogue—but as far as Jewish writing and publishing were concerned the major accomplishments were shared by New York and Charleston. In the next generation the gifted and prolific pen of Isaac Leeser was to shift the center of American Jewish culture to Philadelphia.

What the early Philadelphians lacked by way of creative Jewish scholarship they seem to have made up for by reading. The native-born Jews bought most of the books of Jewish interest issued in other communities. Simon and Hyman Gratz collected substantial libraries.[8] Aaron Levy, Jr., following his uncle's interests, supplemented his small Hebrew collection with works on American history.[9] The Hays and Etting families were wide readers.[10] Jacob I. Cohen acquired the books of the learned Moses M. Mordecai when he married his widow, and to these he added his own purchases to form one of the most important early libraries which, through the care of his nephew Dr. Joshua I. Cohen, has survived.[11] And Jacob Mordecai, the son of Moses, not content with educating polite ladies for whom he conducted a seminary in the South, pursued his biblical studies. The basic Jewish education which he had acquired as a boy in Philadelphia from his father and the other older men who remembered their

European heritage enabled him to compose an unpublished two-volume theological defense of Judaism[12] and to make extensive notes on Maimonides,[13] which clearly demonstrate his grasp of the ethics of the fathers.

Where the subject was more general the Philadelphia Jews as a whole showed more interest. They followed the arguments of Tom Paine and the deists against revealed religion, and when David Levi took up cudgels to defend the Old Testament against Paine and Priestley, first Benjamin Gomez, and later Naphtali Judah republished his works in New York, and both Simon Gratz and Solomon Etting bought copies as soon as they appeared.[14] In Northumberland, Pennsylvania, where he had exiled himself, the famous scientist and free-thinker Priestley published his *Address to the Jews* to supplement his earlier *Letters*,[15] and wrote Simon Levi in Philadelphia, urging him to buy copies of his book and distribute them among his "countrymen."[16] Religious controversies which raged throughout the first part of the century found many who read both sides of any argument with refreshing broadmindedness. Frey's turgid missionary tracts and the effective rebuttals to them, the George Bethune English-Edward Everett debate on Jewish and Christian messianic beliefs, and similar writings found earnest readers among the Jews.[17]

There was one major exception to the local unproductivity in the field of Hebrew letters. Only three months before the British burned Washington, a cultural event of great significance took place in Philadelphia; the first Hebrew Bible printed in America was announced for sale by the publisher Thomas Dobson, at No. 41 South Second Street.[18] The history of the publishing of Bibles in America is as fascinating as it is curious. The Book of Psalms—with Hebrew words in the preface and a complete Hebrew alphabet in the 119th Psalm—had appeared in an English version, as early as 1640, from the pioneer press of Cambridge, Massachusetts,[19] and other editions in English and German were printed frequently in various American cities during the eighteenth century. However, the publication of complete Bibles in English had been by government license only, and the printers in England who enjoyed the monopoly saw to it that the lucrative privilege was not extended to colonial printers. As a result, the only native-printed Bibles produced in the British colonies were John Eliot's translation of both Testaments into the Indian language, which the Cambridge press first issued in 1661-63, and a number of German editions which were printed by the Saur family in Germantown from 1743 on.

Hardly had victory over the British seemed assured when Robert Aitken, a Philadelphia printer, publisher and bookseller, appealed to Congress to support his venture of printing an English Bible to fill the need created by the cutting off of English importations during the Revolution. With the official permission of Congress, the first American edition was issued in 1781-82, and, once a precedent had been established, a whole stream of American-printed Bibles flowed on to the market. An undiminished interest in biblical studies and the establishment of religious freedom encouraged the issuing of different versions in the printing centers of the country. In 1790 Irish-born Mathew Carey, with his partner Stewart, published a handsome Roman Catholic version in Philadelphia, and the following year in Worcester Isaiah Thomas issued an edition of the King James text. A Trenton printing contained the first American appearance of the Apocrypha, and Thomas, going somewhat further afield, produced a New Testament in Greek in 1800.[20]

Meanwhile, in 1787, the Presbyterian Synod in Philadelphia considered a resolution making the study of Hebrew a part of the curriculum of its religious education.[21] As previously for its Bibles, so in the field of Hebrew studies too, the United States had been almost entirely dependent upon the importation of foreign texts. But with the growth and spread of theological seminaries the demand became so great that the publication of Hebrew grammars and lexicons in this country became both feasible and profitable. In the decade preceding the outbreak of the War of 1812, at least eight different American printings of Hebrew linguistic handbooks appeared,[22] the most notable of which was Clement Clarke Moore's *Lexicon*, 1809, the first of its kind written in America. Moore is, however, rather better known for his later poem, *'Twas the Night Before Christmas*, than his Hebrew studies.

None of these works had been published in Philadelphia. But in an effort to carry out the wishes of the Presbyterian Synod, the Reverend James P. Wilson, pastor of the First Presbyterian Church of Philadelphia, undertook to prepare a simple introduction to the study of Hebrew based on Parkhurst's method, then current in England. While Wilson was in the midst of his labors, there arrived in Philadelphia a man who had toured the theological seminaries of New England and New York, carrying with him a prospectus, plans and manuscripts for a complete Hebrew grammar and an American edition of the Bible in Hebrew. At Harvard University and Andover Theological Seminary he had met with considerable interest for his projects, and received no less than forty subscriptions from each institution for his contemplated Bible.[23]

The newcomer was Jonas, later Jonathan, Horwitz, a Jew of Polish extraction, who had lived successively during the almost thirty years of his life in Germany, Holland and England. Upon his arrival in Philadelphia, he quickly made the acquaintance of Dr. Wilson whose text-book, *An Easy Introduction to the Knowledge of the Hebrew Language*, was published in Philadelphia in 1812, the first work on Hebrew to appear in the city.[24] In it Wilson gave his new friend quite a commendation:

Mr. Horwitz, a learned foreigner now in America, permits me to say that he has also an English-Hebrew grammar; which is nearly ready for the press. The highest expectations may be entertained by the critical Hebrew scholar, from his uncommon proficiency in oriental learning.[25]

Wilson's object in putting out his own book was, as he stated, the encouragement of the study of Hebrew among the American clergy, even at the risk of poor sales.[26] Two years after its appearance copies of his book were still available for sale in the hands of several booksellers. The "highest expectations" entertained for Horwitz's grammar were never realized; perhaps he felt that the limited market had been saturated; his work is not known ever to have been published.

As far as the Bible was concerned, Horwitz did not have the field to himself. In 1809 a Hebrew Psalter had been issued at Cambridge,[27] and a year later an attempt had been made in New Haven by the publisher Mills Day to obtain subscriptions for an American edition of the Bible in Hebrew,[28] but the plan never went beyond the prospectus stage. Wilson in his work also mentioned the Bible project of the foreign scholar:

As Hebrew Bibles are very scarce, those who wish to be supplied are hereby recommended to Mr. Horwitz, mentioned before on page 231 [sic], who contemplates editing in Philadelphia a copy of Vander-Hoogt's celebrated edition, and who is fully equal to so great a work.[29]

Wilson's book was inspiring comment in the local theological journals by men anxious to further Hebrew studies. Typical of these, one "W.A." wrote:

Is Latin of more importance than Hebrew? I would ask, does it become us to employ months and years in learning a heathen tongue, and yet not to allot even a solitary day to the sacred Hebrew language, I would ask, sir, does it comport with the duties of religion, is it consistent with those precepts inculcated by the doctrines of Christianity, to elevate men above his Maker, and prefer his works to those of Omnipotence? I would ask, can Horace, Juvenal, Virgil, Homer, and the whole catalogue of Pagan authors, produce one work or passage which can vie with many of the Old Testament in sublimity, beauty of imagery, purity of morality, and the importance and magnificence of the subject discussed?[30]

It is noteworthy that the Jews of Philadelphia evinced no interest in the project which received such enthusiastic support from non-Jews. The Pentateuchs and Scriptures supplied by David Levi of London, printed from texts edited by Jewish scholars, filled their needs, and an edition based principally on Christian scholarship would not have appealed to them even though printed in their sacred language. Still, as Wilson had noted, the scarcity of Hebrew Bibles for the clergy made the publishing of an edition an attractive venture. The recommendations of many ministers and the considerable number of subscriptions secured in advance by Horwitz virtually assured its success.

Most enthusiastically a prospectus was issued, stressing the fact that Mr. Horwitz had been "induced" to proceed with his plans "from finding the great scarcity of copies of the Hebrew scriptures in this country."[31] "There are probably not a dozen copies for sale in the whole United States," it stated. "He knows from personal and particular inquiry, that the bookstores of Boston cannot supply a single copy, those of New York but four, and those of Philadelphia but two." The printing was to be done by William Fry "in two octavo volumes, on superfine paper, with a new pica Hebrew type, cast for the purpose at the foundery of Binny and Ronaldson." Simon Gratz and Brothers may have supplied the lead from which this very font was cast.[32] The recommendations were signed by twelve clergymen of Philadelphia and New York, including the Rector of Christ Church, James Abercrombie, and William Harris, President of Columbia College. It was further announced that the proof sheets would be revised and compared with Van der Hooght's own edition by Horwitz's friend, the Reverend James P. Wilson.

Then, suddenly, in New York appeared an advertisement by Whiting and Watson, stating that they had made arrangements to begin work on:

a *stereotyped edition* of the *Hebrew Bible,* from the text of Van der Hooght's celebrated edition, *with the points,* to which will be added the various readings, selected by Doederlin and Meisner from the voluminous works of Kennicott and De Rossi.[33]

What disturbed Horwitz was that this edition was announced as being under the joint patronage of the Theological Seminary of New York and the Andover Theological Seminary. On January 16, 1813, he had printed a notice to the patronizers of his edition urging them not to confuse the new project with the edition which he was "now about publishing."[34]

Perhaps because it was apparent that if he did not get into print someone else would, Jonas Horwitz, without public explanation, gave up all further interest in the project, and transferred "his right to the edition, together with his list of subscribers" to Thomas Dobson.[35]

Other factors too may have impelled Horwitz to give up his responsibility for the project. One was his decision to enter another field, for about this time he entered the Medical College of the University of Pennsylvania. Another may have been his contact with the community of Jews, who might have pointed out the incongruity of Horwitz's association in the venture.

Whatever the reason, the Hebrew Bible which Horwitz had planned, the proofs of which he may have read, was announced by Dobson as in "progress" on May 27, 1813.[36] The announcement further stated that

this edition will be unencumbered with the Masoretical points now generally exploded by the best Scholarship in the Hebrew language.

In contradiction to the opinions of the backers of the New York project who had promised the help of points, they were spoken of by local theologians as a Jewish scheme to make the acquisition of Hebrew difficult,[37] a rather untenable position, for actually they make reading by a student much easier.

The first volume appeared at the beginning of March, 1814,[38] without a title-page, but with a short account of the origin of the undertaking, giving Horwitz due credit for his initiation of the work. On May 21st the second volume was completed, and with it were included the title-pages for both volumes. Proudly Dobson boasted:

This arduous undertaking, the first of the kind attempted in the United States, is now happily accomplished. The work is considered as one of the finest specimens of *Hebrew Printing* ever executed.[39]

Several months later, Jonathan Horwitz graduated from medical school, and instead of being the publisher of the first American edition of the Bible in Hebrew, his first American production was an unimportant dissertation on colic, for which he received his degree.[40]

No contemporary Jewish opinion of the Dobson Bible has been found, and while the Christian clergy awaited its appearance eagerly, the work was not reviewed in the important theological journals. More than seventy years later, when asked to comment on it, Sabato Morais, then minister of Mikveh Israel and one of the foremost Hebrew scholars of the country, wrote briefly:

The edition is good, and I think as correct as others. The marginal annotations are helpful and copious. They occur more frequently in the Pentateuch and historical books than in the prophets and Hagiographa, where they are found only on each chapter or psalm.[41]

It was not until 1845, when the first volume of Isaac Leeser's Hebrew-English Pentateuch was issued, that any portion of the Bible was published in this country under Jewish auspices.

While Jonathan Horwitz was studying medicine in Philadelphia, he became acquainted with the Andrews family, who had moved to Philadelphia at about that time.[42] Joseph Andrews, who had married Haym Salomon's daughter Sarah, was earning his living as a petty trader and part-time Hebrew teacher. In 1817 the thirty-four-year-old Dr. Horwitz married their daughter Deborah, who was half his age. He opened an office on Vine Street,[43] in an area where most of the Jews lived, and was appointed a staff physician to the Northern Dispensary.[44]

He was, however, still seeking greater prestige than he could expect to find with a neighborhood medical practice in a not too fashionable section of town. He had somehow made the acquaintance of Judge Thomas Cooper, the English lawyer and scientist who had left his native land during the anti-French period of repression at the end of the eighteenth century and settled in Pennsylvania. And Cooper, impressed by his erudition, had mentioned him to Jefferson, then busy gathering together a faculty for the newly established University of Virginia. Early in 1818, Horwitz wrote Jefferson:

> Judge Thos. Cooper, informed me, that when in Virginia, he mentioned my name to you as professor, of Oriental literature, in the College of Char-lotte-Ville under your auspices, & that you replied to him; if it could be joined with the German language, such a professorship might be instituted. This induces me, to take the liberty of addressing you, the German is my vernacular tongue; & am not only master of it, but have actually now in my possession, a manuscript of a German Grammar, which I composed some years ago (an abridgement of Adelung the Johnson of Germany) for the use of Englishmen.
>
> Respecting the Hebrew &c. the enclosed proposals; & its recommendations which were written 7 years since may speak for themselves; but if required, I can obtain a letter of recommendation, signed by most of the Clergy, Advocates, & other literary characters of this City; & I may say of almost half the Union (who had attended my lectures) in favour of both my talent for teaching, & proficiency in Oriental learning. . . .[45]

Jefferson did not rush to take advantage of the opportunity of obtaining for his college this extraordinarily versatile gentleman, and in the fall Horwitz wrote to Judge Cooper asking for his intervention once more.[46] Meanwhile, he advertised in Philadelphia that he would commence two classes in the Hebrew language, "one with the points and one without," each to be given three times a week, the lessons to be:

> interspersed with observations, Biblical, Talmudical, Rabbinical, and Philosophical (particularly the Philosophy of Language), which five branches are requisite to constitute a complete Hebruist.[47]

In 1820, upon the conclusion of a series of lectures to the ministers of the Methodist Episcopal Church which had lasted a month, sixteen of them paid him a public tribute in the press.[48] And yet, as long as Horwitz remained in Philadelphia, he maintained his ties with the Jewish community.

In 1823 he applied to the State of Maryland for an official medical post,[49] which he did not receive; but three years later he began dividing his time between Philadelphia and Baltimore, and early in 1830 moved permanently to the latter city. He was a man of great and varied talents, and some ambivalence. He continued his interest in both medicine and Hebrew, and in 1839 there was published at Baltimore *A Defence of The Cosmogony of Moses,* "By J. Horwitz, M.D.," in which from a traditional Jewish point of view, and with a knowledge of rabbinics that was extraordinary, he pitted his knowledge of midrashic literature and of Maimonides' theories of cosmogony against the interpreters of evolutionary geology.[50] Whether or not he himself abandoned Judaism for Christianity is not known. When he died in 1852,[51] he was buried in an Episcopalian cemetery, and his children, from whom are descended the Horwitz and Bullitt families of Philadelphia, were all brought up in that faith.

If the clergymen of America were delighted to have a Hebrew Bible for their scholarly use, polite literature, the popular *belles lettres* of the day, was—as at present—the main book diet of Philadelphians. Among the Jews it was the Gratzes who left behind a body of correspondence which reveals their literary tastes and literary associations. Through it personal glimpses can be seen of many of the foremost American writers—Washington Irving, James Fenimore Cooper, James K. Paulding and John P. Kennedy—who were their, and especially Rebecca's, friends. Irving in particular was close to the lovely Philadelphia Jewess—"I am gratified to hear that Washington thinks well of me. The friendship of such men I esteem a happiness"[52]—and his courtship of Rebecca's dear friend Maria Fenno Hoffman's stepdaughter, Matilda, was followed by her with loving solicitude.[53] When Matilda died tragically of consumption in 1809, Rebecca was grief-stricken and Irving so shattered that he remained faithful to Matilda's memory all his life, and never married.

Much as the Americans admired Irving, the most avidly read novelist of the day was Sir Walter Scott, whose *Ivanhoe*, with its romantic portrayal of the Jewess Rebecca, appeared in 1820. For many years Rebecca Gratz has been fancifully associated with Scott's Rebecca, the story being that the Scottish author took as the model for his character the lovely Philadelphian, an account of whose life and goodness Washington Irving was reputed to have given him.[54] Rebecca Gratz in her own frequent references to *Ivanhoe* never identified herself with the heroine, although in a letter to Maria Hoffman she showed herself a competent critic of the tale's Jewish feeling.

I am glad to find you have been as much interested in Ivanhoe as I have— and as great an admirer of it. I believe I felt a little extra pleasure from the circumstance of Rebecca's being a hebrew maiden, but she is certainly the most lovely female character he ever drew and indeed I admire the whole work as much as either of its predecessors. Bois Guilbert too is an admirably drawn character—and almost every scene would make a good picture, or be fine in dramatic representation. I am surprised it is not an universal favorite, we have some critics here too who "would d--n it, with faint praise," but I hope we shall have a series of english tales as agreeable as the scotch ones — You may believe I feel grateful for this justification of the jewish character, even old Isaac's avarice is more the effect of persecution than natural baseness of mind, and the goodness of heart sometimes glanced at, and his strong attachment to his daughter, shews that other times, and other circumstances would have made him a humane being—It is worthy of Scott, at a period when persecution has re-commenced in Europe, to hold up a picture of the superstition and cruelty in which it originated.[55]

In another letter to her sister-in-law Maria Gratz, she calls Rebecca "just such a representation of a good girl as I think human nature can reach."[56] Yet to none of her closest friends did she say that she was the model for such a representation. Until such time as a letter from either Irving or Scott is found mentioning the conversation which was supposed to have taken place, the matter must remain merely a pleasant legend.

If such books were the chosen reading of the native-born American Jews, a decade or two would have to pass by before such volumes would be found on the shelves of the Polock, Bomeisler or Hyneman households. The immigrant generation, a surprisingly large number of them well-educated according to European Jewish standards, could not assimilate this strange, new culture; their children grew up on it.

Most of the best books, plays, poems and novels, as well as more serious scholarly works, were bought as they came out in England and America by the Library Company of Philadelphia. Long before the organization of a public library system, the private subscription libraries, of which the Library Company was the oldest in the country, provided the major book resources of a community. They lent books only to their members, but permitted the general reading public to frequent their rooms. So universally was the Franklin-founded library on Fifth Street used that it was known diversely as the Philadelphia Library, the City Library, and the Public Library. From 1757, when David Franks had become a member, a number of Jews had been subscribers, including old Aaron Levy, Hyman and Jacob Gratz, Samuel and Isaac Hays, and Zalegman and Jonas B. Phillips, and they supported this important institution with their annual subscriptions as well as by occasional gifts.[57] A non-member, Mathias Lopez, for some years a resident of the city, gave the library two extremely interesting items: a beautifully written manuscript of prayers for counting the *Omer*, or pentecostal days; and a long autograph letter written in 1773 by Ezra Stiles, the President of Yale, to the travelling sage Haym Isaac Carigal.[58]

Jacob Gratz was outstanding among those who were active in forming other new libraries to meet the demands of the growing population. He represented a new kind of Jew in the city, one who had inherited wealth and had been financially successful, so that he had the leisure to devote himself to cultural pursuits. When the Athenaeum of Philadelphia was founded in 1814, Jacob Gratz was one of its first directors,[59] held that position for many years, and was treasurer in 1816. In 1817 his cousin, Joseph Simon Cohen, was the new institution's acting secretary,[60] and in 1820 there were fifteen Jewish subscribers, including Lt. Uriah Phillips Levy, who made a present of some of his books to the library.[61] When a more practical library was planned for tradesmen and artisans, Joseph Gratz offered his support. He was on the first board of managers of the Apprentices Library, founded in 1820, and was active there for a number of years.[62] And another Gratz relative, Benjamin Etting, then associated with the Board of Education, was elected secretary of the similar Mercantile Library.[63]

However public-spirited the part a handful of Philadelphia Jews played in the formation and management of libraries, it cannot be said that they exerted much influence on the creative writing of the period. The itinerant, restless Joshua Montefiore, in Philadelphia for a few years, published editions of his *Commercial Dictionary* and *Commercial and Notarial Precedents* in 1803, and eight years later applied his knowledge of forms and procedures in the compilation of *The American Trader's Compendium*, a valuable guide to the commercial regulations of the United States.[64] But these were hardly of literary merit. Slightly more so, but still not a work of original genius, was Charlotte Lennox's *Shakespeare Illustrated*, a reissue of a popular work of Shakespearean criticism, with "Critical Remarks" and biographical sketches by young Mordecai Manuel Noah, which was published in Philadelphia in 1809.[65] Two volumes were intended, but only one appeared, for, as Noah wrote many years later, he had not been "able to collect the materials for the other," and subsequently had "been prevented by the pressure of other occupations."[66]

One of these occupations may have been his connection with the short-lived scandal and gossip magazine, *The Trangram, or Fashionable Trifler*, three numbers of which appeared in 1809. The historian of Philadelphia magazines noted that the publisher told William Duane "that the editors were Mordecai M. Noah, Alexander F. Coxe, a son of Tench Coxe, and a third person 'whose named he seemed unwilling to mention!' "[67] After three numbers the triple team quarrelled, and publication ceased.

Except for young Noah's *Sorrento* the only other creative literary work produced by a Philadelphia Jew was by Jonas B. Phillips, a grandson of old Jonas. In 1827 his *Tales for Leisure Hours*, which had originally appeared serially in the *Saturday Evening Post*, were collected and published in book-form.[68] Twelve Gothic tales of minor importance, stilted and typical of mediocre Victorianism, constituted the second belle-lettristic effort of a Jew in the city. Later Phillips became moderately successful as a playwright. Compared to the New Yorker, Samuel B. H. Judah, and the Charlestonians, Isaac Harby and Penina Moise, all of whom received major critical consideration, the Philadelphia Jewish literary scene was bare.

One other work, although written by a New Yorker, deserves mention, for its author was born in Philadelphia and the subject matter of his essays was the city of his birth. In 1828 there appeared in the *New York Gazette*, and were subsequently reprinted in *Poulson's Advertiser*, a delightful series of sketches of a boyhood lived in Revolutionary Philadelphia, relived for a new generation of Americans, by "An Old Philadelphian."[69] The anonymous author has been identified as Naphtali Phillips.[70] His writing is full of a charming nostalgia for old landmarks and forgotten folks, who hitched their horses to iron posts which rose from cobble-stoned alleys.

In one essay he took his readers on a tour through the historic city of his youth, from the edge of the Delaware to the Schuylkill-bordered west, through the outlying districts of Southwark and Northern Liberties, in churchyards and cemeteries, and across forgotten creeks. These vivid recollections of a bygone age preceded John Watson's famous annals of old Philadelphia.

It had taken a good many years to establish the theater in Philadelphia both as a regular and an acceptable feature of the city's life. The Puritan tradition of England, which had looked upon the playhouse as a source of evil and corruption, had taken firm root in America. But time, and the gradual recognition of the drama as a beneficent cultural influence, blunted the opposition of those who looked on the candlelit stage as the fiery mouth of hell. The anti-theater propaganda, which raged in Philadelphia since the 1760s, largely conducted by frivolity-shunning Quakers, and which in the mid 1790s had thrown out one somewhat anti-Semitic dart, had subsided by the end of the century.[71] With the opening of the Chestnut Street Theater, among the original subscribers to which were the Prager brothers, Isaac Franks and Samuel Hays,[72] regular theatrical seasons provided entertainment for Philadelphians.

The change of attitude on the part of the citizenry and the place the theater filled in its life are well described by Mordecai Manuel Noah, who, reminiscing of his youth for William Dunlap, the historian of the American stage, said that he had been a regular attendant of the Chestnut Street Theater.

I seldom missed a night, and always retired to bed, after witnessing a good play, gratified and improved: and thus, probably, escaping the haunts of taverns, and the pursuits of depraved pleasures, which too frequently allure and destroy our young men.[73]

Noah recalled that he had been a member of a society of amateur actors, the Thespian Club, which produced its pieces at a theater on South Street. He had shared with a man named Helmbold the honor of cutting the plays, substituting new passages, casting parts and writing couplets for the exits.

Our little company soon dwindled away, the expenses were too heavy for our pockets; our writings and performances were sufficiently wretched, but as the audience was admitted without cost, they were too polite to express any disapprobation. We recorded all our doings in a little weekly paper, published, I believe, by Jemmy Riddle, at the Corner of Chestnut and Third-street, opposite the tavern kept by that sturdy old democrat, Israel Israel.

Such was the boyhood initiation of one who was to become a firm supporter of the American stage and American plays, and himself a most successful playwright.

English drama, however, was and remained for many years the main source of theatrical entertainment. Richard Cumberland's *The Jew* was one of the favorites from the time it was first produced at the New Theatre in Philadelphia in 1795, becoming part of succeeding seasons' standard repertoire. It was printed in Boston, Philadelphia and New York the same year.[74]

Cumberland's work brought to the audiences of his day a most sympathetic portrayal of the Jew. In the first scene, the principal character, Sheva, a kind-hearted Jewish philanthropist and moneylender, voiced in a dignified manner the tragedy of his people:

We have no abiding place on earth—no country, no home. Everybody rails at us, everybody points us out for their may-game and their mockery. If your playwrights want a butt, or a buffoon or a knave to make sport of, out comes a Jew to be baited and buffetted through five long acts, for the amusement of all good Christians. Cruel sport! merciless amusement! Hard dealings for a poor stray sheep of the scattered flock of Abraham! How can you expect us to show kindness, when we receive none?[75]

This was followed on the stage by a similar work by Thomas Dibdin, *The Jew and the Doctor*, in which Abednego was a kind and generous Jew of the Sheva type. It too, somewhat later, was printed in Philadelphia.[76]

With these plays came English acting companies, which enjoyed tremendous successes throughout the United States, and brought with them the first Jewish actors to appear professionally on the American stage. Miss K. Solomons and a Mrs. Solomons were part of a stock company which was billed regularly at the Old Southwark Theatre in 1794 and at the New Theatre for ten years thereafter.[77] In 1801 Miss Solomons is listed as taking such roles as Donalbaine in *Macbeth* and as appearing with Edgar Allan Poe's mother, Miss Arnold, in an added attraction, "a Pantomimical Dance."[78]

Another touring Englishman, who appeared in prominent roles in 1812 and 1813, was Mr. Jacobs. "Jacobs was an English Jew and a clever vocalist, but was no actor," wrote one chronicler of the Philadelphia theater.[79] Nothing further has been learned of him. But the "dashing young Israelite from London," William Dinneford, left a more colorful record. He made his American debut at the Chestnut Street Theater in 1823. Durang records that:

He was added to the stage corps, during the season, as a leading actor. This gentleman, who came to this country for mercantile purposes, and at one time, at the East, was engaged in the billiard table business, made subsequently some bustle and noise in the theatrical world as an enterprising manager, leaving no town, village or city untouched by his energetic speculative genius.[80]

With E. A. Marshall he took over the management of the

Walnut Street Theatre after the retirement of the famous Wemyss. Dinneford died about 1851 in Panama, on his way to seek his fortune in California.

In spite of the great popularity of the English companies and English plays, a new generation of American actors and dramatists was growing up to challenge their dominance. In Philadelphia various members of the large Phillips family played a leading part in this native effort. Mordecai Manuel Noah, a grandson of Jonas Phillips, saw his first play published in New York, but it was never acted.[81] Then, his diplomatic career in Tunis interrupted his literary production. Meanwhile, Aaron J. Phillips, Noah's uncle, was acquiring a fine reputation as an actor and manager. Before he returned to the city of his birth, he "had been acting at the west doing tragedy with all his might," gathering experience and fame in the new cities of the frontier hungry for any of the crumbs of eastern culture.[82] Aaron was still "touring the provinces" when the first of his nephew's plays made its appearance in Philadelphia.

On Christmas Eve of 1819, Noah's *She Would Be a Soldier, or the Plains of Chippewa*, celebrated its first night in Philadelphia.[83] The first play by an American Jew to have been performed on the stage had been Isaac Harby's *The Gordian Knot*, which Placide's company produced in a garbled form in 1810.[84] The second was the same author's *Alberti*, which was played at the Charleston Theatre in 1818.[85] Then came Noah's American historical drama, which had opened in New York on June 21, 1819, and made nearly $2400 in two performances.[86] The fourth was Samuel B. H. Judah's *The Mountain Torrent*, which, after having been performed in New York in the spring of 1820, made its debut in Philadelphia at the Winter Tivoli Theatre late in the same year.[87]

Harby, Noah, Judah and their contemporaries were doing much to reduce the American stage's dependence on British plays by offering in their place popular American drama. Between 1820 and 1830, Noah reached his dramatic peak and one success followed another. In January, 1822, Philadelphia audiences warmly praised his patriotic play, *Yuseff Caramalli; or the Siege of Tripoli*, based on the author's personal experiences in North Africa.[88] Then, on the following Washington's Birthday, his *Marion; or, the Hero of Lake George*, deemed most appropriate for the occasion, opened at the Walnut Street Theatre,[89] where

Mathias Lopez was stage prompter. For some time Lopez was a fixture in town, getting such a reputation that in 1826 he began to issue a series of plays in a collection which he called the *Acting American Theatre,* "corrected from the prompt books of the Phila. Theatre, by M. Lopez."[90] Shortly afterwards he left town, and was killed in a duel in New Orleans in 1833.

An unusual opening took place on April 15, 1829. Aaron J. Phillips, back in Philadelphia and intending to settle down, undertook to provide the city with the best in theatrical entertainment by opening the Arch Street Theatre under his management. Every preparation was taken to guarantee the success of the venture. Cumberland's popular comedy, *The West Indian,* with a choice cast, played the first night. One nephew, Jonas B. Phillips, the author and later playwright, wrote the poetical prologue for the evening; another, Moses B. Phillips, was in the cast. "Mr. Phillips had certainly engaged a very fine and talented company," we are told, "and indeed every department was adequately filled, and our friend Aaron really deserved a better fate than that which ended in disaster to his management."[91] His attempt at running the Arch Street Theatre failed, but Aaron Phillips continued in the theatrical world, and distinguished himself as a character actor. And his three nephews, Jonas B. and Moses B. Phillips and Mordecai M. Noah, all too remained associated with the stage.

For Jonas it was an avocation, for he had been admitted to the bar in 1826.[92] Nonetheless, he had a moderately successful career, although his plays were not judged to be uniformly good. Phillips' first melodrama, *The Evil Eye,* with Mr. Sarzedas, a French Jew, in one of the parts, was well received in New York in 1831,[93] but his *Camillus,* which opened at the Arch Street Theatre in 1833, according to a contemporary observer, "went off poorly, with a thin house."[94] Except for Noah, the Phillips family in the theater were more hard-working and persistent than brilliant.

Related to the theatrical world was Philadelphia's first musical group, the Musical Fund Society, established in 1820. That year, the same in which he received his medical degree, Isaac Hays became one of its first twelve managers.[95] He was joined as an "amateur" in the society by Nathan Nathans, John Moss and Henry Solomon, while Abraham Hart, the music-seller,[96] and Samuel Cantor[97] were listed as "professors." The first concert was held in 1821, and, while its primary purpose was to provide benefits for the musicians of the city, it at the same time added a new asset to the social and cultural life of the community.

A once great figure in the musical world made a few fleeting appearances in Philadelphia. Lorenzo Da Ponte, Mozart's librettist, now an old, irascible man, bitterly complaining of the world's neglect, came to town in 1818 in hopes of restoring his fortune by selling to the Library Company a large collection of Italian books.[98] He had been born an Italian Jew, but the opportunity of preferment induced his family to embrace Catholicism and although Lorenzo married an English Jewess he had little or no interest in his ancestor's people or their religion.[99] After a career in Europe marked equally by rascality and brilliance, he emigrated to America in 1805, where he tried to support himself teaching Italian, keeping a store and selling books. Disgusted with New York, he went to Sunbury, Pennsylvania, and there established a distillery which failed through mismanagement. Da Ponte's only Jewish association was with Daniel Levy,[100] who foreclosed his mortgage on some property in Sunbury. That was indeed a peripheral contact with the Jewish community, for Levy, like Da Ponte, had removed himself from Jewish life. After some years again in New York, where he published a number of books in Italian and English and taught his native language both privately and at Columbia, he came back to Philadelphia, in 1829 launched an opera season at the Chestnut Street Theater,[101] and once more returned to New York. Although it met with little support at the time, his attempt to introduce Italian opera in America is recognized as a pioneer effort.

In another field of the arts—painting—Jews were early among the patrons of native artists. Like other successful men of the time, the colonial Jewish merchants had their portraits painted, and when they were outstandingly successful they had their wives and children painted too. The charming portrait of young David Franks, with a parakeet on his finger and his little sister Phila beside him, was a work of some unknown American artist.[102] However, as in the field of the drama, there was in colonial days little regard for American work. The English painters were hailed as the masters, and Americans were commissioned only because they were on the spot.

But after the Revolution, the English-trained Gilbert Stuart achieved a reputation which challenged that of the English artists. Mrs. Michael Gratz was painted by him, and so were her daughters Rebecca and Rachel Moses and her husband Solomon Moses.[103] Stuart was a friend and neighbor of Isaac Franks in Germantown in 1802, and at that time painted him.[104] Portraits of Jonas Phillips and his wife Rebecca are attributed to Charles Willson Peale,[105] and a miniature of David Salisbury Franks was done by the same artist.[106] One of Peale's sons James did the Reuben Ettings;[107] another, Rembrandt, portrayed Jacob I. Cohen[108] and the Moses Levys;[109] Charles Peale Polk made a strong character study of old Barnard Gratz;[110] and Anna Claypoole Peale did a delicate miniature of Rebecca.[111]

Late in the year 1807 Thomas Sully, after a few months in Stuart's studio, came to town bearing a letter of introduction from Washington Irving to Rebecca Gratz:

> I hardly need introduce the bearer, Mr. Sully to you, as I trust you recollect him perfectly. He purposes passing the winter in your city and as he will be a mere "stranger & sojourner in the land," I would solicit for him your good graces. He is a gentleman for whom I have a great regard, not merely on account of his professional abilities, which are highly promising, but for his amiable character and engaging manners. I think I cannot render him a favor for which he ought to be more grateful than in introducing him to the notice of yourself and your connections. . . .[112]

Immediately he was commissioned to paint a portrait of Rebecca from a miniature by Malbone, whom she had met through the Hoffmans of New York,[113] and it was not long before other Philadelphians began to patronize the young artist, who was so well sponsored. Six months after he arrived Rebecca wrote Irving of his progress:

> Sully has at length got established here and is every day gaining friends and reputation. He is painting thirty portraits at a reduced price. I think he has improved greatly since I saw him in New York and is generally preferred to Peale, who is a favorite here. Gouvernour Morris is sitting to Sully. His picture will be exhibited in the Academy of Arts and I do not doubt from the interest he has excited that he will be successful in his profession. . . .[114]

One of the great American portraitists was launched on his career. Sully remained friendly with the Gratz family and made canvases of many of them: the venerable Michael Gratz in his sixty-eighth year,[115] Rebecca several times in 1830-31,[116] her brother Benjamin and his wife,[117] Rachel Gratz Etting and her daughter Sally, young Mrs. Isaac Hays,[118] and Rachel Gratz Moses.[119]

It is surprising how many of the leading Philadelphia Jews of the eighteenth and early nineteenth century did sit for their portraits; the Manuel Josephsons to Jeremiah Theus,[120] Solomon Etting to Benjamin Trott,[121] Samuel Hays to James Sharples,[122] both the Solomon Ettings again to John Wesley Jarvis,[123] Mrs. Barnard Gratz to Robert Feke,[124] Aaron Levy and his wife to Robert Edge Pine,[125] and the Joseph Andrews to an unknown painter.[126] Miniatures have survived of Solomon Marache,[127] Benjamin Nones,[128] Mrs. Zalegman Phillips[129] and her son Jonas Altamont Phillips,[130] and there is a wonderful silhouette of John Moss, attributed to the famous William Henry Brown.[131]

The logical step which followed the encouragement of American artists was the establishment of a school to train them. The first of these in the country was the Pennsylvania Academy of the Fine Arts which was founded in 1805, and among the first twelve directors was Moses Levy,[132] who was incidentally also a trustee of the University of Pennsylvania.[133] The project received encouraging support from a small group of Philadelphians and others who saw the need for a native academy. In the first subscription book the names of Simon and Hyman Gratz, Samuel Hays, Sampson Levy and Benjamin and Zalegman Phillips can be read along with those of Francis Hopkinson and Thomas Jefferson.[134] In the Academy's first building, erected in 1807, the center stone of the lobby "of a quality equal to the Kilkenny, viz. of fine jet black with an occasional sprinkling of pure white," was a present from Simon Gratz, and since it was one of the few features picked out for special mention it must have been considered an outstanding gift.[135]

It was the Gratzes who, as in other fields, seem to have participated more fully than any others. From the time that Rebecca helped bring Sully to the attention of their friends in the city, one or another of them was a patron of artists. It was Hyman who became the family's chief representative in art circles. He first became a director of the Academy of the Fine Arts in 1834, and later was chosen its treasurer.[136]

The Academy held its first exhibition in 1811, and Abraham I. Nunes was the first Jewish exhibitor.[137] Nunes was a professional drawing-master and painter of botanical subjects, whose English background and unusual field made him stand out from most of the Philadelphians. In 1810, he had advertised that he would paint portraits at eight and ten dollars each at his "Drawing Academy" on Race Street.[138]

When a group of artists in 1812 decided to form a professional society, Nunes joined with them. He signed the petition requesting the incorporation of the Society of Artists of the United States, and was one of its original members.[139] Although this society differed in its composition from the lay-managed Academy, the two groups held jointly sponsored annual exhibitions. In the second exhibition Nunes again displayed his work,[140] and in later years the youthful Joseph B. Nones, prior to his entrance into the Navy, showed his first crayon sketches,[141] and Mrs. Lopez, believed to be the wife of the dentist Moses Lopez, was permitted to exhibit her portraits.[142]

But none of these Jews chose art as a main career. Nunes, suffering from the neglect that was the lot of many artists, gave up painting as a livelihood, went to Jamaica, and returned to Philadelphia again in 1819 to busy himself in the more lucrative West India trade. At first he was in partnership with Raphael De Cordova, and later advertised himself as a distiller with many years of experience.[143]

One non-Jewish artist, who later distinguished himself, owed his start to David G. Seixas and his Institution for the Deaf and Dumb. The story is told that one day in May, 1820, a High Street crowd gathered about to watch a little boy of eleven sketch views of the city with a piece of chalk. The child, an abandoned deaf-mute, attracted such attention with his skill that Bishop William White, one of the onlookers, at once recommended that he be admitted to Seixas' new school so that he would have an opportunity of developing his ability.[144]

Through the interest of Seixas, the boy, Albert Newsam, was instructed by George Catlin, whose paintings of American Indians were to achieve international fame. Newsam, under the guidance of Seixas and Catlin, became one of the early American masters of lithography.

🐦 17

Medicine and Science

T HE Medical School of the University of Pennsylvania, the American Philosophical Society, and later the Academy of Natural Sciences and the Franklin Institute, made Philadelphia during the first half of the nineteenth century the center of scientific teaching and research in the United States. The Medical School, which had acquired international reputation under the direction of Benjamin Rush, was attracting students from all the states of the Union. Patterning itself upon the great school at Edinburgh, where Morgan, Rush and other early American physicians received their training, the University set high standards of medicine and offered a faculty of distinguished teachers. Only one Jew born in Philadelphia, Joel Hart, is known to have gone abroad to study medicine; he graduated from the Royal College of Surgery in London, and became a prominent physician in New York.[1]

From 1792, when Moses Sheftall studied under Dr. Rush,[2] until 1838, at least seventeen Jews attended the Medical School in Philadelphia.[3] Six were from South Carolina, one from North Carolina, one from Georgia, four from Virginia, four from Philadelphia and one from Easton. The first Philadelphia-born Jew to become a doctor, as we have noted, was Solomon Bush about whose medical education, presumably in England, nothing is known; but the first to attend an American institution was Manuel Phillips, who finished his studies in 1807. His interest in medicine extended itself beyond the routine duties of his profession. In 1808 he was secretary of the Philadelphia Medical Lyceum,[4] and the following year he was appointed an assistant surgeon in the United States Navy.[5] He seems to have spent most of the rest of his life in the service, although between cruises he apparently maintained a Philadelphia practice.

Less than a year after he joined the Navy, Phillips requested a furlough to go to India, where he stayed for four years, reporting his return to the United States in March, 1815. His career was spotted with extended leaves, but he made several cruises; in 1817 in the *U. S. S. Congress* and in 1819 in the *U. S. S. Constellation.* Finally, in 1823, when he was once more ordered to sea, he began to take steps to submit his resignation, and after some trouble, on February 19, 1824 he was informed that it had been accepted.[6] He appears in 1825 as an M.D. at 41 North Fourth Street, where his accountant brother, Joseph, lived.[7] Manuel Phillips died at Vera Cruz in 1826.

Jonathan Horwitz, who had decided to abandon Hebrew studies for medicine, followed Phillips from the Medical School in 1815, and has the distinction of being the only foreign-born Jew who attended the University in those early days. But by far the most outstanding Jewish doctor of the period was Isaac Hays. He graduated from the University in 1816, giving one of the six commencement orations on that occasion, at which his cousin Gratz Etting was awarded his master's degree.[8] In spite of the fact that the subject of his discourse then was American literature, Hays' future lay in the field of medicine. After a brief period in business with his father, he entered the Medical School and, in two years, with characteristic sophomoric wisdom, felt he knew as much as some of his professors. Rebecca Gratz wrote that he "had had the comfort of abusing two of Dr. Hare's lectures."[9] In 1820, having submitted a thesis on "Sympathy," Hays graduated as M.D.,[10] whereupon he began his sixty-year career in medicine by opening an office[11] and offering his services to the Female Hebrew Benevolent Society and the Bikur Holim, the two Jewish philanthropic institutions then operating in the city.[12]

This was an era which saw the establishment of important new American scientific institutions, created and guided by men whose knowledge of various sciences was broad enough to enable them to understand the importance of co-relating different disciplines. One of these was Isaac Hays. Although he maintained a general practice, he began soon after his graduation to specialize in ophthalmology, in which field he acquired his greatest reputation. He may be regarded as the first ophthalmologist in America to prescribe cylindrical lenses to correct astigmatism; he was the first to make observations upon non-congenital color-blindness; and he invented a knife-needle for operating on cataract.[13]

In addition to being an expert physician, Isaac Hays was a man of great energy, strong social conscience and wide interests. He was appointed physician to the Orphan Asylum of which his aunt, Rebecca Gratz, was secretary,[14] and in 1822 he was among the founders and one of the first surgeons of the Pennsylvania Infirmary for Diseases of the Eye and Ear.[15] A year later he was chosen one of the six city physicians for the Philadelphia Dispensary, a post previously held by Dr. Horwitz.[16]

His contributions, moreover, went far beyond the field of medicine. In 1821 he joined the newly founded Academy of Natural Sciences, to which he had donated a collection of fossils in two earlier years,[17] lectured there regularly on natural science,[18] and helped see through the press the second volume of its *Proceedings*.[19] Working side by side with William Maclure the geologist, Thomas Say the entomologist and conchologist, and Titian Peale who combined art with studies in natural history, Hays helped to promote the work of the infant institution. From 1822, for some years, he was one of its curators,[20] and in 1828, as a result of his connection with the Academy, which with the help of Audubon had been fostering an intensive study of American birds, he produced a new edition of Wilson's standard *American Ornithology*, which led to an interesting correspondence with Charles Lucien Bonaparte.[21]

During the same period he became one of the original members of the Franklin Institute[22] and, by 1829, was its corresponding secretary and on its important committee on publications.[23] Such comprehensive devotion to science was honored by the American Philosophical Society which elected him to membership and before which, in 1829 and 1830, he read papers on the bones of a mastodon, later published in its *Transactions*.[24]

It was, however, as an editor that Hays made a contribution to American science equal to his in the field of ophthalmology. In 1827 he took over the editorship of the *Philadelphia Journal of the Medical and Physical Sciences*, which his former teacher and friend, Professor Nathaniel Chapman, had founded seven years before, changed its name to the *American Journal of Medical Sciences,*[25] and continued as its sole editor until 1869, when his son, Dr. Isaac Minis Hays, became associated with him. It was said of Isaac Hays "that by reason of his position as editor of this journal, he was the arbiter of the disposal or destiny of medical manuscripts, and in consequence it was the desire and ambition of every practitioner to have his paper appear in this journal."[26] *The American Journal,* the forerunner of the *Journal of the American Medical Association,* was so much the product of its editor that it is commonly known in the history of medicine as "Hays' Journal."[27] The distinguished Sir William Osler praised it as "one of the few great journals of the world, and one from which one can almost write the progress of American medicine during the past century."[28]

In addition to his editorial work, Hays wrote both monographs and books. His first published article in the field of his specialization, "Observations on Inflammation of the Conjunctiva," appeared in the *Philadelphia Journal* in 1826.[29] Three years later he issued at Philadelphia an edition, with additions, of Arnott's *Elements of Physics,* and in 1831 Carey and Lea put out his and Dr. Griffith's translation of Broussais's *History of Chronic Phlegmasiae.*[30] And as time went on these were followed by an impressive number of other publications.

The legacy of James Wills, a grocer who had died in 1823, provided funds for a hospital for the lame and blind, which, through the efforts of Councilman John Moss as one of a committee representing the city, was eventually established as the Wills Eye Hospital. It absorbed the Infirmary with which Hays was associated, and he became and remained a staff surgeon at the Hospital from 1834 to 1854.[31] During his career, he was the only Jew connected with the major eye hospital in the country. Most of the accomplishments of Isaac Hays belong to a later period, but it should be mentioned that he was one of the founders of the American Medical Association in 1847, and wrote its code of ethics.[32] He was without question the outstanding American Jewish physician of the period.

It was still possible in those days to practice medicine without a formal medical education. Quackery, patent medicines and panaceas, which for ages had seduced the credibility of the sick, were still serious competitors of the medical profession. Abraham Solis, who was in Philadelphia at the beginning of the century, was closer to an itinerant cure peddler, who sold his remedies from town to town, than a professional doctor.[33] But the first really successful quack in town was Samuel Solomon, a handsome Liverpool Jew, who claimed a medical degree from Aberdeen and was a Fellow of the Royal Humane Society.

In 1800 he issued his *Guide to Health* which was sold in New York and which, playing upon the sexual fears of young men and women, was interspersed with attestations to the cures wrought by his "Cordial Balm of Gilead."[34] Shortly thereafter he arrived in Philadelphia where he sold his patented elixir,[35] from which he is said to have amassed a fortune. After 1805 he seems to have returned to England, and not until Doctor Swaim advertised the amazing features of "Swaim's Panacea" two decades later, did the city witness another such successful fraud. It is frequently forgotten that some of the great Philadelphia fortunes were founded in the first half of the nineteenth century on the sale of patent pills, nostrums and tonics.

In the absence of restrictions governing the preparation of medicines and pharmaceutical products, there were many unqualified mixers of potions and pills who, without training or experience, entered the field. More often, after a brief apprenticeship with one who claimed to be an apothecary or druggist, a man with a single mortar and pestle would set himself up in a shop. In most cases real scientific background did not exist. It was different, however, in the case of Abraham M. Cohen and his brother Eleazar. They were sons of Solomon Myers Cohen, and hence first cousins of the Gratzes. In 1809 Eleazar had begun learning the elements of pharmacy under local apothecaries and finally entered the drug business on his own. Before 1817 he formed a partnership with his brother Abraham, and the two conducted a successful apothecary shop for more than two decades, where they sold "a variety of basic pharmaceuticals in quantity" and "a general assortment of Fresh Drugs and Medicines."[36] When it was found necessary to replace haphazard methods with standards based upon knowledge and training, Eleazar L. Cohen met with the sixty-odd men who came together at Carpenters' Hall on February 23, 1821, to establish the Philadelphia College of Pharmacy, the first American school

of its kind.[37] It is noteworthy that when the Pennsylvania Infirmary for Diseases of the Eye and Ear was first established,
Messrs. A. M. and E. L. Cohen supplied it with medicines.[38]

There is a bare mention of a Dr. Solomon De Bruin, who
applied for membership in Rodeph Shalom in 1821, but he does
not seem to have practiced medicine.[39] For a brief period, in
1827–31, two well-trained German physicians were resident in
the city, William, or Wenzel, Leo-Wolf and his son Morris, or
Moritz.[40] Late in 1827 Isaac Hays announced that "Drs. Leo-
Wolf and Maehring, two talented German physicians, who now
reside here, and who are in correspondence with the most distinguished medical men in Germany," would send into the
Journal notices of the most important developments in Germany.[41] The elder Leo-Wolf had received his medical degree
at Erlangen, had been physician to the German and Portuguese Hebrew Societies of Altona, was a frequent contributor
to medical journals, and, after he moved to New York, in
1835 published an attack on the "Abracadabra" of homoeopathic medicine as recommended by the Philadelphian Con-
stantine Hering.[42] Leo-Wolf had been one of the "commissioners" for Hamburg appointed in Noah's *Proclamation to the
Jews* of 1825, urging them to settle in the homeland he projected
at Ararat, New York. It is said, however, that the main purpose
of Leo-Wolf's emigration to America was to arouse interest
in the principles of the "Philalethen," a group of Jewish liberals
whose ritual-free religious ideas antedated those of the Ethical
Culture Society.[43] His son had apparently just finished his studies
at Heidelberg when the family came here, and his medical dissertation, not printed until 1832, mentions that he was in Philadelphia.[44] Both Leo-Wolfs moved on to New York and within
a comparatively few years returned to Hamburg.

Dentistry was still not professionalized, and there is no
evidence of the competence or skill of the early Jewish dentists.
The first we know of was Moses Lopez, who advertised himself
as bleeder and dentist, and who presented a handsome ritual chair
to Mikveh Israel.[45] He was followed as early as 1819 by Zachariah Florance,[46] and, at least by 1825, by E. Carvalho,[47] both
of whom opened offices in town. By 1828 Florance was in New
Orleans, where he seems to have made a fortune before returning
to Philadelphia.[48]

It is worth mentioning in treating of science in general that Hyman Gratz, during the period when he was exploiting the natural resources of Mammoth Cave, also took an interest in the archaeological remains which were discovered there. He sent to the eminent Dr. Samuel Latham Mitchill specimens of cloth and artifacts which had been dug out of "that unparalleled natural excavation." With these went a note which was published in *The Medical Repository* for 1817, describing the cloth and mentioning other discoveries.

> We have, also, an Indian bowl, or cup, containing about a pint, cut out of wood, found also in the cave; and lately there has been dug out of it the skeleton of a human body, enveloped in a matting similar to that of the *kinniconecke* pouch.[49]

At the period when the scientific study of aboriginal American life was in its infancy, discoveries of this sort were of great importance. Simon Gratz had some interest in an allied field; he was a director of the Pennsylvania Botanic Garden.[50]

One other Jewish contribution to science is significant. Lieutenant Uriah P. Levy, then in Washington, in 1823 sent in to the *National Intelligencer* of that city a short note on a natural phenomenon which had attracted the attention of Benjamin Franklin and was to be studied even more fully by the great American oceanographer, Matthew F. Maury.

Seeing a notice in the paper that a bottle, which he had thrown into the Gulf Stream with a request that its finder notify him, had been beached at Nassau, Levy figured that it had drifted 3,420 miles in two years, at the rate of four and five-eighths miles per day, on a west by south course. He made the suggestion that knowledge of the flow of the Gulf Stream after it left the Grand Banks would be greatly increased

> if every master of a vessel would, after he had cleared land, put his latitude and longitude together, with the day of the month, into a bottle, and request the finder to publish it.[51]

Even in this age of scientific advances ocean currents are still being charted by the bottle method.

David G. Seixas represented a part of that genius which was characteristic of America in the early years of the nineteenth century. He "tinkered" about with a great variety of ideas and in a practical way helped introduce new inventions and new methods. He manufactured crockery, which had formerly been imported from England, and has been called "the father of this art in America." He made sealing wax and printer's ink. He discovered the secret of fabricating enameled-surface visiting-cards, then the latest fashion. He established a brewery. He helped introduce daguerreotypes into the country. He invented axilla shields. He offered a solution to the problem of burning anthracite coal which had long been regarded as useless because of its hardness.[52] And he pioneered in methods of teaching deaf-mute children to read, write and communicate.

The arts and sciences, pure and practical, then coming under the broad head of "philosophy," were receiving an unprecedented emphasis in the young, expanding country, which was just beginning to understand the strength of its people and its other resources. Societies for the promotion of the economy of the land through new inventions and better methods were springing up throughout the nation, and particularly in Philadelphia which, since Franklin's day, had been a center of American scientific research. The influences of the cotton-gin and the steamboat are better remembered than the equally important fight for universal vaccination or investigations into the chemical functioning of the stomach. A boundless energy was being devoted to the improvement of man's well-being. And an important part of this movement was an attempt to ameliorate the condition of those afflicted with incurable ailments.

In the United States there were unknown hundreds of deaf-mutes who were doomed to spend their lives uselessly and alone, because they were unable to communicate or be communicated with. In Europe, at least three centers had been established to remedy the situation by instructing children in sign language. Paris had been one of the first cities seriously to approach the problem, and its first teacher was the former Marrano, Jacob Rodriguez Pereira. His system was approved by the Royal Academy of Sciences in Paris in 1747, and because of its success he was elected a member of the Royal Society in London. But Pereira's position as a Jew was insecure in a country which had not as yet granted equal rights to Jews, and he was replaced in the Paris institution by the Abbé Épée.[53]

French and English institutions had been in existence for about half a century before a Deaf and Dumb Asylum was organized in the United States at Hartford in 1815.[54] A year later, Abbé Sicard of the Paris school, anxious to introduce his system into this country, toured the large cities of the United States, demonstrating the aptitude of one of his pupils who had made great strides with the French method. His demonstration was influential in founding a school in New York; but in Philadelphia his visit was received politely and, after a feeble attempt to organize a school, it was quickly forgotten.

An appeal for funds from Philadelphians to promote the Hartford Asylum as a national institution in 1816 was met with resentment.[55] Humanitarian Philadelphians pointed out that there were so many calls upon them for charity at home that "they ought not to be pressed upon with too many solicitations for distant places;" they stressed the need for a local institution of the same nature, and called upon the mayor to organize a meeting that would lead to its establishment. A pious note was added by the suggestion that the lack of education for deaf-mutes would prevent them from inheriting a future Christian state.[56] In December, 1816, a general meeting to raise funds locally was sponsored by the city; but this initial attempt petered out through lack of enthusiasm.[57]

There was one exception to the general lethargy. Sometime during 1818 or 1819, the tin and crockery merchant,[58] David G. Seixas, turned his attention away from mechanical invention and trade to the training of several deaf-mutes living in the neighborhood of his shop. The "natural and philosophical talents," described by his eminent father, the New York *hazan*, had come to fruition. Seixas invented a manual system of his own, gathered up eleven children "deserted by both parents, and thrown aside as useless lumber," boarded them at his own expense in his home and instructed them in his method of manual speech.[59]

By 1820 Seixas' "Deaf and Dumb School," in a small brick house on the south side of Market Street near 21st, had attracted so much attention that many citizens, only half-heartedly moved four years before, became whole-heartedly stirred by actually seeing "their fellow-beings, destitute of hearing and speech, exhibiting a love of learning, an acuteness of observation, and an excellency of comprehension." Letters to the press urged the good people of Philadelphia to contribute to the "disinterested benevolence of an individual of this city," and asked that a society be incorporated by the state legislature. David Seixas' single-handed endeavor was attracting widespread attention.[60]

Rebecca Gratz, herself deep in the philanthropic work of the city, wrote her sister-in-law Maria in the spring of 1820:

Tell Ben his old acquaintance David Seixas is distinguishing himself among the benefactors of mankind, and is likely to reap the reward due to his talents and humanity—he has been privately engaged six or seven months teaching a class of indigent Deaf & Dumb children—and has succeeded so well as to attract the notice of our humane & scientific citizens to whom he has recently exhibited his school—they approve his system, which the Abbe Corree, who has visited the European Schools, says is on a truly philosophical plan—they are about establishing an Institution—of which this ingenious and philanthropic young man will be the principal.[61]

Rebecca was right; within three weeks after she sent this news to Kentucky, at a meeting held at the Hall of the American Philosophical Society on April 12, 1820, the Pennsylvania Institution for the Deaf and Dumb was constituted.[62] Two of her brothers, Joseph and Jacob Gratz, were elected to the original board of directors, and the latter assumed, in addition, three important committee assignments.[63]

It was about this time that the public school system was being introduced into Philadelphia, and its organizers were called in to assist with the formation of the new, specialized school. Roberts Vaux and Thomas Cadwalader conferred with Seixas, agreed to use his schoolroom for the time being, although it could not possibly house the seventy children who had applied for admission, and hired Seixas as the principal at a salary of $1000 a year, which was understood to include the services of his two sisters and brother as assistants.[64] With this as a beginning, the entire community was called upon to contribute to further the project. A ladies' committee of twelve was formed to help, which included Rebecca Gratz and Elkalah Cohen.[65] Twelve Jews, most of them related to the Gratzes, were among the initial contributors, and half of them became life members at once.[66]

The press sang the praises of Seixas and the institution.[67] It received such favorable and widespread publicity that the school blossomed. By the end of the year, the committee of admissions was able to announce that

the Directors have fitted up and furnished a large and commodious building, situated on the south side of High Street, between Schuylkill Sixth & Seventh streets, for the present residence of Pupils entrusted to their care; the house is capable of accommodating sixty Pupils.[68]

In January, 1821, Jacob Gratz, who served on both the admissions committee and the legislative committee, spent three weeks successfully pleading the cause of the institution before the legislature in Harrisburg. A charter was obtained, and a state grant of $8000 a year was approved.[69]

Everything promised well for the future of the Pennsylvania Institution for the Deaf and Dumb. Then, suddenly, a hidden conspiracy—as quiet in its beginnings as the innocent mutes—burst upon the institution, its founders and the principal. David Seixas was accused of taking uncommon liberties with the girl students of the school. The proceedings of the board, containing the accusations and the hearing granted to Seixas, were kept from the public for many months, and only after Seixas' dismissal and an investigation of the matter by the legislature did they become public knowledge, and then only at the insistence of Seixas himself.[70] With more than half the members of the board present, expulsion had been voted by a majority of only one. The group which voted against Seixas were personally unfriendly to him and disapproved of the way he conducted the school, so they were easily convinced that the charges against him were true. On the other hand, his supporters, including Jacob Gratz, Robert Patterson, William Meredith, William Price, William J. Duane, Callender Irvine, James N. Barker and William W. Fisher, were certain that the principal was completely innocent and should be publicly exonerated.[71] As Rebecca Gratz commented,

after he had devoted himself to establish such a school, to be turned off, destitute on the world, I think so cruel, that unless he were guilty, it is unpardonable.[72]

At first Seixas was silent, but after he discovered that the affair was the result of connivance he wrote:

I was fearful that a full disclosure from me would injure the Institution, but from the subsequent errors of the majority, I perceive that my formerly prosperous Institution is plunged deeper and deeper into danger, and that total silence on my part will countenance its ruin.[73]

He asked two of the directors in his public statement whether they had dispassionately weighed the effects of his dismissal upon the afflicted community and upon the benevolent character of

Philadelphia. He refuted the false charges in full. And when the matter was brought before the legislature at the instance of the minority of the board, a "solemn verdict of acquittal" was pronounced by that body.[74] For a year or more, comment continued in the columns of the newspapers and a number of pamphlets and broadsheets were issued on the controversy.[75] Even when an affidavit was obtained from the mother of the girl supposed to have been involved, stating that her charges against Seixas had originated in a "dream," and that she had been urged to make her complaint by the matron,[76] the anti-Seixas faction bitterly refused to reinstate him.

Roberts Vaux, in a confidential letter to John Wurts, referred to Seixas' supporters as "deluded men," and gave evidence that there were some political and religious overtones to the action. He stubbornly held to the opinion that Seixas was guilty, and looked upon the belief of the minority members in his innocence as due to factors having nothing to do with the merits of the case.

As to Meredith's course, it is unaccountable but by supposing that he was under the necessity of keeping fair weather with the Jews. The weakness of old age may explain in some degree R. Patterson's conduct. Price I believe, was desirous of bringing himself into notice in the amiable light of the defender of the oppressed. . . . Gratz was naturally disposed to sustain the Jews at all hazards, and unfortunately had so much influence over the mind of his intimate acquaintance, Henry J. Williams, as to incline him to listen to the suggestion of *mercy,* and to blind for a moment his better judgment which would have told him that in showing mercy to Seixas he could not do *justice* to the helpless and exposed beings under his charge.

But Vaux was not sure he might not weaken, for he added,

I have no desire to encounter Seixas and his supporters, since such a conflict in the actual temper of the times would only end in a victory over myself and what would be of greater evil, a victory over *truth.*[77]

The few directors whom Vaux so mercilessly castigated were, however, not the only friends that Seixas had. Even while the argument was going on, newspapers carried articles praising the work of a new school established by the citizens of Philadelphia, the Philadelphia Asylum for the Deaf and Dumb.[78] Like the first institution, this one received liberal support from the entire community, and the list of contributors published in 1825 included as many as fifty Jewish names. It is interesting to note that the largest single gift was from Harmon Hendricks, one of the leaders of Shearith Israel in New York, who not only became a life member but donated $100 in addition. The Gratzes, of course, gave it solid support; but other very influential men, such as Dr. Richard Bache, Mathew Carey, Irenée duPont, the Lippincotts and the Wetherills, one of whom was president, also showed that they had faith in Seixas.[79]

The New Jersey legislature, impressed by the results of Seixas' teaching methods, allowed him to present before it an examination of one of his pupils so that they could observe what he was doing.[80] As a result, funds were appropriated by that state for a similar institution. In New York, where Seixas' activities had also commanded attention, an account of the cruel treatment which he had received was printed and an extensive account of his school given, which, as related in the childish words of one of the youngsters, gave evidence of kind treatment from Seixas and his sister Rachel, as well as the friendliness of Zalegman Phillips, who permitted the child to visit his "Piano house," so termed by her because he owned two pianos.[81]

The father of this pupil appealed to the legislative body in Harrisburg for funds for the new school, and a counter-appeal was made by Bishop White not to divide the funds between two similar institutions.[82] At first the legislature was inclined to help both schools, but finally, in February, 1825, it was announced that its subvention would go only to the Pennsylvania Institution for the Deaf and Dumb.[83] As a result, the Philadelphia Asylum operated for the next three years on private funds, and shortly thereafter it quietly disappeared from the scene.

The end of this phase of David Seixas' career marked the beginning of his restless experiments in many other fields. The Philadelphia Jewish community continued its faith in him, and his helpful participation in its affairs is best evidenced by his signing of the 1824 charter of Mikveh Israel.

✎ 18

Industry, Trade, and Commerce

ARL Sandburg poetically described what the moon might have told seven-year-old Abe Lincoln it saw as it looked down on the world he lived in:

> That year of 1816 the moon had seen sixteen thousand wagons come along one turnpike in Pennsylvania, heading west, with people hungry for new land, a new home, just like Tom Lincoln. Up the Mississippi River that year had come the first steamboat to curve into the Ohio River and land passengers at Louisville. The moon had seen the first steamboat leave Pittsburgh and tie up at New Orleans. New wheels, wagons, were coming, an iron horse snorting fire and smoke. Rolling-mills, ingots, iron, steel, were the talk of Pennsylvania; a sheet copper mill was starting in Massachusetts.[1]

To the vast resources of undeveloped land and mineral and agricultural wealth, the War of 1812 had added the freedom of the seas. In competition with the infant native industries which had grown up and flourished during the years of embargo and blockade, fleets of fast American clippers poured on to the docks heavy cargoes of goods from all over the world. Square-rigged Yankee ships sailed to Canton and Calcutta, anchored in all the ports of the West Indies and shuttled back and forth from the great tidewater harbors of Europe. Suffering periodically from the economic pains of rapid growth, but steadily building and expanding, the United States became a factor in the commerce of the world.

Domestic manufactures competed with the foreign imports

338

for the vast markets which were created by the steady rise in population—12,866,020 in 1830 compared to 5,308,483 in 1800[2]—and by the settlement of new areas being incorporated into the Union as new states. A host of new consumers in the West needed goods from the East, and the new West, stretching from the Great Lakes to the Gulf of Mexico, had its own products to offer in return. The merchants and tradesmen of Philadelphia, Jewish and non-Jewish, some big, mostly small, shared in the rewards and the disappointments which accompanied this great movement of people and goods.

The methods of business which the elder Gratz brothers had used in a pioneer country were revised and modernized when Simon and Hyman Gratz set up for themselves. During the next three decades, they and their three younger brothers improvised, as they went along, to keep abreast of the practices of the new century. They took their first step up from the status of shopkeepers when, in 1798, they moved from a fringe location on Sassafras (now Race) Street and opened up their wholesale grocery store in the developing business area at the southwest corner of Seventh and Market Streets.[3]

The Gratzes, however, were more than merely grocers. They were committed to the western lands as the heirs of Michael Gratz, who died intestate in 1811.[4] They carried on the B. and M. Gratz tradition as commission merchants and real estate brokers.[5] They entered the booming shipping trade and engaged in business with the Far East, their ships adding to the others which crowded the Philadelphia wharves, bringing their exotic cargoes from the Indian and China Seas.[6]

From Brazil they imported coffee[7] and from the West Indies rum, wines, sugar and cocoa.[8] Precious spices, such as black pepper, came into their warehouse in bulk quantities sufficient to supply a town.[9] It was this bulk trade and the variety of goods which they carried that identified them as outstanding merchants. Food products and liquors were supplemented by a diversity of stock which would have challenged the most fertile imagination of the previous century. They carried the products of local factories, such as sheet-iron and ammunition.[10] And even the valuable Chinese and Indian goods were of secondary importance in quantity to the staples from the South and West. Tobacco, hemp, whisky, and saltpetre from Kentucky[11] were shipped down the Mississippi River to New Orleans, where bales of cotton were added to the cargo of ships sailing for Philadelphia, and ultimately for the Gratz store on Market Street.[12]

This increase of trade in Philadelphia led to the foundation of essential new services. To provide security for the valuable cargoes while in transit, the Insurance Company of North America was founded, and the Gratzes among others protected their investments with policies issued by that company.[13] Among the fifteen men who petitioned the Pennsylvania Assembly for a charter for the Insurance Company late in 1792 had been Michael Prager, who takes a place as one of the founders of a great American institution.[14] To stimulate commerce and at the same time to provide for quick settlement of trade claims by arbitration, the Philadelphia Chamber of Commerce was founded in 1801. A monthly committee of five regularly handled a variety of cases involving claims for losses or damage to goods shipped into the port. In 1805 Samuel Hays, Haym Salomon's old clerk, who was active in the import trade from the Far East as well as other lands, became the first Jew to serve on the committee,[15] and later Simon Gratz was appointed to carry out the same responsibility.[16]

The loose partnerships for specific ventures—not unlike present-day ad hoc corporations—which had been a common feature of mercantilism in the previous century were continued, to enable individuals to take advantage of favorable opportunities or expand their interests without committing their entire capital. Simon Gratz entered into a joint partnership with his brother-in-law, Reuben Etting, to help him get a start, and in 1805 they offered for sale "one hundred pipes 4th proof Cogniac Brandy."[17] The following year, when young Joseph was old enough to carry his share of the family business, the Gratzes announced the dissolution of the old firm of Simon and Hyman Gratz and stated that in the future the enlarged partnership would be known as Simon Gratz & Co.[18] With Joseph in the home office, Simon and Hyman were freed to assume on-the-scene management of the extensive Gratz land interests, and they began to spend more and more time in Kentucky and in the county areas of Pennsylvania, becoming so expert in the handling of real estate that they, and particularly Hyman, were entrusted by others with their affairs as executors or trustees.[19] On the eve of the War of 1812, the partnership was once more enlarged to include Jacob and Benjamin, and the firm became Simon Gratz and Brothers,[20] which increasingly took on side interests in the name of one or more of the family.

The estate of Michael Gratz had been left on his death in the hands of Simon, Joseph and Jacob as administrators, and in 1822 it became the object of bitter family litigation which dragged the Gratz-Cohen-Simon relatives through the courts for decades.[21] Simon chiefly had charged himself with the responsibility for managing the vast and complicated land holdings which they had received by inheritance, but the others went out periodically to cope with particular problems. When Benjamin was old enough to handle matters, he was sent to Lexington, Kentucky, to watch the western end of the business and, at the same time, see if he could not salvage something from the pre-Revolutionary claims of the Gratzes in the Middle West. For a while, in 1819, he was in Vincennes, Indiana; and Rebecca, always concerned about the long and arduous business trips of her brothers, hoped that he would not have to suffer the discomforts of the frontier too long. To Benjamin, out west, she wrote shortly after the Masonic Hall, next door to the Gratz House, had been destroyed by a sensational fire:

> The Illinois & Wabash claim, of which I have all my life heard of so much, seemed like a romance—I never expected to see anything but maps & pamphlets of the subject, or that it would cost us your society, for so long a time —but since it has proceeded so far—I catch a little of the mania and frame wishes for its success at any rate hope you will not permit it to engage years of toil on an uncertain event & that after satisfying your curiosity with every thing worth visiting you will bend your course homeward.[22]

In December of that year, Ben married Maria Gist, settled in Kentucky and, except for occasional visits home, spent the rest of his long life in that state with which his history is connected.

The opportunities which the bustling trade of Philadelphia offered persuaded many to enter commerce or enlarge the scope of their businesses. Jacob Gratz opened up his own store around the corner from the old S. and H. Gratz establishment, and advertised dry-goods, like satin, damask, crepe, pongee and sarsnet, together with brown Havana sugar.[23] Joseph from another address, a counting-house first on South Eighth Street, and later on Front, told the public that he was a merchant specializing in East India goods, but carried as well gunpowder "from one of the best manufactures of this country," hempen yarns, and Madeira wine.[24] Simon, whose marriage to Mary Smith could

not be countenanced by the Jewish community and was therefore pointedly not mentioned—Rebecca Gratz makes no reference to Mrs. Simon Gratz nor to their many children—was living
at his country seat, Willington, an estate which covered many
acres on Broad Street north of Ridge Road. In the winter of
1822 he thanked the Engine and Hose Company for having
saved his house at Broad and Poplar when the kitchen roof
caught on fire.[25]

Hyman, who was taking a leading role in the management of
the affairs of the Jewish community, entered the financial world
and seems to have devoted less time to the day-to-day mercantile
affairs of the firm. His status was recognized by the Philadelphia
Directory which, in the polite vernacular of the day, gave his
occupation as "merchant."[26] The unmarried brothers, with Rebecca keeping house for them, lived in an elegant mansion on
Chestnut Street near Seventh.[27] The family had attained the
status of settled, solid prosperity.

In the early part of the nineteenth century, it was but a step
from handling goods as a merchant to handling money as a
banker. In Philadelphia, the brilliant career of Stephen Girard
was evidence of the metamorphosis from a ship-owner to a
merchant prince and banker. On a much smaller scale the careers
of the Gratzes paralleled his. They never possessed his imagina-
ative ability or achieved Girard's success, but all progressed
through the same interests in much the same manner. Girard's
Bank was one of the chief financial institutions of the city. The
call to organize the Schuylkill Bank at Simon Gratz's counting-
house on December 31, 1813, led to the founding of a far smaller
bank, but a good one.[28] In it, Gratz became a close associate and
warm friend of William Meredith, the two serving for many
years as directors and Gratz occasionally as its treasurer.[29] The
Schuylkill Bank survived the banking crises of the early 1830s
when many banks throughout the country shut their doors and
left their creditors ruined, and it was only in 1839, the year of
Simon Gratz's death, that, as a result of embezzlement on the
part of an employee and the resumption of specie payment, the
Schuylkill Bank failed, surviving by a few months Nicholas
Biddle's once-great Bank of the United States.[30]

This former federal bank, which Jackson disenfranchised, had
had one Jew associated with it during its period of influence.

Solomon Etting, with close family ties in Philadelphia, had represented the State of Maryland as a director.[31]

The expansion of credit which resulted from the establishment of many banks—and which, overextended recklessly, brought on the banking crisis—did help to build the maze of roads and canals which the growing country needed. The merchant and banker, who had considerable stakes in bettering the means of communication so that goods could travel more inexpensively and more quickly, and who benefited from the access these arteries brought to land on which they had loaned money, played a major part in creating stock companies to build turnpikes and cut through canals to connect natural waterways. As Joseph Simon and Levy and Franks had earlier shown interest in the improvement of the Lancaster Pike, which was their main trade route, so one of the survivors of colonial days continued that interest. Solomon Marache, who after the Revolution drifted away from the Jewish community, had been for many years secretary of the Pennsylvania Population Company,[32] in which Solomon Lyons and Isaac Franks had invested. In 1808 Marache appeared as treasurer of the Bustleton and Smithfield Road,[33] while Isaac Franks was the manager of a lottery for the improvement of navigation in the Lehigh River.[34]

But again, it was the Gratzes who, among the Jews of Philadelphia, played leading roles. Simon Gratz became one of the directors of the Philadelphia and Pittsburgh Transporting Company,[35] which owned a toll-road that ran to and through Gratz land, and was connected with at least two other turnpike companies.[36] In the scramble for trade with its neighbors, New York and Baltimore, Philadelphia was rushing to build a vast network of canals to channel cargoes into the Schuylkill and Delaware Rivers. One of the biggest of these, the Chesapeake and Delaware Canal Company, fostered by Stephen Girard and Mathew Carey, numbered Simon Gratz and John Moss among its early directors,[37] and in its building Daniel Levy, an Irish Jew, was killed.[38] After the historic Union Canal was built, Jacob Gratz took part in its management, was one of its regularly elected managers and in 1834 became its president.[39]

Hyman Gratz, in another field, was achieving equal distinction. In 1818 he was elected a director of the young Pennsylvania Company for Insurance on Lives and Granting Annuities.[40] Not

only did Mikveh Israel recognize his ability and integrity by
electing him treasurer in 1824,[41] but the Pennsylvania Company
did likewise by electing him president in 1837.[42] Both offices he
continued to hold until his death in 1857. During the same
period his brother Joseph was a director of the Atlantic Insurance Company.[43]

However, in those days of inflated credit and unsound bank-
notes even so substantial a family as the Gratzes suffered.
When merchants borrowed money to buy goods which had
to come by ship from halfway round the world, when land-
owners mortgaged their lands at inflated values to secure money
for other ventures, when every large business flirted with danger
during an era of basic financial instability, the spectre of bankruptcy—the inability to meet notes when they fell due—stood in
the corner of each counting-house. Bank notes fluctuated so violently almost from day to day that men fully solvent at the beginning of one month were ruined by the beginning of the next.

To this national problem, there was added in Philadelphia a
special one. In 1825 the city was dealt a severe commercial blow;
the Erie Canal was opened. Goods formerly shipped from the
Middle West to the Delaware port could now go fifty percent
more rapidly for half the price by way of the Great Lakes to the
Hudson and Erie Canal.[44] The subsequent shift of trade away
from Philadelphia hurt the commercial life of the city to such
an extent that its effect was felt in the business philosophy of
Philadelphians for almost a century.

Like others, the firm, named once again Simon Gratz and
Brother, found itself in severe trouble. Early in the year 1826,
Rebecca mentioned to Ben that her brothers had no doubt kept
him informed of business, "and a gloomy record no doubt it is
of the mercantile world."[45] In July the worst happened. The
brothers Simon and Hyman Gratz went into bankruptcy. There
was no social stigma attached to such a failure in those days,
when it was the misfortune that befell so many; but it was at
best a bitter experience. Rebecca reported that the anticipation
had been more distressing than the fact, and that her brothers

received too so universal a sympathy—so much respect and consideration
from the whole community as well as those who might expect to suffer by
their misfortune as those who only knew them as enterprising citizens—that
their hearts must be steel not to have melted at such kindness—indeed we
have shed more tears of gratitude rather than grief.[46]

The most touching evidence of consideration amid "so many alleviating circumstances," "so much confidence & moderation," "so much sympathy," that Rebecca wept "from sensibility of generous forbearance—but not once for change of fortune," came from Abraham Elkin, a devoted member of Mikveh Israel. As she wrote Maria Gratz:

> ...I need tell you of one act which penetrated us most because it was from a person whose character was before unknown to us. Mr. Elkin whom our dear Ben may remember as an emigrant from the West Indies—he married and settled in Phila. where he encreases the product of his Island property by lending money on Mortgages and other securities—he was a creditor of our brothers and on the day of their failure Simon sent a message to him begging he would not be alarmed, & the next day he walked out to his place, told him, his visit was not to enquire about his property but to express his sympathy & to offer his services, that he had not much in his power, but had 3 or 4000 in bank which was at his command—that his debt was of no consequence—he would withdraw the note and tear it up and that he might pay when it was convenient—if not for ten years he should not complain—indeed it would gratify the first wish of his heart if he could redeem that beautiful spot (Willington) for him—Poor Simon wept like a child when he related this anecdote to me—Mr. Elkin is a Jew, when he first came here he consulted our brothers about the disposition of his affairs and seemed much attached to Hyman, but there has never been any intimacy between them and as he bears the character of a man close to his interests, lives retired & prudent—tho' highly respectable, we had no idea he was so noble & generous.[47]

On January 1, 1827, the firm of Simon Gratz and Brother was formally dissolved, and Simon took his son Edward in with him to begin a new partnership.[48] The family house on Chestnut Street, next to which the patent medicine king, Swaim of Panacea fame, had just moved with the intention—to Rebecca's horror—of converting a wing of his new house into a cake shop, was put up for sale.[49] Within eighteen months, Rebecca, Hyman and Jacob were ensconced in a much smaller and not so fashionable establishment in Boston Row, on Chestnut Street, two doors from Twelfth.[50] But the position in the city which the brothers had attained they continued to enjoy. It was some while before they were able to disentangle their affairs and rebuild their fortunes, but that too they did. Meanwhile, No. 2 Boston Row was visited, as the Chestnut Street house had been before, by the elite of the literary, social and business worlds. The Gratzes remained the leading Jews of Philadelphia.

Such a leading role was not attained by many other Jewish merchants, but there were others who enjoyed a modicum of success. Moses H. Levy was also in the India trade,[51] and West Indian staples were handled by Isaiah Nathans,[52] Abraham C. Peixotto,[53] Raphael De Cordova,[54] and Wolf Benjamin.[55] Benjamin dealt more heavily in rum and molasses than the others, for having been a distiller in England before he came to America, he ran a small but lucrative distillery in Philadelphia until his death in 1835.

One item that was exported from the city, although commercially of the least importance, was—from a Jewish point of view—of great interest. It will be remembered that in 1767 Michael Gratz had shipped kosher meat to the Jews of the West Indies. In 1807, possibly for the flourishing Jewish community of Bombay, where the famous Sassoon family of England later made their fortunes, or even for that ancient group of Jews in Kai-feng Fu, the rumors of whose existence had just reached the western world,[56] Isaac Lazarus, of 63 North 8th Street, advertised:

Jewish Provisions, Beef & Sausages fit for the West and East-India markets, put up in the nicest order, and for sale on the best terms (accompanied with a certificate).[57]

Exactly who the ultimate consumers were is not known, but enough interest must have been shown in these export wares of Mikveh Israel's *shohet* to have made it worth his while to continue his advertisement for several months.

Among those active as merchants were also several of the Gratz brothers-in-law. When Reuben Etting began in business in his own name, it was as a trader of miscellaneous dry goods, groceries and china, with some dependence upon West Indian imports.[58] In 1809 he became a partner of John Humes as an auctioneer,[59] a trade which, in spite of the protest of Jonas Phillips in 1791, was still restricted to a handful of firms licensed by the Governor. However, Etting's partnership lasted only two years, and he again found himself on his own.[60] His unsuccessful venture into politics, his inability to sustain himself in business, and recurrent bouts of ill-health which might have been the cause of his business difficulties, made him increasingly dependent upon his brother-in-law Hyman Gratz.[61] Poor Reuben, with a large family of children to bring up and provide an education for, did not have an easy time during his years in Philadelphia.

Another Gratz brother-in-law, Solomon Moses, was, however, successful where Etting had not been.[62] Trained in the New York counting-house of his father, Isaac Moses, who had been active in the building of the first synagogue of Mikveh Israel in 1782, Solomon settled in Philadelphia after he married Rachel Gratz in 1806. At first he was merely an agent for the New York firm of which he was a junior partner; but, after three years in the city, he was able to announce that in the future he would transact business as Solomon Moses & Co.[63] His stock included the now familiar variety of Bengal, Madras and Calcutta goods, Guatemala and Louisiana indigo, and, like the Gratzes, sugar, tobacco and cotton from the southern Mississippi River area.

Perhaps it was the pre-war difficulties which an importer faced that decided him to enter "the Auction and Commission Line" in partnership with Frederick Montmollin. From 1811 until 1818, when their license was not renewed by the Governor, the two men conducted one of the most active businesses of its kind in the city.[64] When the partnership was dissolved "by its own limitation," Moses went back to his former trade as merchant.[65]

The most successful Jewish importer in the city was English-born John Moss, who had arrived in Philadelphia in 1796 and immediately announced that he was going to follow his craft of glass-engraving, trusting, with the enthusiasm of a twenty-five-year-old, that "he will find succor in this city, where the arts and sciences are in a flourishing state."[66] But he did not long practice his trade. Within ten years, John Moss had become a dealer in dry goods, then an importer, and finally a shipping merchant. His story is typical of that of many immigrants, except that Moss prospered far above the average. Two-and-a-half months after he put his first notice in a Philadelphia newspaper, he married Rebecca Lyons.[67] In the yellow fever epidemic of 1798, both their children were stricken, and one new-born must have died, for his surviving children included one daughter, Sarah, who was born towards the end of 1797, and a second one, Miriam, born in 1800.[68] By 1820 the family had grown to nine children.

John Moss' career seems to have been assured when, in 1807, he moved from a North Second Street address to a more important location on Market, between Second and Third, "where he intends to keep a general assortment of Dry Goods,

which he will sell as usual at reduced prices."[69] In the new location the stock was quickly enlarged to include most commodities, and within a short time Moss was a full-fledged importer.[70]
As the business increased, he took his brother Samuel in with
him and by 1822 J. and S. Moss were not only chartering ships,
but having them built specially for them.[71]

On April 2, 1822, the ship *Moss* was launched from the yard
of Tees, Vanhook, Bowers and Vandusen at Kensington "to the
glorification of a numerous concourse of spectators." It was
an elegant ship of about 330 tons, designed as a regular London
packet, with uncommon pains taken in its structure and no expense spared to make the accommodations for passengers equal
to any in the European trade.

The event was hailed with pride by the local press, and specific
note taken of the carved figurehead which was "a striking like-
ness of the lady of J. Moss."[72] It is more than likely that this was
one of the masterpieces of the famous carver William Rush, whose
magnificent decorations made Philadelphia ships recognizable
in any harbor in the world.[73] It is said that John Moss had been
responsible for the erection of the fountain of a "Nymph with
a Swan on her Shoulder," carved by Rush, which in 1809 was
placed in front of the Water Works Building in Centre Square.[74]
He was certainly one of the early art patrons of the city.

Somewhat later, he imported from Italy two marble lions,
copied from those by Canova for the tomb of Clement XIII in
St. Peter's, and had them placed on the steps of the Merchant's
Exchange at Third and Dock Streets. In 1923, when the building
was altered, the lions were moved, and they are now to be
seen on the steps of the Philadelphia Museum of Art.[75]

On the pavement in front of his house, at No. 189 Spruce
Street, the first anthracite coal destined for domestic use was
piled. It was said that some of his fellow-citizens expressed the
opinion "that John Moss had gone crazy, dumping black stones
to burn." But he persevered, built a special grate, and enlarged
his chimney in order to prove his point. He was the first to ship
abroad a cargo of Pennsylvania anthracite.[76] Still young and still
energetic, John Moss at the end of 1823 retired from business
and left the control of the firm in his brother's hands.[77] He became a capitalist in the best sense of the word at a time when the
free enterprise system was laying the foundation of the country's
industrial growth. He turned his attention to inland navigation,

turnpike systems, banking and insurance—the same activities in which the four Gratz brothers had been active for more than a decade.

In 1823 he was elected a director of the Pennsylvania Company, on which board he served with Hyman Gratz.[78] The following year, he was chosen a director of two great Philadelphia corporations, the Lehigh Coal and Navigation Company and the Chesapeake and Delaware Canal Company,[79] and sometime later also of the Commercial Bank of Pennsylvania.[80]

Like Hyman Gratz, John Moss remained closely identified with the Jewish community and played a leading role in the management of synagogal and philanthropic affairs. These two men, with lawyer Zalegman Phillips, used the respect which they had earned as men of business to further the welfare of their fellow-Jews. They were men, fully a part of the American life around them, who did not feel it either necessary or desirable to surrender their Judaism or Jewish associations. The more they became involved with the new synagogue of Mikveh Israel, and the little sectarian charities which had just come into being, the more they devoted themselves to general civic projects. A subscription for yellow fever victims,[81] the introduction of a new water system into the city,[82] a solicitation of funds for all the impoverished,[83] a campaign against arson,[84] the improvement of wharves,[85] service on a Grand Jury of the Mayor's Court,[86] and a local anti-slavery society,[87] all found a Gratz, a Moss or a Phillips willing to help. When the newly-founded Franklin Institute, established to encourage American skills, held its second exposition, John Moss acted as the judge of the engraved glass.[88] The cycle had run its full course.

A third Moss, Jacob, was the first Jewish bookseller in the city. His trade, according to the practice of the day, included supplies for young ladies who were taught water-coloring as a matter of course in their genteel schools and who busily decorated their precious albums and scrap-books. Such a stock came over from London in the *Tontine*, owned by the other Mosses, in 1821, when Jacob announced that there had just arrived in his store, at No. 65 South Third Street

a large and elegant assortment of Akerman's colors, ditto Bristol Boards, beautiful colored Medallions, from Akerman's Repository, London; fine Cutlery of every description; Palmer's royal portable Pens, pen-cutters to the royal family; fancy Paper of every description; warranted Razors.

His specialty, however, was the manufacture of quill pens, which he boasted were "warranted superior to any manufactured in America."[89] It is interesting that, in addition to jig-saw puzzles, rosewood work boxes, magic lanterns and magnetic toys, he also offered the effective pamphlet, *Israel Vindicated*, which attacked the calumnies of the missionaries, then enjoying their brief moment of popularity.[90]

Because of their older history and widespread activity, and chiefly because their voluminous family papers were preserved, the Gratzes have in the past over-shadowed the careers of other Philadelphia Jews in the field of trade and commerce. Yet it was others who gave solidity and form to the community, others about whom but fragmentary information has survived, for they were a part of the almost anonymous middle-class who left few records. However, one of the socio-economic phenomena which can be noted was the quick integration of the English-speaking immigrants like John Moss, Robert and Isaac Phillips, and Isaiah Nathans. Unhampered by language difficulties, they, like other Englishmen, were able to fit into the American pattern with ease. They were not considered foreigners, for their names and ways were indistinguishable from those of the great mass of Philadelphians. This same homogeneity also accounts for the ability of the American-born second generation to move up from rank to rank in the still uncrystallized strata of nineteenth-century American society.

In addition to the advantage of knowing the language, these English Jews had family and business connections in England which were most useful. In spite of the emphasis on American manufactures, British goods both before and after the War of 1812 were imported in considerable quantity. And the cultural influence of the mother country remained dominant. The social and commercial relationship maintained by the Moss family was reflected in letters about synagogal affairs. R. and I. Phillips became the Philadelphia agents of the great international banking house of Rothschild.[91] The Nathans were associated with the composer who set Lord Byron's *Hebrew Melodies* to music.[92]

There were three different families of Jewish Phillipses, in addition to a number of non-Jewish ones: the many children of Jonas,[93] Levy Phillips,[94] and the brothers Robert and Isaac, the last of whom married John Moss' oldest daughter. Zalegman

Phillips, who served as *parnass* of Mikveh Israel for twelve years, had a very extensive legal practice. As we have seen, he was a politically active Democrat, defended Jewish rights in court, and took time out to invent a machine for making pins. Announcing in 1825 that he had for sale the patent for it, Phillips stated:

> The machine, with the assistance of a boy twelve years of age, will manufacture at the rate of three thousand six hundred pins an hour, delivering the pin with head and point completely made. The machine can be set in motion and worked by water, by steam, or by horse power, and one steam engine, of 10 horse power, is sufficient to work 60 of the machines.[95]

That same year, his eldest son, Jonas Altamont Phillips, received his master's degree at the University of Pennsylvania, at the same ceremony during which an honorary degree of Doctor of Laws was conferred on Lafayette,[96] and the following year was admitted to the bar,[97] joining Zalegman in what was the outstanding Jewish law firm of the city for a generation.

There was always a large number of Cohens in town. At the beginning of the century Abraham M. Cohen advertised in the most flowery language what seems to have been the first Jewish pawnshop in Philadelphia:

> *No Puff:*
> *'A Friend in Need is a Friend in Deed.'*
> The subscriber having experienced how pleasing it is to meet with a friend in distress, as also urged by the utmost philanthropy to himself and fellow citizens—takes this method of informing them that they can be accommodated with any
> Sum of Money
> *From 5 Dollars to 10,000 & upwards*
> Only by depositing what may be esteemed the value thereof, On the most reasonable terms, by either written or personal application, made at his Office, No. 115 Chesnut-street, opposite the Bank of Pennsylvania— . . .[98]

Abraham was one of the sons of Solomon Myers Cohen and a grandson of old Joseph Simon of Lancaster. He had a brother Eleazer L. with whom he entered into partnership when they opened an apothecary shop, and another brother, the lawyer Joseph S. Cohen.[99] A second Eleazer Cohen was a merchant, in business after 1815 with Michael Nisbet.[100] The unrelated sons of Israel I. Cohen, who were conducting a large lottery and exchange business in Baltimore, maintained a Philadelphia branch.[101] But one of the most unusual trades was followed by

Abraham Haim Cohen, the *shohet* and son of the *hazan*. He supplemented the income he received from the congregation by bottling and selling mineral waters at his Hygeian Fountain and Philadelphia Mineral Water Ware House at No. 31 South Second Street.[102] It was this business which he suspended to take over his father's duties temporarily after his death and which he later resumed again. Cohen is credited with having invented seltzer water and popularized the use of sodas. His product received the formal approval of some of the city's most eminent physicians, among them Benjamin Rush, William P. Dewees, Thomas Parke, and the Frenchman Mongez.

A number of Philadelphia Jews conducted stores which ranged in size from what must have been little one-room shops run by Widow Barnett on Cherry Street near the synagogue[103] and by Widow Keys at Seventh and Noble,[104] a neighborhood into which more and more Jews were moving, to the plain and fancy dry goods stores of Lyon J. Levy[105] and Goldsmit and Goudkop.[106] The Lyon J. Levy establishment which was later to move to the important corner at Fifth and Chestnut was a forerunner of the modern department store, and by mid-century was one of the largest of its kind in the country. Few of the storekeepers, however, did business on a large scale, and so we know nothing about them except an entry in the Directory which simply says "storekeeper," "dry goods store," or "store." Jonas Horwitz's father-in-law Joseph Andrews was one of these.[107]. Aaron and Joseph Asch,[108] Simon Brolaskey,[109] Judah L. Hackenburg,[110] Elias Hyneman and two of his sons, Leon and Benjamin,[111] Aaron Levy, Jr., who was succeeded by his son Joseph and in turn by his grandson Elias,[112] Michael Seeligson[113] and F. and S. Stork[114] were some of the others.

Another was Abraham Hart.[115] Dry goods, groceries, a number of partnerships and an early death summarize his career. His wife continued the business with the help of her teen-age son, also Abraham, whose remarkable energy and ability enabled the Harts to build up a successful book and stationery store. The lad attracted the attention of a local auctioneer who recommended him to the city's outstanding publishers, the company founded by Mathew Carey, and in 1829 operated under the name of Carey, Lea and Carey. The Careys were just in the process of dividing their firm in two, and so impressed were they with the young Jew that they admitted Abraham Hart, then only nineteen years old, to partnership in the junior firm.[116] Within a week, one of James Fenimore Cooper's popular novels appeared in the bookstores bearing the new imprint, Carey & Hart.[117] Hart became one of the most successful and highly esteemed book-publishers in the country, and in the next generation he was without question the leading Jewish layman of Philadelphia.

The Philadelphia Jewish community was being increased to a greater degree by men from different lands. Raphael De Cordova and his son Joshua sold rum and other products from their native Jamaica.[118] For a while they had Abraham I. Nunes, another Jamaican, in partnership with them, and after Raphael retired from active business Joshua seems to have continued as a distiller of bitters.

A French Jew, Lyon Cadet, formed a partnership with English-speaking Alexander Phillips, and their business affairs were administered by the German Abraham Gumpert.[119] When later Cadet entered into a venture with a Hollander, Benedict Nathan, they found they were wrongly accused of theft, since the criminal was heard to speak "Low Dutch, French and High French."[120]

Most of the men, however, who had small local businesses were of German origin. They had little need to go out of their own neighborhood to secure customers, and it is more than probable that they were patronized by neighborhood people. One Isaac Abram was a tailor on North Eighth Street, another man by the same name was a butcher on North Second, and Abraham Abram kept a tavern at the corner of Third and Poplar.[121] In the same northern section of the city, Morris Cohen was a clothier;[122] Jacob Canter, once a cabinet-maker, sold china;[123] the *shohet* Abraham Forst enjoyed the distinction of being called a "Jew-victualler;"[124] Aaron Moses dealt in second-hand clothes;[125] Hyman Polock sold watches and jewelry;[126] and another Abraham Hart had a shoe store.[127]

The trades of the Philadelphia Jews were varied. A. B. Cohen was a carver and gilder;[128] Barnet and Philip Eytinge handled fancy goods at wholesale;[129] M. Isaacson was a furrier and cap manufacturer;[130] Emanuel Moses made combs;[131] Jacob Nathans made brushes;[132] Joseph Pereyra was a candlemaker;[133] Mrs. Solomon, a widow, was an umbrella-maker;[134] Moses Spyers was a watchmaker;[135] Gustavus Pesoa was a bookbinder, and David Pesoa a saddler;[136] John (Levite) Moss was a dyer;[137] Barnett

Cohen was a cabinetmaker;[138] Herman Van Beil, at first a second-hand clothes dealer, became a pawnbroker;[139] and the Christian sons of Lion Van Amring took over their father's grocery store.[140]

There are some figures which can be gathered to give at least a partial picture of Jewish economic life. In 1824 there were seventeen Jewish importers of foreign merchandise in a list of approximately 1,000 firms which did some import business in Philadelphia;[141] in 1827 there were twenty-five out of 1,300.[142] These included, in addition to the leading merchants already mentioned, such newer arrivals as Simeon Dreyfous, who imported jewelry and watches;[143] Aaron Stork, a grocer and wine merchant;[144] Isaac Stuttgart, who of all the Jewish businessmen seemed to have had the greatest difficulty in establishing himself;[145] Mayer Ullman, a tavernkeeper;[146] and later Lewis Allen,[147] Joseph Andrade, a French merchant, who had a reputation for eccentricity for, although he was a wealthy man, he dressed shabbily and lived most parsimoniously,[148] and Louis Bomeisler, who came to Philadelphia in 1817 as supercargo, was stricken with yellow fever, attended by Dr. James Rush, and persuaded by that distinguished physician to settle here.[149]

As compared to the period immediately after the Revolution there were few brokers, some of whom dealt principally in lottery tickets, and of these only five were resident Philadelphians,[150] the Cohens of Baltimore[151] and the Solises of Wilmington[152] merely maintaining offices here. By 1830 a number, like Eleazer Cohen, whose daughter married his partner Nisbet, were retired and listed as "gentlemen." These included Abraham Elkin, who had offered to help the Gratzes in their misfortune, Sol Marache's non-Jewish son Nicholson, Andrew Rodrigues, formerly in partnership with Bomeisler, and, as noticed, Hyman Gratz and John Moss.[153] These, together with the professional men and the merchants, formed the upper stratum of the economic level.

However, the majority of the Jews of Philadelphia in the first three decades of the nineteenth century were small shopkeepers and tradesmen, with the artisans selling direct the shoes, watches and umbrellas they made. There were well over a hundred of them who advertised in the newspapers or were listed in the Directories. It is still impossible to determine the numbers who ran such small shops that they were unlisted, or who began their business careers as peddlers.

In a later period, a majority of the new immigrants may have begun life in America with packs on their backs. Mayer Ullman, before he settled down in his tavern, was the victim of a theft during his peddling days when his trunks were broken open and pilfered,[154] and a similar misfortune befell Barnet Jonas.[155] By the large, however, these men who braved the hardships of the open road were anonymous. But to the towns and villages of the interior the arrival of "the Jew" was an occasion to celebrate, for he brought hard-to-get necessities and rare luxuries in his knapsack, saddlebags or pot-bellied trunks. From the shops and warehouses of his co-religionists in the big cities the peddler distributed throughout the country those little articles of manufacture which made all the difference between bare existence and civilized life. He was a vital part of pioneer America.

One of the marked features of American—and American Jewish life—was the mobility of the population. Men arrived from Europe, stayed in Philadelphia for a while and moved on south and west. Many of the pioneers in cotton towns in the South, in river towns along the Mississippi and in the growing trade centers of the Ohio River Valley had stayed long enough in Philadelphia to become oriented to the American way of life.

When Joseph Jonas came to America from Plymouth, in the autumn of 1816, he lived for a while in the city with the family of Samuel Joseph. Levy Phillips, Mikveh Israel's *parnass*, tried to persuade him to stay on, and not go to Ohio as he planned. "In the wilds of America, and entirely among gentiles, you will forget your religion and your God," the Philadelphian warned him. But Jonas, like others after him, went just the same, and became the founder of the Jewish community of Cincinnati.[156] Somewhat later, his erstwhile host, Samuel Joseph, moved to Cincinnati too,[157] and the ties were made even closer when Joseph Jonas and his brother Abraham married two daughters of Gershom Mendes Seixas, who were then living with their brother David in Philadelphia.[158]

In 1818, the year before Benjamin Gratz moved permanently to Lexington, his nephew, Gratz Etting, announced that he had set up his office in Bellefonte, and would practice law in Centre, Mifflin and Huntington Counties.[159] There is a strong possibility that he too was impelled to move to be the on-the-spot representative of the Gratz interests, for Bellefonte was but a short distance from Aaronsburg and the central Pennsylvania land holdings of Aaron Levy which were now in the hands of Simon Gratz.

Another Philadelphia firm, the brothers Simon and Jacob Phillipson, pushed even further west to the new territory of Missouri. With an Indian trading post in St. Louis and an outlet in Philadelphia, these two early members of Rodeph Shalom handled quantities of furs and skins, "Missouri Beaver, Dressed Buffalo Hides, Racoon, Muskrat, Bear and other Skins, shaved, in the hair and Indian Dressed Deerskins."[160] One of their suppliers was John Jacob Astor, who became the fur king of the country.[161] To supply the tanners of the East, buffalo hunting had begun on a large scale; and to conduct their business more efficiently between the two distant points, Simon Phillipson with his family of seven moved to the St. Louis outpost,[162] while Jacob maintained the Philadelphia branch. They were among the many Jews who, as noted before, settled first in Philadelphia, but moved one by one, or family by family, to the new cities and towns of the vast interior.

Jacob S. Solis, who in 1816 told the merchants of Philadelphia that he was opening an auction business at Wilmington, Delaware,[163] was in New York state in the early 1820s,[164] and went down to New Orleans in 1827.[165] That boom-town, cotton shipping center, attracted a number of Philadelphians. Haym Salomon's son Ezekiel became cashier of the branch of the United States Bank there.[166] Solis, the dentist Zachariah Florance and A. H. De Yonge, who contributed to Rodeph Shalom in 1824, were among the incorporators of Louisiana's first synagogue in 1828.[167] And perhaps others of the first Jewish community there, whose Philadelphia origin cannot definitely be traced, did in fact go South from the Quaker City.

Jamaica-born Jacob R. De Cordova, after doing business for some years on South Front Street, left town because of his health and returned to the West Indies. Later he came back to this country, passed through New Orleans, and established himself in Galveston, where he organized De Cordova's Land Agency, one of the largest promotion companies for Texas land. His brother Phineas, who had been born in Philadelphia in 1819, afterwards joined him in business.[168] Joseph Osterman, a member of Mikveh Israel in 1822, moved to Baltimore a few years afterwards, and he too eventually settled in Galveston, where he ran a most successful dry goods store.[169] Another former Philadelphian, Michael Seeligson, was an even more prominent citizen of that Texas city, eventually becoming its mayor.[170] And Moses A. Levy, who had received his medical education at the University of Pennsylvania, was Surgeon-General of Sam Houston's army which won the independence of Texas.[171]

A few other Jews from other cities came to Philadelphia from time to time, but there was none who has left a more human picture of life there than Raphael Jacob Moses. It is one of the weaknesses of a history such as this that so few personal reminiscences are extant. Business advertisements, government documents, synagogal records and fleeting references in many places are the pieces which make up the jigsaw puzzle, but the warm personal comments—with the single exception of Rebecca Gratz's letters—are notably lacking. Therefore, it is all the more important to record a fragment which does have a real and living quality. Raphael Jacob Moses, born in Charleston in 1812, was the son of Israel and Deborah, a daughter of Jacob Raphael Cohen, and hence a sister of Michael Hart's widow Esther. He was brought up to Philadelphia when he was in his teens, and has left a vivid picture of his relatives and friends.

Soon after I quit school I went to Philadelphia with my parents and stayed with my aunt, Mrs. Esther Hart, the grandmother of Louisa Lyons, née Hart, who is the mother of Rachel Huestes. They left me in Philadelphia.

I nominally stayed in Bacon & Hart's music store in the daytime and attended law lectures at night, given by Judge Hopkins[on], and I was very much interested in them. They were altogether on commercial law, but my mind was too much on pleasure bent. I was not much older than thirteen. My companions were generally several years older than myself. I had the very free use of money and used it. I always thought my father was wealthy. He was then in the auction business, kept horses, and lived up to his means, if not beyond them, as I discovered in later years, and being an only child whose wishes were law, I was not very particular about what might or might not be his bank balances so that my purse was not empty.

. . . I had an old-maid cousin, Anna Hart, who late in life married Mr. Bacon, of the firm of Bacon & Hart. She was a typical old maid and a model housekeeper, always kept the rooms darkened to keep the sun and flies out, and I always opened them to let the sun and air in, irrespective of how many flies might come with me. Of course, I was her horror. Then I had another cousin, Louisa, a very cultivated and charitable woman, and as ugly and outré in her style of dressing as she was intelligent and benevolent. And she found out that I had said, or somebody had said that I had said, I would not walk with her on Chestnut Street because of her ill-favored face and want of taste in dressing. And, of course, with her my fat was in the fire and sizzled as bad as if I really had said it, which, by the way, at this late date I am not prepared to deny.

I soon quit attending law lectures at night, much preferring the theater, for which I had a passion. The next year, when father went north, as he did every summer, I returned with him . . . Again I went to Philadelphia with father; I suppose I was about fifteen. We dined with Mr. Peixotto, a West Indian. He had been quite wealthy, but was less so because of the emancipation of his slaves, but he was still well off. [He] had no children, but had adopted two nephews and two nieces and a very sweet girl, Betsy Shaw. The latter was a Christian, and although he was a very Orthodox Jew, he was scrupulously exact in her attendance of church. He was a very arbitrary man. His wife, who we all called "Gam," an abbreviation for grandma, was as kind as she could be.

Much to my surprise and satisfaction—anything to stay North—father arranged with Mr. P. for me to stay in his office and be an inmate of his house. He did a large business in Kingston, Jamaica, and had a copy of his daybook sent by vessel to Philadelphia. There the entries were journalized and posted, so that he always had before him the daily transaction of his West India business. The books were kept in £, s. d., and it was with him that I learned practical bookkeeping.

I think I must have stayed with him about two years. It was to me a very happy home. I was really one of the family and very fond of Betsy Shaw, but never thought of engaging myself to her, for I knew that Mr. Peixotto would never consent to her intermarriage. Besides, we were both too young for serious love. Gam was like a mother to me; she was a warmhearted West Indian. Mr. Peixotto, as I have already indicated, was a very benevolent man but very dictatorial. I was then, as much as it may contrast with my present habits, very fond of dress and fashion. Chestnut Street was the fashionable street. I generally walked that way home, wore gloves, and twirled a rattan. One day about dinnertime he came into the office and said: 'Ralph, I have bought a pair of turkeys; they are on Front Street, and I must take them home. You come with me, and I will take one, and you will take the other.'

I was amazed. Our path home would be right down Chestnut Street. I respectfully declined the 'hazardous adventure.' Mr. Peixotto insisted; I resisted. At last he said: "When I hire a boy, he must do what I tell him." I replied: "You employ me to keep your books: I am no *hired* boy." "Well, sir," said he, "hired or employed, you will carry that turkey or quit." "Then, sir, it is quit, for I shan't carry it," and quit I did. We always remained friendly, but with him it was absolute obedience; with me it was anything but toteing a gobler and we split on the turkey. . . .

From Mr. Peixotto I went back to my aunt's. And soon after, as I was very much troubled with dispepsia, I got from Simeon Dreyfous (who boarded there and was an importer of Swiss watches) an assortment of Swiss watches and a traveler's trunk, made to carry samples, and started for Easton, Pennsylvania, where my mother had lived in her early life. I went by stagecoach and stopped at Redding, Allentown, and other small places between Philadelphia and Easton, exhibiting my watches at the different small towns, and made more than enough to pay all my travelling expenses. . . .

I stayed in Easton some time and then went on the Mauch Chunk R. R. to the mines and went into the mines and saw the miners at work. The R. R. was propelled to the mines by horse power, hauling the cars upgrade empty, and then they came back loaded, down a gradual incline, by their own momentum. Contrast that mule team with the great Pennsylvania R. R. I went to the Delaware Gap and other places of interest, was charmed with the beautiful scenery, and returned to Philadelphia sound in health and purse.

I then clerked for Dreyfous and boarded at Mrs. Reynolds' on Chestnut Street, and the way I happened to go to Mrs. Reynolds was this: I saw a very pretty girl on Chestnut Street and followed her home. She went into a house just opposite the Mint. I took another opportunity to look at the doorplate and found Mrs. Reynolds. Then ascertained that she kept a boardinghouse and, to make the story short, I left my aunt's and went there to board. [I] made the acquaintance of pretty Kate, for such was her name, attended her wedding soon after, and there became acquainted with a lot of good fellows, all seven or eight years older than myself, and all in business and able to spend freely. . . .

It was while I was living at Mrs. Reynolds' that I walked, one night, down Chestnut Street with Hetty Pisoa and her cousin, Henry M. Phillips. When we were between Second and Third Streets, near an alley, someone from an upstairs window cried out: "The house [is] on fire!" I ran round the alley, got over the back fence and into the back door. The front room, on fire, was a cigar store. I rushed up the stairs and at the second story called aloud to the inmates, but received no reply. . . . I have not the least idea of how I escaped, but when I woke up I was lying in the yard, bleeding. Someone came to my assistance and I asked to be carried to my aunt's. I was taken there and had something like pneumonia. . . .

My trips to and from the North were so frequent that I am a little confused in dates, but think this is a trip I made by stage, via Washington and Richmond. At the latter place Abraham Cohen lived. He was quite a talented man and was rabbi (then called hazan) for a number of years. His father, my grandfather, for whom I was named, was minister for about thirty years in Philadelphia, and my mother inherited all of their Orthodox ideas, so that all the influence of birth and education were with me on the religious side, but I never became indoctrinated with their views. . . .[172]

Such was part of the saga of the grandson of Mikveh Israel's second *hazan*, who was to become an unreconstructed Southerner even before the Civil War and then an officer in the Confederate Army.

✎ 19

The Second Synagogue of Mikveh Israel

As in every religious community which had increased in size and in which more and more members had attained high civic, social and economic positions, a house of worship befitting the size and the status of its congregation became a matter of both pride and necessity. The little thirty-foot square synagogue on Cherry Street had been big enough, and more, for the Jews remaining in Philadelphia after the exodus of the Revolutionary exiles from other cities. That was in 1782. A generation later, with the sons of the former leaders now managing synagogue affairs, something bigger and better was desired. The Jews of Philadelphia wanted an edifice which would match the respect in which they were held by their fellow-citizens.

After the difficulties both Mikveh Israel and Rodeph Shalom encountered in their attempts to conduct lotteries for funds to repair and build synagogues, the idea was abandoned by the latter. However, the more experienced and more influential members of Mikveh Israel, aware that some of the churches of the city were having their requests approved in spite of increasing public sentiment against lotteries for such purposes, persisted in their appeals. Their first petition having been held up when the commissioners appointed to conduct the lottery refused to act,[1] Benjamin Nones addressed a letter to Governor Simon Snyder, an old personal friend of Aaron Levy of Aaronsburg, asking his intercession.[2]

After the facts were presented to the legislature, it declared that they seemed to be "to the serious inconvenience of the congregation." The petition was therefore reintroduced, and after running its long legislative course, ended up as a bill signed by the Governor on February 28, 1810, authorizing the

members of the Hebrew congregation of the city of Philadelphia to raise by way of lottery, a sum of money for the repairs of their synagogue and burial place and for other purposes of relief.[3]

This was a small affair of not more than $4,000—as compared to the grandiose scheme of $100,000 which had been turned down—and was seemingly privately run, for the only record of a religious body conducting a publicly advertised lottery at this time concerned the Universalist Church.

As a maintenance fund, this would have tided the congregation over for a few years, but this was not what Mikveh Israel was really seeking. The deteriorating synagogue continued to need repairs. On November 1, 1818, the *adjunta* appointed a committee of three to determine how much it would cost to put the old building in condition and how much to rebuild the synagogue completely.[4] A new application for a lottery was considered, but more practically a subscription was begun among the members.[5] At the Passover meeting of the congregation in 1819, Joseph Gratz, the treasurer of the new building fund, announced that over $6,000 had been pledged.[6]

Conducted in the atmosphere of the "Era of Good Feelings," as Monroe's administration following the War of 1812 was known, at a period when hopes were high even though economic recovery from the effects of the war was not up to expectations, this was one of the most effective fund-raising campaigns ever entered into by Mikveh Israel. With the promise that contributions could be deducted from the price of seats in the new synagogue, a city-wide appeal was made. John Moss and his wife and one of his in-laws gave $1,300; Simon Gratz gave $1,000, and four of his brothers and his sister Rebecca together matched his gift. Other Gratz-connected families, the Hays and the Ettings of Baltimore, were generous in their support. Ninety-two individuals, representing forty-three Mikveh Israel families, and, surprisingly enough, thirteen Rodeph Shalom families, made up the Philadelphia list.[7]

To assure the success of the campaign, letters were addressed to other congregations in the United States, in the West Indies and abroad, as well as to a few individual Jews of world-famed wealth. Abraham R. Brandon, the *parnass* of Nidche Israel in Barbados, then in New York on business, was the recipient of one of these appeals, and after his return home he succeeded in raising over $800 which was sent on to Philadelphia in the form of a bill of exchange to be cleared through Moses Myers of Norfolk.[8] Abraham Touro of Boston was told by Simon and Joseph Gratz, John Moss and Hyman Marks that they,

aware of the interest you take in advancing the respectability of our Holy religion, believe they could not address one more likely to forward their views, by a liberal contribution.[9]

Even after the cornerstone was laid, but before the edifice was dedicated, the mail campaign continued. The same aggressive committee, with Solomon Moses in the place of Hyman Marks, wrote to the almost legendary Nathan Meyer Rothschild of London, appealing for help to the founder of the banking firm "so universally known for acts of beneficence."[10] With what must have been a degree of pride, they gave Rothschild the London banking houses of Baring Brothers and Bainbridge and Brown as references. The Spanish and Portuguese Synagogue of London had already sent the Philadelphians fifty pounds,[11] and the largest out-of-town contribution, $1,000, had been received from Judah Touro on behalf of himself and other Jews in New Orleans.[12] By the fall of 1823, the international building fund campaign had received cash and pledges amounting to almost $8,000.[13]

Even before all these generous gifts were received from far away, with just over $6,000 subscribed, the building committee had been instructed to pull down the old synagogue and commence building a new one "not to cost more than $2,000—over and above the amount subscribed,"[14] but things did not move as fast as the first success of the campaign would seem to have warranted. Three and a half years elapsed from the first decision to tear down and rebuild anew, and the actual demolition. Two plans for a new structure had been submitted, considered and rejected.[15] Finally, on September 6, 1822, the committee approved the proposal of William Strickland, one of the leading architects of the country, whose designs for the Second Bank of the United States (now the Old Customs House), then going up on Chestnut Street, had been chosen in an open competition. Stipulating "that the whole cost of the building completed, shall not exceed Eight thousand Dollars," they ordered Strickland to commence work forthwith.[16]

On September 8th a committee of three was appointed to superintend the removal of the ritual objects of the synagogue and to procure a temporary place of worship.[17] They made arrangements to rent the old Masonic Hall, almost next door to the fashionable Gratz home on Chestnut Street, and found themselves in immediate trouble. Almost the whole Gratz family, Benjamin Nones, Samuel Hays, Benjamin I. Phillips and others promptly protested, in spite of the connections some of them had with masonic lodges, that such a place could not be consecrated to the worship of the God of Israel.[18] After some debate, an acceptable substitute was found in the home of the part-time *hazan*, Jacob Bensadon, and there for a few years the services of the congregation were conducted.[19]

That knotty problem having been settled, the congregation got down to the more important business connected with a new synagogue, the auctioning off of the honors. Notices of this event had been passed on to the members of Rodeph Shalom and of Shearith Israel in New York,[20] and Solomon Moses, one of the city's popular auctioneers, agreed to cry the sale. The southeast cornerstone went to John Moss for $50. Benjamin Nones and Jacob I. Cohen, two Revolutionary soldiers and the sole surviving participants in the first cornerstone laying, bid in the northeast and northwest stones; and Hyman Gratz, continuing the family tradition in the second generation, purchased the remaining one. Two members of Rodeph Shalom, Louis Bomeisler and Isaac Stuttgart, bought the doorposts; and another one, Joseph Dreyfous, for $5, secured the honor of the original marble inscription which Jonas Phillips had insisted be cut and placed above the door in 1782.

There were more than enough honors to go around, and the sale must have been a most satisfactory occasion for all concerned. Haym Salomon's son-in-law, Joseph Andrews, obtained the sill stone; and Hyman Marks, the son of another of the Revolutionary generation, the new inscription stone. Three women— Mrs. Bell Cohen, the daughter of the Lancaster pioneer Joseph Simon; Mrs. Rebecca Phillips, the aged widow of Jonas; and Mrs. Judith I. Cohen, the widow of Israel I. Cohen of Richmond— successfully bid for three of the six pillars, and Henry H. and

Hillel Marks and Lazarus Hackenburg secured the other three. The stone doorposts went to Isaiah Nathans and Simeon Dreyfous; the six steps to Isaac B. Phillips, Mrs. Leah Phillips, Elias Hyneman, Joseph Levy, David Nathans and Joseph J. Andrews; the placing of the Ten Commandments near the ark to Levy Phillips; the hanging of the perpetual light to Hyman Polock; the lighting of it to Joseph Osterman; the placing of the candlesticks around the ark and the lighting of them to Joseph Andrews, Michael Oppenheimer, David Pesoa, Levi M. Goldsmit, Moses I. Goudcop and Emanuel Oppenheimer; the placing and lighting of the two candlesticks by the reader's desk to Leon and Benjamin Hyneman; and finally the hanging and lighting of the candles to Michael E. Cohen.[21]

On September 26, 1822, the official laying of the cornerstone took place. In the southeast stone a cavity was hollowed out in which was placed a volume containing the Constitution of the United States and those of the several states, the coins of the country, and a plate neatly engraved by the well-known Philadelphia artist, William Kneass, with the inscription:

> The Corner Stone of a House consecrated to the worship of Almighty God Jehovah, by the Congregation Kal Kodesh Mickve Israel, is placed in its bed by John Moss, on the eleventh day of Tisri, Anno Mundi 5583, corresponding to the 20th day of September, in the 47th year of the Independence of the United States of America.
> James Monroe being President, and Daniel D. Tomkins Vice President of the United States of America, and Joseph Hiester, Governor of the Commonwealth of Pennsylvania.
> This happy Country in which Religious and Civil Liberty is secured to its inhabitants, is now at Peace with the whole World—may that enjoyment long endure, and the integrity of this Government, and the reign of "Virtue, Liberty, and Independence" be triumphant "until the wreck of matter and the crush of worlds."[22]

It was duly noted that the building committee consisted of John Moss, Simon Gratz, Hyman Marks, Solomon Moses and Joseph Gratz, and that William Strickland was architect, Daniel Groves master mason, Samuel Baker master carpenter, and John Strothers master marble mason. By December, the *Philadelphia Gazette* reported that "the building had risen to its proper height, is now under roof and progressing to its completion."[23]

The membership of Rodeph Shalom was impressed by these material signs of progress, and the trend towards Mikveh Israel increased. Between 1812 and 1818, a significant number of former members of the German congregation had applied for admission into the Portuguese one. Men who had been drafters and signers of the constitution of Rodeph Shalom, the Goldsmit, Oppenheimer, De Lange, Stork and Hyneman families, one by one switched their memberships, and some of their allegiance by ceasing to contribute to the poorer congregation.[24] There were few like Louis Bomeisler and Isaac Stuttgart who remained consistently faithful to Rodeph Shalom, and at the same time made contributions to Mikveh Israel.[25] Many of the individuals who moved over to the more socially attractive group, beckoned by the rising structure, became important leaders in the life of Mikveh Israel and were signatories to the charter and by-laws of 1824. Only one member of Mikveh Israel, Levy Phillips, who was *parnass* in 1820–21, occasionally contributed to the German congregation, although he was never a member of it.[26]

In 1822 the defections increased and Rodeph Shalom, even more desperately in need of a new building than Mikveh Israel, again petitioned the legislature for "authority to raise, by way of lottery, the sum of $6,000, to enable them to purchase a lot and erect a house for public worship."[27] The petition was tabled. One can only speculate on the extent to which this influenced Wolf Benjamin in 1823 to recommend that Rodeph Shalom begin to save small sums of money towards a "Fund for the Erection of a new synagogue."[28] As soon as ten dollars was in the fund, it was deposited in the Philadelphia Saving Fund Society to draw interest. At the end of the year only $120 had been collected,[29] and, although the congregation began looking for a site, nothing more came of the first definite attempt by the Ashkenazic congregation to build its own synagogue.

Out of the land of Egypt had come the designs which William Strickland had drawn for the new synagogue of Mikveh Israel. After Nelson's victory at the Battle of the Nile in 1798, Egyptian motifs enjoyed a widespread popularity in England, and Napoleon's expedition in Egypt, culminating in the Battle of the Pyramids, brought back to France a similar taste for the newly discovered antiquities. The research of archaeologists, beginning for the first time serious studies in Egyptology, further stimulated the interest, and it is significant that Champollion's important work on hieroglyphics, based on the famous Rosetta stone, was first published as the walls of Mikveh Israel were rising.[30] Neo-Egyptian was the most modern style in architecture; the synagogue was the first example of it built in Philadelphia.

The two-storied building, with its slate-roof and a skylight, about twice the size of the original synagogue, faced Cherry Street. Its basic construction was of native stone from the Falls of the Schuylkill. The Egyptian tone was given by the inclined jambs which formed the doorway and the two windows which flanked it, and the cornice on which was sculptured a winged globe. Inside, the seats were arranged in two semi-circular blocks on either side of the ark facing which stood the reader's table. The ark, approached by three steps, was of course in the east. It was decorated by pilasters which supported a curved cornice on which was a marble tablet of the Ten Commandments with the winged globe design above it. The galleries, semi-circular along the north and south, were supported by columns, copied from the temple at Tentyra, which extended up to and in turn supported the dome.[31] All in all, it was a handsome example of the work of a great architect, using the newest style for the first time in his career.

It was not until the autumn of 1824 that the Strickland building stood proudly as a completed work. Meanwhile, Simon Gratz and the *adjunta* had been writing frantically to every possible source which might turn up a permanent *hazan* for the congregation.[32] When Abraham Israel Keys responded to the call of a city with coal, gas-lights and a new synagogue, the members of Mikveh Israel proceeded with plans for an elaborate but dignified installation service for their new minister, combined with the consecration of their new building. Jacob Seixas of New York undertook to train a choir of mixed voices, a most unusual adjunct to a Jewish religious service in those days.[33] Samuel Jackson, the Jewish printer and editor, was ordered to publish 400 copies of a special bi-lingual order of services.[34] And Moses Peixotto of Shearith Israel was invited to assist *Hazan* Keys in the consecration.[35]

As soon as Keys arrived in town, invitations were sent to Rodeph Shalom and to the congregations in New York, Baltimore and New Orleans to attend the dedication ceremonies.[36]. J. Andrew Shulze, the Governor of Pennsylvania, was invited, but could not attend because of other business,[37] but Chief Justice William Tilghman accepted,[38] as did the venerable Bishop William White and other dignitaries of the state and church whom Zalegman Phillips, as *parnass*, had asked to join their fellow-citizens on the happy, solemn occasion. The date for the ceremony was set for January 21, 1825.

No financial cloud hung over the building, as had been the case in 1782. Although the completed structure cost $13,000,[39] considerably more than had been authorized, seats sold on an advance payment basis,[40] the donations from out-of-towners,[41] and another lottery brought in several thousand dollars more. This last lottery, possibly pushed through the legislature through the influence of Zalegman Phillips, then somewhat of a power in the Democratic Party, was arranged in a most business-like manner. Instead of conducting it in the name of Mikveh Israel, the congregation sold its legislative permit to a professional lottery operator, Archibald McIntyre, for $7837.50, and was able to get the money it needed without the work and publicity which would have been necessary had the members sold the tickets themselves.[42]

Everything to make the dedication day an auspicious one was there. At this period in American life, few events were looked upon more favorably than the sanctification of a house of worship, and one to be consecrated by "those ancient people of the Lord" had the added attraction of a novelty. The people of Philadelphia, looking forward to a day of interest and excitement, had a kind of pride in the fact that such an event was taking place in the United States, that it was part of their community. Admission to the synagogue was by invitation only, and by the time the congregation finished the afternoon prayers, at half-past three, every one of the 192 seats downstairs and 164 in the gallery was filled.[43]

Rebecca Gratz, in a delightful letter to her brother Benjamin, "alone in a land of strangers," has left the only description of the service as seen through Jewish eyes:

I have never witnessed a more impressive or solemn ceremony or one more calculated to elevate the mind to religious exercises—the shool is one of the most beautiful specimens of ancient architecture in the city, and finished in the Stricklands best manner—the decorations are neat yet rich and tasteful—and the service commencing just before the Sabbath was performed by lamp light—Mr. Keys was assisted in the service by the Hazan from New York, Mr. Peixotto a venerable, learned & pious man who gave great effect to the solemnity—the doors being opened by our brother Simon and the blessing pronounced at the entrance—the processions entered with the two Reverends in their robes followed by nine copies of the Sacred Rolls—they advanced slowly to the Tabah while a choir of five voices chanted the appointed psalms most delightfully when the new Hazan had been inducted into office and took his place at the desk. Mr. P in slow and solemn manner preceded the Sephers in their circuit round the area of the building between the desk and the ark— whilst such strains of sacred songs were chanted as might truly be said to have inspiration in them—between each circuit, the prayers appointed (as you will see in the book our brother sent you) to be performed by the Hazan and the congregation were said and among the most affecting parts of the service —Mr. Keys in a fine full voice and the responses by Mr. Peixotto in a voice tremulous from agitation and deep feeling. I have no hope of conveying by description any idea of this ceremony—you must have seen the whole spectacle—the beautiful ark thrown wide open to receive the sacred deposit, with its rich crimson curtains fringed with gold—the perpetual lamp suspended in front with its little constant light like a watchman at his post—and with the humble yet dignified figure of the venerable Mr. P. as he conducted the procession in its seven circuits and then deposited the laws—after which Mr. Keys recited with an effect amounting almost to eloquence that impressive prayer of King Solomon—the whole audience was most profoundly attentive and tho' few were so happy as to understand the language—those who did—say they have never heard Hebrew so well delivered as by Mr. Keys—the bishop expressed this opinion—and all who were there acknowledge there has never been such church music performed in Phila—you will wonder where "these sweet singers in Israel" were collected from—the leader, teacher and principal performer is Jacob Seixas and his female first voice his sister Miriam, they were fortunately on a visit to their sister Mrs. Phillips and induced a class to practice for some weeks . . .[44]

If Rebecca Gratz was so deeply moved by what she saw that she could not hope to convey her feelings in a letter, she was not alone in her sense of inadequacy. Four different accounts, all struggling to express the solemnity of the event, were featured in the Philadelphia newspapers.[45] The *Philadelphia Gazette* considered the consecration of such importance that it devoted one article to a description of the ceremony, and another to the architectural design of the synagogue. To Philadelphians who had never heard the like before, the music evoked the most comment. Sephardic melody and intonation were compared to the chants of the Catholic Church. The Episcopal Bishop White stated that he had never heard such a Hebrew rendition, and others observed with Rebecca Gratz "that there had never been such church music performed in Philadelphia." Criticism of devotional music, or music of any kind, rarely appeared in the contemporary press, and so the following notice is of unusual interest:

The music was of a very devotional cast, and interested us much at the time; but this interest has since been greatly increased by hearing that much of it is so very ancient that the date of its origin cannot be ascertained, while its antiquity is fully verified by the fact that it is used in almost all the synagogues throughout the world. It is not written, at least no copies of it are known to be extant in America; but it has descended from father to son, and such harmonies as were added to the original airs, were added by the choristers pretty much *ad libitum*. If this had been generally known, it would have added greatly to the interest which the Christian part of the congregation took in the service. But even as it was, they were highly gratified . . .[46]

The account was correct; there was still no American printing of Jewish liturgical music. The order of service followed closely that of Shearith Israel as conducted at its dedication in 1818.[47] Mikveh Israel, however, must have possessed European printings of synagogal chants, for the New York congregation requested their use several years later. The first published arrangements of Jewish liturgical music in America were the work of a member of Mikveh Israel, E. Roget, shortly after the arrival of Isaac Leeser.[48]

Great as the interest was in the music, the chief attraction of the dedication was the Strickland-designed building. Since he was largely responsible for the introduction of neo-Egyptian architecture in the United States, those culturally-minded folks who appreciated artistic innovations took pride that this example of modernity had been erected in Philadelphia. One commentator regretted that the synagogue "did not stand in a better situation, especially as it is the only specimen of Egyptian Architecture we have in Philadelphia."[49] But the Jews preferred to have their synagogues in the immediate vicinity of their homes and shops for the convenience of daily and Sabbath worship. However, if the reporter was sorry that the building was huddled against others in a solidly built-up section of the city, he was very impressed with the beauty of the interior, in which, he remarked, "the architect, Mr. Strickland, had free scope for his taste and his judgment, and the liberality of the congregation has enabled him to display both to the best advantage." The rich, crimson silk curtains of the ark and covering of the reader's desk, as well as the Brussels carpet which lay on the floor, were favorably commented on. "Everything is made to correspond," was the summary, "and the *tout ensemble* is very pleasing."[50]

If aesthetically the new synagogue and its dedication service were noteworthy, equally so were the civic implications of the event. Another newspaper called it a more than gratifying spectacle and

for those who duly estimate the happy equality of our religious rights, and the prevailing harmony among our religious Sects, the scene was productive of higher emotions. Among the audience and in conspicuous stations on the floor of the building, we observed the venerable and excellent Bishop White, with several other of the Christian clergy, the Chief Justice and the Associate Judges of the Supreme Court and many other distinguished citizens, all manifesting by their presence and demeanour, that, however we may differ upon certain points, the great truth is recognized and acted upon, that we are all children of a common and eternal Father. For the Europeans who were present the spectacle must have been a highly instructive one; and there are states at no great distance from us to whom it may be useful, to behold in this commonwealth members of the Jewish persuasion are eligible to all public offices, and possess every political right with Christians; that some of our most estimable citizens profess that creed; and withal, that the Christian faith is at least as warmly cherished and as assiduously cultivated here as in any other part of the world.[51]

Pennsylvania had much to be proud of insofar as civil rights were concerned; the bordering state of Maryland was still denying full political equality to Jews. The news items about the dedication ceremony were picked up by other newspapers throughout the country, and the account of Philadelphia's second synagogue consecration was printed in almost every large paper up and down the Atlantic seaboard.

This tangible accomplishment of Mikveh Israel played a not inconsequential role in strengthening the Philadelphia Jewish community. It may have been a recognition of this strength which prompted Joel Angell to offer his services as *shohet* as a "community" employee.[52] And certainly there was pride in the presentation of a new *shofar* to Mikveh Israel by a man who begged for the privilege of continuing the honorable task which he had performed in the past.[53] Even the *shamash*, Abraham E. Israel, felt that a new era had come, and requested a raise in salary because of the additional duties assigned to him, which raise, in this time of expansive optimism, was granted together with the free use of the house behind the synagogue.[54] Mrs. Sarah Carvalho was graciously presented with a seat for life in memory of her husband's service to the congregation.[55] And finally, new rules were drawn up and publicly proclaimed to govern decorum during worship, a number of which dealt with the behaviour of the growing community of children. One such read:

Parents are requested not to bring their children to synagogue unless they are of sufficient discretion to be under their control & remain quiet in their seats; their running in and out will not on any account be suffered; and the *shamash* is strictly enjoined to prevent their interruption.[56]

With a new synagogue, an energetic *hazan*, a growing membership, no debts, and a feeling of accomplishment, Mikveh Israel looked forward to constructive years ahead.

Meanwhile, Rodeph Shalom was continuing its efforts to get its own building. One lot of ground had been purchased, but because of disagreement among the membership as to its fitness it was resold.[57] From the end of 1826 until early in 1829, the German congregation searched carefully for a suitable site, and with their meager savings, then amounting to $1800, finally bought a lot on St. John Street between Callowhill and Noble, in the heart of the German section of Northern Liberties.[58] But with all their money invested in land, the congregation had nothing left to build with. Worried that despair might induce some to sell, a special resolution was introduced forbidding the resale of the ground or its use for anything other than the original purpose—a synagogue.[59]

Alas, nature intervened, and the plot, in spite of the determination to the contrary, had to be abandoned; the old Cohoquinoque Creek which flowed alongside undermined the land and it sank to such an extent that building was out of the question.[60] Rented quarters, inadequate and without distinction, were the best that Rodeph Shalom could afford. It was not until the increase of German-Jewish immigration after 1830 that the congregation gained a more solid footing. Two other congregations were to be established in Philadelphia before Rodeph Shalom finally consecrated its own synagogue in 1847.

∾ 20
End of an Era

Just prior to the high holidays in the fall of 1829, a meeting of Congregation Mikveh Israel was held to choose a *hazan* to take the place of Abraham Israel Keys, who unhappily died in October, 1828. Two candidates were to be voted upon, E. S. Lazarus, who had come from New York the previous Passover to fill in for that special occasion, and young Isaac Leeser, of Richmond. Leeser, then only twenty-three years old, had been brought to America by his uncle Zalma Rehiné to help in his shop. Born in Westphalia, he had attended school at Munster, and while he worked for his uncle he spent his leisure hours in further study, at the same time helping the Richmond *hazan*, Isaac B. Seixas, with his classes for the children of the congregation. Leeser first emerged into prominence in 1828, when a strong, well-written article by him appeared in the Richmond *Whig* in answer to aspersions cast on Jews and Judaism in the *London Quarterly Review*. Perhaps it was Leeser's enthusiasm for teaching, perhaps the positive Jewish spirit of this article, perhaps the strong recommendation of Jacob Mordecai, which moved the Philadelphians to choose the young German over the more experienced New Yorker. As of Rosh Hashanah, 1829, Isaac Leeser became *hazan* of Mikveh Israel.

With his coming, a new era opened for the Jews of Philadelphia. Leeser emerged as the leading Jew, not only of the city, but of the whole country. The years of American Jewish history from 1830 until the close of the Civil War are, in fact, the "Age of Leeser." He wrote schoolbooks for children, prayer-books for his congregants, an English translation of the Bible, and treatises on Judaism. He published the most influential and most widely-read Jewish periodical, the first really national Jewish magazine in the United States: *The Occident.* He worked to promote Jewish education on all levels, from a Hebrew Sunday School Society to Maimonides College, the first American Jewish theological seminary. He fostered a plan to unite all the Jewish congregations in the country into a single national body. He stimulated and guided new philanthropic institutions in Philadelphia, the Hebrew Education Society, the Jewish Hospital, and the first Jewish Publication Society. And he was the effective and tireless defender of traditional Judaism against the incursions of the new spirit of liberalism, as well as of all Jews against invasions of their rights at home and persecutions abroad. In brief, a formless, drifting, haphazardly growing American Jewish community was given leadership and direction and substance by Isaac Leeser.

The Philadelphia community into which he moved had been in existence for not quite a century. It was small, both in terms of present-day urban Jewish communities and in relation to the total population of its day, but to Judaism, which has thought historically in terms of a surviving remnant, its importance cannot be estimated in numerical terms. In recent years commentators on contemporary Jewish life have placed emphasis on numbers, overlooking the fact that the creation of pioneer synagogues, charities and schools in a new land within the framework of democracy, and the adaptation to a way of life which was completely without precedent in the centuries of Jewish existence, were not only the foundations upon which successive waves of Jewish immigration built, but the patterns adopted by the immigrants themselves.

The Americanization of the twentieth-century immigrant Jew has been looked upon as a phenomenon. The first phase, the period of the hardships and struggles of the newcomers, has been recorded in a now rich corpus of folk stories, and the new phase, assimilation into the higher level of American suburbia, is the subject of many articles, frequent discussions, and much thought on the part of Jewish leaders today. And yet, the Philadelphia Jewish community into which Leeser came was on a miniature scale at the end of exactly the same kind of cycle.

The few Jews of Colonial days had bought ground for a cemetery, formed a congregation, and built a synagogue. Their successors in the Federal period and in the early decades of the
following century had perfected the synagogal organizations,
founded small charitable agencies and fought for the status of
Jews in the new nation. A pioneer generation of immigrants, to
most of whom English was but an imperfectly acquired tongue,
established a religious life for themselves and their children, and
at the same time became a part of the mainstream of the land in
which they lived. The elder Gratzes, Mordecai Mordecai and
Jonas Phillips, Yiddish-speaking Jews, had shared with their
fellow-Americans the birth pangs of a nation. Their children
reaped the rewards; they were free-born American citizens with
the inalienable rights of life, liberty and the pursuit of happiness.
Because their fathers had been proudly and reverently Jewish,
they were, under the basic law of the land, able to worship
proudly and reverently as Jews.

The native-born generation quickly and easily made its way
in the social and business life of the city. Like other leading
Philadelphians, they were of colonial stock. They achieved position and affluence, but they also inherited and maintained the
respect which the Christian majority tendered them as Jews.
Not handicapped by language difficulties, they were able to participate fully in the typically American game of politics as soon
as they had the qualifications of age. They went to universities,
and became doctors and lawyers; they were placed on the boards
of directors of Philadelphia corporations; they helped found art
academies and libraries, joined the army and navy when a war
came, and promoted and contributed to civic enterprises of all
kinds. And, when these same men built for themselves a new
synagogue, their non-Jewish associates joined with them in hail-
ing and celebrating the occasion.

Meanwhile, a steady, if small, influx of immigrants was adding
to the nucleus of integrated Philadelphia Jews. There were in
1822 approximately two hundred and twenty-five foreign-born
Jews in Philadelphia, mainly adult males who had arrived in
the city after 1800. An examination of sixty-two immigration
records—about one-quarter of the probable total—shows that
twenty-eight claimed German allegiance, thirteen Dutch, ten
English, four Polish or Russian, three French, two Jamaican
English, one Belgian and one Italian. Most of them were in

their twenties and had come alone; when they had established themselves, relatives followed. Of these, all but three were, like the overwhelming majority of the earlier Philadelphia Jews, of Ashkenazic origin. By 1830, the recent arrivals outnumbered the native-born, but the process of integration had continued without change. The numbers were not so great that they presented a problem to the settled Jewish community or to the city as a whole.

The newcomers found a second synagogue, which a handful of Dutch and German Jews had established before the turn of the century, where they felt more at home than in Mikveh Israel with its traditional Sephardic ritual, and they found small charities which could help them in case of emergency. But, like the colonial Jews, they smelled the fresh air of freedom and found it good. The naturalization act of 1795 enabled immigrants to apply for citizenship, and one of the first Jews who took advantage of it was Dr. David Nassy of Surinam. A regular stream of petitions for citizenship followed.

In a period when there was no social or economic pressure to force an immigrant to become naturalized and when great numbers did not take advantage of that privilege, the rate at which Jewish immigrants became citizens was remarkably high. They saw other Jews voting, and they wanted as soon as possible to take advantage of that right denied them in Europe. Citizenship to those who had been deprived of it was more precious than to those who had formerly enjoyed it as a matter of course.

Moses Spyers arrived in Philadelphia in 1806, was naturalized in 1811, and was active in ward politics before 1820. John Moss, who had come to town in 1796 and become a citizen in 1803, was a member of the Common Council in 1828. They saw the Gratzes, Ettings, Phillips and Cohens, worshipping as Jews, and yet moving easily among and working on the best of terms with non-Jews. This was the revelation of America, and the newcomers wanted to make themselves as much like the members of the older families as quickly as they were able. In fact, this desire to be American carried over into religious life. The Portuguese congregation somehow seemed more American than the German one, and a steady flow of immigrants, who had joined Rodeph Shalom upon their first arrival, changed their allegiance to Mikveh Israel after they had been in the city for a number of years.

There were not yet social barriers within the Jewish community which created snobbishness and an answering resentment. The accretion of numbers had been slow and gradual. There were not so many foreign-speaking Jews with uncouth European manners at any one time that the integrated Jews felt their status in the city was being threatened by the newcomers. It was not yet fashionable for "Portuguese" Jews of German origin who belonged to Mikveh Israel to look down their noses at the "German" Jews of Rodeph Shalom. The great immigration was yet to come; and within a comparatively short while after Leeser's arrival in Philadelphia it did come, and it made itself felt. As the over-all German immigration to the United States increased, the German Jewish immigration increased with it. In the period from 1821 to 1830, 7,583 Germans were recorded as having entered the country; from 1831 to 1840, the number jumped to 148,204. This very considerable influx, more even than Leeser's presence in Philadelphia, changed the character of the Philadelphia Jewish community.

The earlier pattern of settlement, economic adjustment and integration had to be repeated all over again, and fortunately for the German Jews who came to Philadelphia in such numbers from 1830 to 1860 that pattern had been established. It was not by any means a perfect one. Leeser was one of those who deplored the lack of Jewish knowledge and Jewish education among American Jews. He was one of those who were concerned by the high rate of intermarriage and subsequent total assimilation of families into the Christian community. The immigrants, intoxicated as they were by the atmosphere of democracy, were shocked by what seemed to them the watered-down Jewishness of the American Jews. With the same kind of energy that Barnard and Michael Gratz had shown in their lives, they built up a broader religious and philanthropic life at the same time that they built up their business fortunes. Gradually, too, they became wholly American as had their predecessors— Jews religiously and philanthropically, yes, but American in the outward semblance of their living. And, by the time the Eastern European immigration arrived at the end of the century, the second cycle had gone its full round; the German Jews were now the integrated American Jews, and the horde of newcomers, scornful of the native Jewish life as the former too had been, became the threat to their position.

The story of the first cycle in American Jewish life comes to a logical end in the year 1830. The heavy German immigration had not begun. Isaac Leeser was just entering upon his ministry. Abraham Hart, who was to be the leading Philadelphia Jew of his generation, had just embarked on his publishing career. Abraham Simon Wolf, the effective organizer of Jewish communal organizations, was running a country store in Kutztown, Pennsylvania. Moses Aaron Dropsie, only nine years old, had not yet come to the age when he would make his own decision whether to follow the religion of his Jewish father or that of his Christian mother. No member of the later influential Fleisher, Teller, Binswanger, Wolf, Gerstley, Gimbel, Lit or Snellenburg families had left Germany. One era of the history of the Jews of Philadelphia was drawing to a close; the next was about to begin.

List of Abbreviations

Acc. Bk....................	Account Book of Michael Gratz, Etting MSS., HSP
Am. Dai. Adv..............	American Daily Advertiser see also Poulson's and Claypoole's
AHR......................	American Historical Register
AJAr.....................	American Jewish Archives
AJHS.....................	American Jewish Historical Society
APS......................	American Philosophical Society
Claypoole's...............	Claypoole's American Daily Advertiser
CR.......................	Pennsylvania Colonial Records
DNB......................	Dictionary of National Biography
Fed. Gaz..................	Federal Gazette
Fr. Jour..................	Freeman's Journal
Fr. Pa...................	Franklin Papers, APS
Gen. Adv.................	General Advertiser
HSP.....................	Historical Society of Pennsylvania
Ind. Gaz.................	Independent Gazetteer
JASNY...................	Journal of the Assembly of the State of New York
JCC.....................	Journals of the Continental Congress
JE......................	Jewish Encyclopedia
LC......................	Library of Congress
LCP.....................	Library Company of Philadelphia
Ma. Pa..................	Madison Papers, LC
MBH.....................	Minute Book of the Hebra Gemilut Hasadim
MBMI....................	Minute Book of Mikveh Israel
MBRS....................	Minute Book of Rodeph Shalom
MIAr....................	Mikveh Israel Archives
NY Documents...........	Documents Relative to the Colonial History of the State of New York, History of the Dutch and Swedish Settlements on the Delaware River (Albany, 1877)
NY Gaz..................	New York Gazette and Weekly Mercury
NY Gaz. Ad..............	New York Gazette and Weekly Advertiser
NYHS...................	New York Historical Society
NYPL...................	New York Public Library
Occ.....................	The Occident
PAr.....................	Pennsylvania Archives
Pa. Chr.................	Pennsylvania Chronicle
PaEP...................	Pennsylvania Evening Post
Pa. Gaz.................	Pennsylvania Gazette
PAJHS..................	Publications of the American Jewish Historical Society

Pa. Jour....................*Pennsylvania Journal*
Pa. Led....................*Pennsylvania Ledger*
Pa. Mag....................*Pennsylvania Magazine of History and Biography*
Pa. Pac....................*Pennsylvania Packet*
PCC.......................Papers of the Continental Congress, LC
PD........................*The Philadelphia Directory*
Pe. Ber....................*Pennsylvanische Berichte*
Phi. Cor....................*Philadelphische Correspondenz*
Phi. Gaz....................*Philadelphia Gazette*
Phi. Pub. Led..............*Philadelphia Public Ledger*
Phil. Sta...................*Der Wochentliche Philadelphische Staatsbote*
Poulson's..................*Poulson's American Daily Advertiser*
RMMI....................Rough Minutes of Mikveh Israel
RSAr.....................Rodeph Shalom Archives
SBMI.....................Subscription Book, Mikveh Israel
SIAr......................Shearith Israel Archives
SIM......................Minutes of Shearith Israel
US Gaz....................*United States Gazette*

Notes

Chapter I

1 Dutch West India Company Papers, MS., Historical Society of Pennsylvania. These are contemporary Dutch manuscript copies of the correspondence between the Council in New Amsterdam and the Directors of the Company in Holland. They are the basic source for the earliest history of the Jews in New Amsterdam. Apparently part of the same group of manuscripts are similar documents in the Lenox Library of the New York Public Library. A detailed study of these manuscripts would seem indicated. The texts have been variously printed at different times, but most authoritatively by Samuel Oppenheim, "The Early History of the Jews in New York, 1654-1664," *PAJHS*, XVIII (1909), 1-91.

2 Petition of Nov. 29, 1655, Oppenheim, *op. cit.*, 27-28, NY Documents, XII, 117.

3 Much of this material was gathered from other printed sources by A. S. W. Rosenbach, "Notes on the First Settlement of Jews in Pennsylvania," *PAJHS*, V (1897), 191-198; but Oppenheim in some instances corrects Rosenbach's assumptions. Oppenheim gives Cardoso's name as Benjamin; Isaac is correct.

4 NY Documents, XII, 136.

5 Oppenheim, *op. cit.*, 33.

6 *Ibid.*, 29.

7 NY Documents, XII, 147-148.

8 *Ibid.*, XII, 158, 160, and 162.

9 *Ibid.*, XII, 450.

10 John Brodhead, *History of the State of New York* (New York, 1853), I, 698.

11 NY Documents, III, 71.

12 An account of this early period also appears in Abram Vossen Goodman, *American Overture, Jewish Rights in Colonial Times* (Philadelphia, 1947), 115-119.

13 Goodman, *op. cit.*, 122-123.

14 George Fox, *A Visitation to the Jews* (London, 1656), and *A Looking-Glass for the Jews* (London, 1674).

15 H. F. Russel Smith, *Harrington and his Oceana* (Cambridge, 1914).

16 Lee M. Friedman, *Jewish Pioneers and Patriots* (Philadelphia, 1942), 153–159. Typical of the contemporary publications was Thomas Thorowgood, *Jews in America, or Probabilities that the Americans are of that Race* (London, 1650); and revised edition (London, 1660).

17 Gabriel Thomas, *An Historical and Geographical Account of Pennsylvania* (London, 1698), 1–2.

18 Charles H. Browning, "Philadelphia Business Directory of 1703," *American Historical Register*, II (1895), 846, from the Account Book of William Trent in HSP. Trent also did business with Jacob Andrade of Barbados, *ibid.*, II, 851. Arnold Bamberger, cited by Hyman P. Rosenbach, *The Jews in Philadelphia prior to 1800* (Philadelphia, 1883), 5, as being the earliest Jewish landholder in the city, which statement was repeated by Henry S. Morais, *The Jews of Philadelphia* (Philadelphia, 1894), 11, was not a Jew. James T. Mitchell and Henry Flanders, *Statutes at Large of Pennsylvania from 1682 to 1801* (Harrisburg, 1897), IV, 57, states that he was "of the Protestant or reformed religion." Still another purported Jew was Jacob Philadelphia: Julius F. Sachse, "Jacob Philadelphia, Mystic and Physicist," *PAJHS*, XVI (1907), 73–83; but no documentary evidence concerning his life in the city exists, and no contemporary statement anywhere that he was a Jew. Jacob R. Marcus, *Early American Jewry* (Philadelphia, 1953), II, 83, merely assumes that Jacob was a Jew.

19 Receipt Book of Thomas Coates, MS., in the possession of Seymour Adelman, Philadelphia.

20 No record of Joseph Monteyro can be found, but it seems probable that he was a West Indian Jew; for molasses was a typical product of that area.

21 Eleazer Valverde died in Barbados in 1725: Samuel Oppenheim, "List of Wills of Jews in the British West Indies prior to 1800," *PAJHS*, XXXII (1931), 60.

22 No record of Samuel Peres can be found, except that William Trent also dealt with him: Browning, *op. cit.*, II, 856.

23 Benjamin Gomez was doing business with Jacob Pinedo, of Curaçao, in 1747: Lyons Collection, *PAJHS*, XXVII (1920), 248.

24 Abraham Haim de Lucena may have been a descendant of Abraham de Lucena, who was refused permission to trade on the Delaware in 1655. A sketch of his life appears in David de Sola Pool, *Portraits Etched in Stone* (New York, 1952), 456–459.

25 *CR*, III, 53.

26 Daniel Gomez (1695–1780) was one of the leaders of the Jewish community of New York, a trustee of the cemetery, and several times *parnass* of Shearith Israel: Leon Hühner, "Daniel Gomez, A Pioneer Merchant of Early New York," *PAJHS*, XLI (1951), 107–126.

27 Letter Book of Jonathan Dickinson, *passim*, MS., LCP. Dickinson wrote

God's Protecting Providence (Philadelphia, 1699), which told of his shipwreck and adventures among the Indians in Florida.

28 Letter Book, 12, contains business correspondence with Isaac Lamego, David Nunez, Abraham Gomez Sampaio, and Jacob Gutteres, all written on Apr. 26, 1715. Lamego, who died in 1767, and Gutteres, who died in 1748, are both mentioned by George Fortunatus Judah, "The Jews' Tribute in Jamaica," *PAJHS*, XVIII (1909), 153–156, and by Oppenheim, *op. cit.*, 62–63. On Dec. 5, 1719, Dickinson wrote to Judith Nunez, who may have been the widow of David, and who may have died in Barbados in 1774: Letter Book, 309, and Oppenheim, *op. cit.*, 59.

29 Cardoso was apparently an old resident of Jamaica: Samuel Oppenheim, "A List of Jews made Denizens in the Reigns of Charles II and James II, 1661–1687," *PAJHS*, XX (1911), 111. He is also mentioned by Judah, *op. cit.*, 152.

30 Letter Book, 308, 320 and 324, dated Dec. 7, 1719, Apr. 25, 1720, and July 1, 1720.

31 Louis B. Wright and Marion Tinling (eds.), *The Secret Diary of William Byrd of Westover, 1709–1712* (Richmond, 1941), 1, the entry for Feb. 7, 1709 *et seq.*

32. Frederick B. Tolles, *James Logan*, shortly to be published, will be the best biography of Logan. Some of the information about his intellectual accomplishments comes from his books now in the Loganian Library of the LCP.

33 Johann Buxtorf, *Lexicon Hebraicum et Chaldaicum* (Basle, 1676), James Logan's copy in LCP.

34 Joannes Leusden, *Lexicon Novum Hebraeo-Latinum* (Utrecht, 1687), James Logan's copy in LCP.

35 William Robertson, שער השני או הפנימי אל לשון הקדש: *The Second Gate, or the Inner Door to the Holy Tongue; being a compendious Hebrew Dictionary* (London, 1655), James Logan's copy in LCP.

36 אבן העור, שלחן ערוך [*Shulhan Arukh*] (Amsterdam, 1698), James Logan's copy in LCP.

37 *Mischna sive totius Hebraeorum Juris* . . . (Amsterdam, 1698–1703); James Logan's copy in LCP.

38 Logan's books are to be found listed in the *Catalogus Bibliothecae Loganianae* (Philadelphia, 1760).

39 Hebrew Note-Book of James Logan, Dickinson MS. 202, LCP.

40 Norman Penney (ed.), *The Correspondence of James Logan and Thomas Story, 1724–1741* (Philadelphia, 1927), 20.

41 סֵפֶר יְשַׁעְיָה . . . *Prophetia Isaiae* (Paris, 1539), and מקרא *Biblia Hebraica* (Geneva, 1618), Isaac Norris, Jr.'s copies in LCP.

42 Marcus, *op. cit.*, II, 4.

43 Account Book of Thomas Chalkley, MS., LCP.

44 James Logan to Henry Goldney, March 7, 1723, *PAr*, 2nd Series, VII, 77.

45 There is some confusion about the date of this. It is headed "Indian Complaint ag't J. Miranda 1730," but bears the date of Aug. 21, 1720, at the end. One or the other date, probably the latter, may be an error, *PAr*, 1st Series, I, 266–267.

46 *Ibid.*, 2nd Series, IX, 738.

47 *Ibid.*, 2nd Series, IX, 632.

48 Rabbi Hayyim Vital, (ספר הגלגולים) (Frankfurt, 1683), James Logan's copy in LCP, with ownership inscriptions of Miranda in Spanish on front and back fly-leaves.

49 This is in two parts, the first, a translation, is signed at the end by Isaac Navarro, and dated Amsterdam, 1658; the second is attributed to Andreas Antonio Abdias ben Israel: James Logan's copy in LCP.

50 Isaac Miranda, Will, MS., Register of Wills, City of Philadelphia, Will No. 401, Book E, 325.

51 The *American Weekly Mercury* commenced publication on Dec. 22, 1719. References to Jews appear in the following early issues: Oct. 27, and Nov. 10, 1720; Aug. 24, 1721; May 10, May 31, and Nov. 8, 1722; March 7, and Oct. 17, 1723.

52 Monis began teaching Hebrew at Harvard in 1722; his grammar was published at Boston in 1735.

53 George Keith, *New England's Spirit of Persecution* (Philadelphia or New York, 1693). It is not known whether the volume was printed in Philadelphia or New York. There are eight Hebrew words on page 8: A.S.W. Rosenbach, *An American Jewish Bibliography* (New York, 1926), 4–10.

54 Rosenbach, *op. cit.*, 29–31.

55 Henry S. Morais, *op. cit.*, 10–11, suggested that Keimer might have been a Jew; but Keimer himself in the *Pa. Gaz.*, Jan. 4, 1729, avowed his adherence to the Church of England.

Chapter 2

1 Day Book of Brewery owned by Freame, Norris and Charles, MS., 31 and 93, LCP. For the New York background of Nathan Levy, see Marcus, *op. cit.*, I, 51, and II, 6. Like many New York Jews he continued to contribute to Shearith Israel, and his name appears frequently in the records of that congregation.

2 *Pa. Gaz.*, Sept. 8, 1737.

3 *Ibid.*, Nov. 27, 1729, Sept. 9, 1731, and Oct. 21, 1736.

4 Philip von Reck, "Reise-Diarium," in Samuel Urlsperger, *Der Ausführ-*

lichen Nachrichten von der Königlich-Gross-Britannischen Colonie Saltz-burgischer Emigranten in America . . . (Halle, 1735), I, 156.

5 *Pa. Gaz.*, Sept. 15, 1737.

6 *Ibid.*, Jan. 3, Aug. 17, and Aug. 24, 1738, and subsequent issues.

7 The Jews of Newport were engaged quite heavily in the slave trade: Marcus, *op. cit.*, I, 126–127.

8 Philadelphia Land Grants, 1684–1772, Penn MSS., VII, 39, HSP.

9 *Ibid.*

10 *CR*, IV, 88; *Pa. Gaz.*, Oct. 18, 1739; and Thomas Penn Bills, 1739, Mc-Allister MSS., LCP.

11 *Pa. Gaz.*, Oct. 2, 1740.

12 For the New York background of David Franks, see Marcus, *op. cit.*, I, 57 ff. Jacob Franks had married Abigail, a daughter of Moses Levy. David Franks was born in New York in 1720.

13 "An Act for naturalizing such foreign Protestants, and others therein mentioned, as are settled, or shall settle, in any of his Majesty's Colonies in America," 13 George II (1740), Cap. VII. The distinctive feature of the Act, which admitted Jews as British subjects after seven years' residence in the colonies, was that it omitted the words "upon the true Faith of a Christian," and allowed the oath to be made on the Five Books of Moses: J. H. Hollander, "The Naturalization of Jews in the American Colonies under the Act of 1740," *PAJHS*, V (1897), 103–117. See also *Pa. Gaz.*, June 3, 1742, for Franklin's comments on the act, and for text, Morris U. Schappes, *A Documentary History of the Jews of the United States, 1654–1875* (New York, 1950), 26–30.

14 *Pa. Gaz.*, Apr. 16, 1741.

15 *Ibid.*, Sept. 16, 1742.

16 "Ship Registers for the Port of Philadelphia, 1726–1775," *Pa. Mag.*, XXIII (1899), 374; XXIV (1900), 220, 351, 359 and 507; XXV (1901), 126. The earliest entry of a Philadelphia ship registered in the name of Jews was on Oct. 10, 1730, when the London merchants Solomon and Elias Depaz, together with a non-Jewish resident of Philadelphia, Alexander Wooddropp, appeared as owners of the *Diligence*. Marcus, *op. cit.*, II, 5, is misleading in implying that the Depazes came to Philadelphia to have their ship built; they more probably bought a share in it through Wooddropp. Other entries from 1737 on are in the names of Rachel and Joseph Marks, but no record of their Jewish origin exists. The famous *Myrtilla* was entered in the registry as 100 tons, described in the *Pe. Ber.*, Sept. 3, 1757, as 200 tons, and in the *Pa. Gaz.*, Feb. 27, and Oct. 18, 1750, and June 6, 1751, as 250 tons.

17 *Pa. Gaz.*, March 22, 1747.

18 *Ibid.*, March 26, 1745, et passim.

19 *Ibid.*, June 27, 1751. Isaac Norris, Jr., Accounts Abroad and Account of Rents, 1734–67, MS., 32–36, LCP, shows that the firm rented the Slate House for £80 a year from June 18, 1751 to July 1, 1755.

20 *Ibid.,* Sept. 28, 1752. The *Myrtilla* left London some time after July 5, and arrived in Philadelphia about Sept. 1. Because of the calendar change which took place at that time, the exact date remains undetermined.

21 Victor Rosewater, *The Liberty Bell Its History and Significance* (New York, 1926), remains the best account to date. It is interesting that, in addition to the Hebraic origin of the motto on the Bell, a Jew, Frank Marx Etting, was chosen official historian at the Centennial Celebration in 1876, and another Jew, Victor Rosewater, for the same post at the Sesquicentennial in 1926. The Levy-Franks association is here noted for the first time.

22 Isaac Sharpless, *Political Leaders of Provincial Pennsylvania* (Philadelphia, 1919), 190.

22a James Logan to John Kinsey, Philadelphia, Dec. 12, 1749, MS., Logan Letter Book, 1747–50, HSP.

23 See chap. I, note 41.

24 The exact date of Joseph Simon's (1712–1804) arrival in Lancaster is not known, but he was naturalized in Lancaster County at the same time as Joseph Solomon, March 25, 1749: Hollander, *op. cit.,* 117, which infers that he had been a resident for at least the previous seven years. He married Rosa Bunn (1727–1796), the niece of Samuel Myers Cohen of New York: Samuel Evans, "Sketch of Joseph Simon," *Publications of the Lancaster County Historical Society,* III, No. 7 (1899), and Henry Necarsulmer, "The Early Jewish Settlement at Lancaster, Pa.," *PAJHS,* IX (1901), 29–44. There has been confusion as to whose niece Rosa Bunn was, Iyda R. Hirsh, "The Mears Family and Their Connections, 1696–1824," *PAJHS,* XXXIII (1934), 209–210.

25 Petition to the King, [1743/44,] MS. copy by Christian Lehman, in John F. Watson, "Annals of Philadelphia," MS., 173, LCP.

26 The date of the arrival of Israel Jacobs (1714–1810) is given in his obituary: *Poulson's,* March 6, 1810. He has been frequently confused with a Christian of the same name.

27 Hollander, *op. cit.,* 117. As in the case of Simon, this would imply that Bush had been in Philadelphia since 1742.

28 Gratz Mordecai, "Notice of Jacob Mordecai," *PAJHS,* VI (1897), 40.

29 These two men were naturalized under the Act of 1740 on Sept. 20, 1753: Hollander, *op. cit.,* 117. Perhaps, we should read "Bunn" for "Bonn"; he may have been a relative of Joseph Simon's wife.

30 *Pa. Gaz.,* May 17, 1750.

31 *Ibid.,* Dec. 27, 1753.

32 *Ibid.,* July 13, 1749.

33 Sampson (or Samson) Levy, Sr. (1722–1781), was a son of Moses Levy of New York by his second wife, Grace Mears: Pool, *op. cit.,* 225–226. In 1744 William Black was in Philadelphia, and went "to Mr. Levy's, a Jew, and very considerable Merch't; he was a Widdower. And his Sister, Miss Hetty Levy, kept his House." If this was Sampson Levy, as Henry

Morais, *The Jews of Philadelphia* (Philadelphia, 1894), 41–42, assumed (he did have a sister Hester), then he remarried. His children, Nathan (1754–?), Moses (1757–1826), and Sampson, Jr., were by a Christian wife, Martha Thompson (1731–1807), whom he married at Old Swedes' Church on Nov. 3, 1753: Lee M. Friedman, *Pilgrims in a New Land* (Philadelphia, 1948), 96.

34 Sampson Levy's Hebrew Bible, still in the possession of his Christian descendants: Friedman, *loc. cit.*

35 Morais, *op. cit.*, 31–34, cites all the evidence known to him, and concludes that Israel "was of Jewish extraction, but was *never* a Jew."

36 Henry Muhlenberg to Israel Israel, New Providence, Mar. 31, 1784, MS., formerly in the possession of Mrs. James Alden Valentine, of East Walpole, Mass.: Hannah R. London, *Portraits of Jews by Gilbert Stuart and Other Early American Artists* (New York, 1927), 29–30. Muhlenberg was in error about Israel's age at the time of his baptism, for he was born in 1743.

37 Hollander, *op. cit.*, 117. The identification of Midrach Israel with Michael Israel has not been made before, but it seems quite obvious.

38 Hyman P. Rosenbach, *op. cit.*, 6, says "as early as 1747." Mikveh Israel now officially sets its founding at 1740. There are no surviving records to show exactly when or where the first services (*minyan*) were held.

39 While the library of Nathan Levy contained "Spanish" prayer-books, it should be remembered that he and other New York-born children of Ashkenazic Jews had been brought up at Shearith Israel. The prayer-books of immigrant colonial Jews, still preserved at Dropsie College, are predominantly of the Ashkenazic *minhag*.

40 Lyons Collection, *PAJHS*, XXVII (1920), 282.

41 Carl Bridenbaugh (ed.), *Gentleman's Progress; The Itinerarium of Dr. Alexander Hamilton, 1744* (Chapel Hill, 1948), 191.

42 Joseph P. Sims, *The Philadelphia Assemblies, 1748–1948* (Philadelphia, 1948), 10, where the names of David Franks and Sampson Levy appear on the list of the original subscribers.

43 Sims, *op. cit.*, 15, lists Joseph Marks as one of 21 new members admitted in 1749.

44 *Pa. Gaz.*, May 26, 1748 and June 22, 1749.

45 Minute Book of the Library Company of Philadelphia, I, 168, MS., LCP.

46 "The Mount Regale Fishing Company of Philadelphia," *Pa. Mag.*, XXVII (1903), 88–89.

47 These were Abigail (1744–1798), John, or Jacob (1747–1814), Mary, or Polly (1748–1774), Moses, and Rebecca (1760–1823): Israel Solomons, "The Genealogy of the Franks Family," *PAJHS*, XVIII (1909), 213–214. David Franks's wife and his daughter Polly were buried in Christ Church-yard.

48 The statement that David Franks himself became a Christian was first made by Isaac Markens, *The Hebrews in America* (New York, 1884), 71,

and repeated thereafter. As a matter of fact, Franks continued his contributions to Shearith Israel, Lyons Collection, *PAJHS*, XXI (1913), 45, 53, and 63, and on Feb. 19, 1769: "Mr David Franks promised Mr Levy that he wou'd pay the Sedaka five Pounds Annually, exclusive of the offering he may make in the Synagogue," *ibid.*, 102. Finally, on Dec. 26, 1792, he made an affidavit "being duly sworn on the five Books of Moses (he being a Jew)": Simon W. Rosendale, "A Document concerning the Franks Family," *PAJHS*, I (1892), 103.

49 Capt. N. Taylor Phillips owned his Hebrew Bible, and in "The Levy and Seixas Families," *PAJHS*, IV (1896), 197, says that he was a proficient Hebrew scholar.

50 *Pa. Gaz.*, Sept. 12 and 19, 1751.

51 John Penn to Mathias Bush, June 21, 1765, MS., Mikveh Israel Archives; and Sketch of the Surveyor John Lukens, Oct. 8, 1765, MS., in the possession of J. Solis-Cohen, Jr.

52 *Pa. Gaz.*, Dec. 27, 1753.

53 Undated and unsigned Hebrew Manuscript, McAllister MSS., LCP. The obituary is based upon *Lam.* 5. 16, and is here published for the first time.

54 Register of Wills, County of Philadelphia, Administration Papers, No. 58, Book F, 527. Transfer of the administration of the estate was made in 1761, when Levy's widow, Michal, was confined in the city's mental hospital: *ibid.*, No. 65, Book G, 276.

55 Almost all the books listed were among the most popular texts of the day, and are found in most colonial American libraries; Edwin Wolf, 2nd, "Franklin and his Friends Choose Their Books," *Pa. Mag.*, LXXX (1956), 11–36.

Chapter 3

1 Barnard Gratz, Account with David Franks, McAllister MSS., LCP. There Gratz records his salary from Franks began on Feb. 1, 1754. Printed in William Vincent Byars (ed.), *B. and M. Gratz, Merchants in Philadelphia, 1754–1798* (Jefferson City, Mo., 1916), 31.

2 Byars, *op. cit.*, 8–9.

3 Agreement signed by Joseph Simon and Jacob Henry, Lancaster, July 6, 1754, MS., Historical Society of Lancaster County; Byars, *op. cit.*, 31–32. This is the first documentary reference to Henry.

4 Barnard Gratz, Account with David Franks, McAllister MSS., LCP.

5 "Day Book of an Old Philadelphia Merchant (Barnard Gratz)," MS., American Jewish Historical Society.

6 See note 3, *supra.*

7 Frances Dublin, "Jewish Colonial Enterprise in the Light of the Amherst Papers," *PAJHS,* XXXV (1939), 20–24; Marcus, *op. cit.,* II, 93.

8 *Pa. Gaz.,* May 29, 1760 to March 15, 1764, carries scattered advertisements of Plumsted and Franks relating to accounts of the western expeditions.

9 George Washington to David Franks, May 1, 1758, John C. Fitzpatrick (ed.), *Writings of George Washington* (Washington, 1931) II, 190; David Franks to George Washington, Philadelphia, June 27, 1758: Leon Huhner, "The Jews of Virginia from the Earliest Times to the Close of the Eighteenth Centrury," *PAJHS,* XX (1911), 91.

10 Samuel Oppenheim, "David Franks as an Insurance Broker, 1757 and 1758," *PAJHS,* XXVI (1918), 268.

11 Agreement between David Franks and Michael Moses, Tallow Chandler, Jan. 1, 1757, McAllister MSS., LCP. This is an unexecuted copy. Franks' "Chandlery Work" was located on Second Street, and Moses kept one slave in the place: *Pa. Gaz.,* Sept. 23, 1762. When Moses died in Oct. 1769, Mathias Bush entered the firm: Mathias Bush to Barnard Gratz, Nov. 7, 1769, Etting MSS., HSP, published in Byars, *op. cit.,* 106. On May 6, 1773 the business, then located on Front Street near Race, was offered for sale by Nathan Bush and David Franks: *Pa. Gaz.,* May 12, 1773.

12 Solomon Henry to his Parents, London, Jan. 28, 1763, Sulzberger MSS., AJHS: Translation from the original Yiddish published by Byars, *op. cit.,* 59–61. This and the other Yiddish letters published by Byars represent the first modern attempt to translate eighteenth-century Yiddish in the United States. The letters in the Sulzberger collection were transcribed from cursive Hebrew to square letters by Phineas Mordell of Philadelphia, and then translated into English by Judge Mayer Sulzberger, with the aid of David Werner Amram. The Mordell transcriptions are accurate, but occasionally incomplete; the translations, in the light of more recent knowledge, require revision, and have been revised in this work.

13 *Pa. Gaz.,* Sept. 1, 1757, carried the first of Henry's advertisements after he returned; a full list of the goods he imported is found in the issues of Sept. 8, and Oct. 6, 1757.

14 Jacob Henry to David Franks and Barnard Gratz, Newport, July 14, 1760, and Jacob Henry to Barnard Gratz, New York, Jan. 1, 1761, McAllister MSS., LCP; Byars, *op. cit.,* 49–52.

15 *Pa. Gaz.,* Dec. 21, 1758; Marcus, *op. cit.,* II, 49.

16 *Pa. Gaz.,* Jan. 1, 1761. Abraham Judah had been a resident of Wilmington for at least eight years: *ibid.,* Jan. 5, 1758. He had registered ships from there as early as 1753: "Ship Registers for the Port of Philadelphia," *Pa. Mag.,* XXV (1901), 405.

17 *Pa. Gaz.,* Dec. 25, 1760.

18 *Ibid.,* Feb. 1, 1759, where Levy advertises for a stray horse.

19 *Ibid.,* Nov. 1, 1759.

20 *Ibid.,* Aug. 12, 1762, "Levy Marks, Taylor, . . . removed from Chestnut-street into Front-street"; *ibid.,* Aug. 23, 1770, speaks of the starch business "at the sign of the Blue Bonnet in Chestnut-street, between Front and Second-streets, or at the Manufactory in the Northern Liberties . . ." Second Will of Michael Gratz, June 15, 1765, Etting MSS., HSP, speaks of his Philadelphia cousins, Henry and Levy Marks: Byars, *op. cit.,* 74–75.

21 Barnard Gratz to Solomon Henry, Philadelphia, Nov. 20, 1758, copy of the original Yiddish with translation made in 1854: Etting MSS., HSP; Byars, *op. cit.,* 36–37.

22 Byars, *op. cit.,* 12.

23 Solomon Henry to Jacob Henry, London, Apr. 5, 1759, McAllister MSS., LCP: Byars, *op. cit.,* 42. When this letter was written Michael had already left London, but he was overtaken by Solomon Henry's messenger with a packet of letters for America. The date fixes his time of embarkation, and the ship *Britannia* on which he sailed is named.

24 *Pa. Gaz.,* Aug. 2, 1759, is B. Gratz's first business advertisement on his own.

25 It had long been said that on Dec. 10, 1760 Barnard married Richea, the daughter of Sampson Mears; but Iyda R. Hirsh, "The Mears Family and Their Connections, 1696–1824," *PAJHS,* XXXIII (1934), 209–210, shows this to have been impossible. Her detailed genealogical chart shows the Cohen family connections. Mathias Bush married Rebecca (Tabitha) Myers Cohen. See also Pool, *op. cit.,* 228–230. Samuel Myers Cohen's son, Solomon, married Bell Simon of Lancaster: *ibid.,* 263.

26 Jacob Henry to Barnard Gratz, New York, Jan. 7, 1761, McAllister MSS., LCP; first published by Hyman P. Rosenbach, *op. cit.,* 6–7; Byars, *op. cit.,* 52–53. The transliteration by Byars of שול as *Shiloh* should read *shul.* The reference to Hambro implies more than the adoption of the Hamburg ritual, but suggests the pattern of an independent synagogue, such as was founded in London in 1702, which defied both the Sephardic and the Ashkenazic authorities: *JE* (New York, 1907), VI, 191.

27 Moses Heymann (Heyman or Hyman) (?–1765) was a member of Shearith Israel in 1750, but moved to New Hanover, Pa., in 1748, and to Philadelphia between 1748 and 1765: *Pe. Ber.,* Dec. 16, 1748 and Feb. 16, 1749; *Phil. Sta.,* Sept. 5, 1763; and *Pa. Gaz.,* June 26, 1760, Sept. 1, 1763, and Nov. 21, 1765. David Franks was an administrator of his estate.

28 Meyer Josephson was closely identified with Reading, Pa., where he lived continuously from 1756 to 1773. The first reference to him is in the Reading tax lists for 1756, as a "single man." He was associated in business with Moses Heymann and Jacob Levy, and in 1762 married Esther ?, by whom he had one son and one daughter. For interesting aspects of the Reading-Lancaster-Philadelphia communal relationship, see Joshua N. Neumann, "Some Eighteenth Century American Jewish Letters," *PAJHS,* XXXIV (1937), 75–106.

29 Receipt by Joseph Simon and others to K. K. Shearith Israel, Sept. 8, 1761, Lyons Collection, *PAJHS,* XXVII (1920), 20–21.

30 Account Book of Michael Gratz, Etting MS., HSP.

31 AJAr. has recorded on microfilm approximately 200 letters in Yiddish in the Gratz Papers between 1755–1800, acquired from the Joseph Family of Montreal; there are abcut 35 in the McAllister MSS. in the LCP; and no count has been made of those in the HSP, the AJHS, or private collections.

32 Meyer Josephson to Michael Gratz, Feb. 19, 1763, Sulzberger MSS., AJHS; transliteration and translation in Neumann, *op. cit.*, 83–84.

33 Michael Gratz to Barnard Gratz, St. Kitts, July 12, 1765, McAllister MSS., LCP; Byars, *op. cit.*, 75, "Being just שבת, I can say no more than enclose three sets of bills . . ."

34 Register of Wills, City of Philadelphia, Will No. 66, Book M, 111; *Pa. Gaz.*, Apr. 2, 1761, notice by David Franks and Mathias Bush, executors of the estate of Jacob Henry.

35 *Pa. Gaz.*, Jan. 18, 1759, Franks as executor of Henry Benjamin Franks, of Mount Holly, N.J., and *ibid.*, Nov. 21, 1765, as executor, with Benjamin Booth, of Moses Heymann.

36 Certificate, Nov. 27, 1761, Miscellaneous MSS., Box 9, HSP.

37 Leon Hühner, "Jews in Connection with the Colleges of the Thirteen Original States prior to 1800," *PAJHS*, XIX (1910), 121.

38 Ship Registers, *Pa. Mag.*, XXVII (1903), 95, 96 and 107.

39 David Hirschel Fraenckel, *Eine Danck-Predigt* (Philadelphia, 1758). It was also reprinted in English the same year in New York and Boston: Rosenbach, *American Jewish Bibliography*, nos. 34–38.

40 David Hirschel Fraenckel, *A Thanksgiving Sermon* (Philadelphia, 1763), 3; Rosenbach, *op. cit.*, no. 42.

41 Marcus, *op. cit.*, II, 55.

42 Charles Norris, Joseph Richardson, and Jacob Shoemaker to Isaac Levy, August 14, 1761, Norris of Fairhill MSS., Griffits Estate, 124, HSP.

43 *Pa. Gaz.*, Jan. 1, 1761.

44 Benjamin Franklin, "Observations concerning the Increase of Mankind," *Gentlemen's Magazine* (London, 1755), 485.

45 *Phil. Sta.*, May 12, 1766 (Supplement).

46 Rev. Thomas Barton to Sir William Johnson, Lancaster, July 22, 1767, Sir William Johnson MSS., LC; Byars, *op. cit.*, 81.

47 *Phil. Sta.*, June 9, 1766.

48 *Pa. Gaz.*, Apr. 10, 1766.

49 *Ibid.*, Aug. 2, 1759.

50 L. S. Hayne to Mourendo (?) & Gratz, Montreal, June 22, 1765, McAllister MSS., LCP.

51 Cornelius Tucker to Barnard Gratz, Mobile, July 31, 1766, Gratz-Croghan Papers, HSP; Byars, *op. cit.*, 80.

52 Henry Cruger, Jr. to Barnard Gratz, Bristol, Oct. 8, 1766, Etting MSS., HSP; Byars, *op. cit.*, 80.

53 James Cuming, Jr., to Barnard and Michael Gratz, Quebec, July 5, 1766, McAllister MSS., LCP.

54 The Gratz's correspondence with agents in Curaçao and St. Eustatia in 1765–66 is printed in Byars, *op. cit.*, 75 and 78–80, and other similar documents are among the McAllister MSS., LCP.

55 *Pa. Gaz.*, Aug. 6, 1761.

56 Non-Importation Agreement of Philadelphia, Oct. 25, 1765, MS., HSP; Schappes, *op. cit.*, 38–40.

57 Byars, *op. cit.*, 77.

58 Isaac Adolphus to Barnard Gratz, New York, Sept. 24, 1765, McAllister MSS., LCP. Franks had just arrived in New York where he remained for over a month.

59 Hebrew Certificate by Abraham I. Abrahams, 1767, Sulzberger MSS., AJHS.

60 English Certificate (in blank), undated, ca. 1767, McAllister MSS., LCP.

61 Levy Andrew Levy to Michael Gratz, Lancaster, Feb. 23, 1768, MS., Gratz Papers, Henry Joseph Collection, AJAr.

62 Joseph Simon to Barnard Gratz, Lancaster, July 7, 1768, McAllister MSS., LCP; Byars, *op. cit.*, 86–87. Mr. Solomon was Joseph Solomon, naturalized in Lancaster County, March 25, 1749, Hollander, *op. cit.*, 117.

63 *Pe. Ber.*, May 25, 1759.

64 *Ibid.*, Feb. 13, 1761.

65 *Phil. Sta.*, Aug. 19, 1765, and the three subsequent issues.

66 Account Book of the Synagogue Building Fund, 1782–84, MS., MIAr.

67 Barnard Jacobs, Circumcision Book, MS., MIAr. Mordecai wrote this note in 1834 when he presented the MS. to Lewis Allen, then *parnass* of the congregation.

68 Michael Gratz to Barnard Gratz, New York, Apr. 4, 1764, McAllister MSS., LCP; Byars, *op. cit.*, 67.

69 Pemberton Papers, XX (1768–69), HSP; *Pa. Gaz.*, Aug. 13, 1767; *PAr.*, 3rd Series, XIV, 164, shows that Levy Marks, living in the Walnut Ward, with one servant, paid a tax in 1769 of £4. It is interesting to note that in the same tax list, 193, Barnard Gratz, also with one servant, paid the same amount, and Michael only £3.10.0.

69a Julius F. Sachse, *Old Masonic Lodges of Pennsylvània* (Philadelphia, 1912), 75. It should be noted that Joseph Miranda, of Jewish extraction, played a prominent part in that lodge as secretary in 1759 and deputy master shortly afterwards: Norris S. Barratt and Julius F. Sachse, *Freemasonry in Pennsylvania, 1727–1907, as shown by the records of Lodge No. 2, F. and A.M. of Philadelphia* (Philadelphia, 1908), 27, 38, 43, 52, 53, 67, 68, 71.

70 *Pa. Chr.*, Dec. 14, 1767, and *Pa. Gaz.*, Sept. 23, 1762 and Dec. 10, 1767.

71 *PAr.*, 3rd Series, XIV, 157, shows Jacobs paid £6.3.4.

72 *Ibid.*, 212. John Franks, who earlier had lived in Germantown, was listed in Mulberry Ward, and paid a tax in 1769 of £9.18.8.

73 *Pa. Gaz.*, May 22, 1760.

74 [Christopher Saur,] *Eine Nützliche Anweisung Oder Beyhülffe Vor die Teutschen Um Englisch zu lernen* (Germantown, 1762). This book, now in LCP, contains three inscriptions: "David Fraencks sein Gramatic, 1762, d. 5te. Aprill, Germantown," "David Salusbury Franks 1762 His Book," and "David Franks." The exact date of his departure for Montreal is not known. His family relationships are not clear. We do not know what his father, John Franks, was to David Franks the merchant. He may have had a brother John of Montreal, another Moses B. who was named an administrator of his estate, and a sister Rebecca, who was living in Philadelphia in 1799: Rebecca Franks to John Franks, Philadelphia, Feb. 5, [1799], MS., John Lawe Papers, State Historical Society of Wisconsin. Rebecca does not mention David Salisbury Franks, who had died in 1793, but she does speak of having lived in Canada and does mention a brother Moses, then in the West Indies. Furthermore, she complains of having been neglected by her brothers, which would indicate that the family ties were not close.

75 Richard Morris, Receipt Book, MS., Oct. 3, 1764, LCP.

76 *Pa. Chr.*, July 27, 1767.

77 Jacob R. Marcus, *Memoirs of American Jews, 1775–1865* (Philadelphia, 1955), I, 29. Joseph Cohen soon went back to Europe, coming back to America for a short time late in the century. His grandson, Henry, returned to Philadelphia in 1837 and became a permanent resident.

78 *Ind. Gaz.*, Oct. 29, 1782, prints a letter to Abraham Levy, which says that the writer understood he had lived in Philadelphia about fourteen years.

79 *PAr.*, 3rd Series, XVI, 209, lists Mordecai Levy as living in Mulberry Ward in 1769 subject to no tax.

80 *Pa. Gaz.*, Jan. 14, 1768.

81 Barnard Gratz to Michael Gratz, New York, June 14, 1769, and Manuel Josephson to Michael Gratz, New York, June 19, 1769, MSS., Gratz Papers, Henry Joseph Collection, AJAr.

82 Isaac Mendez Seixas to Joseph Simon, New York, June 20, 1769, Lyons Collection, *PAJHS*, XXVII (1920), 170–171.

83 Frank Willing Leach, "Old Families of Philadelphia (Gratz)," *Philadelphia North American*, Dec. 1, 1912 (Sunday Magazine).

84 Barnard Gratz to Michael Gratz, London, Sept. 11 and Nov. 16, 1769, MS., Gratz Papers, Henry Joseph Collection, AJAr.

85 Barnard Gratz to Michael Gratz, London, Oct. 31, 1769, MS., Gratz Papers, Henry Joseph Collection, AJAr.

86 Non-Importation Agreement, Philadelphia, March 10, 1769, Du Simitière MSS. (Scraps), LCP.

87 Mathias Bush to Barnard Gratz, Philadelphia, Nov. 7, 1769, Etting MSS., HSP; Byars, *op. cit.*, 106–107.

88 Solomon Henry to Barnard Gratz, London, Nov. 11, 1762, Etting MSS., HSP; Byars, *op. cit.*, 58, "I condole with the loss of your daughter."

89 Isaac Adolphus to Barnard Gratz, Sept. 24, 1765, McAllister MSS., LCP, "I heard from Mr. David Franks that it has pleased the almighty to take Mr. Moses Heyman out of this troublesome world."

90 *Pa. Chr.*, Apr. 4 and 11, 1768.

91 Mathias Bush to Barnard Gratz, Philadelphia, Nov. 7, 1769, Etting MSS., HSP; Byars, *op. cit.*, 106–107.

92 See chap. 2, note 51.

93 Second Will of Michael Gratz, June 15, 1765, Etting MSS., HSP; Byars, op. cit., 74–75.

94 *Pa. Gaz.*, Feb. 16, 1769.

95 For Kals, *Pa. Gaz.*, March 8, 1759, and June 25, 1761; for Keyl, *ibid.*, Nov. 27, 1766.

96 Rachel Moses to the Rev. Richard Peters, July 11, 1769, Peters MSS., VI (1763–1770), HSP.

96a See note 91, *supra.*

97 Andreas Henry Groth to Barnard Gratz, Exeter, Oct. 24, 1770, Mc-Allister MSS., LCP; Byars, *op. cit.*, 113.

98 Minute Book of Congregation Shearith Israel, May 16, 1768, Lyons Collection, *PAJHS*, XXI (1913), 99.

99 Jacob Melhado to Michael Gratz, Kingston, Jamaica, Aug. 22, 1770, McAllister MSS., LCP.

100 Lyons Collection, *PAJHS*, XXVII (1920), 18–20.

101 Printed Circulars, addressed to Michael Gratz, Sulzberger MSS. (Series IV), AJHS.

102 Lyons Collection, *PAJHS*, XXVII (1920), 250, reference in the Ledger of Benjamin Gomez.

103 *Pa. Jour.*, March 22, 1770. The first printed reference to Lyon Nathan, in business with his brother Benjamin in Reading, is in the *Pe. Ber.*, Nov. 25, 1758.

104 *Pa. Gaz.*, Apr. 19, 1770.

105 *Ibid.*, Sept. 12, 1771.

106 *Ibid.*, July 2 and Sept. 2, 1772.

107 *Ibid.*, Jan. 9, 1772.

108 *Pa. Pac.*, March 2 and 9, 1772.

109 I. D. Rupp, *A Collection of Upwards of Thirty Thousand Names of German, Swiss, Dutch, French and other Immigrants in Pennsylvania from 1727 to 1776* (Philadelphia, 1927), 403.

110 *Pa. Gaz.*, Sept. 2, 1772.

111 Aaron Levy is supposed to have come to America as early as 1760, but the earliest official record of his presence is his application for a lot in Sunbury, July 3, 1772: Sidney M. Fish, *Aaron Levy, Founder of Aaronsburg* (New York, 1951), 4–5.

112 *Ind. Gaz.*, Nov. 12, 1782, where Nones speaks of himself as having been engaged in the city's trade "for ten years past."

113 *N.Y. Gaz.*, July 13 and 27, 1772; Samuel Oppenheim, "Three Pre-Revolutionary Items," *PAJHS*, XXVIII (1922), 255.

114 Manuel Josephson to Michael Gratz, New York, July 17, 1771, McAllister MSS., LCP; Marcus, *op. cit.*, II, 44.

115 Joseph Simon to Michael and Barnard Gratz, Lancaster, Nov. 17, 1771, Sulzberger MSS., AJHS; transliteration of the original Yiddish and translation, Neumann, *op. cit.*, 99–102.

116 *Pa. Gaz.*, July 29, 1772. The notice appeared simultaneously in most of the Philadelphia English and German press. See also Case of Edward Batchelder vs. Isaac Jacobs, and Thomas Assheton vs. Emanuel Lyon, June 9, 1772, James Read Papers, HSP.

117 Mathias Bush to Barnard Gratz, Philadelphia, Nov. 7, 1769, Etting MSS., HSP; Byars, *op. cit.*, 106–107, "My ship is launched but not up yet;" "Ship Registers for the Port of Philadelphia," *Pa. Mag.*, XXVIII (1904), 235; the ship *Priscilla* built in Sussex County, Delaware, was registered on July 10, 1770.

118 Myer Polock to Michael Gratz, Newport, Jan. 8, 1771, Etting MSS., HSP; Byars, *op. cit.*, 114–115; and Myer Polock to Michael Gratz, Newport, Jan. 15, 1770 [1771], MS., Gratz Papers, Henry Joseph Collection, AJAr.

119 Byars, *op. cit.*, 259n. Solomon died in childhood.

120 *Phil. Sta.*, July 30, 1771.

121 Barnard Gratz to Michael Samson, Philadelphia, Oct. 15, 1771, Etting MSS., HSP; Marcus, *op. cit.*, II, 57–58.

122 Myer Myers to Michael Gratz, New York, Jan. 26, 1772, Etting MSS., HSP; Byars, *op. cit.*, 121. Two pairs of *rimonim* were made by Myers for Mikveh Israel; for descriptions of these and the New York and Newport ones, see Jeanette W. Rosenbaum, *Myer Myers, Goldsmith, 1723–1795* (Philadelphia, 1954), 99–100.

123 *Pa. Pac.*, May 17 and 24, June 7, 1773.

124 Frederick William Hunter, *Stiegel Glass* (Boston and New York, 1914), 45, 73, 200, 201 and 240.

125 Stiegel Account Books, HSP; Samuel Oppenheim, "Three Pre-Revolutionary Items," *PAJHS*, XXVIII (1922), 255–256.

126 Hyman P. Rosenbach, *op. cit.*, 16–17, quotes from the "minute from the proceedings in 1773." The minute was also printed in full by J. Thomas Scharf and Thompson Westcott, *History of Philadelphia, 1609–1884* (Philadelphia, 1884), II, 1437. The original document which they cited cannot now be found in the Archives of Mikveh Israel.

127 Indenture of Apprenticeship of Solomon Marache to Isaac Hays, New York, May 15, 1749, New York City Hall of Records, File No. PL–1754–1837 A 307; Schappes, *op. cit.*, 30–32.

128 Solomon Marache to Barnard Gratz, Lancaster, March 20, 1774, MS., Gratz Papers, Henry Joseph Collection, AJAr.

129 Levy Andrew Levy to Michael Gratz, Lancaster, May 28, 1774, William Henry MSS., II, HSP; Byars, *op. cit.*, 141–142.

130 Receipt Book of Abraham Hydrick of Philadelphia, MS., in the possession of George R. Loeb, of Philadelphia. An entry of Jan. 7, 1774, is the earliest reference to the Philadelphia residence of Phillips. He began advertising in the following year, *Pa. Led.*, July 8, 1775.

131 Barnard Gratz to Michael Samson, Philadelphia, Oct. 15, 1771, Etting MSS., HSP.

132 For a sketch of the career of Phillips before he came to Philadelphia, see N. Taylor Phillips, "Family History of the Reverend David Mendez Machado," *PAJHS*, II (1894), 51–55.

133 Phillips married Rebecca Machado on Nov. 10, 1762. The wedding was in Philadelphia, because about 1753, after her father David Mendez Machado died, her widowed mother Zipporah married Israel Jacobs; *ibid.*, 49 and 51.

134 Thomas Balch, *Letters and Papers relating chiefly to the Provincial History of Pennsylvania* (Philadelphia, 1855), lxxiii.

135 *Pa. Gaz.*, Aug. 24, 1774.

136 University of Pennsylvania, *Biographical Catalogue of the Matriculates of the College . . . 1749–1893* (Philadelphia, 1894), 18.

137 *Pa. Gaz.*, Sept. 14, 1774.

138 Levy Andrew Levy to Michael Gratz, Lancaster, 1784, Ms., Gratz Papers, Henry Joseph Collection, AJAr.

139 William Murray to Barnard and Michael Gratz, Pittsburgh, May 15, 1773, Etting MSS., HSP; Byars, *op. cit.*, 130–131.

Chapter 4

1 Charles Matheson to Michael Gratz, Pittsburgh, Apr. 10, 1776, Etting MSS., HSP; Byars, *op. cit.*, 154.

2 The history of the early western land companies is a confused one. The best overall study is Thomas Perkins Abernethy, *Western Lands and the American Revolution* (New York, 1937), and many documents relating to them are printed in Byars, *op. cit.*, and Kenneth P. Bailey (ed.), *The Ohio Company Papers, 1753–1817* (Arcata, Cal., 1947). Two more recent studies, still unpublished, which have used the new material in the Gratz Papers of the Henry Joseph Collection, as well as the vast corpus of documents and letters in the Croghan, Trent, and Gratz Papers in HSP, are biographies of George Croghan by Nicholas B. Wainright, and of Barnard and Michael Gratz by Sidney M. Fish. These both correct and supplement much of the older research.

3 Bailey, *op. cit.*, 36–173, prints the papers of the "Suffering Traders of 1754."

4 Benjamin Franklin, "Plan for Settling Two Western Colonies in North America," in Albert Henry Smyth (ed.), *The Writings of Benjamin Franklin* (New York, 1905–07), III, 358–366.

5 David Franks to Michael Gratz, Philadelphia, June 12, 1763, McAllister MSS., LCP; Byars, *op. cit.*, 64. According to a diary kept by Lt. James MacDonald during the siege of Detroit, a "Mr. Levey" was taken captive by the Wyandots after having been promised a safe conduct to Fort Pitt, Dublin, *op. cit.*, 16. Levy, presumably Levy Andrew Levy, was not killed as stated by Dublin.

6 Samuel Wharton, *View of the Title to Indiana, a Tract of Country on the River Ohio* (Philadelphia, 1775), and his *Plain Facts; being an Examination into the Rights of the Indian Nations of America, to their respective countries* (Philadelphia, 1781), give a detailed account of the origin of the claims of the "Suffering Traders of 1763," the treaty at Fort Stanwix, and a justification of the right of the Indiana Company to a clear title to the Ohio lands. David Franks, Joseph Simon and Levy Andrew Levy are named as original proprietors of the Indiana Company.

7 Albert T. Volwiler, *George Croghan and the Western Movement, 1741–1782* (Cleveland, 1926), 169.

8. Edward Shippen, Jr., Joseph Morris, Benjamin Levy, David Franks, Thomas Lawrence, and Samuel Wharton to Moses Franks, Philadelphia, Jan. 4, 1769, Etting MSS., HSP; Bailey, *op. cit.*, 211–213, where Moses Franks' Memorial to the King for the Indiana Company follows.

9 Invoice of Simon, Levy and Company to George Croghan, Fort Pitt, Mar. 23, 1765, with receipts signed by David Franks, Feb. 26 and May 3, 1766 and May 7, 1767, McAllister MSS., LCP; Byars, *op. cit.*, 69–71.

10 William Murray to Barnard Gratz, Carlisle, June 8, 1768, Etting MSS., HSP; Byars, *op. cit.*, 84.

11 William Murray to Barnard and Michael Gratz [Fort Pitt, June, 1768], Etting MSS., HSP; Byars, *op. cit.*, 86.

12 B. and M. Gratz to William Murray, Philadelphia, Aug. 31, 1768, Letter Book of Michael Gratz, HSP; Byars, *op. cit.,* 88–89.

13 Receipt, Kaskaskia, June 10, 1768, Etting MSS., HSP; Byars, *op. cit.,* 85, where a note gives an account of Morgan's fight with Prather.

14 Byars, *op. cit.,* 120.

15 *PAr,* 5th Series, I, 374–379.

16 The deed for 9,450 acres of New York land was executed by Croghan to Michael Gratz, March 1, 1770, Byars, *op. cit.,* 90; also Barnard Gratz to Michael Gratz, New York, June 14, 1769, Gratz Papers, Henry Joseph Collection, AJAr. On Oct. 3, 1770 Barnard, in London, sent a copy of the deed to William Emerton, asking his help in disposing of some tracts— "Should you meet with a purchaser and sell, you will be allowed a good commission"—Byars, *op. cit.,* 112–113. A broadside dated at Albany, May 26, 1773, offered the Mohawk River lands for sale: Rosenbach, *op. cit.,* 61–63.

17 Carl Van Doren, *Benjamin Franklin* (New York, 1938), 394–396.

18 Bailey, *op. cit.,* 280.

19 Extract from the Minutes of the Grand Ohio Company, London, Dec. 27, 1769, *ibid.,* 283–284.

20 Case of Barnard Gratz and Others, *ibid.,* 386–389. "Croghan being indebted to Barnard Gratz in the Sum of £11839–12–9 and having various resources of payment, but none which appear'd more certain or better Grounded by Deeds, duly executed, prov'd and recorded," conveyed to Gratz the land. Gratz "entertain'd no hope of immoderate gain, nor did he blindly accept of a Deed from Croghan before he had investigated the foundation of his Claim."

21 Byars, *op. cit.,* 216–217, and 351.

22 *Ibid.,* 136–137.

23 William Murray to Barnard and Michael Gratz, Pittsburgh, May 15, 1773, Etting MSS., HSP; Byars, *op. cit.,* 130–131.

24 Petition of David Franks, J. Murray and John Campbell to the Earl of Dunmore, Philadelphia, Apr. 19, 1774, Public Record Office, London, MS., C.O.5:1352; Marcus, *op. cit.,* II, 38–41.

25 William Murray to Barnard Gratz, Philadelphia, May 16, 1774, Etting MSS., HSP; Byars, *op. cit.,* 140–141.

26 John Campbell to Levy Andrew Levy (to be forwarded to Michael Gratz), Pittsburgh, May 30, 1774, Etting MSS., HSP; Byars, *op. cit.,* 142–143.

27 Michael Gratz to Barnard Gratz, Philadelphia, Aug. 5, 1774, MS., in possession of Edwin Wolf 2nd.

28 Michael Gratz to Bernard Gratz, Philadelphia, May 30, 1775, McAllister MSS., LCP; Byars, *op. cit.,* 149–150.

29 Robert Campbell to Barnard Gratz, Pittsburgh, July 6, 1775, Gratz-Croghan Papers, HSP; Byars, *op. cit.*, 151.

30 Michael Gratz to Barnard Gratz, Philadelphia, July 24, 1776, McAllister MSS., LCP; Byars, *op. cit.*, 158.

31 Barnard Gratz to Michael Gratz, Pittsburgh, Aug. 17, 1776, MS., Gratz Papers, Henry Joseph Collection, AJAr.

Chapter 5

1 The statement sometimes made that David Franks was a member of the legislative Assembly of Pennsylvania is a confusion with his membership in the social Philadelphia Assembly.

2 Carl and Jessica Bridenbaugh, *Rebels and Gentlemen* (New York, 1942), 18.

3 Articles of Agreement between Michael Gratz and Abraham and Ezekiel Levy, Philadelphia, June 18, 1776, Ms., Gratz Papers, Henry Joseph Collection, AJAr.

4 Joseph E. Fields, "Birthplace of The Declaration," *Manuscripts*, VII (1955), 140–149.

5 *JCC*, VI, 1046, Dec. 27, 1776.

6 Benjamin Levy to Maj. Horatio Gates, Baltimore, May 25, 1775, Ms., Gates Papers, New York Historical Society; Samuel Oppenheim, "Some Revolutionary Letters," *PAJHS*, XXV (1917), 143.

7 *Pa. Gaz.*, July 19, 1775; Morris Jastrow, "Notes on the Jews of Philadelphia, from Published Annals," *PAJHS*, I (1892), 60.

8 Petition of David S. Franks, May 12, 1789, Library of Congress, Division of MSS., U.S. Applications for Office under Washington; Oscar S. Straus, "New Light on the Career of Colonel David S. Franks," *PAJHS*, X (1902), 102–105. This is an autobiographical petition, summarizing Franks' services. See also, Marcus, *op. cit.*, I, 251–254.

9 Minutes of New York Provincial Congress, June 29, 1776, Peter Force (ed.), *American Archives*, 4th Series, VI (1846), 1437–1438. Franks had secured certificates from Samuel Brewer, an aide-de-camp at Chambly, and from Abraham Yates, Jr., chairman of the Albany Committee of Safety.

10 *Pa. Pac.*, Dec. 18, 1776.

11 Jonas Phillips to Gumpel Samson, Philadelphia, July 28, 1776, Ms., Public Record Office, London; transliteration and translation in Samuel Oppenheim, "Letter of Jonas Phillips," *PAJHS*, XXV (1917), 128–131.

12 JCC, V, 517–518, July 4, 1776.

13 MS. (Aug. 20, 1776), Franklin Papers, LC; Julian P. Boyd (ed.), *The Papers of Thomas Jefferson* (Princeton, 1950), I, 494, where a full account of the work of the committee is given.

14 JCC, V, 689–691, Aug. 20, 1776, when it was read and tabled.

15 PaEP, Sept. 10, 1776.

16 *Ibid.*, Sept. 24, 1776.

17 *Ibid.*, Sept. 26, 1776.

18 Thompson Westcott, *Names of Persons who took the Oath of Allegiance to the State of Pennsylvania* (Philadelphia, 1865), xv–xvi; Marcus, *op. cit.*, II, 521.

19 Allan Nevins, *The American States during and after the Revolution 1775–1789* (New York, 1924), 151.

20 *The Constitution of the Common-wealth of Pennsylvania* (Philadelphia, 1776), 13.

21 CR, XVI, 316. Levy was not paid until Apr. 5, 1790, for the supplies furnished in Dec. 1775.

22 *Ibid.*, X, 473.

23 JCC, VII, 188, March 21, 1777. Marks moved to Lancaster late in 1776, but maintained his business connections in Philadelphia: *Pa. Pac.*, May 13, 1778. He took the Oath of Allegiance on Jan. 5, 1779, Westcott, *op. cit.*, 3.

24 *JASNY* (New York, 1792), 162; and *ibid.* (1795), 21 and 48.

25 Levy Andrew Levy to Maj. Ephraim Blaine, Lancaster, June 7, 1776, Blaine MSS., LC; Byars, *op. cit.*, 157.

26 Col. Aeneas Mackay to Barnard Gratz, Pittsburgh, Sept. 16, 1776, McAllister MSS., LCP; Byars, *op. cit.*, 162.

27 JCC, IV, 396, May 27, 1776.

28 *Ibid.*, XIV, 844–845, July 17, 1779.

29 *Ibid.*, III, 315, Nov. 2, 1775.

30 Joseph Simon to Barnard Gratz, Lancaster, Apr. 4, 1777, McAllister MSS., LCP; Byars, *op. cit.*, 163.

31 Alexander Abrahams to Michael Gratz, Philadelphia, Sept. 2, 1776, Etting MSS., HSP; Byars, *op. cit.*, 159–160.

32 Nathan Bush to Michael Gratz, Philadelphia, Sept. 3, 1776, Etting MSS., HSP; Byars, *op. cit.*, 160–161.

33 CR, XII, 140.

34 Mrs. Harry Roger and Mrs. A. H. Lane, "Pennsylvania Pensioners of the Revolution," *Pa. Mag.*, XLII (1918), 31.

35 Solomon Bush to Henry Lazarus, Chestnut Hill, Nov. 15, 1777, MS.,

HSP; Samuel Oppenheim, "Two Letters of Solomon Bush," *PAJHS*, XXIII (1915), 177.

36 *Pa. Led.*, Feb. 4, 1778.

37 *Ibid.*, Oct. 15, Dec. 13 and 20, 1777, and frequently thereafter; *Royal Pennsylvania Gazette*, March 27, 1778, and frequently thereafter. Phillips was selling both at retail and by auction, and would accept paper money in part payment.

38 *Pa. Led.*, Nov. 12, 1777, lists Solomon Marache, Solomon Aaron, Joseph Solomon Cohen, Moses Mordecai, Barnard Solomon, Israel de Lieben and David Franks among those who signed a petition favoring the continuance of colonial currency to relieve the financial embarrassment of the British troops in Philadelphia.

39 Israel de Lieben came from Ireland, but was a native of Bohemia. He found employ with Aaron Levy as a personal *shohet* in Northumberland County. Cf. Israel de Lieben to Aaron Levy, Oct. 18, 1773, MS., Gratz Accounts, 1760–96, Etting MSS., HSP. He came to Philadelphia in the same capacity; but his qualifications were disputed by the Gratzes, and in 1776 he was replaced by Levy. Many years later he turned up in Charleston: Charles Reznikoff and Uriah Z. Engelman, *The Jews of Charleston* (Philadelphia, 1950), 57, 95, 96, and 291.

40 Gratz Mordecai, "Notice of Jacob Mordecai," *PAJHS*, VI (1897), 41.

41 *Pa. Led.*, Jan. 21, 1778.

42 Minute Book of Shearith Israel, Dec. 2, 1783, Lyons Collection, *PAJHS*, XXI (1913), 141.

43 Separate Sheet from the Bureau of Pensions, enclosed in letter from Green B. Raum, Commissioner, to Philip M. Russell, Washington, June 25, 1891, photostat in AJAr, gives a history of Russell's services, with the statement that his official papers were burned, and so his record was given from memory when he applied for a pension in 1818, at which time "from his age and impaired health, (he) was unfitted to furnish a statement of his appointment," and from the recollections of his widow and witnesses. Mrs. Russell probably supplied the story of the Washington letter.

44 J. M. Toner, *Medical Men of the Revolution* (Philadelphia, 1876), 106, cites Russell as being on the pension rolls. On Nov. 2, 1776, Russell had married Esther, the daughter of Mordecai M. Mordecai, Morais, *op. cit.*, 29. His obituary in the *Herald and Free Press*, Aug. 17, 1830, said he "served his country with fidelity and honor as an officer during the whole of the Revolutionary War, and discharged since then all the duties of a private citizen with an exemplary exactness." He left ten children.

45 Marcus, *op. cit.*, II, 75.

46 Solomon Bush to Timothy Matlack, Chestnut Hill, Sept. 27, 1779, MS., HSP; *CR*, XII, 140.

47 *Ibid.*, XII, 151. In the interim, on July 5, 1777, Bush had been appointed Deputy Adjutant-General of the Pennsylvania Militia, *ibid.*, XI, 240.

48 *JCC*, III, 309, Dec. 2, 1775.

49 George Washington to John Hancock, President of Congress, Cambridge, Feb. 9, 1776; Fitzpatrick, op. cit., IV, 313.

50 JCC, VIII, 422, June 6, 1777. The deputies were to be allowed the pay and ration of majors.

51 Marcus, op. cit., II, 94. This position was accepted by Congress, for Franks is referred to in the JCC, IV, 116, Feb. 7, 1776, as "agent to the contractors for victualling the troops of the king of Great Britain."

52 Attestation of Myer Hart, March 19, 1778, MS., Mendes Cohen Collection, AJHS; Marcus, op. cit., II, 100–101.

53 The inability to supply specie as demanded by both sides led to the downfall of Franks; he was in an impossible situation.

54 JCC, VI, 901–902, Oct. 24, 1776.

55 Joseph Simon to Elijah Etting, Lancaster, Jan. 29, 1778, PCC, 1778, XX, 179, LC; Byars, op. cit., 168.

56 Joseph Simon to David Franks, Lancaster, Apr. 9, 1778, McAllister MSS., LCP; Byars, op. cit., 168–169.

57 Joseph Simon to David Franks, Lancaster, May 12, 1778, McAllister MSS., LCP; Byars, op. cit., 169–170.

58 Elizabeth F. Ellet, The Women of the Revolution (New York, 1848), I, 178–188.

59 Barnard Gratz to Michael Gratz, Philadelphia, July 7, 1778, MS., Gratz Papers, Henry Joseph Collection, AJAr.

60 Michael Gratz to Miriam Gratz, Williamsburg, July 15, 1778, McAllister MSS., LCP; Byars, op. cit., 171–172.

61 JCC, XII, 1032–1033, Oct. 21, 1778; Pa. Pac., Oct. 22, 1778.

62 George Washington to the President of Congress, Fredericksburg, Oct. 26, 1778; Fitzpatrick, op. cit., XIII, 158.

63 Joseph Simon to the Board of War, Philadelphia, Nov. 5, 1778, PCC, 1778, XX, 335, LC; Byars, op. cit., 173.

64 JCC, XII, 1070, Oct. 28, 1778, and XII, 1076, Oct. 29, 1778.

65 PAr., III, 395–396.

66 Pa. Pac., Apr. 29, 1779.

67 Ibid., May 13, 1779.

68 Ibid., Apr. 13, 1779, contains a bitter criticism of Lee based on his correspondence with Rebecca Franks.

69 Rebecca Franks to Anne Harrison Paca [Philadelphia], Feb. 26, 1778, MS., Maryland Historical Society; Henry F. Thompson, "A Letter of Miss Rebecca Franks, 1778," Pa. Mag., XVI (1892), 216–218.

70 Moses Franks to Sir Grey Cooper [London], Dec. 22, 1778, Bancroft MSS., NYPL; Harold Korn, "Three Early Letters," PAJHS, XXVIII (1922), 254.

71 *CR*, XI, 679 and 683. The Supreme Executive Council referred the matter to Congress on Jan. 28, and after receiving its approval ordered a pass to be given Rice on Feb. 2.

72 *JCC*, XIII, 123, Jan. 29, 1779.

73 *PAr.*, VII, 180.

74 *CR*, XII, 141.

75 Marcus, *op. cit.*, II, 108–109.

76 *Pa. Gaz.*, June 2, 1779, and Jan. 12, 1780.

77 *CR*, XII, 199.

78 *Ibid.*, XII, 495–496.

79 *Ibid.*, XII, 499, 502, 505, 509, and 547. Franks was permitted to remain until Nov. 23 to get his affairs in order.

80 An auction of the books of David Franks was advertised in the *Pa. Pac.*, Oct. 31, 1780, on the strength of which a printed catalogue is listed by Charles H. Hildeburn, *A Century of Printing, The Issues of the Press in Pennsylvania, 1685–1784* (Philadelphia, 1886), II, no. 4002. No copy has been located.

81 Marcus, *op. cit.*, II, 112–113.

82 Winfield Scott, *Memoirs of Lieut.-General Scott, LL.D.* (New York, 1864), I, 172–174.

83 *By the Hon. Major General Arnold, Commander in Chief of the forces of the United States of America, in the city of Philadelphia, &c. . . . June 19, 1778* (Philadelphia, 1778), broadside: Rosenbach, *An American Jewish Bibliography*, 80–81.

84 *CR*, XI, 325.

85 See note 8, *supra*.

86 A. S. W. Rosenbach, "Documents relative to Major David S. Franks while Aide-de-Camp to General Arnold," *PAJHS*, V (1897), 158–173. The court-martial took place at Raritan on June 1, 1779.

86a *CR*, XII, 141; Scharf and Westcott, *op. cit.*, I, 401–403.

87 Benjamin Rush, MS. Ledger B, 69, LCP.

88 David S. Franks to Joseph Reed, Philadelphia, March 27, 1780, *CR*, XII, 296.

89 David S. Franks to Maj. Gen. Baron von Steuben, Camp, July 18, 1780, Steuben Papers, New York Historical Society; Samuel Oppenheim, "Some Revolutionary Letters," *PAJHS*, XXV (1917), 142.

90 David S. Franks to Gen. George Washington, Philadelphia, July 4, 1778, Letters of Washington, XXIV, 257, National Archives; Herbert Friedenwald, "Jews mentioned in the Journal of the Continental Congress," *PAJHS*, I (1892), 77.

91 David S. Franks to Col. Lamb, Headquarters, Robinson's House, Aug.

15 and 16, 1780, and West Point, Sept. 15, 1780, Lamb Papers, NYHS; Oppenheim, *op. cit.*, 142–143.

92 *CR*, XII, 495–496.

93 Benedict Arnold to Gen. George Washington, On Board the Vulture, Sept. 25, 1780, Letters to Washington, National Archives; *Pa. Gaz.*, Oct. 4, 1780.

94 George Washington to Maj. Gen. William Heath, Robinson's House, Sept. 26, 1780; Fitzpatrick, *op. cit.*, XX, 89.

95 *Pa. Pac.*, Oct. 14, 1780. It is curious that Franks was hailed before the Supreme Executive Council for neglecting to perform his tour of militia duty (an absurd statement applied to a man who a week before had been at West Point) the same day the other David Franks was arrested, *CR*, XII, 495–496. Major Franks was merely ordered to return immediately to the army.

96 David S. Franks to Gen. George Washington, Robinson's House, Oct. 16, 1780, Letters to Washington, XLII, 351, National Archives; Friedenwald, *op. cit.*, 77–78.

97 H. P. Johnston, "Colonel Varick and Arnold's Treason," *Magazine of American History*, VIII (1882), 717–733; Rosenbach, "Documents relative to Major David S. Franks," *op. cit.*, 173–187.

98 The appointment of Franks as lieutenant-colonel has not been found, but the earliest reference to that rank is on Jan. 15, 1784, *Journal of the United States In Congress Assembled* (Philadelphia, 1784), 35–36, where it was resolved "That a triplicate of the ratification of the definitive treaty, be sent to our ministers plenipotentiary, by lieutenant-colonel David S. Franks."

99 They were enrolled in Capt. George Honey's Company, Jan. 2, 1777, *PAr.*, 6th Series, I, 591. It should be noted that many of the men said to have served in the Revolution are not here noted because, upon examination of the references given, it was found that they appeared on the draft lists with specific notations that they did not serve. In the record it states that Hayman Levy, who was said even at the age of sixty to have shouldered a rifle, was most logically excused because of age, *PAr.*, 6th Series, I, 285.

100 Leon Hühner, "Some Additional Notes on the History of the Jews of South Carolina," *PAJHS*, XIX (1910), 152, 154, and 155. Both returned to Philadelphia, Cohen until he moved to Richmond, Aaron until he announced in the *Pa. Pac.*, June 28, 1785, that he was going to "depart for Europe in a few months."

101 There may have been more than one Ezekiel Levy; see Marcus, *op. cit.*, II, 150, although the pattern set by Cohen and Aaron makes it seem possible that the Philadelphian fought in South Carolina, Hühner, *op. cit.*, 152 and 154.

102 This account is given in the Philadelphia County pension applications, *PAr.*, 5th Series, IV, 566.

103 On Oct. 31, 1778, Phillips joined Capt. John Linton's Company, *PAr.*, 6th Series, I, 58.

104 Solomon Myers Cohen had been in Capt. Thomas Bradford's Company of the 1st Battalion in 1777–78, *PAr.*, 6th Series, I, 46; on Sept. 20, 1781, he and his brother joined Capt. Andrew Geyer's Company of the 3rd Battalion, *ibid.*, I, 261. Solomon (1744–1796) was a brother-in-law of Gershom Mendes Seixas, who married his sister Elkalah, and of Barnard Gratz who was married to his wife Bell's sister. He had been *parnass* of Shearith Israel in 1773, Pool, *op. cit.*, 262–263.

105 Lyon Moses was in Capt. Isaac Austin's Company of the 5th Battalion, from Aug. 10, 1780 to May 31, 1781, *PAr.*, 6th Series, I, 368.

106 Lazarus Levy was in Capt. George Esterly's Company of the 3rd Battalion from July 1777 to Sept. 23, 1778, *ibid.*, I, 188 and 195; and in Lt. Henry Meyer's Company on Sept. 14, 1778, *ibid.*, I, 63.

107 Isaac Moses (1741/2–1818) was born in Germany, and married Hayman Levy's daughter Reyna. He was the leading New York Jewish merchant in the post-war period, Pool, *op. cit.*, 384–392. He was in Capt. Andrew Burkhard's Company of the 3rd Battalion in 1780, *PAr.*, 6th Series, I, 744.

108 Benjamin Judah was in Capt. Humphrey's Chestnut Ward Company on Aug. 1, 1780, *ibid.*, I, 81. He is not to be confused with Benjamin Judah, formerly of Georgetown, who died at Philadelphia in 1763.

109 Marcus, *op. cit.*, II, 184–185.

110 Westcott, *op. cit.*, 23–24. Abraham M. Seixas (1751–1799) was a brother of Gershom and Benjamin, Pool, *op. cit.*, 347. He was a lieutenant and fought in South Carolina, Hühner, *op. cit.*, 152 and 154.

111 Mordecai Sheftall (1735–1797) had been one of the leading merchants of Savannah. He had been appointed Commissary General for the Georgia Militia in 1777 and, the next year, was made Deputy Commissary of Issues for the Southern Department, Edmund H. Abrahams, "Some Notes on the Early History of the Sheftalls of Georgia," *PAJHS*, XVII (1909), 174–184. His own account of his capture and imprisonment appeared in George White, *Historical Collections of Georgia* (New York, 1854), 340–342. His petition is in PCC, No. 78, XX, 629, LC; Marcus, *op. cit.*, II, 364. For various references to him, see *JCC*, XII, 572–573, June 29, 1780, 592, July 7, 749, Aug. 21, 824, Sept. 13, 846, Sept. 22, 854, Sept. 25, 955, Oct. 19, 1069, Nov. 18, 1074, Nov. 20, 1079, Nov. 22, and 1112–1113, Dec. 1.

112 Abrahams, *op. cit.*, 182; *JCC*, XII, 1183, Dec. 23, 1780.

113 Benjamin Nones to the Printer of the Gazette of the United States, Philadelphia, Aug. 11, 1800; Cyrus Adler, "A Political Document of the Year 1800," *PAJHS*, I (1892), 112.

114 Markens, *op. cit.*, 127. Contrary to frequently printed statements to that effect, there is no evidence that Nones was ever a major, or on Washington's staff.

115 Isaac Franks, Statement of Military Career, Philadelphia, Apr. 6, 1818; Morris Jastrow, "Documents relating to the Career of Colonel Isaac Franks," *PAJHS*, V (1897), 25–27. He was commissioned an ensign, and mustered out an ensign, *ibid.*, 16–17; he was not a lieutenant-colonel during the Revolution.

116 Minute of the New Amsterdam Council on the Petition of Jacob Bar-
    simson and Asser Levy, Nov. 5, 1655; Oppenheim, "Early History of the
    Jews of New York," *PAJHS*, XVIII (1909), 25.

117 Benjamin Rush, Commonplace Book, MS., 77, LCP; George W. Corner
    (ed.), *The Autobiography of Benjamin Rush* (Princeton, 1948), 119.
    This has been widely misquoted as "The Jews were generally Whigs
    in every stage of the revolution."

Chapter 6

1 Phillips, "Family History of the Reverend David Mendez Machado," 56–
    57; Lyons Collection, *PAJHS*, XXVII (1920), 252.

2 *Pa. Gaz.*, July 5, 1780.

3 *PAr.*, 3rd Series, XV, 340.

4 *Ibid.*, XV, 237.

5 *Ibid.*, XV, 213, 240, 277, 324 and 328. Michael Gratz's assessment must have
    been for the firm, for he is listed twice, and Barnard's name appears with-
    out any figure. The other Jews who appeared on this return were Ben-
    jamin Levy's estate (so designated because he was in Baltimore), £28,000;
    Levy Marks, £19,400; Zipporah Mordecai, no value; Moses Gomez, £6,
    400; Sampson and Moses Levy, £30,800; Sampson Levy's estate, £17,
    000; Lyon Nathan, £3,800; Abraham Levy, £1,000; Manuel Josephson,
    £7,600; David Solomon, £2,400; Solomon Marache, £9,000; David Franks'
    estate, £60,000; Moses Mordecai, £7,700; Isaac Levy, no value; Moses D.
    Nathans, £3,300; Lyon Moses, £8,000; Moses Judah, no value; Isaac Abra-
    hams, £6,000; Seixas & Levy, £4,000; Samuel Judah, no value; Hayman
    Levy, £11,400; Simon Judah, £2,400; Solomon Lyons, £6,500; and Haym
    Salomon, £1,200: *ibid.*, XV, 205, 206, 212, 248, 260, 271, 276, 278, 293, 310,
    312, 315, 316, 322, 324, 338, 339, 340, 341, and 355.

6 *Ibid.*, XV, 637.

7 *Ibid.*, XV, 714.

8 *Ibid.*, XV, 607 and 614.

9 The Jews on the tax lists for 1781 and 1782 are as follows: Lyon Moses,
    £105 and £100; Jacob Cohen, £105 and £105; Moses Cohen, £255 and
    £386; Benjamin Seixas, £642 and £75; Isaac Abrahams, £100 and £100;
    Coshman Pollock, £650 and £150; Hannah Levy, no value; Abraham
    Levy, £50 and £253; Ezekiel Levy, no value (1781); Manuel Josephson,
    £124 and £94; Isaac Da Costa, £243 and £160; Gershom Seixas, no
    value; Eleazar Levy, £100 and £96; Esther Mordecai, no value and £12;
    Marache, Pratt & Davidson, £1,105 (1781) and Solomon Marache, £300
    and £156; Solomon and Myer Myers Cohen, £485 and £293; Samuel
    Judah, £169 (1781) and his widow, £69 (1782); Isaac Moses, £2,904

and £1,120; Simon Judah, £100 and £75; Solomon Lyons, £150 and £275; Simon Nathan, £624 and £612; Abraham Cohen, no value; Lyon Nathan, £50 and £100; Mordecai Levy, no value; Haym Salomon, £172 and £340; Hayman Levy, £175 and £1,258; Samuel De Lucena, no value (1781); Zipporah Mordecai, no value (1781); Benjamin Levy, £406 and £410; Rachel Marks £325 (1781); Henry Moses, £225 (1781); Jonas Phillips, £2,829 and £2,272; Moses Nathans, £462 and £1,595; Sasportas & Le Boeuf, £3,600 and £1,680 and M. Sasportas, £115 (1782); Henry Marks, £800 (1781), Sampson Levy's estate, £300 and £300; Moses Gomez, no value; Jacob Hart, £100 (1782); Solomon Moses, £150 (1782); Asher Myers, £109 (1782); and Mordecai Mordecai, £50 (1782): *ibid.*, XV, 581, 582, 583, 588, 594, 595, 604, 605, 607, 609, 621, 622, 623, 635, 637, 638, 639, 641, 648, 650, 651, 676, 681, 694, 695, 707, 727, 730, 732, 736, 741, and 758, and XVI, 282, 287, 290, 292, 315, 334, 340, 361, 362, 397, 398, 404, 405, 409, 415, 416, 423, 426, 427, 437, 445, 446, 448, 449, 456, 465, 466, 468, 470, 473, 475, 480, 484, 486, 488, 490, and 494.

10 Judah died in Philadelphia, and his obituary in *Pa. Gaz.*, Oct. 24, 1781, described him as "formerly an eminent merchant of New York; and has left an inconsolable widow, with twelve hapless children."

11 *Pa. Gaz.*, Jan. 13, 1779.

12 *Pa. Pac.*, July 15, 1779.

13 For a sketch of Josephson's early career, see Marcus, *op. cit.*, I, 76–79. He had been *parnass* of Shearith Israel in 1763, Lyons Collection, *PAJHS*, XXI (1913), 211.

14 For sketches of Da Costa, see Marcus, *op. cit.*, II, 233–240, and for Sasportas, Reznikoff and Engelman, *op. cit.*, 37, 69, 272 and 275. No detailed study has yet been made of the Jewish emigrés in Philadelphia during the Revolution.

15 George Walton, W. Few, and Richard Henly to the Continental Congress, Philadelphia, Oct. 24, 1780, MS., Rosenbach Collection, AJHS.

16 Benjamin Levy to Robert Morris, Baltimore, Dec. 13, 1776, Rosenbach Collection, AJHS; Edward D. Coleman, "Benjamin Levy," *PAJHS*, XXXIV (1937), 271.

17 Isaac Seixas to Hayman Levy, Stratford, Conn., Nov. 13, 1778, Lyons Collection, *PAJHS*, XXVII (1920), 171–172, asking consent for his son to marry Levy's daughter. They were married on Jan. 27, 1779: *ibid.*, 162.

18 Phillips, *op. cit.*, 49; *Independent Gazetteer*, Nov. 9, 1782. For a few notes on Moses, who later became *shohet* of the Charleston congregation, see Reznikoff and Engelman, *op. cit.*, 46, 51, 245, 271, and 272.

19 Jacob Hart (1756–1822) came from Fürth, Germany; in 1800 he became *parnass* of Shearith Israel: Pool, *op. cit.*, 411–413.

20 *Ibid.*, 288.

21 *Ibid.*, 414–418. Simon Nathan (1746–1822) was born at Frome, England.

22 Samson Mears to Aaron Lopez, Newport, Feb. 16 and 23, 1779, Lopez Letter Books, Newport Historical Society; Jacob R. Marcus, "Light on Early Connecticut Jewry." *AJAr*, I, 2 (1949), 12 and 40–42.

23 Westcott, *op. cit.*, 68.

24 Benjamin Rush, MS. Ledger B, 191. He later returned, for in 1792 he signed a petition for the purpose of forming an independent militia company: Petition, Apr. 17, 1792, MS., HSP. He is not to be confused with the *shohet* Abraham Forst who did not come to America until the nineteenth century.

25 *Ibid.*, 153, 165, 176 and 180. Josephson seems to have been under care for a long while in 1781–82, and Cohen was charged £45.5 "To Sundry Operations upon his leg & dressing it every day for one month & every other day for above two months with sundry applications to it."

26 First *hashcabah* list, to be read on Yom Kippur Eve, MS., MIAr; MBMI, MS., Nov. 12, 1782.

27 The origin of many of the erroneous statements concerning the "loans" of Salomon (also Salomons and Solomon) was due to a misunderstanding of his role as a broker. His son, Haym M. Salomon, convinced enough congressmen that his father had not been repaid for "loans" to Congress so that legislation was introduced, but never passed, to compensate his descendants. By 1847, the petitions of Haym M. Salomon and the congressional reports had established the premises as facts. A complete account of this was published in the Philadelphia *Saturday Courier*, Oct. 30, 1847. Several biographies of Salomon and hosts of articles about him have been published, but almost without exception they are a compound of fact and fiction, largely the latter. The best study from original sources is Max Kohler, *Haym Salomon, the Patriot Broker of the Revolution* (New York, 1931). In spite of the denial of the myth and the presentation of the facts by such competent historians as Marcus, *op. cit.*, II, 132–164, and Schappes, *op. cit.*, 578–580, the fictitious story flourishes.

28 Isaac Rivkind, "Early American Hebrew Documents," *PAJHS, XXXIV* (1937), 69.

29 Haym Salomon, Ledger Account, 1782–83, has an entry showing the payment to Kosciusko of $142, Charles Edward Russell, *Haym Salomon and the Revolution* (New York, 1930), 246.

30 In the receipt book of Judah Hays in the Virginia State Historical Society is a voucher signed by one Haym Solomons at New York on July 10, 1764; but there is no documentary evidence to show that Haym Salomon of Lezno was here that early: Harold Korn, "Receipt Book of Judah and Moses M. Hays," *PAJHS*, XXVIII (1922), 225–226.

31 On July 30, 1776, "Hyam Solomon, the distiller," appeared as an interpreter for Dr. Joseph Gerreau, a Frenchman, before the New York Provincial Congress, Lyons Collection, XXVII (1920), 392.

32 Leonard Gansevoort to Maj. Gen. Philip Schuyler, New York, June 12, 1776, MS., Schuyler Papers, NYPL; Schappes, *op. cit.*, 579.

33 Memorial of Haym Salomon to the Continental Congress, Philadelphia, Aug. 25, 1778, PCC, No. 41, IX, 58–59, LC; Friedenwald, *op. cit.*, 87–88.

34 *Ibid.*

35 *Royal American Gazette*, Jan. 1 and June 18, 1778; *NYGazAd.*, Jan. 12 and 19, 1778.

36 Certificate in Hebrew, July 6, 1777, MS., Rosenbach Collection, AJHS.

37 Memorial of Haym Salomon, *supra.*

38 *Ibid.*

39 *JCC*, XI, 840, Aug. 27, 1778.

40 Draft payable to Haym Salomon, Philadelphia, Dec. 14, 1780, MS., AJHS; *PAJHS*, XXIX (1925), xlii. This is so far the earliest known record of Salomon's commercial activity in Philadelphia, and is on the regular form printed by Franklin at Passy, and signed by Francis Hopkinson, Treasurer of Loans.

41 *Pa. Jour.,* Feb. 28, 1781.

42 *Pa. Pac.,* March 24, 1781.

43 *Ibid.,* July 26, 1781.

44 Robert Morris, Diaries in the Office of Finance, 1781–84, MS., LC, June 8, 1781; Russell, *op. cit.,* 139.

45 No documents relating to Salomon's appointment as the French agent have been discovered, but Morris mentions it in his diary as above, and Salomon states it in his authorized advertisements.

46 Peter Stephen Du Ponceau, Autobiography, MSS., HSP, Sept. 20, 1837; *Pa. Mag.,* LXIII (1939), 327–328.

47 On June 8, 1781, Morris and Salomon had agreed upon the commission rate, Morris, Diaries, *supra.*

48 Peletiah Webster, *An Essay upon Credit, in which the Doctrine of Banks is considered* (Philadelphia, 1786), 21.

49 Lawrence Lewis, Jr., *A History of the Bank of North America* (Philadelphia, 1882), 134.

50 *Pa. Pac.,* Jan. 1 to July 16, 1782.

51 Morris, Diaries, July 12, 1782.

52 *Pa. Pac.,* July 20, 1782.

53 Morris, Diaries, Aug. 16, 1782.

54 James Madison to Edmund Randolph, Philadelphia, Aug. 27, 1782; Henry D. Gilpin (ed.), *The Papers of James Madison* (Washington, 1840), I, 163.

55 Haym Salomon, Ledger Account, 1782–83; Russell, *op. cit.,* 246.

56 James Madison to Edmund Randolph, Philadelphia, Sept. 30, 1781; Gilpin, *op. cit.,* I, 178–179.

57 *Pa. Pac.,* Apr. 19 and 22, 1783; *Ind. Gaz.,* Apr. 19, 1783.

58 *Pa. Pac.,* Jan. 15, 1784.

59 *Ibid.,* Feb. 7, 1784.

60 The furnishings in Salomon's Front Street house are listed in the Administration Papers of his estate, Register of Wills, County of Philadelphia, No. 106, Book I, 141.

61 *Pa. Pac.*, June 3, 1783.

62 *Ibid.*, Jan. 15, 1784.

63 *Pa. Jour.*, May 7, 1784.

64 Full-column bi-lingual advertisements appeared in the *Pa. Pac.*, May 29, June 8, 12 and 22, July 13 and 22, Aug. 3, 12, and 26, Sept. 4, 16, 21, 23, 24, 27, 28, 29, 30 and thereafter in 1784. The *Ind. Gaz.*, *Pa. Jour.* and *Phi. Cor.* also carried the large advertisement during the same period.

65 Lewis, *op. cit.*, 137–143.

66 Webster, *op. cit.*, 25.

67 Morris, Diaries, Feb. 10, 1784.

68 Of the seven Jewish brokers then in business in Philadelphia—Haym Salomon, Moses Cohen, Isaac Franks, Moses D. Nathans, Benjamin Nones, Lazarus Barnett, and Lyon Moses—only Salomon was involved in the banking structure. See *Ind. Gaz.*, Aug. 14 (Nones), Aug. 24 (Cohen, Moses, Nathans, Salomon, and Barnett), Sept. 4 (Salomon, Barnett, and Nathans), and Sept. 18, 1784 (Salomon, Moses, Franks, and Barnett).

69 *Ind. Gaz.*, Dec. 24, 1785, printed a signed letter of Moses Cohen defending Oswald and referring to the Battle of Monmouth.

70 *Ind. Gaz.*, March 13, 1784.

71 *Ibid.*, March 20, 1784.

72 As a result of Franklin's account of balloon ascensions in France which was transmitted by Benjamin Rush to the American Philosophical Society on March 19, 1784, a public appeal to support a large "subscription balloon" was made by Dr. John Morgan, *Pa. Pac.*, June 29, 1784, and *Pa. Gaz.*, June 30, 1784. Among those who signed it were, what Butterfield terms, "the intellectual elite of Philadelphia," including Salomon, Phillips and Nones. When the Philadelphians heard of the successful ascension of Peter A. Carnes, of Bladensburg, Md., which had occurred on June 24, their plans were temporarily suspended, and Carnes came to Philadelphia to demonstrate on July 17. A full account of his attempt was given by Benjamin Rush in a letter to his sister on July 30, 1784: Lyman H. Butterfield, "Further Letters of Benjamin Rush," *Pa. Mag.*, LXXVIII (1954), 22–25, where the background of the event is given.

72a *Pa. Pac.*, Oct. 30, 1784.

73 J. P. Brissot de Warville, *New Travels in the United States of America, performed in 1788* (London, 1794), 340.

74 Thomas Paine, *Dissertations on Government, the Affairs of the Bank, and Paper Money. By the Author of Common Sense* (Philadelphia, 1786).

Chapter 7

1 No scientific attempt to estimate the colonial Jewish population has ever been undertaken. Figures given are pure guesses. Our figure, however, is based on a decade to decade count of heads of families, considering five to be the average family. All available genealogical data would seem to indicate that five is a conservative figure, because men with ten children were not uncommon. Deaths and removals from the city have been taken into consideration. Any absolute figure, however, would be impossible to give, because of the difficulty of identifying Jews by name only when they are not otherwise so identified.

2 N. Taylor Phillips, "Family History of the Reverend David Mendez Machado," *PAJHS*, II (1894), 57.

3 MBMI, 1782–1791, MS., March 17, 1782, MIAr. "Mikveh (also Mickve and Mikve) Israel", for uniformity, we use the spelling now preferred by the congregation.

4 The list of names has been variously given, sometimes to include men who later subscribed to the building fund. The signatures on the original document, in the order in which they appear, are as follows: Isaac Da Costa, Benjamin Seixas, Michael Gratz, Simon Nathan, Jonas Phillips, Isaac Moses (Jr.), Abraham Levy, Barnard Gratz, Jacob Mordecai, Mordecai Sheftall, Coshman Pollock, Jacob Hart, Sol Marache, Solomon Myers Cohen, Haym Salomon, Hayman Levy, Gershom Seixas, Samuel De Lucena, Israel Jacobs, Moses D. Nathans, Barend Moses Spitzer, Jacob Myers, Manuel Josephson, Ezekiel Levy, Henry Marks, Lyon Nathan, Benjamin S. Judah, Asher Myers, Judah Myers, Isaac Abrahams, Benjamin Nones, Mordecai M. Mordecai, Isaac Moses (Sr.), Mordecai Levy, Myer M. Cohen, and Jacob Cohen.

5 MBMI, March 24, 1782. Minutes sometimes exist in three forms; a rough set of on-the-spot notes were made, and then transferred to a formal book, 1782–1791, and an additional copy of this book was transcribed by a professional 18th century amanuensis; but this last is unreliable and occasionally inaccurate.

6 Isaac Da Costa was the dean of the refugee community. He had been a most successful merchant in Charleston, and when Congregation Beth Elohim was formed in 1749 he was its first *hazan*: Reznikoff and Engelman, *op. cit.*, 13, 15–16.

7 MBMI, March 25, 1782.

8 This was the last matter of business taken up on March 24th.

9 MBMI, Apr. 14, 1782.

10 Mordecai had been in Northampton Town (Allentown) as early as 1760, and was in Easton four years later: Joshua Trachtenberg, *Consider the Years* (Easton, 1944), 37–38. He first appears in the Philadelphia tax-lists in 1782, chap. 6, note 9, but he remained there until 1790. In 1791 he appears in the records of the newly founded Congregation Beth Shalome of Richmond, and after 1800 he served in a rabbinical capacity in Baltimore, where as the officiating minister at a wedding he was referred to as "the Rev. Rabbi Mordecai:" *Pa.Gaz.*, March 12, 1807. Mor-

decai Moses Mordecai is not to be confused with Moses Mordecai, who died in 1781.

11 Account Book of the Synagogue Building Fund, 1782–84, MS., MIAr; a copy kept by one of the Gomezes: Lyons Collection, *PAJHS*, XXVII (1920), 461–462.

12 MBMI, Apr. 14, 1782.

13 *Ibid.*, Apr. 25, 1782.

14 Fish, *op. cit.*, 25.

15 Isaac Moses, Barnard Gratz, Jonas Phillips, Benjamin Seixas, and Simon Nathan to the President and Vestry of the Reformed German Congregation, May 1, 1782, MS., MIAr. This was the second letter; no copy of the first has survived.

16 MBMI, Apr. 25, 1782.

17 The rough draft of the minutes detailing the sale of the cornerstones is undated.

18 MBMI, June 9, 1782.

19 *Ibid.*, June 23, 25, 27, and 30, 1782.

20 *Ibid.*, May 28, 1782.

21 Jonas Phillips to the Congregation, Philadelphia, May 30, 1782, MS., MIAr. No mention of a *mikvah* earlier than this has been found, and the first proposal for additional buildings, as well as Phillips' dissenting opinion concerning the placing of the door, are contained in this letter.

22 MBMI, June 2, 1782, "We examined the Dinim respecting that matter & are fully satisfied & convinced therfrom that a door in a synagogue (in places where our prayers are said to the Eastward) ought to be in the west, and is not to be deviated from when there is a sufficiency of ground."

23 Contract between Congregation and John Donahue, carpenter, and Edward McKegan, bricklayer, Apr. 22, 1782, MS., MIAr.

24 MBMI, June 23, 1782.

25 *Ibid.*, June 30, 1782. Mordecai M. Mordecai composed the Hebrew letter to Surinam; the *parnass* wrote the others.

26 *Ibid.*, Aug. 18, 1782.

27 The records are full of references to the bond and requests on the part of the signers to be released. When the debt was finally paid, the signatures were clipped from the document, thereby cancelling it. These six signatures, with wax seals, are now in the McAllister MSS., LCP.

28 *Ind. Gaz.*, June 15 and 29, 1782.

29 *Pa. Pac.*, Aug. 15, 1782.

30 MBMI, Aug. 29, 1782. There is no contemporary reference to Salomon's gift of a Torah; but many years later, when his son, Haym M. Salomon,

asked for its return, it was then stated that the scroll had been an out-right gift; see chap. 13.

31 *Ibid.*, Oct. 9, 1782.

32 *Ibid.*, March 30, 1783. Capt. Lyon, who gave the lustre, may have been the grocer who advertised in the *Pa. Pac.*, Aug. 15, 1782; he was certainly the Philip Lyon, "Ship Captain belonging to Philadelphia," who took the oath of allegiance on Oct. 3, 1782: Westcott, *op. cit.*, 91. Whether he was Jewish or not is not known.

33 Subscription List, Nov. 3, 1782, MS., MIAr. This subscription was handled by Mrs. Jonas Phillips and Mrs. Simon Nathan.

34 MBMI, Aug. 4, 1782.

35 Gershom Mendes Seixas, Order of Consecration, MS., Rosenbach Collection, AJHS.

36 MBMI, Sept. 12, 1782; *CR*, XIII, 367.

37 MBMI, Sept. 12, 1782, where all the plans were discussed in detail.

38 Seixas, Order of Consecration, *supra*.

39 *Ibid.*

40 Coshman Polock (Polack and Pollock) advertised that he was returning to Georgia in the *Pa. Pac.*, Nov. 9, 1782. He returned to Philadelphia in 1796, MBMI, Sept. 25, 1796, and died in 1798: *Claypoole's*, June 12, 1798, and Register of Wills, County of Philadelphia, Letters of Administration, No. 92, Book H, 312. He was buried in the Spruce Street Cemetery.

41 David Sarzedas was a Georgian, but fought in the siege of Charleston. His name appears on the petition to General Lincoln, May 10, 1780, concerning the defence of the city: Leon Hühner, "The Jews of South Carolina from the Earliest Settlement to the End of the American Revolution," *PAJHS*, XII (1904), 53, 55, 57.

42 Most of the New Yorkers returned before the end of 1783. At the first meeting of the reorganized Shearith Israel on Dec. 9, 1783, five of the eight men present—Hayman Levy, Myer Myers, Isaac Moses, Solomon Myers Cohen, and Benjamin Seixas—had been in Philadelphia: Lyons Collection, *PAJHS*, XXI (1913), 141. Hayman Levy was then elected *parnass*.

43 Moses Myers to B. and M. Gratz, London, May 10, 1783, Gratz Papers, Henry Joseph Collection, AJAr.

44 Gershom Seixas to Hayman Levy, Philadelphia, Dec. 21, 1783, MS., SIAr; Marcus, *op. cit.*, I, 97–98, printed from a copy, location of original not known to him.

45 Hayman Levy to the Parnass and Adjunta of Mikveh Israel, New York, March 22, 1784, MS., MIAr.

46 Gershom Seixas to the Parnass and Adjunta of Mikveh Israel, Philadelphia, Feb. 15, 1784, MIAr. Seixas had accepted Shearith Israel's terms in January: Lyons Collection, *PAJHS*, XXVII (1920), 129.

47 MBMI, March 14, 1784.

48 Hayman Levy, March 22, 1784, *supra.*

49 Morais, *op. cit.,* 18, states that Cohen may have come from the Barbary States, but this has never been established. His knowledge of English and the style of his penmanship indicate that he was educated in England. His itinerary prior to his arrival in Philadelphia can be found in his MS. Circumcision Record Book, which also contains marriage records, in MIAr. He has noted the same itinerary in some of his prayer-books now at Dropsie College.

50 MBMI, Aug. 4, 1782, records the call for a *shamash.* His salary and duties were outlined on Aug. 18, and the applicants were asked in advance if they were satisfied with the conditions. Abraham E. Cohen was acting *shamash* when Lyon Nathan was elected on Aug. 27. The salary of £37.10, then agreed to, was an increase over that paid to Cohen.

51 SIM, March 6, 1768, Lyons Collection, *PAJHS,* XXI (1913), 96.

52 MBMI, Mar. 30, 1783.

53 General Offerings Book, Jul. 7, 1786, MS., MIAr, lists a payment of £37.10 for three quarters' salary to Levy.

54 Certificate to Solomon Etting, signed by Barnard Gratz and Aaron Levy, 1782, MS., Jewish Theological Seminary; Rivkind, *op. cit.,* 66–69. Solomon Etting (1764–1847) was the son of Elijah Etting of York. He married first Joseph Simon's daughter Rachel, and after her death Barnard Gratz's daughter, Rachel, in 1791. He was associated in business with Simon in Lancaster, and moved to Baltimore some time in the 1790s. The fifteen-year-old Rachel Gratz (1764–1831) had been in Lancaster during the British occupation of Philadelphia, and wrote a delightful letter to her father which is printed in Byars, *op. cit.,* 182.

55 Ezekiel Levy was in the dry goods business with his father in Philadelphia and Baltimore. They became involved in a bitter business controversy with Benjamin Nones at about this time, *Ind. Gaz.,* Oct. 12, 22, and 29, and Nov. 9, 12, 23, and 26, 1782, see chap. 9.

56 MBMI, Sept. 15, 1782. While the charge was Sabbath-breaking, nothing was said about shaving, which in itself was an infraction of orthodox law. A Lithuanian Jew (Mordecai) was bringing charges against a Polish Jew (Levy) before a German Jew (Phillips), while a French Jew (Nones) was bitter against Levy's father for being "bearded" and speaking languages—Polish and Yiddish—that Nones could not understand.

57 John Samuel, "Some Cases in Pennsylvania wherein Rights claimed by Jews are affected," *PAJHS,* V (1897), 35.

58 MBMI, May 29, 1782.

59 *Ibid.,* June 9, 1782.

60 *Ibid.,* Aug. 12, 1782.

61 *Ibid.,* Aug. 25, 1782. The morning meeting was adjourned in order to have Cohen present; it was resumed late in the afternoon, and at that time the instructions to Seixas were recorded.

62 *Ibid.,* Sept. 5, 1790.

63 *Ibid.,* July 15, 1793. Nathans' letter, dated July 8, was read to the *adjunta* by Nones.

64 SIM, Jan. 4, 1784, Lyons Collection, *PAJHS,* XXI (1913), 143.

65 Benjamin Nones to the *Beth Din* of London, Philadelphia, Aug. 7, 1793, MIAr. This is a hitherto unnoted American *she'elah.*

66 Jacob Raphael Cohen, Marriage Record Book, May 18, 1794, MS., MIAr.

67 *Ibid.,* May 1, 1792. Elkalah (Eleanor) Bush was married to Moses Sheftall three weeks later, *ibid,* May 21, 1792. The *halitzah* was witnessed by Barnard Gratz and *Hazan* Cohen, and presupposes some unknown problems present in the Bush or Sheftall families.

67a Moses Sheftall to Mordecai Sheftall, Philadelphia, Dec. 1, 1791, MS., Sheftall Papers, AJHS.

68 See note 10, *supra.*

69 Myer Hart was one of the founders of Easton, a business associate of David Franks, Joseph Simon, the Gratzes and other Jewish merchants of Pennsylvania and New York: Trachtenberg, *op. cit.,* 55–67. While the relationship between Mordecai and Hart's wife, the former Rachel de Lyon, is not definitely known, it must be assumed that Mordecai's wife, Zipporah, was Rachel's sister, because the account of the affair, note 71 *infra,* said his "wife is the sister of the girl's mother." The same account also stated that Barnet Levy's deceased wife was Zipporah Mordecai's sister.

70 James Pettigrew (1755–1793) had been retired from the army on June 17, 1781. He and Judith Hart (1762–1844) were supposed to have met at a ball given to General Washington in Easton: "The Descendants of James Pettigrew," *The Saint Charles,* I (1935), 133–137.

71 Manuel Josephson and Joseph Wolf Carpeles to Rabbi Saul (Löwenstamm) of the Ashkenazic Community of Amsterdam, Philadelphia, March 20, 1785, MS., MIAr. This is the Yiddish letter which outlines the cases of both Mordecai and Clava, and in the form of a *she'elah* gives all the details.

72 Barnet (Barnard Lazarus or Baer) Levy first appeared at Easton in 1772, and stayed there until about 1793, when he moved to Philadelphia: Trachtenberg, *op. cit.,* 43–47.

73 Mordecai M. Mordecai to Barnard Gratz and the Officers and *Adjunta* of Mikveh Israel, May 16, 1784, MS., MIAr.

74 MBMI, Oct. 24, 1784.

75 Mordecai M. Mordecai to the *Parnass* and *Adjunta,* Oct. 30, 1784, MS., MIAr.

76 MBMI, Dec. 12 and 28, 1784, and Jan. 9, 1785.

77 *Ibid.,* March 13, 1785.

78 Jonas Phillips, Henry Marks and Moses D. Nathans to the Congregation,

March 16, 1785, MS., MIAr, asked that a meeting be called to discuss the question.

79 MBMI, March 16, 1785.

80 *Ibid.*, March 20, 1785.

81 See note 71, *supra.*

82 Benjamin Nones to Manuel Josephson, Philadelphia, Jan. 19, 1786, MS., MIAr, tells Josephson that it was resolved "That the Hebrew Letters lately received from the Hahamim of Amsterdam and the Hague should be translated into the English Language so soon as a Person can be found to undertake it." Solomon Calmer was paid on May 22, 1786, for making the translation: General Offerings Book, MS., MIAr. However, neither the original nor the translation has been found at Mikveh Israel.

83 "The Descendants of James Pettigrew," 135–136.

84 See note 71, *supra.*

85 Manuel Josephson, Will, Register of Wills, County of Philadelphia, No. 256, Book X, 401, by a codicil he gave his brother Aaron "that part of my Library which consists of Hebrew Books to be sent to him by the first Vessel which shall sail either for Bremen or Hamburgh;" the rest of his library was to be sold at auction. No record of a sale can be found. Josephson's obituary notice, *American Daily Advertiser,* Feb. 4, 1796, described him as "skilled in different languages of the world." Sheftall Sheftall to Mordecai Sheftall, Philadelphia, July 8, 1792, MS., AJHS; Isidore S. Meyer, "John Adams Writes a Letter," *PAJHS,* XXXVII (1947), 201n, speaks of books imported by Josephson.

86 MBMI contains no entries from Sept. 4, 1785 to June 28, 1789, which section has been lost, but correspondence shows that Josephson was *parnass* in 1785–1790.

87 Manuel Josephson to Stephen Chambers, Philadelphia, May 31, 1787, Dreer MSS., HSP; and *ibid.*, Oct. 12, 1787, Stauffer MSS., HSP.

88 Note by Benjamin Nones on letter from him to Manuel Josephson, Philadelphia, Sept. 1, 1793, MS., MIAr. Nones had written to ask for the loan of the *shofar,* Abraham Cohen had certified that he had delivered the letter, and Nones noted down Josephson's oral reply. He was virtually excommunicated as a result, MBMI, Sept. 1, 1793.

89 Manuel Josephson to Moses Seixas, Philadelphia, Feb. 4, 1790, Lyons Collection, *PAJHS,* XXVII (1920), 185–190.

90 Rabbi Saul Löwenstamm of Amsterdam on the letter of Haym Salomon, referred to below, made an affidavit, stating that he knew "the perfect scholar Reb Joseph the son of Wolf Carpeles of Prague." Carpeles was in Philadelphia only from 1783 to 1786.

91 An original Latin document, attested to by officials of the synagogue of Lissa in Poland, Aug. 9, 1783, establishes the fact that Jacob Abraham of Lissa was the brother and heir of Ephraim Abraham, who wrote from Charleston, South Carolina, in 1778, to his family in Lissa telling them of his business and the wealth he had acquired. This MS. is in the possession of George R. Loeb, of Philadelphia.

92 Haym Salomon (*per* Joseph Wolf Carpeles) to Rabbi David Tevele Schiff, Philadelphia, Aug. 19, 1784, MS., Jewish Theological Seminary; Hyman B. Grinstein, "A Haym Salomon Letter to Rabbi David Tevele Schiff, London, 1784," *PAJHS*, XXXIV (1937), 107–116. Grinstein did not know that the deceased's name was Ephraim Abraham, nor that his executor was Jacob I. Cohen. These facts, Abraham's residence in Virginia, and the amount of the bond are contained in the original arbitration agreement, Philadelphia, Aug. 27, 1784, the original of which has not been located, but a typed copy of which was sent to Dr. A.S.W. Rosenbach by its owner, Mrs. Coale of Baltimore, 1927.

93 Haym Salomon to Watson and Cossoul, Philadelphia, Sept. 4, 1782, Haym Salomon Letter Book, MS., Rosenbach-Oppenheim Collection, AJHS; Marcus, *op. cit.*, II, 144.

94 Eleazer Levy to Samuel Myers, Philadelphia, Jan. 9, 1783, Haym Salomon Letter Book; Marcus, *op. cit.*, II, 147–148. Eleazer Levy (d. 1811) was Hayman Levy's son. He had a mortgage on the land which the army took over for the fort at West Point, and spent many years trying to get some compensation for the loss in his equity: Pool, *op. cit.*, 322–325. Levy took the Pennsylvania oath on Oct. 18, 1779: Westcott, *op. cit.*, 18. He, together with Thomas Fitzsimons, Matthew Clarkson and Joseph Carson, was an administrator of Haym Salomon's estate: *Pa. Jour.*, Jan. 15, 1785.

95 Haym Salomon to Israel Myers, Philadelphia, Apr. 29, 1783, Haym Salomon Letter Book; Marcus, *op. cit.*, II, 149.

96 Haym Salomon to Joseph Elis (?), Philadelphia, July 10, 1783, Haym Salomon Letter Book; Marcus, *op. cit.*, II, 153–154.

97 Michael Gratz to Solomon Henry, Philadelphia, Apr. 17, 1769, Michael Gratz Letter Book, MS., HSP; Byars, *op. cit.*, 92–93.

98 Solomon Henry to Michael Gratz, London, February 25, 1784, Etting MSS., HSP; Byars, *op. cit.*, 225–226.

99 MBMI, Sept. 26, 1783, approval noted for making a *mishaberach* every second day in the name of "the Habrah of Hazrat Orechim;" and Promissory Note from Abraham de Ely Azuby, Dec. 14, 1783, MS., MIAr. These are the two earliest records of the Ezrath Orechim.

100 Receipt signed by Simon Benjamin for £1, Nov. 6, 1791, Receipt Book, MS., MIAr.

101 MBMI, Nov. 3, 1782.

102 *Ibid.*, Oct. 24, 1790.

103 Receipt signed by Mordecai Moses for £1, Aug. 24, 1792, Receipt Book, *supra*.

104 Subscription List "for the porpos of Radiming two Infortunate strangers which are now on bord the Brig Toze from Hombourg," Sept. 21, 1795, in the autograph of Benjamin Nones, MS., MIAr.

105 Cash Offerings Book, Jan. 16, 1792, MS., MIAr.

106 General Offerings Book, MS., MIAr. This volume contains records of both expenditures and receipts.

107 "Sedaka" Account Book, Sept. 17, 1784, et seqq., M.S., MIAr.

108 Ind. Gaz., Aug. 6, 1785, carries an announcement that Bush was about to leave for Charleston.

109 Moses Cohen and Benjamin Nones to the Administrators of the Estate of Haym Salomon, Philadelphia, Sept. 7, 1785, MS., MIAr.

110 Receipt Book, supra, gives the names of Jews in Philadelphia who appear nowhere else, such as Moses Wallach, Colman Levy, Uriah Levy, Judah bar Moshe, Judah bar Gabriel and Barnard Joseph.

111 Receipt from Nidchi (Nidhe) Israel to Michael Gratz, 1787, Etting MSS., HSP.

112 Lyons Collection, PAJHS, XXVII (1920), 42, a list of the debts due the Sedaka Fund of Shearith Israel, March 27, 1787.

113 Account with Levy Phillips, Aug. 3, 1788, MS., MIAr.

114 Pa. Pac., Aug. 16, 1788. Abraham Yaari, שלוחי ארץ ישראל (Jerusalem, 1951), the most comprehensive study of Palestinian messengers, does not mention these.

115 Isaac Moses to Simon Nathan, Philadelphia, Oct. 28, 1783, and Jan. 18, 1784, MSS., MIAr.

116 MBMI, Nov. 17, 1783, Jan. 11, 1784, June 28, 1789, and Apr. 10, and Sept. 25, 1791. On July 18, 1784, it was reported that a judgment for the bond had been brought against Levy, Gratz, Phillips, Seixas, Nathan and Moses.

117 Moses Levy to Michael Gratz, [Philadelphia, ca. 1783], Gratz Papers, Henry Joseph Collection, AJAr. Levy asks that Gratz surrender the lots adjoining the burial ground so that they can be sold to make good Phillips' bond. The minutes of Oct. 26, 1783 (?) state that Phillips acted contrary to the constitution in bringing suit.

118 Jonas Phillips to Manuel Josephson, [Philadelphia,] June 5, 1786, MS., MIAr.

119 MBMI, March 16, 1784.

120 General Offerings Book, May 2, 1786, and Apr. 6, 1787, "Matzo for the Hazan."

121 Ibid., Apr. 15, 1786.

122 "Excerpts from the Day-Books of David Evans, Cabinet-Maker, Philadelphia, 1774–1811," Pa. Mag., XXVII (1903), 49–50.

123 General Offerings Book, Jan. 2, 1787.

124 Pa. Pac., Dec. 23, 1784.

125 Petition to the Parnass and Adjunta, May 21, 1784, MS., MIAr.

126 Michael Gratz to Barnard Gratz, Philadelphia, Apr. 3, 1785, Gratz Papers, Henry Joseph Collection, AJAr.

127 MBMI, Apr. 24, 1785.

128 Subscription for Building a *Mikvah*, Sept. 9, 1785, MS., MIAr.

129 MBMI, May 11, 1786.

130 General Offerings Book, Mar. 1, May 9 and July 31, 1786, *et seqq.*, payments to "Mary Snyder Lighting Candles."

131 MBMI, March 30, 1783.

132 General Offerings Book, May 24, and Dec. 11, 1786.

133 *Ibid.*, May 1, 1786.

134 Jacob Raphael Cohen, Circumcision Book, 1775–1811, MS., MIAr.

135 General Offerings Book, July 7, 1786, three quarter's salary was £37.10; MBMI, June 28, 1789; Mordecai Levy, Will, Philadelphia, Oct. 1, 1786, Register of Wills, County of Philadelphia, No. 242, Book T, 414; copy in Gratz Papers, Henry Joseph Collection, AJAr.

136 Abraham Eleazer Cohen, Will, Philadelphia, Nov. 9, 1785, MS. copy, MIAr; Register of Wills, County of Philadelphia, No. 170, Book T, 286.

137 A prayer-book of the Bush family is in the possession of Maxwell Whiteman, and their Pentateuch is in the Philip H. and A.S.W. Rosenbach Foundation; Etting and Phillips family prayer-books are in the AJHS; some which belonged to the Gratzes and the Ettings are at Gratz College; and others are at Dropsie College.

138 *Evening Service of Roshashanah, and Kippur* (New York, 1761), and *Prayers for Shabbath, Rosh-Hashanah, and Kippur* (New York, 1766), Rosenbach, *American Jewish Bibliography*, 51–52, and 56–58.

139 *Ind. Gaz.*, Aug. 6, and Oct. 8, 1785. It is interesting to note that a non-Jewish merchant, John Murgatroyd, who bought them directly from Pinto, presented copies of both volumes to the Library Company of Philadelphia in 1789.

140 *Pa. Pac.*, March 1, 4, 6, 9, and 11, 1790.

141 *Ibid.*, Feb. 23, 1788.

142 Subscription for the Payment of Jacob Cohen's Salary, June 28, 1789, MS., MIAr.

143 Transcription of MBMI, Nov. 8, 1789, MS., LCP, "Resolved that the Hazan should be requested to go three times in the week with some of the Congn. on the Colection of Donations from the Citizens."

144 Subscription List, Apr. 30, 1788, MS., MIAr; Morais, *op. cit.*, 19–20.

145 Smyth, *op. cit.*, I, 325.

146 *Minutes of the Second Session of the Twelfth General Assembly of the Commonwealth of Pennsylvania* (Philadelphia, 1788), 115.

147 *Pa. Pac.*, Aug. 5, 1790 *et seqq.*

148 *Minutes of the Second Session of the Fourteenth General Assembly* (Philadelphia, 1790), 261–262.

149 *Pa. Pac.*, Aug. 11 to Sept. 23, 1790, frequently.

150 *Ibid.*, Sept. 16, 1790.

151 *Ibid.*, Sept. 21, 1790.

152 *Ibid.*, Oct. 7, 16, 18, and 19, 1790.

153 *CR*, XVI, 489. On Oct. 11, 1790, the Supreme Executive Council agreed to permit its lottery wheels to be used upon the application of Manuel Josephson. The prizes were announced in *Pa. Pac.*, Oct. 29, 1790.

Chapter 8

1 Varnum Lansing Collins, *The Continental Congress at Princeton* (Princeton, 1908), 87–89, and 263 ff.

2 Philip S. Foner (ed.), *The Complete Writings of Thomas Paine* (New York, 1945), II, 263–265, and 1219–1220.

3 Leon Hühner, "Jewish Signers to a Patriotic Address to Congress in 1783," *PAJHS*, XXII (1914), 196–197; Schappes, *op. cit.*, 61–63, and 581–582.

4 MBMI, Nov. 17, 1783.

5 *The Constitutions of the Several Independent States of America* (Philadelphia, 1781), 102, note in the autograph of Gershom Mendes Seixas, in his copy in the Philip H. and A.S.W. Rosenbach Foundation. There are nineteen other comments by Seixas in the volume.

6 MBMI, Nov. 20, 1783.

7 Simon Nathan (1746–1822) had been elected *parnass* on Sept. 22, 1783. Born in Frome, England, he had come to Philadelphia from Richmond, but had been in Havana, New Orleans and other places before that. In March, 1780, he married the *hazan's* sister, Grace Mendes Seixas, and after the war he returned to New York, where he became *parnass* of Shearith Israel in 1785: Pool, *op. cit.*, 414–418.

8 Asher Myers, also came from New York and returned there. He had been *parnass* of Shearith Israel in 1765 and 1771, Lyons Collection, *PAJHS*, XXI (1913), 211.

9 *Fr. Jour.*, Jan. 21, 1784; Schappes, *op. cit.*, 63–66.

10 *Journal of the Council of Censors* (Philadelphia, 1783), 20.

11 *Fr. Jour.*, *supra; Ind. Gaz.*, Jan. 17, 1784; and *Pa. Pac.*, Jan. 17, 1784.

12 *Ind. Gaz.*, *supra.*

13 *Fr. Jour., supra.*

14 George Fox, *A Looking-Glass for the Jews* (Philadelphia, 1784), vi-vii.

15 Herbert Friedenwald, "A Letter of Jonas Phillips to the Federal Convention," *PAJHS*, II (1894), 108–110; Max Farrand (ed.), *The Records of the Federal Convention of 1787* (New York, 1911), III, 78–79.

16 Farrand, *op. cit.*, II, 335.

17 As presented it was the third article, as passed the first. It begins, "Congress shall make no law respecting an establishment of religion," *Laws of the United States of America* (Philadelphia, 1791), I, 123.

18 *Pa. Pac.*, July 9, 1788, where a full account of the "Grand Federal Procession" is given.

19 [Benjamin Rush,] "Observations on the Federal Procession on the Fourth of July, 1788," *The American Museum*, IV (1788), 77.

20 Naphtali Phillips to John McAllister, New York, Oct. 24, 1868, MS., McAllister MSS., LCP; "The Federal Parade of 1788," *AJAr*, VII, No. 1 (1955), 65–67. This Isaac Moses is not to be confused with the New York merchant.

21 Myer Polock to Michael Gratz, Newport, Jan. 8, 1771, Etting MSS., HSP; Byars, *op. cit.*, 114–115.

22 *Pa. Pac.*, June 20, 1786, advertises the sale of the Brig *Rising Sun* at auction.

23 *Laws of the United States of America*, I, 13. This is Article IV, Section 2, of the Constitution.

24 *The Proceedings relative to Calling the Conventions of 1776 and 1790* (Harrisburg, 1825), IV, 163. The only record of this petition is the entry in the journal of the Convention, "a letter from Jonas Phillips, in behalf of himself and others, Israelites, was read, and ordered to lie on the table."

25 *Ibid.*, IV, 376.

26 Isaac Moses and Solomon Simson to the Congregation at Philadelphia, New York, June 20, 1790, MS., MIAr; the identical letter sent to Newport is printed in Lyons Collection, *PAJHS*, XXVII (1920), 217–218.

27 Moses Seixas to the Parnassim and Adjuntos of Yeshuat Israel, Newport, July 2, 1790, MS., Lyons Collection, *PAJHS, ibid.*, 218–220.

28 Hebrew Congregation of the City of Savannah to the President of the United States, Savannah, May 6, 1789, Letter Book, Washington Papers, LC, 129–130; Schappes, *op. cit.*, 77–78. These addresses have been reprinted many times, but the best texts are those of Schappes.

29 Hebrew Congregation in Newport to the President of the United States, Newport, Aug. 17, 1790, Letter Book, Washington Papers, 17–18; Schappes, *op. cit.*, 79–80.

30 Philip Hart and I. Cohen to Isaac Moses and Solomon Simson, Charleston, Nov. 20, 1790, MS.: Lyons Collection, *PAJHS*, XXVII (1920), 221.

31 N. Taylor Phillips, "Items Relating to the History of the Jews of New York, *PAJHS*, XI (1903), 156.

32 Solomon Simson to Manuel Josephson, New York, Nov. 25, 1790, Phillips, *op. cit.*, 156–157.

33 Manuel Josephson to Solomon Simson and the Trustees of Shearith Israel, Philadelphia, Dec. 14, 1790, MS.: Lyons Collection, *PAJHS*, XXVII (1920), 221–222.

34 Hebrew Congregations in the Cities of Philadelphia, New York, Charleston, and Richmond to the President of the United States, Philadelphia, Dec. 13, 1790, Letter Book, Washington Papers, 30–31; Schappes, *op. cit.*, 82–83. Josephson's draft is in MIAr. The letter and Washington's answer were published in *Pa. Pac.*, Dec. 15, 1790.

35 George Washington to the Hebrew Congregation in Newport (Newport, August, 1790), MS., in the possession of the Morris Morgenstern Foundation; Schappes, *op. cit.*, 80–81. The retained copy is in the Letter Book, Washington Papers, 19–20.

36 George Washington to the Hebrew Congregation of the City of Savannah (New York, May, 1789), retained copy in Letter Book, Washington Papers, 131–132; Schappes, *op. cit.*, 78.

37 George Washington to the Hebrew Congregations in the Cities of Philadelphia, New York, Charleston and Richmond (Philadelphia, Dec. 13, 1790), MS., MIAr; Schappes, *op. cit.*, 83–84. The retained copy is in the Letter Book, Washington Papers, 32–33.

38 Gov. Robert Dinwiddie, Proclamation, Williamsburg, Feb. 19, 1754: Kenneth B. Bailey (ed.), *The Ohio Company Papers, 1753–1817* (Arcata, Cal., 1947), 25–26.

39 At the Pension Bureau there is a bounty-land grant to Franks issued on Jan. 28, 1789: Herbert Friedenwald, "Jews Mentioned in the Journal of the Continental Congress," *PAJHS*, I (1892), 85.

40 Account Book of the Synagogue Building Fund, 1782–84, MS., MIAr. Bush gave £6.

41 Solomon Bush to the Continental Congress, Philadelphia, Dec. 8, 1780, MS., PCC, LC; photostat AJAr.

42 Solomon Bush to the Supreme Executive Council of Pennsylvania, Nov. 24, 1784, MS., "Individual Petitions," 38, HSP.

43 Bush had been issued £811.15.0 in depreciation certificates on which £48.13.9 interest was ordered paid May 1, 1783: CR, XIII, 567. In 1784 and 1785 the principal was given as £752.2.6 and the interest £45.2.5: *ibid.*, XIV, 126 and 410.

44 Norris S. Barratt and Julius F. Sachse, *Freemasonry in Pennsylvania, 1727–1907* (Philadelphia, 1908), I, 425; Samuel Oppenheim, "The Jews and Masonry in the United States before 1810," *PAJHS*, XIX (1910), 42. Moses Michael Hays of Boston had been appointed Deputy Inspector-General of Masonry for North America by Henry Andrew Francken, Dec. 6, 1768, by virtue of which he had the right to make other appointments: Oppenheim, *op. cit.*, 7.

45 *The Mirror and Keystone,* III (1854), 212; Marcus, *op. cit.,* II, 81–82. The letter was submitted to the Philadelphia lodge on Dec. 7, 1785: Oppenheim, *op. cit.,* 44.

46 *Pa. Pac.,* March 7, 1788.

47 *Ibid.,* Oct. 1, 1788.

48 Oppenheim, *op. cit.,* 42.

49 *Ibid.,* 46.

50 Barratt and Sachse, *op. cit.,* I, 426–428; Oppenheim, *op. cit.,* 45.

51 Oppenheim, *op. cit.,* 45.

52 *Ibid.,* 47.

53 Solomon Bush to George Washington, London, July 20, 1789, United States Applications for Office under Washington, Division of MSS., LC.

54 Solomon Bush to George Washington, London, Aug. 5, 1789, *ibid.*

55 R. Claiborne to George Washington, London, July 23, 1789, *ibid.*

56 George Washington to Solomon Bush, New York, Nov. 24, 1789: Fitzpatrick, *op. cit.,* XXX, 465–466.

57 *Pa. Pac.,* Sept. 24, 1790, lists among the arrivals on the *Pigou,* from London, "Doctor S. Bush."

58 *Am. Da. Adv.,* Apr. 7, 1791. Bush thereby became the brother-in-law of Zaccheus Collins who at the beginning of the next century was to be one of the outstanding communal leaders of the city.

59 Solomon Bush to George Washington, Alexandria, Oct. 24, 1793, United States Applications for Office under Washington, Division of MSS., LC.

60 Solomon Bush to George Washington, Whitemarsh, Nov. 12, 1793, *ibid.*

61 Frederick A. Muhlenberg to George Washington, Providence Township, Montgomery County, Oct. 20, 1793, *ibid.*

62 Solomon Bush to George Washington, Philadelphia, Jan. 8, 1795, *ibid.*

63 *Fed. Gaz.,* May 16, 1793; *Ind. Gaz.,* May 18, 1793.

64 Solomon Bush, Will, June 8, 1795, Register of Wills, County of Philadelphia, No. 188, Will Book X, 297. In addition to his wife and brother-in-law Collins, Bush mentions a son Mathias and a brother Joseph.

65 *Pa. Pac.,* July 23, 1788.

66 Memorial of David S. Franks to John Hanson, President of Congress, Aug., 1782, MS., PCC, No. 41, III, 268; Friedenwald, *op. cit.,* 79–80.

67 John Jay to Benjamin Franklin, St. Ildefonso, Sept, 14, 1781, MS., Fr.Pa., XXII, 146, APS. An account of Franks' experiences in France in 1781–82 is given in Hersch L. Zitt, "David Salisbury Franks, Revolutionary Patriot," *Pennsylvania History,* XVI (1949), 77, but quotations from the Franklin-Franks correspondence are here printed for the first time.

68 William Carmichael to William Temple Franklin, St. Ildefonso, Sept. 21, 1781, MS., Fr.Pa., CIII, 104, APS. This talk against Franklin refers to the bitterness of the Lees and Izard, and to the fact that John Adams and Laurens were coming abroad as commissioners: Carl Van Doren, *Benjamin Franklin* (New York, 1938), 624–625.

69 Sarah Bache to Benjamin Franklin, Philadelphia, July 12, 1781, MS., Fr.Pa., V, 29, University of Pennsylvania.

70 David S. Franks to William Temple Franklin, Nantes, May 22, 1782, MS., Fr.Pa., CIV, 45, APS.

71 David S. Franks to William Temple Franklin, Brest, Dec. 23, 1781, MS., Fr.Pa., CIII, 157, APS, in which Franks asks Franklin to take his part in the matter.

72 David S. Franks to Benjamin Franklin, Brest, Dec. 10, 1781, MS., Fr.Pa., XXIII, 113, APS.

73 David S. Franks to William Temple Franklin, Brest, Dec. 10, 1781, MS., Fr.Pa., CIII, 149, APS.

74 Benjamin Franklin to David S. Franks, Passy, Dec. 17, 1781, MS., Franklin Letter-Book, LC.

75 David S. Franks to Benjamin Franklin, Brest, Dec. 20, 1781, MS., Fr.Pa., XXIII, 129, APS.

76 David S. Franks to Benjamin Franklin, Brest, Dec. 23, 1781, MS., Fr.Pa., XXIII, 137, APS.

77 Ferdinand Grand *l'aîné* to Benjamin Franklin, (Paris,) Dec. 12, (1781,) MS., Fr.Pa., XXIII, 118, APS.

78 David S. Franks to Benjamin Franklin, L'Orient, Jan. 26, 1782, MS., Fr.Pa., XXIV, 44, APS.

79 David S. Franks to William Temple Franklin, Nantes, May 26, 1782, MS., Fr.Pa., CIV, 48, APS.

80 In his memorial Franks complained that he had been deranged from the army, in spite of the fact that Morris stated that he was to receive no other pay than that to which he was entitled as a major. Congress resolved that he should get pay until Jan. 1, 1783, when he was to be considered as retiring, *Journals of the Congress, and of the United States In Congress Assembled* (Philadelphia, 1782), VII, 511, Oct. 22, 1782.

81 *A Synopsis of the Records of the State Society of the Cincinnati of Pennsylvania* (Philadelphia, 1891), 37.

82 Petition of David S. Franks, May 12, 1789, United States Applications for Office under Washington, Division of MSS., LC; Oscar S. Straus, "New Light on the Career of Colonel David S. Franks," *PAJHS*, X (1902), 103.

83 Thomas Jefferson to James Madison, Baltimore, Feb. 14, 1783, MS., Ma.Pa., LC; Julian P. Boyd (ed.), *The Papers of Thomas Jefferson* (Princeton, 1952), VI, 241.

84 Thomas Jefferson to James Madison, Baltimore, Jan. 31, 1783, MS., Ma. Pa., LC; Boyd, *op. cit.*, VI, 226.

85 *Ind. Gaz.*, May 3, 1783.

86 Robert R. Livingston to Elias Boudinot, President of Congress, Philadelphia, June 5, 1783; Straus, *op. cit.*, 105.

87 The endorsement signed by a number of merchants points out that Franks had had experience in the mercantile line and, through his residence in Canada, could speak French, PCC, No. 79, III, 271. Franks sent it with a letter which he wrote to Livingston from Philadelphia in May, offering his services as a consul, *ibid.*, 267; Friedenwald, *op. cit.*, 81.

88 Petition of David S. Franks, *supra; Journal of the United States In Congress Assembled* (Philadelphia, 1784), IX, 35–36, Jan. 15, 1784; Charles Thomson to Benjamin Franklin, Annapolis, Jan. 15, 1784, MS., Fr.Pa., XXXI, 27, APS, telling him that Franks was on the way with the treaty— "I need not recommend Col. Franks to your notice as you are already acquainted with him. He has great Merit for the early part he took & the sacrifices he has made in the late controversy & for his steady adherence to our cause."

89 Thomas Balch (ed.), *Letters and Papers relating chiefly to the Provincial History of Pennsylvania* (Philadelphia, 1855), lix–lx.

90 David S. Franks to William Temple Franklin, Nantes, Nov. 2, 1784, MS., Fr.Pa., CVI, 106, APS.

91 David S. Franks to William Temple Franklin, (Paris,) June 22, 1784, MS., Fr.Pa., CVI, 182, APS. The loan of twenty guineas was still unpaid two years later, Benjamin Franklin to William Temple Franklin, (Philadelphia,) Apr. 26, 1787, MS., Fr.Pa., XLV, 209, APS.

92 Jonathan Williams to William Temple Franklin, Paris, July 23, 1784, MS., Fr.Pa., CVI, 54, APS.

93 Thomas Barclay to Thomas Mifflin, President of Congress, L'Orient, Sept. 17, 1784; *The Diplomatic Correspondence of the United States* (Washington, 1837), I, 352.

94 Petition of David S. Franks, *supra*.

95 David S. Franks to Thomas Jefferson, Paris, June 17, 1785, MS., LC; Boyd, *op. cit.*, VIII, 225.

96 Thomas Jefferson to David S. Franks, Paris, June 17, 1785, MS., Letter-Book, LC; Boyd, *op. cit.*, VIII, 225 and note.

97 Petition of David S. Franks, *supra*, where he gives his itinerary.

98 David S. Franks to Thomas Jefferson, (Paris, Dec. 1786,) MS., LC; Boyd, *op. cit.*, IX, 651–652.

99 Thomas Jefferson to James Monroe, Paris, Jan. 30, 1787; Paul Leicester Ford (ed.), *The Writings of Thomas Jefferson* (New York, 1894), IV, 365.

100 David S. Franks to George Washington, New York, June 11, 1789; Straus, *op. cit.*, 106.

101 William S. Baker, "Washington After the Revolution, 1784–1799," *Pa. Mag.*, XIX (1895), 454.

102 "New York and Philadelphia in 1787, Extracts from the Journal of Manasseh Cutler," *Pa. Mag.*, XII (1888), 102.

103 David S. Franks to Thomas Jefferson, New York, Feb. 8, 1790; Straus, *op. cit.*, 106–108.

103a *CR*, XVI, 513.

104 David S. Franks to John Kean, Cashier of the Bank of the United States, New York, Nov. 2, 1792, MS., Simon Gratz Collection, HSP, shows that Franks had charge of bringing a shipment of gold valued at over $100,000 from New York to Philadelphia. He is listed as "assistant cashier" in James Hardie, *The Philadelphia Directory* (Philadelphia, 1793), 181.

105 Mathew Carey, *A Short Account of the Malignant Fever, lately prevalent in Philadelphia: . . . Fourth Edition, Improved* (Philadelphia, 1793), 134.

Chapter 9

1 Edgar Stanton Maclay, *A History of American Privateers* (New York, 1899); Charles Oscar Paullin, *The Navy of the American Revolution* (Chicago, 1906).

2 Leon Hühner, "Jews Interested in Privateering in America during the Eighteenth Century," *PAJHS*, XXIII (1915), 171–174.

3 Carter Braxton to Michael Gratz (Account), 1777, Lenox Miscellaneous MSS., NYPL; Hühner, *op. cit.*, 176; Carter Braxton to Michael Gratz, March 31, 1781, Etting MSS., HSP; Byars, *op. cit.*, 204–205.

4 *Pa. Pac.*, Nov. 19, 1782.

5 Hühner, *op. cit.*, 172; *Pa. Gaz.*, May 16, 1781.

6 *Pa. Pac.*, March 7, 1780.

7 *Ibid.*, May 28, 1782.

8 *Ibid.*, Sept. 5, 1782.

9 *Ind. Gaz.*, Feb. 18, 1783.

10 *Pa. Pac.*, June 18, 1782; *Ind. Gaz.*, June 15, 1782.

11 *Ind. Gaz.*, July 27, 1782.

12 *Pa. Pac.*, Aug. 15, 1782.

13 *Ibid.*, Aug. 17, 1782.

14 *Ind. Gaz.*, July 15, 1786; *Pa. Pac.*, July 18, 1786; Deed Poll, Alice Supplee to Isaac Franks, Philadelphia, Nov. 6, 1787 and March 3, 1792, MS., in the possession of Maxwell Whiteman. It conveyed a tract of land in Northumberland County to Rush; Bradford and James Mease were involved in the transaction.

15 *Pa. Pac.*, Jan. 29, 1787.

16 *CR*, XVI, 1.

17 Franks and Rachel Salomon were both children of Moses B. Franks. Isaac married Mary Davidson on July 9, 1782, and they had two children, Samuel D. Franks, who was a Judge of the Court of Common Pleas for Schuylkill, Lebanon and Dauphin Counties, and Sara Eliza, who married Peter Huffnagle: Morris Jastrow, Jr., "Documents relating to the Career of Colonel Isaac Franks," *PAJHS*, V (1896), 10–11.

18 See note 11, *supra.*

19 *Ind. Gaz.*, Oct. 12, 1782.

20 *Ibid.*, Oct. 22, 1782.

21 *Ibid.*, Oct. 29, 1782.

22 *Ibid.*, Nov. 9, 1782.

23 *Ibid.*, Nov. 12, 1782.

24 *Ibid.*, Nov. 23, 1782.

25 *Ibid.*

26 *Ibid.*, Nov. 26, 1782.

27 *Ibid.*, Sept. 27 and Oct. 4, 1783.

28 *Pa. Pac.*, July 27, 1782.

29 *Ind. Gaz.*, July 27, 1782.

30 *Ibid.*, June 14, and Nov. 15, 1783.

31 Lazarus Barnett was one of the rolling-stones who came to Philadelphia briefly. "Having resided here upwards of ten months," he applied for membership in Mikveh Israel: Lazarus Barnett to the Parnass and Mahamad, Philadelphia, Oct. 26, 1783, MS., MIAr. His creditors advertised in the *Pa. Pac.*, Dec. 1, 1784 and Feb. 22, 1785, the latter one hinting fraud. A notice of his bankruptcy, describing Barnett as "late of Philadelphia, in N. America, but now in Somerset-street, Whitechapel," appeared in the *St. James Chronicle*, Feb. 3, 1785.

32 *Pa. Pac.*, Jan. 29, 1784.

33 Letters of Administration of the Estate of Haym Salomon, Register of Wills, City of Philadelphia, No. 106, Book I, 141. Salomon died on Jan. 6, 1785, and when the administrators filed an inventory of his estate it showed assets of $353,729.33 against which were approximately $45,-000 in debts. However, the assets were largely in Loan Office certificates and Continental currency whose face value was far greater than their real value. The final account, filed on Dec. 23, 1789, showed

assets of $44,732, debts of $45,292, and hence a deficit of $560. All the widow got out of the estate were the household goods, furniture and personal effects of the deceased to which she was entitled by Pennsylvania law: Russell, *op. cit.*, 272-275.

33a *Ind. Gaz.*, Jan. 8, 1785.

34 They were married on Aug. 24, 1786: *Ketubah* Records, MS., MIAr.

35 *Pa. Pac.*, Aug. 15, 1782, Feb. 14, 1784, and Dec. 1, 1784. By 1787 he was back again on Market St.: *Pa. Pac.*, Jan. 9, 1787.

36 *Ind. Gaz.*, March 6, 1784, and Oct. 30, 1784, and *Pa. Pac.*, June 19, 1786.

37 *Pa. Pac.*, June 27, 1782.

38 *Ibid.*, July 4, 1782.

39 *Ibid.*, Jan. 29, 1784.

40 *Ibid.*, July 14, 1790.

41 *Ibid.*, Nov. 17, 1790. On Apr. 11, 1802, Solomon Lyons married a convert; their first son had been circumcised by *Hazan* Cohen on Nov. 29, 1801: Records of Marriages, Births and Deaths, MS., MIAr.

42 *Ibid.*, Feb. 17, 1785.

43 *Ibid.*, May 23, 1785, "Moses Cohen, Broker, Will receive in payment the New Emission of Paper Money, for any kind of Merchandize, or Public Securities, equal to Gold or Silver." *Ibid.*, June 19, 1786, where Phillips states the same.

44 *Ind. Gaz.*, July 9, 1785, Nathans says that he was making his asseveration of solvency because he had "been informed, that some evil minded people endeavored to injure his credit and reputation as an honest man." *Ibid.*, Apr. 23, 1785, Lyons says that he was making his statement because it had been maliciously reported that he "had delivered up my books to Creditors."

45 Thomas Jefferson to Simon Nathan, Monticello, May 18, 1783, MS., Massachusetts Historical Society: Boyd, *op. cit.*, VI, 270.

46 *Pa. Pac.*, Oct. 21, 1785, Hays advertised that he will act as a broker at his office in Front Street, opposite the Custom House.

47 *Ind. Gaz.*, Jan. 7, 1786, Benjamin Nones publicly denied having recommended Manuel Noah to Levi Hollingsworth. *Pa. Pac.*, Feb. 3, 1786, contains a call for a meeting of the creditors of Noah, and *ibid.*, Feb. 15, 1786, a statement by some of the creditors that goods in the possession of Solomon Aaron and Moses Jacobs, mistakenly attached as Noah's property, are rightfully purchased goods.

48 Notice of Nathan's bankruptcy appeared in the *Pa. Pac.*, Feb. 17, 1787; of Nones' *ibid.*, Nov. 10, 1787; of Homberg's *ibid.*, Mar. 13, 1787.

49 Benjamin Rush, Letters, Facts, and Observations upon a Variety of Subjects, MS., LCP, 154-155; George W. Corner (ed.), *The Autobiography of Benjamin Rush* (Princeton, 1948), 203.

50 *Ibid.*, 155; Corner, *op. cit.*, 203.

51 Articles of Agreement between William Plunket and Benjamin Rush and Isaac Franks, Philadelphia, Apr. 2, 1784, MS., Rush Papers, XXXI, 49, LCP, provided that Plunket should lay claim to the land, he and his associates take one-half of the tract, and Rush and Franks share the other half. Stephen Chambers to Benjamin Rush, Lancaster, June 24, 1787, MS., Rush Papers, XXVI, 24, LCP, tells of the difficulties with regard to the title to the land, because Plunket and a man named Reese both applied for and received warrants for the same land on the same day.

52 Rush, Letters, Facts, etc., 160; Corner, *op. cit.*, 206.

53 Nathan must have maintained a Philadelphia office which failed, for he was *parnass* of Shearith Israel in 1785: see note 7, chap. 8.

54 See note 40, *supra*.

55 *Pa. Pac.*, Nov. 28, 1788, July 4, 1789, and Jan. 23 and Feb. 4, 1790.

56 Abraham Ritter, *Philadelphia and her Merchants* (Philadelphia, 1860), 165, "Benjamin Nones, a highly respectable Hebrew, was favorably known as a dealer in dry goods, and celebrated for vending Madras handkerchiefs."

57 *Ind. Gaz.*, Oct. 9, 1784.

58 *Ibid.*, July 23, 1785.

59 *Ibid.*, July 26, 1783, in which Josephson issued a statement on behalf of Jacques Garat.

60 *Pa. Pac.*, Mar. 25, 1788.

61 Edmund Hogan, *The Prospect of Philadelphia* (Philadelphia, 1795), 54, on 6th St. north of Market.

62 Printed Form of the Pennsylvania Population Company, Mar. 14, 1796, Nead Papers, HSP.

63 Agreements between Solomon Marache and Mary Marache and John Nicholson, Jan. 18, 1794, MSS., in the possession of Edwin Wolf, 2nd.

64 He does not seem to have played any role in the affairs of Mikveh Israel after his resignation as *gabay;* MBMI, Jan. 23, 1785. In 1766 Marache had married Rebecca Myers in New York; after her death he remarried, this time to a Christian.

65 *Pa. Pac.*, Feb. 2, 1782, Dec. 4, 1784, July 10, 1786, Oct. 20, 1789, and Jan. 5, 1791; *Ind. Gaz.*, Aug. 17, 1782.

66 *Pa. Gaz.*, Dec. 6, 1786, carries an extract from the Minutes of the 1st Session of the 11th Assembly.

67 License by Mayor James Duane, New York, July 7, 1786; N. Taylor Phillips, "Family History of the Reverend David Mendez Machado," *PAJHS*, II (1894), 58–59.

68 Jonas Phillips to the General Assembly of Pennsylvania, Philadelphia, Jan. 9, 1791, McAllister MSS., LCP.

69 *Pa. Pac.*, May 26, 1789, and Feb. 2 and Apr. 5, 1790.

70 In 1795 Phillips offered 18/6 as his New Year's offering, and after some correspondence about it with Benjamin Nones, then *parnass*, he wrote, "I must beg Mr. Nones to take the money as I send it for I am determined to open no [accounts] with the Congregation. If you refuse this you will not take it amiss if any one of my family offers but 6d for the Parnass & K.K.", Jonas Phillips to Benjamin Nones (Autumn, 1795), MS., MIAr.

71 Pool, *op. cit.*, 297.

72 *Ibid.*, 409.

73 Isaac Goldberg, *Major Noah* (Philadelphia, 1936), 15.

74 MBMI, Sept. 15, 1816. Noah was proposed as an elector, residency requirements being waived, because he had been a member of the congregation before he left the country in 1797.

75 *In the Supreme Court of the United States. To the Honorable John Jay, Esquire, Chief Justice and His Associates* (Philadelphia, 1791). Among the plaintiffs listed are Simon Nathan, David Franks, Joseph Simon and Levy Andrew Levy, as holders of shares in the Indiana Company. Nathan's shares were assigned by Barnard Gratz, who had bought them from William Trent, *op. cit.*, 25.

76 Byars, *op. cit.*, 369–376.

77 *Ibid.*, 350.

78 Minute Book of the Illinois and Wabash Companies, MS., McCormick Collection, Princeton University Library; Byars, *op. cit.*, 177–179.

79 Byars, *op. cit.*, 368.

80 *Pa. Gaz.*, Jan. 12, 1780.

81 Minutes of the Indiana Company, May 8, 1783, Etting MSS., HSP; Bailey, *op. cit.*, 340–342; Matthias Slough to Michael Gratz, Lancaster, Apr. 20, 1783, MS., Gratz-Croghan Papers, HSP; Byars, *op. cit.*, 214.

82 Richard Graham to Michael Gratz, Dumfries, Aug. 17 and Sept. 7, 1779, and Feb. 16 and Apr. 12, 1780, MSS., Gratz-Croghan Papers, HSP; Byars, *op. cit.*, 183–184, 186, 195–196, and 198–199.

83 Barnard Gratz to the Governor and Council of Virginia, Richmond, Dec. 20, 1782, Etting MSS., HSP, and Petition of Michael Gratz to the House of Delegates of Virginia, May 17, 1783, MS., Virginia State Library; Byars, *op. cit.*, 210 and 215.

84 John Gibson to B. and M. Gratz, Lancaster, March 9, 1784, Etting MSS., HSP; Byars, *op. cit.*, 226.

85 Barnard Gratz to Michael Gratz, Richmond, June 10, 1784, Etting MSS., HSP; Byars, *op. cit.*, 227–228.

86 For a detailed account of Nathan's troubles with Virginia, see Boyd, *op. cit.*, VI, 321–324.

87 CR, XIII, 2.

88 Edmund Randolph to Michael Gratz, Philadelphia, Aug. 4, 1791, Etting MSS., HSP; Byars, *op. cit.*, 240–241.

89 The Eleventh Amendment, stating that federal judiciary power does not extend to a suit by a citizen of one state against another state, was adopted in 1793 after vehement protest against the Supreme Court's decision on the case of *Chisholm vs. Georgia.*

90 Petition of Michael Gratz to the Mayor, Recorder, Aldermen, and Common Council of Philadelphia, Philadelphia, May 1, 1789, Etting MSS., HSP; Bailey, *op. cit.,* 478–479.

91 Clement Biddle, *Philadelphia Directory for 1791* (Philadelphia, 1791), 48.

92 Miriam Gratz to Barnard Gratz (Philadelphia), Sept. 26 (1790), Etting MSS., HSP; Byars, *op. cit.,* 239–240.

93 Agreement between John Harvie and Barnard and Michael Gratz, Richmond, July 23, 1783, Etting MSS., HSP; Byars, *op. cit.,* 218. This covered 81,135 acres.

93a *Pa. Pac.,* Jan. 27, 1784.

94 Stephen Austin to Michael Gratz, London, Aug. 14, 1795, Etting MSS., HSP; Byars, *op. cit.,* 248–249.

95 In 1794–96 the Gratzes were involved with William Du Val in the sale of various tracts, one of which contained 162,607 acres: Byars, *op. cit.,* 247–248. A schedule of lands in Virginia and Kentucky belonging to the North American Land Company shows 47,325 acres sold to Robert Morris by Gratz in June and July, 1794. For all of these Gratz had patents from the State of Virginia, dated 1787–90: MS., ca. 1820, in possession of Edwin Wolf, 2nd.

96 Certificate by Jacob Morris, Clerk of Otsego County, New York, Feb. 14, 1793, Etting MSS., HSP; Byars, *op. cit.,* 244.

97 Richard Edwards to Simon Gratz, Cherry Valley, N. Y., Apr. 15, 1796, Etting MSS., HSP; Byars, *op. cit.,* 249, "Mr. Cooper has said to me that he has purchased all your father's right in the land in question."

98 Will of George Croghan, Philadelphia, June 12, 1782, Etting MSS., HSP; Byars, *op. cit.,* 209. He left Barnard 5,000 acres on Chartier's Creek, "adjoining the tract of land I have heretofore conveyed to him." Bond of Barnard Gratz to Simon Gratz, Sept. 22, 1800, MS., in possession of Edwin Wolf, 2nd. This conveys land in Bucks County which Croghan had assigned as early as 1769.

99 *Ind. Gaz.,* June 26, 1784, and *Pa. Pac.,* July 1, 1784.

100 The children of Michael Gratz who survived to adulthood were Frances (1771–1852), Simon (1773–1839), Richea (1774–1858), Hyman (1776–1857), Sarah (1779–1817), Rebecca (1781–1869), Rachel (1783–1823), Joseph (1785–1858), Jacob (1789–1856), and Benjamin (1792–1884): Byars, *op. cit.,* 259.

101 These textbooks were at Gratz College in 1949.

102 Simon Gratz to Michael Gratz, Philadelphia, March 7, 1791, MS., in the possession of Edwin Wolf, 2nd. The master for whom Simon worked is not named: "I have served him with diligence, punctuality & with Honesty two Years & 5 Months & Some days for which I have got nothing."

103 Miriam Gratz to Simon Gratz, Philadelphia, July 11, 1793, MS., in the possession of Edwin Wolf, 2nd, shows that both Simon and Hyman were then in Lancaster working for Joseph Simon.

104 Barnard Gratz to Simon Gratz, Philadelphia, Aug. 6, 1795, and Baltimore, March 7, 1798, MSS., in the possession of Edwin Wolf, 2nd.

105 Solomon M. Myers to Barnard Gratz, New York, May 14, 1786, Gratz Papers, Henry Joseph Collection, AJAr.

106 J. Solis-Cohen, Jr., "A Famous Family Fight about Real Estate: Gratz vs. Cohen," *PAJHS*, XXXVII (1947), 348–352.

107 Barnard Gratz to Michael Gratz, Philadelphia, Aug. 19, 1785, Etting MSS., HSP; Bailey, *op. cit.*, 474–475: "A Relation came that Solomon Henry sent here."

108 Jonas Hirschel Bluch to the "High-Mighty Lords, Supreme Lords of the Republic of America in Philadelphia," Langendorf, Silesia, May 5, 1797, official translation by Charles Erdmann, Philadelphia, Jan. 3, 1798, MS., in the possession of Edwin Wolf, 2nd. The land was given to Henry on Nov. 10, 1789; he died on May 10, 1793; and the Gratzes sent the news on Nov. 1, 1795.

109 Simon and Hyman Gratz to Jonas Hirschel Bluch (Philadelphia), Sept. 15, 1799, MS., Sulzberger Collection, AJHS; Byars, *op. cit.*, 251–252.

110 Joseph E. Fields, "Birthplace of The Declaration," *Manuscripts*, VII (1955), 140–149. The Gratzes bought the house shortly after Hiltzheimer's death, in 1798, and added the adjoining building (702) to their store in 1802.

111 Deed from Aaron Levy to Joseph Henry, Philadelphia, Dec. 31, 1787, MS., in the possession of Edwin Wolf, 2nd.

112 Aaron Levy, *To the Public*, May 23, 1786, broadside; Rosenbach, *American Jewish Bibliography*, 83–85; Pa. Pac., Nov. 24, 1786, according to which the drawing took place on Oct. 4.

113 Agreement between Aaron Levy and Robert Morris, Aug. 22, 1792, MS., Philip H. and A.S.W. Rosenbach Foundation; Fish, *op. cit.*, 72–73.

114 Fish, *op. cit.*, 32–33.

115 Simon Gratz to Isabella H. Rosenbach, Philadelphia, Nov. 28, 1893, MS., in the possession of Edwin Wolf, 2nd. Gratz repeated what he had heard from his father who had had it from his father Simon Gratz I.

116 Aaron Levy, Power of Attorney, Philadelphia, Nov. 18, 1802, and Aaron Levy, Will, Philadelphia, June 28, 1802, MSS., in the possession of Edwin Wolf, 2nd; Isabella and A.S.W. Rosenbach, "Aaron Levy," *PAJHS*, II (1894), 162–163.

117 Hogan, *op. cit.*, 22, 39, 47, 72, 73, 121, 124, and 139.

118 *Aurora*, July 22, 1794.

119 James Hardie, *PD* (Philadelphia, 1794), 29.

120 *Ind. Gaz.*, Nov. 6, 1784.

121 Hogan, *op. cit.*, 50.

122 *Claypoole's*, Dec. 1 and 8, 1796.

123 Hardie, *op. cit.*, 111.

124 James Hardie, *PD* (Philadelphia, 1793), 76.

125 Hardie, *op. cit.* (1794), 110.

126 *Pa. Pac.*, Dec. 23, 1785.

127 Hardie, *op. cit.* (1793), 89.

128 Hogan, *op. cit.*, 35.

129 *Ibid.*, 68.

130 *Ibid.*, 58.

131 *Ibid.*, 67.

132 Biddle, *op. cit.*, 105.

133 License to Solomon Raphael, signed by Benjamin Franklin, Philadelphia, March 23, 1787, MS., AJHS.

134 Solomon Raphael to Levy Phillips, Philadelphia, Oct. 12, 1788, MS., MIAr.

135 Stephen's *PD* (Philadelphia, 1796), 151. Raphael moved to Richmond by 1798: Herbert T. Ezekiel and Gaston Lichtenstein, *The History of the Jews of Richmond from 1769 to 1917* (Richmond, Va. 1917), 78. He there continued his progress and became a "merchant": *ibid.*, 133.

136 Hogan, *op. cit.*, 40.

137 David Samuel to Maria Phillips, Philadelphia, Oct. 1858, MS., in the possession of Edwin Wolf, 2nd. Rachel Levy's maiden name was Phillips, and this is obviously a family tradition.

138 Agreement between Isaac Solomon and Aaron Levy, Philadelphia, Jan. 4, 1788, MS., in the possession of Edwin Wolf, 2nd.

139 *Poulson's*, July 31, 1801.

140 *Pa. Gaz.*, Jan. 28, 1807, announces Moss' removal from No. 9 North 2nd St. to Market between 2nd and 3rd, "where he intends to continue to keep a general assortment of Dry Goods."

141 Hardie, *op. cit.*, (1795), 32.

142 "Naphtali Phillips," *PAJHS*, XXI (1913), 172–173. Phillips was working for Claypoole in 1796. A partnership with his brother Benjamin was dissolved two years later: *Claypoole's*, Feb. 16, 1798. In 1801, he advertised a ship for sale or charter from No. 14 Chestnut St.: *Poulson's*, Sept. 18, 1801; and shortly after that moved to New York, where, within a few years, he became the proprietor of the *National Advocate*.

Chapter 10

1 *Pa. Pac.*, May 2, 1788.

2 *Ibid.*, Sept. 2, 1789.

3 *Ibid.*, Aug. 5, 1787.

4 *Ibid.*, Feb. 20, 1786.

5 *Ibid.*, Sept. 17, 1788.

6 *Ibid.*, March 8, 1788.

7 *Ibid.*, Jan. 12, 1790.

8 *Am. Dai. Adv.*, May 19, 1791.

9 *Ibid.*, July 27, 1791.

10 *Gen. Adv.*, Jan. 27, 1794.

11 The Pragers came to Philadelphia shortly after the Revolution. According to N. I. Hyman, of Haifa, Israel, Michael was born in County Cork, Ireland, in 1740. He died in 1793. Benjamin Rush treated three members of the family in 1783–87, and in his Ledger C, 8–9, MS., LCP, names them as Michael Prager, Sr., Michael Prager, Jr. "of Holland," and Mr. Prager, "Relation of Mr. Prager Senr." In 1798–99, he treated Mark Prager: Ledger D, 161; and in 1796–1799 a John Prager: *ibid.*, 94. They were in business as Pragers, Liebaert & Co., as early as 1784: *Pa. Pac.*, Sept. 25, 1784. Although born Jews, they were never professing Jews in America. Later, the firm went under the name of Pragers & Co., *Am. Dai. Adv.*, Aug. 8, 1791.

12 Scharf and Westcott, *op. cit.*, II, 970n.

13 *Pa. Pac.*, Oct. 27, 1778.

14 *Ibid.*, Oct. 22, 1790.

15 *The Constitution of the Pennsylvania Society for Promoting the Abolition of Slavery* (Philadelphia, 1787).

16 Pennsylvania Abolition Society, Manumission Book A, 46, MS., HSP.

17 Marcus, *op. cit.*, I, 126.

18 *Ibid.*, II, 322–323 and 328.

19 *Ind. Gaz.*, Sept. 11, 1784; *Pa. Pac.*, Jan. 6, 1789.

20 Pennsylvania Abolition Society, Manumission Book C, 52, 54 and 57.

21 *Ibid.*, Manumission Book A, 86.

22 *Ibid.*, 87.

23 *Ibid.*, 134–135.

24 *Ibid.*, Manumission Book D, 37 and 78.

25 *Ibid.*, 21 and 46.

26 *Ibid.*, 25.

27 *Ibid.*, Manumission Book B, 239–240 and 267–268.

28 *Ibid.*, Manumission Book A, 161.

29 *Ibid.*, Manumission Book B, 170.

30 *Ibid.*, 37.

31 *Ibid.*, 38.

32 *Pa. Pac.*, Dec. 3, 1790, offering a reward for her return.

33 Alexander Abrahams to Michael Gratz, Sept. 2, 1776, Etting MSS., HSP; incompletely published in Byars, *op. cit.*, 159–160.

34 George Nagel to Barnard Gratz, Reading, March 2, 1772, McAllister MSS., LCP.

35 Simon Gratz to Michael Gratz, Philadelphia, March 7, 1791, MS., in the possession of Edwin Wolf, 2nd: "Its reported here that Mr. Etting intends to move to Baltimore."

36 *Gen. Adv.*, June 13, 1794.

37 *Votes and Proceedings of the House of Delegates of the State of Maryland, November Session 1797* (Annapolis, 1798), 69, and 71–72.

38 *Address of the Maryland State Colonization Society, to the People of Maryland; with the Constitution of the Society* (Baltimore, 1831).

39 John H. Powell, *Bring Out Your Dead, The Great Plague of Yellow Fever in Philadelphia in 1793* (Philadelphia, 1949), 4–7, and 13–16.

40 *Ibid.*, 104.

41 *Ibid.*, 142–144.

42 *Ibid.*, 234.

43 *Ibid.*, 114–139.

44 *Ibid.*, 153–164.

45 Bernard Felsenthal and Richard Gottheil, "Chronological Sketch of the Jews in Surinam," *PAJHS*, IV (1896), 3–6. The Nassy family had been among the leading Jews of the Dutch colony from 1664 when Dr. Nassy's ancestor of the same name founded a community there of Jews who had come from Brazil by way of Cayenne. Dr. Nassy had been one of the *regenten* of the Jewish community of Surinam and had come to Philadelphia by way of St. Thomas: Sigmund Seeligmann, "David Nassy of Surinam and his 'Lettre Politico-Theologico-Morale sur les Juifs'," *PAJHS*, XXII (1914), 27 and 29.

46 David Nassy to James Hutchinson and John Williams, Corresponding Secretaries of the American Philosophical Society, Philadelphia, Feb. 1, 1793, MS., APS, apologizing for being unable to attend a meeting.

47 *Transactions of the American Philosophical Society*, I (1771), xxiii, lists

among those elected Jan. 18, 1771, "Mr. Joseph Ottolenge, of Georgia." At this same time Ottolenghe published *Directions for Breeding Silk-Worms* (Philadelphia, 1771), which describes him on the title-page as "Late Superintendent of the Public Filature in Georgia." Marcus, *op. cit.*, II, 307–315, writes of Ottolenghe, but did not know of his membership in the Philosophical Society or his book.

48 Benjamin Rush, Family & private Account Book, MS., LCP, 47 and 51.

49 David Nassy, *Observations on the Cause, Nature, and Treatment of the Epidemic Disorder, prevalent in Philadelphia* (Philadelphia, 1793), 24.

50 *Ibid.*

51 Powell, *op. cit.*, 200.

52 Nassy, *op. cit.*, 18n.

53 The importance of this book in American Jewish bibliography has not hitherto been noted.

54 MBMI, Sept. 1, 1793 (twice).

55 Barnard Gratz to Michael Gratz, Baltimore, Sept. 9, 1793, Gratz Papers, Henry Joseph Collection, AJAr.

56 William Bradford to Mrs. William Bradford, Easton, Sept. 26, 1793, MS., Wallace Papers, II, HSP.

57 Mathew Carey, *A Short Account of the Malignant Fever, lately in Philadelphia . . . Third Edition, Improved* (Philadelphia, 1793), "List of Names of Persons Buried," 1 and 16. There has always been some confusion because David Franks and David Salisbury Franks both died of the fever. Carey lists the latter without his middle name as buried at Christ Church, and the former as a Jew. Carey, *ibid.* (Fourth Edition), 134, lists both Franks, and in addition, 148, " . . . . . . Pragers," who was Michael Prager.

58 Benjamin Rush to Julia Rush, Philadelphia, Oct. 7, 1793, MS., Trent Collection, Duke University; Butterfield, *op. cit.*, II, 706. Apparently, earlier Rush had been caring for Franks, for in his Ledger C, 383, is an entry ending Sept. 1793.

59 Benjamin Rush to Julia Rush, Philadelphia, Oct. 9, 1783, MS., Trent Collection, Duke University; Butterfield, *op. cit.*, II, 711.

60 *Fed. Gaz.*, Sept. 27, 1793.

61 Powell, *op. cit.*, 106–107.

62 *Ibid.*, 260–264.

63 The house, known as the Deshler-Morris House, is 4782 Germantown Avenue. It was built by Deshler in 1774–75, used by the British Army during the Battle of Germantown, and bought by Franks in 1782. In 1804, he sold it to Elliston and Samuel Perot: Townsend Ward, "The Germantown Road and its Associations," *Pa. Mag.*, VI (1882), 141–148.

64 Copy of Bill from Isaac Franks to George Washington, Jastrow, *op. cit.*, 32–33; "Washington's Household Account Book, 1793–1797," *Pa. Mag.*,

XXX (1906), 172, contains an entry of the payment of $75.56 on March 26, 1794 to Franks for "house rent etc."

65 *Ibid.*, 321, contains another entry of the payment of $201.60 on Sept. 24, 1794 again to Franks for "house rent etc."

66 Jastrow, *op. cit.*, 12.

67 Commission as Lieutenant-Colonel, Philadelphia, July 15, 1794, Jastrow, *op. cit.*, 18.

68 *Poulson's*, Apr. 22, 1801.

69 Commission as Justice of Peace, Philadelphia, Sept. 25, 1795, Jastrow, *op. cit.*, 19.

70 Original Painting in the Pennsylvania Academy of the Fine Arts; Hannah R. London, *Portraits of Jews by Gilbert Stuart and Other Early American Artists* (New York, 1927), 53.

71 Isaac Franks to Benjamin Rush, Reading, Sept. 12 and 15, 1803, MSS., Rush Papers, V, 79–80, LCP.

72 Isaac Franks to Benjamin Rush, Ephrata, June 25, 1810, MS., Rush Papers, V, 81, LCP. Rush had been Franks' doctor for a long time. In his Ledger C, 3, MS., LCP, are thirty-six entries for medical services to Franks, his wife, children and father between 1783 and 1792, part of which were "Probably settled by Services, Goods &c.," and the rest "Settled by an exchange of receipts on the (–) of Sepr: 1800 in full." There were further entries in Ledger D, 188, MS., LCP, between Oct. 1800 and Mar. 1805.

73 Isaac Franks to Benjamin Rush, Reading, Aug. 28, 1804, MS., Rush Papers, V, 75, LCP.

74 Isaac Franks to Benjamin Rush, Reading, Feb. 27 and March 6, 1805, MSS., Rush Papers, V, 77–78, LCP.

75 Isaac Franks to Benjamin Rush, Lancaster County, "5 miles from Litiz," Nov. 9, 1812, MS., Rush Papers, V, 73, LCP.

76 Isaac Franks to Benjamin Rush, Ephrata, Dec. 23, 1812, MS., Rush Papers, V, 74. Rush's prescription is on the back of Franks' letter to him.

77 Isaac Franks to Richard Rush, Ephrata, May 10, 1813, Jastrow, *op. cit.*, 23–25, condoling with Rush on the death of his father and asking help in securing employment at the Mint.

78 John Hill Martin, *Martin's Bench and Bar of Philadelphia* (Philadelphia, 1883), 26.

79 *Poulson's*, March 5, 1822.

80 Rush was the Phillips family's regular physician. In his Ledger C, 191 and 399, are thirty-seven entries for various members of the immediate family of "Jonas Philips Jew market st" between June, 1787, when Rush made the entry "To sundries for wife £5.15–," and May, 1795; and in Ledger D, 8 and 192, are many more covering the period between 1795 and 1801. A later entry, *ibid.*, 258, shows a charge to Widow Phillips in

Apr. 1805. In addition, in Ledger C, 65, there is the record of the treatment of Manuel Noah, "Jonas Phillips son in law," in July 1790 and Sept. 1791, with the credit column marked "Gone to S Carolina;" *ibid.*, 191, services "given" to Mr. Levy, "son in law to Jonas Philips," in May 1789; *ibid.*, 177 and 347, the care of Israel Jacobs, "Jonas Phillips father in law," in 1795; Ledger D, 63 and 222, treatment of "Mr. Pisso [Isaac Pesoa] —No 112 Vine Street, married Miss Philips," in 1796 and from 1803 to 1806; and finally, *ibid.*, 220, services to Zalegman Philips in Feb. 1803.

81 Benjamin Rush to Julia Rush, Philadelphia, June 27, 1787, MS., in the possession of Gordon A. Block, Jr., of Philadelphia; Lyman H. Butterfield (ed.), *Letters of Benjamin Rush* (Princeton, 1951), I, 429–432.

82 Benjamin Rush, Commonplace Book, MS., APS; Corner, *op. cit.*, 222–223. Corner misread Mrs. "Norris" for Mrs. Nones. Cf. Abraham I. Abrahams to Moses Seixas, New York, June 1, 1772, MS., Phillips Collection, AJHS; Frank Zimmerman, "A Letter and Memorandum on Ritual Circumcision," *PAJHS*, XLIV (1954), 58–63.

83 David Nassy, *Essai Historique sur la Colonie de Surinam* (Paramaribo, 1788).

84 Benjamin Rush, Commonplace Book; Corner, *op. cit.*, 223.

85 Benjamin Rush, Ledger C, 380, MS., LCP, shows nineteen entries in the account with Nones from Aug. 1792 to Nov. 1794, including "Consultation with a french physician" in Aug. 1792. Rush remained Nones' physician, and in Ledger D, 27 and 240, are records of services rendered in mid-1795 and from Dec. 1803 to Oct. 1805.

86 Powell, *op. cit.*, 211.

87 *Gen. Adv.*, Feb. 11, 1794.

88 David Nassy, Discours, Feb. 20, 1794, MS., APS.

89 David Nassy to the American Philosophical Society, Philadelphia, May 30, 1794, MS., APS.

90 David Nassy to the American Philosophical Society, Philadelphia, June 19, 1795, MS., APS; Samuel Oppenheim, "A Letter of David Nassy, of Surinam," *PAJHS*, XIII (1915), 185.

91 David Nassy to Messrs. Brown, Benson & Ives, Philadelphia, Apr. 26, 1795, MS., John Carter Brown Library.

92 David Nassy to the American Philosophical Society, Paramaribo, Surinnam, Aug. 18, 1799, MS., APS; Oppenheim, *op. cit.*, 185–186. The copies which Nassy sent to the Philosophical Society and the Library Company are still in those collections.

93 Moses Sheftall to Benjamin Rush, Savannah, Jan. 24, 1795, Rush MSS., XXXVIII, 51, LCP.

94 Leon Hühner, "The Jews of New England," *PAJHS*, XI (1903), 86–87.

95 *Am. Dai. Adv.*, Aug. 1, 1800.

96 Manuel Phillips attended, but did not graduate from, the Medical School of the University of Pennsylvania. He is not listed as having received a

degree, but he joined the Navy in 1809 as an Assistant Surgeon, and thereafter practised in Philadelphia: Morais, *op. cit.,* 416 and 477.

97 *Ibid.,* 38–41.

98 *Ibid.,* 431.

99 *Ibid.,* 432.

100 Dr. Negley K. Teeters provided this information.

101 Board of Inspectors' Minutes of the Walnut Street Jail, Apr. 4, 1797; Negley K. Teeters, *The Cradle of the Penitentiary* (Philadelphia, 1955), 55.

102 *Gen. Adv.,* March 21, 1794, where the address of the Academy is given as "in Cherry Alley, between Third and Fourth Streets, No. 9, near the Synagogue and the sign of the White Lamb."

103 *The Rise and Progress of the Young Ladies' Academy of Philadelphia* (Philadelphia, 1794), 5, 6, 13, 16, 29, 37, 47, where the Rev. Jacob Cohen is listed as a "Visitor" from 1787 to 1791, together with ten other divines and six educators.

Chapter II

1 George Washington to Charles Cotesworth Pinckney, Philadelphia, Aug. 24, 1795, MS., formerly in the possession of The Rosenbach Company.

2 For a brief, illustrated survey of the period, see Roger Butterfield, *The American Past* (New York, 1947), 16–25.

3 *Ibid.,* 21.

4 Democratic Society of Philadelphia, Minutes, Aug. 8, 1793, MS., HSP, 30–31, and 54.

5 Democratic Society, Minutes, 129 and 132. Solomon was the son of Solomon Marks of Lancaster and Philadelphia, who was a haberdasher in 1782: Norris Family Accounts, III, 41, HSP. Solomon, Jr., after setting up in business in Philadelphia, moved to Richmond: *Claypoole's,* May 2, 1797; he was there by August: Herbert T. Ezekiel and Gaston Lichtenstein, *The History of the Jews of Richmond from 1769 to 1917* (Richmond, 1917), 77. He later came back to Philadelphia where he died: Letters of Administration, Register of Wills, County of Philadelphia, No. 61, Book O, 117.

6 The records of most of these societies have not survived, but in the light of Nones' later activity, it seems reasonable to assume that he had joined them almost as soon as they came into existence.

7 *Porcupine's Gazette,* March 17, 1798.

8 James Morton Smith, "The Aurora and the Alien and Sedition Laws,"

Pa. Mag., LXXVII (1953), 3–23, gives a detailed account of Bache's editorship and his troubles with the administration.

9 Smith, *op. cit.*, 18–19.

10 *Claypoole's*, Aug. 16, 1797, *et seqq.*

11 *Ibid.*, Sept. 4, 1797.

12 *Ibid.*, Oct. 28, 1797.

13 Richard Folwell, *A Short History of the Yellow Fever* (Philadelphia, 1798), 58.

14 Smith, *op. cit.*, 22.

15 *Ibid.*, 123–124.

16 *Claypoole's*, Aug. 31, 1798.

17 *Ibid.*, Sept. 14, 1798.

18 Nathan C. Goodman, *Benjamin Rush, Patriot and Citizen* (Philadelphia, 1934), 216–222.

19 *Gaz. US*, July 16, 1800; Smith, *op. cit.*, 151

20 *DNB*, XXX, 14. Johnson had married Rebecca Franks on Jan. 17, 1782.

21 Smith, *op. cit.*, 145–148.

22 *The Rush-Light* (New York, 1800), No. I, 1.

23 *Ibid.*, No. II, 78n; Morris U. Schappes, "Anti-Semitism and Reaction," *PAJHS*, XXXVIII (1948), 129–130.

24 *The Rush-Light*, No. III, 116.

25 Benjamin Rush, Ledger D, 39, MS., LCP, marks the account from July 1795 to July 1798 settled in full.

26 Charles Nisbet to Charles Wallace, Philadelphia, Dec. 11, 1797; Eugene Perry Link, *Democratic-Republican Societies, 1790–1800* (New York, 1942), 51n.

27 See chap. 2, note 36.

28 *Gaz. US*, Aug. 5, 1800; Schappes, *op. cit.*, 132–133.

29 Benjamin Nones to William Duane, Philadelphia, Aug. 11, 1800, *Aurora,* Aug. 13, 1800; Schappes, *A Documentary History*, 93–96.

30 Benjamin Nones to the Printer of the Gazette of the United States, Philadelphia, Aug. 11, 1800, printed broadside, only copy known in the possession of Maxwell Whiteman.

31 *Aurora*, Aug. 13, 1800.

32 Printed for the first time from the broadside, *supra*. Cyrus Adler, "A Political Document of the Year 1800," *PAJHS*, I (1892), 111–115, took his text from Nones' autograph draft, then in the possesion of John M. Noah. Schappes, in his *PAJHS* article, *supra*, mentioned, and in *A Documentary History*, 92–96, used the *Aurora* printing.

33 *Phi. Gaz.*, Aug. 13, 1800.

34 Joseph Bloomfield and James Morgan to the People of New Jersey, *Aurora*, Oct. 7, 1800.

35 Abercrombie preached his sermon at Christ Church and St. Peter's Church on Aug. 24, 1800.

36 *Aurora*, Sept. 1, 1800.

37 *Phi. Gaz.*, Sept. 5, 1800. This whole incident is here discussed for the first time.

38 *Aurora*, Sept. 10, 1800.

39 *Phi. Gaz.*, Sept. 10, 1800.

40 *Ibid.*, Sept. 11, 1800.

41 *Aurora*, Sept. 13, 1800.

42 *Ibid.*, Oct. 7, 1800.

43 Smith, *op. cit.*, 154–155.

44 *Aurora*, Apr. 29, 1802.

45 *Poulson's*, March 6, 1813.

46 [William Maclure,] *To the People of the United States* (Philadelphia, 1807), 345, where Nones' loss is listed.

47 Letters of Administration, Register of Wills, Philadelphia County, 218, Y-105.

48 *Journal of The Senate of The United States of America; being the Second Session of the Sixth Congress* (Washington, 1821), 148.

49 Simon Wolf, *The American Jew as Patriot, Soldier and Citizen* (Philadelphia, 1895), 48.

50 *Poulson's*, Aug. 11, 1801, in the list of presidential appointments, "Reuben Etting, Marshall of the district of Maryland—in the room of David Hopkins—dismissed;" Reuben Etting, Receipt Book as Marshall, June 18, 1801 to May 23, 1804, MS., LC.

51 Reuben Etting (1762–1848) was the son of Elijah Etting of York. He married Frances Gratz, the first cousin of his brother Solomon's wife. He has been confused with another Reuben Etting, son of Asher Etting, who was taken prisoner by the British at Charlestown and died May 24, 1778: Solomon Solis-Cohen, "Note concerning David Hays and Esther Etting his Wife, and Michael Hays and Reuben Etting, their Brothers, Patriots of the Revolution," *PAJHS*, II (1894), 66.

52 Benjamin H. Hartogensis, "Unequal Religious Rights in Maryland since 1776," *PAJHS*, XXV (1917), 95–99.

53 *Aurora*, Oct. 19, 1804, in which Etting advertises part of a cargo for sale; *Phi. Gaz.*, July 10, 1805.

54 *Phi. Gaz.*, March 22, 1809 carried an advertisement of Humes and Etting, auctioneers; *ibid.*, Oct. 29, 1811, announces the dissolution of the firm.

55 *Poulson's*, Feb. 23, 1802.

56 *Phi. Gaz.*, Apr. 5, 1803.

57 *Ibid.*, July 11, 1803; *ibid.*, March 8, 1805, "Notary Office. The Merchants and Shippers of the city of Philadelphia are respectfully informed, that the Subscriber will issue from his Notarial Office Proofs of Property, in the Spanish Language, in addition to those issued by him in English and French, being duly commissioned and appointed Sworn Interpreter of Foreign Languages for the Commonwealth of Pennsylvania; *ibid.*, Aug. 9, 1809, "In conformity with the new arrangement of the department of State of the United States respecting Passports", Nones announced they may be obtained from him.

58 *Ibid.*, Dec. 8, 1808.

59 *Aurora*, March 29, 1804.

60 *Phi. Gaz.*, July 8, 1805.

61 *Poulson's*, Oct. 7, 9, and 16, Nov. 17 and 21, and Dec. 24, 1806.

62 William J. Duane, A Book of Original Entries, 87, MS., LCP.

63 *Phi. Gaz.*, Sept. 19, 1805.

64 *Martin's Bench and Bar*, 76 and 78. Levy served as Recorder until 1808; he was commissioned Presiding Judge of the District Court in 1822. The Recorder presided in the Mayor's Court.

65 *The Trial of the Boot & Shoemakers of Philadelphia, on an Indictment for a Combination and Conspiracy to Raise Their Wages* (Philadelphia, 1806); Moses Levy's charge to the jury, in Schappes, *op. cit.*, 103–112.

66 *Journal of the Seventeenth House of Representatives of the Commonwealth of Pennsylvania* (Lancaster, 1806), 58, 443, 682–684, and 747–748; *Journal of the Senate* (Lancaster, 1806), 230, 267, 274, 339, and 367–369.

67 Thomas Jefferson to Albert Gallatin, Monticello, Sept. 1, 1804, Henry Adams (ed.), *The Writings of Albert Gallatin* (Philadelphia, 1879), I, 206.

68 Albert Gallatin to Thomas Jefferson, Treasury Department, Sept. 18, 1804, Adams, *op. cit.*, I, 208.

69 The Jeffersonians were furious at his charge to the jury in Shoemakers' Case, *Aurora*, March 31, 1806, "never did we hear a charge to the jury delivered in a more prejudiced and partial manner." *Phi. Gaz.*, Oct. 10, 1807, lists Moses Levy as one of six Federalist "Friends of the Constitution."

70 *American Eagle* (Easton), July 6, 1805; Trachtenberg, *op. cit.*, 78.

71 *Poulson's*, Sept. 2, 1806.

72 *Phi. Gaz.*, Sept. 30, 1807, Oct. 7, 1808, and Sept. 23, 1809.

73 *Ibid.*, June 30, 1807.

74 *Ibid.*, July 2, 1807.

75 Morais, *op. cit.*, 407.

76 Fish, *op. cit.*, 33–39.

77 Simon Snyder to Aaron Levy, Lancaster, July 30, 1806, MS., Gratz Collection, HSP.

78 Simon Snyder to Aaron Levy, Jan. 13, 1796, MS., Gratz Collection, HSP.

79 Simon Snyder to Aaron Levy, Feb. 13, 1804, and Jan. 17, 1805, MSS., Gratz Collection, HSP.

80 Simon Snyder to Aaron Levy, Harrisburg, Feb. 13, 1804, MS., Gratz Collection, HSP.

81 Simon Snyder to Aaron Levy, July 30, 1806, MS., Gratz Collection, HSP.

82 *Aurora*, Sept. 5, 10, 13, 14 and 16, 1808.

83 Goldberg, *op. cit.*, 34–35.

84 *Aurora*, Sept. 19, 1808.

85 *Ibid.*, Sept. 29, 1808.

86 *Ibid.*, Sept. 23, 1808, and *ibid.*, Oct. 8, 1810.

87 *Ibid.*, Sept. 23, 1808.

88 *Phi. Gaz.*, Sept. 25, 1809.

89 *Poulson's*, Sept. 26, and 27, 1810.

90 *Aurora*, Sept. 25 and 27 and Oct. 6, 1810.

91 *Ibid.*, Oct. 10, 1808.

92 Schappes, *op. cit.*, 122–125 and 597–598.

93 *The American Speaker; A Selection of Popular, Parliamentary and Forensic Eloquence* (Philadelphia, 1814), 279–282.

94 *Poulson's*, June 13, 1810.

Chapter 12

1 MBMI, Sept. 3, 1792.

2 Draft of Constitution, Jan. 21, 1798, MS., MIAr, has Section 9, concerning Sabbath-breaking, crossed out, and no such provision appears in any of the subsequent constitutions.

3 David Nassy, *Essai Historique*, 43; Seeligmann, *op. cit.*, 34–35. Solomon Marache was one of the founders of Mikveh Israel, but his second wife was a non-Jewess: see chap. 9, note 64. Lion Van Amring (also Leon Amringe) was one of the founders of Rodeph Shalom; he married a non-Jewess, Elizabeth, and had three children, George O., Rachel Sophia, and Augustus, none of whom had any Jewish associations. Moses Hom-

berg was the innkeeper who died of the yellow fever in 1793. MBMI, Sept. 9, 1792, shows that he had applied for membership in the congregation. After his death his widow Ann continued his business of "tavern keeper & livery stable": Hardie, *Philadelphia Directory* (1794), 71. Haim Reuben Wallach was a contributor to Mikveh Israel in 1784, 1785 and 1787, and also to the Ezrath Orechim, and Moses Wallach signed a receipt for a gift from the *tsedaka* fund. Charity Solis appeared on a list of women who sewed the Torah covers about 1782: MS. Scrap, MIAr, but no other record of the Solis family has been found this early.

4 Mrs. John Warder, Diary, "12 mo. 15, 1786," MS., HSP; "Note," *PAJHS*, III (1894), 150. She calls him "Martin," but it must be Mark Prager.

5 "Extracts from Washington's Diary, kept while attending the Constitutional Convention of 1787," *Pa. Mag.*, XI (1887), 301.

6 See chap. 2, note 48.

7 Both Abraham Gumpert and Abraham Moses appeared as contributors to Mikveh Israel on the 1799–1800 Subscription List, MS., MIAr.

8 Kenneth and Anna M. Roberts (eds.), *Moreau de St. Mery's American Journey, 1793–1798* (New York, 1947), 337.

9 Hyman B. Grinstein, *The Rise of the Jewish Community of New York, 1654–1860* (Philadelphia, 1945), 40–49.

10 Constitution (1798), *supra*, Section 8, provides that any person residing in Philadelphia or the two adjoining townships may, when approved, become a member by paying $3.00 and signing the constitution.

11 Abraham Rice, Letters and Homilies, (1844), MS., Jewish Theological Seminary, ". . . it is because of our many iniquities that there is no ritual bath in Philadelphia about 49 years, and the daughters of Israel are estranged and children of the ritually unclean." Rice was not quite accurate, for there are references to a *mikvah* between 1795 and 1844; it was in that latter year that Rodeph Shalom decided to establish a permanent one, see chap. 13, note 107.

12 Deed from Thomas Warwick and his Wife to Lion Van Amring, Isaiah Nathans, Isaac Marks, Aaron Levy, Jr., Abraham Gumpert, and Abraham Moses, Philadelphia, Nov. 23, 1801, MS., RSAr. לוח לשנת תרכא ולפיק *Hebrew Calendar, for A.M. 5621* (Philadelphia, 1860), 54, lists the first burial ground of Rodeph Shalom as "in Duke Street, now Thompson, late District of Kensington." The site is not now known.

13 Ketubah Book, MS., MIAr.

14 Aaron Levy, Jr., the son of Aaron of Aaronsburg's brother Moses Hayyim, came to Philadelphia late in 1795, Fish, *op. cit.*, 2.

15 See note 7, *supra*.

16 Constitution, Oct. 10, 1802, MS., RSAr; Edward Davis, *The History of Rodeph Shalom Congregation, 1802–1926* (Philadelphia, 1927), 13–14, which omits Articles 22 and 23, and is not always a fully accurate translation of the Yiddish.

17 Constitution, "Middle days of Passover," 1810, MS., RSAr, Article 14.

From the preamble to Article 8 the original manuscript of the constitution has not survived, but the text is available in a certified copy of the Charter, By-Laws and Constitution, attested to by the Secretary of the Commonwealth of Pennsylvania, Oct. 13, 1887. Those who signed a declaration to support this constitution were A. B. Cohen, Michael Levy, Abraham Hart, Abraham Gumpert, Abraham Moses, Aaron Stork, Lewis Allen, Moses Abraham, Isaac Marks, Elias Hyneman, Benedict Nathan, Lyon Cadet, Alexander Benjamin, Abraham Eleazer Israel, Levy Abraham, Jacob de Lange, Levi M. Goldsmit, Mayer Arnold, Simon Cauffman, Emanuel Oppenheimer, Mayer Ullman, Isaac Stuttgart, Abraham Joseph, A. Schoger, Moses Spyers and Abraham Lazarus.

18 How rapidly this took place can be judged by the fact that before 1810 Aaron Levy, Jr. and Isaiah Nathans were both active in Mikveh Israel, and that, of those who signed the 1810 document, in 1813 Hart, Israel, De Lange and Goldsmit, in 1814 Spyers, and in 1815 Hyneman applied for membership in the other congregation.

19 MBMI, Nov. 9, 1799. A docket note on the 1798 Constitution reads, "Draught of Constitution presented to the Congregation by Naphtali Phillips Jany. 21, 1798."

20 He was *parnass* fourteen times, for the first time in 1804 and the last time in 1823: Lyons Collection, *PAJHS*, XXI (1913), 212.

21 Salomon died in 1785, Bush in 1790, Josephson in 1796, Barnard Gratz in 1801, Phillips in 1803, and Michael Gratz in 1811.

22 Constitution (1798), Section 7, "The Parnass shall keep in a book for that purpose fair records of the transactions of the Congregation & Adjuntos at all their meetings."

23 Gershom Mendes Seixas, Rules concerning Prayers, Minhag, Conduct, Hours of Worship, etc., MS., MIAr.

24 *Ibid.*, 19.

25 Moses Lopez, *A Lunar Calendar, of the Festivals, and other Days in the Year, Observed by the Israelites* (Newport, 1806); Rosenbach, *American Jewish Bibliography*, 127–128.

26 Articles concerning Religious Worship, Iyar 2, 1810, MS., RSAr. The original is in Yiddish; a translation was published in Davis, *op. cit.*, 133–135.

27 It is interesting that the change at Mikveh Israel from the Hebrew calendar in the Minute Book to the western one coincided with the departure of Seixas.

28 Constitution (1798), *supra*; *Rules and Regulations of the Congregation of* ק״ק מקוה ישראל (Philadelphia, 1813), Rosenbach, *op. cit.*, 152; *Constitution of the* ק״ק מקוה ישראל (Philadelphia, 1823), *ibid.*, 216 and 218; *Charter and Bye-Laws of* ק״ק מקוה ישראל *Kaal Kadosh Mickve Israel, of the City of Philadelphia* (Philadelphia, 1824), *ibid.*, 227–228.

29 At the beginning there were five *adjuntos*: MBMI, March 24, 1782; the number was reduced to three the next year; *ibid.*, Sept. 30, 1783; the fourth was added in 1823: *Constitution* (1823), Article I, Section 1; and the secretary was added in 1824: *Charter* (1824), Article I, Section 12.

30 Constitution (1798), Section 1, "to be elected by the Congregation by ballot on the first Sunday after Rosh Hodes Elul in every year to serve for one year from Rosh Hashonah."

31 Constitution (1798), Section 2; *Charter* (1824), Article III, Section 1.

32 Constitution (1798), Section 3; *Rules* (1813), Article VI; *Constitution* (1823), Article III, Section II.

33 Constitution (1798), Section 3, "to transact such business as may be necessary during the recess of the Congregation"; *Constitution* (1823), Article I, Section 2, "shall be entrusted with the administration of the affairs of the Congregation."

34 Constitution (1798), Section 2; *Constitution* (1823), Article III, Section III.

35 Refusal to accept the position of *parnass* was from the beginning subject to a fine of £10: MBMI, March 24, 1782; apparently the first fine paid was by Haym Salomon who paid £5 for refusing to serve as *Hatan Bereshit:* MBMI, Sept. 15, 1782. Fines were recorded in the regular account books.

36 Constitution (1798), Section 8.

37 *Ibid.,* Section 12.

38 Isaiah Nathans and Aaron Levy, Jr. to the Parnass and Adjunta, Philadelphia, June 14, 1812, MS., MIAr.

39 *Rules and Regulations* (1813), Article V.

40 *Constitution* (1823), Article II, Section 1.

41 Constitution (1798), Section 8; *Rules and Regulations* (1813), Section 1; *Constitution* (1823), Article II, Section 1; *Charter* (1824), Article II, Section 1.

42 Moses Lopez to Hyman Marks, Philadelphia, June 16, 1816, MS., MIAr, in which he asked that after "near three Years application you will be pleased to investigate the reason." The minutes for 1816 are not in existence, but Lopez was apparently admitted; Moses Lopez to Hyman Marks and Levy Phillips, Philadelphia, Sept. 2, 1816, MS., MIAr, in which he presented "a Chair adapted to hold the Ewer and Basin with Four Damask Napkins for the use of the   כהנים   which I crave your acceptance."

43 James Robinson, *The PD for 1816* (Philadelphia, 1816), in list of dentists in front, unpaged.

44 Constitution (1810), *supra.*

45 Charter, By-Laws & Constitution, 1810, see note 17, *supra.*

46 MBMI, Feb. 22, 1824; the Judges of the Supreme Court refused to approve the charter unless the first section of the fourth article was expunged, which was done: MBMI, Apr. 25, 1824. This section forbade the sale, mortgaging or closing up of the synagogue or burial ground. A simple clause permitting the congregation to hold lands, rents, annuities, or other hereditaments was substituted for it.

47 MBMI, Oct. 24 and Nov. 10 and 14, 1784.

48 Constitution (1810), Article 2.

49 *Ibid.*, Article 5.

50 *Ibid.*, Article 6.

51 Morais, *op. cit.*, 272. The firm, Hyman and Simon Gratz, went into bankruptcy in July, 1826, see chap. 18, note 46.

52 Constitution (1810), Article 19.

53 *Ibid.*, Article 10, "a specific sum, not less than four Dollars."

54 Articles (1810), where a curious provision reads, "The Mitzvos should be sold to the highest bidder but no bids should exceed that of the Parnos."

55 MBMI, Apr. 25, 1824, first-class seats downstairs were priced at $100, and second-class ones $50, while in the upstairs ladies' gallery they were $30 and $20 respectively.

56 Constitution (1810), Article 11, stating that any member who has not paid his dues for two years shall be expelled, "unless such members shall be too poor, and in such case shall give information thereof to the President, stating his inability, of which the President shall make a memorandum on the subscription paper with the words *poor* opposite to the member's name, which shall be kept private by the Officers."

57 By-Laws, Oct. 8, 1820, MS., RSAr.

58 *Ibid.*, Article 6.

59 *Ibid.*, Article 7.

60 *Journal of the Nineteenth House of Representatives of the Commonwealth of Pennsylvania* (Lancaster, 1808), 22, 50, 152, 757, 850, and 856.

61 *Journal of the Twentieth House of Representatives of the Commonwealth of Pennsylvania* (Lancaster, 1809), 176–177, where the history of the lottery is given.

62 *By Authority. Scheme of a Lottery for the Benefit of the Hebrew Congregation of the City of Philadelphia*, Nov. 10, 1808, printed broadside, Rosenbach, *op. cit.*, 133–134, and 136.

63 Benjamin Nones to Governor Simon Snyder, Philadelphia, June 21, 1810, MS., MIAr; *Journal of the Twentieth House*, 155, 176–177, 195, 247, 255–256, 257, 268–269, 534, 565, 642, 658, and 885.

64 *Phi. Pub. Led.*, Apr. 9, 1839, where the account of the fire at No. 7 Pear Street appears on the front page.

65 Jeanette W. Rosenbaum, "Hebrew German Society Rodeph Shalom in the City and County of Philadelphia (1800-1950)," *PAJHS*, XLI (1951), 85–86.

66 Jacob Ezekiel to Dr. Henry Berkowitz, Cincinnati, Jan. 24, 1899, MS., RSAr; Davis, *op. cit.*, 38.

67 *Rules and Regulations* (1813), Article 12; By-Laws (1820), Article 13.

68 Constitution (1810), Articles 15, 16 and 17.

69 Articles (1810), Article 1; Davis, *op. cit.*, 27-28.

70 See note 2, *supra*.

71 Constitution (1810), Article 12.

72 John Samuel, "Some Cases in Pennsylvania wherein Rights claimed by Jews are Affected, " *PAJHS*, V (1897), 35.

73 William J. Duane, A Book of Original Entries, 73, MS, LCP.

74 Anna Barnett to the Members of the Hebrew Congregation, Philadelphia, Nov. 13, 1794, MS., MIAr.

75 Marcus, *op. cit.*, II, 504 and 506.

76 *Ibid.*, II, 509.

77 Cecil Roth, *Anglo-Jewish Letters* (London, 1938), 125 ff.

78 Constitution (1798), Section 10.

79 RMMI, Nov. 11, 1805.

80 Sarah Sophia Deacon to Hyman Marks, Philadelphia, Aug. 25, 1816, MS., MIAr, asking for conversion.

81 L. G. Isaacs to Hyman Marks, London, June 9, 1824, MS., MIAr.

82 MBRS, Nov. 11 and 18, 1827, *et seqq.*

83 *Ibid.*, Apr. 26, 1829. Abraham Cuyk had come to Philadelphia from Holland about 1823, and some time later moved to Baltimore. According to his statement given to the Commissioners of Immigration in Baltimore in 1855, he was an agent to send German immigrants to the West: John P. Sanderson, *The Views and Opinions of American Statesmen on Foreign Immigration* (Philadelphia, 1856), 64-65.

84 See chapter 7, note 65.

85 Anna Nones to the Parnass and Adjuntos, Philadelphia, June 22, 1818, MS., MIAr.

86 Hannah [Anna] Nones to the Parnass and Adjuntos, Philadelphia, Aug. 31, 1818, MS., MIAr, stating that she and her three sons had complied "with the Sacred Rules and regulations of the Law of Moses agreeable to *Dinn Torach*."

87 David B. Nones to Hyman Marks, Philadelphia, Sept. 1, 1818, MS., MIAr.

88 Hyman Marks to David B. Nones, (Philadelphia), Sept. 4, 1818, MS., MIAr.

89 RMMI (August or September, 1826).

90 MBMI, Sept. 10, 1826.

91 Isaiah Nathans married Sarah Abrahams (the ritual name given to a

female convert), Feb. 4, 1802, Records of Marriages, Births and Deaths, MS., MIAr.

91a Mrs. S. J[ane Picken] Cohen, *Henry Luria; or, The little Jewish Convert: being contained in the memoir of Mrs. S. J. Cohen* (New York, 1860).

92 Certificate of Conversion (in Hebrew and English), Philadelphia, Nov. 22, 1819, MS., Lyons Collection, *PAJHS*, XXVII (1920), 231.

93 Certificate by Naphtali Phillips, New York, Nov. 26, 1819, MS., *ibid.*, 232.

94 Gratz Van Rensselaer, "The Original of Rebecca in Ivanhoe," *Century Magazine*, XXIV (1882), 682.

95 Lucy E. Lee Ewing, *Dr. John Ewing and Some of His Noted Connections* (Philadelphia, 1924), 55.

96 Invitation to the City Dancing Assembly, Feb. 22, 1802, Rollin G. Osterweis, *Rebecca Gratz, A Study in Charm* (New York, 1935), 79.

97 Rebecca Gratz to Maria Fenno Hoffman, Philadelphia, Oct. 20, 1817, MS., AJHS; Schappes, *op. cit.*, 137–139.

98 *Poulson's*, Dec. 13, 1819, "Married at Canewood, Clark County Kentucky on the 24th of November, Benjamin Gratz, Esq. of this city, to Miss Maria C. Gist, of the former place."

99 Rebecca Gratz to Maria Gist Gratz, (Philadelphia,) Dec. 25, 1819, MS., AJHS; Philipson, *op. cit.*, 21–22.

100 Max J. Kohler, "Some Jewish Factors in the Settlement of the West," *PAJHS*, XVI (1907), 31.

101 Simon Gratz, Will, Register of Wills, County of Philadelphia, No. 131, Book XIII, 598, mentions his sons Edward, Simon, Theodore and David, and his daughters Louisa, Caroline, Mary and Elizabeth. He does not provide for his wife, who presumably predeceased him. Her name, according to Rabbi Malcolm Stern, Genealogist of the American Jewish Archives, was Mary Smith.

102 Sabato Morais, Judah L. Hackenburg and Abraham Finzi to Louisa Gratz, Philadelphia, July 3, 1857, MS., Gratz Papers, HSP, "we ... have suffered you to undergo the religious purification, required by our laws for the admission of proselytes."

103 Jacob Gratz, Will, Register of Wills, County of Philadelphia, No. 10, XXXVII, 191, speaks of his son Robert Henry Gratz. There is no mention of a wife, and Morais, *op. cit.*, 432, says he was unmarried.

104 MBRS, Apr. 18, 1826.

105 Thomas Armstrong to Henrietta, daughter of Solomon Marache, *Poulson's*, May 24, 1806; Daniel Addis to Sophia, daughter of L. Van Amringe by the Rev. Dr. Smith, *Phi. Gaz.*, Jan. 8, 1808; John V. Cowell to Hannah, daughter of Solomon Marache, by the Rev. Mr. Engles, *ibid.*, Nov. 6, 1823; Wilson Jewell to Rachel, daughter of Solomon Lyons, by the Rev.

Dr. Staughton, *ibid.*, Apr. 26, 1824; George O. Van Amringe to Abby Ellis, by the Rev. Robert White, *ibid.*, Sept. 18, 1824; Jacob Crownin-shield to Harriet, daughter of Moses Wallach, by the Rev. Mr. Young, *Columbian Observer*, June 14, 1825; John Curry to Elizabeth, daughter of Joseph Levy, by the Rev. P. F. Mayer, *Poulson's*, March 7, 1826; Kar-man Levy to Katherine Shields, by Mayor Joseph Watson, *ibid.*, March 16, 1826; H. Emanuel Leviestein to Mrs. Sarah Ann Jackson, by Mayor Watson, *ibid.*, March 30, 1826; John Stoddart to Sarah, daughter of Abraham Moses, by the Rev. Stephen Smith, *ibid.*, Aug. 23, 1827. These were mostly the children of mixed marriages. Louis Bomeisler, who married a non-Jewess, had great difficulties in 1844 in having his children "made" Jews: MBMI, July 30, 1844. One of the most interesting cases was that of Abraham Gumpert, whose wife was not Jewish, but whose daughter Rebekah, "not born within the pale of Judaism," as Morais, *op. cit.*, 329, put it, was converted, married Benjamin Hyneman and be-came a noted author of poems and stories on Jewish themes.

106 When Levy Phillips proposed a by-law depriving of all synagogal honors "a Jew or Jewess who marries a Christian, and the son of a Jewess who is not made a Jew according to the law of Moses," it was voted down, MBMI, Oct. 16, 1823.

107 MBRS, Apr. 26, 1829.

107a Charles Crawford, *An Essay upon the Propagation of the Gospel* (Philadelphia, 1799), 33. In the LCP copy there is a contemporary note saying the man was later discovered to have been an imposter.

108 *Phi. Gaz.*, Jan. 3, 1823.

109 *Ibid.*

110 *Ibid.*, March 18, 1824.

111 Solomon Henry Jackson, *The Jew; being a Defence of Judaism against all Adversaries* (New York, 1823), Rosenbach, *op. cit.*, 224–226.

Chapter 13

1 Constitution (1798), Section 5.

2 MBMI, Apr. 24, 1785, June 28, 1789, July 3, 1791, Sept. 3, 1792, Sept. 16, 1795, Dec. 23, 1798, and Nov. 9, 1799; Agreement with Jacob Cohen, Sept. 3, 1792, MS., salary $200; Subscription List for Salary of Jacob Cohen, Sept. 16, 1795, MS., specifically as *hazan* and *shohet;* Subscription List for Salary of Jacob Cohen, Nov. 9, 1799, MS., MIAr.

3 RMMI, Jan. 11, 1806.

4 Seixas received $500 in 1803: Lyons Collection, *PAJHS*, XXVII (1920), 73; and received an increase of $250 in 1808: *ibid.*, *PAJHS*, XXI (1913), 162.

5 Jacob Cohen to Naphtali Phillips, [1800,] MS., MIAr.

6 Jacob Cohen to Naphtali Phillips, July 24, 1800, MS., MIAr.

7 Receipt of Abraham Cohen to Jonas Phillips, Tammuz 1, 1792, MS., MIAr, for teaching his child.

8 *Pa. Pac.*, March 1, 4, 6, 9 and 11, 1790.

9 Jacob Cohen to the Parnass, Gabay and Members of Mikveh Israel, July 7, 1800, MS., MIAr.

10 Jacob Cohen to Isaac Pesoa, May 30, 1804, MS., MIAr.

11 Agreement between Jacob Cohen and Isaac Pesoa, undated, MS., MIAr.

12 Simon Gratz to Moses Nathans, Samuel Hays and Benjamin I. Phillips, (January, 1805), MS., MIAr.

13 Aaron Levy to Simon Gratz, New York, Jan. 14, 1805, MS., MIAr. This Aaron Levy (1771–1852) was the son of Hayman Levy of New York; in 1805 he was *parnass* of Shearith Israel: Pool, *op. cit.*, 384.

14 *Shehita,* or License, for Isaac Lazarus by Jacob Hart, Sr. and Jacob Abrahams, New York, Jan. 13, 1805, MS., MIAr.

15 See note 12, *supra.*

16 Jacob Cohen to Simon Gratz, Jan. 21, 1805, and *ibid.*, Shebat 20, 1805, MSS., MIAr.

17 Isaac Lazarus to Isaac Pesoa, July 14, 1805, MS., MIAr.

18 RMMI, July 26, and Aug. 29, 1805.

19 *Ibid.*, Jan. 16, 1806.

20 *Ibid.*

21 *Ibid.*, Oct. 26, 1806.

22 Draft of Agreement between Isaac Lazarus and Zalegman Phillips, Jan. 14, 1807, MS., MIAr.

23 RMMI, Oct. 6, 1811.

24 Abraham H. Cohen to Benjamin I. Phillips, Philadelphia, May 12, 1812, MS., MIAr.

25 MBMI, Dec. 18, 1814 and July 16 and Oct. 1, 1815.

26 Abraham H. Cohen to Hyman Marks, Philadelphia, July 9, 1815, MS., MIAr.

27 Abraham H. Cohen to Benjamin I. Phillips, Feb. 28, 1814, and *ibid.*, Apr. 3, 1814, MSS., MIAr.

28 Gershom Seixas to Benjamin I. and Levy Phillips, New York, Sept. 9, 1814, MS., MIAr.

29 MBMI, Feb. 13, 1814, Cohen was requested to make up a new Hashkabah Book.

30 *Ibid.*, Oct. 29, 1815.

31 This Abraham Forst was born in 1782, and died Dec. 1, 1830: *Poulson's,* Dec. 3, 1830.

32 Abraham Forst to the Adjunta and Members, Sept. 12, 1813, MS., MIAr.

33 *Ibid.*

34 Davis, *op. cit.,* 35.

35 Alexander Wertheim, Circumcision Book, 1810-1829, MS., MIAr.

36 MBMI, Oct. 29, 1815.

37 Edward S. Daniels, "Extracts from Various Records of the Early Settlement of the Jews in the Island of Barbados, W.I.", *PAJHS,* XXVI (1918), 252. Carvalho had been discharged in 1805, was temporarily reinstated, and left finally in 1808.

38 Lyons Collection, *PAJHS,* XXI (1913), 161-164; Reznikoff and Engelman, *op. cit.,* 290. The contract was made with Carvalho on May 26, 1808, and he left in 1811, although he had been offered the Charleston post as early as March 15, 1809.

39 Reznikoff and Engelman, *op. cit.,* 114-115.

40 Mordecai Manuel Noah to Naphtali Phillips, Charleston, May 10, 1812; Goldberg, *op. cit.,* 51-53.

41 Emanuel Nunes Carvalho מפתח לשון עברית *A Key to the Hebrew Tongue* (Philadelphia, 1815), Rosenbach, *op. cit.,* 157, 159-160.

42 Emanuel Nunes Carvalho, *A Sermon, preached on Sunday,* י״א בתמוז ה׳ת׳ק׳ע׳ו *July 7, 1816, on Occasion of the Death of the Rev. Mr. Gershom Mendes Seixas* (Philadelphia, 1816), Rosenbach, *op. cit.,* 164-165.

43 Parnass and Adjunta to Emanuel Nunes Carvalho (in third person), (1816), MS., MIAr.

44 RMMI, Apr. 7, 1816.

45 *Ibid.,* Sept. 16, 1816.

46 Carvalho died March 20, 1817: *Poulson's,* March 21 and 25, 1817.

47 MBMI, Oct. 17, 1819. Morpurgo was then in Amsterdam; he later went to London, and in 1822 came to New York by way of Surinam to teach at Shearith Israel: David and Tamar de Sola Pool, *An Old Faith in the New World* (New York, 1955), 220-221. He returned to Surinam in 1829: Morpurgo MSS., Dutch West Indies Collection, AJAr.

48 J.M.S., Hebrew Acrostic Poem, (ca. 1818-20), MS., MIAr.

49 Naphtali Phillips, Naphtali Judah, Moses L. M. Peixotto, Jacob Hart, and M. L. Moses to the Parnass of Mikveh Israel, Sept. 30, 1816, MS., MIAr.

50 For five years before Carvalho came, and for four years after he left, Charleston's Beth Elohim had to get along with lay readers: Reznikoff and Engelman, *op. cit.,* 113-114 and 290.

51 From 1816 until 1828 there were no regular *hazanim;* Isaac B. Seixas served from 1828 to 1839; Lyons came in 1839, Lyons Collection, *PAJHS*, XXVIII (1920), 264–265.

52 RMMI, March 22, 1818.

53 Morais, *op. cit.*, 44. Hartwig Cohen (1783–1861) was *hazan* in Charleston from 1818 to 1823. Bernard M. Baruch is his great-grandson: Reznikoff and Engelman, *op. cit.*, 290 and 319.

54 MBMI, Sept. 14, 1817 and Apr. 18, 1819, at the latter of which compensation of $100 was voted to Bensadon "for his services in reading the Parasa."

55 Isaac B. Seixas (1782–1839) was a son of Benjamin and Zipporah Levy Seixas, and had been born in Philadelphia: N. Taylor Phillips, "The Levy and Seixas Families of Newport and New York," *PAJHS*, IV (1896), 211. He was acting *hazan* in Richmond sometime before 1806; Ezekiel and Lichtenstein, *op. cit.*, 241. He was asked first for the High Holy Days: MBMI, Sept. 14, 1817; and then to be *hazan* at $800 a year: *ibid.*, Oct. 5, 1817; which offer he turned down: *ibid.*, Oct. 26, 1817.

56 Eleazar S. Lazarus was the son of Samuel and the grandfather of the poetess Emma Lazarus. He was the Hebrew editor of the first Hebrew-English prayer book published in this country, Solomon Henry Jackson's *The Form of Daily Prayers* (New York, 1826): Pool, *Portraits*, 278. He was asked to officiate at the High Holy Days in 1821: RMMI, Sept. 23, 1821; and he was asked to be *hazan* three years later: Zalegman Phillips, Simon Gratz and Isaac Hays to Eleazar S. Lazarus, Philadelphia, May 9, 1824, MS., MIAr.

57 Jacob Mordecai to Zalegman Phillips, Simon Gratz and Isaac Hays, Richmond, June 15 (1824), MS., MIAr.

58 Morais, *op. cit.*, 72; Ullman died in 1829. MBRS, Jan. 25, 1824, records thanks to Moses Content for having officiated at services during the illness of Jacob Lippman.

59 MBRS, Apr. 26, 1818; Davis, *op. cit.*, 26.

60 MBRS, June 1, 1819.

61 *Ibid.*

62 Jacob Ezekiel to Dr. Henry Berkowitz, Cincinnati, Jan. 24, 1899, and P. de Cordova to Dr. Henry Berkowitz, Austin, Jan. 13, 1900, Davis, *op. cit.*, 38 and 40–41.

63 MBRS, Apr. 14, 1822.

64 Zalegman Phillips to Abraham Forst, Philadelphia, Sept. 15, 1829, "you are permitted to resume killing with John Hentz, and in no case with any of the butchers are you to leave the slaughter house until the meat is sealed;" Zalegman Phillips to Daniel Solis, Philadelphia, July 12, 1832, "George Waltman agrees that you shall kill with him every Sunday, Monday, Tuesday, Wednesday and Thursday which I desire you to do so that the Congregation will constantly have beef from one butcher every day in the week;" Samuel Runner to Zalegman Phillips, Philadel-

phia, Jan. 1, 1834, MSS., MIAr.: "i shall give up killing und less Mr. Solis will take thirty Dollars a year."

65 Zalegman Phillips to Daniel Solis, July 12, 1832, MS., MIAr.

66 "An Elector" to Zalegman Phillips, Philadelphia, Nov. 29, 1822, MS., MIAr.

67 Zalegman Phillips to Naphtali Phillips, Philadelphia, Dec. 12, 1830, MS., MIAr. His brother Jacob had applied for the position before: Jacob da Silva Solis to Simon Gratz, Greensburgh, N. Y., Dec. 9, 1822; but Gratz told him that the congregation did not need a *shohet:* Simon Gratz to Zalegman Phillips, Dec. 18, 1822, MSS., MIAr. Jacob da Silva Solis (1780–1829) came from England in 1803, and was engaged in business with his brother Daniel in Wilmington, Del. He moved to New Orleans in 1826, and was one of the founders of Congregation Shanarai Chasset in 1827: Schappes, *op. cit.,* 609.

68 *Shehita,* or License, for Daniel Solis by Isaac B. Seixas, Joseph Samuel and Naphtali Phillips, New York, Dec. 14, 1830, MS., MIAr.

69 MBMI, Nov. 1, 1818.

70 Isaac B. Seixas to Zalegman Phillips, Simon Gratz and Isaac Hays, Richmond, June 18, 1824, "under no circumstances would I accept an annual appointment, a competency to support my family unaided by a resort to other business is all that is desired that should have at least the appearance of permanency during satisfactory performance in office."

71 Zalegman Phillips, Simon Gratz and Isaac Hays to Eleazar S. Lazarus, Philadelphia, May 9, 19 and 23, 1824, and Eleazar S. Lazarus to Zalegman Phillips, Simon Gratz and Isaac Hays, New York, Apr. 16 and May 11 and 17, 1824, MSS., MIAr.

72 *Phi. Gaz.,* Dec. 11 and 12, 1823.

73 Simon Gratz to Abraham R. Brandon, Philadelphia, June 21, 1824, MS., MIAr.

74 MBMI, June 20, 1824; Zalegman Phillips, Simon Gratz, and Isaac Hays to Abraham Israel Keys, Philadelphia, June 21, 1824, MS., MIAr.

75 Isaac de Peza Massiah to the President and Adjunta, Barbados, Nov. 23, 1824, MS., MIAr.

76 Rebecca Gratz to Benjamin Gratz (Philadelphia,) Feb. 27, 1825, MS., AJHS; Philipson, *op. cit.,* 74–75.

77 Joseph J. Andrews (1753–1824) was born at Strassburg. Exactly when he came to this country is not known, but before 1798 he married Sarah (Sallie), the daughter of Haym Salomon. He was a member of Shearith Israel and was still in New York in 1808 when he made a complaint about the *shohet:* Lyons Collection, *PAJHS,* XXI (1913), 162–163. He appears in the *Philadelphia Directory* for 1813 as a teacher at 25 Sansom Street, and as a merchant in 1816. On Oct. 29, 1815, he applied for membership in Mikveh Israel, was admitted the following year, and became an elector on Sept. 27, 1818. His children were Eve (1798–1884) who married Abraham Elkin on July 10, 1816, Deborah (1800–?) who married Jonas Horwitz in Dec. 1817, Joseph J. (1801–1875) who married

Miriam Nones in 1849, Haym M. (1803–?) who married Clarissa King, Zalegman (1805–?) who married Esther Abrahams, Esther (1807–1894) who married Simeon Dreyfous, Miriam (1809–1880) who married Solomon Soher, Salomon (1811–1848) unmarried, Eleazer Lewis (1812–1848) who married Jessie Judah, Rachael (1814–?) who married Henry Morrison, Emily (1816–1819), and Samuel Elkin (1818–1846).

78 Abraham E. Israel (1773–1852) was *shamash* from 1824 until his death: Morais, *op. cit.*, 53. He left Amsterdam on June 13, 1804, and a journal of his trip to America is in the possession of Maxwell Whiteman. He arrived in Philadelphia in 1804, and declared his intention of settling on Jan. 9, 1811: Declaration Dockets, Oct. 1810–Sept. 1820, Department of Records, Archives Division, City of Philadelphia, 18. He signed the Rodeph Shalom constitution in 1810, and became an elector of Mikveh Israel on Oct. 1, 1815. He is listed as the "collector" for the *hebra* in the *Charter* (1824).

79 MBMI, Sept. 19, 1824.

80 Barnard Gratz to Simon Gratz, Baltimore, March 7, 1798, MS., in the possession of Edwin Wolf, 2nd.

81 Rebecca Gratz to Benjamin Gratz, March 7, 1819, MS., AJHS; Philipson, *op. cit.*, 17.

82 MBMI, March 16, 1784, mentions flour for the poor at Passover.

83 *Ibid.*, Oct. 6, 1811, speaks of getting insurance for the "Shool, House & Kitchen."

84 Netlad & Hyatt to the President and Managers of Mikveh Israel (1834), MS., MIAr.

85 Cash Book, 1823–1847, MS., RSAr, lists $8.80 paid to Watson for 100 pounds of *matzoth*.

86 Grinstein, *op. cit.*, 307.

87 Receipt from Isaac Rheinstrom, 1845, MS., MIAr. In the advertising section of *The Occident*, XIV (1857), 3, Rheinstrom calls himself "The oldest and best Matzah-baker in Philadelphia." *Jewish Exponent*, Dec. 22, 1899, gives the obituary of Isaac S. Cohen (1813–1899), who "came to this country in 1841, locating in Philadelphia, where he engaged in the Matzoth business, and had ever since resided."

88 Jacob I. Cohen, Will, Register of Wills, County of Philadelphia, No. 162, Book 8, p. 93.

89 Joseph Simon, Will, Lancaster, Feb. 15, 1804, MS., Archives of Lancaster County; Byars, *op. cit.*, 271. He left his silver plate "used or appropriated for the purposes of religious worship in my family and the two rolls containing the five books of Moses" to Mikveh Israel after the death of his son-in-law Levy Phillips who was to have the use of them during his lifetime.

90 The split of Bnai Jeshurun from Shearith Israel was brought about by a personal fight between Barrow E. Cohen and the officers of the synagogue. Haym M. Salomon sided with Cohen, and became one of the founders of the new congregation, Grinstein, *op. cit.*, 40–44.

91 Haym M. Salomon to Zalegman Phillips, New York, June 23, 1825, MS., MIAr.

92 Zalegman Phillips to Haym M. Salomon, Philadelphia, Oct. 17, 1825, MS., MIAr.

93 Haym M. Salomon to Zalegman Phillips, New York, Nov. 10, 1825; Zalegman Phillips to Haym M. Salomon, Nov. 13, 1825, MSS., MIAr.

94 Haym M. Salomon to Zalegman Phillips, New York, Nov. 30, 1825, MS., MIAr.

95 *Order of Service For Sabbath Evening* (פרשה יתרו) 5576, printed broadside, MIAr.

96 Abigail de Lyon to Benjamin Nones, Philadelphia, Oct. 2, 1795, MS., MIAr.

97 Raphael De Cordova to the Congregation, Aug. 5, 1816, MS., MIAr.

98 Michael E. Cohen to Zalegman Phillips, Philadelphia, Sept. 1, 1825, "Being honnored for many years past, in the time of the old Synagogue to be the תוקע and the same renew'd in the present one," he makes his donation.

99 MBRS, Nov. 4, 1810.

100 Michael E. Cohen to Zalegman Phillips, March 11, 1827, MS., MIAr, "Mr Hyman Gratz invited Christian Ladies (whom was in our synag. at time of worship) before the היכל and show'd them the ספרים . . ."

101 See chap. 12, note 11.

102 Jonas Phillips to the Adjunta (ca. 1792), MS., MIAr.

103 *Phi. Gaz.*, Aug. 6, 1800.

104 Jacob R. Cohen to Isaac Pesoa, March 15, 1802, MS., MIAr., "it is Impossible to live any longer in the House unless something be done with that Cistern." The cistern took the overflow from the *mikvah*.

105 MBMI, Feb. 13, 1814.

106 Certificate by Morris Spyers and S. de Wolff, Philadelphia, Aug. 15, 1836, MS., MIAr.

107 MBRS, Dec. 1, 1844, "Mr. Schoger proposed to the congregation to Establish a school & *Mikwe* for the use of our Religion and to appoint a committee to submit a plan." This was the first time Rodeph Shalom considered such a building of their own.

108 See chap. 2, note 8.

109 "An Extract from the Minutes," Oct. 9, 1825, MS., MIAr. The statement merely says that an interment had taken place then, but does not identify the person buried. It may well have been an infant.

110 See chap. 2, not 51.

111 Indenture between Samuel Hays, Simon Gratz, Zalegman Phillips and Abraham Myers Cohen and John Wilson Moore, Philadelphia, Sept. 13,

1831, MS., in the possession of Edwin Wolf, 2nd, speaks of the grant on March 30, 1782, of five lots to Michael Gratz—recorded in Patent Book I, p. 137—"which said lots the said Michael Gratz had purchased with the moneys for and on behalf of the Jewish Congregation of Philadelphia, as appears by the minutes of the said Congregation, and the covenant of the said Michael Gratz executed to the Trustees of the said Congregation bearing date the nineteenth day of September seventeen hundred and eighty two, intended to be recorded."

112 Indenture, *supra*. On Dec. 2, 1782, Michael Gratz and his wife conveyed the deed to Joseph Simon, Manuel Josephson, Barnard Gratz, Solomon Lyons and Samuel Hays as trustees, duly recorded in Deed Book, No. 31, p. 254.

113 Affidavit by David Franks, Philadelphia, Nov. 30, 1791, MS., MIAr; Sabato Morais, "Mickvé Israel Congregation of Philadelphia," *PAJHS*, I (1892), 21; MBMI, Nov. 27, 1791.

114 Indenture between Benjamin and Rachel Levy and Manuel Josephson, Joseph Simon, Barnard Gratz, Solomon Lyons and Samuel Hays, Philadelphia, May, 1793, MS., MIAr. This was not signed, so perhaps it was not valid.

115 Marcus, *op. cit.*, II, 69.

116 Hetty Levy to Simon Gratz, Baltimore, Nov. 26, 1812, MS., MIAr, "About eighteen years ago when my mother and aunt were in Philadelphia an offer was made my mother for this lot which she was advised by Mr. Benjamin Chew, not to accept as the time would come when it would be of considerable importance to herself or those she should leave behind her."

117 Moses Levy to Simon Gratz, Chestnut Hill, Jan. 1, 1813, MS., MIAr.

118 MBMI, Sept. 12, 1813.

119 *Ibid.*, Nov. 26, 1826. On Dec. 24, 1826, the resolution was amended to limit the height of the "barrier" to nine inches.

120 Pool, *op. cit.*, 81–87.

121 RMMI, Jan. 14, 1826; Morais, *op. cit.*, 202, where the Act, dated Apr. 14, 1828, is quoted in full.

122 Indenture, Sept. 13, 1831, *supra*. Payments of the $70 semiannual rent from Dr. Moore are recorded by Hyman Gratz on the lease from Apr. 12, 1832 to Aug. 1, 1851.

123 Morais, *op. cit.*, 203.

124 As in the case of Benjamin M. Clava, MBMI, March 16 and 20, 1785.

125 Scharf and Westcott, *op. cit.*, II, 1440; RMMI, July 24, 1814, when Benjamin I. Phillips and John Moss were appointed a committee to supervise the building of a "House in the Beth Chaim which is to be of Brick Two stories high."

126 *Constitution and By-Laws of the* חברה של בקור חולים וגמילות חסדים (Philadelphia, 1824), 12. Rosenbach, *op. cit.*, 222–223.

127 Grinstein, *op. cit.*, 323–324.

128 Leon H. Elmaleh and J. Bunford Samuel, *The Spruce Street Burial Ground* (Philadelphia, 1906), 11, 15, 17 and 18, note the removal of the remains of members of the Hackenburg family, including Mrs. Lewis Allen, to Mt. Sinai.

129 RMMI, Nov. 26, 1816, consideration of the "propriety of burying David Nathan who by a verdict of the Coroner's Jury was found to have destroyed himself by taking Laudanum."

130 Judith Pettigrew was buried along the fence: Elmaleh and Samuel, *op. cit.*, 15.

131 MBRS, Nov. 7, 1811, Rosetta de Jung asked to have her son buried, "but since she did not marry in accordance with The Law of Moses and Israel, we could not give our consent that such a son be buried in our Cemetery."

132 Morais, *op. cit.*, 203. Rebecca Gratz to Lewis Allen, May, 1841, MS., MIAr, writes on behalf of the burial of the Negro.

133 MBMI, Sept. 10, 1829.

134 *Pa. Gaz.*, Sept. 12 and 19, 1751, Levy's notice to vandals in which he said that the fence had been destroyed, and that there was a "brick wall now erected."

135 Scharf and Westcott, *op. cit.*, II, 1440.

136 RMMI, 1803; Simon Gratz and Benjamin Nones, "Committee for Building Wall round Burial Ground," Note to the Order of Aaron Levy, Philadelphia, Apr. 30, 1804; Lyons Collection, *PAJHS*, XXVII (1920), 229.

137 William J. Duane, A Book of Original Entries, MS., 69, LCP.

138 See chap. 12, note 12.

139 *The Laws of Pennsylvania, in Relation to The Board of Health and the Health Laws of the City & County of Philadelphia* (Philadelphia, 1848), 32–33.

140 MBRS, Oct. 6, 1811.

141 Committee Report, Philadelphia, Jan. 13, 1850, MS., RSAr.; Davis, *op. cit.*, 63–64.

Chapter 14

1 Benjamin Franklin, "Observations concerning the Increase of Mankind, Peopling of Countries, etc.," Smyth, *op. cit.*, III, 72.

2 Directors of the Dutch West India Company to Peter Stuyvesant,

Amsterdam, Apr. 26, 1655, Oppenheim, *op. cit.*, 8, gave the Jews permission to stay "provided the poor among them shall not become a burden to the company or to the community, but be supported by their own nation."

3 *Rules for the St. Andrew's Society in Philadelphia* (Philadelphia, 1751), 3.

4 *Rules and Constitutions of the Society of the Sons of St. George* (Philadelphia, 1772), 5–6.

5 *Charter and By-Laws of The Society of the Sons of St. George* (Philadelphia, 1840), 7.

6 *Ibid.*, 6.

7 Grinstein, *op. cit.*, 103, Bernard Hart.

8 *Charter* (1840), 44–56.

9 No other reference to Lindo in Philadelphia has been found. For Moses Lindo, see Reznikoff and Engelman, *op. cit.*, 24–34.

10 Joseph Ricardo was listed as a merchant on North 3rd St. in Hogan, *op. cit.*, 36; he was obviously of English origin, and may even have been one of the brothers of David Ricardo. George Alexander Kohut, "A Subscription List of the Year 1773," *PAJHS*, VI (1897), 155, notes a Joseph Ricardo of Philadelphia who subscribed to David Levi's *Seder ha-Tephilot;* however, there is no record of a Ricardo participating in Jewish communal activities. *Am. Dai. Adv.*, July 10, 1794, announced that Ricardo's partnership with Henry Capper had been broken up in February.

11 John Moss (1774–1847) came to Philadelphia in 1796 and married Rebecca, the daughter of Eleazer Lyons, on Feb. 15, 1797: Sanford A. Moss, *Genealogy of John Moss and his Wife Rebecca (Lyons) Moss* (Rutland, 1937), 6–8. He petitioned for naturalization on July 14, 1803. Moss became a member of the St. George Society in 1810 and was a Steward in 1826–29.

12 Samuel Moss, John's brother, followed him to America some years later. He became a member of the Society in 1813.

13 Jacob Moss, another brother, born in 1791, arrived in Baltimore in 1811, and on May 28, 1813, declared his intention to settle in Philadelphia: Declaration Dockets, Oct. 1810–Sept. 1820, MS., Department of Records, Archives Division, City of Philadelphia, 394. He applied for membership in Mikveh Israel in 1815 and became a member of the Society in 1819.

14 Joseph Lyons Moss (1804–1874) was a son of John. In 1828 he married Julia Levy, the daughter of Solomon Hyam and Rebecca Hendricks Levy, of New York: Moss, *op. cit.*, 14–15. He became a member of the Society in 1828 and was Steward in 1830–40.

15 Joseph Moravia Moss was a son of Samuel. He became a member of the Society in 1836.

16 Isaac B. Phillips (1794/5–1851) was apparently no relation of the Jonas Phillips family. He and his brother Robert applied for membership in Mikveh Israel in 1813, shortly after their arrival from England. Isaac

married John Moss' daughter Sarah on Jan. 16, 1822: Moss, *op. cit.*, 8; and became a member of the Society in 1819. It is interesting to note that he was a member of the *hebra* before 1818 and its treasurer in 1823–24.

17 Lyon J. Levy arrived in Philadelphia some time before 1830, where he is listed in *Desilver's PD* (Philadelphia, 1830), 112. He joined the Society in 1832.

18 Wolf Benjamin (1770–1835) was born at London, arrived in New York from Jamaica in 1816, and on Feb. 24, 1818, declared his intention of settling in Philadelphia: Declaration Dockets, Oct. 1810–Sept. 1820, 851. He became active in Rodeph Shalom and was for some years both reader and *parnass:* Davis, *op. cit.*, 40–41. He became a member of the Society in 1829, and was, according to his will, a "rectifying distiller."

19 James Hardie, *PD* (Philadelphia, 1793), 206.

20 Israel Abrahams, *Jewish Life in the Middle Ages* (Philadelphia, 1896), 333–335.

21 Pool, *op. cit.*, 96–104.

22 *Constitution* (1810), Article 15.

23 *Ibid.*, Article 16.

24 List of Burials, MS., RSAr; Davis, *op. cit.*, 14.

25 *Constitution* (1810), Article 17.

26 *Constitution and Rules to be Observed and Kept by the Friendly Society of St. Thomas's African Church* (Philadelphia, 1797).

27 *Stephen's PD* (Philadelphia, 1796), supplement, 18; *Claypoole's,* Oct. 8, 1796.

28 *Constitution of the Hebra* (1824), says on its title-page that the society was organized in the month of *Heshvan, 5574,* which would have been the fall of 1813. The Minute Book begins Oct. 6, 1813.

29 MBMI, Feb. 13, 1814.

30 *Constitution* (1824), Article 2.

31 MBH, Feb. 20, 1820, MS., MIAr.

32 *Constitution* (1824), Article 19.

33 *Ibid.*, Article 2.

34 *Ibid.*, Article 10.

35 *Ibid.*, Article 3.

36 MBH, March 31, 1816.

37 *Constitution* (1824), Article 14.

38 Receipt Book of the *Hebra,* 1819, MS., MIAr. Lyon Jacobson first appears on the Rodeph Shalom subscription list the same year: Davis, *op. cit.*, 143.

39 *Constitution* (1824), Article 13.

40 MBH, July 1, 1821.

41 *Constitution* (1824), 13–14.

42 *Ibid.,* 12–13.

43 *Ibid.,* Article 14 and p. 13.

44 *Ibid.,* 12.

45 Joseph Simon Cohen (1788/90–1858) was the son of Solomon and Bell Simon Cohen. He went to the University of Pennsylvania and graduated in 1813: *Poulson's,* Aug. 8, 1813.

46 *Constitution* (1824), Article 14.

47 *Hebra* Committee Report, Philadelphia, May 2, 1830, MS., AJHS.

48 MBH, Sept. 18, 1814. This was, of course, Abraham Haim Cohen, the acting *hazan.*

49 *Ibid.,* and Jan. 1, 1815.

50 *Ibid.,* Oct. 8, 1826, the request was made by David Othias of Morocco to Levy Phillips.

51 Morais, *op. cit.,* 144–145.

52 MBH, March 20, 1817.

53 *Ibid.,* Oct. 11, 1823; and *Poulson's,* Oct. 14, 1823.

54 Morais, *op. cit.,* 145.

55 For the general background of philanthropy in Philadelphia, see O. A. Pendleton, "Poor Relief in Philadelphia, 1790–1840," *Pa. Mag.,* LXX (1946), 161–172.

56 W. C. Heffner, *History of Poor Relief Legislation in Pennsylvania, 1682–1913* (Philadelphia, 1913), 171.

57 Pendleton, *op. cit.,* 163.

58 See note 27, *supra.*

59 See chap. 3, note 96.

60 *The Constitution of the Female Association of Philadelphia, for the Relief of Women and Children, in Reduced Circumstances* (Philadelphia, 1803), 2–3.

61 *Ibid.,* 32.

62 Pendleton, *op. cit.,* 163.

63 *Constitution and By-Laws of The Orphan Society of Philadelphia* (Philadelphia, 1815), 10; *Fourth Annual Report* (Philadelphia, 1819), 9; *Fifty-Fifth Annual Report* (Philadelphia, 1870), 6–7, containing an obituary of Rebecca Gratz, the last survivor of the original board.

64 William White, *A Sermon on The Drawing of Moses out of the Waters. Delivered Before the Orphan Society of Philadelphia, On Sunday, the 5th of March, 1815* (Philadelphia, 1815).

65 *Phi. Gaz.*, Jan. 30, 1822.

66 Rebecca Gratz to Maria Gist Gratz, (1832,) MS., AJHS; Philipson, *op. cit.*, 145–146.

67 *Fifty-Fifth Annual Report*, 7.

68 *Constitution*, 13, 15, 19, 20; *First Annual Report* (Philadelphia, 1816), 24, 30, 32; *Second Annual Report* (Philadelphia, 1817), 12.

69 *Constitution*, 19 and 25; *First Annual Report*, 27.

70 *Second Annual Report*, 15.

71 *Fourth Annual Report*, 15.

72 *First Annual Report*, 47.

73 *Third Annual Report*, 10; *Seventh Annual Report* (Philadelphia, 1822), 10.

74 *Eighth Annual Report* (Philadelphia, 1823), 3–7.

75 Rebecca Gratz to Maria Gist Gratz, Feb. 9, 1822, MS., AJHS; Philipson, *op. cit.*, 53.

76 *Poulson's*, Jan. 28, 1822.

77 *Ibid.*, Feb. 20, 1822.

78 Aaron Levy Jr., to Benjamin Phillips, March 30, 1814, MS., MIAr.

79 Mrs. Levy to Hyman Marks, July 13, (1815); Subscription List, Philadelphia, July 23, 1815, MSS., MIAr; and RMMI, July 16, 1815.

80 Hirsch Mendelson to the Parnass, Sept. 1, 1815, MS., MIAr.

81 Lewis Lewis to Hyman Marks, June 3, 1817, MS., MIAr.

82 David Montefiore to Hyman Marks, Feb. 16, 1819, MS., MIAr.

83 *Rules of the Philadelphia Dispensary for the Medical Relief of the Poor . . . and the Annual Report for 1815* (Philadelphia, 1816), 2.

84 *Ibid.*, 5.

85 *Rules and Regulations of the Northern Dispensary for the Medical Relief of the Poor . . . And the Annual Report for 1817* (Philadelphia, 1818), 12; *Poulson's*, Jan. 20, 1818.

86 MBH, Feb. 20, 1820.

87 *Poulson's*, Apr. 14, 1830, gives Wertheim's obituary, stating that he had been "an active officer to the Board of Health, for almost ten years."

88 MBH, Apr. 27, 1823. Hays had graduated from the Medical School in 1820, *Catalogue of the Medical Graduates of the University of Pennsylvania* (Philadelphia, 1839), 36.

89 *Phi. Gaz.*, Jan. 19, 1822.

90 Pendleton, *op. cit.*, 164–166.

91 *Ibid.*, 166.

92 Morais, *op. cit.*, 127; *Occ.*, I (1843), 451.

93 *The Constitution of The Female Hebrew Benevolent Society of Philadelphia*, (Philadelphia, 1825); Rosenbach, *op. cit.*, 233–234.

94 *Ibid.*, 7–8.

95 *Ibid.*, 6.

96 *Loc. cit.*

97 *Ibid.*, 8.

98 *Loc. cit.*

99 *Ibid.*, 6.

100 *Ibid.*, 7–8, "And that every delicacy may be secured to those who have seen 'better days,' a select committee will be formed at the next session, through which hands relief may be secretly bestowed on reduced families, should such unhappily be found in our congregation." Because of this provision, still adhered to, the minute books of the Society were not permitted to be used for this history.

101 Rebecca Machado Phillips was the widow of Jonas Phillips.

102 Mrs. Bell Cohen was the widow of Solomon Myers Cohen, and the daughter of Joseph Simon, of Lancaster.

103 Mrs. Bravo was the widow of Jacob M. Bravo, of Jamaica, who was buried in Spruce Street, Apr. 29, 1812. In his Commonplace Book under date of Dec. 15, 1812, Benjamin Rush noted that he received $20 for attendance on her husband, who died in the city; "I did not expect the payment of this bill, having seldom, or perhaps never received the payment of a bill under equal circumstances. Mrs. Bravo was a Jewess. Blush Christians! who forget or neglect to practice similar acts of justice": Corner, *op. cit.*, 310; also Mrs. S. Bravo to Benjamin Rush, Kingston, Jamaica, Nov. 9, 1812, Rush MSS. B I, 89, LCP. She must have returned to Philadelphia some time before 1819.

104 *Constitution*, 9–12.

105 *Ibid.*, 11.

106 This is based upon Edwin Wolf, 2nd's recollection of what he saw in the original minute book of the United Hebrew Benevolent Society.

107 Wolf Benjamin to the President and Managers of Mikveh Israel, Sept. 22, 1822, MS., MIAr, requested permission to ask for offerings in the synagogue; and Wolf Benjamin to the Officers and Junto of Rodeph Shalom, (1823,) MS., RSAr, thanking them for allowing offerings to be solicited.

108 Bernard D. Rosenblum, *History of Jewish Philanthropy in Philadelphia* (1940), unpublished typescript. Rosenblum had access to the original constitution of 1822 and the first minute book, both of which have since been lost or misplaced, and could not be located for examination.

109 *Constitution and By-Laws of the "United Hebrew Beneficent Society of Philadelphia"* (Philadelphia, 1829); Rosenbach, *op. cit.*, 316–317.

110 *Ibid.*, Article 2.

111 Rosenblum, *op. cit.*, 6.

112 *Loc. cit.*

113 *Constitution,* Articles 2 and 10.

114 *Ibid.*, Article 10, Section 2.

115 MBH, July 5, 1829. This was in conflict with the amendment to the Constitution made on Feb. 20, 1820, which opened membership to non-members of Mikveh Israel.

116 *Constitution of the United Hebrew Benevolent Society,* Article 8.

117 *Ibid.*, Article 9.

118 *Ibid.*, 18.

119 Rosenblum, *op. cit.*, 6.

120 *Rules of the Philadelphia Dispensary for the Medical Relief of the Poor . . . and the Annual Report for 1823* (Philadelphia, 1824), 7; *Constitution of the U.H.B.S.,* 14, "The Society shall subscribe to the City Dispensary *five dollars,* annually, and to the Northern and Southern Dispensaries *three dollars* each, annually."

121 *Rules of the Southern Dispensary for the Medical Relief of the Poor . . . and the Annual Report for 1823* (Philadelphia, 1824), 6; according to Rosenblum a $5.00 subscription to the Northern Dispensary was also paid, but the *Report* of that branch does not list the Society as a member.

122 Pendleton, *op. cit.*, 169.

123 This is based solely on negative evidence; no mention of Jews in the Almshouse has been found.

124 *Poulson's,* Jan. 16, 1829; *Constitution of the United Hebrew Benevolent Society,* 18. Abraham Elkin was elected treasurer, Joseph J. Andrews secretary, and Jacob Phillips, John Moss, Simpson Morris, Michael E. Cohen, Lewis Allen, Simeon Dreyfous, David Pesoa and Hart Stork managers.

125 Zalegman Phillips and Wolf Benjamin to the Parnass, Treasurer, and Junta of Mikveh Israel, Philadelphia, Oct. 12, 1825, MS., MIAr.

126 MBRS, Apr. 14, 1811.

127 Louis Bomeisler, Mayer Ullman and A. B. Cohen to Bnai Jeshurun, Philadelphia, Jan. 25, 1827, MS., RSAr; Davis, *op. cit.*, 44–45.

128 John T. Hart, M. M. Noah, M. Marks, and Rowland Davies to the Parnass and Adjuntos of Rodeph Shalom, New York, Jan. 14, 1827, MS., RSAr; Davis, *op. cit.*, 43–44.

129 Naphtali Phillips to Hyman Marks, New York, Aug. 21, 1817; and Naphtali Phillips, Naphtali Judah, M. L. Moses, Eleazer S. Lazarus, M.L.M. Peixotto, and Aaron Levy to Mikveh Israel, New York, Aug. 21, 1817, MSS., MIAr.

130 J. Levi to the Parnass, Adjuntos and Committee of Mikveh Israel, Barbados, Apr. 15, 1819, MS., MIAr.

131 Subscription Book of the New Synagogue, 1819–1825, MS., MIAr.

132 MBMI, Sept. 11 and Oct. 9, 1825.

133 J[oseph] J[onas], "The Jews in Ohio," *The Occident*, II (1844), 40.

134 MBMI, *loc. cit.*

135 *Ibid.*, Oct. 15, 1826.

136 Davis, *op. cit.*, 127.

Chapter 15

1 For the general background of the period in brief form, see Butterfield, *op. cit.*, 52–59.

2 *Poulson's*, June 15, 1812.

3 *Poulson's*, Aug. 26, 1812. Henry Solomon was the son of Myer S. and Catherine Bush Solomon. Zalegman Phillips married his sister Arabella (1786–1826) at Baltimore in 1805, *Phi. Gaz.*, Oct. 29, 1805.

4 *Poulson's*, July 4, 1812. Elijah Gratz Etting (1795–1849) was the son of Reuben and Frances Gratz Etting: Morais, *op. cit.*, 393. The whole Reuben Etting family moved back to Baltimore about 1825.

5 See chap. 11, note 74.

6 *Poulson's*, Jan. 9, 1812. Among the Jews mentioned as dead and missing in the same paper on Jan. 4, 1812, were Joseph Jacobs and his daughter Elizabeth, Mrs. Mordecai Marks, Charlotte, the daughter of the erstwhile Philadelphia peddler, Solomon Raphael, and a child of Barack Judah.

7 *Phi. Gaz.*, Sept. 26, and Oct. 7, 1811, lists Joseph Gratz as a member of the American Republican Committee of Vigilance for the Middle Ward.

8 Rebecca Gratz to Benjamin Gratz, Aug. 21, (1812,) MS., AJHS; Philipson, *op. cit.*, 4.

9 Nassy, *Lettre Politico-Theologico-Morale sur les Juifs*, 101; Seeligmann, *op. cit.*, 36.

10 Abram Kanof, "Uriah Phillips Levy: The Story of a Pugnacious Commodore," *PAJHS*, XXXIX (1949), 1–66, gives an accurate story of his life. The material used here concerning his early career was taken by Kanof from a transcript of the Proceedings of the Court of Inquiry of 1857 from the original records in the National Archives, and is based on Levy's own testimony.

11 Kanof, *op. cit.*, 3.

12 *Ibid.*, 4.

13 *Ibid.*, 4–5.

14 *Ibid.*, 5.

15 *The Naval Monument, containing Official and Other Accounts of all the Battles Fought between The Navies of the United States and Great Britain . . . To which is annexed A Naval Register of the United States* (Boston, 1816), Levi Harby, midshipman, June 18, 1812, Uriah Levy, sailing master, Oct. 21, 1812, J. B. Nones, midshipman, Feb. 1, 1814, and Ezekiel Salomon, purser, May 26, 1814.

16 Kanof, *op. cit.*, 5–7.

17 Leon Hühner, "Jews in the War of 1812," *PAJHS*, XXVI (1918), 194. These included Harby, Manuel Joseph, and Morris Russel and William Wolf of Savannah.

18 Mordecai M. Noah, *Travels in England, France, Spain, and the Barbary States, in the Years 1813–14 and 1815* (New York, 1819) is an autobiographical account of Noah's adventures from the time he sailed on May 28, 1813.

19 Goldberg, *op. cit.*, 34–41.

20 Mordecai M. Noah to Naphtali Phillips, Baltimore, June 10, 1811, Goldberg, *op. cit.*, 45–46.

21 Noah, *op. cit.*, 2.

22 Goldberg, *op. cit.*, 48–67.

23 Scharf and Westcott, *op. cit.*, II, 1137.

24 Noah, *op. cit.*, 2.

25 *Ibid.*, 2–59.

26 Scharf and Westcott, *op. cit.*, I, 563.

27 *Poulson's*, May 8, 1813.

28 See chap. 11, note 16.

29 *Phi. Gaz.*, Nov. 18, 1811.

30 Byars, *op. cit.*, 278.

31 Horace Carter Hovey and Richard Ellsworth Call, *Mammoth Cave of Kentucky, an Illustrated Manual* (Louisville, 1899), 11.

32 *Book of the First Troop of Philadelphia City Cavalry, 1774–1914* (Philadelphia, 1914), 79; *By-Laws, Muster-Roll, and Papers selected from the Archives of the First Troop Philadelphia City Cavalry* (Philadelphia, 1840), 26.

33 *PAr*, 6th Series, VII, 60 and 860.

34 *Ibid.*, VII, 94, 523, 529, and VIII, 570 and 592.

35 *Poulson's*, July 22 and Sept. 17, 1813.

36 *Ibid.*, July 31, 1813.

37 *Ibid.*, Sept. 22, 1813.

38 *Ibid.*, Sept. 23, 1813.

39 *Ibid.*, Oct. 2, 1813.

40 Isaac De Young (Jung) (1795–1868) came to America with his father about 1803: Morais, *op. cit.*, 460.

41 Morais, *op. cit.*, 460; *The Constitution and Register of Membership of the General Society of the War of 1812* (Philadelphia, 1908), 45. The 100th Anniversary of De Young's enlistment was celebrated by the Society of the War of 1812 and the Admiral DuPont Post, No. 24, G.A.R.: *Jewish Exponent*, June 7, 1912.

42 Morais, *op. cit.*, 460.

43 *Ibid.*, 459.

44 *Catalogue of the Medical Graduates of the University of Pennsylvania* (Philadelphia, 1839), 55; *Poulson's*, Aug. 27, 1812; Thomas H. S. Hamersly, *Complete Army and Navy Register of the United States of America, from 1776 to 1887* (New York, 1888), 71. His commission in the 2nd Regiment of Artillery was dated May 1, 1812.

45 Hamersly, *op. cit.*, 567. His commission as Assistant Surgeon in the Navy was dated July 18, 1809; Phillips resigned in 1824.

46 *Poulson's*, Aug. 31, 1814.

47 *PAr*, 6th Series, VIII, 398.

48 *Ibid.*, VII, 75 and 603.

49 Daniel Bowen, *A History of Philadelphia . . . including the names of over 2000 patriotic officers and citizen soldiers who volunteered their services in defence of this city, when threatened by an hostile army in 1812–13 & 14* (Philadelphia, 1839), 45.

50 *Poulson's*, Sept. 6, 1814.

51 *PAr*, 6th Series, VII, 92, 206, and 633.

52 Joseph B. Nones, Naval Reminiscences From the Years 1812 to 1822, MS., AJHS. All this information about Nones is contained in these autobiographical notes.

53 The commission as midshipman was dated Feb. 1, 1814, Hamersly, *op. cit.*, 533.

54 *Hebrew Leader*, Aug. 22, 1879; *Army and Navy Journal*, Sept. 6, 1879; *New York Times*, Apr. 2, 1877; *New York Ledger*, Dec. 8, 1860 and Jan. 5, 1861; *New York Herald*, Nov. 1, 1875.

55 *PAr*, 6th Series, VII, 481, 487, VIII, 398, and IX, 143.

56 Nones, Naval Reminiscences, *supra*.

57 Hühner, *op. cit.*, 186–188.

58 Rebecca Gratz to Benjamin Gratz, (1814,) MS., AJHS; Philipson, *op. cit.*, 5.

59 Rebecca Gratz to Benjamin Gratz, (Sept., 1814,) MS., AJHS; Philipson, *op. cit.*, 7–8.

60 Rebecca Gratz to Benjamin Gratz, Philadelphia, Sept. 20, 1814, MS., AJHS; Philipson, *op. cit.*, 6–7.

61 "Extracts from the Diary of Thomas Franklin Pleasants, 1814," *Pa. Mag.*, XXXIX (1915), 326, 330–332, and 416–417.

62 *PAr*, 6th Series, VII, 94.

63 *Poulson's*, Sept. 15 and 19, 1814.

64 *Ibid.*, Sept. 22 and Oct. 3, 1814. Among these were Eleazer Cohen, Jacob David, Joseph I. Cohen, Aaron Levy, Joseph Levy, Samuel Moss, Abraham Wolf, and the firm of Levy and Hyneman.

65 MBH, Sept. 18, 1814, and Jan. 1, 1815.

66 MBMI, Dec. 18, 1814.

67 Bowen, *op. cit.*, t.p.

68 The "Act passed at the December session of the Assembly of 1824," was enacted into law on Feb. 26, 1825, and confirmed on Jan. 5, 1826: Hartogensis, *op. cit.*, 96–98.

69 *Phi. Gaz.*, June 4, 1811. Gratz gave a commencement oration on the Schools of Ancient Greece and Rome, and received his B.A.

70 *Poulson's*, Jan. 2, 1813.

71 *Ibid.*, May 27, 1813.

72 *Ibid.*, Feb. 26, 1818. He was mentioned as being on committees, *ibid.*, Feb. 23, 1816, Feb. 24, 1817, and March 9, 1819.

73 *Martin's Bench and Bar*, 273.

74 *Poulson's*, June 1, 1816.

75 *Ibid.*, Nov. 11, 1819.

76 Nathan Nathans was the son of Moses Nathans (1749–1815), who appointed Meredith his son's guardian in his will. He died on Feb. 24, 1815: *Poulson's*, Feb. 25, 1815.

77 Samuel B. How to William Meredith, New Hope, Dec. 14, 1815, MS., in the possession of Dr. S. Weir Newmayer, of Philadelphia.

78 Nathan Nathans to William Meredith, Brighton, May 21, 1815, MS., in the possession of Dr. S. Weir Newmayer, of Philadelphia.

79 *Poulson's*, Sept. 27, 1815, July 30, 1816, Sept. 17, 1817, and July 31, 1818.

80 *Ibid.*, Aug. 9, 1816.

81 *Ibid.*, Oct. 4, 1816.

82 Butterfield, *op. cit.*, 70–72.

83 Marshall B. Davidson, *Life in America* (Boston, 1951), II, 346–347.

84 *Phi. Gaz.*, Oct. 21, 1823.

85 *The World Almanac* (New York, 1955), 633.

86 These included Joseph Lyons, Benjamin, Jacob, Joseph, Simon and Hyman Gratz, Henry Solomon, Abraham M., Joseph S., and Michael E. Cohen, Moses Spyers, Jacob, David, and Isaiah Nathans, Isaac Hays, Hyman Marks, Robert Phillips, Levy Arnold, Jonas Weinberg, Abel Lazarus, Abraham L. and Naphtali Hart, John Moss, Isaac Moses, Jr., Edward Dreyfous, and Samuel Davis: *Poulson's*, Sept. 21, 27, and 28, 1815, July 30, Aug. 1, and Sept. 16, 1816, Sept. 17, and 26, 1817, July 20, and 31, Aug. 19, and Oct. 1, and 12, 1818, July 1, Sept. 23, and 28, and Oct. 1, 1819, Sept. 22, and 25, 1820, July 30, and Sept. 28, 1821, July 31, 1822, Sept. 19, and Oct. 9, 1826, Aug. 21, and 25, and Sept. 5, 13, and 23, 1828, and Sept. 29, and Oct. 2, 1829; *Phi. Gaz.*, July 17, and Sept. 13, 18, 19, 25, 27, and 29, 1823; *United States Gazette*, Sept. 23, 26, and 28, 1825.

87 These included Zalegman Phillips, Samuel M. Solomon, Wolf Benjamin, Solomon Joseph, Reuben Etting, Aaron Levy, Jr., Joseph Phillips, and Nathan Nathans: *Aurora*, Sept. 7, and 23, 1816; *Phi. Gaz.*, Aug. 29, Sept. 13, and 19, 1823; *The Democratic Press*, Feb. 2, 6, 7, and 17, 1826. In addition, David B. Nones and S. B. Lasalle, not otherwise active, supported an independent candidate for sheriff: *Poulson's*, Oct. 2, 1829.

88 *Poulson's*, Oct. 16, 1817. He won against the Democrat, William Shaw, 2827 to 1604.

89 *Ibid.*, Sept. 23, and Oct. 14, 1819.

90 Elkan Nathan Adler, *London, Jewish Community Series,* (Philadelphia, 1930), 168.

91 *Poulson's*, Nov. 24, 1819.

92 *Phi. Gaz.*, Oct. 21, 1823.

93 Zalegman Phillips, *To the Electors of the Second Congressional District of Pennsylvania* (Philadelphia, 1828), 6–7.

94 Scharf and Westcott, *op. cit.*, I, 611.

95 *Columbian Observer*, Jan. 11, 1825.

96 Rebecca Gratz to Benjamin Gratz, Feb. 27, 1825, MS., AJHS; Philipson, *op. cit.,* 76, and xiii. Anna Gratz married Thomas Hart Clay.

97 Phillips headed the Hickory Club committee for the celebration of the 49th anniversary of American independence, *Columbian Observer,* June 24, 1825.

98 *The Balance,* Jan. 22, 1825.

99 *USGaz.,* March 9, 1825.

100 *Ibid.,* Jan. 26, and 29, June 15, and July 9, 1825.

101 *Ibid.,* March 14, 1825.

102 *Columbian Observer,* Jan. 26, 1825.

103 Marquis de Lafayette to Joseph Wheaton, La Grange, Dec. 20, 1823, from unidentified clipping which said it was reprinted from the *National Intelligencer.*

104 Kanof, *op. cit.,* 56–57: *USGaz.,* March 31, 1825.

105 *USGaz.,* July 22, 1825.

106 *Ibid.,* March 8, 1825.

107 MBMI, July 23, 1826.

108 *The Democratic Press,* Feb. 2, 1826.

109 *Ibid.,* Feb. 6, 7, and 17, 1826.

110 *USGaz.,* Sept. 28, 1825.

111 *Aurora,* Oct. 3 and 16, 1828. He won against John B. Linn, 4568 to 3763.

112 Scharf and Westcott, *op. cit.,* I, 619.

113 Phillips, *To the Electors, supra.*

114 *The Democratic Press,* Aug. 29, 1828.

115 *Poulson's,* Sept. 29, 1829.

116 *Ibid.,* Jan. 17 and 21, 1829.

117 *Ibid.,* March 14, 1829.

Chapter 16

1 See chap. 10, notes 47 and 49.

2 See chap. 3, notes 39 and 40.

3 See chap. 13, note 41.

4 Rebecca Gratz to Mrs. Ogden Hoffman, March 9, 1818, MS., Rosenbach Collection, AJHS; S. I. Cohen, *Elements of Jewish Faith. Translated from the Hebrew* (Richmond, 1817) and (Philadelphia, 1823), Rosenbach, *op. cit.*, 172–173 and 210–211. Simon Gratz's copy of the Richmond edition is at Gratz College. It is not certain whether S. I. Cohen was the same as H. Cohen, who advertised that he taught Hebrew at Mr. Hart's on Vine St.: *Poulson's*, July 7, 1818.

5 A large collection of these, many with early notes of ownership of Philadelphia Jews, is at Dropsie College. No study has yet been made of the liturgical books used in the early days of this country, based on the actual books owned by American Jews. It is interesting to note that among other Hebrew text books the bookseller N. G. Dufief advertised "Levi's form of Prayers, according to the custom of the German and Polish Jews, 6 vol. royal 8vo, *splendid,*" *Poulson's,* July 2, 1813.

6 See chap. 13, note 42.

7 Rosenbach, *op. cit.*, 56–60, 170, 190, 226, 235, and 240–241.

8 Some of these were at Gratz College, Philadelphia, but in comparatively recent years some were sold; others are in the AJHS, and in private collections.

9 A small collection of his Hebrew books is in the Pennsylvania Historical Society: Fish, *op. cit.*, 3.

10 These are scattered in various collections.

11 The collection of Dr. Joshua I. Cohen at Dropsie College is richer in books of an early American Jewish provenance than any other.

12 MS., AJAr.

13 MS., in the possession of Maxwell Whiteman.

14 David Levi, *Letters to Dr. Priestley, in Answer to those he addressed to the Jews* (New York, 1794), Rosenbach, *op. cit.*, 98. Simon Gratz's copy is in the possession of Edwin Wolf, 2nd. David Levi, *A Defence of the Old Testament, in a Series of Letters addressed to Thomas Paine* (New York, 1797), Rosenbach, *op. cit.*, 112–114. Solomon Etting's copy is at Gratz College.

15 Joseph Priestley, *A Comparison of the Institutions of Moses with those of The Hindoos and Other Ancient Nations; . . . and An Address to the Jews on the present state of the World and the Prophecies relating to it* (Northumberland, 1799).

16 Joseph Priestley to Simon Levi, Northumberland, Jan. 9, 1800, MS.,

formerly in the possession of Walter R. Benjamin; "Notes," *PAJHS,* XXVIII (1922), 252.

17 Rosenbach, *op. cit.,* 149, 160–162, 164–166, 170–174, 196, 205, 210, and 212–213, and see note 7, *supra.*

18 *Poulson's,* May 17, 1814.

19 *The Whole Booke Of Psalmes Faithfully Translated into English Metre* (Cambridge, 1640), Rosenbach, *op. cit.,* 1–3. This is the famous Bay Psalm Book, the first book printed in British America.

20 An account of these Bibles and others may be found in E. B. O'Callaghan, *A List of Editions of the Holy Scriptures and parts thereof, Printed in America Previous to 1860* (Albany, 1861).

21 *A Draught of the form of the Government and Discipline of the Presbyterian Church in the United States of America* (New York, 1787), 18.

22 These were lexicons and grammars by Samuel Pike, Stephen Sewell, John Smith and Clement C. Moore: Rosenbach, *op. cit.,* 120, 121, 122–123, 127, 140–141, 143, 147, and 149.

23 *New York Evening Post,* Jan. 16, 1813; M. Vaxer, "The First Hebrew Bible Printed in America," *Journal of Jewish Bibliography,* II (1940), No. 1, 23.

24 James P. Wilson, *An Easy Introduction to the Knowledge of the Hebrew Language without the points* (Philadelphia, 1812); Rosenbach, *op. cit.,* 149.

25 Wilson, *op. cit.,* 233.

26 *Ibid.,* 276.

27 ספר תהלים   *Liber Psalmorum Hebraïce cum Notis Selectis* (Cambridge, Mass., 1809); Rosenbach, *op. cit.,* 138–139.

28 *Proposals By Mills Day, New-Haven, for publishing by subscription, an edition of the Hebrew Bible, from the text of Van-Der-Hooght* (New Haven, 1810); Rosenbach, *op. cit.,* 140 and 142.

29 Wilson, *op. cit.,* 276.

30 *The Quarterly Theological Magazine,* II (1813), 92–95.

31 [Prospectus for The first American edition of Van der Hooght's Hebrew Bible, without the points. By J. Horwitz, Philadelphia, 1813], copy in the Alderman Library, University of Virginia.

32 Bill from Simon Gratz & Brothers to Binny & Ronaldson, Philadelphia, Aug. 24, 1814, McAllister MSS., LCP, for "112 Pigs of Lead."

33 *New York Commercial Advertiser,* Dec. 21, 1812.

34 *New York Evening Post,* Jan. 16, 1813; Vaxer, *op. cit.,* 23.

35 This appeared on a page, containing a history of the project, inserted in the first volume of the Bible in lieu of the title-page, which a note said would be supplied with the second volume. It is dated February, 1814. Vaxer, *op. cit.,* 22 and 24, states that Horwitz sold Dobson the

Hebrew type used, but in his advertisement in *Poulson's*, May 21, 1814, Dobson says the Bible was "Elegantly printed by William Fry, with a new Fount of Hebrew types, cast on purpose for the work, by Binney and Ronaldson."

36 *Poulson's*, May 27, 1813.

37 *The Quarterly Theological Magazine*, III (1814), 168.

38 *Poulson's*, March 5, 1814.

39 *Ibid.*, May 21, 1814. תורה נביאים וכתובים *Biblia Hebraica, secundum ultimam editione Jos. Athiae, a Johannie Leusden denuo recognitam, recensita variisque notis Latinis illustrata ab Everardo Van Der Hooght* (Philadelphia, 1814); Rosenbach, *op. cit.*, 155–156.

40 *Catalogue of The Medical Graduates of the University of Pennsylvania* (Philadelphia, 1839), 39.

41 John Wright, *Early Bibles of America* (New York, 1894), 122–124.

42 See chap. 13, note 77.

43 Paxton's *PD* (Philadelphia, 1819).

44 See chap. 14, note 85.

45 Jonathan Horwitz to Thomas Jefferson, Philadelphia, Jan. 12, 1818, MS., Alderman Library, University of Virginia. In the letter Horwitz enclosed the prospectus for his Hebrew Bible.

46 Jonathan Horwitz to Thomas Cooper, Philadelphia, Sept. 11, 1818, MS., Alderman Library, University of Virginia.

47 *Poulson's*, Sept. 21, 1818.

48 *Ibid.*, Aug. 16, 1820.

49 Statement from Dr. Jacob R. Marcus to Maxwell Whiteman, April 30, 1955.

50 Jonathan Horwitz, *A Defence of The Cosmogony of Moses* (Baltimore, 1839); Rosenbach, *op. cit.*, 334–335.

51 *Baltimore Sun*, July 1, 1852.

52 Rebecca Gratz to Maria Fenno Hoffman, May, 1808, MS., Rosenbach Collection, AJHS; Osterweis, *op. cit.*, 114.

53 Osterweis, *op. cit.*, 115–121.

54 Gratz Van Rensselaer, "The Original of Rebecca in Ivanhoe," *Century Magazine*, XXIV (1882), 678–682. This article was the true beginning of the story. It was analyzed by Joseph Jacobs, "The Original of Scott's Rebecca," *PAJHS*, XXII (1914), 53–60, who came to no very definite conclusions, but presented such facts as were known.

55 Rebecca Gratz to Maria Fenno Hoffman (March, 1820), MS., Rosenbach Collection, AJHS.

56 Rebecca Gratz to Maria Gist Gratz, May 10 (1820), MS., AJHS; Philipson, *op. cit.*, 32.

57 According to the Minute Books of the Library Company, David Franks was admitted as a member in 1757: I, 168; Aaron Levy in 1795: IV, 17; Hyman Gratz in 1807: IV, 148; Zalegman Phillips in 1808: IV, 250; Samuel Hays in 1815: IV, 344; Isaac Hays in 1826: V, 203; and Jonas B. Phillips in 1829: V, 221.

58 *Ibid.*, V, 86, Apr. 28, 1814.

59 *Poulson's*, Feb. 8, and 17, 1815, note that the first annual report was pre-pared and delivered by Jacob Gratz and Jonah Thompson. *Charter and By-Laws of the Athenaeum of Philadelphia* (Philadelphia, 1820), 4–6.

60 *Poulson's*, Feb. 25, 1817.

61 *Charter*, 21–24, and 28–29.

62 *Poulson's*, Feb. 28 and March 3, 1820.

63 *Poulson's*, Jan. 22, 1829. Etting and Michael E. Israel were elected Direc-tors of the Public Schools: *Poulson's*, Jan. 17 and 21, 1829.

64 Joshua Montefiore, *Commercial and Notarial Precedents* (Philadelphia, 1803 and New York, 1822), *The Commercial Dictionary* (Philadelphia, 1803), and *The American Trader's Compendium* (Philadelphia, 1811). Joshua Montefiore (1762–1843) was born in London, a first cousin of Sir Moses, came to America about 1803, when his book was published, stayed in Philadelphia about ten years, and in 1835 moved to Vermont: Lee M. Friedman, "Joshua Montefiore of St. Albans, Vermont," *PAJHS*, XL (1950), 119–134.

65 Charlotte Lennox, *Shakespeare Illustrated; or, The Novels and Histories On Which The Plays of Shakespeare are Founded. . . . With Critical Remarks and Biographical Sketches of the Writers by M. M. Noah* (Philadelphia, 1809).

66 Mordecai Manuel Noah to Thomas P. Barton, New York, Dec. 28, 1842, MS., Barton-Ticknor Collection, Boston Public Library; Goldberg, *op. cit.*, 37n.

67 Albert H. Smyth, *Philadelphia Magazines and their Contributors 1741–1850* (Philadelphia, 1892), 181–183.

68 [Jonas B. Phillips,] *Tales for Leisure Hours* (Philadelphia, 1827). The volume was published anonymously, but the copy presented by the author to the Library Company gives his name.

69 Charles A. Poulson, Historical Illustrations of the History of Philadel-phia in the Olden Time, Scrap Book with MS. Notes, LCP, V, 61, and VI, 5 and 15. These are the Poulson reprints of the articles which appeared in the *New York Gazette*, March 24 and Dec. 15 and 28, 1828.

70 *Ibid.*, IV, 5, contains a brief note on Naphtali Phillips, stating that, from information given Poulson by John McAllister, Jr., "This gentle-man was the author of the papers signed an 'old Philadelphian.'"

71 See chap. 10, note 10.

72 See chap. 10, note 12.

73 Mordecai Manuel Noah to William Dunlap, New York, July 11, 1832;

William Dunlap, *History of The American Stage* (New York, 1832), 380–382.

74 Richard Cumberland, *The Jew: or, Benevolent Hebrew,* A Comedy (Boston, Philadelphia, and New York, 1795); Rosenbach, *op. cit.,* 102, 104–105.

75 Montagu Frank Modder, *The Jew in the Literature of England to the End of the 19th Century* (Philadelphia, 1939), 121–122.

76 Thomas Dibdin, *The Jew and the Doctor, A Farce* (Philadelphia, 1823); Rosenbach, *op. cit.,* 210.

77 George O. Seilhamer, *History of the American Theatre* (Philadelphia, 1891), III, 104–106, 175, 189; *Poulson's,* Oct. 7, 1800.

78 "Playbills of the American Theater, 1799–1802," collection in The Alderman Library, University of Virginia; *Shakespeare Quarterly,* VI (1955), frontis., 428, 434, 454, 482 and 483.

79 Charles Durang, *The Philadelphia Stage, from 1749 to 1821,* clippings from articles which appeared in the *Sunday Dispatch,* LCP, I, 91.

80 *Ibid.,* II, 36.

81 See chap. 11, note 83.

82 Durang, *op. cit.,* II, 2.

83 *Ibid.,* I, 119.

84 N. Bryllion Fagin, "Isaac Harby and The Early American Theatre," *American Jewish Archives,* VIII (1956), 4; Isaac Harby, *The Gordian Knot* (Charleston, 1810).

85 Isaac Harby, *Alberti, A Play, in Five Acts* (Charleston, 1819); Rosenbach, *op. cit.,* 179, 182–183.

86 Mordecai Manuel Noah, *She Would Be A Soldier, or the Plains of Chippewa; An Historical Drama, in Three Acts* (New York, 1819); Rosenbach, *op. cit.,* 185-186.

87 Samuel B. H. Judah, *The Mountain Torrent, A Grand Melodrama, interspersed with Songs, Choruses, &c. in Two Acts* (New York, 1820); Rosenbach, *op. cit.,* 190–191; Scharf and Westcott, *op. cit.,* II, 974.

88 Durang, *op. cit.,* II, 4. *Yuseff Caramalli* does not seem to have been printed.

89 *Ibid;* Mordecai Manuel Noah, *Marion; or, The Hero of Lake George: A Drama, in Three Acts, founded on events of the Revolutionary War* (New York, 1822); Rosenbach, *op. cit.,* 205–206.

90 James N. Barker, *Lopez and Wemyss' Edition. The American Acting Theatre. Tragedy of Superstition* (Philadelphia, 1826), James N. Barker, *Marmion* (Philadelphia, 1826), Richard Brinsley Sheridan, *Pizarro* (Philadelphia, 1826), and possibly others.

91 Durang, *op. cit.,* II, 92; *Poulson's,* Apr. 17, 1829. Aaron J. Phillips (d. 1846) was a son of Jonas. Jonas B. Phillips (1805–1867) was the son of

Benjamin I. and hence the grandson of Jonas. Moses S. Phillips (1798–1854) was the son of Naphtali, and also a grandson of Jonas.

92 *Poulson's,* Apr. 29, 1826.

93 Jonas B. Phillips, *Clayton's Edition. The Evil Eye: A Melodrama, In Two Acts* (New York, 1831); Rosenbach, *op. cit.,* 276.

94 Joseph Sill, Diary, MS., HSP, I, 295. Jonas B. Phillips, *Clayton's Edition. Camillus; or, The Self-Exiled Patriot. A Tragedy, in Five Acts* (New York, 1833); Rosenbach, *op. cit.,* 290.

95 *Constitution of the Musical Fund Society of Philadelphia* (Philadelphia, 1822), 20, 23–25.

96 Abraham Hart (1781–1823), born in Hanover, came to Philadelphia in 1804, was a member of Rodeph Shalom by 1810, transferred to Mikveh Israel in 1813, in which year he declared his intention of settling in Philadelphia: Declaration Dockets, Oct. 1810–Sept. 1820, Department of Records, City of Philadelphia, 539. He married Sarah, daughter of Aaron Stork, and their son Abraham was born on Dec. 15, 1810: Morais, *op. cit.,* 54–55.

97 Samuel Cantor was admitted a member of Rodeph Shalom in 1817, MBRS, May 6, 1817.

98 Austin K. Gray, *The First American Library* (Philadelphia, 1936), 43–46.

99 He had been born Emmanuel Conegliano, and was baptized Lorenzo da Ponte in 1763 at the age of fourteen: *Grove's Dictionary of Music and Musicians* (New York, 1935), IV, 227.

100 Lorenzo da Ponte, *Memorie* (New York, 1830), II, 46. Daniel Levy of Northumberland County, was admitted to the Philadelphia bar in 1787, and was Prothonotary of the county from 1800 to 1809: Morais, *op. cit.,* 410–411. Levy is not known to have had any Jewish associations.

101 Gray, *op. cit.,* 46.

102 Hannah R. London, *Portraits of Jews by Gilbert Stuart and Other Early American Artists* (New York, 1927), 10–11. There were two versions of this portrait, both formerly in the possession of Capt. N. Taylor Phillips and now in AJHS.

103 London, *op. cit.,* 53–54. These pictures are in the possession of the Joseph family of Montreal.

104 *Ibid.,* 53. Now in the Pennsylvania Academy of the Fine Arts.

105 *Ibid.,* 22–23. The portrait of Phillips and a copy of that of his wife are in AJHS. The original of Mrs. Phillips was in 1927 in the possession of Mr. Isaac Graff, of New York.

106 Hannah R. London, *Miniatures of Early American Jews* (Springfield, Mass., 1953), 15–16. Now in the possession of Mrs. Clarence I. De Sola, of Montreal.

107 *Ibid.,* 66. Now in the Pennsylvania Academy of the Fine Arts.

108 *Ibid.*, 66. Now in the possession of Mrs. Harriet Cohen Coale, of Baltimore.

109 London, *Portraits*, 25. Formerly in the possession of Mr. J. J. Milligan, of Baltimore.

110 *Ibid.*, 34. Now in AJHS.

111 London, *Miniatures*, 45. Now in the possession of Mrs. Andrew Van Pelt, of Radnor, Pa.

112 Washington Irving to Rebecca Gratz, New York, Nov. 4, 1807, MS., HSP; Osterweis, *op. cit.*, 110.

113 London, *op. cit.*, 39. Now in the possession of Mrs. John Heard Hunter, of Savannah. The Sully copy is described in London, *Portraits*, 56. It is now in the possession of the Joseph family, of Montreal.

114 Rebecca Gratz to Maria Fenno Hoffman, April, 1808, MS., Rosenbach Collection, AJHS; Osterweis, *op. cit.*, 113.

115 London, *Portraits*, 56–57. Now in the possession of the Joseph family, of Montreal.

116 *Ibid.*, 70. One of these is in the possession of the Clay family of Lexington, Kentucky, the other in that of the Gribbel family, of Philadelphia.

117 *Ibid.*, 57. In the possession of the Clay family, of Lexington.

118 *Ibid.*, 70. Present location unknown.

119 *Ibid.*, 71. In the possession of the Nathan family, of New York.

120 *Ibid.*, 32–33. In the possession of Congregation Mikveh Israel.

121 London, *Miniatures*, 32. Now in the Pennsylvania Academy of Fine Arts.

122 London, *Portraits*, 34–35. Present location unknown.

123 *Ibid.*, 38–39. Now in the Maryland Historical Society.

124 *Ibid.*, 34. Present location unknown.

125 *Ibid.*, 30–31. Now in HSP.

126 *Ibid.*, 35–36. Formerly in the possession of Mrs. E. L. Goldbaum, of Memphis.

127 London, *Miniatures*, 13–14. Formerly in the possession of the Rev. Rufus Henry Bent, of Philadelphia.

128 *Ibid.*, 14. In the possession of Miss Miriam Goldbaum, of New Orleans.

129 *Ibid.*, 32. In the possession of Mrs. William Moran, of Sumter, South Carolina.

130 *Ibid.*, 49. Now in the Pennsylvania Academy of the Fine Arts.

131 London, *Portraits*, 31–32. Present location unknown.

132 *Charter, By-Laws, and Standing Resolutions, of the Pennsylvania Academy of Fine Arts* (Philadelphia, 1813), 5.

133 Morais, *op. cit.*, 38.

134 Subscription Book, MS., Pennsylvania Academy of the Fine Arts.

135 *Phi. Gaz.*, March 14, 1807.

136 Morais, *op. cit.*, 272; *Twenty-Third Annual Exhibition* (Philadelphia, 1834), 2.

137 *First Annual Exhibition of The Society of Artists and the Pennsylvania Academy* (Philadelphia, 1811), 17, No. 344, "A Deception," and 45.

138 *Poulson's,* Oct. 18, 1810.

139 Minute Book of the Society of Artists, MS., Pennsylvania Academy of the Fine Arts.

140 *Second Annual Exhibition* (Philadelphia, 1812), 29.

141 *Third Annual Exhibition* (Philadelphia, 1813), 6–7; *Fourth Annual Exhibition* (Philadelphia, 1814), 8.

142 *Fourth Annual Exhibition,* 8; *A Catalogue of the Paintings, Statues, Prints, &c. Exhibiting at the Pennsylvania Academy of the Fine Arts* (Philadelphia, 1818), No. 7.

143 See chap. 18, note 54.

144 Scharf and Westcott, *op. cit.*, II, 1064–1065.

Chapter 17

1 S. R. Kagan, *Contributions of Early Jews to American Medicine* (Boston, 1934), 10. Joel, the son of Ephraim Hart and Manuel Noah's sister, Frances, was born in Philadelphia in 1784. He was a charter member of the New York County Medical Society: Pool, *op. cit.*, 290.

2 See chap. 10, note 48.

3 *Catalogue of the Medical Graduates of the University of Pennsylvania* (Philadelphia, 1839) lists Abraham De Leon of South Carolina, 1811; D. De Leon of the same state, 1836; Philip De Young of North Carolina, 1838; Morris Emmanuel of Virginia, 1831; Isaac Hays of Pennsylvania, 1820; Jonathan Horwitz of Pennsylvania, 1815; Moses A. Levy of Virginia, 1832; Isaac Lyons, Jr., of South Carolina, 1831; Frederic Marx of Virginia, 1835; Solomon Mordecai of the same state, 1822; S. Gratz Moses of Pennsylvania, 1835; Jacob De La Motta of South Carolina, 1810; Mordecai C. Myers of the same state, 1827; and Solomon Etting Myers also of South Carolina, 1829. Not listed were Moses Sheftall, Manuel Phillips, and Henry S. Hart of Easton, who attended, but did not take a degree. Henry (1796–1817) was the son of Michael Hart: Trachtenberg, *op. cit.*, 84–85.

4 *Phi. Gaz.*, Dec. 29, 1808.

5 See chap. 15, note 45.

6 The files of the Department of the Navy, National Archives, contain letters received by the Secretary of the Navy from Dr. Phillips of Oct. 22, 1810, June 19, 1811, March 2, 1815, and June 11, 1815; and copies of letters sent by the Secretary of the Navy to Dr. Phillips (Appointments, Orders and Resignations) of Dec. 5, 1815; Nov. 25, 1817; July 1, 1819; Sept. 23, 1819; May 1, 1823; May 15, 1823; Sept. 23, 1823; Dec. 27, 1823; and Feb. 19, 1824; and (Letters to Officers, Ships of War) of July 18, 1809; June 22, 1811; Nov. 4, 1823; Feb. 7, 1824; and Feb. 17, 1824.

7 Thomas Wilson, *PD* (Philadelphia, 1825), 110.

8 *Poulson's*, Jan. 15, 1816.

9 Rebecca Gratz to Benjamin Gratz, (Nov. 12, 1818,) MS., AJHS; Philipson, *op. cit.*, 14.

10 See note 3, *supra*.

11 Rebecca Gratz to Benjamin Gratz, June 12, 1820, MS., AJHS; Philipson, *op. cit.*, 35, "Isaac has just opened an office."

12 See chap. 14, notes 88 and 97.

13 William Campbell Posey and Samuel Horton Brown, *The Wills Eye Hospital of Philadelphia* (Philadelphia, 1931), 50–51.

14 Adolph Carl Peter Callisen, *Medicinisches Schriftsteller-Lexicon der jetzt lebenden Verfasser* (Copenhagen, 1840), XXVIII, 421, calls him "Arzt am Philad. Orphan Asylum."

15 Posey and Brown, *op. cit.*, 17. The original minute book of the organization is in the handwriting of Isaac Hays.

16 *Poulson's*, Jan. 23, 1823; *US Gaz.*, Jan. 27, 1825.

17 *Journal of the Academy of Natural Sciences of Philadelphia*, II (1821), 395.

18 *Report of the transactions of the Academy of Natural Sciences of Philadelphia, during the year 1824* (Philadelphia, 1825), 20; and *ibid., 1825–26*, 15.

19 *Journal of the Academy of Natural Sciences*, II (1821), 1.

20 *Ibid.*, 193; and *Poulson's*, Dec. 27, 1827, Jan. 3, 1829 and Jan. 5, 1830.

21 Alexander Wilson, *American Ornithology; or The Natural History of the Birds of the United States* (Philadelphia, 1828). Although Hays' name is not signed to the editor's preface, the *Dictionary of American Biography* (New York, 1932) VIII, 462, noting his correspondence with Bonaparte, states he was the editor.

22 *Charter of Incorporation, Constitution and By-Laws of The Franklin Institute of The State of Pennsylvania for the Promotion of the Mechanic Arts* (Philadelphia, 1824), 21.

23 *Poulson's*, Jan. 21, 1829 and Jan. 23 and Feb. 15, 1830.

24 *Transactions of the American Philosophical Society*, III, New Series (1830), vi, where Hays is listed as a new member, and *ibid.*, 471–477, "Description of a Fragment of the Head of a New Fossil Animal, dis-

covered in a Marl Pit, near Moorestown, New Jersey," noted as read Dec. 4, 1829 and Jan. 1, 1830.

25 *The American Journal of the Medical Sciences,* I (1828), which notes that in the issue of Aug. 1827 the change of title from the *Philadelphia Journal of the Medical and Physical Sciences* had been announced.

26 Posey and Brown, *op. cit.,* 48.

27 Francis R. Packard, *History of Medicine in the United States* (New York, 1931), II, 1169.

28 *Ibid.,* II, 1005n–1006n.

29 *Philadelphia Journal of Medical and Physical Sciences,* IV (1826), No. 5, 1–9.

30 Neil Arnott, *Elements of Physics, or Natural Philosophy, General and Medical . . . First American from the Third London Edition, With Additions, By Isaac Hays* (Philadelphia, 1829), and later editions; and François J. V. Broussais, *History of Chronic Phlegmasiae, or Inflammations . . . Translated from the French of the Fourth Edition, By Isaac Hays, M.D. and R. Eglesfield Griffith, M.D.* (Philadelphia, 1831).

31 *Poulson's,* Nov. 1, 1830; Packard, *op. cit.,* II, 1162 and 1175.

32 *The Transactions of the American Medical Association,* I (1848), 9, 16, 25–31, 37, and 289–290; *Code of Ethics of the American Medical Association. Adopted May 1847* (Philadelphia, 1848). Hays was elected the first treasurer of the AMA, and was chairman of the committee which drew up the Code of Ethics.

33 See chap. 10, note 79.

34 Samuel Solomon, *A Guide to Health* (Stockdale, and sold in New York, 1800).

35 *Aurora,* Oct. 24, 1801, where Solomon calls himself "of the University and College of Physicians." "Solomon's Cordial Balm of Gilead" was advertised for many years for sale by various druggists: *Phi. Gaz.,* Jan. 2, 1807, *et. seqq.*

36 *Poulson's,* Oct. 9, 1817 and Oct. 21, 1820; *National Gazette,* Jan. 25, 1827.

37 *First Century of the Philadelphia College of Pharmacy* (Philadelphia, 1922), 56.

38 Posey and Brown, *op. cit.,* 17–18.

39 MBRS, Oct. 13, 1821. De Bruin died in 1826: Records of Births, Deaths and Marriages, Mikveh Israel, 19. *Directory* (1825), 41, lists him as "vender of jewelry" at 10 Wood St.

40 Adolph Carl Peter Callisen, *Medicinisches Schriftsteller-Lexicon der jetzt lebenden Aertze, Wundärtze, und Naturforscher aller gebildeten Völker* (Copenhagen, 1832), XI, 248–250.

41 *American Journal of the Medical Sciences,* I (1828), "To Readers."

42 William Leo-Wolf, *Remarks on the Abracadabra of the Nineteenth Century; or on Dr. Samuel Hahnemann's Homoeopathic Medicine* (New York, 1835).

43 Letter from Dr. H. G. Reissner to the authors, March 20, 1955. Declaration Dockets, Oct. 1828–Oct. 1832, 180, includes that of Lewis Leo-Wolf, born at Hamburg in 1806, who migrated from Germany to New York in 1828, and declared his intention of settling in Pennsylvania the following year. Dr. Reisner states that Morris emigrated in 1829, but he did not know that the father was in Philadelphia by Nov. 1827 as attested to by Hays.

44 Moritz Leo-Wolf, *De Morbo qui laesiones in Cadaveribus dissecandis haud rare sequi solet* (Heidelberg, 1832), viii–ix.

45 See chap. 12, notes 42 and 43.

46 *Poulson's*, Apr. 2, 1819.

47 *Directory* (1825), 29 "surgeon dentist 23 S 7th."

48 Zachariah Florance was in Charleston in 1801–02: Barnett A. Elzas, *A History of Congregation Beth Elohim, of Charleston, S. C., 1800–1810* (Charleston, 1902), 8. He applied for membership in Mikveh Israel on Sept. 10, 1816: MS., MIAr; and he was one of the original members of Congregation Shanarai Chasset in New Orleans in 1828: Schappes, *op. cit.*, 609. The Florance family name was originally Levy: Evelina Gleaves Cohen, *Family Facts and Fairy Tales* (Wynnewood, Pa., 1953), 92–93.

49 *The Medical Repository*, XVIII (1817), 187–189.

50 *Poulson's*, Feb. 4, 1817, and March 3, 1818.

51 *Phi. Gaz.*, Aug. 8, 1823, reprinted from the *Washington City Gazette* which reprinted it from the *National Intelligencer*.

52 *Occ.*, XXII (1864), 95–96. David (1788–1864) was the oldest child of Gershom Seixas by his second marriage with Hannah Manuel.

53 *JE* (New York, 1901–1906), IX, 597–598, for an account of Pereira; *The Encyclopaedia Britannica* (New York, 1910), IX, 666–667, for an account of L'Épée.

54 *Poulson's*, May 29, 1815.

55 *Ibid.*, Dec. 5, 1816.

56 *Ibid.*, Dec. 14, 18 and 20, 1816.

57 *Ibid.*, Jan. 15, 1817, carrying a notice that at the general meeting on Dec. 7 a committee was appointed to collect funds.

58 *Phi. Gaz.*, Aug. 19 and Sept. 16, 1811, contain Seixas' advertisements for tin-plate and copper; he appears in Edward Whitely, *PD* (Philadelphia, 1820), as "queensware manuf. High W. Sch. 7th."

59 *Poulson's*, Nov. 23 and 26, 1819, and Feb. 9 and Mar. 2, 1820.

60 The letter of March 2, 1820, *supra*, is an eloquent plea for the establishment of a state-chartered school.

61 Rebecca Gratz to Maria Gist Gratz, Apr. 4, 1820, MS., AJHS; Philipson, *op. cit.*, 28.

62 *Poulson's*, Apr. 25, 1820; *An Account of the Origin and Progress of the Pennsylvania Institution for the Deaf and Dumb* (Philadelphia, 1821), 3.

63 Rebecca Gratz to Maria Gist Gratz, May 10, 1820, MS., AJHS; Philipson, *op. cit.*, 32; *An Account of the P.I.D.D.*, 5.

64 Thomas Cadwalader to Roberts Vaux, May 4, 1820, MS., HSP, sending a draft of the proposed agreement with Seixas.

65 *An Account of the P.I.D.D.*, 10.

66 *Ibid.*, 27–38. These were Jacob, Joseph, Simon and Rebecca Gratz, Samuel Hays and his wife, Abraham M., Joseph Simon, Sarah M. and Elkalah Cohen, and John and Samuel Moss.

67 *Poulson's*, June 7, 1820.

68 *The Village Record, or Chester and Delaware Federalist*, Dec. 27, 1820.

69 Rebecca Gratz to Maria Gist Gratz, Jan. 1821, MS., AJHS; Philipson, *op. cit.*, 44; *Phi. Gaz.*, March 13, 1821.

70 *Documents in Relation to the Dismissal of David G. Seixas, from the Pennsylvania Institution for the Deaf and Dumb; Published . . . In Pursuance of a Resolution of the Board of Directors, passed the 3d of April, 1822* (Philadelphia, 1822); Rosenbach, *op. cit.*, 199–200.

71 David G. Seixas, *Letters to C. C. Biddle, Wm. M'Ilvaine, Mary Cowgill, and John Bacon: connected with the Dismissal of David G. Seixas* (Philadelphia, 1822); Rosenbach, *op. cit.*, 200–201.

72 Rebecca Gratz to Maria Gist Gratz, Dec. 29, 1821, MS., AJHS; Philipson, *op. cit.*, 51–52.

73 Seixas, *op. cit.*

74 *Deaf and Dumb, From the Columbian Observer, Apr. 20, 1822* (Philadelphia, 1822). This is a two-page leaflet in defense of Seixas.

75 *Deaf and Dumb School by Anti-Persecutor* (Philadelphia, 1822), a printed broadside in support of Seixas; *A Sketch of the Origin and Progress of the Institutions for the Instruction of the Deaf and Dumb in Pennsylvania* (Philadelphia, 1823), with many excerpts from newspapers praising Seixas' work; *Phi. Gaz.*, Jan. 27, 1823.

76 *Deaf and Dumb, From the Columbian Observer, supra.*

77 Roberts Vaux to John Wurts, Philadelphia, Feb. 12, 1823, MS., Vaux Papers, HSP.

78 *Poulson's*, May 24, June 7 and 22, and Nov. 8, 11 and 27, 1822.

79 *Constitution and By-Laws of the Philadelphia Asylum for the Deaf and Dumb* (Philadelphia, 1825), 7–14.

80 *USGaz.*, Nov. 11, 1825. Seixas had by then established a school in Gloucester County, N. J.

81 *New York Commercial Advertiser,* Jan. 23, 1823, where a letter from the little girl, Janet Houston, is printed in full.

82 *Phi. Gaz.*, Mar. 10, 1823.

83 *Journal of the Thirty-Third House of Representatives of the Commonwealth of Pennsylvania* (Harrisburg, 1822–23), 316, 368, 444, 569, 570, 573 and 583; and *Journal of the Thirty-Fifth House* (Harrisburg, 1824–25), 326–327.

Chapter 18

1 Carl Sandburg, *Abraham Lincoln, The Prairie Years* (New York, 1926), I, 34.

2 *The World Almanac* (New York, 1955), 258.

3 See chap. 9, note 110.

4 Letters of Administration of the Estate of Michael Gratz, Register of Wills, County of Philadelphia, No. 251, Book K, 456.

5 *Poulson's,* Apr. 29, May 17, and July 6, 1814, only by way of example.

6 *Ibid.,* March 5, 1801, lists imports from Canton; Oct. 6 and 31, 1801, details such commodities as cloves, tea, nutmegs and spices; June 26, 1817, contains an invoice of China goods; Apr. 14, 1819, offers Canton silks; and there are a great many more similar advertisements.

7 *Ibid.,* Apr. 13, 1802, "10,000 lbs. First Quality Brazil Coffee."

8 *Ibid.,* Dec. 8, 1801, "15,000 lbs. of St. Domingo Cocoa:" *Phi. Gaz.,* Oct. 3, 1803 and July 25, 1808, many liquors including rum; *Poulson's,* Feb. 8, 1806, "Havannah Sugars"; and many more.

9 *Poulson's,* Oct. 18, 1802, "50,000 lb. heavy black Pepper."

10 *Phi. Gaz.,* Nov. 13, 1805, 20 tons of sheet-iron and ten tons of patent shot; *Poulson's,* Jan. 4, 1817, "a quantity of single and double F Gunpowder from one of the best manufactories of this country."

11 *Poulson's,* Jan. 1, 1814, "100 Barrels Refined and Crude Salt Petre from the Mammouth Cave of Ky.," Jan. 13, and Aug. 20, 1814, and July 26 and Aug. 14, 1815, "100 bbls Fine Kentucky Rye Whiskey," as well as other Kentucky products.

12 *Ibid.,* Aug. 24, 1803, July 23, 1810, and July 8, 1815, "Prime New Orleans Cotton:" *Phi. Gaz.,* Apr. 1, 1803, "Mississippi cotton."

13 *Poulson's,* Nov. 21, 1801.

14 Petition of the Directors of the Insurance Company of North America to the General Assembly of Pennsylvania, (Philadelphia, December, 1792), McAllister MSS., LCP.

15 *Phi. Gaz.*, Feb. 21 and Apr. 16, 1805.

16 *Ibid.*, June 4, 1821.

17 *Ibid.*, Apr. 1, 1805.

18 *Poulson's*, Feb. 1, 1806.

19 *Phi. Gaz.*, Sept. 11 and 30, 1803, Simon as executor of the estate of John Duffield; *Poulson's*, May 17, 1806, Simon as assignee of the estate of Hugh Kiernan; *Phi. Gaz.*, Jan. 26, 1808, Hyman as assignee of estate of Thomas Bennet of Harrisburg; *ibid.*, June 24, 1808, Simon Gratz & Co. as executor of the estate of Abel Humphries; *Poulson's*, Feb. 8, 1819, the firm as agent for the estate of Richard Davenport of Danville, Ky.

20 *Poulson's*, Apr. 2, 1812.

21 Solis-Cohen, *op. cit.*

22 Rebecca Gratz to Benjamin Gratz, March 24, 1819, MS., AJHS; Philipson, *op. cit.*, 19. *Poulson's*, March 11, 1819, carries a public letter of thanks from the Gratzes to the Fire and Hose Companies for having saved their property.

23 *Poulson's*, Nov. 28, 1820, at No. 2 South Seventh St.

24 *Ibid.*, Jan. 4 and June 26, 1817.

25 *Ibid.*, Nov. 26 and 28, 1822.

26 *Robinson's PD* (Philadelphia, 1817), 193.

27 Thomas Wilson, *PD* (Philadelphia, 1825), 59, lists Hyman, Jacob and Joseph Gratz's home address as 219 Chestnut.

28 *Poulson's*, Dec. 31, 1813.

29 *Ibid.*, May 30, 1814, Nov. 28, 1815, Nov. 25, 1817, Nov. 23, 1819, and Nov. 28, 1820.

30 Scharf and Westcott, *op. cit.*, I, 653–654.

31 *Claypoole's*, Feb. 20, 1796.

32 *Ibid.*, Jan. 2, 1797, and *Poulson's*, Jan. 2, 1801 and Jan. 6, 1802.

33 James Robinson, *PD* (Philadelphia, 1808), xxxii.

34 *Poulson's*, Feb. 10, 1803; *ibid.*, May 3, 1803, advertised "Lottery Tickets and shares, warranted undrawn, in the Lehigh Navigation, St. Augustine Church, and Easton Delaware Bridge lotteries for sale."

35 *Ibid.*, Apr., 3, 1817.

36 *Aurora* (country edition), June 8, 1811, an incorporator of a road from Sunbury to Aaronsburg; *Poulson's*, July 13, 1825, a commissioner of the Milesburg and Smithsport Turnpike Company.

37 *Poulson's*, Feb. 11, 1822, and *USGaz.*, Oct. 12, 1825.

38 *Poulson's*, Aug. 25, 1826, the obituary of Daniel Levy, "a native of Ireland," who died at the hospital on the Chesapeake and Delaware Canal after having worked on it for several months.

39 *Annual Report of the Managers of the Union Canal Company of Pennsylvania* (Philadelphia, 1834), 2.

40 *Poulson's*, Jan. 23, 1818.

41 See chap. 12, note 51.

42 Harrison S. Morris, *A Sketch of the Pennsylvania Company for Insurance on Lives and Granting Annuities* (Philadelphia, 1896), 38–41. Among the original subscribers for stock in the company in 1809 were E. Solomon for 50 shares and Simon Gratz for 20 shares: *ibid.*, 75–76.

43 *USGaz.*, March 23, 1825; *Poulson's*, Jan. 18, 1827.

44 Marshall B. Davidson, *Life in America* (Boston, 1951), II, 218.

45 Rebecca Gratz to Benjamin Gratz, Feb. 26, 1826, MS., AJHS; Philipson, *op. cit.*, 79–80.

46 Rebecca Gratz to Maria Gist Gratz, Aug. 6, 1826, MS., AJHS; Philipson, *op. cit.*, 84–85.

47 Rebecca Gratz to Maria Gist Gratz, Sept. 10, 1826, MS., AJHS; Philipson, *op. cit.*, 86–87.

48 *Poulson's*, Jan. 24, 1827.

49 *Ibid.*, Jan. 4, 1827, "House and lot, No. 219, on the North side of Chesnut-street, the fourth west of Delaware (from) Seventh-street, 28 feet front, extending in depth 176 feet to Lodge Alley. This House is built of the best materials in the modern style with mahogany folding doors, marble mantles, &c. the apartments are spacious, main building 56 feet in depth, extensive buildings, bathhouse, cistern and a large stable and carriage house." Rebecca Gratz to Maria Gist Gratz, March 12, 1826, MS., AJHS; Philipson, *op. cit.*, 81–82, "Tell Ben—the renowned Panacea Swain (*sic*) has bought both Moses Levy's and Wm Waln's fine houses—he is to be our neighbor—and will convert a wing of the great house into a cake shop! is not this too bad . . ."

50 Rebecca Gratz to Maria Gist Gratz, Aug. 3, 1828, MS., AJHS; Philipson, *op. cit.*, 91: ". . . I must introduce you to our new habitation in Boston-row, for so Mr Brooke denominates the stone buildings he was erecting opposite our Sister Hays' residence in Chestnut Street, when you were last here—ours is No. 2 from 12th Street, the house is small compared with the one we left our two parlours being nearly covered by the mat taken from the floor of the back room but then there is a small dining room besides—a Library & bathroom above it—and very comfortable chambers—. . ."

51 *Poulson's*, Apr. 14, 1802. Levy was "of the House of James M. Taggart & Co. Merchants, Calcutta."

52 *Poulson's*, July 6, 1819.

53 *Freeman's Journal,* Sept. 20, 1825. Peixotto arrived from Jamaica at the age of 48 in 1823, and on July 8, 1823, declared his intention of settling in Philadelphia: Declaration Dockets, Oct. 1814–March 1824, Department of Records, City of Philadelphia, 228. He did, however, go back to Kingston, after severe financial losses in Philadelphia: *Occ.,* XVII (1860), 306.

54 Raphael De Cordova applied for membership in Mikveh Israel in 1816, MBMI, Sept. 15, 1816. He had come with his sons Joshua R. and Jacob from Jamaica in 1816. On Jan. 25, 1820, Joshua, having reached the age of twenty-one, declared his intention of remaining in Philadelphia: Declaration Dockets, Oct. 1810–Sept. 1820, 990. Raphael was *parnass* of Mikveh Israel for a brief period in 1820. They advertised as R. De Cordova & Son in *Poulson's,* June 20, 1817, and announced the formation of De Cordova, Nunes & Co., *ibid.,* Feb. 1, 1820.

55 See chap. 14, note 18.

56 Solomon Grayzel, *A History of the Jews* (Philadelphia, 1947), 744 and 748–749.

57 *Phi. Gaz.,* Feb. 23, 1807. Shortly after he arrived in this country, Lazarus married Esther Lyons, and hence was a brother-in-law of John Moss: Sanford A. Moss, *op. cit.,* 14. He took out his citizenship papers on June 2, 1806, after two years' residence in the city: MS., Department of Records, City of Philadelphia.

58 *Aurora,* Oct. 19, 1804, and *Phi. Gaz.,* July 10, 1805, and Jan. 3, 1809.

59 *Phi. Gaz.,* March 22, 1809.

60 *Ibid.,* Oct. 29, 1811.

61 Reuben Etting to Hyman Gratz, Philadelphia, Sept. 19, Oct. 15 and 22, Nov. 6 and 18, and Dec. 12, 1823, and Jan. 15, (Feb. 21), and May 6, 1824, MSS., in the possession of Edwin Wolf, 2nd. The general tenor is as of the last, "It is truly distressing to be so troublesome to you, but I really cannot help it, therefore must ask you for $10 on accot of this Month altho it has just commenced—I am out of Wood and several other articles—"

62 Solomon Moses had married Rachel Gratz, who died at the age of 40 in 1823, leaving nine children, *Phi. Gaz.,* Oct. 2, 1823. The young Moses' were brought up by their aunt Rebecca Gratz: Philipson, *op. cit.,* xvi–xvii.

63 *Phi. Gaz.,* Jan. 4, 1809.

64 *Ibid.,* Aug. 13, 1811.

65 *Poulson's,* Apr. 16, 1818; the firm of Montmollin & Moses had been stricken from the Governor's list, *ibid.,* March 24, 1818.

66 *Claypoole's,* Dec. 1 and 8, 1796.

67 Sanford A. Moss, *op. cit.,* 8.

68 *Ibid.,* 8 and 14.

69 *Phi. Gaz.,* Jan. 28, 1807.

70 *Ibid.*, Feb. 22, 1808 and Jan. 24, 1809, and *Poulson's* June 14 and Dec. 7, 1815 and many other issues in successive years.

71 *Phi. Gaz.*, Feb. 15, 1822.

72 *Poulson's*, March 30, and Apr. 2, 3 and 17, 1822, and *National Gazette*, March 30, 1822.

73 Henri Marceau, "William Rush," *The One Hundred and Fiftieth Anniversary Exhibition, The Pennsylvania Academy of the Fine Arts* (Philadelphia, 1955), 18–19.

74 Moss, *op. cit.*, 3.

75 *Ibid., loc. cit.*

76 Lucien Moss, "Memoir of John Moss," *PAJHS*, II (1894), 172.

77 *Phi. Gaz.*, Dec. 31, 1823.

78 Morris, *op. cit.*, 67. Moss served from 1823 to 1847.

79 *USGaz.*, Jan. 11 and Oct. 12, 1825.

80 *Poulson's*, Nov. 25, 1828 and Nov. 24, 1829.

81 *Claypoole's*, Aug. 31, 1798.

82 *Phi. Gaz.*, Aug. 6, 1800; the subscribers included Simon and Hyman Gratz, Eleazer Cohen, Solomon Lyon, Moses Levy, and the Pragers.

83 *Political and Commercial Register*, Jan. 24, 1805.

84 *Poulson's*, Dec. 17, 1816.

85 *Phi. Gaz.*, Jan. 16, 1821.

86 *Poulson's*, June 22, 1827.

87 *Ibid.*, Nov. 26, 1819.

88 *USGaz.*, Oct. 4, 1825.

89 *Phi. Gaz.*, Apr. 4, 1821. Jacob Moss died in 1830, *Poulson's*, Nov. 16, 1830.

90 *Phi. Gaz.*, Feb. 22, 1821.

91 Sanford A. Moss, *op. cit.*, 8; see chap. 14, note 16. The firm of R. and I. Phillips, "merchants," did business at 20 Chestnut St.: *PD* (1820). It was dissolved on Jan. 1, 1825, *Phi. Gaz.*, Dec. 7, 1824.

92 I. Nathan, who in 1829 wrote a book, *Fugitive Pieces and Reminiscences of Lord Byron:* Elkan Nathan Adler, *Jewish Community Series, London* (Philadelphia, 1930), 174.

93 Jonas' sons were David M., Naphtali, Benjamin I., Manuel, Joseph, Aaron J. and Zalegman. Of his daughters, Phila married Isaac Pesoa, Rachel married Michael Levy, Esther married Myer Moses, and Zipporah married Manuel Noah. Other children died in infancy and childhood: N. Taylor Phillips, *op. cit.*, 60–61.

94 Levy Phillips, who had married Joseph Simon's daughter Leah, had long been active in Mikveh Israel, serving as *parnass* in 1788, 1793, 1796, 1819 and 1820. Benjamin Rush, who treated him from Nov. 1792 to Apr. 1795, noted that he was a shopkeeper on 3rd St.: Ledger C, 392, LCP. He was in business by himself: *Phi. Gaz.*, Dec. 13, 1810 to Feb. 9, 1811; later went into partnership with Robert Phillips, and then once more maintained his own store: *Poulson's*, Dec. 1 and 3, 1817.

95 *Poulson's*, July 18, 1825.

96 *USGaz.*, July 18, 1825.

97 *Martin's Bench and Bar*, 302; *Poulson's*, Apr. 29, 1826.

98 *Claypoole's*, Aug. 1, 1800.

99 Solomon had eight children, Abraham M., Samuel M., Eleazer L., Joseph S., Sarah, Rachel, Rebecca, and Elkalah, *To the Honorable the Judges of the Circuit Court of the United States, in and for the Third Circuit in the Eastern District of Pennsylvania* (Philadelphia, 1839), 15.

100 *PD* (1810), 64, "merchant 75 north Fourth;" *Poulson's*, July 7, 1815, Feb. 24, 1817, and May 24, 1820. According to Morais, *op. cit.*, 445n, Cohen married a Christian and his daughter married his partner Nisbet.

101 This was a Baltimore firm, but they advertised extensively in Philadelphia where they maintained an agency: *Poulson's*, Aug. 27, 1817, and Sept. 15, 1825; *USGaz.*, March 9, 1825; and *National Gazette*, Jan. 18 and 31, 1827. The firm was known as I. I. Cohen, Jr. & Brothers. They were not the sons of Jacob I. Cohen, who had no children.

102 *Political and Commercial Register*, Dec. 7, 1808, and May 23, 1809, *Phi. Gaz.*, March 25, 1811, and *Poulson's*, May 13, 1814.

103 *PD* (1830), 10. She may have been the widow of Nathan Barnett, who died in 1797: *Claypoole's*, Nov. 3, 1797.

104 *Ibid.*, 103, "store keeper 7th n Noble."

105 *Ibid.*, 112, where he is listed as "dry goods st(ore)." He became one of the leaders of the Philadelphia Jewish community: Morais, *op. cit.*, 50–51.

106 Levi M. Goldsmit was elected a member of Mikveh Israel in 1813, MIMB, Sept. 19, 1813. He had signed the constitution of Rodeph Shalom in 1810, Davis, *op. cit.*, 23. Moses I. Goudkop, who was born in Amsterdam in 1798, came to this country in 1815, and declared his intention of becoming a permanent resident ten years later: Declaration Dockets, Oct. 1820–May 1827, 349. They were in business at 68 North 2nd St.: *PD* (1825), 58.

107 *Ibid.*, 11. He was at the corner of 2nd and Callowhill, and within five years had moved to 14 No. 3rd St.: *PD* (1830), 4.

108 *PD* (1830), 6. The Aschs were Polish, as the obituary of a third brother, Moses M. stated: *Poulson's*, June 17, 1829. Joseph Asch died in 1866: *Occ.*, XXIV (1866), 192.

109 *Ibid.*, 22.

110 *Ibid.*, 77. Judah Lazarus Hackenburg, born at Coblentz in 1793, was the first of that family to emigrate to America, arriving in Philadelphia in

1815. On Oct. 8, 1818, he filed his declaration of intent: Declaration Dockets, Oct. 1810–Sept. 1820, 902. He married Maria, daughter of Lewis Allen, and they had several children, among them William B., Isaac E., and Rebecca, who married David Teller: Morais, *op. cit.*, 273–274; and he died in 1862: *Occ.*, XIX (1862), 569.

111 *PD* (1825), 72, where Elias Hyneman is described as a "gent." at 210 No. 6th St. *Ibid.* (1830), 94, lists the father and two sons at 4th St. north of Arch. According to Morais, *op. cit.*, 327, the father first settled in a country town in Montgomery County, and after his oldest son Leon was born moved to Philadelphia. His son Benjamin was born in Philadelphia on Sept. 25, 1806: Records of Births, Deaths and Marriages, MS., MIAr, 23. Elias was a subscriber to Rodeph Shalom in 1811, but joined Mikveh Israel four years later. He was at first in partnership with Abraham Hart: *Phi. Gaz.*, Aug. 28, 1811, announcing the dissolution of the firm, and later a partner in Smith & Hyneman, grocers: *Poulson's*, Oct. 1, 1817.

112 *PD* (1810), 169, where Aaron was listed alone. For a while he had been a partner of Isaac Lyons: *Phi. Gaz.*, May 11, 1808. On June 10, 1801, Aaron Levy married Fanny Joseph: Records of Births, Deaths and Marriages, 57. *PD* (1830), 111–112, lists his sons Benjamin and Joseph at his address, but earlier he had announced that he had sold out to Joseph: *Phi. Gaz.*, March 1, 1824. The latter is not to be confused with another Joseph Levy, an exchange broker: *PD* (1810), 169; *Phi. Gaz.*, May 1, 1805 and Nov. 8, 1811, and *Poulson's*, May 6, 1816.

113 *PD* (1830), 172.

114 *Ibid.*, 188.

115 *PD* (1816), "merchant S.W. corner 3d & Race." See chap. 16, note 96. After his partnership with Hyneman was concluded, see note 111, *supra*, Hart went with Michael Nisbet who later became Eleazer Cohen's partner: *Poulson's*, July 3, 1815, announcing the dissolution. Hart went bankrupt in 1816, and his father-in-law took charge of his affairs: *ibid.*, Nov. 27, 1816. He is not to be confused with Abraham Luria Hart, the proprietor of a music-store at 30 So. 4th St.: *PD* (1820), who was the son of Michael Hart of Easton, nor with another Abraham Hart, who ran a shoe-store: *ibid.* (1830), 82.

116 *Poulson's*, Nov. 2, 1829.

117 James Fenimore Cooper, *The Wept of Wish Ton Wish* (Philadelphia, 1829): *Poulson's*, Nov. 7, 1829. For other advertisements of the new firm, see *ibid.*, Nov. 30 and Dec. 8, 1829.

118 See note 54, *supra*.

119 *Aurora*, June 13, 1804. Lyon Cadet took out his citizenship papers on June 1, 1807, and signed his name in Hebrew characters. His son Judah was born on May 11, 1808: Records of Births, Deaths, and Marriages, 24. He signed the 1810 constitution of Rodeph Shalom, and remained active there until 1827. He conducted a dry-goods store in partnership with Jacob Hipple at 160 No. 2nd St.: *PD* (1816), and later set up for himself at 82 No. 4th St.: *PD* (1820). Abraham Gumpert was one of the first members of Rodeph Shalom, and remained active there for over twenty

years. However, when he died in 1849 at the age of 87, he was buried in the Mikveh Israel Cemetery: Elmaleh and Samuel, *op. cit.*, 7. Gumpert was in partnership with Moses: *PD* (1810), 121, but later joined with his brother Samuel, at 263 No. 2nd St.: *PD* (1820). Alexander Phillips is not otherwise known.

120 *Poulson's*, Feb. 17, 1806.

121 *PD* (1830), 1.

122 *Ibid.*, 36.

123 *PD* (1825), 28, and (1830), 29.

124 *PD* (1820), and see chap. 13, note 31.

125 *PD* (1830), 137.

126 *PD* (1820), "dealer 11 Key's Alley."

127 *PD* (1830), 82, and see note 115, *supra*.

128 *PD* (1820), with G. Cohen at 262 So. Front St., and later by himself at 159 Cedar St.: *PD* (1825), 33. A. B. Cohen was one of the signers of the 1810 constitution of Rodeph Shalom, and remained a member for more than twenty years.

129 *PD* (1825), 49, and (1830), 60. There were four Eytinges, possibly brothers, Barnet and Philip as noted, Simon a jeweller, and Solomon a merchant: *loc. cit.* Simon was in partnership with E. I. Philip: *Poulson's*, March 16, 1819, and Dec. 25, 1826. Solomon, born in 1792, and Barnet, born in 1782, migrated from Holland, landing in Baltimore in 1816 and 1820 respectively. They both declared their intention to settle in Pennsylvania in 1833: Declaration Dockets, Sept. 1832–Apr. 1834, 240 and 288. In 1822–23, Barnet was a subscriber to Rodeph Shalom. David Eytinge, probably their father, born in 1765, landed in New York in 1828, and six years later appeared at City Hall to make his declaration: Declaration Dockets, Jan. 1834–Sept. 1835, 553.

130 *PD* (1830), 94.

131 *Ibid.*, 137.

132 *Ibid.*, 140. Another Jacob Nathans was a broker.

133 *Ibid.*, 150. Joseph lived at 5 Bryans Court with Henry Pereyra, an accountant. A third Pereyra, Peter, was listed as a merchant in Baker's Alley: *PD* (1820). They were probably sons of Jeshurun Rodriguez Pereyra, who had died on Apr. 10, 1806: Records of Births, Deaths, and Marriages, 18. D. R. Pereyra was a broker at 24 St. John Str.: *Census Directory* (1811), 252. He may have been a brother of Jeshurun.

134 *PD* (1825), 131. She was Frances, the widow of Alexander Solomon.

135 *PD* (1810), 266, "dealer 66 Callowhill." Moses Spyers, born at Amsterdam in 1763, stated most internationally that he was born a member of the German nation and owed allegiance to the King of Holland and Emperor of France. He migrated from London, and arrived at New York in 1806. On Jan. 9, 1811, he declared his intention of settling in Philadelphia: Declaration Dockets, Oct. 1810–Sept. 1820, 17. He applied

for admission in Mikveh Israel in 1813, although three years earlier he had signed the constitution of Rodeph Shalom. He was listed as a watchmaker in 1830: *PD* (1830), 184.

136 *PD* (1830), 151, where Gustavus, David and their widowed mother Phila were all listed at 154 No. 4th St. David was born Feb. 9, 1801, and Gustavus June 17, 1805: Records of Births, Deaths, and Marriages, 23. Their father Isaac, *parnass* of Mikveh Israel in 1800–1804 and also a binder, had died in 1809: *ibid.*, 18. In 1829, Gustavus was elected secretary of the Provident Association of Journeymen Bookbinders: *Poulson's*, March 13, 1829.

137 *PD* (1830), 137. John Moss, distinguished from the merchant of the same name by the appellation "Levite," was also an Englishman, born at Liverpool in 1787. He arrived in Philadelphia in 1823, and made his statement of intent on Dec. 11, 1828: Declaration Dockets, Oct. 1828–Oct. 1832, 112. He was active in Rodeph Shalom.

138 *PD* (1830), 36.

139 *PD* (1825), 143, and (1830), 200. Van Beil, a Dutchman born in 1799, came to Philadelphia in 1820, and made his statement of intent on Sept. 19, 1826: Declaration Dockets, Oct. 1820–May 1827, 425. He joined Rodeph Shalom, was its secretary in 1827, and became president in 1831: Davis, *op. cit.*, 50–51. He died Dec. 26, 1865: *Occ.*, XXIII (1866), 528.

140 George, Samuel, and Augustus Van Amring (or Van Amringe) were the sons of Lion by his Christian wife Elizabeth. Lion was a merchant by 1801: James Robinson, *PD* (Philadelphia, 1801), 89, and George by 1815: *Poulson's*, Dec. 22, 1815. The brothers were in business together at 57 Chestnut St.: *PD* (1825), 143; but later operated three separate stores, the chief one being under the name of Augustus Van Amringe & Co.: *Poulson's*, Jan. 15, 1827 and *PD* (1830), 200.

141 *Phi. Gaz.*, Nov. 24, 1824.

142 *Poulson's*, Nov. 17, 1827.

143 Simeon and Joseph Dreyfous were both in the jewelry business in neighboring stores on South 4th St.: *PD* (1825), 44. They were Alsatians. Joseph arrived at New York in 1816, and on June 30, 1820, declared his intention of settling in Pennsylvania: Declaration Dockets, Oct. 1810–Sept. 1820, 1001. Both were members of Rodeph Shalom. According to Morais, *op. cit.*, 143, Joseph was the first president of the United Hebrew Beneficent Society. In the summer of 1830 Simeon announced that he was closing out his business: *Poulson's*, Aug. 31, 1830.

144 *PD* (1810), 272. Aaron Stork signed the 1810 constitution of Rodeph Shalom, having arrived in the country from Holland three years before: Morais, *op. cit.*, 54–55. He died in 1842, and was buried in the Spruce Street Cemetery: Records of Births, Deaths, and Marriages, 40.

145 Isaac Stuttgart born in Amsterdam in 1785, arrived in Philadelphia in 1807, and stated that he was going to settle permanently on Feb. 19, 1811: Declaration Dockets, Oct. 1810–Sept. 1820, 23. He was one of the signers of the Rodeph Shalom constitution in 1810, and was secretary in 1817. After Levy Ancker went bankrupt in 1808: *Phi. Gaz.*, June 13, 1808, he went into partnership with Stuttgart, but the firm only lasted a few years

and was dissolved in 1815: *Poulson's,* July 13, 1815. Stuttgart himself later had to assign the stock of his "fancy dry goods store" to his creditors: *PD* (1825), 136; *Poulson's,* March 29, 1826. He died in 1830, and was buried in the Spruce Street Cemetery: Records of Births, Deaths and Marriages, 29.

146 Mayer Ullman was also a signer of the 1810 constitution, at about which time he came to Philadelphia. His tavern was on Shippen (now Bainbridge) St.: *PD* (1816). He died in 1828.

147 According to Morais, *op. cit.,* 242-243, Lewis Allen, Sr., (1771-1815) came over to Philadelphia from London with his twelve-year-old son Lewis, Jr. in 1805. He called himself a native of Germany when he took out his citizenship papers on Sept. 25, 1809, and there stated that he had resided in the United States upwards of eight years, and within Pennsylvania upwards of two years. He was listed as a "trader 398 North Third": *PD* (1810), 16. The father was a member of Rodeph Shalom, was elected its president in 1811: Davis, *op. cit.,* 139, and died in 1815: *Poulson's,* March 1, 1815. His son, who married Anna, daughter of Michael Marks, on Dec. 10, 1823, succeeded him in business as a "merchant," on High Street: *PD* (1816). Lewis, Jr. became president of Mikveh Israel in 1834, and died in 1841.

148 *PD* (1820), and Morais, *op. cit.,* 53.

149 Morais, *op. cit.,* 252-253, where it is stated that Louis Bomeisler was born in 1790 and came to the country in 1819. His declaration of June 20, 1820: Declaration Dockets, Oct. 1814–March 1824, 163, states that he was born in Bavaria in 1792, and arrived Philadelphia in 1817. He had been preceded by a younger brother, Michael, who came to America the year before: *ibid.,* 142, and was followed by another brother Joseph in 1823: Declaration Dockets, Mar. 1824–Oct. 1825, 64. Both Louis and Michael are listed as subscribers to Rodeph Shalom in 1818, and Louis was president in 1827. For a while they did business in partnership with the widow of Isaac Rodrigues under the name of Rodrigues, Bomeisler & Co.: *PD* (1820), and also as Louis Bomeisler & Co.: *ibid.,* and finally, when Bomeisler & Brother was set up by Michael and Joseph, Louis continued on alone: *PD* (1830), 18. Louis died in 1856.

150 Moses B. Seixas and Benjamin I. Phillips: *Aurora,* Jan. 22, 1825; Hyman Marks: *Poulson's,* Apr. 22 and June 20, 1816, and Apr. 4, 1820; Isaac Franks: *Phi. Gaz.,* May 3, 1803; and Benjamin Nones, *ibid.,* Dec. 8, 1808.

151 See note 101, *supra.*

152 *Poulson's,* Apr. 28, 1818.

153 *PD* (1830), 36, 56, 74, 126, 137, and 165.

154 *Poulson's,* July 22, 1816.

155 *Ibid.,* Sept. 27, 1816.

156 Jacob Rader Marcus, *Memoirs of American Jews 1775-1865* (Philadelphia, 1955), I, 205. These are the reminiscences of Joseph Jonas.

157 *Ibid.,* 209.

158 *Phi. Gaz.,* Dec. 11, 1823; and Pool, *op. cit.,* 372.

159 *Poulson's*, Sept. 3, 1818.

160 *Poulson's*, July 18, 20 and 21, 1812, and *Aurora*, Jan. 2, 1816.

161 John Jacob Astor to Simon Phillipson, New York, Oct. 19, 1814, MS., Missouri Historical Society. According to recently discovered bills in the same archives, the Phillipsons were also engaged in business with August Chouteau, the founder of St. Louis.

162 *Poulson's*, Feb. 15, 1822, carries a notice of the death of Simon's wife in St. Louis.

163 *Poulson's*, Dec. 4, 1816. He married Charity Hays, and their daughter, Judith Simha Solis, became the wife of Myer David Cohen, from whom the Solis-Cohens are descended.

164 Some time in the early 1820s, Jacob S. Solis issued a printed circular from Mount Pleasant, West Chester County, calling for the establishment of a school called "The American Jewish Asylum," a copy of which is in the possession of Edwin Wolf, 2nd.

165 Schappes, *op. cit.*, 609.

166 Isaac Markens, *The Hebrews in America* (New York, 1888), 92; *Memoirs of Lodge No. 51, F. & A.M. of Pennsylvania* (Philadelphia, 1941), 1038–1039, says Salomon was also the first bookkeeper in the Philadelphia Bank, and in 1807 went as an American diplomatic representative to Leghorn.

167 Schappes, *loc. cit.*

168 Henry Cohen, "The Jews in Texas," *PAJHS*, IV (1896), 9–14.

169 *Ibid.*, 15–16. Osterman applied for membership in Mikveh Israel on Sept. 8, 1822, MS., MIAr. In 1830 he was one of the incorporators of the Baltimore Hebrew Congregation, and in 1839 he moved to Galveston.

170 Henry Cohen, "Settlement of the Jews in Texas," *PAJHS*, II (1894), 150. Seeligson is listed as a contributor to Rodeph Shalom in 1823–24: Davis, *op. cit.*, 144; and he appears in the *PD* (1830), 172, as the owner of a dry-goods store at 109 N. 2nd St.

171 Cohen, *op. cit.*, 151; Solomon R. Kagan, *Jewish Contributions to Medicine* (Boston, 1934), 5–6, 44.

172 Jacob R. Marcus, *Memoirs of American Jews* (Philadelphia, 1955), I, 153–158.

Chapter 19

1 *Journal of the Twentieth House of Representatives of the Commonwealth of Pennsylvania* (Lancaster, 1809), 176–177, where the previous history of Mikveh Israel's earlier requests is reviewed.

2 Benjamin Nones to Governor Simon Snyder, Philadelphia, June 21, 1810, MS., MIAr.

3 *Journal of the Twentieth House*, 155, 176–177, 195, 247, 255–256, 257, 268–269, 534, 565, 642, 658, and 885.

4 MBMI, Nov. 1, 1818.

5 *Ibid.*, Nov. 8, 1818.

6 *Ibid.*, Apr. 18, 1819, Report No. 1, Subscription Book for Building New Synagogue, 1818–1825, MS., MIAr.

7 Subscription List, Nov. 8, 1818, MS., MIAr.

8 Joseph Gratz to Abraham R. Brandon, Philadelphia, Nov. 26, 1818, with enclosure; Levy Phillips, Jacob I. Cohen, Samuel Hays, John Moss, and Joseph Gratz to the Parnass and Adjuntos of the Hebrew Congregation in the Barbados, Philadelphia, Nov. 20, 1818; Joseph Gratz to Abraham R. Brandon, Philadelphia, Feb. 8, 1820; and Joseph Gratz to Messrs. M. E. Montefiore Co., Philadelphia, June 9, 1820, MSS., SBMI. There was some difficulty encountered in cashing the Barbados note, and additional correspondence refers to this.

9 Simon Gratz, John Moss, Hyman Marks, and Joseph Gratz to Abraham Touro, Philadelphia, Apr. 19, 1819, MS., Subscription Book. Abraham Touro (1774–1822) was the older brother of the famous New Orleans merchant Judah Touro, who remained in Boston when Judah moved and became one of the prominent merchants of New England: Leon Hühner, *The Life of Judah Touro* (Philadelphia, 1946), 43, and 64–65.

10 Simon Gratz, John Moss, Solomon Moses and Joseph Gratz to Nathan Meyer Rothschild, Philadelphia, Feb. 4, 1824, MS., SBMI. A similar letter was sent to B. A. Goldsmidt of London on March 19, 1824.

11 Joseph Gratz to S. Almonsino, Secretary of the Spanish and Portuguese Jews of London, Philadelphia, Jan. 8, 1824, MS., SBMI.

12 Joseph Gratz to Judah Touro, Philadelphia, March 15, 1824, MS., SBMI. The individual contributions were R. D. Rochelle $250, A. M. Nathan $250, Samuel Herman $100, H. M. Shiff $100, and Judah Touro $300. It is an interesting commentary on the mobility of early 19th-century Jews that, except for Touro, not one of these was apparently still in New Orleans four years later, for their names do not appear among the contributors or incorporators of Congregation Shanarai Chasset in 1828: Schappes, *op. cit.*, 609. Reuben D. Rochelle and Abraham Nathan both returned to Philadelphia and both were buried in the Spruce Street Cemetery, Rochelle in 1824, and Nathan in 1841.

13 Report No. 3, Aug. 5, 1823, SBMI.

14 Report No. 1, Apr. 18, 1819, SBMI; MBMI, Apr. 18, 1819.

15 The two rejected plans are still in the MIAr; the accepted Strickland plan cannot be located. It has recently been reconstructed by Alfred Bendiner from the available information: Rachel Wischnitzer, *Synagogue Architecture in the United States* (Philadelphia, 1955), 29–30.

16 SBMI, Sept. 6, 1822.

17 MBMI, Sept. 8, 1822.

18 Protest to Zalegman Phillips, David Nathans, and Levi M. Goldsmit, Philadelphia, Sept. 11, 1822, MS., MIAr.

19 MBMI, Dec. 8, 1822, places a special meeting of the congregation "at the house of Mr. Bensadon back of the shool." Michael E. Cohen to the Committee of the Congregation, Philadelphia, Sept. 15, 1822, MS., MIAr, speaks of the *sepharim* deposited in the house of Bensadon.

20 MBMI, Sept. 8, 1822.

21 MMI, Sept. 22, 1822.

22 SBMI, Sept. 26, 1822. The transliteration of the sacred tetragrammaton is a most un-Jewish practice, and would seem to have been done by the engraver.

23 *Phi. Gaz.*, Dec. 27, 1822, where an account of the earlier cornerstone laying is also given.

24 Aaron Stork, Abraham E. Israel, Elias Hyneman, Abraham Hart, Levi M. Goldsmit, Emanuel Oppenheimer, Jacob De Lange and Moses Spyers, all appeared as contributors to Rodeph Shalom in 1812, and, with the exception of Oppenheimer who maintained his contributions until 1816, they all disappear from the records that year: Davis, *op. cit.*, 141–142. From 1813 to 1817 they made application for admission to Mikveh Israel.

25 Isaac Stuttgart was a regular contributor to Rodeph Shalom from 1812 to 1824, and Louis Bomeisler from 1818 to 1833: Davis, *op. cit.*, 141–146. Stuttgart eventually became a member of Mikveh Israel and was buried in the Spruce Street Cemetery in 1830: Elmaleh and Samuel, *op. cit.*, 14.

26 It is interesting that Levy Phillips made his donations in 1821–22, when the members of Rodeph Shalom were contributing to Mikveh Israel: Davis, *op. cit.*, 143–144.

27 *Journal of the Thirty-Third House of Representatives of the Commonwealth of Pennsylvania* (Harrisburg, 1822), 48.

28 Davis, *op. cit.*, 34.

29 Cash Book, 1823–1847, MS., RSAr. On Nov. 18, 1824, the money was deposited in the Saving Fund.

30 *The Encyclopaedia Britannica, Eleventh Edition* (New York, 1910), IX, 39 and 57; Rachel Wischnitzer, "The Egyptian Revival in Synagogue Architecture," *PAJHS*, XLI (1951), 61–62; Rachel Wischnitzer, *Synagogue Architecture in the United States* (Philadelphia, 1955), 28–32.

31 *Philadelphia in 1824*, (Philadelphia, 1824), 55; Agnes Addison Gilchrist, *William Strickland, Architect and Engineer* (Philadelphia, 1950), 17, 62 and 63.

32 MBMI, Feb. 22 to May 23, 1824. This is discussed in detail in chap. 13.

33 Apparently Isaac B. Seixas had been asked to form a choir as early as 1824: Isaac B. Seixas to Zalegman Phillips and Solomon Moses, New York, May 7, 1824, MS., MIAr, in which he suggests that a group be formed and rehearsals begun, so that he would be able to perfect the group during

visits. MBMI, May 27, 1825, orders a note of thanks to Isaac B. Seixas for organizing the singing class which performed at the consecration. Apparently his nephew, Jacob Seixas, took over the work. According to Rebecca Gratz, *infra*, Jacob (1794–1854), the son of Benjamin M. Seixas, was in town with his sister Miriam, the wife of David M. Moses, visiting their sister Abigail, the wife of Benjamin Phillips, and decided to remain in Philadelphia.

34 *Form of Service at the Dedication of the New Synagogue of the "Kahal Kadosh Mickvi Israel,"* (New York, 1825); Rosenbach, *op. cit.*, 236–238.

35 Zalegman Phillips to Moses L. Peixotto, January 25, 1825, MS., MIAr., thanking him for his "very polite and prompt assistance in the Consecration of the Synagogue," and inclosing a check for $75.

36 RMMI, Dec. 30, 1824.

37 J. Andrew Shulze to Zalegman Phillips, (Harrisburg,) Jan. 17, 1825, MS., MIAr.

38 William Tilghman to Zalegman Phillips, (Philadelphia,) Jan. 11, 1825, MS., MIAr.

39 MBMI, March 6, 1825, contains a report of the building committee which gives the cost as $11,875.03 to that date with an additional $1000 still required.

40 MBMI, Apr. 25, 1824.

41 Report No. 5, SBMI, Jan. 7, 1825, states that there had been paid into the hands of the treasurer of the Building Committee $8,884.35. This did not include the proceeds from the lottery.

42 RMMI, Oct. 10, 1824. No other references could be found in the newspapers or the Journal of the Pennsylvania Assembly.

43 *Phi. Gaz.*, Jan. 24, 1825; on Jan. 2nd it had been ordered that 350 downstairs and 250 upstairs tickets be issued. According to the plan the seating capacity was as given: Rachel Wischnitzer, *Synagogue Architecture in the United States* (Philadelphia, 1955), 33.

44 Rebecca Gratz to Benjamin Gratz, Feb. 27, 1825, MS., AJHS; Philipson, *op. cit.*, 72–77.

45 *Phi. Gaz.*, Jan. 22 and 24, 1825; *Aurora*, Jan. 24, 1825; and *Poulson's*, Jan. 25, 1825.

46 *Phi. Gaz.*, Jan. 24, 1825.

47 *Form of Service at the Dedication of the New Synagogue of the "Kahal Kadosh Shearith Israel"* (New York, 1818); Rosenbach, *op. cit.*, 177–178.

48 *Occ.*, I (1843), 143.

49 *Phi. Gaz.*, Jan. 22, 1825.

50 *Ibid.*

51 *Poulson's*, Jan. 25, 1825.

52 See chap. 13, note 34.

53 See chap. 13, note 98.

54 Abraham E. Israel to the Adjunta, Philadelphia, Adar 11, 1825, MS., MIAr; Minute Book of the "Junto," Oct. 10, 1824.

55 Minute Book of the "Junto," July 29, 1824, MS., MIAr.

56 Regulations for the Government of the Congregation during Divine Worship, Jan. 28, 1825, MS., MIAr.

57 Davis, *op. cit.*, 31. This was a lot in Crown Street, sold in 1817.

58 *Ibid.*, 48. The lot was bought on July 29, 1829.

59 MBRS, Aug. 10, 1829; Davis, *op. cit.*, 48–50.

60 Davis, *op. cit.*, 50.

Index

וּקְרָאתֶם

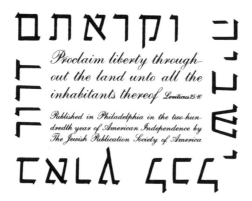

Proclaim liberty through-
out the land unto all the
inhabitants thereof *Leviticus 25:10*

Published in Philadelphia in the two-hun-
dredth year of American Independence by
The Jewish Publication Society of America

דְּרוֹר

בָּאָרֶץ לְכָל־

יֹשְׁבֶיהָ

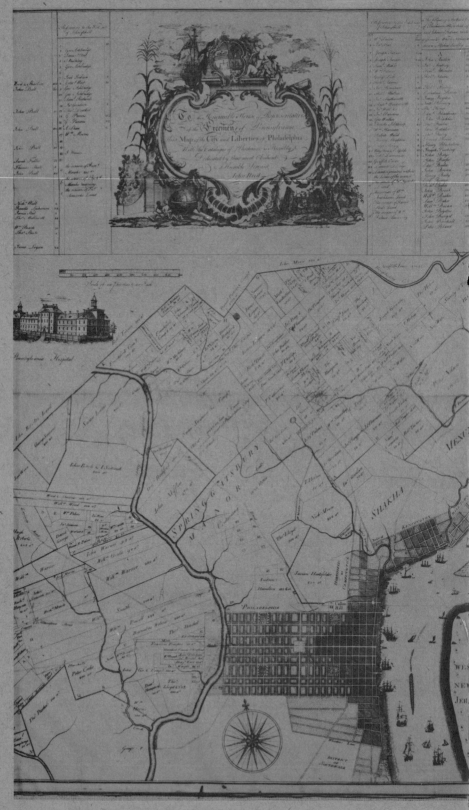

John Reed's map of the city and liberties of Philadelphia, with a list of land purchasers, 1774